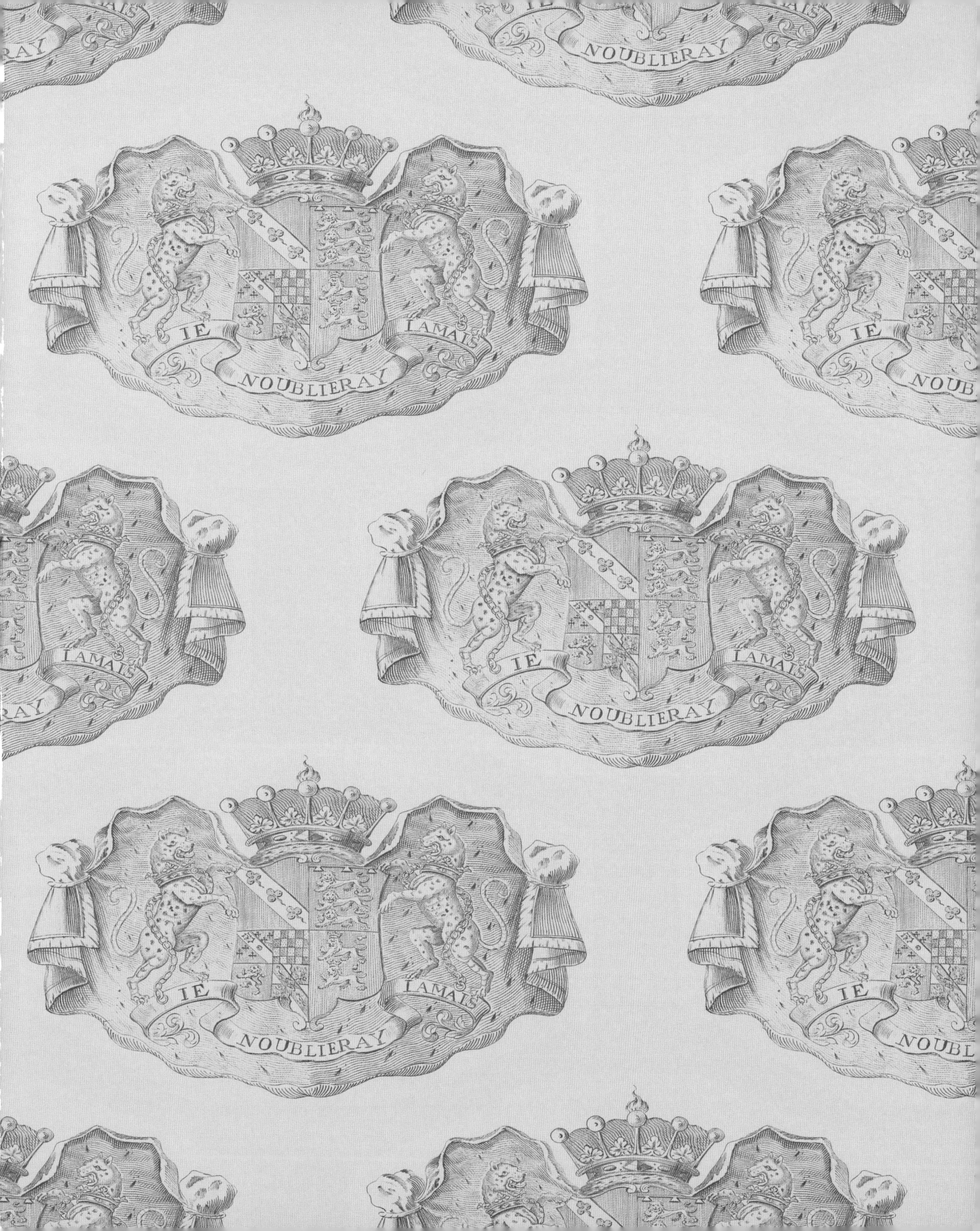
IE
IAMAIS
NOUBLIERAY

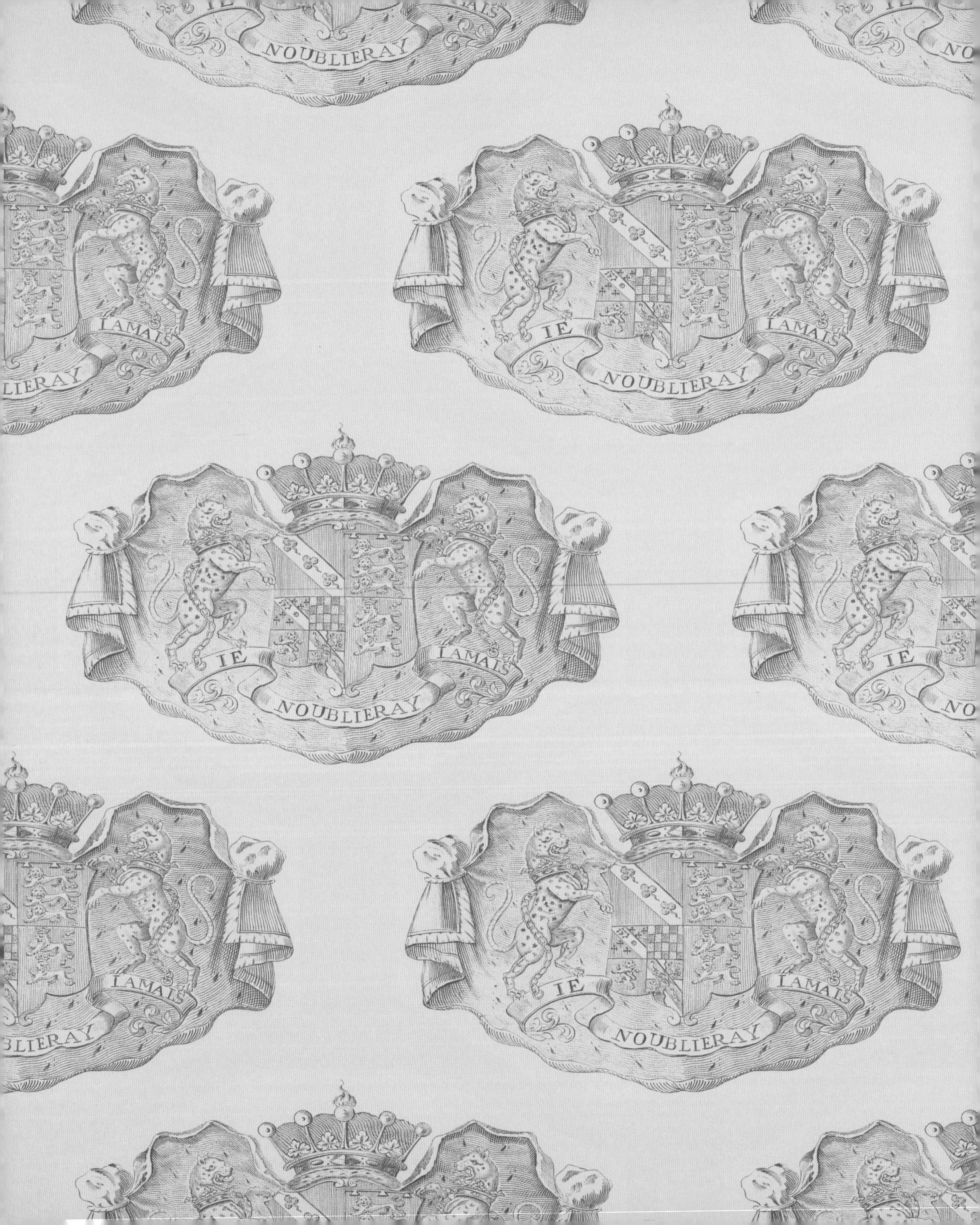
IE
IAMAIS
NOUBLIERAY
IE
IAMAIS
NOUBLIERAY
IE
IAMAIS
NOUBLIERAY

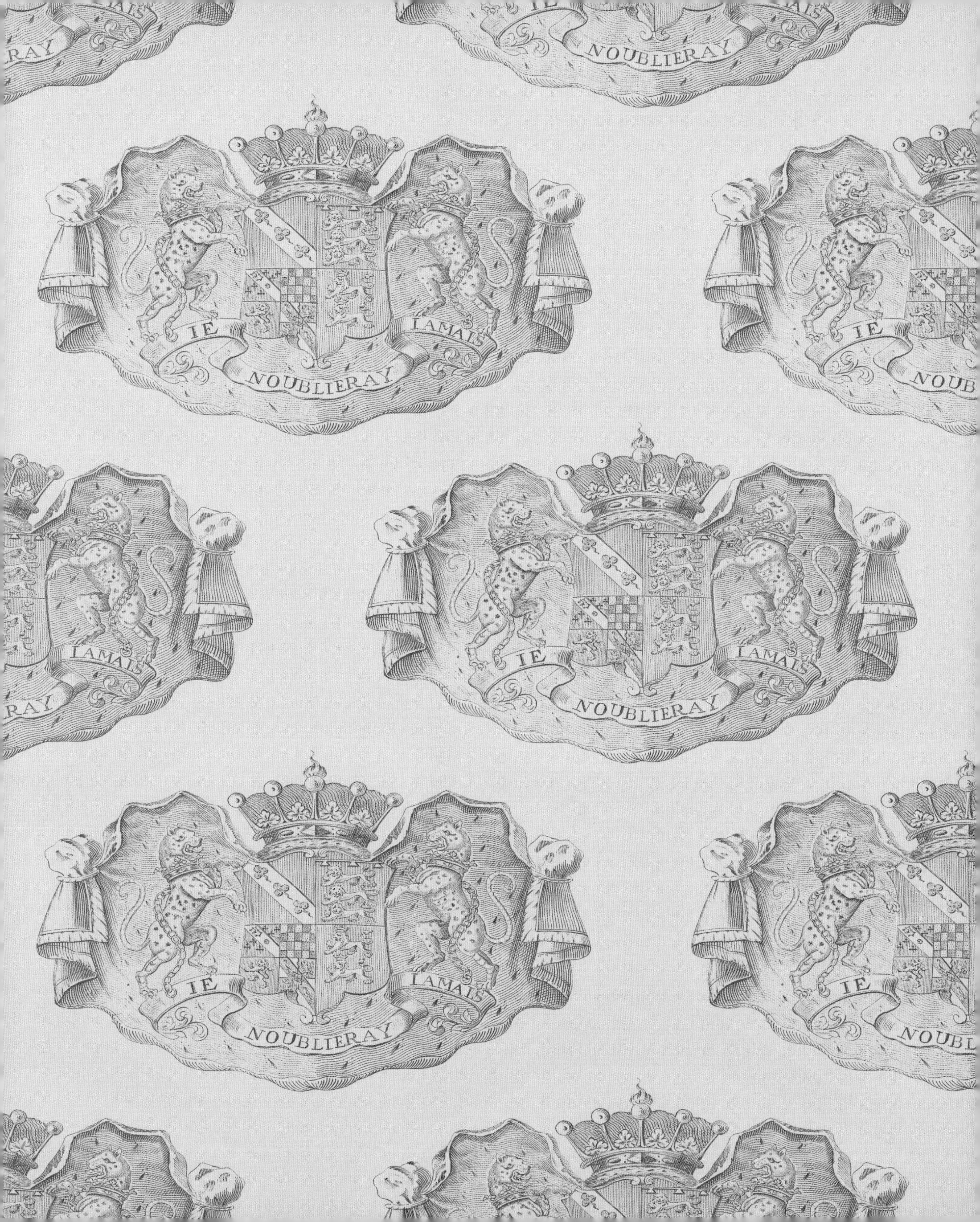
IE IAMAIS
NOUBLIERAY

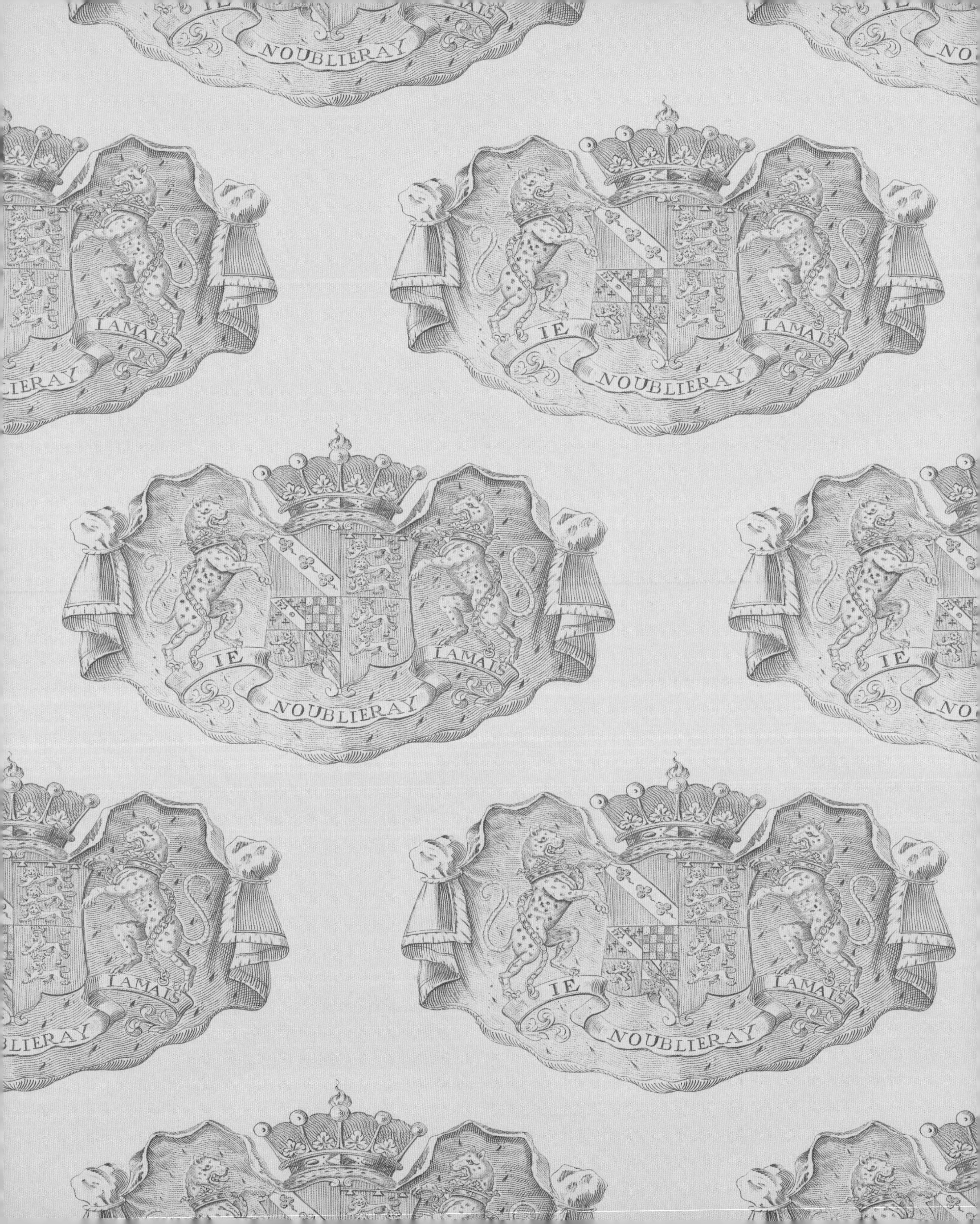
IE
IAMAIS
NOUBLIERAY

SILVER FOR ENTERTAINING

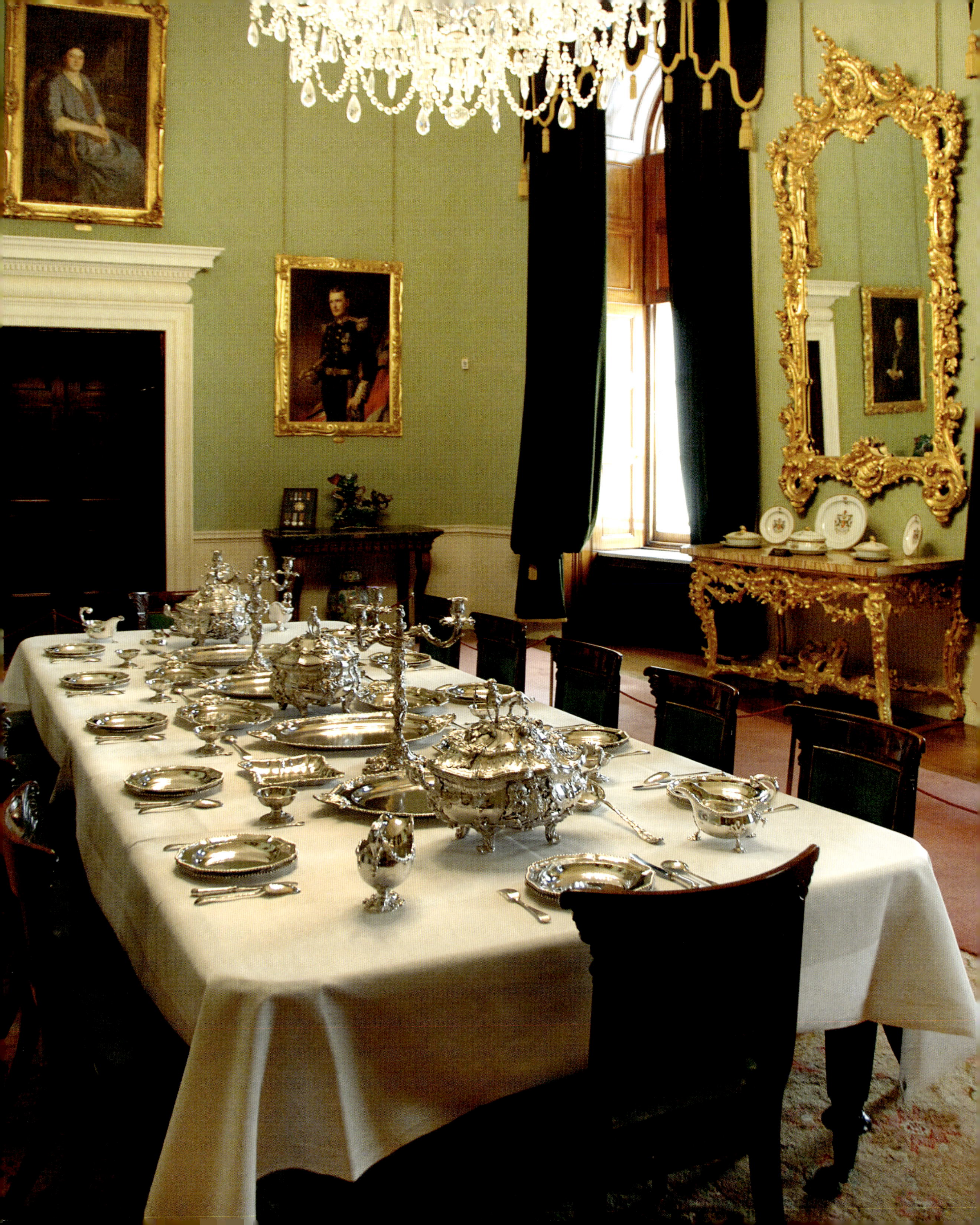

SILVER FOR ENTERTAINING

THE ICKWORTH COLLECTION

JAMES ROTHWELL

PWP

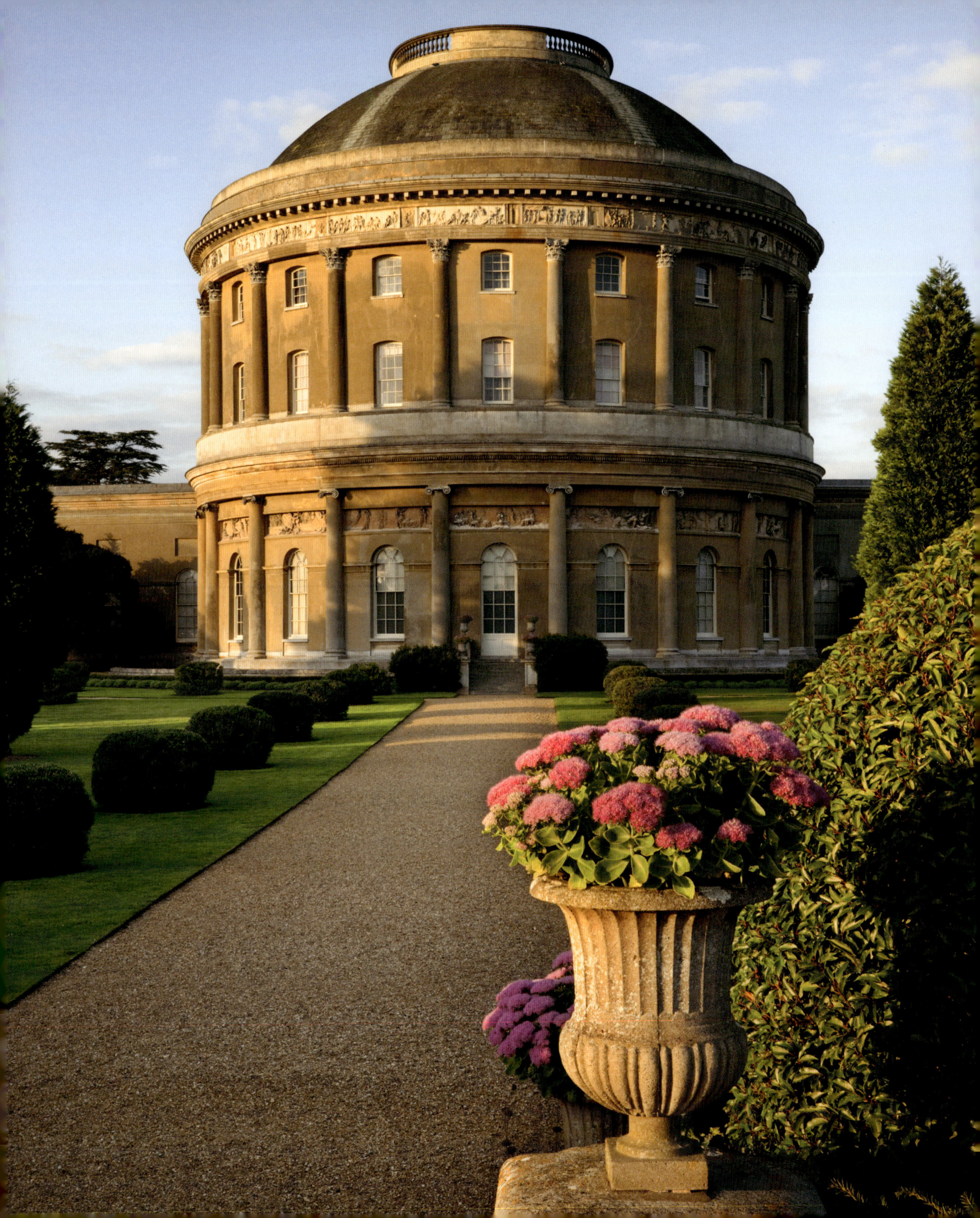

To my father, David Rothwell

Published in 2017 by Philip Wilson Publishers
An imprint of I.B.Tauris & Co. Ltd
London · New York

www.philip-wilson.co.uk

ISBN: 978 1 78130 042 8

A full CIP record for this book is available from the British Library
A full CIP record is available from the Library of Congress
Library of Congress Catalog Card Number: available

Designed and typeset in Garamond by E&P Design
Printed and bound in the UK by Gomer Press Ltd

FSC www.fsc.org MIX Paper from responsible sources FSC® C114687

Frontispiece: The dining room table at Ickworth laid with some of the Bristol plate.
Dedication: The Rotunda at Ickworth.

CONTENTS

PREFACE

The great house at Ickworth, wildly extravagant in its oval form and grandiose in its extent, epitomises the character of its creator, Frederick Hervey, 4th Earl of Bristol and Bishop of Derry. He was Walpole's Earl-Bishop, a man of inexhaustible energy who sought to realise his own view of perfection in building and collecting and would tolerate nothing or no one that stood in his way. As the most extreme of a tribe of eccentrics, he proved an impossible husband and father, a visionary prelate and Irish nationalist, and a remarkable patron of the arts. What he created at Ickworth is so powerful that it is easy to forget that he left only an empty shell on his death in 1803, and that his years of manic yet discerning collecting for his temple of the arts in Suffolk, fascinating though they are to art historians, came to virtually nothing. The French, when they swept into Rome in 1798, confiscated the lot and in spite of the Earl-Bishop's attempts to retrieve it, and the appeals of the countless artists he had patronised, his hoard was scattered by auction in 1804. It was left to his contrastingly placid and likeable son, the 5th Earl and 1st Marquess of Bristol, to make sense of the immense but awkward space within the house during the 1820s and to place there, instead of the Earl-Bishop's Titians, Raphaels and Caraccis, his own less numerous but nevertheless high-quality acquisitions mixed with the accumulated treasures of earlier Herveys.

The strengths of the Ickworth collection in general are from the tenures of the 1st and 2nd Earls and of the 1st Marquess, and that mix is reflected in the superb collection of silver. The earliest survival is the great wine cistern of 1680 by Robert Cooper, originally the property of Baptist May, confidant of Charles II, and a second-hand purchase by the 1st Earl. Another such acquisition by the same Earl forty years later brought all but one of the Paul de Lamerie pieces at Ickworth. This catalogue reveals for the first time that together they represent the earliest surviving substantial remnants of an English epergne, the one commissioned by the 4th Earl of Scarsdale in the early 1720s along with the monumental cistern now in the Hermitage. The rest of the 1st Earl's plate is of the archetypally sober but sophisticated form that predominated in the early decades of the eighteenth century and was so effectively interpreted by the Huguenot goldsmiths whom he seems exclusively to have patronised. The alternative was the rich surface treatment of the *Régence* and that was favoured by the Earl's son, John, Lord Hervey. Though only a handful of items commissioned by him survive they are amongst the finest from the time, being big, decorative pieces from the de Lamerie and Crespin workshops of the early 1730s.

Lady Hervey, like her father-in-law, seems to have had a plainer, more domestic taste in silver, but her eldest son, George, 2nd Earl of Bristol, fully embraced the rococo and it is his new and reworked plate that dominates the silver collection at Ickworth today. He was single-minded in his ambition to elevate himself and the Herveys through dedication to a diplomatic and political career and it is not inconceivable that he could have become prime minister in the 1760s. As it was he rose to be Britain's most senior diplomat in a Europe engulfed by the Seven Years War and he used his spectacular plate, much of it by that master of the sculptural form in the mid-century, Frederick Kandler, as a critical tool in his diplomatic armoury. When it proved not enough in the face of stiff French competition, he simply acquired yet more and being in Turin at the time he went to the best of the goldsmiths there, Andrea Boucheron and Paolo Antonio Paroletto. Thus it is that Ickworth contains one of the largest assemblages of mid-eighteenth century Turinese silver from a single patron surviving anywhere in the world.

The huge quantities of perquisite plate that flowed into British aristocratic collections in the eighteenth century from the Jewel Office did not pass Ickworth by, and the 2nd Earl's appointment as ambassador to Madrid in 1758 brought the customary grant of nearly 7,000 ounces. Of particular note is the largest, earliest and most lavish set of candelabra from the period to survive, extending to twelve pieces with the capacity for no fewer than forty-eight candles. The candelabra are one of many examples in the collection which elucidate the practices of goldsmiths and the complex web of suppliers and retailers about which there is still so much to learn. Though supplied by Simon Le Sage they appear to have been made by James Peltro, a figure presumably rendered shadowy because he was never a direct retailer. He is mooted in this work as a possible candidate for the skilled chaser who seems to have worked on a number of sets of candlesticks of this model from the late 1740s.

By his death in 1775 the 2nd Earl had sufficient plate to dazzle as many as forty dinner guests, all of whom would have been able to eat off silver. Fortunately, the family circumstances of the late Georgian period dictated against the dramatic refashioning that happened in many other collections and which would have left us with the sort of chaste neoclassical or puffed-up Regency services that have survived elsewhere in greater numbers. Those additions that were made by the 1st Marquess, including fine pieces by Paul Storr, were either in harmony with the collection or stood safely alone without overshadowing what had come before. His steadfast determination to maintain the heirloom plate and to put the whole estate on a sound financial footing ensured that the collection passed unscathed into the twentieth century, and the equal determination of Theodora, Marchioness of Bristol, that it should not be sacrificed to the ravages of taxation, brought it to the National Trust in 1956 and thus to public view.

It is not only the survival of the silver itself that makes this collection so extraordinarily significant but its combination with rich archival sources, many of which have been explored for the first time in preparing this catalogue. From the 1st Earl of Bristol's diary, accounts and letters to the scrapbooks of Geraldine, Marchioness of Bristol, via the state papers of Britain and the Kingdom of Sardinia, the accumulation, use and preservation of the Ickworth silver is brought to life and explained. And in a wider context it stands as a clear example of how the decorative arts played their part in the social, cultural and political history of this nation and of Europe as a whole.

ACKNOWLEDGEMENTS

This book would not have been possible without the assistance of the Paul Mellon Centre for Studies in British Art. In 2013 they funded my research costs during a three month sabbatical, including time in Turin, and then in 2015 I was awarded a mid-career fellowship which gave me a further four, uninterrupted months to concentrate on writing. I am enormously grateful to the staff and the members of the Centre's Advisory Council for their support of and faith in me, and in particular to Mary Peskett Smith whose vision it was to open up opportunities for curators as well as academics. Of equal significance to the success of my project has been the National Trust's scholarly publishing programme, put on a firm footing by Sir William Proby Bt during his chairmanship and since then ably and productively steered by David Adshead, Head Curator. He has helped and guided me throughout the long gestation of this book together with, in more recent years, Claire Forbes, the Trust's specialist editor, who has shown patience beyond measure. They have fostered a successful partnership with Philip Wilson Publishers who could not have been more straightforward and professional to deal with and I am indebted especially to Anne Jackson as commissioning editor, Clare Martelli as production editor, Henry Howard for copy editing, and Ian Parfitt for the design. The end result is something of beauty as well as being, I hope, informative.

Silver is the most reflective of natural substances and the consequentially difficult task of photographing the Ickworth collection for this catalogue – from the vast cistern down to the minutest of hallmarks – was ably undertaken by Robert Thrift, with some additional shots by Robert Morris. External images were tracked down from all over the world by Susannah Stone – her success rate was astonishing and well beyond my expectations. Certain items of the collection needed technical analysis to understand their evolution and that was carried out by Dave Merry and Chris Walne from the London Assay Office, their infectious enthusiasm and clarity of expression helping me overcome a general scientific ignorance. In addition, Rod Kelly discussed the practical silversmithing of such complex items as the Kandler tureens and he and Sheila McDonald inducted me in the craft at their Shetland workshop.

James Lomax, whose research and publications have done so much to advance the understanding of silver, generously acted as external reader and I also owe him much for having helped me cut my teeth as a silver scholar and an author at the beginning of my curatorial career. He is an inspiration. Certain aspects of the text have, in addition, been read and commented upon by specialists, in particular Timothy Schroder (the Le Sage candelabra), Peter Cameron (Frederick Kandler and Lewis Hamon), Vanessa Brett (toymen) and Ann Eatwell (nineteenth century silver). Christopher Hartop looked at the collection with me on a number of occasions, answering endless queries and he and Juliet Nusser provided hospitality and respite on several of my visits to East Anglia. Tessa Murdoch (Victoria and Albert Museum), too, has helped throughout, being key to the commissioning of the book in the first place and generously standing aside when it became apparent that my researches were straying into areas that she might otherwise have tackled.

At Ickworth, my constant visits and requests over some eight years have provoked nothing but enthusiasm and helpfulness from past and present staff and volunteers including Anna Forrest, Jan Summerfield, Neil Robinson, Chloe Woodrow, Caroline Pons, Helena Rodwell, Fiona Terrington, Sarah Madgett, Kate Hills, Sue Borges, Jo Dean and Geoff Ochs as well as all the members of the housekeeping team. Others from the National Trust to whom I am indebted are Steve Lang, Christopher Rowell, Dr Wolf Burchard, Alastair Laing, David Taylor, Mark Purcell, Yvonne Lewis, Sash Giles, Katie Taylor, Nicola Whyton and Jess Conridge. Of the many archives and libraries I have visited I am particularly grateful to the staff of the Suffolk Record Office in Bury St Edmunds and the Archivio di Stato di Torino, Sezione Corte. Professor Alistair Rowan introduced me at the latter, and to Turin in general. Others who assisted my researches relating to the city and its silver were Edoardo Piccoli (Politecnico di Torino), Gianfranco Fina and Luca Mana (Museo di Arti Decorative Accorsi-Ometto), Tomaso Ricardi (Veneria Reale), Annarita Colturato (Università degli Studi di Torino), Karin Wolfe (British School at Rome) and Dr Toby Osborne (University of Durham).

Many more have given their help over the years including Philippa Glanville who, as always, was unfailingly generous with her time and expertise, Jane Ewart, Patricia Ferguson, Dr Sarah Rutherford, Rosemary Ransome Wallis and David Beasley (Goldsmiths' Company), Olivia Horsfall-Turner, Nicholas Webb and Maria Sienkiewicz (Barclays Group Archives), Pamela Hunter (Hoare's Bank), Professor Anthony Geraghty (University of York), Rupert Harris, Isabel Keating (Duke of Northumberland's archives), Dr David Mitchell, Jane Eddleston, Edward and Natasha Rowland, Michéle Bimbenet-Privat (Musée du Louvre), Lorenz Seelig (Bayerische Nationalmuseum), José Manuel Cruz Valdovinos (Universidad Complutense de Madrid), Lucy Wood, Annabel Westman and Jonathan Ellis.

ONE

SILVER PATRONAGE DURING THE RESTORATION AND THE EARLY EIGHTEENTH CENTURY JOHN HERVEY, 1ST EARL OF BRISTOL

In 1456 Elizabeth Drury, widow of Henry and tenant for life of the Ickworth estate, inherited from her father-in-law a 'silver bowl with the cover graven with a molet [mullet]'.[1] By her own will, drawn up in 1475, she made specific bequests of a silver spoon, a covered goblet, a salt and, to her brother-in-law Roger Drury, the same 'cou'ed [covered] cuppe of silver which I had of his father'.[2] Thus commences the recorded history of silver at Ickworth and although references are scant over the ensuing two hundred years the precious metal clearly maintained an important presence, as it would continue to do up to the present day.

The early Herveys of Ickworth

Elizabeth and Henry's grandson, William Hervey (1464–1538), was the first of that family to possess the Ickworth estate, and though there are no inventories detailing the contents of the manor house which then stood by the church, successive wills, such as that of John Hervey who died in 1556, do refer to plate in general passing from one generation to the next.[3] The family's wealth was not on the scale of the Kytsons of nearby Hengrave Hall, who owned 4,400 ounces of silver in 1548, but they might have been expected to have had a quarter of that amount, as did Sir John Gage of Firle Place in Sussex in 1555.[4] A typical gentry collection of plate at that time would have consisted of drinking cups, some of them covered, standing salts, ewers and basins, nests of goblets, a set of bowls, perhaps a chafing dish, chapel plate and a relative profusion of spoons. George Collier, Warden of Manchester Collegiate Church, only had one hundred or so ounces of silver on his death in 1558 but that included 'Sixe meate spoones' and thirteen 'other spoones'[5] and the great Lincolnshire magnate, William, 11th Lord Willoughby de Eresby, had some two dozen silver-gilt spoons and a further two dozen not gilt in 1526.[6] A relatively high proportion of silver in the sixteenth century was either gilt or parcel-gilt.[7]

John Hervey would have seen considerable magnificence at Hengrave, where he is sure to have dined as a neighbouring landowner, but it would have been nothing compared to that experienced by his courtier younger brother, Sir Nicholas Hervey (d. 1532). In 1520 he accompanied Henry VIII to the Field of the Cloth of Gold where, according to Edward's Hall's near-contemporary *Chronicle*, 'all noblemenne, gentlemenne, squiers, knights, and every honeste officer of the kynge was richly apparrelled, and had chaynes of golde, greate and marvelous waightie,' whilst at the feast before the jousting 'all the noble men were served in gilt vessel, and all other in silver vessel.'[8] Sir Nicholas would no doubt have been wearing the gold chain again at the jousting that was put on for the French ambassadors at Greenwich in 1527, when he was described as the King's 'valiaunt Esquier', and he went on to experience another of the great courts of Europe on being sent to Augsburg in 1530 as ambassador to the Holy Roman Emperor, Charles V.[9] The practice had not yet been established of supplying ambassadors with perquisite plate (see chapter 3) but it was customary for them to receive gifts of precious metal or jewels from the monarch they were attending on departure. Given that Sir Nicholas was forlornly pleading Henry VIII's case to divorce the Emperor's aunt, Catherine of Aragon, he may not have done as well as a subsequent English representative to the Imperial court, Lord Digby, who in 1621 received a solid gold ewer and basin from Ferdinand II.[10]

Gold chains became highly fashionable under Elizabeth I, who favoured jewellery and elaborate costume over plate,[11] and amongst the many men shown wearing them in portraits of the second half of the sixteenth century is Francis Hervey (1534–1602) (fig. 1), Sir Nicholas's nephew and the younger brother of William Hervey of Ickworth (1526–92). Francis had been appointed to the corps of Gentlemen Pensioners, the monarch's personal bodyguard staffed by scions of noble houses, by Queen Mary and he managed to remain in favour under Elizabeth through his close association with the Earl of Essex.[12] His portrait, which was painted in 1564 and is the earliest authentic image of a Hervey at Ickworth, shows him bedecked with precious metal: several jewel-encrusted gold rings are prominently displayed on the hand in which he holds the gold-tasselled battleaxe of the Gentlemen Pensioners, his costume sparkles with gold and silver thread and three bands of a heavy gold chain rest on his chest. A comparable chain of just over 44 ounces was purchased a decade later by the younger Sir Thomas Kytson (1540–1603) of Hengrave. He had probably exchanged his father's gold cup of nearly the same weight for it, paying in addition 2s 9d per ounce fashion.[13]

For much, if any, of the silver at Ickworth in the sixteenth century to have survived not only wear and tear and changes in fashion but also the turbulence of the Civil War years would have been highly unlikely and John Hervey (1616–80), to whom the estate was passed in 1642, probably had to replenish the family's store of plate following the Restoration in 1660. He was dubbed 'the founder of our family' by his nephew, the 1st Earl of Bristol, because of his considerable expansion of the estate both by purchase and through marriage to his irascible cousin Elizabeth (*c.* 1615–1700), daughter and heiress of Lord Hervey of Kidbrooke.[14] As another in the long line of Hervey courtiers, serving as Treasurer to the Queen from 1662, John was principally resident in London and the manor house at Ickworth was let to a farmer. In 1677 he took advantage of his position as a trustee of the Earl of St Albans' London development to acquire for £5,100 a recently constructed house in St James's Square (No. 6) which was to remain the family's town residence until 1955.[15] He was clearly very wealthy indeed, making specific bequests in his will over and above his landed estate amounting to nearly £12,000 and instructing that a further £20,000 be outlaid in purchasing additional lands, the income to go to his wife for her life.[16] In this context his silver is likely to have been both expansive and of the highest quality but sadly nothing whatsoever is known of it beyond how it was devised:

> *I do also give and bequeath unto my Entirely beloved and ever deare wife Elizabeth Hervey All my Jewells Plate Houshold Stuffe and implements of houshould only desiring her that my Brother Sr Thomas Hervey may att her decease have all my Gould Silver and Brasse Medales which I give bequeath unto him after her life That they may remain to him and his heires and the owners of Ickworth.*

Thus, although Elizabeth had a life interest in the estates as she did in the St James's Square house, she was given the plate, excepting the medals, outright. That was unusual and may be a further indication that all of it had been acquired by John Hervey, perhaps even with his wife's money, rather than being inherited from his father. John pleaded in his will for his brother and his wife, who were his executors and clearly not on good terms, to be 'kind and friendly to one another' and for Elizabeth furthermore to remember that she was a part of the family 'by blood as well as marriage'. This seems to have fallen on deaf ears, however, and as the antipathy between them deepened over the years there was little prospect of anything under Elizabeth's personal control ever reaching her Hervey relations. By the time of her death in 1700 she had anyway managed to alienate her entire personal estate to one of her 'meniall servants' and no silver would have passed with possession of the estates to her nephew, the younger John Hervey.[17]

John Hervey, 1st Earl of Bristol

John Hervey (fig. 3) was born on 27 August 1665, the eldest surviving son of Sir Thomas (1625–94) by his wife Isabella May (1625–86) and the ultimate heir presumptive from birth of his childless uncle, the elder John Hervey. His first years were spent in London amongst a profusion of influential relations, many of them courtiers, parliamentarians and placemen – his father was a Navy Commissioner, his paternal uncle John was a Member of Parliament as well as being Treasurer to the Queen, three of his maternal uncles were also Members of Parliament and two of them, Sir Algernon and Baptist May, were respectively Equerry to the Queen and Keeper of the Privy Purse. Most notably of all, his cousin, Henry Jermyn, Earl of St Albans, was Lord Chamberlain and one of Charles II's most influential advisers. From 1668, when Sir Thomas resigned his Navy post in the wake of a Commons inquiry into the conduct of the Second Dutch War,[18] the family resided principally in Bury St Edmunds. Sir Thomas's house there was in School Hall Street (now Lane) which was then on the outskirts of the town, on the Ickworth side.[19] John Hervey was educated at Bury Grammar School and Cambridge[20] and in November 1688, aged 23, he married Isabella Carr (1670–93) (fig. 2), the heiress of considerable estates in Lincolnshire. Thenceforth, until his death at the age of 85 in 1751, he kept detailed notes of disbursements in two successive books of accounts which also doubled as diaries and these, together with his copious surviving correspondence, give a clear picture of the context in which he acquired silver.[21]

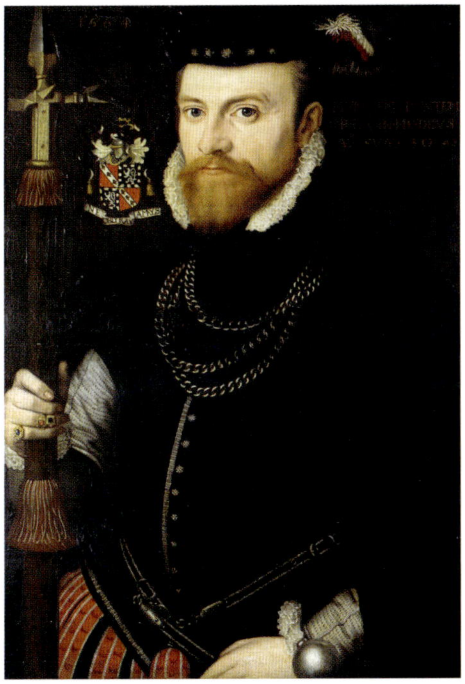

FIG. 1 / *Francis Hervey*, Anglo-Flemish School, 1564. Oil on oak panel: 67.3 x 46.4 cm (26½ x 18¼ in). National Trust, Ickworth.

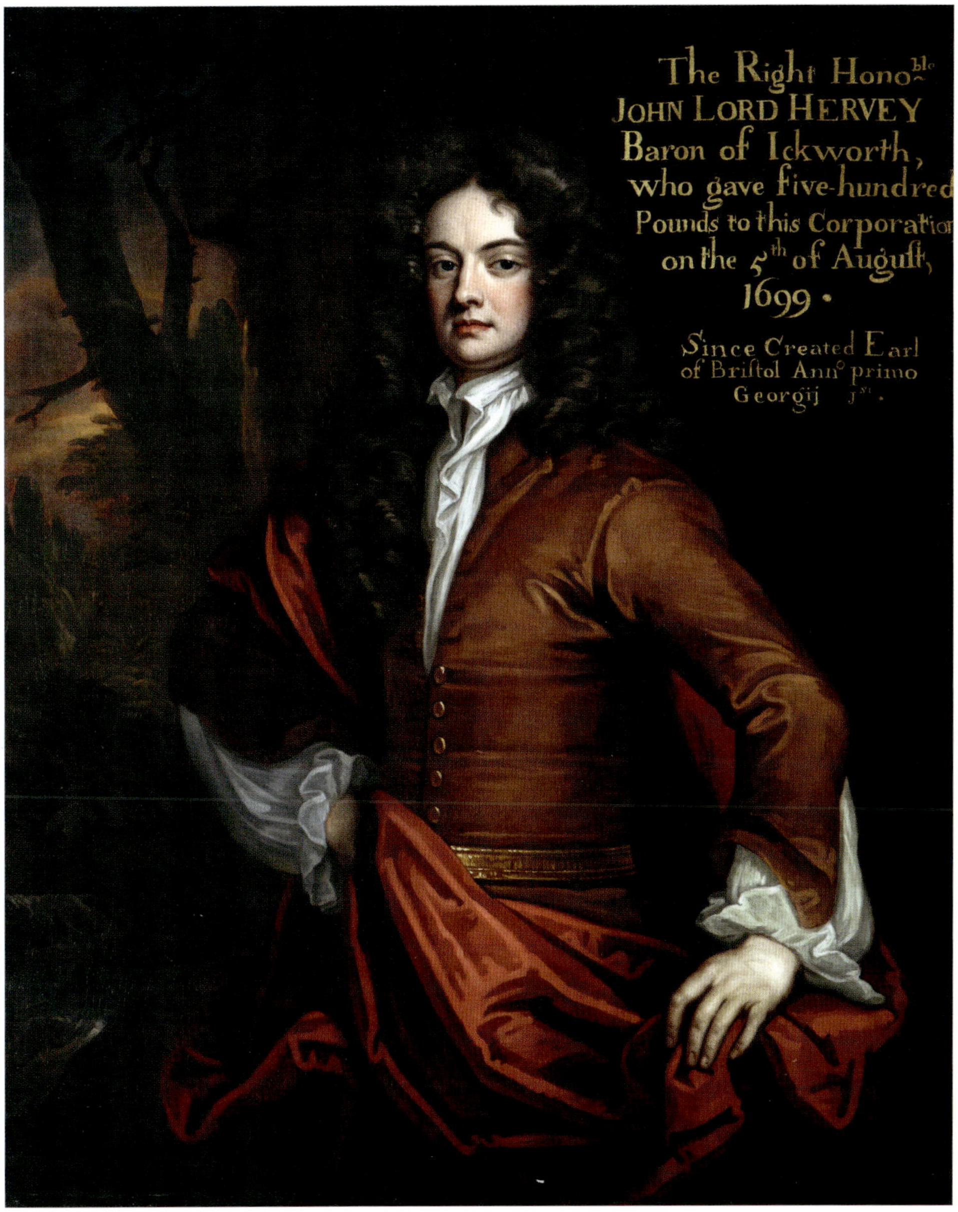

FIG. 3 / *John Hervey, 1st Earl of Bristol* by John Fayram after Sir Godfrey Kneller, *c.*1715. Showing the Earl as a young man. Oil on canvas: 123 x 100 cm (48⅜ x 39⅜ in). National Trust, Ickworth, on loan from St Edmundsbury Borough Council.

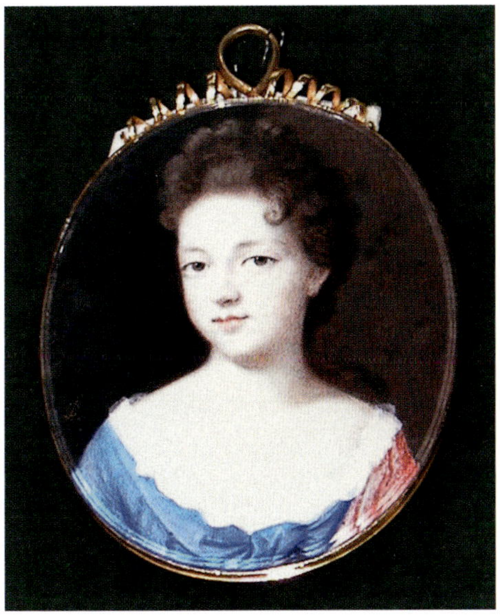

FIG. 2 / *Isabella Carr, Mrs John Hervey* by Peter Cross after Joseph Brook, *c.*1693. Portrait miniature, watercolour on vellum: 8 x 6.5 cm (3⅛ x 2½ in). National Trust, Ickworth.

EARLY SILVER PURCHASES

On marriage John Hervey received an allowance of £1,000 from his father and an additional £912 in the right of his wife, giving him a healthy income of just under £2,000. That allowed the young couple, after residing initially with Lady Carr in Pall Mall, to set up house in King Street off St James's Square, renting from the Earl of Berkeley and also taking the 'french Embassadours stables'.[22] Fashionable furnishings were acquired including gilt leather and brocatelle hangings, the latter for Isabella Hervey's antechamber, '2 great jarrs', 'two other less', beakers, basins, fish and much other china, Dutch chairs, twelve leaves of 'cutt Jappan' made up into a screen, a 'Tea Table', a full set of lacquered chairs, stools and couch, 'Glasses, Tables, Stands &c' from Gerrit Jensen (d. 1715) and four tapestries from the merchant Gerard van Heythuysen. Sashes were introduced to three windows, probably including the principal bedchamber which was upholstered by Francis La Pierre (d. 1717).[23] He was paid £55 on 27 November 1689 for 'making up The Bed, Chairs, hanging ye Room, & my wife her Closett & other things', and he probably used the sumptuous 'orange & Silver stuff' lined with scarlet[24] paid for on 16 October and the 'Fringe of ye Bed, Edging for the window Curtains, &c' which had come at the same time from 'Frenoye, ye silk man' at a cost of £205.[25] Wrought silver formed part of the ensemble too with £13 5s being expended on 'a pair of Silver Andirons for my dear wife her Closett Chimney' on 24 January 1690 and what was probably Isabella Hervey's toilet service being overhauled by 'boyling' and varnishing in October 1689 for a total cost of £1 15s 6d.[26]

This show of magnificence was effected in anticipation of the birth of their first child on 3 October, a daughter Isabella Carr Hervey (1689–1711) who was known as Binny. She would have been presented to the world during the official lying-in, her mother receiving guests from the La Pierre bed, and when not being paraded the baby enjoyed the reassuring light cast from a 'silver hanging candlestick for the nursery weighing 17 ounces 10 penny weight' which had been purchased on 4 October 1689 for £5 11s. Silver in the form of a basin would also have been needed for the child's christening which occurred in the house on 31 October and an existing piece, most likely a wash-hand basin, must have been utilised as no relevant purchase is to be found in the accounts.[27] Six months later, on 14 March 1690, the goldsmith-banker Abraham Chambers (d. 1693) was paid £1 10s 'for a Corrail Sett in Gold' (see cat. 124 for a nineteenth-century example) which would have been for use during teething. That evidently did not go smoothly as, rather gruesomely, in December of the same year, 'Franklin ye Surgeon' was paid 10s 9d 'for cutting ye childs Gums'.[28]

Other silver items purchased during the four and a half years of John Hervey's first marriage included a silver candlestick in November 1689, gold and silver snuff boxes in January 1690, the latter possibly being that still in the collection (cat. 2), and an inkstand from Mrs Harache[29] later the same year. A 'sillver ege thing worth tenn ginnes', perhaps a frame for boiled eggs as that of 1740 by Peter Archambo at Dunham Massey,[30] was a gift from him to his wife on 3 February 1690, probably for her twentieth birthday (20th January), and more andirons, described as large, were purchased with a pair of silver scales for £88 5s 6d from Robert Fowle (d. 1705), a goldsmith banker,[31] in December, 1692. The andirons must have been considerably more magnificent, even allowing for the scales, than those for Mrs Hervey's closet and may have been a further embellishment of the principal bed-chamber in readiness for the birth of the couple's third child. That occurred on 7 March 1693 but there was to be no lying-in on this occasion as Isabella, in her distraught husband's words, 'died ye very moment she was deliver'd of my daughter Elizabeth'.[32]

The lack of dining plate amongst purchases in these early years is almost certainly explained by either Sir Thomas Hervey or Lady Carr, or even both, equipping the couple on setting up a household, as John Hervey himself was to do for his second son Jack following his marriage in 1720 (see appendix 1). The fact that Mrs Hervey's toilet plate was being overhauled just months into her marriage suggests that it was not new, and it may well have been her mother's, perhaps dating from around 1665 when she married Sir Robert Carr, 3rd Bt. Also likely to have been old were Mrs Hervey's inkstand, for the gilding and mending of which John van Collema[33] was paid £1 1s 6d on 1 May 1691, and Hervey's shaving pot, perhaps passed on from his father or the Carrs, which was exchanged for 'a new shaving Bason & Pott' in October 1689.

A very significant purchase of new silver was made at the end of this period, John Hervey paying £420 to Robert Fowle on 3 February 1693. This was the largest single payment in the first five years of his accounts by a long way and would have equated to 1,400 ounces or so if charged at 6s an ounce to include fashion, but frustratingly no details are given, Hervey merely noting that the payment was for 'several pieces of Plate'. Fortunately he is more explicit over some of the costume and harness incorporating precious metal, and amongst his acquisitions whilst married to Isabella were a 'black sadle with silver Galloone', 'plate furniture, and a sadle, Hoose, Capps, and baggs, with Silver galloone & fringes', a 'Brown & Silver westcoat', 'silver fringd Gloves' and a silver-headed cane.[34]

EXPANDING THE STORE OF PLATE

John Hervey was so grief-stricken by his wife's death, followed in May 1694 by that of his father, Sir Thomas, that he abandoned keeping his accounts for eighteen months, only resuming when some *joie de vivre* was returned by the beautiful Elizabeth Felton (1676–1741) (fig. 4) who he probably encountered at Boxted Hall in Suffolk, the home of her aunt, Lady Poley, just ten miles to the south of Ickworth.[35] Added to her personal charms were the prospect of an enormous fortune and a close proximity to one of the most distinguished of English noble families, Elizabeth being the granddaughter of James Howard, 3rd Earl of Suffolk. John's first entries on resuming his accounts, in June 1695 were payments to 'Charles Mather (ye Cane-man in ffleet Street) for a silver snuff box, a Table-Book, a Pockett Case & a silver wove-Hatband' and to 'William Remon (a french Embroiderer) for my Cloak' and these were perhaps the hatband and cloak he wore when he and Elizabeth married on 25 July in Boxted church, and again a few days later when the couple was met at Bury St Edmunds Guildhall 'by ye Corporation in their gowns'.[36]

John and Elizabeth established themselves in a house in Jermyn Street in London, again on his cousin, the Earl of St Albans' estate, and, as in 1689, the focus of attention were the principal rooms including his pregnant wife's apartment. The royal cabinet maker, Gerrit Jensen, was paid £70 for 'for ye black sett of Glass, Table & Stands, and for ye Glasses &c over ye Chimneys, & elsewhere in dear wifes Apartment' on 25 May 1696. Elizabeth herself received eight diamond buckles for her bodice the same month, and on 7 October John Hervey paid £34 10s to 'Mr James Seamers (ye Goldsmith's) man Tho. Outlaw, for ye great silver chasd Baskett, weighing 128ou:04dwt, at 5s:5d pr ounce'. This piece, the price per ounce of which suggests it was second-hand, is likely, given the impending birth, to have been a layette basket intended for the linen and clothes of a newborn child. These were often made in Holland where the practice was more common, and surviving examples include one of *c.*1670, possibly London-made, in the Gilbert Collection at the Victoria and Albert Museum (fig. 5).[37] Another was amongst the plate of the 2nd Earl of Warrington, 'a large Silver Basket Chased Work' weighing 175oz 15dwt recorded in 1750/4 probably having been acquired for the birth of his daughter and only child, Lady Mary Booth, in 1704.[38] Hervey was evidently increasing the level of domestic grandeur in response to the additional status and wealth brought to the family by his second marriage and this was also reflected at the christening in the house of his second son John (the future Lord Hervey, always known as Jack, 1696–1743) (fig. 6), for whom the layette basket was acquired, on 25 October, 1696: whereas his children by his first wife

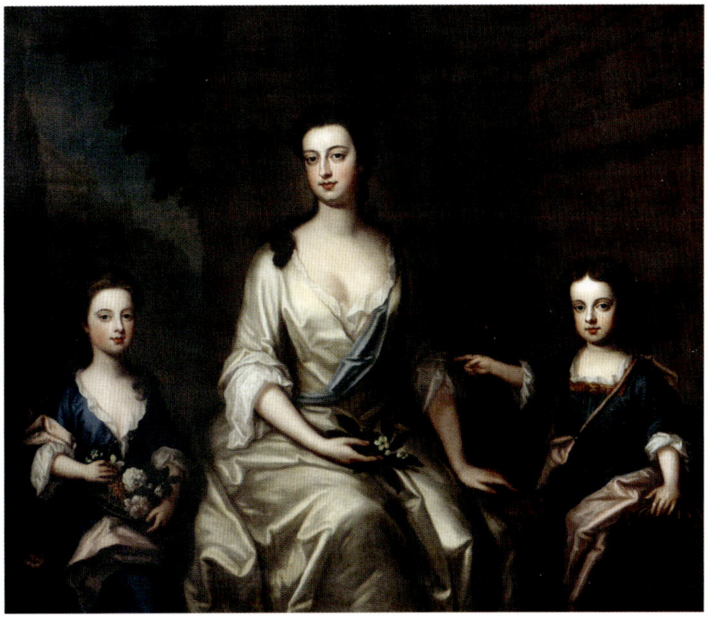

FIG. 4 / *Elizabeth Felton, Countess of Bristol with Lady Henrietta Hervey and the Hon. Charles Hervey* by Charles d'Agar, 1709. Oil on canvas: 137.2 x 157.5 cm (54 x 62 in). National Trust, Ickworth.

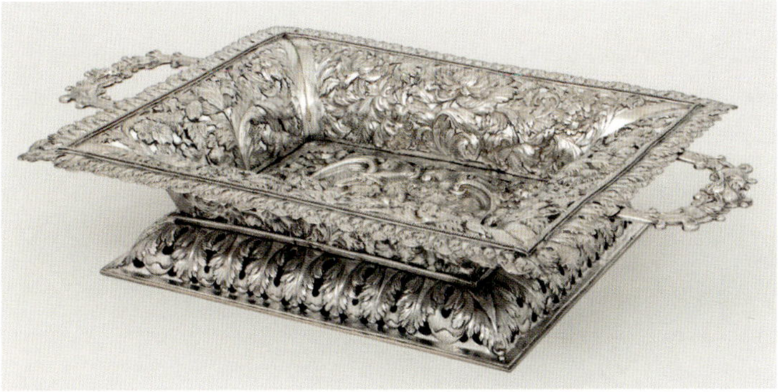

FIG. 5 / Layette basket, *c.*1670. Silver: 12 x 64 x 42 cm (4¾ x 25¼ x 16½ in); weight 3680 g. The Rosalinde & Arthur Gilbert Collection, Victoria and Albert Museum.

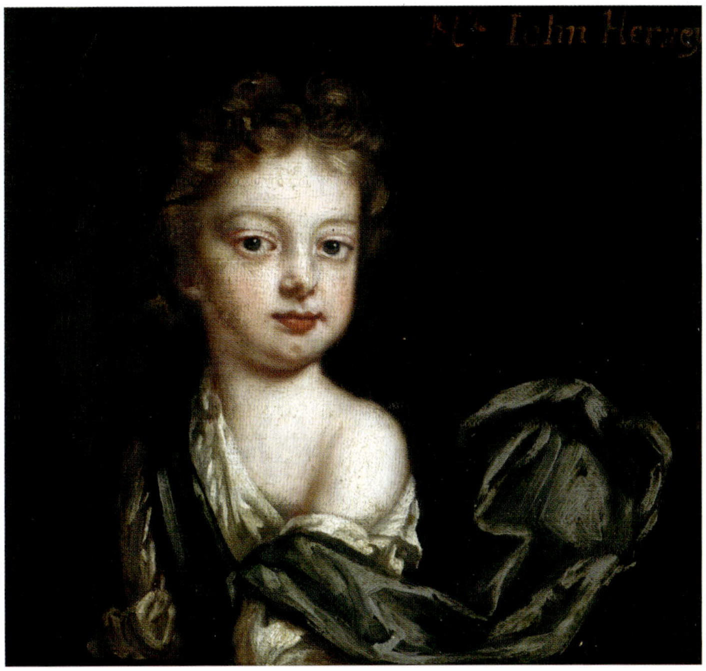

FIG. 6 / *John Hervey, 2nd Lord Hervey as an infant* by Joseph Brook, 1701. Oil on canvas: 29.2 x 24.1 cm (11½ x 9½ in). National Trust, Ickworth.

had near relations as godparents, Jack's female sponsor was the Duchess of Lauderdale.[39]

Amongst other silver acquisitions in 1696 were two 'Table Stands' plus a monteith and chafing dish also from Seamer,[40] a basin and ewer and 'Eleven Dishes, 1 dozen of Plates, a Coffee Pott & a porridg Ladle weighing [in total] 802 ounces' from Edward Waldegrave[41] and a pair each of branch candlesticks and gilt sconces from Richard Hoare (d. 1719). Another supplier, however, was emerging as the favourite, in the form of James Chambers (d. 1733) who was one of the antecedents of Goslings Bank. From him some £115 worth of unspecified plate was acquired on 6 May followed by 'an other Dozen of silver Plates' at £62 2s 6d on the 18th of the same month, a silver stand and salvers in June and two dishes weighing 154½ ounces in November. In total John Hervey spent £544 5s 8d on plate within the twelve-month period, bringing the total since 1688 to over 4,000 ounces if one assumes a conservative cost per ounce of 5s 6d where unspecified. He had also that year gained possession of his father's plate following the death of his sister, Isabella Elwes, to whom a life interest had been left along with the Bury St Edmunds house,[42] and when old Lady Carr died in October 1696 any silver she had retained would have come his way as well. Even allowing for the 950 or so ounces of old plate traded in against the 1696 purchases this all represented a significant augmentation of the family silver.

Given that John Hervey already had a reasonable quantity of silver these purchases are likely to have brought the overall store of plate up to at least 5,500 ounces and as such it ranked alongside those of the wealthiest of landowning families of the period, if not quite being up at the dizzying heights of the princes of the aristocracy.[43] At Dunham Massey in 1693 there were 3,694 ounces[44] and there were similar amounts at Lyme Park in 1687[45] and at Belton in 1698.[46] Dunham was the seat of an earl and the silver there included six dozen and eight plates whilst Belton, occupied by an extremely wealthy baronet, had four dozen plates plus another dozen gilt for dessert. Lyme (which had hosted the future James II in the 1670s) had three dozen plates, but a much more lavish provision of serving dishes. John Hervey probably also had three dozen plates by the end of 1696, twenty-four being added during the year, and as such he was equipped to follow the fashion of serving food *à la Française* to up to twelve diners, their plates being changed for the different courses or 'removes'. At Lyme and Belton there were only a dozen each of silver spoons and forks and this suggests, interestingly, that diners would have been expected to keep their cutlery, as was, and remained, the custom in France.[47] By the early eighteenth century the grandest and most fashionable of British families were, in contrast, changing their knives and forks with the plates and consequently many more were required (see cat. 69). Though we only have scant records of John Hervey's acquisitions of flatware and cutlery, it is very likely that he too would have had a dozen of each in the late seventeenth century and augmented the number over the ensuing years as the fashion evolved.

SECOND-HAND PLATE

All but two of the purchases up to the end of 1696 of ungilt silver for which rates are given were at less than six shillings an ounce, the exceptions being the branch candlesticks from Richard Hoare which were charged at 7s 6d and the chafing dish from James Seamer at 6s 6d. Of the rest some pieces were of such simplicity that the fashioning was minimal, such as the two dishes from James Chambers which were no doubt plain and circular and were charged at 5s 2d for the metal and 4d for fashion, 5s 6d in total. Others however were clearly quite ornate, such as the 'great silver chasd Baskett' from James Seamer, but were still charged at a low rate, in this case 5s 5d per ounce. The reason for this is that they were being purchased second-hand which was quite acceptable at the time and continued to be so, provided the pieces were in good condition and were not rendered hopelessly old-fashioned by their style. No acknowledgement of the craftsmanship or effort of manufacture went beyond the first acquisition, so almost all that was being paid was the cost of the metal, and that could always be redeemed thereafter.[48] The purchaser had the satisfaction of gaining items for which somebody else had previously paid significantly more and which could be put to good use whilst remaining a secure investment.

John Hervey exhibited a thrifty approach to the accumulation of plate from the beginning of his independent adulthood, and he always bought second-hand as well as new. Although this went for other goods as well, such as in April 1697 when he paid £22 10s to 'La Pierre ye Upholsterer in full of his Bill for severall Goods bought of him at second hand'[49] it was with silver that this tendency was most marked, and the following month saw one of his most spectacular single purchases. As he recorded in his accounts for 7 May, he

> *Paid Mr Duncombe & Mr Pigeon (as Execs: of Mr Bapt May) for a large silver Cystern, 2 Dozen of nurld plates, 1 large Cup & Cover, 1 Bason, 1 Chamber pott, 1 Ladle & 1 Skimer, all weighing – 1128 ounces 15 peny weight which at 5s:4d p ounce came to 301 £*

All but one of these pieces must subsequently have been exchanged or melted as they do not survive at Ickworth but fortunately the exception is the great bottle cistern (cat. 1), one of the earliest still in existence. Though it had been made in 1680 and was no longer at the cutting edge of fashion it was still perfectly presentable, and very similar vessels continued to be made, such as that by George Garthorne of 1694 in the Bank of England collection (fig. 68). Much work had gone into the piece, and as it weighed 314 oz, 15 dwt, the saving on fashion would have been considerable, as much as £20 if a charge for new making of 7s per ounce is assumed. The piece would anyway have been seen at a distance, being placed by the sideboard during dinner, and that is probably what enabled it to survive numerous opportunities for exchange or melting during the eighteenth century, together with the huge fashion cost of obtaining a replacement.

Taking advantage of the pick of a near-relation's goods before the remainder was dispersed by public auction or otherwise was something John Hervey was to do several times during his long life, including in 1709 following the death of his father-in-law and in 1727 from the estate of Lady Howard of Effingham, his wife's aunt.[50] He also bought second-hand pieces directly from goldsmiths, as already touched upon, and in later life he got a taste for auctions as well. The account books record three that he attended, the first being that of Brigadier Munden in April 1726 at which he bought 'a Copy of Rubens's Bacchanal', ten black leather chairs, 'a sett of Knives & Forkes at 18s' and 'a Case of 12 Agatt handled Knives, 12 Forkes Ditto, & 12 silver spoons at 10£:10s'.[51] A year later he bought '12 gilt Knives, 12 Spoons & 12 Forks, weighing 131 ounces at 5s.8½d' at the Duchess of Shrewsbury's sale[52] and, most momentously of all, in 1737, he acquired the Earl of Scarsdale's weighty epergne of 1724–5 by Paul de Lamerie[53] of which the casters, cruets and central dish survive (see cat. 11–13). All of these pieces of silver were ornate or in some other way distinctive and they were also considerable bargains, it being likely that on the epergne alone Lord Bristol (as John Hervey was by then) saved between £55 and £70 against the price of having such a piece new-made (see cat. 11).

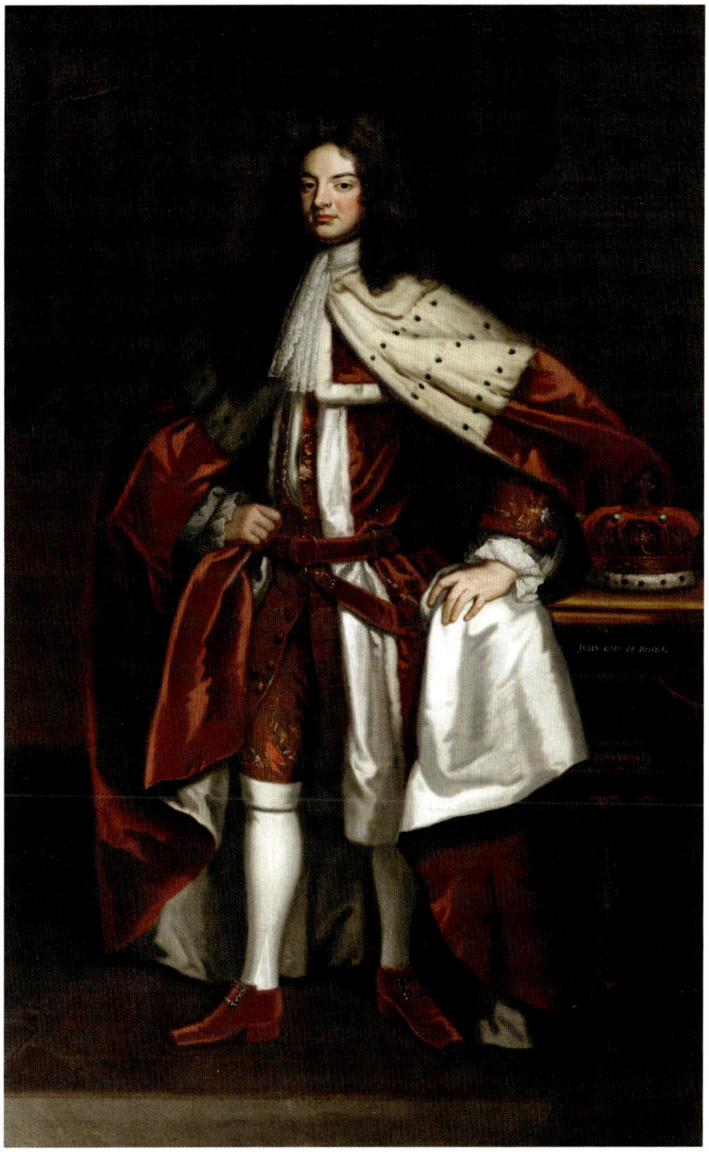

FIG. 7 / *John Hervey, 1st Earl of Bristol* by Eenoch Seeman the younger after Sir Godfrey Kneller, 1738. Showing the Earl in his robes for the coronation of George I including the coronet acquired from Louis Cuny (see appendix 1). National Trust, Ickworth.

NEW PLATE

John Hervey could not have satisfied all his silver requirements through second-hand plate even if he had wanted to, and the majority was bought new, particularly where the occasion required the very best and most up-to-date. Thus on moving into the Hervey town house in St James's Square in December 1698[54] he immediately acquired from David Willaume I what must have been a magnificent series of sconces.[55] There were eight of silver-bordered glass with two matching 'Chimney Sconces' for the drawing room and a further set of eight plus chimney sconces, described as 'great' and without glass, which were probably for the principal bedchamber as were the surviving 'very large sconces' supplied to Lord Warrington for Dunham Massey in 1730 by Peter Archambo.[56] The silver for the glass sconces was charged at 6s 6d per ounce and that for the 'great' sconces' at 7s, indicating that all were new. As in his previous houses, Hervey also spent lavishly on trimmings for the hangings which, coming from Dufresnoy again and costing the enormous sum of £160, must have contained precious metal thread.[57] The need for an impressive display of silver would have been kept sharply in focus in succeeding years by the burgeoning collection of his next door neighbour in St James's Square (at No. 5), Thomas Wentworth, 3rd Lord Raby and 1st Earl of Strafford (1672–1739). In 1701–2 he had acquired plate worth just over £556, also from David Willaume I, and to that was added two lots of perquisite plate (see chapter 3 for an explanation) as ambassador successively in Berlin and at The Hague and a magnificent set of silver furniture from Augsburg.[58]

The patronage of the Duchess of Marlborough resulted in Hervey's political and social star rising rapidly in the early years of Queen Anne's reign, bringing a peerage in 1703, as Baron Hervey of Ickworth, and the company of some of the greatest in the land. He dined with the Duke of Devonshire at Chatsworth and the Earl of Carlisle at Castle Howard in 1706, his daughter Ann had as godparents the following year the Queen, the Duchess of Somerset and the Marquess of Kent (Lord Chamberlain), and on New Year's Day, 1712, 'ye day after ye queen had taken ye command of ye army from ye Duke of Marlborough' he had the Duke dining with him at St James's Square together with Lords Somers, Cowper, Godolphin, Sunderland, Halifax, Portland, Wharton and Scarborough and the Duke of Devonshire. Marlborough returned the following week with Prince Eugene of Savoy and in November 1714, just weeks after being created Earl of Bristol (fig. 7), King George I 'did me ye honour to supp with me at my house in St James's Square'.[59] It must have been to bring his dining plate up to a sufficient quantity and quality that in 1703 James Chambers had supplied Hervey with '22 new Dishes & 3 Doz: of Plates weighed in all 1668 ou: 05 dwtt at 10d ffashion' (see appendix 1). These were of a sufficient weight and thick grade to be able to be converted to fashionable new plates for his grandson in the early 1750s (see cat. 35) whereas no evidence survives of those acquired in the 1690s, nor of any he might have inherited from his father or from the Carrs. It is likely, therefore, that some had been exchanged already and others were not robust enough to be reworked without melting after his death.

The accumulated collection of the 1st Earl

The quantity of dinner plates Lord Bristol had at his disposal following the 1703 purchase is impossible to prove in the absence both of inventories and of consistently detailed accounts but it is likely to have been at least five dozen. That was what was held by both Thomas Coke (subsequently 1st Earl of Leicester)[60] and George Lee, 2nd Earl of Lichfield,[61] contemporaries of similar wealth and position. In addition they both had twenty-one dishes compared to Lord Bristol's twenty-two of 1703; around twenty seems to have been a typical quantity to accompany five to six dozen plates, as witnessed by a number of cases amongst George Wickes' clients. Sir Jacob Bouverie, 3rd Bt (subsequently Viscount Folkestone) in 1738 and Joseph Ledson in 1742, for instance, purchased five and six dozen plates respectively with eighteen and twenty-one dishes.[62] In contrast Lord Montfort's nine dozen plates were accompanied by thirty-three dishes in 1743 and the Earl of Kildare's seven dozen by thirty in 1747.[63]

Lord Bristol must also have augmented his cutlery over the years and most probably had the same number of knives and forks as plates. He also had dessert silver, including the set of gilt cutlery acquired from the Duchess of Shrewsbury's sale, and there must have been salts and all the other accoutrements of the table, which expanded in range as the century progressed. For the sideboard there was display plate, including the ewer and basin acquired in 1696, the cup and cover bought from Baptist May's estate, 'a great silver nurld Dish' which came in 1708 and the 'large gilt cup, cover and salver' received as a royal christening gift from the Jewel Office in 1716, George I having stood sponsor to his daughter Louisa the previous year.[64] Plenty of silver for lighting is referred to in the accounts, such as the sconces already mentioned and some of the surviving candlesticks (see, for instance, cat. 3), along with salvers, items for serving tea (cat. 14), coffee (cat. 15) and chocolate (cat. 5), culinary wares (cat. 10 and 16), inkstands or standishes and some chamber plate. Unlike Dunham Massey, where there was sufficient of the latter for the occupants of all ten principal bedrooms to perform their ablutions using silver vessels,[65] only four pieces are named in Lord Bristol's accounts, a shaving basin and pot in 1689 and two chamber pots, one in 1697 and the other in 1716.

SILVER IN LONDON AND AT ICKWORTH

There probably was a certain amount more chamber plate than is articulated but the impression given by the accounts and what survives today is that investment was concentrated on items for use in public rather than private spaces. Once again this is in contrast to Dunham Massey where silver was provided liberally for every conceivable domestic use, whether on display or not. This is in part explained by another key difference between the two collections: Lord Warrington's plate was kept in its entirety in the country, the Earl never having a town house and only ever visiting briefly, whereas the Hervey silver was almost all in London, with 6 St James's Square serving as the primary residence of the family until the completion of the Earl-Bishop's vast new house at Ickworth in the 1820s. House guests would be comparatively rare in London, those coming to dinner and supper being able to return to their own abodes at night, whereas in the country that would not often have been practicable. The emphasis was on London for the Herveys because, although Lord Bristol increasingly retreated to Suffolk after 1715, many of the rest of the family remained inextricably linked with the Court, Parliament and society. The Countess of Bristol was Lady-in-Waiting to Caroline of Ansbach as Princess of Wales and Queen, Lord Hervey was an MP then Vice-Chamberlain of the Household and finally Lord Privy Seal, and his younger brothers Thomas and Felton both had minor Court appointments as well as serving successively as Members of Parliament for Bury St Edmunds.[66]

Some silver would, of course, have been required at Ickworth and guests other than close family did occasionally stay, such as the Duke and Duchess of Grafton and Sir Thomas Hanmer in September, 1709, plus there were occasions when display was required such as on 31 August, 1710 when Grafton, Sir Philip Parker, 3rd Bt '& ye whole Corporation of Bury St. Edmunds dined with me at Ickworth'.[67] It was not, however, a great show-place like Blenheim or Castle Howard, or even Ditchley and Dunham Massey. The house that Lord Bristol finally gained possession of on the death of his aunt in 1700 had been reduced to near-ruin by many years of neglect and was subsequently demolished, a farmhouse (Ickworth Lodge) being patched up for the family to reside in when in Suffolk. Lord Bristol clearly intended building a suitable seat, visiting many of the finest houses of the period to gain ideas and employing Sir John Vanbrugh to whom he gave a present of plate worth £65 in 1702 (see appendix 1). He got as far as laying out a new garden[68] (fig. 8) and having the eminent architect 'sett out ye scituation of my new house, leaving a plan with me for ye same' (which, sadly, does not survive) but for one reason or another nothing happened. Reputedly an enormous loss at cards by Lady Bristol was the reason[69] but there was also no great imperative with his family so intent on being in London. Ickworth Lodge gradually expanded and improved, and there was also a very respectable house in Bury.[70] Furthermore, in the 1730s his wife built herself a fashionable and commodious residence in Bury too.[71] Even where a family did have a splendid seat in addition to a great London house it was quite common for the bulk of the silver to be kept in town, as was the case with the 1st Duke of Montagu in 1709. He had just 264 ounces of silver at Boughton in Northamptonshire in comparison to 16,229 ounces at Montagu House in Bloomsbury.[72] Suitable quantities of plate could be transported to the country on the few occasions that it might be needed there.

OVERALL WEIGHT

As to the weight of plate that Lord Bristol accumulated an analysis of the accounts shows that between 1697, when he had around 5,500 ounces (see above) and 1741, when the bulk was handed over to Lord Hervey, he had acquired another 5,800 ounces or so.[73] Taking account of the 1,236 ounces of old plate he had turned in during the same period the overall total would have been in the region of 10,000 ounces. That was a perfectly respectable quantity for a man of his position and wealth at the time, comparing favourably for instance with the Earl of Lichfield's 5,253 ounces 3dwt in 1743.[74] It might seem to pale into insignificance when contrasted with the 26,589 ounces 9½ dwt – more than three quarters

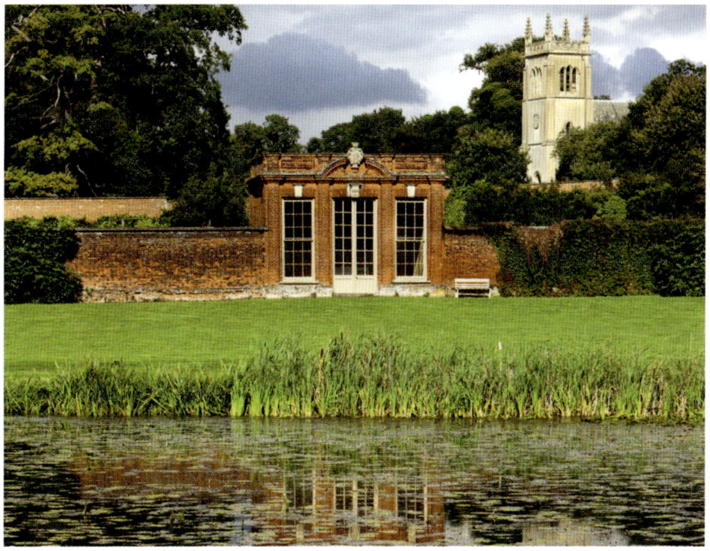

FIG. 8 / The summer house and canal created by the 1st Earl of Bristol at Ickworth in the early 18th century as part of the setting for a new house that was never executed.

of a ton – amassed by the 2nd Earl of Warrington but that was exceptional and superior even to many ducal collections.[75] Having turned around his family's fortunes Lord Warrington was using silver as a safe way of holding his burgeoning wealth, as well as for use and display, and with only one daughter he had very little call on his income beyond his own comparatively parsimonious requirements.

Lord Bristol was just as acutely attuned towards economy but, conversely to Lord Warrington, saw his financial position gradually deteriorate over his life. It was at its strongest in the last years of the seventeenth century when he was the beneficiary of numerous legacies and stood as a mortgagee. As his multitudinous family grew, however, they had to be supported and his younger sons in particular had inherited their mother's disregard for financial restraint, so there were also regular debts and gaming losses to pay off. Lord Bristol soon found himself the mortgagor, borrowing his first sum in 1717 and owing an astonishing £29,000 by 1727.[76] Thus, having equipped himself with sufficient plate to hold his own in society by 1710 he did not have the wherewithal to make as many purchases thereafter, and he had an even more acute eye for a bargain, as in the case of the epergne.

Goldsmiths as bankers, retailers and manufacturers

During John Hervey's first and most frenetic decade of silver purchasing, from 1688 to 1698, not one of those who supplied him (detailed in appendix 2) had a registered maker's mark at Goldsmiths' Hall. Domestic plate came predominantly from well-known goldsmith-bankers – the brothers Abraham and

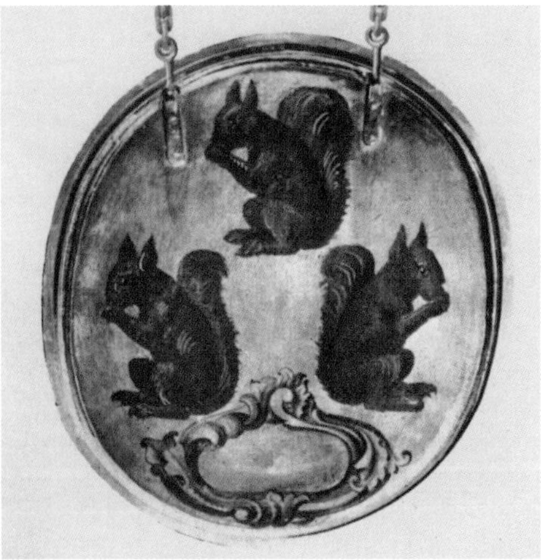

FIG. 9 / The early 18th century sign from the premises on Fleet Street occupied by the goldsmith-banker James Chambers. Oil on pewter. Barclay's Group Archives, Manchester.

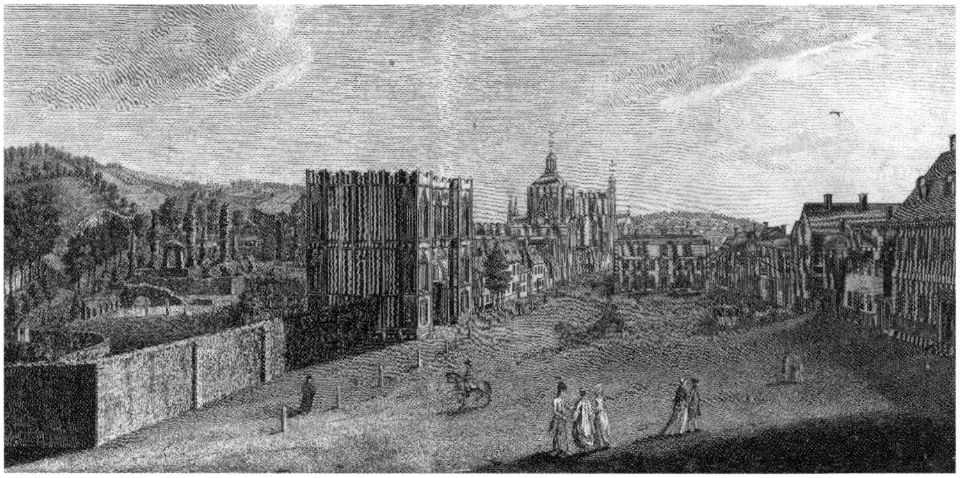

FIG. 10 / *Angel Hill in St Edmund's Bury* by P.S. Lambourn after J. Kendall, 1774. Engraving: 38.1 x 63.5 cm (15 x 25 in). Suffolk Record Office, Bury St Edmunds.

James Chambers, Robert Fowle and Richard Hoare – who would have contracted with working goldsmiths, and thus there would have been no direct contact between manufacturer and client. The only items surviving at Ickworth that might relate to these purchases are the four candlesticks by John Laughton (cat. 3) which were probably amongst the unspecified plate for which payment was made on 6 May 1696 to James Chambers (see appendix 1). He had taken over the business, based at the Sign of the Three Squirrels (fig. 9) 'over against St Dunstan's Church, Fleet Street' (appendix 2), in 1693 on the murder of his brother Abraham by highwaymen and also acted as banker to the Herveys, as did his successors into the nineteenth century.[77] James Seamer, Edward Waldegrave and Walter Compton may have had a similar business but judging by the charges per ounce they specialised in second-hand plate as certain goldsmiths are known to have done.[78] Finally, the mysterious Mrs Harache, from whom an inkstand was bought in 1690, was possibly the wife of Peter Harache I, acting as his agent, and she is also recorded as having supplied plate to the 6th Duke of Somerset the same year.[79]

All but Mrs Harache were based in or near Fleet Street and one gets the impression from the accounts that Hervey was visiting the various establishments himself – very regularly in 1696 – and mostly choosing from stock. For smaller items, in the 1690s and thereafter, he visited two of the finest toyshops of the period, those of John Deards and Charles Mather which were both also on Fleet Street.[80] As Vanessa Brett's researches have fully clarified, toys at this time were 'small and desirable luxury items' which were for adults more than for children and were predominantly metalwares.[81] Lord Bristol's purchases from Deards and Mather entirely conform to this, being a silver-headed cane, a gilt etui, gold and silver snuff boxes (see cat. 2) and gold buckles for use at George II's coronation. Other gold and silver came from clock and watchmakers (in the form of watch cases and chains), saddlers, gunsmiths, fringe-makers and tailors (gold and silver thread).

In 1699 and 1700 Hervey made purchases from David Willaume I who did have a mark registered, though whether in these cases he was supplying work stamped by him or by others is impossible to tell in the absence of surviving pieces. Given that he is known to have had a banking business the plate he sold, if not supplied by other goldsmiths, was presumably mostly made by journeymen and apprentices, particularly Huguenots, with him acting as sponsor. The other major purchase in 1700, of two pairs of andirons, was definitely not from the hand of the vending goldsmith, George Lewis, as they were imported French silver, then referred to as 'French plate' and not to be confused with the later silvered brass and copper known by the same name.

On the first occasion that Hervey definitely commissioned new plate rather than buying second hand or from stock, in 1703, he did so through James Chambers and, fortunately, on this occasion there is evidence to show that the work was carried out by John Jackson I (see cat. 35). When a new flagon was acquired for Ickworth church (cat. 6) three years later Jackson was again employed and it is probable that he was Chambers' favoured supplier, though Hervey clearly had no concept of anyone else being involved, noting in his accounts for 19 November 1696 that two dishes he had purchased were 'made by Mr Chambers'. From 1718, when the surviving bank ledgers commence, Simon Pantin seems to have dealt with most of the commissions received, as well as buying old plate that had been turned in.[82] Goldsmith-bankers were rapidly retreating from the plate business, however, and Lord Bristol's last significant purchase in this way had been in 1716. Chambers retired that year which suggests that his successors,

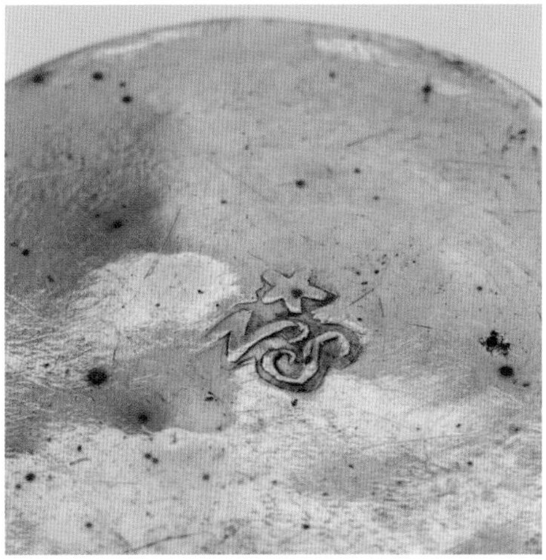

FIG. 11 / Nicholas Sprimont's maker's mark on a re-used nozzle from a later set of candlesticks. National Trust, Ickworth.

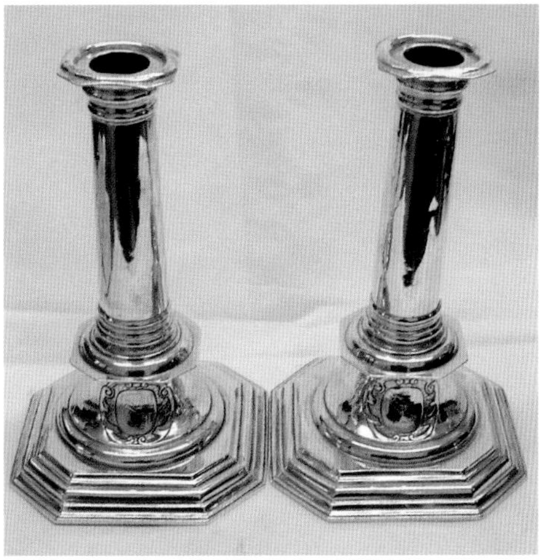

FIG. 12 / Pair of candlesticks by Ambrose Stevenson, London, 1710. Given by Carr Hervey. Silver: h. 25.4 cm (10 in). Clare College, Cambridge.

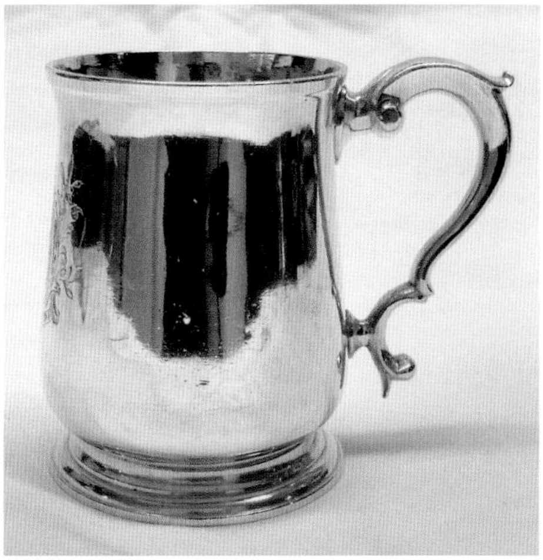

FIG. 13 / Pint mug, English, *c.*1715. Inscribed 'John Harvey'. Silver: weight 15 oz, 16 dwt. Clare College, Cambridge.

George Wanley[83] and George Cradock and, from 1720, Richard Nicholls and Abraham Fowler, did not have the requisite experience and skills to serve the Earl in the same fashion.[84] It is symptomatic of this change, which was general in the eighteenth century, that Lord Bristol began to refer to Fowler as 'my Banker' rather than 'my Goldsmith', this first occurring against the entry dated 16 October 1732.

As the major banking houses ceased supplying plate to concentrate on the business of money some retail goldsmiths broadened their spheres to provide the requisite service themselves. Essentially this was a specialisation which allowed for the growth of banking and goldsmithing, both of which were burgeoning in the eighteenth century as a consequence of Britain's increasing prosperity. Most famous of all the retail businesses today, because of the survival of a near-complete run of ledgers from 1735 (now in the Victoria and Albert Museum), is that begun by George Wickes in the 1730s which eventually became Garrards, erstwhile Crown Jewellers. Others are more shadowy but amongst them were Crespin and de Lamerie (see cat. 18) and the Willaumes acting with Edward Jordens. Given that Wickes himself was from Bury St Edmunds[85] it might have been expected that Lord Bristol would have favoured him, but he did not and there is only one related purchase in the accounts, of a coffee pot in 1733 which does not survive. He had turned to Anthony Nelme in 1721 to have the coronets on his plates and dishes rather belatedly updated following his elevation to an earldom seven years previously, but it was David Willaume I who was to get his regular custom and after a gap of some twenty-five years a succession of purchases were made from him, his son and Edward Jordens between 1725 and 1737 (see appendices 1 and 2). From surviving accounts and silver of the period it is clear that the Willaumes and Jordens had a substantial retail business in the mid-eighteenth century, significant clients other than Lord Bristol including the 4th Duke and Duchess of Beaufort and the 2nd Earl of Warrington.[86]

Though the great bulk of Lord Bristol's plate came from the smartest goldsmiths and toymen in London he had always made some purchases in Bury St Edmunds which was a comparatively sophisticated and well served regional centre in the 18th century in which the gentry and nobility of the locality would congregate for assemblies and for the two annual fairs (fig. 10).[87] Thus in October, 1700 he paid one of the town's shopkeepers, Samuel Lanseter, for two silver jars which had been delivered at St Matthew's Fair the previous month, and in 1709 mourning rings in respect of the Earl's lately deceased father-in-law came from the Bury goldsmith John Chamberlain. The major tradesman in Bury to receive Lord Bristol's patronage, however, was Peter Rogers who is described as 'silversmith' in the accounts and was evidently quite successful, being ranked as a gentleman by the time of his death in 1791.[88] He supplied numerous of the customary gifts given at the Bury fairs as well as domestic plate and, fortunately, two pieces in the latter category survive; a coffee pot bought in 1735 (cat. 15) and a saucepan which followed in 1746 (cat. 16). Both are by London makers indicating that Rogers acquired at least some of his stock from the capital and could get hold of it quite quickly, the saucepan bearing the date letter for 1745–6.

The Earl did not entirely abandon direct contact with London after becoming a permanent resident at Ickworth, however, and one intriguing purchase was made in the last decade of his life. On 14th July 1743 Nicholas Sprimont, that most spirited of eighteenth-century designers whose *oeuvre* is so limited, was paid £25 4s 4d 'for two Pair of Silver Candlesticks'. Tragically they do not survive and may well have been exchanged relatively soon after the Earl's death in 1751 for a rather flimsy set of twelve filled candlesticks (cat. 62), at least three of the reused nozzles of which bear Sprimont's mark (fig. 11). It is possible, perhaps probable, that Lord Bristol was completing a purchase initiated by his eldest son, Lord Hervey, who by July 1743 was fatally ill at Ickworth, incapable of writing and thus of executing business.[89]

Silver of the 1st Earl's children

The only silver to survive that is associated with Lord Bristol's children by his first wife is the pair of candlesticks of 1710 by Ambrose Stevenson (fig. 12) presented that year to Clare College, Cambridge by Carr Hervey (1691–1723). The college also has a pint mug (fig. 13) inscribed 'John Harvey' which was probably given by Lord Bristol's eldest son by his second union, to Elizabeth Felton, on his entry in 1713.[90] Two of Lord Bristol's daughters by Elizabeth, Ann (1707–71) and Louisa (1715–70), were godchildren of the reigning monarch, and as such there was an entitlement to gifts of silver-gilt engraved with the royal arms. According to the Jewel Office delivery book Pierre Platel provided 'two large gilt Sallvers' weighing 110 ounces (the allowance for a baron) on 2 April 1708[91] in respect of Ann Hervey but her father noted in his accounts that he paid Platel 'ye french silversmith' £63 10s 'more than ye office allowd for Nanns [Ann's] silver frame & ye 5 covers to it' (see appendix 1). Thus the gilt salvers were shown to the Jewel Office for form's sake and the value was actually put towards a plate ring and five plates, the additional cost being made up in cash. Although Lord Hervey, as the Earl then was, referred to the frame as his daughter's the gifts were in fact directed to the parents rather than the children and this allocation plus the 'large gilt Cup Cover and Salver' weighing 130 ounces (the allowance for an earl) of 1716 relating to Lady Louisa[92] would have been subsumed into the family plate.[93] Lady Ann, who remained a spinster and was set up in her own house near Ickworth by her father, did however have her own silver, paying tax on 600 ounces[94] and mentioning a set of gilt dressing plate and a coffee pot in her will as well as two gold snuff boxes with portraits of Lord Bristol and her brother William.[95]

Of the Earl's five younger sons by Elizabeth Felton who survived childhood, all are likely to have had some silver. The querulous and scandalous Thomas (he ran off with his cousin's wife), who lived in Old Bond Street in London, paid excise on 800 ounces of plate in the 1760s,[96] his next brother William was given a case of a 'Dozen Spoons, Knives & Forks' by Lord Bristol in 1726 (appendix 1), Henry would have had use of the family plate of his heiress wife, Catherine Aston, and Felton, the youngest, inherited a life interest in Lady

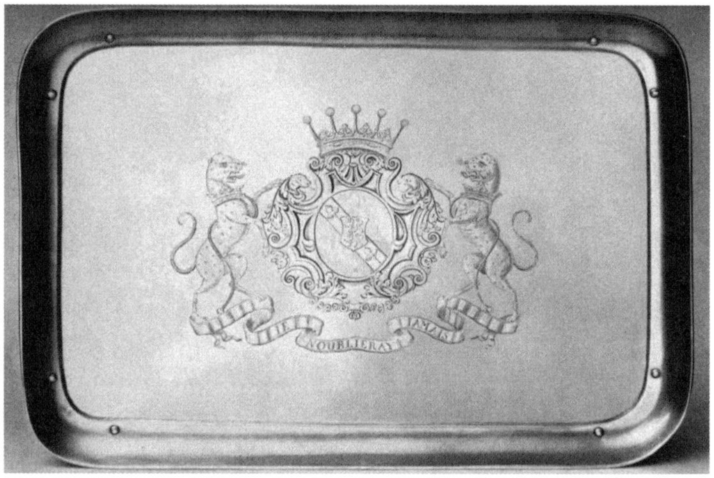

FIG. 14 / Salver by Robert Cooper, London, 1712. Engraved with the arms of the 1st Earl of Bristol. Silver: w. 43.8 cm (17¼ in); weight 62 oz, 4 dwt. Sotheby's.

Bristol's Bury house along with all the plate 'therein at the time of my [the Countess's] decease'.[97] Amongst the latter must have been the large oblong salver by Robert Cooper of 1712 (fig. 14) which subsequently descended with other of Felton Hervey's silver to the Lords Cottesloe and was sold at Sotheby's in London on the 4th March, 1965.[98] Because of this chance alienation from the rest of the family plate the salver escaped melting or re-engraving in the 1750s and is the only piece of silver still to bear the arms of Lord Bristol as an earl.[99]

LORD HERVEY

In a letter to Lady Mary Wortley Montagu written from Bath on 12 September 1741, John, Lord Hervey (fig. 15), Lord Bristol's eldest son and heir, requested her to address future correspondence 'to my House in St. James's Square, wch. my Father has given me with all his Pictures, Medals, Books, Plate & Furniture, & will be ready to receive me, by the help of forty men I have now at work there, at my return from this place'.[100] The Earl had been released from an obligation to maintain a London establishment by the death of his wife in the spring. Even before this happened, however, Lord Hervey had amassed an impressive collection, as can be seen from the records and from the few pieces of his silver that survive at Ickworth either intact (cat. 17–20) or refashioned (cat. 35–40).

In 1720, when John Hervey was still a younger son but was the heir to his mother's Felton estates, Lord Bristol had given him £315 'to buy him silver Plates & Dishes' (appendix 1) on setting up a household after marriage. That would have been enough to have secured 900 ounces at a charge of say seven shillings per ounce, perhaps equating to two dozen plates, eight or so dishes and flatware and cutlery.[101] A further dozen plates came from Lord Bristol in February 1726 and the following year he also bought for Lord Hervey a cistern weighing 317 ounces, about the same as his own (cat. 1), from the estate of Lady Howard of Effingham (appendix 1). Hervey seems to have begun making his own purchases around 1730 and the surviving ice pails by Philip Rollos (cat. 18) and bread basket by Paul de Lamerie (cat. 19) show that his acquisitions included plate of the most spectacular and fashionable form by the finest makers of the period. More dishes and plates followed in the 1730s and 1740s (see cat. 35–40), many of them marked by Paul Crespin who was probably acting as his principal supplier in much the same way as the Willaumes and Jordens did for his father (see cat. 18 for a discussion). A final and substantial addition of silver could have come in the year of Lord Hervey's death when he was bequeathed a life interest in Buckingham House and its plate by the Duchess of Buckingham, but it appears that he immediately passed it on to the ultimate heir, the Duke's natural son Charles Sheffield.[102]

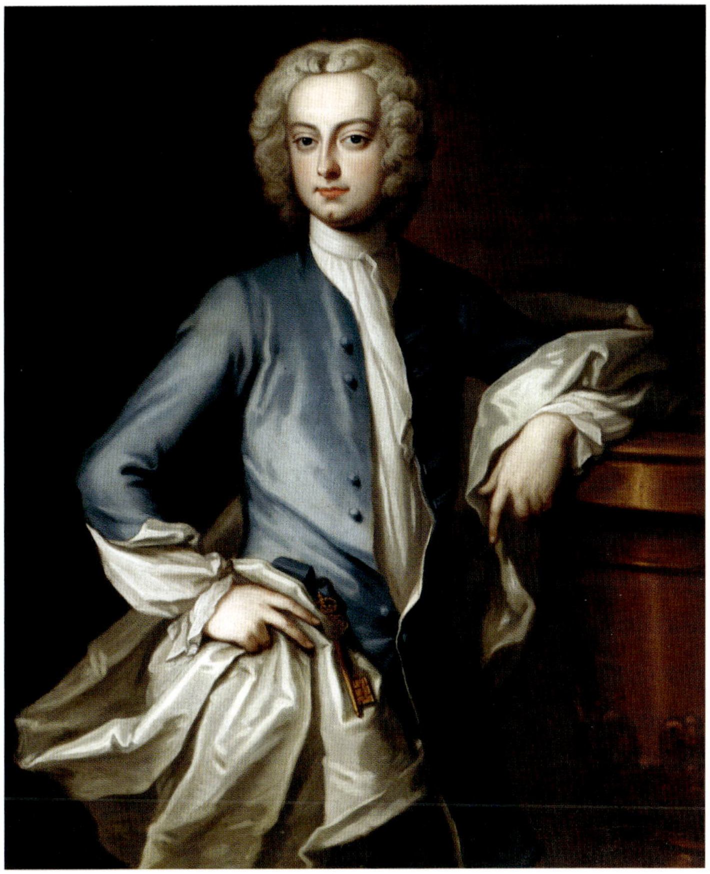

FIG. 15 / *John, Lord Hervey* by John Fayram, *c.*1737. With the Vice Chamberlain's gold key of office at his waist. Oil on canvas: 127 x 101.6 cm (50 x 40 in). National Trust, Ickworth.

LADY HERVEY

A woman in the eighteenth century was probably at her most independent as a well provided-for widow and Lady Hervey (fig. 16), who was in that position following the death of her husband in 1743, made the absolute most of it after what cannot have been the easiest of marriages.[103] This charming and vivacious individual was described in eulogistic terms by a number of her contemporaries including the 4th Earl of Chesterfield who, as late as 1750, wrote that she had been 'bred all her life at courts, of which she has acquired all the easy good-breeding, and politeness, without the frivolousness ... No woman ever had more than she has, le ton de la parfaitement bonne compagnie, les manières engageantes, et le je ne sais quoi qui plaît'.[104] In her widowhood she regularly visited Ickworth to see her father-in-law, of whom she was fond, went for long spells to France and built herself a smart new London house to the design of Henry Flitcroft in St James's Place overlooking Green Park.[105] She described it and its 'altering, fitting up and completing' as her chief 'amusement'[106] and it was there that she entertained a select group of witty and intelligent friends including Lord Chesterfield, David Hume, Horace Walpole, William Pulteney, Earl of Bath and the French philosopher, Claude Adrien Helvétius.[107] Lady Hervey employed a French cook, Jacques Lalliet, and select dinners were given, such as that described by the Earl of March (subsequently 4th Duke of Queensberry, 'Old Q') in 1762:

> *I have just returned from the* Hôtel de Milady. *At dinner Lord and Lady Stormont, Mrs Dives, Stanley, Morris, Augustus [Hervey] and myself. Never was anything so French as her dinner and the manner of its being served. It is a charming house, and as I have rather a partiality for the French I am very glad to have the entree.*[108]

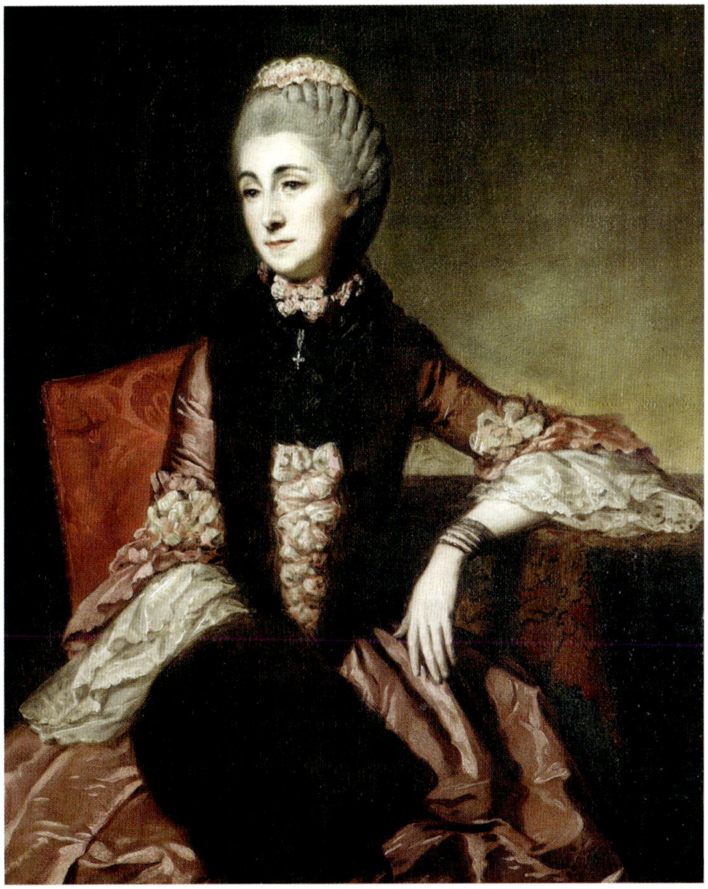

FIG. 16 / *Mary Lepel, Lady Hervey in old age* by Johann Zoffany, *c.*1765. Oil on canvas: 43.2 x 35.6 cm (17 x 14 in). National Trust, Ickworth.

Lady Hervey purchased furniture from Pierre Langlois and Paul Saunders, fireplaces from Thomas Carter, luxuries from the jeweller and toyman Susanna Passavant[109] and for plate, which was very much needed in the context of her entertaining, she went to Frederick Kandler. He was fast establishing a large retail business (see chapter two) and Lady Hervey's account with Goslings reveals that between 1752 and her death in 1768 she paid Kandler £665 2s, all but £34 of it in the 1750s (appendix 3). This would have equated to about 1,500 ounces if taken at a generous 8s per ounce, and Lady Hervey already had some silver which her husband had high-handedly permitted her 'to dispose of' in his will.[110] In total she declared 2,000 ounces for Plate Tax which seems about right and for which she paid £5 per annum between 1757 and 1767.[111] Only a few pieces now remain at Ickworth (cat. 21–4), with her arms engraved in a lozenge as is correct for a woman, but they suggest that her taste was for simple, good quality and practical pieces to serve their respective purposes in receiving guests at St James's Place.

On the 2nd September 1768, just a few months after her last purchase of silver, Lady Hervey died and bequeathed a life interest in the house and its contents to her eldest son, the 2nd Earl of Bristol, with the stipulation that all the 'Goods, ffurniture, Plate, Books and pamphlets, pictures, China and all other Ornaments' should be kept with it. He took no notice of this and some at least of the china was taken to St James's Square,[112] furniture went to Leasingham Hall[113] on his Lincolnshire estate and most of the silver was probably despatched back to Kandler's workshop to be melted. The little that survives was presumably passed to other family members or tolerated to remain because it was useful.

---

1. Copinger 1911, p. 69. The mullet in English heraldry is the five-pointed star representing the spiked revolving disc of a spur. Mullets are the principal charges of the Drury coat of arms.
2. Gage 1838, pp. 203–5.
3. Copinger 1911, p. 73.
4. Glanville 1990, pp. 48–9.
5. Earwaker 1884, p. 21.
6. Lincolnshire Archives, 2ANC3/A/41, Last will and testament of William, 11th Lord Willoughby de Eresby, 4 May, 1526.
7. See Rothwell 2012, pp. 64–5.
8. Hervey 1857, p. 367.
9. http://www.historyofparliamentonline.org/volume/1509-1558/member/harvey-nicholas-1491-1532, accessed 29 December 2015.
10. Glanville 1990, p. 103.
11. Rothwell 2012, p. 65.
12. Strachey 1998, p. 37.
13. Gage 1822, p. 203.
14. Hervey 1857, p. 386.
15. Ibid. and 'St. James's Square: No 6', in *Survey of London*, Vols 29 and 30: St James Westminster, part 1, ed. F.H.W. Sheppard (London, 1960), pp. 103–109 http://www.british-history.ac.uk/survey-london/vols29-30/pt1/pp103-109, accessed 28 December 2015.
16. TNA, PROB 11/363/4, Will of John Hervey of Ickworth, proved 14 February 1679/80. Elizabeth also received the income from his existing lands, including Ickworth.
17. TNA, PROB 11/455/358, Will of Dame Elizabeth Hervey, proved 11 May, 1700. She appears already to have alienated her personal estate to a servant, Thomas Hall, who had subsequently acted 'unfaithfully and treacherously' towards her.
18. http://www.historyofparliamentonline.org/volume/1660-1690/member/hervey-sir-thomas-1625-94. Sir Thomas was assessed by his colleague Samuel Pepys as 'such an idle fellow as he have £500 a year for nothing'.
19. TNA, PROB 11/420/420, Will of Sir Thomas Hervey, proved 26 June 1694.
20. Hervey 1894b, vol. 1, p. xiv.
21. All these papers are in the Suffolk Record Office. The diary and extensive extracts from the accounts are transcribed in Hervey 1894a and the letters in Hervey 1894b.
22. Hervey 1894a, pp. 88–9 and 132–3. The stables may have been those associated with the single, large house at the end of King Street which was not then open to St James's Street. See 'King Street', in *Survey of London*, Vols 29 and 30, pp. 295–307, http://www.british-history.ac.uk/survey-london/vols29-30/pt1/pp295-307, accessed 3 January 2016.
23. Bristol Accounts 1688–1742, disbursements for 1689 and 1690. Many but not all of these are cited in Hervey 1894a, pp. 136–141. The sash windows, by John Yeates at a cost of £9, were paid for on 9 August 1689. Gerrit Jensen was paid £57 for the glasses, tables and stands on 19 September 1689.
24. Ibid., 16 October 1689. Only 15½ yards of the 'orange and Silver stuff' was supplied by Paul Clowdsley which would not have been enough on its own for the bedchamber but may have been additional to a quantity already procured.
25. Ibid. Frenoye was paid in two instalments, £50 on 1 October 1689 and £155 on the 31st. He was Paul Dufresnoy who was one of the principal suppliers of silk and metal thread trimmings in London from the 1660s, including to the Duke of Lauderdale for Ham House and the Earl of Exeter for Burleigh and for Drayton House. Information from Annabel Westman. See Westman 2013, pp. 250 and 255 and Beard 1997, p. 17.
26. See appendix 1 for these payments. Boiling in this context is likely to mean pickling, involving the placing of the silver in a solution of sulphuric acid to remove stains.
27. Private baptisms were prohibited under a Royal Order of 1560 but they had become the norm for wealthy Anglicans during the Commonwealth when fonts were considered trappings of Popery, and they were tolerated thereafter. I am grateful to Philippa Glanville for this information. Surviving baptismal basins from churches, such as that from St Paul's, Deptford (see Oman 1957, plate 146a), are very close in form to wash-hand basins. That at Uppark in Sussex of 1692 by Anthony Nelme (NT inv. no. 2900041) is recorded as having been used for the Christening of Sir Harry Fetherstonhaugh, 2nd Bt, in 1754. See also Schroder 2009, cat. 231, pp. 624–7.
28. Bristol Accounts 1688–1742, 31 December 1690.
29. Mrs Harache must be the silversmith recorded at the corner of Great Suffolk Street in 1694. See Grimwade 1990, p. 533.
30. Lomax and Rothwell 2006, cat. 21, pp. 70–1.
31. See Mitchell 1994 for a discussion of the Fowle family's business.
32. Hervey 1894a, p. 19.
33. John van Collema was a Dutch merchant who is known to have also supplied 'India' goods and china to Queen Mary and the Dukes of Montagu and Somerset. See Ferguson 2016, p. 116.
34. Bristol Accounts 1688–1742, 17 April 1691, 17 July 1691, 24 December 1689, 10 and 17 December 1692.
35. Hervey 1894b, vol. 1, p. xv.
36. Hervey 1894a, p. 23.
37. Schroder 1988b, cat. 25, pp. 112–15.
38. Lomax and Rothwell 2006, p. 171.
39. Hervey 1894a, p. 25.
40. Heal 1935, pp. 239–40, gives James Seamer/Seamour/Seymour at the sign of 'Flower-de-luce [fleur-de-lis], near Serjeant's Inn, Fleet Street' 1695–1709 and at the same sign 'corner of Mitre court, Fleet street' 1693–1734.
41. Heal 1935, p. 262, Edward Waldegrave, at the sign of the 'Anchor, or Anchor & crown, Russell street, Covent Garden' 1690–1721.
42. TNA, PROB 11/420/420, Will of Sir Thomas Hervey, proved 26 June 1694. Isabella Elwes' date of death is given in Hervey 1894a, p. 310.
43. At the very highest levels the quantities of silver owned were already immense, the future 1st Duke of Devonshire acquiring 4,740 ounces in 1687 alone, including a cistern that weighed 3,496 ounces on its own. See Hayward 1959, pp. 76–7. In contrast, at the lower end of the scale, the Massingberds of Gunby had only 100 ounces of silver as late as 1723 and there was about the same at Canons Ashby in 1717.
44. Lomax and Rothwell 2006, p. 184.
45. Chetham's Library, Manchester, Raines Bequest, vol. 38, p. 465, 'An Inventory of all the Goods etc. of Richard Legh of Lime in Hanley Co Cest. Esq. decd. taken 3 Jac. 2d 1687 [31 August, 1687]…'. Only a value is given and the weight has been estimated based on 5s 2d per ounce. This is the amount given for the plate John Hervey exchanged in 1696.
46. Transcript of plate from the 1698 inventory of Belton in the National Trust curatorial files at Clumber Park. Only a value is given and, as with the Lyme inventory the weight has been estimated based on 5s 2d an ounce.
47. Dunham had slightly more, with 50 spoons and 20 forks, but still not enough to allow changes with each course.
48. Old pieces would be bought in by a goldsmith at slightly less than the metal charge on new pieces, around 5s 2d at this period, and if sold on would be charged at a few pence more per ounce, varying according to the desirability of the piece.
49. Bristol Accounts 1688–1742, 6 April 1697. These could well have had gold or silver thread in their upholstery.
50. Bristol accounts 1688–1742, 6 October 1709 and 21 January/23 April, 1727. The latter purchase included another cistern, this time for Lord and Lady Hervey. It does not survive.
51. Ibid., 9 April 1726. Richard Munden (d.19 September 1725) had served under Marlborough and was still in the army at the time of his death.
52. Ibid., 17 April 1727. This was Adelhida Paleotti, widow of the Duke of Shrewsbury. She died on the 29 June 1726. The agate-handled knives and forks could have been those that survived at Ickworth in 1951, described as *c.*1695, although at that time they were said to have been given to the 1st Viscount Templetown by the King of Prussia. They do not seem to have passed to the National Trust and are not in the house today. See Death duties list *c.*1951, p. 14.
53. Ibid., 1 April 1737. Nicholas Leke, 4th and last Earl of Scarsdale died on 17 July 1736.
54. Hervey 1894a, p. 29. 'Dec. 22. – Thursday, dear wife with ye whole family removd from Jermyn Street to my house in St James Square'. Initially he was the tenant of his aunt, Elizabeth Hervey, who had a life interest but on her death in 1700 it became his outright.
55. Bristol accounts 1688–1742, 17 and 20 January and 21 February 1689/90.
56. Lomax and Rothwell 2006, cat. 46, pp. 104–8.
57. Bristol accounts 1688–1742, 8 May 1699.
58. Lomax 2014, pp. 66–86.
59. Hervey 1894a, pp. 45–6, 55 and 62.
60. Mortlock 1997, p. 555, silver acquired from Paul de Lamerie in 1718.
61. Murdoch 2006, p. 152, from the transcript of the 1743 inventory of Ditchley in Oxfordshire.
62. Wickes Ledgers, VAM 1 1735–40, f. 142, 10 February 1737/8 and VAM 2 1740–8, f. 69, 16 August 1742.
63. Ibid, VAM 2 1740–8, f. 86, 12 February 1742/3 and

VAM 3 1747–50, f. 1.
64. Jewel Office Delivery Book 1698–1732, f. 211. See appendix 1 for the other items.
65. Lomax and Rothwell 2006, p. 97.
66. Hervey 1894b, vol. 1, pp. xv–xxi.
67. Ibid., pp. 50 and 52.
68. Ibid., p. 66, 25 October 1717, 'I narrowly escaped from being drowned in my new Canall at Spring Garden in ye parke'.
69. Strachey 1998, p. 50.
70. The Bury house, presumably that inherited from his father, was good enough for the Duchess of Grafton to stay there for a week in December 1716. Lord and Lady Bristol 'waited on her there to entertain her all ye time'. See Hervey 1894a, p. 64.
71. The Manor House, Honey Hill, Bury St Edmunds. Lord Bristol recorded in his diary that he and Lady Bristol spent their first night in the house on 25 September, 1738.
72. Murdoch 2006, p. 61 and NRO, MH6 / Table 17, 'His Grace the late Duke of Montague's Plate Weighed and Valued by Geo. Lewis March 28th 1709'. As late as 1860 some 15 pages were devoted to a partial list of the Cavendish plate at Devonshire House whereas everything at Chatsworth was able to be fitted within four pages. 'An Account of Plate belonging to His Grace, The Duke of Devonshire, at the Several Residences, 1860', Devonshire Collection, Chatsworth House.
73. Where rates per ounce are not given a conservative 6s has been assumed.
74. Murdoch 2006, p. 152.
75. Lomax and Rothwell 2006, pp. 24 and 173. Even the proverbially lavish 1st Duke of Chandos could not beat this, having about 20,600 ounces at Cannons and his house in St James's Square in 1725. See Jenkins 2005.
76. Bristol accounts 1688–1742, 5 March 1717 and 30 March, 1 April, 29 April, 6 June and 9 February 1727–8. His principal mortgagee was the Duke of Marlborough.
77. Matthews and Tuke 1926, pp. 80 and 82. The bank was known from 1794 as Gosling and Sharpe and amalgamated with Barclays in 1896 (pp. 89–90). A complete run of bank ledgers survives from 1718.
78. John Hopkins, who supplied to Lord Bristol in 1739, is a case in point: see Grimwade 1990, p. 551.
79. Cousins 2005, p. 74.
80. In early 1729 he also made a purchase from another toyshop, that of Paul Girard.
81. Brett 2014, p. 16.
82. See for instance Goslings ledgers, 130/8, f. 120, Simon Pantin's account for February 1724 to March 1726.
83. George Wanley was James Chambers' nephew but predeceased him: Will proved October 1729. TNA, PROB 11/633/16. Chambers' great-niece (and Wanley's niece), Dorothy Hutton, married Simon Yorke 1 of Erddig and the Hutton plate now forms part of the collection there.
84. Matthews and Tuke 1926, p. 82. Lord Bristol did make one final purchase of plate through his bankers, acquiring a new-made 'Scollop Plate' in April, 1726 for £8 13s 4d (see appendix 3).
85. Barr 1980, p. 1.
86. See Sale 1995, pp. 386–7 and 390–1 and Lomax and Rothwell 2006, p. 29.
87. When the Duchess of Grafton stayed with Lord Bristol in Bury in 1716 it was for two assemblies during the December fair. Hervey 1894a, p. 64.
88. TNA, PROB 11/1204/46, Will of Peter Rogers, proved 9/4/1791.
89. *Daily Gazetteer*, London, Friday 22 July 1743, 'The Right Hon. the Lord Hervey, son to the Earl of Bristol, lies dangerously ill at his Father's Seat at Ickworth in Suffolk.' Lord Hervey's brother Felton patronised Sprimont after he had set up the Chelsea porcelain manufactory, paying him £25 5s 6d on 12 December 1757 and subsequently settling £1 18s 1½ of 'Charges on china ware sent to Hamburgh'. He was presumably acting as an agent for someone abroad.
90. Jones 1939, pp. 20–1 and 48, plate IX.
91. Jewel Office delivery book 1698–1732, f. 114.
92. Ibid., f. 211. The weights of christening plate given to different ranks were strictly codified (with some slight variations up to the accession of George II) as follows: a gentleman, knight or baronet received 100 oz, a baron 110 oz, a viscount 120 oz, an earl or the son of a duke if of lower rank 130 oz, a marquess 160 oz and a duke 200 oz. Occasional grants at a lower rate were made to ambassadors and other resident foreigners, the Marquis of Tabuerniga from Spain receiving 120 oz in 1748, see Jewel Office Delivery Book 1732–93, f. 95. A variance of a few ounces (usually above) was tolerated.
93. They do not survive and were almost certainly melted by the 2nd Earl in the early 1750s.
94. Plate tax lists 1757–62, p. 813. A tax on plate owned was introduced in 1756 and lasted until 1777. Payments were on a sliding scale according to weight owned up to a maximum of 4,000 oz. See Sale 2008, pp. 114–5.
95. Partial transcript of the Will of Lady Ann Hervey, proved 1771, in the family scrapbook of Geraldine, Marchioness of Bristol, National Trust, Ickworth House. Lady Ann had inherited the toilet service from her mother, see Hervey 1894a, p. 234.
96. Plate tax lists 1757–62, p. 150. The rate for 800 oz was £2 per annum.
97. Hervey 1894a, p. 232. The bequest to the Hon. Felton Hervey took effect on Lord Bristol's death in 1751.
98. The salver was recently with S.J. Shrubsole, New York.
99. Sotheby's, 4 March 1965, lot 169.
100. Transcript by Gervase Jackson-Stops of SRO 941/47/2, National Trust, Westley Bottom.
101. Two dozen plates might have weighed 450 ounces and eight dishes 330 ounces based on those supplied to Everard Fawkener by George Wickes in 1735. See Wickes ledgers, VAM 1 1735–40, f. 38.
102. Stuart 1936, p. 118. The Duchess's grandson Constantine Phipps had recently married Lord Hervey's daughter Lepel.
103. Another woman who did the same was Barbara Hutton, mother of Dorothy Yorke of Erddig. She had the use of the family house and carriage and used her plentiful income to commission some superb pieces of silver, now at Erddig.
104. Dobson 1896, p. 315–6, quoting Lord Chesterfield's letter to his son of 22 October 1750.
105. Payments to Flitcroft in Lady Hervey's account with Goslings commence in 1748 and continue intermittently until 1761. Goslings ledgers, 130/21 ff. 168–9, 130/23 f. 244, 130/25 f. 218, 130/27 f. 185 and 130/29 f. 171. The house, no. 25, was destroyed in the Second World War.
106. Croker 1821, p. 261
107. Dobson 1896, pp. 319–22.
108. Stuart 1936, p. 179.
109. Goslings ledgers, 130/23 f. 244, 130/25 ff. 218–9, 130/27 f. 185 and 130/29 f. 171.
110. SRO, HA 507/5/7 – Will of John, Lord Hervey. Witnessed 23 June 1743, proved 18 August 1743.
111. Plate Tax lists 1757–62, p. 150, and Plate Tax defaulters 1768.
112. TNA, C 103/174, 'An Inventory of the Rt. Honble the Earl of Bristol's China taken in St. James's Square', 1 March 1768 to 6 June 1773.
113. Ibid, 'Goods Apprized at Leasingham for the Right Honourable the Earl of Bristol', 12 May 1775.

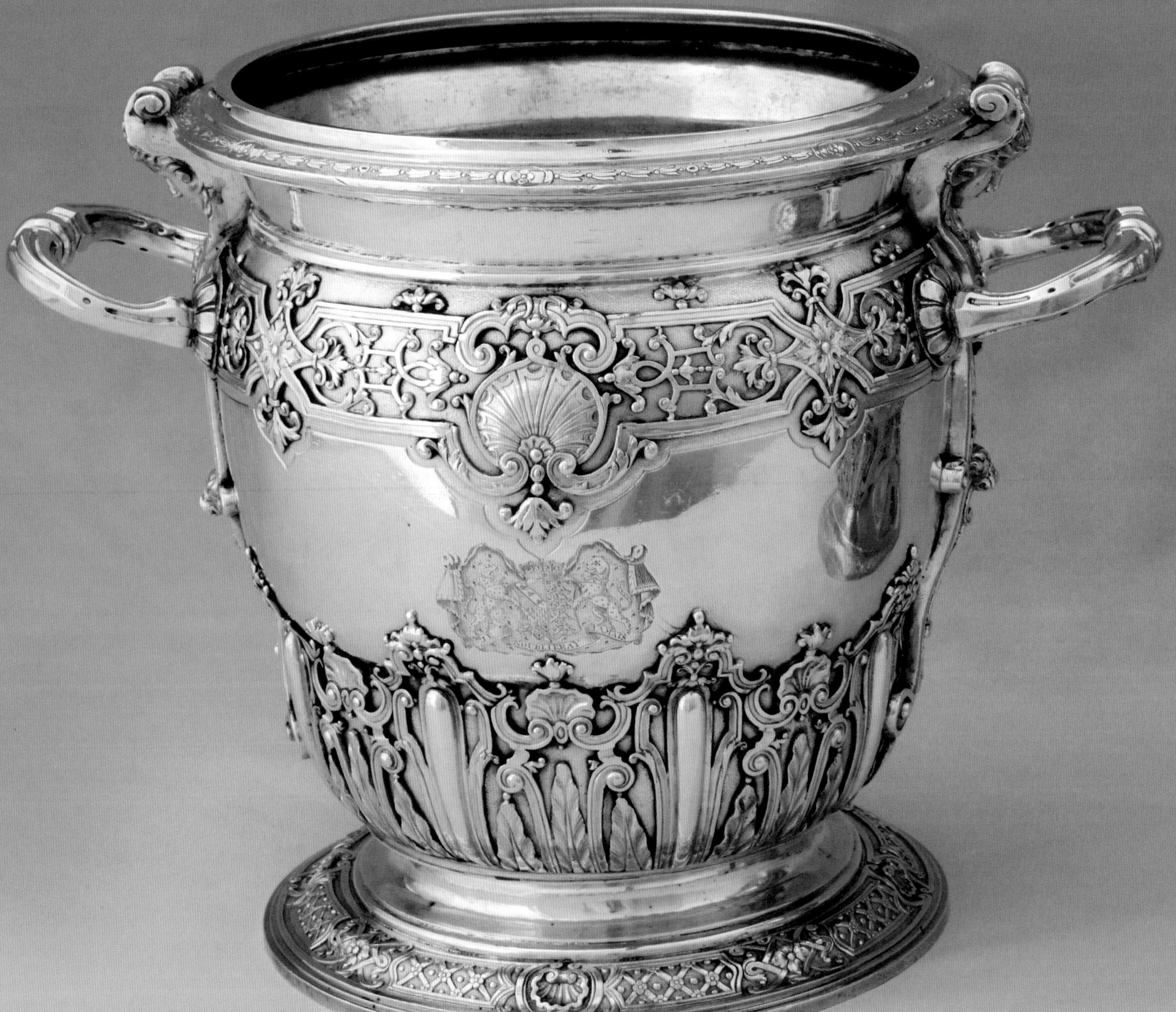

A pair of ice pails (Philip Rollos II, *c.*1730) from the silver of John, Lord Hervey and Mary Lepel, Lady Hervey (see cat. 18)

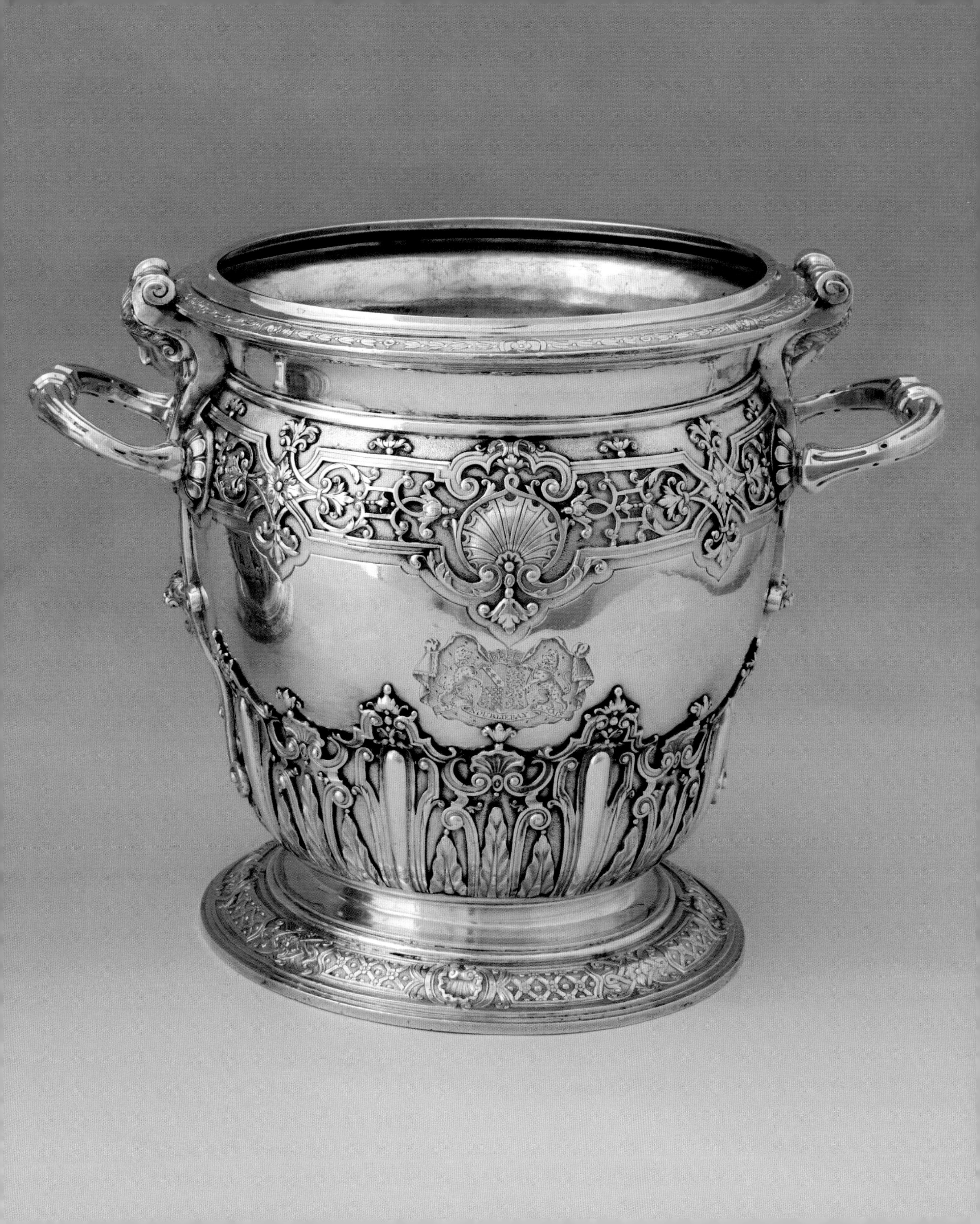

TWO

SILVER FOR THE INTERNATIONAL STAGE
THE 2ND EARL OF BRISTOL

George William Hervey (1721–75), the principal patron of the Ickworth silver collection, was born on 3 August 1721 and though not then the certain heir to his grandfather, the 1st Earl of Bristol,[1] his family was so much at the heart of court affairs that he had not one but two royal godparents: King George I and the Princess of Wales. His father, John Hervey, received the customary gift of silver-gilt from the Jewel Office and as he was under the rank of baron the lowest weight was applicable and he received 81 oz, 15 dwt.[2] It came in the form of a 'Gilt Ewer-Enchaced' which, for some reason, was not delivered until July 1724.[3]

John and his wife Mary (or Molly), dubbed the 'Birds of Paradice' by Lady Mary Wortley Montagu, showed remarkably little interest in their baby and sent him with his wet-nurse to his grandfather in Suffolk when just a month old whilst they went off to stay with that 'lively ready wit', William Pulteney.[4] Lord Bristol was unimpressed, particularly as he had just learnt of the Countess of Stamford having to fight off highwaymen in Marlborough Forest, and as it was the coachman lost his way and headed off towards Norwich. All was well in the end, however, and George arrived safely at Ickworth on 6 September 1721, proceeding to make his presence thoroughly known by screaming the house down whenever his mouth was 'not stoppd with the bubby'. He soon responded to the benign environment and to his grandfather's warm heart, however, and within a week Lord Bristol could report to the Countess that 'our grandson is so wonderfully altered for the better, both as to his looks and humour, since he came hither as is not to be imagined … yesterday … he laughed near half an hour incessantly.'[5] These characteristics of dogged determination to get what he wanted and a responsiveness to attention were to remain with George throughout his life.

EDUCATION TO BE A COURTIER

Following the death of the dissolute Carr, Lord Hervey in 1723 George was in direct line for the earldom and family estates and in the expectation that he would follow the centuries-old tradition of the Herveys and pursue a career at court, he was given a suitable education at the expense of his grandfather.[6] From the age of five he was sent to Monsieur Dennis Delaplace's 'french schoole' in London[7] which was evidently an establishment favoured by the sophisticated aristocracy as Edward Coke, the future 1st Earl of Leicester's son and heir, was there at the same time.[8] In 1731 George progressed to Westminster School, the nursing ground of countless leading figures of the eighteenth century including four prime ministers,[9] and whilst there he had additional tuition in speaking and writing French and in arithmetic from a Monsieur F.A. Pillissier, a Huguenot.[10] He would undoubtedly also have had fencing, dancing and riding lessons as had his father and uncles earlier in the century.[11]

On 7 September 1738, when just seventeen, 'my hopeful grandson George', as Lord Bristol noted in his diary, 'sett forward from London on his journey towards Geneva (by Paris) to study there' and thus to complete his education.[12] Geneva (fig. 18) was at that time an independent city-state, not yet part of Switzerland, and it had the great advantage for the aspiring British aristocrat who wanted to perfect the courtly manners of Europe, and particularly those of France, that as well as being highly cultured and French-speaking with close ties to Paris, it was also Protestant.[13] The Academy, in addition, had the reputation for being one of the finest universities in Europe. Little is known of George Hervey's time in Geneva but it is apparent from his grandfather's letters that the intention, contrary to Lord Bristol's strongly

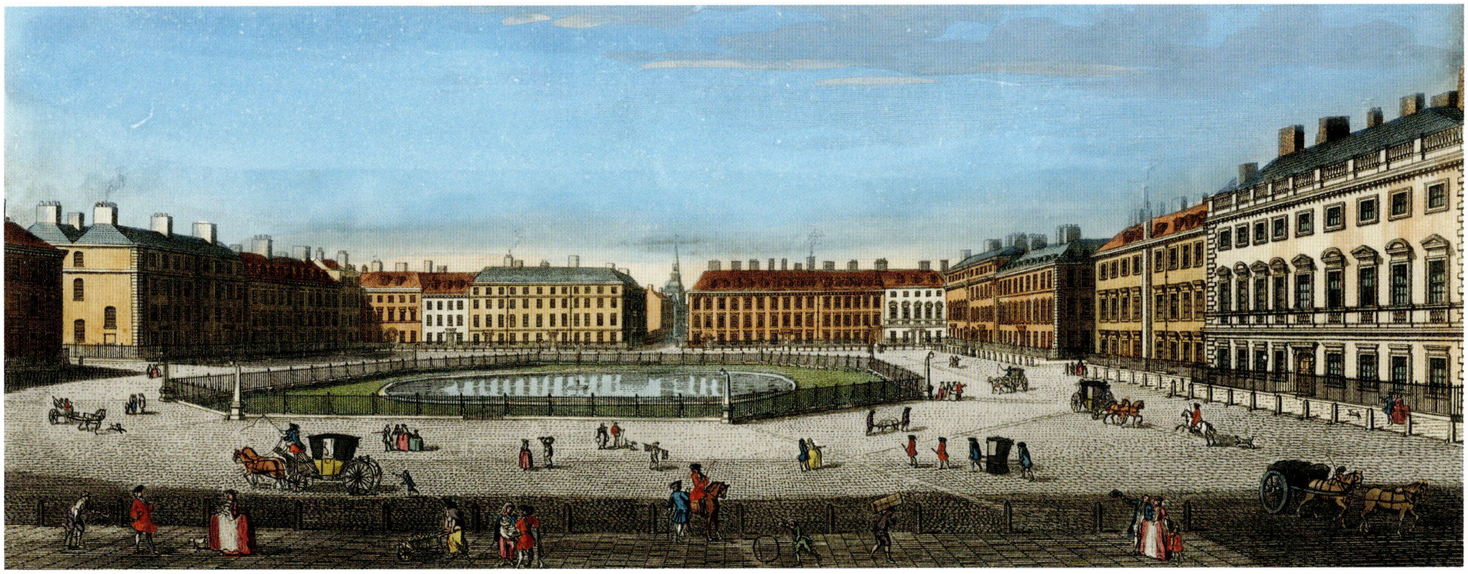

FIG. 17 / *A View of St James's Square London* by Thomas Bowles, 1753. The townhouse of the Herveys is top right, one in from the corner. Engraving. Historic England.

expressed wishes, was to train him up for the army.[14] He probably followed a similar course of tuition to that of the 3rd Duke of Richmond who was there in the early 1750s and stated in a letter to the Duke of Newcastle that 'Riding, Fencing, Drawing, & Mathematicks, I now learn, & will particularly apply to Landscips, Gunnery & Fortifications.'[15]

Having had his fill of education, Hervey set off on a tour of Italy in the summer of 1740 and visited Venice before going on to Rome where he was to be found in January 1741.[16] He was probably then in Naples but was back in Rome in March, borrowing the Countess of Pomfret's 'antiquarian', Parker, for a few days[17] before proceeding to Florence where he attracted considerable attention. Sir Horace Mann, the British Minister there, described to Horace Walpole how the conceited Count Kaunitz, Austrian diplomat and future foreign minister, 'sat three hours at his toilette every morning' but in spite of that most people thought 'that the Inglisino (Harvey) was much handsomer'.[18] Hervey left Florence at the same time as Walpole, returning via Paris to London where he arrived on 17 June 1741 to take up his commission as a captain in the 34th Regiment of Foot.[19] In October 1742, encouraged by his father who had in turn been bribed to the tune of £10,000 by Lord Bristol, he gave up his commission and thereby avoided ever seeing any active service.[20]

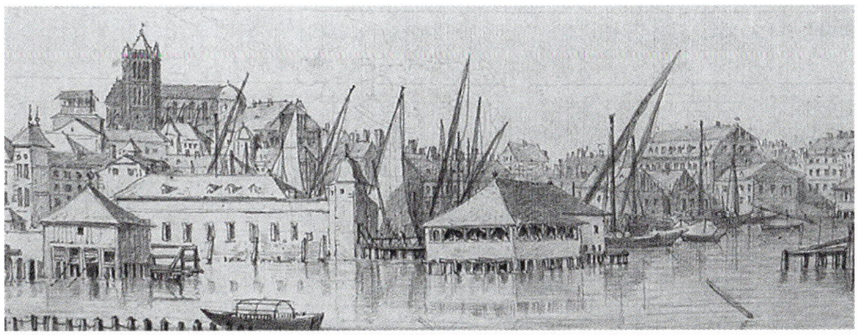

FIG. 18 / *View of Geneva from the Lake* by Louis-François Cassas, *c.*1777. Graphite on paper: 15 x 30.4 cm (5⅞ x 12 in). National Trust, Ickworth.

POLITICS, SOCIETY AND MATRIMONY

On the untimely death of his father in August 1743 George succeeded to his property, including the St James's Square house (fig. 17) and the family plate, and to a seat in the House of Lords.[21] No doubt coloured by his adoring grandfather's antipathy towards involvement in government and his own father's sacking as Lord Privy Seal in 1742, he became thick with the opposition 'Patriot' Whigs and in particular with William Pitt the Elder. In January 1745 he spoke against the government in a debate relating to British payment for Hanoverian troops and he did not mince his words. 'Nothing', he declared, 'seems to me more incontrovertibly manifest, than that the interest of Hanover is contrary to that of England,' and he went on to express the desire that the author of the proposals to saddle the country with such unnecessary and futile expense should 'not long escape punishment'.[22] That author was the Duke of Newcastle and as neither he nor the King, who loved both his troops and Hanover, were quick to forgive, Hervey's chances of preferment were, for the moment at least, rendered negligible.

Over the next few years he bided his time, proving himself an astute estate manager in helping his increasingly infirm grandfather, making improvements to 6 St James's Square to the design of Henry Flitcroft[23] and entering into society. Horace Walpole mentions his presence on various occasions and he paid particular attention to one incident that tested the mettle of Lord Hervey (fig. 21) at the beginning of 1750. He was attending one of Lady Cobham's Wednesday assemblies in London and, as recited by Walpole,

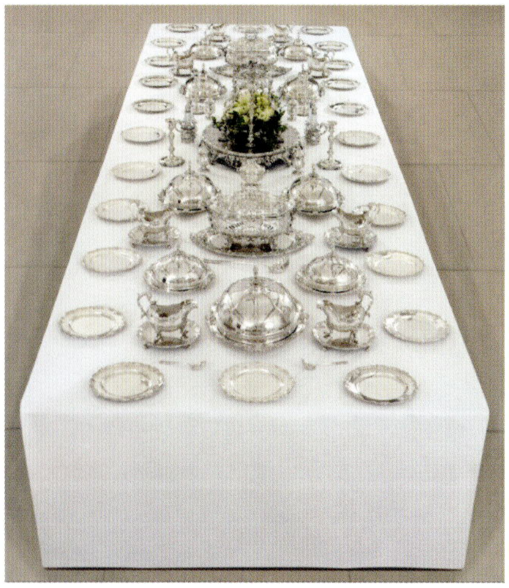

FIG. 19 / Part of the dinner service supplied by George Wickes to the 20th Earl of Kildare (subsequently Duke of Leinster) in the 1740s. Christie's.

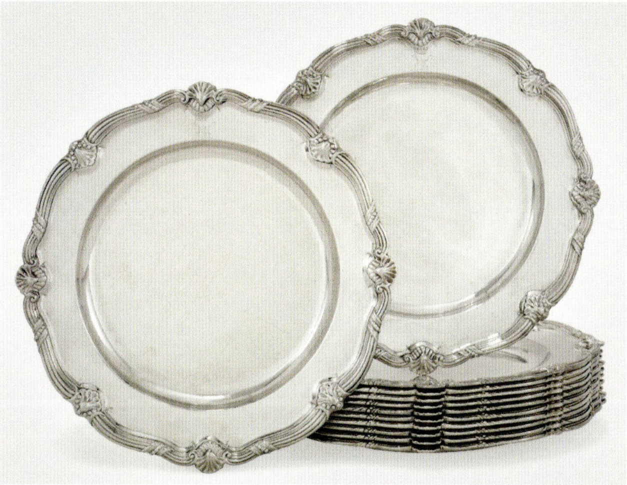

FIG. 20 / Dinner plates from the Leinster service by George Wickes, London, 1745–56. Silver: diam. 25.4 cm (10 in). Christie's.

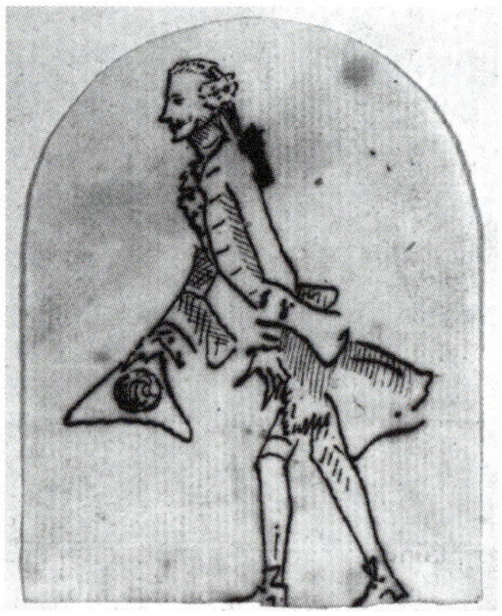

FIG. 21 / *George William Hervey, 2nd Earl of Bristol* by George, 4th Viscount and 1st Marquess Townshend, *c.* 1750. This sketch may have been prompted by the incident involving Lord Hervey's hat in 1750. Pen and ink on paper: 8 x 5.7 cm (3⅛ x 2¼ in). National Portrait Gallery.

> *was leaning over a chair talking to some women, and holding his hat in his hand – Lord Cobham [the future Earl Temple] came up and spit in it – yes, spit in it! – and then with a loud laugh, turned to Nugent and said, 'Pay me my wager'. In short, he had been laid a guinea that he committed this absurd brutality, and that it was not resented. Lord Hervey with great temper [control] and sensibly, asked if he [Cobham] had any farther occasion for his hat? – 'Oh! I see you are angry!' – 'Not very well pleased', Lord Cobham took the fatal hat and wiped it, made a thousand foolish apologies, and wanted to pass it for a joke.*

Lord Hervey, who was nothing if not proud, and brave too in spite of a slight stature and an apparently effeminate appearance,[24] declined to receive the offending pair the next morning and challenged one or other of them to a duel. He only backed down when Cobham agreed to write an abject apology in his own hand.[25] Walpole dubbed Hervey 'the fair conqueror' and Lady Hervey wrote to her second son Augustus in Paris proudly recounting the whole affair as well as society's commendation of 'Lord H's coolness and conduct throughout'.[26]

Another important aspect of Lord Hervey's life in the 1740s was his attempt, albeit half-hearted, at seeking a wealthy bride. In 1743, according to Horace Walpole, John, Lord Hervey had despatched his eldest daughter Lepel to Constantine Phipps 'at a day's notice' and next threatened her trembling brother to be 'ravished to bed to some fortune or other'.[27] On that occasion his father's death took off the pressure but old Lord Bristol was equally determined to see his heir married, and profitably too, and proceeded to direct the young man to various suitable prospects. George dutifully visited Petworth in 1748 to pay court to one or other of the Ladies Frances and Charlotte Seymour, daughters of the ailing 6th Duke of Somerset and both considerable heiresses,[28] but that came to nothing and Lord Bristol turned his attention instead to Gilbert Jodrell's daughter, worth £12,000 per annum. Lord Hervey, however, was at the same time wooing a mysterious 'Lady C' who it seemed he was close to proposing to in the spring of 1750 although negotiations came to an unsuccessful conclusion in May. The Earl, by now somewhat exasperated, nevertheless spirited up yet another prospect, a Miss Archer from Lincolnshire with 'an immense fortune', and berated his grandson for having already let three such heiresses 'slip through your fingers'. Once again, however, death intervened and with the old Earl breathing his last on 20 January 1751 any real prospect of George ever marrying disappeared.[29]

Refashioning the family plate

One of George Hervey's first acts on succeeding as 2nd Earl of Bristol was to deliver the bulk of his inherited silver to Frederick Kandler for refashioning and re-engraving with his own arms. Many other heirs acted similarly but in the new Lord Bristol's case he had actually already owned the plate for more than seven years, since inheriting it from his father in 1743. So restrained was he in the intervening period that he does not even appear to have acquired any additional pieces, there being no payments to goldsmiths in his bank account before 1751. This was thus a carefully considered plan that he must have had in mind for some time but desisted from executing in order to save any bad feeling between him and his grandfather, with whom there was evidently mutual love and affection. The old Earl would undoubtedly have seen the refashioning as an unnecessary cost and perhaps even have been hurt at much of what he had gathered disappearing into the melting pot. A contemporary case where such sensitivity was expressed is that of Sir Horace Mann and the evidently elaborate coffee pot given to him by Horace Walpole. Mann despatched it in 1744 in order to purchase dining plate and begged Walpole's forgiveness stating it was too fine for him, he had nothing else fit to be seen with it and that he would inscribe 'ex dono Horatij Walpole' on 'every plate and dish I buy'.[30]

The 2nd Earl was, in fact, far from being wantonly extravagant and he took care to provide himself with a suitably fashionable and magnificent assemblage of silver without spending any more than he really needed to. A brasher and more carefree spender might have been prepared to have everything entirely new and in the richest of contemporary styles. One such was James FitzGerald, 20th Earl of Kildare (and subsequently 1st Duke of Leinster) who inherited from his father in 1744 and within three years had lavished £4,044 on 7,263 ounces of silver (fig. 19) without turning in anything old as part of the equation.[31] That averages at more than 11s per ounce, an extraordinarily high charge overall for such a large commission of silver. Taking for example dinner plates, which as a whole were the weightiest single component of most collections, Lord Kildare's (fig. 20) were shaped in the conventional manner but their French-inspired reed and tie borders were more deeply modelled than was the norm and they were embellished with additional shell 'ornaments'.[32] Not only did this add to the weight, each plate being an ounce or so heavier than usual, but it also resulted in a charge per ounce of 8s 7d. By comparison, in 1749 the Dowager Duchess of Somerset was charged 7s 4d for standard shaped and gadrooned plates[33] made new and Lord Bristol, by having his old plates refashioned, would have paid even less. George Wickes' rate for such refashioning was consistently 1s 2d per ounce at this time (see cat. 35) and duty was only charged, if at all, on the added weight of the gadrooning. If the 2nd Earl was not asked to pay duty, which he might not have been given the careful retention by Kandler of old hallmarks, he could have been charged as little as 6s 6d, including a nominal 5s 4d for the silver he turned in, and he would only have had to find about £100 in cash for his six dozen plates.[34] In contrast, for the same number the Duchess of Somerset paid £495 and Lord Kildare £660.[35] Completely plain plates, of course, would have cost Lord Bristol even less but they would not have been acceptable at the table of a man aspiring to reach the highest levels of power and influence. He had to show himself to be abreast of the fashions and to be able to hold his own amongst his peers both at home and abroad.[36]

Further prudence was shown by Lord Bristol in his clever transformation of a variety of meat dishes inherited from his father to which he had handles added in the form of magnificent shells (cat. 38–40). This unified them and brought them right up to date at a fraction of the cost

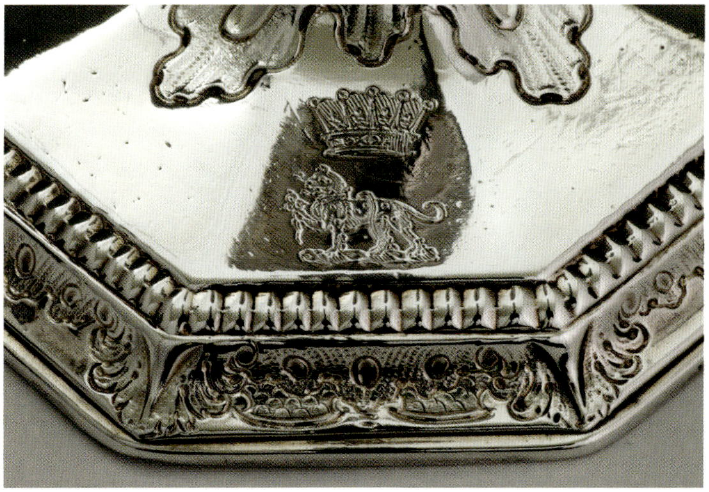

FIG. 22 / Rococo chasing of *c.*1752 on one of the candlesticks by Louis Mettayer, London, 1708 (cat. 8). National Trust, Ickworth.

of completely new pieces. Similarly he had the least ornate of his inherited candlesticks (cat. 8 and 9) embellished with rococo chasing (fig. 22) whilst such items as the Rollos ice pails (cat. 18) and the de Lamerie bread basket (cat. 19) were evidently considered sufficiently showy and stylish to be retained exactly as they were and indeed, in the case of the basket, to be copied (cat. 45). The baroque ponderousness of the 1720s epergne, also by de Lamerie, may have done for it as an ensemble at this stage but many of its component parts, with their rich *Régence* decoration, survived (cat. 11 and 12) and one, the main dish (cat. 13), was another subject of replication (cat. 28). Other items, for use behind the scenes or in private, such as the preserving basin (cat. 10), the saucepan (cat. 16) and his grandfather's battered old chocolate pot (cat. 5) had no need to be updated and, once again, demonstrate the Earl's considered and frugal approach.

Perhaps the most surprising of the Earl's retentions was the 1680 bottle cistern (cat. 1), bought second-hand in 1697 and certainly not capable of passing for fashionable in the 1750s. It is most unlikely that Lord Bristol was driven by an antiquarian spirit or by familial reverence as the application of such sentiments to his plate seems incompatible with his pragmatism and focus on the present and on future advancement. Instead the decision was probably based on the substantial cost of getting a replacement made and the fact that it would anyway be placed at a distance from the company, by the sideboard and perhaps even partly in shadow, and would primarily make an impression through being a large lump of precious metal of indeterminate detail performing the task for which it was intended.

Some items could either not be rendered acceptable by refashioning, were insufficient in number or had not existed within the Hervey plate previously, and in such cases new plate was commissioned. The Daniel Piers sauce boats (cat. 30), circular salad dishes (cat. 31), the mazarines (cat. 33) and the Kandler salts (cat. 46) are examples, as are the most spectacular pieces of silver in the entire collection, the pair of oval tureens of 1752 by Frederick Kandler (cat. 43). As the principal players of the Earl's dining table he concentrated his investment in them to ensure that through their massy and sculptural form and meticulously cast armorials they expressed him as the owner as well as his taste and wealth. They are amongst the finest to survive from the period and must have made a considerable impression, so very much more exuberantly Continental are they than most of what was being produced by London goldsmiths at the time.

Up to the end of 1753 Lord Bristol had only paid Kandler £446 12s (see appendix 3) which falls far short of what would have been needed to cover the cost of the first batch of newly made and refashioned silver. The total bill for what survives today would have been something in the order of £545,[37] excluding engraving, cases and suchlike, and a number of objects have certainly been lost since then, most obviously almost all the flatware and knife handles. The shortfall is likely therefore to have been at least £100, and probably significantly more, and must have been settled by turning in further inherited pieces to be melted. These would have been credited at 5s 6d judging by the Wickes ledgers[38] so over 400 ounces would have been needed. What does not survive of the epergne – 325 ounces – would have gone a good way towards it and there must also have been at least a pair of inherited tureens which would no longer have been needed. The remaining purchases, mostly of new-made silver, before the Earl went to Turin in 1755 (cat. 48–51) would have cost in the region of £135[39] and as that is easily covered by the £151 cash paid to Kandler in 1755 (see appendix 3) it is unlikely that any further old plate was turned in at this stage.

FREDERICK KANDLER

Apart from for his ambassadorial plate the 2nd Earl of Bristol exclusively patronised Frederick Kandler (fig. 25). Why he was chosen is not known for certain but it may simply have been the proven reputation of his workshop for the finest of craftsmanship and for design that was closely connected to the latest developments on the Continent. Lord Bristol clearly demanded quality and fashionability. There is also some evidence pointing towards a connection between Kandler and Paul de Lamerie as explored by Timothy Schroder in relation to the two sets of matching figural candlesticks in the Ashmolean, one by de Lamerie with branches by Kandler, and the other exclusively by Kandler.[40] Given that Lord Hervey had patronised de Lamerie (cat. 19) it is possible that the ailing and aged goldsmith (he died August 1751) passed Lord Bristol on to Kandler who also happened to be only a stone's throw from the Earl's St James's Square house, in Jermyn Street.[41]

There has been much debate over whether Charles Kandler, who first entered a mark in 1727, and (Charles) Frederick Kandler, who died in 1778, were one and the same man. Dr Penzer considered they were not after investigating the Jernagan cistern by Charles Kandler but Arthur Grimwade came down in the opposite camp in his biographical dictionary of London goldsmiths.[42] The careful researches of Peter Cameron in the 1990s, however, clarified the situation and it is now clear that they were two individuals, possibly both coming together from Saxony in the 1720s and the younger of them, Frederick, taking over the business and premises in Jermyn Street in the 1730s on Charles's perhaps returning home.[43] There is certainly a clear stylistic link between the two as is exhibited in the vertical flutes or creases, plasticity and overall form of the Ickworth tureens of 1752 (cat. 43).

Both the Kandlers were Catholic and Charles's clientele was markedly so, as well as including Jacobite Anglicans, but as the retail side of the business expanded around the middle of the century under Frederick a broader range became evident. Prominent Catholics such as the 9th Duke and Duchess of Norfolk and the 14th Earl of Shrewsbury remained but were joined by such stalwarts of the established church and the Hanoverian succession as Lord Bristol, albeit that his mother, who exasperated him with her dabbling in romantic Jacobitism, was another of Kandler's major clients.[44] The retail business must have been extensive by the 1760s judging by the evidence from clients' accounts so far uncovered, including those of John Chute of The Vyne in Hampshire[45] and the 5th Duke of Beaufort,[46] both of whom patronised Kandler over a long period like Lord Bristol. The scale of the enterprise may well have vied with Parker and Wakelin but as none of the business records survive it is impossible to be sure. Frederick Kandler died in 1778, three years after Lord Bristol, and his son, another Charles (d. 1807), carried on the business until at least 1793.[47]

Much of the plate that came from Kandler bears his mark and must have been made in his workshop or under his sponsorship but evidently he was also supplied by a large circle of other goldsmiths to fulfil his commissions. Surviving at Ickworth there are pieces representing Daniel Piers, Dru Drury, Edward Feline, John Robinson, Ebenezer Coker, Elizabeth Aldridge and the Chawners.[48] It is noticeable that the generalists amongst these names are grouped at the commencement of Lord Bristol's patronage whereas from the 1760s and 1770s there are only the specialist makers, Elizabeth Aldridge for pierced work and the Chawners for flatware. Though the Bristol silver is too small a sample to form any firm conclusions it could be that the burgeoning of Kandler's business in the early 1750s, perhaps following the death of Paul de Lamerie, resulted in him needing the services of other working goldsmiths for a wide range of plate but that thereafter he expanded the capacity of his workshop and reduced external help to specialists.

Envoy to Turin

By 1751 the fruitlessness of opposition in terms of advancement, particularly in the light of the apparent unassailability of the Pelham administration, caused Lord Bristol to have a strategic change of heart. His grandfather was no longer present to extol the virtues of opposition and George became 'totally inclined to go [over] to the Court', as his brother Augustus disapprovingly recorded in his journal on the very day of the 1st Earl's death. Within weeks approaches were made through the 1st Duke of Dorset, then Lord President of the Council, and the response was promising.[49] He was selected to be one of the six earls who acted as pallbearers at the funeral of Frederick, Prince of Wales in April 1751[50] and the same month he was offered the post of Lord of the Bedchamber to young Prince George. He refused that, no doubt prudently assessing that the Walesian court was often in dispute with the King and in such circumstances any further progression would be blocked.[51] A diplomatic career was, in any event, a surer route, suiting Lord Bristol's education and character and having a good record for leading to high political office at home; the Earls of Harrington, Granville, Chesterfield and Holderness had all been ambassadors before becoming Secretaries of State under George II. In October, whilst staying with his sister Lepel Phipps at Mulgrave Castle in Yorkshire and enjoying a 'very merry … time', Lord Bristol announced to Augustus Hervey that 'he had asked to go Envoy to Portugal, and that the Duke of Newcastle had hinted the Embassy to Spain.'[52]

At court George II (fig. 23) frequently turned his back on or 'rumped'[53] Lord Bristol who was clearly not forgiven for his past misdemeanours, and Newcastle was no natural friend to him either, having been loathed and ridiculed by John, Lord Hervey. The Duke, however, also had his eye on building support in Parliament and Bristol, as well as having a vote in the House of Lords, controlled one of the Bury St Edmunds seats in the Commons. This proved not quite enough on its own, the Herveys previously having been too entrenched in opposition to be entirely trusted, and reminders by Lord Bristol of the promises made in 1751 initially met with evasive responses.[54] He played the trump card, however, when he offered the Duke his proxy vote should he be sent abroad and in August 1754 it was suggested that he go to

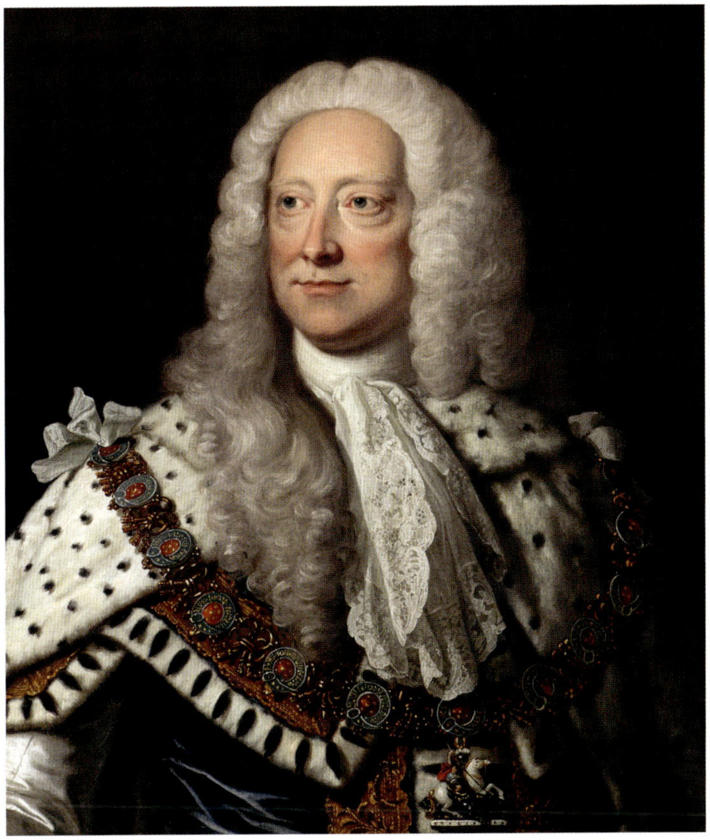

FIG. 23 / *King George II* by Thomas Hudson, *c.*1744. Oil on canvas: 74.9 x 62.2 cm (29½ x 24½ in). National Trust, Ickworth.

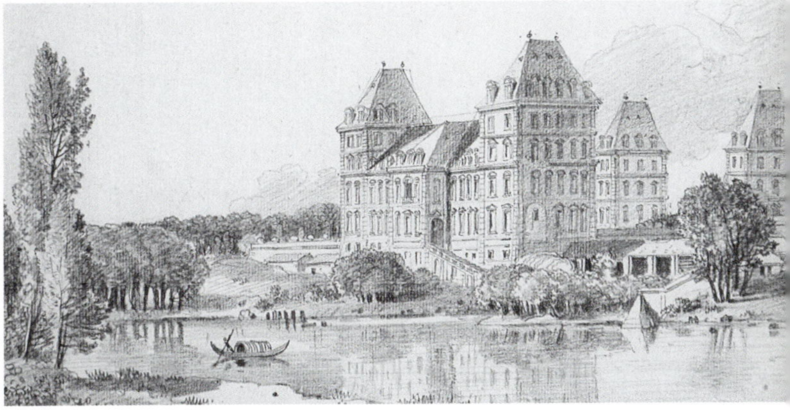

FIG. 24 / *Royal Residence of Valentine, near Turin on the Po* by Louis-François Cassas, 1780. One of Turin's many magnificent 17th and 18th-century buildings. Lord Bristol recorded discussing business with the King of Sardinia in the gardens here. Graphite on paper: 20.8 x 31.2 cm (8⅛ x 12¼ in). National Trust, Ickworth.

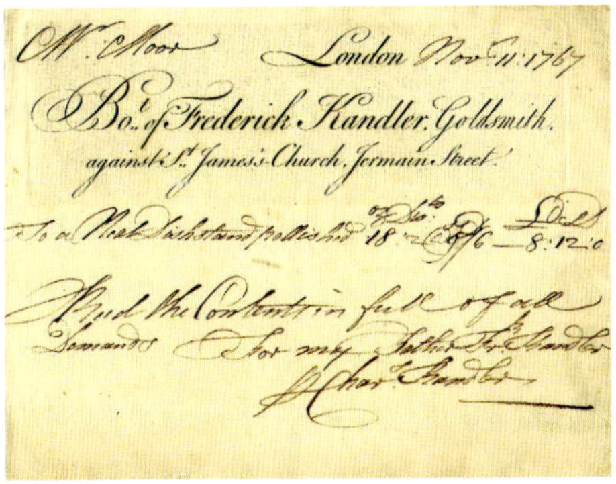

FIG. 25 / Printed bill-head of circa 1760 with Frederick Kandler's name and address. Ink on paper. Heal collection, British Museum.

Portugal as Envoy.[55] The death of the 2nd Earl of Albemarle in December, however, changed the course of events as Lord Rochford, in spite of opposition by Newcastle who considered him quite unsuitable, was appointed Groom of the Stole in Albemarle's place and recalled from Turin where he had been serving as envoy.[56] Lord Bristol promptly wrote to both Newcastle and the King's mistress, Lady Yarmouth, requesting to be sent there instead of Lisbon and he also garnered the support of the Sardinian envoy to London, Count Perrone.[57] At last his efforts met with success and after some resistance from the King he was named for the post on the 3 April 1755, kissing hands the following day.[58]

Though Lisbon was very desirable to many Englishmen because of its climate, sociability and long-standing alliance with Britain, Turin was undoubtedly a more elevated appointment. The capital of the Kingdom of Sardinia was critically placed between the Austrian dominions and France making it the focus of much diplomatic attention and at times the most important posting after France and Spain. Turin, too, was a thoroughly modern European capital city and its court was considered amongst the politest in Europe. Like Geneva, there was an academy of high repute favoured for the sons of the British aristocracy and Turinese diplomats, according to Lord Chesterfield writing in 1748, were 'the ablest, the politest and les plus déliés [the most free/untied]' in Europe.[59] Lord Bristol is bound to have had first-hand experience of the place on his travels in Italy in 1740–1 and his brother Augustus had responded favourably when he was there in 1747, finding the town 'regular, clean and pretty,' the people civil and amusing and the palace richly furnished and 'very well planned'.[60] A visitor later in the eighteenth century went so far as to describe Turin as 'one of the finest cities in Italy for the magnificence of its buildings (fig. 24), the beauty of its streets and squares, the number and sociable temper of its inhabitants, and for all the conveniences of life.'[61]

Just as the Earl was enthusiastic about going to Turin so were the Turinese about receiving him. Count Perrone, on hearing that he was likely to be appointed, made enquiries in London in February 1755 and reported back to King Carlo Emanuele III (1701–73) (fig. 26) that 'non seulement il est trés noble et fort riche, mais qu'il a aussi beaucoup d'esprit et un caractère fort doux et honnête [not only is he very noble and extremely rich, but he also has much spirit and a very gentle and honest character].' Neither side was to prove disappointed, Lord Bristol's letters home showing that he took to the role with great ease and gained the confidence of the King and his minister, Giuseppe Osorio, whilst they sent rapturous reports to Count Perrone, stating that the Earl had much merit and had met with 'l'estime generale'.[62] They were to be even more delighted when Henry Fox, an intimate of John, Lord Hervey, became Secretary of State for the Southern Department in November, Count Viry, who had replaced Perrone, informing Osorio that 'Mr Fox est fort dans les interests de Milord Bristol [Mr Fox is strongly in the interests of Lord Bristol].'[63] A year later the situation was yet further improved when the Earl's strongest political ally and mentor, William Pitt the Elder, succeeded Fox.

SILVER BEFITTING THE KING'S REPRESENTATIVE

Lord Bristol's rank, wealth and refinement were very important both in complimenting the Sardinian King and in holding George II's and Britain's own against the ministers of all the other courts represented. To this end it was incumbent upon the Earl to display 'magnificence', a concept which had great potency in eighteenth-century monarchical and aristocratic Europe and is vividly demonstrated in the description of Robert Darcy, 4th Earl of Holderness's public entry as ambassador to the Venetian Republic in 1744:

> *The whole ceremony was conducted with the greatest order & magnificence; Nothing was wanting on the part of the Republick that could tend to demonstrate how sensible they are of the Honour done them by his Majesty in this Embassy: The Senators appointed to attend, were chose out of the Principal Families & Chief men of the State; At Night great numbers of the most considerable of the Venetian Nobility of Both Sexes came in Mask to pay their Compliments to the Ambassador & Ambassadress. I take the Liberty to add, in justice to the Ambassador, that he supported his Character with Dignity, magnificence & Politeness. His Palace was finely illuminated, Concerts of musick in several rooms, & the Company entertained with Chocolate Iced waters &c for two days, during which time the Palace was crowded with Masks. His Liveries & Equipage were numerous & splendid.*[64]

The Duke of Newcastle specifically instructed Lord Bristol to act in the same fashion, albeit there was no public entry for an envoy, and the Earl later wrote of 'the many thousand pounds I have drawn for since I left England' in pursuit of this general goal.[65] He also recorded his particular intention of not letting 'the French Minister live with more splendor or magnificence than his Majesty's representative'.[66] Horace Walpole ridiculed him for his pomposity and described him as 'a very Spaniard in formality and pride'[67] but these characteristics were positive advantages in his chosen career path, provided that they were checked by intelligence and sensitivity as appears, with him, to have been the case.

Costume, carriages, houses and their furnishings, plate, the size of the household, the sumptuousness of liveries[68] and the scale and sophistication of entertaining all had their parts to play in creating the requisite magnificence. Lord Bristol did his best on all fronts and Sir Horace Mann wrote from Florence in 1758 that he 'gives £500 a year for his house, and has everything in it equal to that expense'.[69] That figure has been shown by Edoardo Piccoli in his study of English residents in Turin in the eighteenth century to have been enormous and probably an exaggeration[70] but Lord Bristol had clearly found a very splendid and expensive house and his bank account corroborates that he was expending a great deal of money in the city. In 1756 alone £4,050 was drawn down through the bankers Paul Torras & Co plus an additional £1,846 paid direct to Count Viry in London.[71] The latter may suggest that Lord Bristol was renting a palace previously occupied by the Count in Turin and paying the additional expenses of a household and stables through him as well. Otherwise it is difficult to conceive why Viry was receiving such large sums.[72] The massively scaled giltwood furniture in the Turinese rococo style now at Ickworth (fig. 27) was probably acquired for the capacious rooms of the Earl's palace and he certainly had the family plate with him, paying £76 4s 6d to insure it on its journey by sea to Genoa.[73]

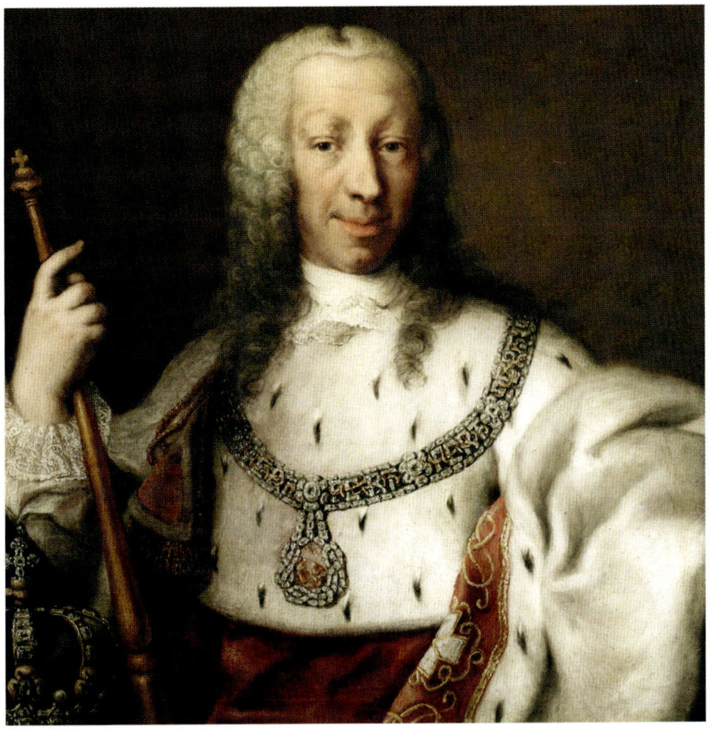

FIG. 26 / *Carlo Emanuele III, King of Sardinia* by Maria Giovanna Clementi and studio, *c.*1758. Probably given by the King to the 2nd Earl of Bristol. Oil on canvas: 74.9 x 62.2 cm (29½ x 24½ in). National Trust, Ickworth.

Silver was an especially important tool in the creation of magnificence because it represented raw wealth as well as taste and it was the focus of attention when entertaining fellow diplomats, government ministers and the indigenous aristocracy. Only ambassadors received a grant of plate from the Jewel Office (see chapter 3) but even those lower than an envoy would be expected to put on something of a show and in 1744 Horace Mann, British Resident in Florence, purchased his predecessor, the 2nd Viscount Fane's plate for '600 or 700 pounds, including knives, forks, spoons, salvers, salts, [and] ladles,' intending to add 'plates and dishes … and creep into a service before I am aware of it'.[74] He stated that there was not even a consul without a dinner service in Florence at the time, though that seems somewhat improbable.

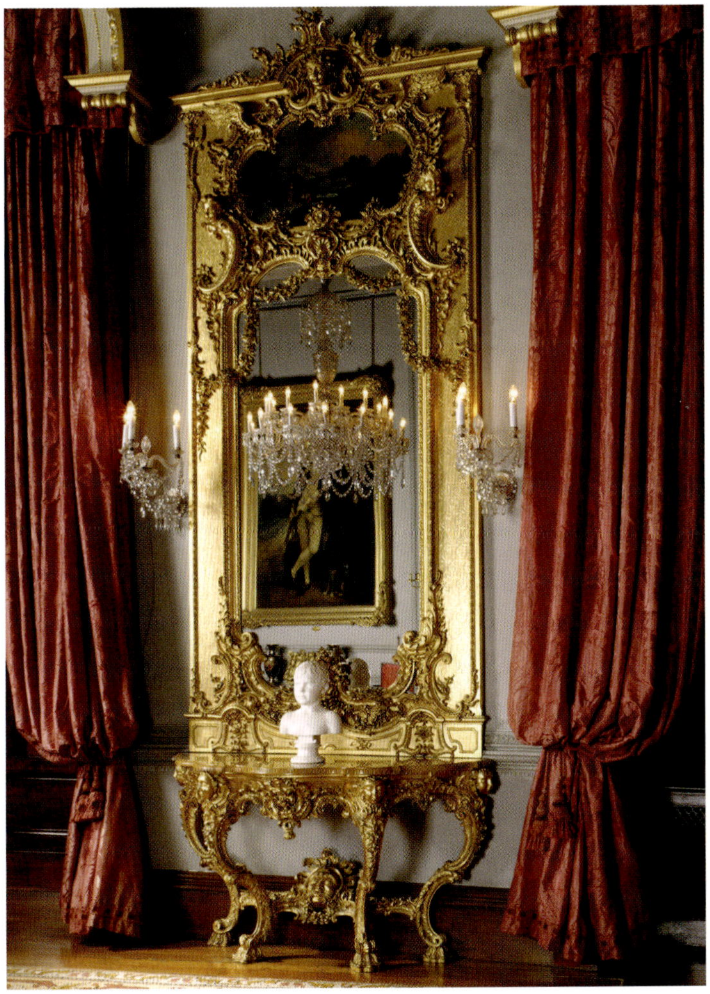

FIG. 27 / One of the series of mid-18th century Turin pier tables and glasses at Ickworth, this one in the Drawing Room. The table: 89 x 153 x 59 cm (35 x 60¼ x 23¼ in). The mirror: 312 x 147 cm (122⅞ x 57⅞ in). National Trust, Ickworth.

A diplomat's plate would inevitably be put to a great deal of use as well and the 1st Earl Waldegrave, ambassador in Paris, complained in 1732 that after five years 'a good deal of it [his plate] must be so battered and worn out … that it is only fit to be melted down; and had I not made use almost constantly on ordinary days of my own plate, to have his majestys for days of Shew, little of it woud be by this time fit for Service.'[75] That would suggest a very careless approach by his guests and servants but there was unquestionably an intense round of dinners and other entertainments expected of a diplomat as evident from the comprehensive series of letters from Benjamin Keene describing life in Madrid between 1749 and 1756. Shortly after arrival he observed that 'it is well for me that I have good appointments, for you can not imagine the luxury in cloaths and tables that is introduced among them [the diplomatic community]. Even the Nuncio gives *quatre services de cuisine* at a dinner.'[76]

COMPETING AT THE DINNER TABLE

Lord Bristol arrived in Turin on 15 June 1755, having stopped in Paris *en route* and, presumably, crossed the Alps via the Mont Cenis pass.[77] His silver had been shipped in April so should have been waiting for him and he would have been glad of it, learning from the departing embassy secretary, George Charles, of the entertainments recently put on by the man who was to be the Earl's chief rival in Turin, the indubitably haughty French ambassador, the Marquis de Chauvelin.[78] He had had Louis xv's cousin, the Duc de Penthièvre, staying with him in April and in spite of being incognito the Duc was treated in accordance with his rank: 'His Table at the French Ambassadors consisted daily of twenty five covers' and besides other diplomats there were army officers present, ministers of the King of Sardinia and senior members of the royal household. The following month the Abbé Bernis, on his way back to France from Venice, received similar treatment though this time the dinners were for thirty 'to which were Invited many Ladies, some of the most distinguished in this City, by their Rank & Beauty'.[79]

The Earl of Bristol would have known immediately that he needed to keep up with this level of hospitality, and it was a necessity made all the more acute by a realisation on acquaintance that he personally loathed M. Chauvelin. After just two months he relayed, in cypher, a vituperative assessment to the Earl of Holderness, then in attendance on George ii in Hanover:

> *I have taken some pains to study his Excellency's Character & by the best judgement I can form of him, he has pride without Dignity, he flatters without persuading, is Verbose without meaning and never scruples to assert an untruth, tho' he knows it can serve his turn but for an hour. His publick Character alone supports him, for his private one is Vain, frivolous and false.*[80]

The two quickly fell into dispute over the protocol of which of them should visit the other first, and Bristol would take any opportunity to report unfavourably on Chauvelin. When the Frenchman made an appearance in the Earl's box at the opera[81] (fig. 29) in December 1755 and 'staid a considerable time' Lord Bristol was especially pleased, as at the beginning of the season Chauvelin had told the Spanish ambassador's wife that he would not step over the threshold 'because I was the Master of it'.[82] He also showed great delight two years later, by which time further edge was given to the personal competition since Britain and France were at war, at a demonstration of Chauvelin's all-consuming pride:

> *The French Embassador on the Duchess of Savoy's Birthday had a Dispute with the two Cardinals Delle Lanze and Rovero about Precedence in the King of Sardinia's Closet, but Monsieur Chauvelin who came in first, notwithstanding a very remarkable Struggle kept the highest Place.*[83]

The sort of dinners that Chauvelin had been reported as giving required a great deal of silver, as is demonstrated by one of Vincent La Chapelle's plans in his 1742 publication *Le Cuisinier moderne* (fig. 28) and by Augustus Hervey's contemporary description of the French ambassador, the

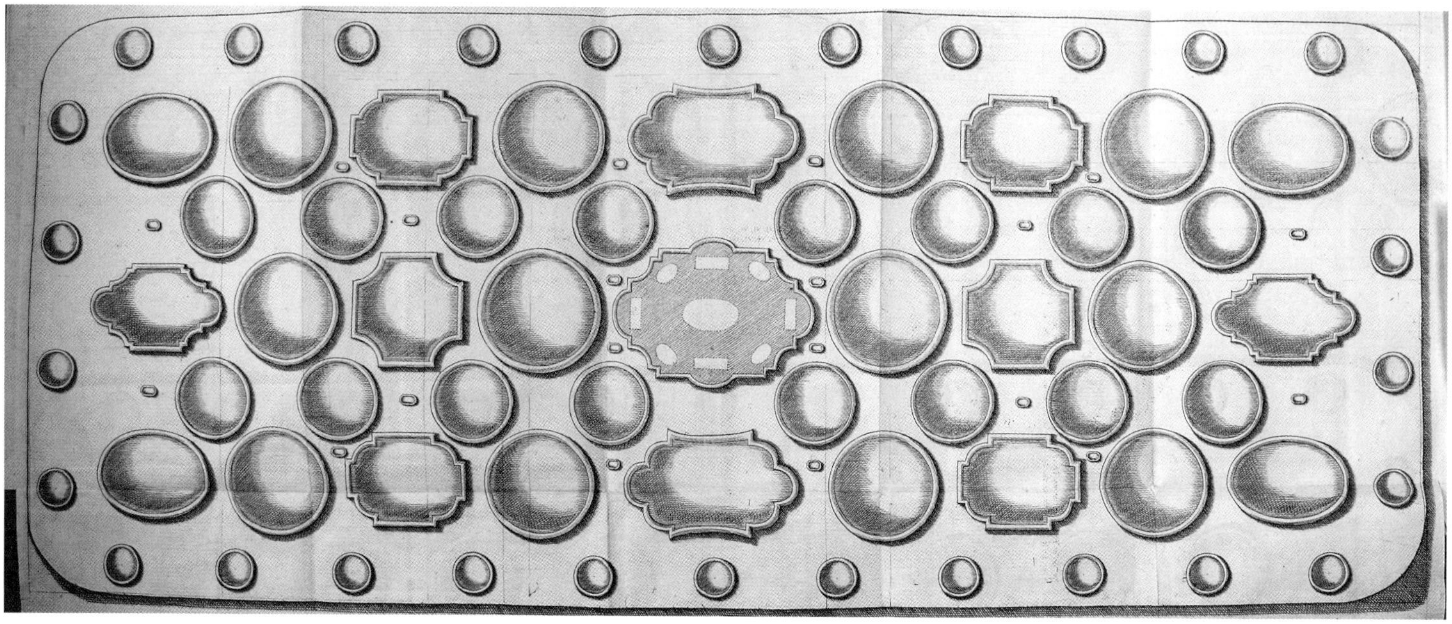

FIG. 28 / 'A Table for Thirty Covers' from Vincent La Chapelle, *La Cuisinier moderne*, Paris, 1742. Forty-two silver dishes are shown as well as the central epergne or plateau. Queen's College Library, Oxford.

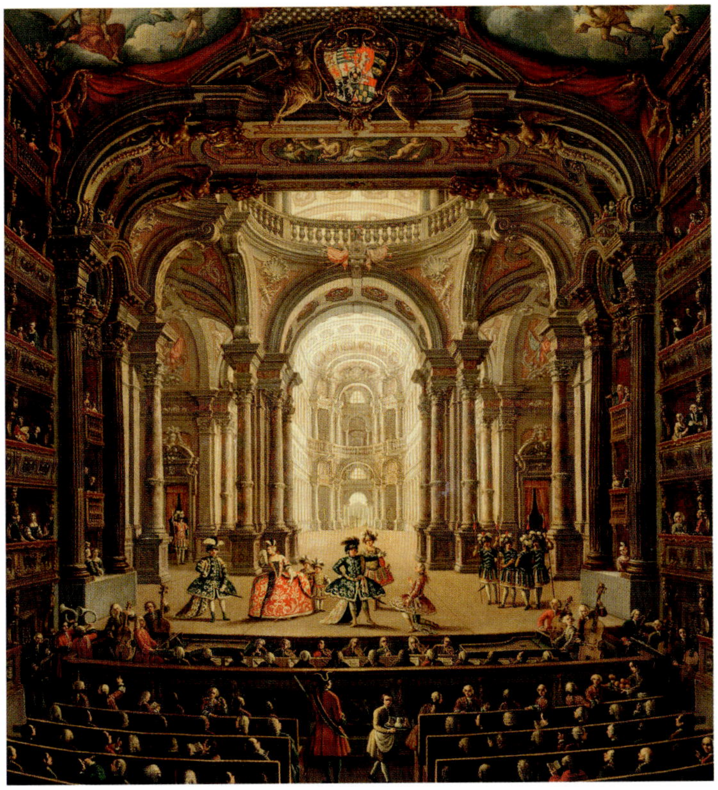

FIG. 29 / *Interior of the Theatre Royal of Turin* attributed to Giovanni Michele Graneri, *c.*1750. Oil on canvas: 128.5 x 114 cm (50⅝ x 44⅞ in). Museo Civico d'Arte Antica, Palazzo Madama, Turin.

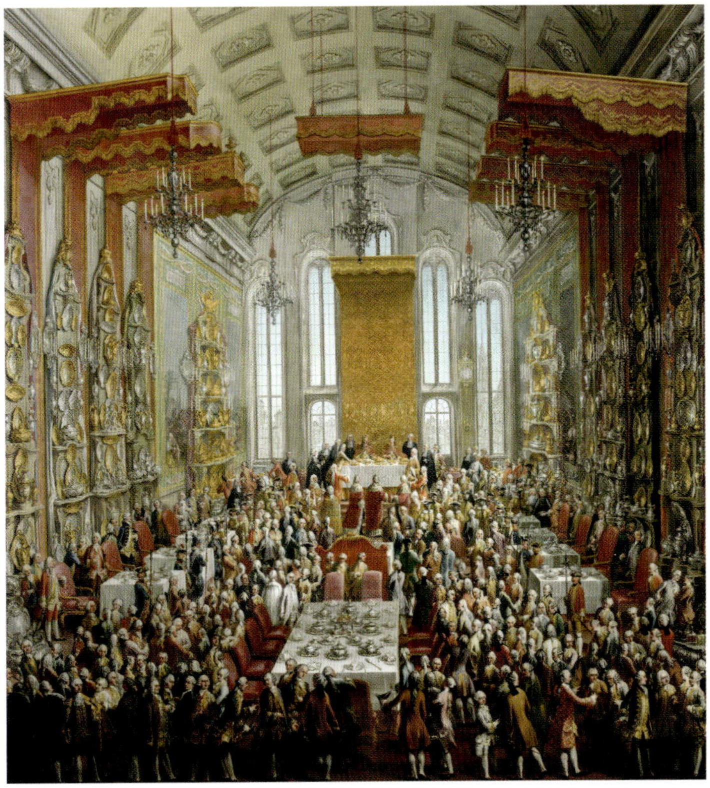

FIG. 30 / *The Coronation Banquet of the Archduke of Austria (the future Joseph II) as King of the Romans at Frankfurt in 1764*, studio of Martin van Meytens (1695–1770). Hofmobiliendepot – Möbel Museum Wien.

Comte de Baschi's table before his public entry in Lisbon in April, 1755:

> *There were thirty-six people at dinner, a table of three services of forty-eight dishes, a dessert of above a hundred, numbers of gentlemen waited, and the service of plate was magnificent, and everything well dressed and delicately served, the King's music playing the whole time …*[84]

This was an extreme occasion but even to accommodate thirty diners, following the English fashion of changing plates with each of the services or courses, Lord Bristol would have required a quantity of ninety plates and he had brought just seventy-two with him (cat. 35). Furthermore, he would have observed that, unlike in Britain, it was *de rigueur* on the Continent to have four tureens,[85] two circular and two oval, and for stands to be provided for them as well plus, ideally, for many of the other service vessels on the table.

Such stands can clearly be seen in the foreground of the depiction of the coronation banquet of the Archduke Joseph as King of the Romans in 1762 (fig. 30). The same painting also demonstrates the pressure for display added to the equation by parts of the Duchy of Savoy falling within the Holy Roman Empire; within that loose federation a plethora of sovereign princes all vied with each other to display the most spectacular tables and buffets of silver.

All of this could have been avoided by mutual agreement, as was the case in Spain where in 1754 Sir Benjamin Keene and the Duc de Duras had put an end to dinners of show, even those for the King's chief minister, Ricardo Wall.[86] There was, however, absolutely no prospect of such prudent amity being shown in Turin and Lord Bristol consequently commissioned another four dozen plates (cat. 56), two round tureens (cat. 53), stands both for these and for the oval tureens (cat. 55) and a number of other items. Turinese hallmarks did not include a year mark so it is impossible to tell exactly when the pieces were delivered but Lord Bristol's expenditure in Turin was markedly higher in 1756 and 1758 than in 1757 so the commission may have been split between those two flanking years.[87]

ANDREA BOUCHERON AND PAOLO ANTONIO PAROLETTO

On realising that he needed to augment his plate the Earl could have sent back to London, but communication over such a distance was neither easy nor quick and a further substantial delay would have been caused by the slow speed of transportation. Cosmopolitan contemporaries including the Earls of Chesterfield and Berkeley had in previous decades sought silver from Paris and such superb craftsmen as the Germains, Jacques Roëttiers and Edme-Pierre Balzac. The war with France, however, put that out of the question and, anyway, Turin had a fine reputation for goldsmithing and such close design links with Paris that Lord Bristol was as well off commissioning there.

Amongst the most distinguished of the craftsmen designers who flowed between Turin and Paris were Juste-Aurèle Meissonnier, François Ladatte, Lorenzo Lavy and Andrea Boucheron and it was with the latter, who had been Royal Goldsmith in Turin since 1737, that the Earl must have placed his order. Many of the pieces bear either his mark or that of the other great Turinese goldsmith of the period, Paolo Antonio Paroletto, and it is probable that the two cooperated on large commissions in much the same way as Paul de Lamerie and Paul Crespin appear to have done in London in the 1730s (see cat. 18). Boucheron had trained in Paris under Thomas Germain and produced pieces of extraordinary virtuosity such as the silver-gilt inkstand of *c.*1753 in the Metropolitan Museum[88] (fig. 31) and a cruet stand of a similar date in a private collection.[89] These and others of Boucheron's pieces have all the sophistication of design and quality of casting and chasing of the Paris masters. Paroletto was almost if not equally as accomplished and had, with his brother, executed the superbly chased silver frontal for the high altar of Turin Cathedral in the 1740s.[90] He went on to produce some fine secular work too, including a pair of tureens (fig. 32) made after 1759 which have similarities to those created for the Earl of Bristol and an oval dish with shell handles of *c.*1760 surely inspired by the English ones (cat. 32) copied for the tureen stands (cat. 55).[91] It is a great tragedy that so little survives from both makers thanks to the ravages of Napoleon's army, though there is, fortunately, sufficient to show that the secular work they produced was fully informed by French fashions and of high technical quality.

Lord Bristol's commissioning of silver in Turin had been anticipated by General Thomas Wentworth whilst in the city in 1747 as a special military envoy with instructions to mediate between the allied but quarrelling courts of Vienna and Savoy prior to the concluding campaign of the War of the Austrian Succession. Wentworth acquired coffee spoons, knives and a set of salts with spoons from Giacomo Antonio Serafino in June 1747 but had little time to use them as he fell ill shortly thereafter and died on the 2nd December. Following his death his goods, including all his silver, were sold in Turin.[92] In London, Turinese silver would have been known through the tables of the Sardinian envoys who seem consistently to have been at the heart of society in the eighteenth century. On the departure of one, the Marquis d'Aix in 1729, there was a sale of his household furniture including 'Clocks, Beurows, Inlaid Commode desks' and a 'large Quantity of Fine Plate' and it is just possible that it was through such a disposal that the Turin elements, some with Boucheron's mark, of the Neptune centrepiece in the Royal Collection entered the London market.[93] A more permanent presence of Turin plate was on display to the Catholic community through the Sardinian embassy chapel in Lincoln's Inn Fields which was favoured for the devotions of the elite before emancipation. Following a fire and reconstruction in the late 1750s a new set of plate was supplied by Andrea Boucheron in the latest French fashion[94] (fig. 33) and the surviving pieces are now in the Victoria and Albert Museum.[95]

Departure from Turin

Irrespective of his relationship with the Marquis de Chauvelin and his success or otherwise on the battlefield of the dining table, Lord Bristol was quite clearly a highly able diplomat, protecting British interests whilst remaining sensitive to the needs of the court of Savoy. He was also proving a very

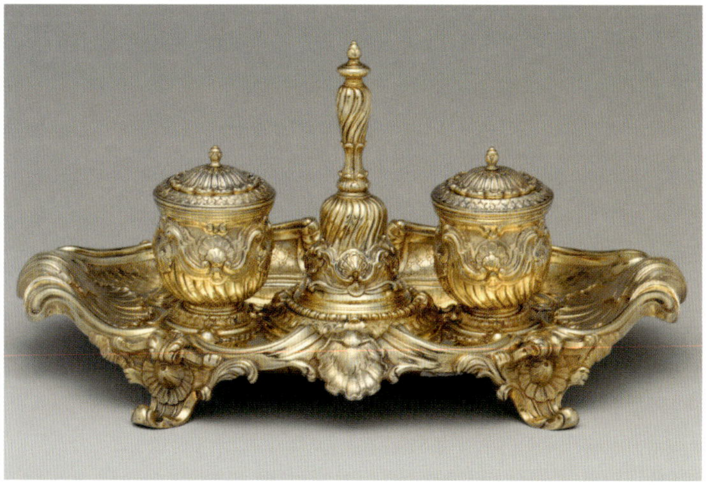

FIG. 31 / Inkstand by Andrea Boucheron, Turin, *c.*1753. Silver-gilt: 15.2 x 33 cm (6 x 13 in). Metropolitan Museum, New York.

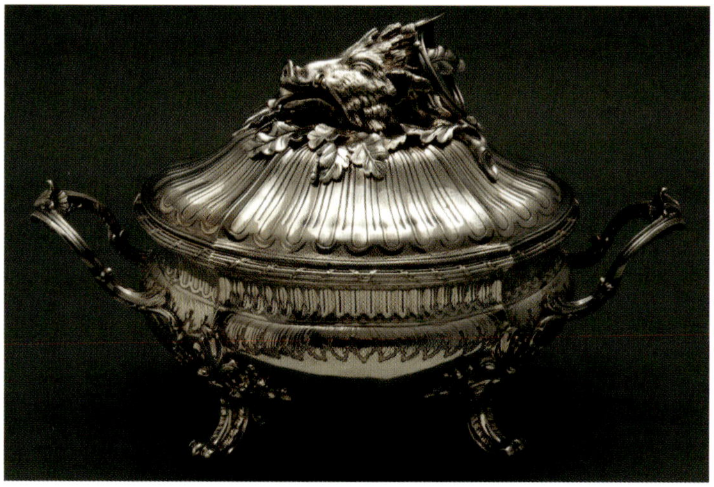

FIG. 32 / Tureen (one of a pair) by Paolo Antonio Paroletto, Turin, *c.*1760. Silver: 26 x 42 x 24 cm (10¼ x 16½ x 9½ in); weight (incl. dish, not shown) 5384 g. Private collection.

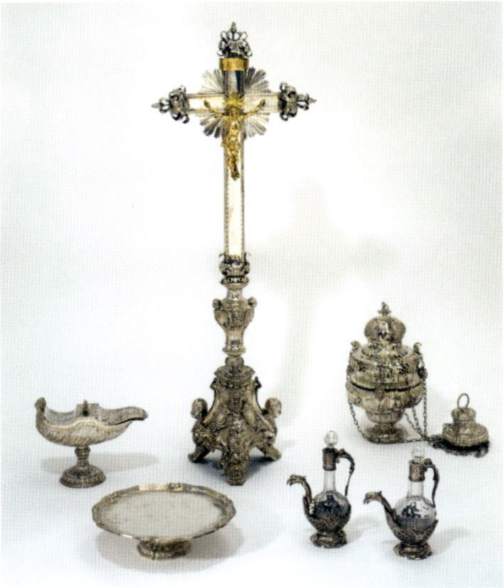

FIG. 33 / The Sardinian chapel plate by Andrea Boucheron, *c.*1760. Victoria and Albert Museum, lent by the Church of St Anselm and St Cecilia, Kingsway.

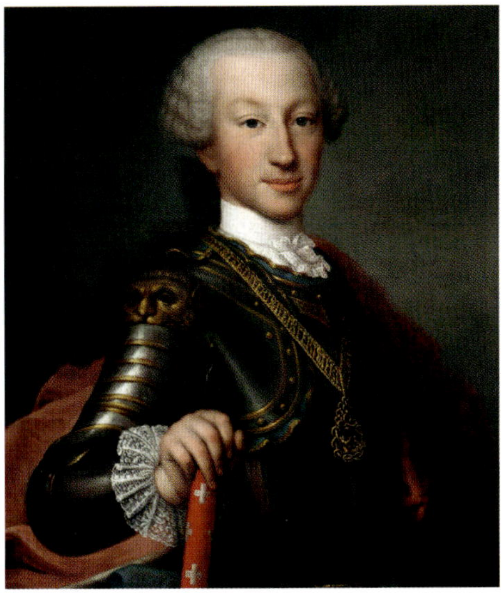

FIG. 34 / *Vittorio Amedeo, Duke of Savoy* (subsequently King Vittorio Amedeo III of Sardinia) by Domenico Duprà, *c.*1758. Oil on canvas: 73.7 x 61 cm (29 x 24 in). National Trust, Ickworth.

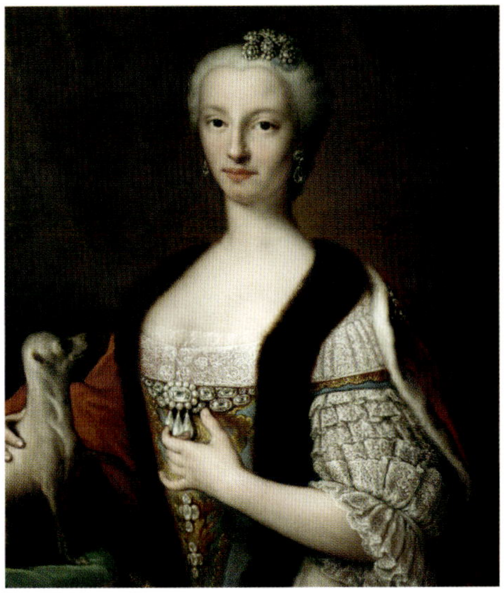

FIG. 35 / *Maria Antonia Bourbon, Duchess of Savoy* (subsequently Queen of Sardinia) by Domenico Duprà, *c.*1758. Oil on canvas: 73.7 x 61 cm (29 x 24 in). National Trust, Ickworth.

effective spymaster for not only did he garner information on naval and army manoeuvres from agents sent over the border into southern France but he also managed to secure a mole in the Neapolitan embassy giving him access to communications to and from the Bourbon court.[96] Although there was no real prospect of an open alliance with Sardinia because of its precarious position between France and Austria,[97] the maintenance of neutrality was of critical importance to British chances of success and Lord Bristol's intimacy with Osorio and Carlo Emanuele undoubtedly contributed towards that.

After less than a year the Earl of Bristol had begun to look towards advancement and appealed to the Duke of Newcastle in April 1756 for elevation to the status of ambassador at Turin, thereby putting him on a par with Chauvelin. In spite of pointing out that 'the establishment of my family [household] is upon a much greater foot than that of the French Embassador,' as well as offering to forego any additional remuneration and less than subtly reminding Newcastle of the allocation of his proxy, he was, however, unsuccessful and had to bide his time.[98] A more realistic opportunity opened up with the death in Madrid of Sir Benjamin Keene on 15 December 1757 and Lord Bristol wasted no time in seizing it. With almost indecent haste, he wrote asking for the appointment and recalling that Newcastle had named the Spanish embassy for him when they first spoke on the subject in 1751.[99] Matters were complicated because multiple promises had been thrown out and Sir James Gray, 2nd Bt, the envoy in Naples, also had the impression the post was his for the asking – which he consequently did.[100] Finally, in March 1758, the decision was made in the Earl's favour, in part at least because of his rank,[101] and on the 28th William Pitt wrote to relay the news that the King was to appoint him 'Ambassador in Ordinary to the Court of Spain'.[102] Bristol was not entirely content as this was a notch down from the highest appointment possible, but he secured that by appealing to George II's proverbial stinginess, foregoing the additional pay and being named Ambassador Extraordinary and Plenipotentiary 'without any additional expence to the King'. He was thus on the same level as his French counterpart in Madrid, the Marquis d'Aubeterre, and his promise 'to support the dignity with the highest eclat' could, without question, be relied upon.[103]

The Earl took his official leave of the Sardinian royal family on 10 August, 1758[104] and he received the customary presents of jewel-encrusted miniatures[105] from the King and from his eldest son, the Duke of Savoy. These, shorn of their diamonds, survive at Ickworth together with oil portraits (fig. 26, 34 and 35) of the same individuals plus the Duchess of Savoy that may also have been gifts or have been purchased by Lord Bristol. Because of the state of war with France the journey to his new posting could not be undertaken overland and arrangements were made for him to be transported from Genoa on his brother Augustus's man-of-war, HMS *Monmouth*. He was accompanied by six servants, two in livery, with a further fifteen plus all his furniture, pictures, plate, coach, chaises and other baggage despatched separately in 'a great Dutch ship he had hired for that purpose'. Apart from a scare when an enemy boat was thought to be approaching, the journey went smoothly and he landed at Alicante on 4 September 1758. He distributed silver-gilt boxes to the officers of the guards 'which was the etiquette' and on finding a tape and seal put on one of his trunks by impertinent customs officials he 'took out his sisars and cut [the tape] before their faces', stepped into his coach and departed the town.[106]

With a fifteen-gun salute resounding in his ears and full of his own self-importance the 2nd Earl of Bristol headed off for what promised to be a very satisfactory posting. He was the most senior British diplomat in Europe, with the wealth and the inclination to live as was demanded at a court presided over by a cultured anglophile king, Ferdinand VI. Furthermore, the Queen, Barbara of Portugal, who had been described by Keene as possessing 'so many and so amiable qualities',[107] was, like Lord Bristol, a great music-lover. She patronised Italian opera and had the famous castrato Farinelli with his singers and an orchestra on hand to perform whenever required.[108]

---

1. His father's elder brother, Carr, Lord Hervey was then still alive.
2. Jewel Office delivery book 1698–1732, f. 265. The normal weight given for a gentleman was 100 oz though there does seem to have been some flexibility prior to the accession of George II. See chapter 1, note 92.
3. The ewer does not survive and must have been exchanged by either Lord Hervey or the 2nd Earl.
4. Halsband 1973, p. 45.
5. Hervey 1894b, vol. 2, pp. 164, 185, 187 and 190.
6. Hervey 1894a, pp. 118–20.
7. Ibid., p. 118.
8. Mortlock 2007, p. 89.
9. The Marquess of Rockingham, the Dukes of Grafton and Newcastle and the latter's brother Henry Pelham.
10. Hervey 1894a, pp. 119–20. Pillissier is noted as having been a godparent at the French church in Soho in 1750. See Huguenot Society 1891–3, p. 412.
11. Ibid., pp. 99–112.
12. Hervey 1894a, p. 85.
13. Black 1999, p. 37.
14. Hervey 1894b, vol. 3, pp. 253 and 258–9.
15. Newcastle papers, Add MS 32726, ff. 145–6, Duke of Richmond to Duke of Newcastle, Geneva, 18 February 1752.
16. Hoare's bank accounts, George William Hervey, ledger 39, f. 73. Hervey ceased drawing on the banker Alexandre Alexander, whom he had been using whilst in Geneva, in June 1740. He received funds in Venice in October 1740 and in Rome in January 1741.
17. Brinsley Ford Archive, Paul Mellon Centre, London, Notes on George William Hervey.
18. Lewis 1937–83, vol. 17, p. 37, Horace Mann to Horace Walpole, 9 May 1741
19. Brinsley Ford Archive, Paul Mellon Centre, London, Notes on George William Hervey.
20. Halsband 1973, p. 276.
21. John, Lord Hervey had been called up to the House of Lords in his father's barony in 1732.
22. Proceedings in Parliament 1743–74, vol. 1, pp. 73–5.
23. Hervey 1894b, vol. 3, p. 349 and 384 and Goslings ledgers, 130/21, f. 191. Lord Bristol had previously employed Flitcroft, in 1742–3, to build a new apartment for his eldest son at Ickworth. See p. 279 and Bristol diary and accounts 1742–51, 15 March 1743/4: 'Repaid Lord Hervey what he had paid to Mr. Flitcroft on Account of the new Building at Ickworth [£]24 06[s.]'
24. Horace Walpole described him as 'little Lord Hervey' and 'delicate', Lewis 1937–83, vol. 19, p. 148 and vol. 20, p. 145. Mrs Montagu wrote in the 1750s of the 'delicacy and effeminacy' of the whole family, Erskine 1953, p. 234, n. 2.
25. Lewis 1937–83, vol. 20, pp. 123–4, Horace Walpole to Horace Mann, 25 February 1750 (NS), Strawberry Hill.
26. Ibid., vol. 26, pp. 29–30. The original of this letter is in the Suffolk Record Office. Augustus Hervey endorsed it 'Lord Cobham alias Lord Gobham'.
27. Lewis 1937–83, vol. 18, p. 185, Horace Walpole to Sir Horace Mann, 3 March 1743.
28. Ibid., vol. 9, p. 98, Horace Walpole to George Montagu, 26 August 1749. See also Hervey 1894b, vol. 3, pp. 366–7. Each of the Seymour girls was provided with toilet plate in 1749 in anticipation of marriage, see Wickes ledgers, VAM 3 1747–50, f. 87.
29. Hervey 1894b, vol. 3, pp. 395–411. The 2nd Earl did propose to Lady Charlotte Tufton and Lady Stawel in early 1767 but was rejected by both. They were heiresses and he was minded to have a vicereine for Ireland. See Lewis 1937–83, vol. 30, p. 241.
30. Lewis 1937–83, vol. 18, p. 472, 17 July 1744.
31. Wickes ledgers, VAM 3 1747–50, ff. 1 and 20. For more on the Leinster service see Barr 1980, pp. 197–205. A significant portion was sold at Christie's 5/7/2012, lot 48.
32. George Wickes often described such embellishments as ornaments though not in this case. See for instance Wickes ledgers, VAM 3 1747–50, f. 164, 'Nurl'd [gadrooned] Plates with Ornments' supplied to the Marquess of Granby at 7s 8d per ounce.
33. Wickes ledgers, VAM 3 1747–50, f. 86 and Christie's, 25 November 1987, lot 170.
34. Calculated on an average weight per plate of 18 oz, 5 dwt, at a charge of 1s 2d plus 2s per plate duty.
35. Lord Kildare actually purchased seven dozen which at £770 work out at £110 per dozen, thus £660 for six dozen.
36. Most of his British contemporaries were quite content with straightforward shaped and gadrooned plates like those he commissioned, for example the 3rd Earl of Bute, for some of whose plates see Christie's, 3 July 1996, lots 86–9.
37. Based on an average charge per ounce on new plate of 9s and an average on old plate refashioned of 1s 2d.
38. See for instance Wickes ledgers, VAM 3 1747–50, f. 122, credits to Lady Caroline Harpur, 1750 and f. 126, credits to Mrs. Harvey (no relation to the Herveys), also 1750.
39. Calculated at 9s per ounce for new plate and 1s 2d for refashioning old.
40. Schroder 2009, cat. 185–6, pp. 476–485. Those by de Lamerie are of 1748 with Kandler branches of 1753. The other set, without branches, is by Kandler, 1752. The female stick was the model chosen by Lord Bristol for his set of twelve candelabra of 1758; see cat. 72.
41. He was near St James's Church. See Grimwade 1990, p. 567.
42. Ibid.
43. Cameron 1996, pp. 495–9.
44. Augustus Hervey recorded in his journal in July 1750 that Lord Hervey (as the 2nd Earl then was) was furious with their mother for making 'rank Jacobites' of their youngest sisters Caroline and Emily, teaching them 'to reverence the Pretender'. See Erskine 1953, p. 105.
45. HRO, 31M57/637–8, John Chute's statements from Frederick Kandler, 1756–8 and 1769–74. Discovered by Vanessa Brett and brought to my attention by Peter Cameron.
46. Sale 1995, p. 391.
47. Grimwade 1990, p. 567. The Duke of Beaufort continued making payments to Charles Kandler up to that year. See Sale 1995, p. 391.
48. From The Vyne can be added John Carter who made a set of waiters supplied by Kandler in 1773.
49. Erskine 1953, p. 111.
50. *The London Advertiser and Literary Gazette*, no. 37, 15 April 1751.
51. Erskine 1953, p. 113.
52. Ibid., p. 115.
53. This blatant mark of royal displeasure was dispensed to numerous of George II's courtiers and even, on occasion, to foreign ministers. See, for instance, Thompson 2011, pp. 158–9.
54. Newcastle papers, Add MS 32726, f. 199, Earl of Bristol to Duke of Newcastle 29 February 1752 and ff. 350–1, Duke of Newcastle to Earl of Bristol 28 March 1752, Add MS 32736, ff. 176–7, Earl of Bristol to Duke of Newcastle 8 August 1754.
55. Ibid., Add MS 32736, ff. 176–7, Earl of Bristol to Duke of Newcastle 8 August 1754.
56. Thompson 2011, pp. 230–1. Both the 4th Earl of Rochford and his countess had reputations for loose morals.
57. Newcastle papers, Add MS 32852, f. 343, Earl of Bristol to Duke of Newcastle 3 February 1755 and f. 555, Earl of Bristol to Lady Yarmouth 20 February 1755; AST, Materie Politiche Estero, Lettere Ministeri, mazzo 59/1, Count Perrone to King Carlo Emanuele III, 13 February 1755. Perrone stated his opinion that Lord Bristol would be very acceptable if appointed.
58. AST, Materie Politiche Estero, Lettere Ministeri, mazzo 59/1, Count Perrone to Cavaliere Giuseppe Osorio [Sardinian foreign minister] 3 and 7 April 1755.
59. Woolf 1961, p. 211.
60. Erskine 1953, pp. 59–60.
61. Pollak 1991, p. 2, quoting Thomas Nugent who was writing in the 1770s.
62. AST, Materie Politiche Estero, Lettere Ministeri, mazzo 59/2, Cavaliere Giuseppe Osorio to Count Perrone, 21 June 1755 and King Carlo Emanuele III to Perrone, 21 June 1755.
63. Ibid., mazzo 59/3, Count Viry to Cavaliere Osorio, 20 November 1755. Management of foreign affairs by the British government was divided between the two Secretaries of State, that for the Southern Department covering southern Europe including France, Spain and the Italian states.
64. TNA, SP 99/64, State Papers Venice 1744–5, Sir James Gray, 2nd Bt to Duke of Newcastle, Venice, 26 February 1745 (NS).
65. Newcastle papers, Add MS 32889, ff. 8–9, Earl of Bristol to Duke of Newcastle, Madrid, 12 March 1759.
66. Chatham papers, PRO 30/8/24, f. 40, Earl of Bristol to William Pitt, Turin, 28 April 1758.
67. Erskine 1953, p. 291, n. 1.
68. Matthew Prior had advised the incoming ambassador to Paris in 1699 'that the beauty of one's coaches and the *bel air* of one's liveries are things essential to a man's reputation in France'. Jacobsen 2012, p. 34. This was clearly the case for the 1st Earl of Portland, ambassador in 1698. The Duc de Saint-Simon wrote of him that 'No one more splendid could possibly have been nominated. He was attended by a vast and magnificent suite, and his expenditure on his table, horses, liveries, carriages, furniture, dress, and silver was most princely and all in exquisite taste.' Norton 1980, p. 43.
69. Lewis 1937–83, vol. 21, p. 175, Sir Horace Mann to Horace Walpole, 11 February 1758, Florence.
70. Piccoli 2016. I am grateful to him for sharing his work with me prior to publication.
71. Goslings ledgers, 130/25, ff. 79–80.
72. For comparison, in the 1770s the 3rd Earl of Bristol's annual expenditure included £2,200 for housekeeping, £1,400 for wages and liveries, £600 for stables and £180 for gardens. SRO, 941/50/6, Income and Expenditure of Augustus John, Earl of Bristol's 'Estates in Suffolk, Lincolnshire, and Essex'.
73. Goslings ledgers, 130/25, f. 77, 29 April 1755.
74. Lewis 1937–83, vol. 18, f. 472, Horace Mann to Horace Walpole, 17 July 1744 (NS), Florence.
75. TNA, SP 78/200, State Papers France, f. 42, Earl Waldegrave to the Duke of Newcastle, 20 February 1731/2, Paris.
76. Lodge 1933, p. 96, Benjamin Keene to Abraham Castres, 20/2/1749, Madrid.
77. State Papers Turin, SP 92/63, ff. 100–2, Earl of Bristol to Earl of Holderness, 21 June 1755, Turin. The 3rd Earl of Essex took the same route in 1732 and sent his baggage and servants by sea to Genoa. See SRO, HA 507/7/7, f. 265, 'Earl of Essex Extraordinaries', October 1732.
78. François Claude Bernard Louis, Marquis de Chauvelin (1716–1773) was a crony of Louis XV and his death at the King's gaming table inspired Alexandre Dumas's novel, *Le Testament de M Chauvelin* (1861). His son, Bernard-François, served as Ambassador from Republican France to Britain and also inspired a literary character – the villain in Baroness Orczy's Scarlet Pimpernel novels.
79. State Papers Turin, SP 92/63, ff. 53–5 and 88–9, George Charles to Sir Thomas Robinson, 12 April 1755 and 31 May 1755, Turin.
80. Ibid., ff. 151–3, Earl of Bristol to Earl of Holderness, 30 August 1755, Turin.
81. For a discussion of opera in Turin in the 1740s and 50s, and of the painting attributed to Graneri see Butler 2009. I am grateful to Annarita Colturato for drawing this to my attention.
82. Ibid., ff. 196–8, Earl of Bristol to Henry Fox, 13 December 1755, Turin.

83. Ibid., SP 92/65, unpaginated, Earl of Bristol to William Pitt, 23 November 1757, Turin.
84. Erskine 1953, p. 179.
85. It is noticeable from the Jewel Office records that those who already had experience of the Continent were much more likely to include a full complement of tureens plus stands in their allocations of plate. Examples include the 4th Earl of Sandwich (who took eight tureens and stands) and the 2nd Earl of Albemarle in 1749 and Benjamin Keene the following year. Jewel Office Delivery Book 1732–93, ff. 101, 108 and 111.
86. Lodge 1933, p. 366.
87. Lord Bristol drew down £4,050 from Paul Torras & Co. in 1756, £2,660 in 1757 and £3,970 in 1758. Goslings ledgers, 130/25, ff. 79–80 and 130/27, ff. 64–5.
88. Metropolitan Museum acc. no. 1997.151.1a, b–.4. See also Fina 2002, p. 38.
89. See Fina and Mana 2012, pp. 44–5 and figs 8 and 8a–c.
90. Fina 2002, pp. 92–3.
91. For the tureens see Fina and Mana 2012, cat. 296–7, pp. 208–11, ill. They bear the assay mark of Carlo Micha who was in post from 1759. For the shell-handled dish see Bargoni, 1963, p. 24, no. 159 and tav. 45. It has the counter-assay mark of Giovan Battista Carron, as found on many of the Bristol pieces.
92. Mazza and Piccoli 2011, pp. 71–3. See Fina and Mana 2012, pp. 238–9 for biographical information on Serafino. References to General Wentworth's purchase of silver in Turin and the disposal of his goods are amongst his papers (Stratford-upon-Avon Record Office), including the bill from Giacomo Antonio Serafino, ref. D 18/5/28. I am grateful to Edoardo Piccoli for drawing my attention to Wentworth's commission and these papers.
93. Winterthur Library, papers of R.W. Symonds, Box 6 /28, *The Daily Post*, no. 3226, 21 January 1729. I am indebted to Tessa Murdoch for this reference and for suggesting the connection with the Neptune centrepiece for which see Jones and Garibaldi 2006.
94. Oman 1966, pp. 500–503. Boucheron's mark was, when Oman was writing, generally thought to be Lorenzo Lavy's.
95. V&A Museum nos. LOAN.ST.ANSELM.1–5.
96. Dutens 1806, vol. 1, pp. 188–9.
97. State Papers Turin, SP 92/65, Earl of Bristol to William Pitt, 9 March 1757, Turin.
98. Newcastle papers, Add MS 32864, ff. 442–3, Earl of Bristol to Duke of Newcastle, April 1756, Turin.
99. Ibid., Add MS 32876, f. 361, Earl of Bristol to Duke of Newcastle, 21 December 1757, Turin.
100. Holderness correspondence, ff. 338–9, Sir James Gray to Earl of Holderness, Naples, received 21 November 1757.
101. State Papers Spain, SP 94/157, ff. 105–6, William Pitt to Ruvigny de Cosne, 28 March 58, Whitehall, 'It is not to be doubted, but that the Appointment of a Nobleman, of His Lordship's Rank, will be considered, in the present Conjuncture, as a Mark of his Majesty's Attention to that Court.'
102. State Papers Turin, SP 92/66, unpaginated, William Pitt to Earl of Bristol, 28 March 1758, Whitehall.
103. Newcastle papers, Add MS 32879, f. 308, Earl of Bristol to Duke of Newcastle, 26 April 1758, Turin.
104. State Papers Turin, SP 92/66, unpaginated, Earl of Bristol to William Pitt, 9 August 1758, Turin.
105. Storrs 2000, p. 247.
106. Erskine 1953, pp. 289–91.
107. Lodge 1933, p. 121. Keene adored the Spanish Queen and eulogised her regularly in his letters.
108. Sadie 1990, p. 331.

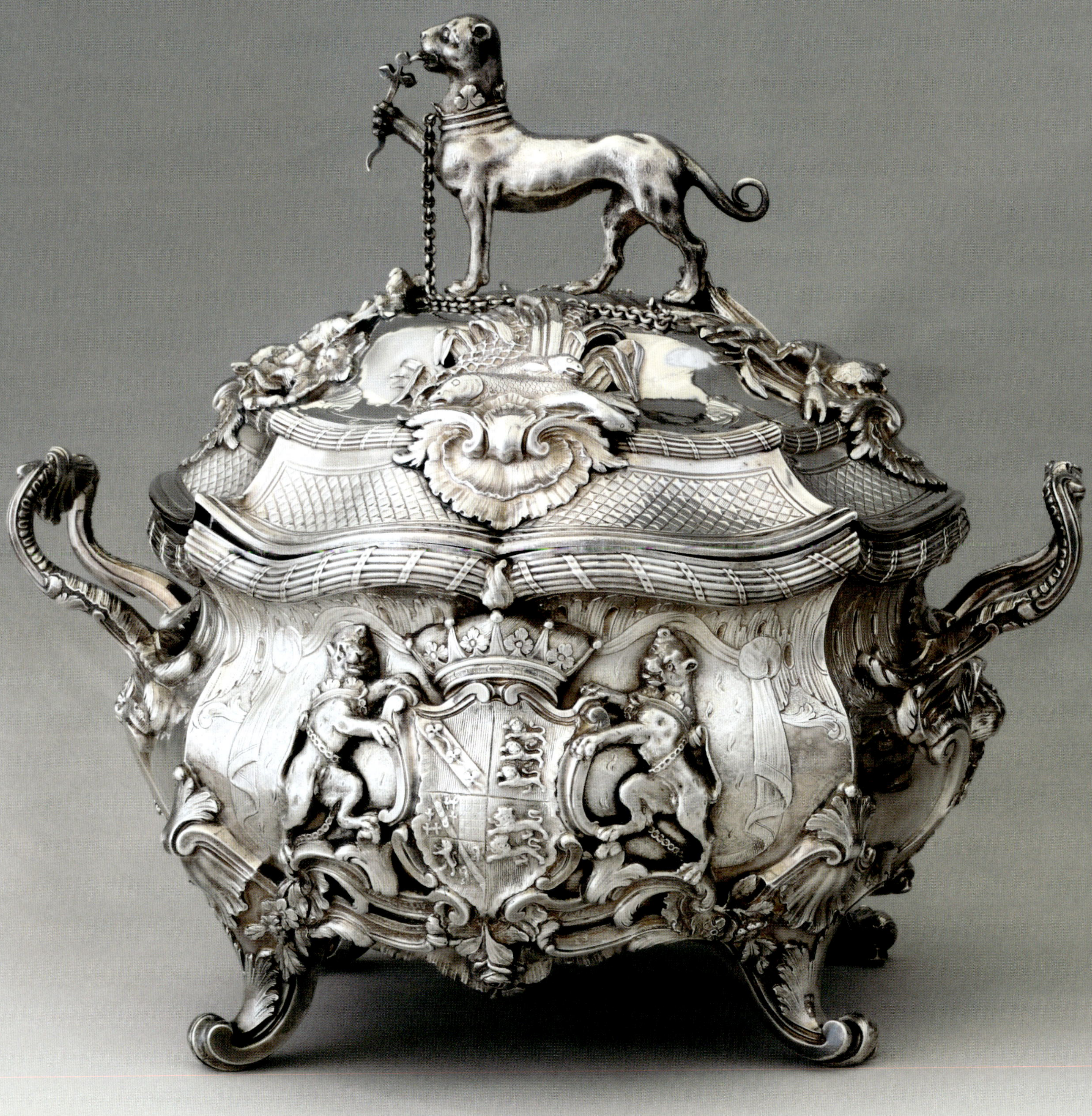

A pair of round tureens (Turin, *c.*1756) from the silver of George William Hervey, 2nd Earl of Bristol (see cat. 53)

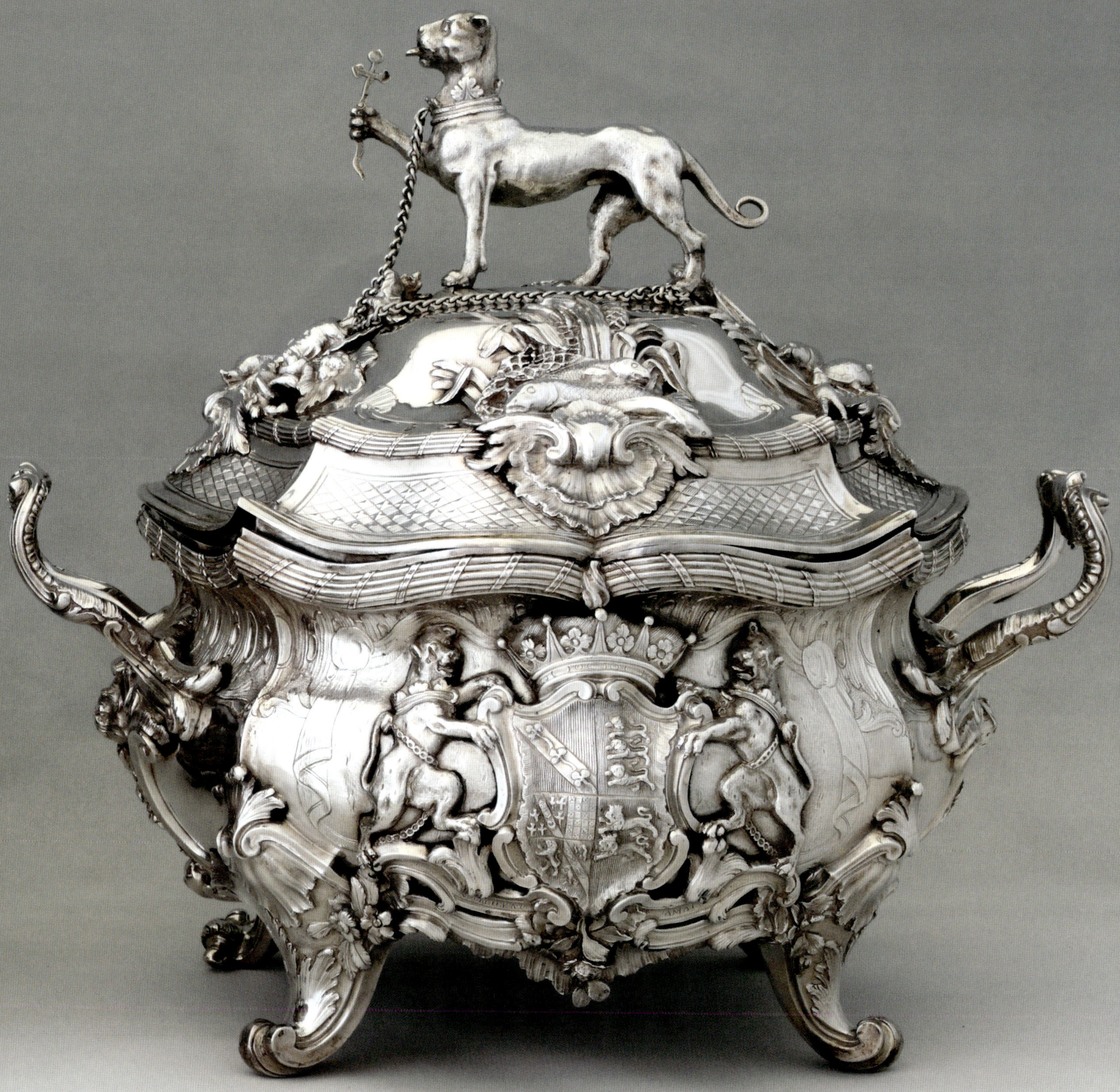

THREE

PERQUISITE PLATE AND THE LATER CAREER OF THE 2ND EARL OF BRISTOL

Ambassadors representing all significant European countries would have been expected to have a substantial quantity of plate to uphold the dignity of their respective monarchs, but it seems that only in Britain did a system develop whereby it was lent, and subsequently given. The Dutch Republic did sometimes make loans but did not discharge plate to the borrower[1] and in France, Prussia and all the other major powers it appears that the ambassador was expected to provide for himself.[2] Thus it was that the Marquis d'Abreu, the Spanish ambassador to London, had to spend his own money with George Wickes in 1756 to augment his plate, acquiring a number of items including a pair of tureens.[3] The Venetian aristocracy in particular saw the costs involved in being a diplomat as an investment, being an effective way of strengthening their pretensions 'to being advanced & in the Government at the Return home'.[4] This approach was obviously cheaper for the country being represented but did narrow the pool of potential candidates, and had it been applied in Britain it would have precluded such gifted diplomats as Sir Benjamin Keene and James Harris (subsequently 1st Earl of Malmesbury) who were from less exalted backgrounds.

On being appointed ambassador to Spain in 1758 the 2nd Earl of Bristol was thus entitled to an allocation of silver from the Jewel Office, the organisation which had been established in the Middle Ages to look after the king's treasure and to supply plate for royal and official use.[5] Others eligible were the great officers of state who carried out the monarch's business at home and ambassadorial secretaries and colonial governors who also represented him or her abroad. By the 18th century this had become clearly codified with colonial governors receiving 180 oz of white chapel plate, ambassadorial secretaries 300 oz white, the Lord Chamberlain,[6] Lord Steward, the Treasurer and the Comptroller of the Household plus the Master of the Horse, Groom of the Stole, and the Secretaries of State all receiving 1000 oz of white plate, the Speaker 4000 oz, also white, and ambassadors 5893 oz white and 1066 oz gilt.[7] These were the only post-holders to receive what was designated as 'indenture plate' by the Jewel Office and it had, by custom, become part of the perquisites of their jobs, starting as a loan but almost always being discharged to the recipient after a seemly period of time.[8] It is thus commonly known as 'perquisite plate' and is marked out by being engraved with the royal arms.

The various stages of allocating and discharging perquisite plate can be closely followed in Lord Bristol's case through the Jewel Office records (appendix 4) and his personal papers. First of all a warrant was issued on the 22 June 1758 by the Lord Chamberlain, the 4th Duke of Devonshire, signifying the King's pleasure that the 'the Usual Allowance' of white and gilt plate be provided and delivered to 'the Earl of Bristol His Majestys Ambassador Extraordinary and Plenipotentiary to the Catholick King [the King of Spain]'.[9] The commission would then have been allocated by Thomas Minors, the principal goldsmith (merely an administrator), to a subordinate, working goldsmith, in this case Simon Le Sage. The Earl may well have had some say in this choice and he would certainly, thereafter, have agreed exactly what was to be provided, it being at his discretion to do so. In fact Lord Bristol was not to find Le Sage so agreeable to work with as Frederick Kandler and he was frustrated by what he considered to be a slow pace, writing to Joseph Richardson, First Clerk in the Southern Department, on 27 November, 1758, 'I am concern'd the silversmith is so dilatory; he made Lady Hervey advance him £100 without which he said he cou'd not go on, pray do not settle his accounts without communicating them to my Mother.'[10] She, Lady Hervey, had made the payment on 16 September and presumably acted as her son's agent in ensuring the commission was executed according to his wishes, her sophistication and taste for all things French making her a safe choice for such a task.[11] The commission being so large and the pressure great, Le Sage subcontracted a good deal to Kandler, David Hennell and James Peltro amongst others, as is evident from the hallmarks of the surviving pieces (cat. 63–78).

Though there is no specific mention of the plate having to be brought to the Jewel Office for inspection this must have been the case, as is corroborated by a Parker and Wakelin ledger entry for the 1st Earl Harcourt in 1769. He had been appointed ambassador to France and was charged 15s 'for Cartage to ye Jewel Office D[itt]o. Back & D[itto]. to ye Inn' (and thence to Paris) on 13 March,[12] just before his plate was officially released.[13] The pieces presented would be listed in the 'Plate Book or Goldsmiths Book', giving descriptions, the rates per ounce charged, weights and the sums payable to the goldsmith.[14] Precise dates are not given in this ledger but as Lord Bristol's pieces appear under 1758 they must have been taken to the Jewel Office at the very end of the year.[15] On 9 January 1759 the plate was handed over to John Turner as agent for the Earl and was listed once again, this time in the delivery book and without costs.[16] Six weeks later a routine note in the warrant book recorded that none of the plate had been returned and that left the way clear for the discharge which is dated 9 April 1759. Being about a valuable commodity, it is a lengthy legal document but the nub of it is contained in one phrase: 'in Consideration of the many good and acceptable Services performed unto Us by the said George William Earl of Bristol to grant unto him the aforesaid plate and to discharge him from the same'.[17] The gap between delivery of the plate and the discharge had rapidly shortened since the beginning of the century and there was scarcely time any more for the recipient to have realistically performed those 'good and acceptable Services' he was being rewarded for. Fees, totalling £64 and including substantial tips to clerks and chamber keepers, were paid for the initial warrant and the discharge of plate[18] and the final act of the Jewel Office was to cross through the list in the delivery book, thereby indicating that the plate no longer belonged to the Crown.

Matters did not end there, however, as the limits on what could be charged for perquisite plate, 10s 6d per ounce for gilt and 8s for white with an overall ceiling of £2,950,[19] would, if adhered to, have precluded such expensively fashioned pieces as Lord Bristol's set of twelve spectacular candelabra (cat. 72). The simplest solution was for the recipient to make an additional, personal payment direct to the goldsmith and that is what Benjamin Keene had done in 1748, noting in a letter to Abraham Castres, the Envoy in Lisbon, that his four 'magnificent' tureens had cost him '£300 out of my own pocket on account of the wrought work'. Alternatively, an excessive weight could be recorded in the Jewel Office ledgers to compensate for the fashion not able to be charged, as happened in 1761 with the Speaker, Sir John Cust's great cistern.[20] This, however, required the officials to be complicit and though they may have been perfectly happy to be so, a more subtle approach appears to have been taken by Le Sage on behalf of Lord Bristol. From the evidence of the surviving pieces it would appear that he presented a number of items, presumably from stock, which were not actually intended for the Earl and in that way extracted the additional payment from the Jewel Office (see cat. 72). There are certainly no private payments beyond the £100 Le Sage had required up front and a great deal more than that would have been required to cover the extra cost on the twelve candelabra alone.

In addition to plate Lord Bristol also received a full-length portrait of George II which was provided by John Shackleton and framed by René Stone, respectively the King's Painter and Frame Maker,[21] plus various items from the Great Wardrobe. There was a richly embroidered state canopy accompanied by a 'Chair of State, 2 High Stools, Foot Stool and 2 Cusheons', all upholstered in crimson silk damask and bedecked with gold tassels and fringe, the latter weighing 244 oz. An altar cloth of crimson velvet paned with gold tissue and with more gold fringe was provided for the chapel together with a finely bound bible and four books of Common Prayer.[22] On ascertaining that the furniture to be placed beneath the canopy was to have plain frames the Earl, not considering them up to the show he intended to put on, requested they be left behind 'as I propose setting up more ornamental ones ... but I wou'd have the damask with the gold fringe belonging to it sent for the covering of the chair and stools I intend making here'.[23] He was also turning his mind to the smooth running of his entertaining and the use of his plate and he asked Richardson to execute a private commission for him:

> *I shou'd be much oblig'd to you if you wou'd order Mr. Hallet the Cabinet-Maker or whoever now keeps that great shop of his in Long-Acre where I us'd to deal, to send me six large mahogany trays quite plain, for servants to bring dishes upon to the eating-room, I hope I explain my-self right, and at the same time to pack up a mahogany eating table that by adding different parts and leaves to it, will hold from eight to four and twenty people; let the cabinet maker furnish me with good wood without knots. I have dealt so much in that shop I hope I may rely on his serving an old Customer well.*[24]

William Hallett, the cabinetmaker referred to, had in fact retired and the business was now run by William Vile and John Cobb to whom the work was given.[25] The pieces were not, however, destined to reach Spain, the Earl's account with the Southern Department being debited on 18 June with £3 3s paid 'To Mr Vile for the Loss on Three Large Mahogoney Tables & Trays'.[26] They must have been destroyed in the fire which devastated the associated workshop of Samuel Norman, Hallett's nephew, in January 1759.[27]

TRANSPORTATION TO MADRID

Having missed the opportunity of bringing the plate, portrait and Great Wardrobe allocations on 'a ship of war coming to the mediterranean' in December, thanks to the continued slow pace, as Lord Bristol judged it, of both Le Sage and Shackleton,[28] the combined hoard was finally dispatched in the spring of 1759. The plate would have been packed in baize bags and placed in chests supplied by Le Sage, probably including those surviving at Ickworth (fig. 37), and there would have been rough outer cases too. That was how the 1st Earl Harcourt's silver for Paris was dealt with a decade later, Parker and Wakelin providing 27 baize bags at 2s each, a baize cushion at the same price, two large and two lesser plate chests for £32 10s and two deal boxes with paper shavings for £1 0s 6d. The chests were matted and corded and secured with padlocks. There were also '30 Plate Brushes & 4 Washleather Skins' at 16s and '12 boxes of Crocus' (ferric oxide, also known as jeweller's rouge) for keeping the silver clean.[29]

Once safely packed Lord Bristol's baggage would have been transported from the Thames by sea to Portsmouth, where the plate was loaded on Admiral Boscawen's flagship, HMS *Namur*, and the rest of the cases on other ships of the squadron.[30] They all set sail from Spithead in the Solent on 13 April and reached Gibraltar Bay on the 27th without encountering storms or enemy vessels.[31] News reached Lord Bristol of the safe arrival around 8 May and he instructed Burrington Goldsworthy, British consul in El Puerto de Santa María, to arrange onward carriage to Madrid.[32] Goldsworthy organised the necessary passports and certificates to prevent the cases being opened, found 'a careful Person to have charge of it all the Way' and was offered a couple of armed men by the Spanish authorities. After some difficulty he also found a carrier 'at the rate of Twenty Nine Rials of Vellon [just under 12 standard reales] the Arrove [equivalent to 25 lbs]', the whole being estimated to weigh 90 Arroves or almost exactly a ton.[33] The fourteen cases were sent in a Royal Navy vessel from Gibraltar to the small Spanish port of Tarifa where the carrier, one Joseph Sempara, was to take charge of them and set out for Madrid.[34] All did not go smoothly, however, and Lord Bristol must have been alarmed to learn that on his arrival at Tarifa Sempara was imprisoned on suspicion of involvement in an illicit trade, and, worse still, having been proved innocent and set out at last for Madrid he then returned to El Puerto without any of the baggage including the silver. It had been impounded at Medina Sidonia, less than fifty miles into the journey. Goldsworthy managed to obtain its release and Sempara reached Madrid around 10 July, blaming the 'Weight, and Bulk of some of the Cases' for a slower pace than he had first quoted.[35] Having been only two weeks at sea from England to Gibraltar it had then taken nearly a month and a half to get the silver and other cases overland to their final destination. Lord Bristol must have been very relieved indeed to see them.

The Earl was to have an even more frustrating time with a picture which was sent on to him after his departure from Turin. As he appears to have taken no interest in subject pictures this may have been one of the three versions of the portrait of him in peer's robes with a chair of state attributed

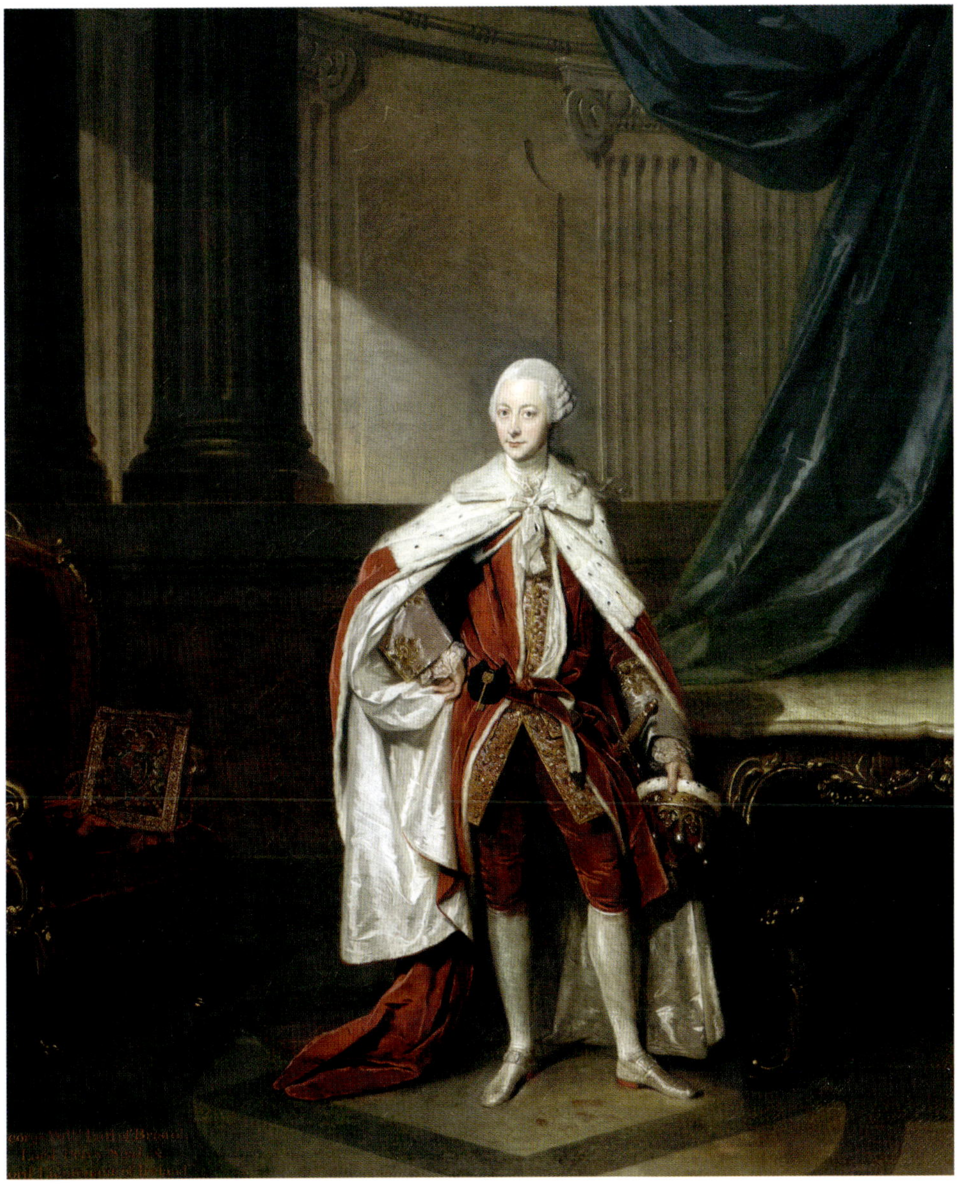

FIG. 36 / *George William Hervey, 2nd Earl of Bristol* attributed to Johann Zoffany, *c.*1758. Oil on canvas: 124.5 x 99.1 cm (49 x 39 in). National Trust, Ickworth.

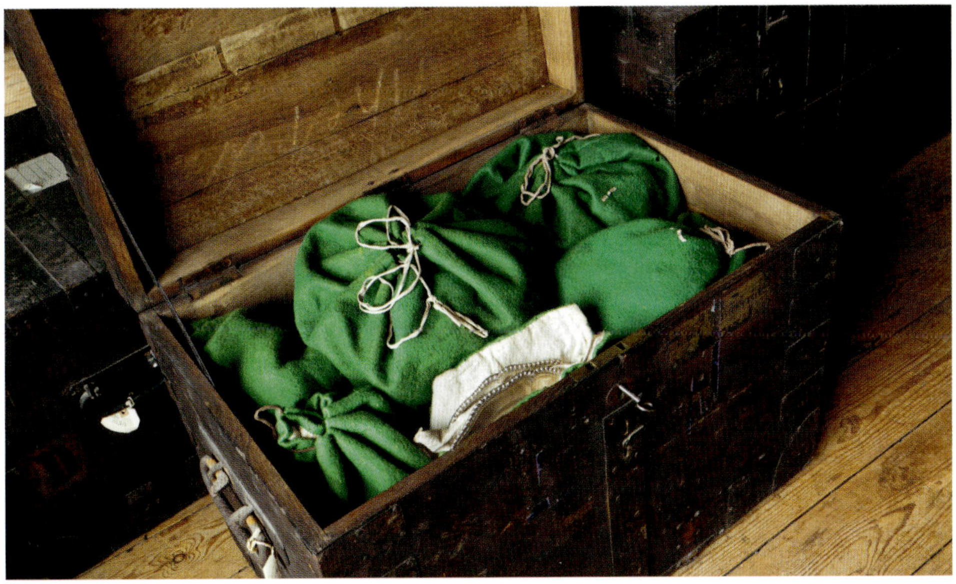

FIG. 37 / One of several plate chests of *c.*1758 surviving at Ickworth, with contemporary baize bags. Oak with iron straps and handles and brass plates engraved 'Earl of Bristol'. National Trust, Ickworth.

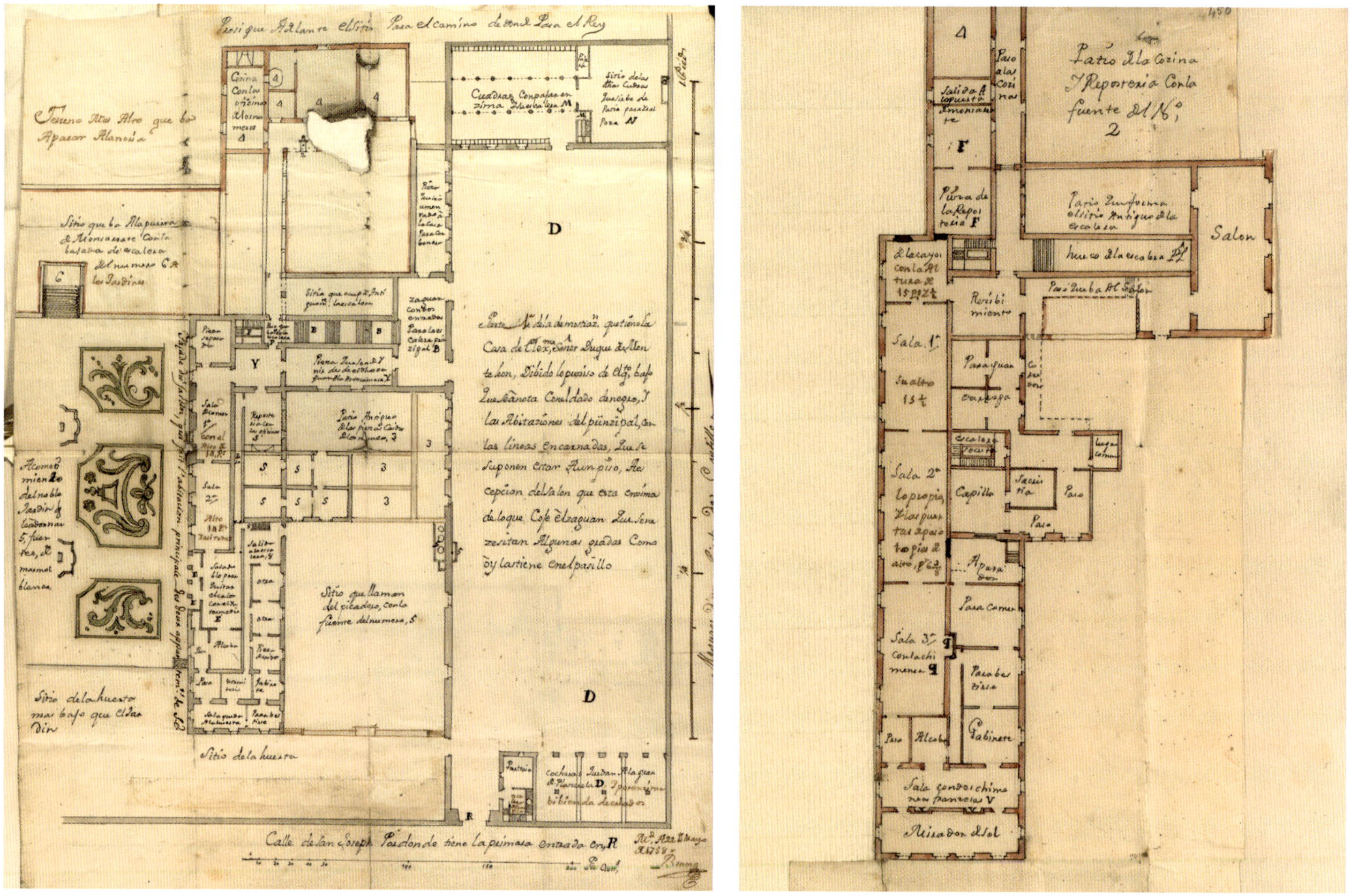

FIG. 38 / Plans of the ground floor and *piano nobile* of the Monteleón Palace, Madrid, *c.*1758. These plans were probably sent to Lord Bristol whilst he was still in Turin. Bristol Papers, Suffolk Record Office, Bury St Edmunds. Ref: 507/7/6, ff. 449–50.

to Johann Zoffany (fig. 36).[36] The artist could well have passed through Turin on his way from Rome to Trier around 1757 and could have been sending either the original or, more likely, one of the two copies. Whether it was this portrait or another picture altogether, it was impounded in Marseilles, finally retrieved by James Holford, the British consul in Genoa, and sent from there to Alicante in October, 1761.[37] It should have had time to have reached the Earl before he left Madrid at the beginning of the following year, though the fact that the whereabouts of what must be the prime version of the portrait are unknown may suggest otherwise.

THE MONTELEÓN PALACE

The painting was destined to join the giltwood furniture from Turin, the greatly augmented Bristol plate and the richly upholstered state canopy with its associated seat furniture, amongst no doubt much else of equal grandeur that had filled the 'great Dutch ship' hired by the Earl in Genoa. All was to be displayed in the vast town house of the Duke of Monteleón (figs. 38–9), situated on the north-eastern edge of the city as it then was, which could not have been more desirable as an ambassadorial residence to a man of the 2nd Earl of Bristol's proud temperament. Built in the 1690s for an intimate of Charles II of Spain, the palace contained grand baroque interiors including a mirrored gallery and a staircase frescoed by the distinguished Spanish painter, Bartolomé Pérez, and there had been a remodelling in the 1720s to allow the building to serve as a residence for Philip V and his second wife, Elizabeth Farnese, whilst the new royal palace was being constructed.[38] The grounds, which adjoined open country, were extensive and included a viewing terrace and an adjoining large and fashionable parterre presumably laid out during royal occupation (fig. 40). A French visitor to Madrid had commented that it 'would be difficult to find a more sumptuous residence'[39] and Sir Benjamin Keene, Lord Bristol's predecessor, who had taken the tenancy in the summer of 1749, described how as he loved 'a *puff*, and as I can afford it and have no useless expenses, I have been tempted to put our Master's arms on a real Palace' as large as a Cambridge college. Sir Benjamin also further embellished the interiors, introducing an English-style fireplace into one of the rooms and obtaining commodes and a set of Gobelins tapestries, presumably for the chamber he used as a drawing room. Having 'spent above twenty thousand dollars' on the place, he anticipated outshining all others in the diplomatic community apart from the Portuguese ambassador, the Viscount Ponte de Lima, 'who lives neatly and nobly'.[40]

Though Lord Bristol had always been personally abstemious[41] he prepared himself for entertaining on a grand scale by securing casks of Malaga and sherry wines from the British consul at Malaga[42] and by establishing a household, or 'family' as it was then termed, on the grandest of scales. His chaplain, the Rev. Edward Clarke, described how the Spanish '*Grandees*, and people of the first fashion' in Madrid lived with great pomp and when taking 'their airing on *gala*, or court days, all their footmen are then dressed in laced [gold braided] liveries, with plumes of feathers in their hats'. He also noted that the number of servants they kept was 'immoderate' and that his master, 'in compliance with the taste of the country, keeps near 100' in a 'large, magnificent and expensive' house [the Monteleón Palace] which would contain an assembly of 'two or three hundred people with ease'.[43] The servants would certainly have included a French chef, and the confectioner and *maître d'hôtel* might also have been French, as those employed by Sir Benjamin Keene appear to have been.[44] Lord Bristol would at the very least have maintained Keene's standards and he had considered his table to be amongst the three finest in Madrid, along with those of the chief minister, Ricardo Wall, and the Dutch ambassador. Before his agreement with the Marquis d'Aubeterre to give up competitive entertaining Keene hosted a number of 'great dinners', including some to the entire *corps diplomatique*, and on the last such occasion, in August 1753, there was so much bustle during the preparation that, in spite of the scale of the Monteleón Palace, Sir Benjamin fled to the country 'to leave my house to cooks and scullions'.[45]

ROYAL MADNESS AND SOBRIETY

With his magnificent and richly furnished house, most elevated of official situations, plate to rival the finest in Europe, and huge personal income Lord Bristol was in a good position to take full advantage of his term at a court that in recent years had been both cultivated and reasonably well-disposed towards Britain. From the moment that he set foot on Spanish soil, however, it would have been evident to him that the situation was changing rapidly. Queen Barbara, who had fallen ill before Lord Bristol left Turin, suffered horribly for over a month and died on 27 August 1758, just days before he landed at Alicante.[46] The King, who was devoted to his wife, was distraught when he entered the palace-fortress of Villaviciosa de Odón for 'the usual 9 days of retirement observed in Spain in such circumstances' but it soon became apparent that his grief had led to some sort of severe mental breakdown and reports emerged that he would not be shaved for fear of having his throat cut, or lie down in case he died.[47] More and more disturbing accounts were relayed by Lord

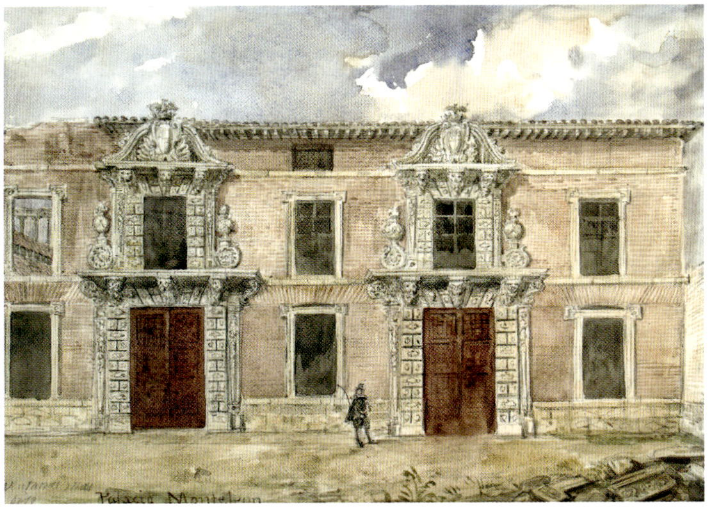

FIG. 39 / *The Monteleón Palace, Madrid*, 1850. Part of the principal façade shortly before demolition. Watercolour on paper. Fundación Lázaro Galdiano, Madrid.

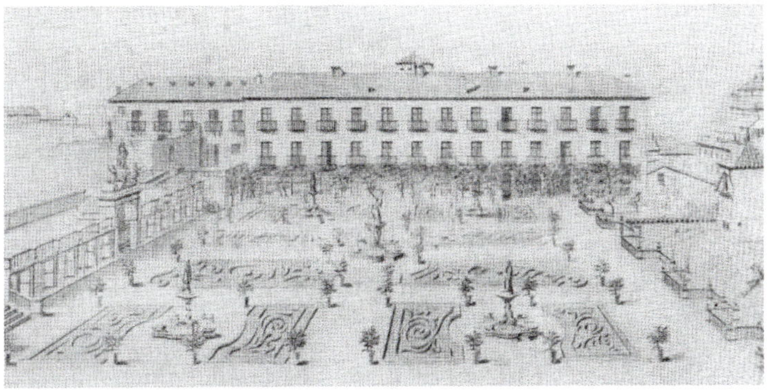

FIG. 40 / Garden front of the Monteleón Palace, Madrid, *c.*1750, as reproduced in Sir Richard Lodge (ed.), *The Private Correspondence of Sir Benjamin Keene*, Cambridge, 1933.

Bristol to William Pitt and government business, along with court ritual, was at a standstill. King Ferdinand carried on in this state for many months and by July 1759 he was having to be sewn into his sheets to prevent him hurting himself, 'yet nothing can hinder his Screams and Howlings, which are heard in most parts of the Castle'.[48] Finally his sufferings were ended by death on 10 August, nearly a year after his wife, and he was succeeded by his half-brother, the King of Naples, who became Charles III of Spain (1716–88) (fig. 41).

Charles III's character and outlook were very different to those of Ferdinand, and that did not bode well for Lord Bristol. The new Spanish king bore a deep grudge against the British for humiliatingly forcing him to withdraw from the War of the Austrian Succession in 1742 under threat of bombardment of Naples and he was far from being charming or cultured, beyond his love of grandiose building.[49] Sir James Gray, still smarting from failing to secure the Spanish ambassadorship, wrote to the Earl that as a lover of music he should, under Charles III, 'suspend the hopes of indulging your taste for it while at Madrid'. He added smugly that at Naples 'Next Friday on the King's name day we are to have an Opera … in which I am assured there is both fire & invention.'[50]

There was, at least, a fully functioning state again and Lord Bristol admired the King's honesty and dedication to business, noting that 'as His Catholic Majesty rises constantly at Five, no Matters are postponed, as formerly, from Day to Day, & then left unexecuted; but ... Affairs are now examined by the Catholick King Himself, & everything dispatched with Accuracy & Expedition.' Bristol presented his credentials to the King and Queen on 24 January 1760 but he did not have a grand public entry with processions of carriages, feasting and entertainment, which he would probably rather have enjoyed, as such events were largely abandoned by the mid-century through agreement between the great powers, in order to defray the enormous costs involved.[51] Nor were there to be intimate and open discussions with the King in his closet or walks with him in the garden, as there had been with Carlo Emanuele in Turin, and the Queen of Spain's death in September made the court even more dour.

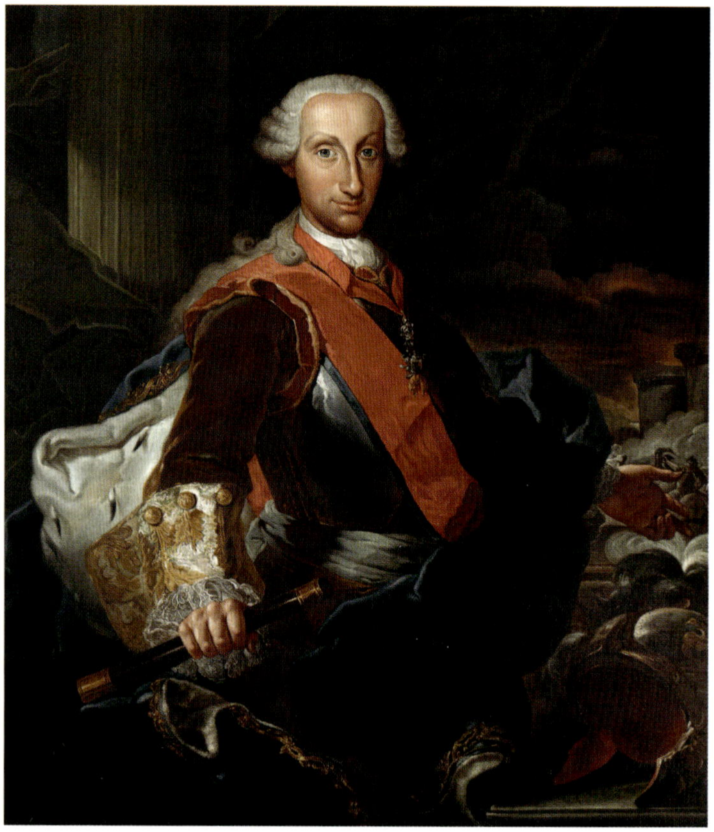

FIG. 41 / *King Charles III of Spain*, studio of Anton Raphael Mengs, *c.*1760. The portrait was probably a gift from the King to Lord Bristol. Oil on canvas: 124.5 x 99.1 cm (49 x 39 in). National Trust, Ickworth.

The year ended badly for the Earl personally too, with a bout of ill health and his determined efforts to secure the Garter finally and firmly rejected by George II. It was common for diplomats to seek honours; Benjamin Keene pursued the 'gew gaw of a red ribbon' (knighthood of the Bath) in the early 1750s[52] as did Sir James Gray later in the decade,[53] and the arguments were always the same, that they deserved reward and the distinction would put them in a better position at the relevant foreign court, particularly with regard to their French counterparts. Few were as determined without achieving success as Lord Bristol, however. He had begun with a salvo of letters to William Pitt[54] and the Duke of Newcastle in the spring of 1759, and pursued an increasingly acrimonious correspondence with the latter over the next eighteen months before resorting to a direct appeal to the King in November 1760.[55] All was to no avail and the Earl had had the added chagrin of learning that one of the vacant Garters went instead to Earl Temple, the man, who as Lord Cobham, had so insultingly spat in his hat in 1750 (see chapter 2).[56]

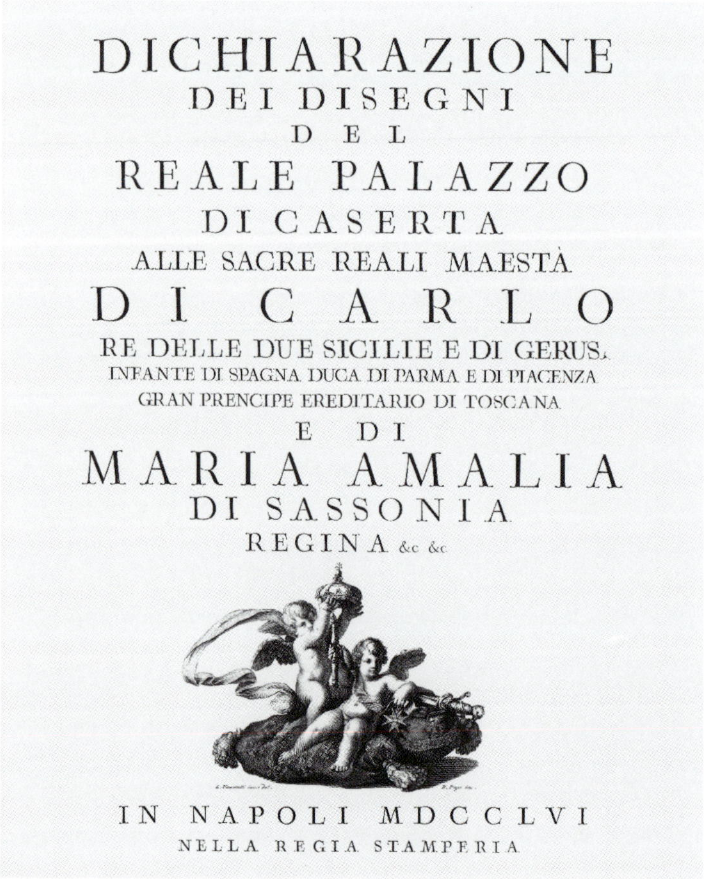

DICHIARAZIONE
DEI DISEGNI
DEL
REALE PALAZZO
DI CASERTA
ALLE SACRE REALI MAESTÀ
DI CARLO
RE DELLE DUE SICILIE E DI GERUS.
INFANTE DI SPAGNA DUCA DI PARMA E DI PIACENZA
GRAN PRENCIPE EREDITARIO DI TOSCANA
E DI
MARIA AMALIA
DI SASSONIA
REGINA &c &c

IN NAPOLI MDCCLVI
NELLA REGIA STAMPERIA

FIG. 42 / Title page of Luigi Vanvitelli's *Dichiarazione dei disegni del reale palazzo di Caserta*, Naples, 1756, given to Lord Bristol by Charles III of Spain in January, 1761. National Trust, Ickworth.

The gift by the King of Spain of a book of plans of the Neapolitan palace of Caserta (fig. 42) in December 1760 was seized upon by Lord Bristol as a particular mark of distinction, and he took further heart from the addition of three volumes 'relating to the Antiquitys of Herculaneum' the following month.[57] There were soon, however, rumours, and then proof, of a renewal of the Family Compact between the Bourbon kings of France and Spain, and the Earl's previously amicable relationship with the Spanish minister, Ricardo Wall, became increasingly strained as the age-old demands of the Spanish court with regard to rights and infringements in North America were pursued with increased vigour. By August 1761 war seemed inevitable and was only temporarily staved off by Pitt being forced from office. Lord Bristol was at his best and most steely when he had confidence in his master and without Pitt's firm resolve he became increasingly forlorn. In November he wrote of the ever more 'haughty Language now held by this Court' and, convinced that his negotiations had failed and that the climate would be the death of him, he asked to be recalled.[58] The request was declined but he did not have to wait long, matters coming to a head the following month, and Lord Bristol, following instructions from London, departed Madrid without taking leave on 17 December. With Spain refusing to answer the categorical question – whether they intended to join with the French – put to Wall on the 8th, Britain had finally lost patience and war was declared on 2 January 1762.

FLIGHT FROM MADRID

It is inconceivable that Lord Bristol managed to take his entire baggage with him when he left Madrid, state canopy and all, but he would have been conscious that whatever he left behind was at risk of being seized and he had at least had time to prepare.[59] Given that there were no purchases of plate back in London in the immediately ensuing years he must have managed to transport that at least, though with some difficulty as Wall would not authorise changes of horses for the 250-mile journey to Elvas just over the border into Portugal.[60] With the ordinary post from Madrid having been stopped since 7 December and no official couriers other than those of the King of Spain allowed to pass, Lord Bristol also had to put his skills for subterfuge into action. He took one King's Messenger, Ardouin, with him to go on with dispatches as soon as they reached Portugal, while the other, Potter, was sent north in disguise. As related by Lord Egremont, who had succeeded Pitt as Secretary of State, Potter had with great daring and 'disguised like a merchant got a pass from the French Ambassador at Madrid; came through France & got his pass renewed at Versailles, & made the whole journey in company with the Spanish Courier coming hither unsuspected & unknown'. He also made careful notes of what he observed whilst passing through enemy territory.[61]

The Earl of Bristol and his much-reduced retinue of seven men and one woman embarked from Lisbon on 19 January on HMS *Portland*, the Earl being put ashore at Falmouth on the 28th whilst the others, plus his baggage, carried on to Portsmouth.[62] Having received a fifteen-gun salute from the *Portland* as the King's representative, Lord Bristol wrote his last official report as ambassador, merely informing the Earl of Egremont of his having landed and forwarding dispatches from the Hon. Edward Hay, the Envoy to Portugal.[63] By 12 February he was back in his house at St James's Square, no doubt very relieved to be home after an absence of nearly seven years.[64]

Lord Lieutenant of Ireland

Though the Duke of Newcastle tried to pass the blame for the collapse of the relationship between Britain and Spain in 1761 onto the 2nd Earl of Bristol[65] the general consensus was that he had performed his duties exemplarily even when under severe duress and his reputation was reinforced when the relevant correspondence with the Secretary of State was published by order of Parliament shortly after his return.[66] Newcastle came off less well and fell from power in May 1762. Though Lord Bristol remained out of office for the next four years he was included in all Pitt's prospective cabinets on the various occasions that the Great Orator came close to being called to power[67] and, according to the newspapers, also had approaches from other parties which he declined.[68]

In early July 1766 Pitt finally acceded to George III's requests for him to form an administration and on the 20th of that month Lord Bristol received at Ickworth 'a long very kind letter from Mr. P[itt] inviting him in & to everything he can wish & desire'.[69] The Earl put off plans for going abroad for his health and hurried to London but it was to be another month before the shape of the administration fully emerged, complicated by Pitt's largely unfulfilled desire to include all those of talent irrespective of party.[70] On 22 August he was again called down from Ickworth and informed of the King's 'intention of appointing him Ld. Lieutenant of Ireland, but expecting his constant residence whilst He holds that Office'.[71] The stipulation as to residence stemmed from the habit of many Lords Lieutenant of at best residing in Dublin only during the sitting of the Irish Parliament, which was of a few months' duration every other year. On 4 September the Earl kissed the King's hand on being officially appointed, and in a clear display of his key place in the administration and his intimacy with its leader he was one of the two peers who introduced Pitt to the House of Lords as Earl of Chatham in November.[72]

Preparations were made for removing to Ireland including the purchase of his predecessor, the Earl of Hertford's six carriages, the 'State Coach, the Leading Coach, the Berlin, the State Chariot, Lady Hertford's New Coach, & the Demé Landau,' as well as suitable horses and a sedan chair. Appointment of a household began, the Lord Lieutenant having his own Master of the Horse and other equivalents to the royal establishment in London, a *batterie de cuisine* was acquired, silver lace commissioned for liveries, the cellar was stocked and plans of Dublin Castle were sent to London so that consideration could be given to the allocation of apartments.[73] Lord Bristol relished being at the heart of affairs again, with access whilst still in England to the King's closet and a place in the Cabinet, and his elevation to a position of power and semi-regal patronage would have resulted in his silver coming fully into its own once more, for grand dinners and on such occasions as the 'numerous and splendid Levee at his Lordship's House in St James's Square' on 8 December 1766.[74]

Several pieces of plate were commissioned at this time (cat. 80–5) and the inclusion amongst them of the mirror plateau (cat. 80) and the set of pierced bottle stands (cat. 81) indicates that the Earl intended to be both fashionable and magnificent in his entertaining. Though mostly engraved with the royal arms these were not official perquisites, Lords Lieutenant of Ireland not being amongst those eligible. Custom had, however, established a precedent for using part of the official allowances of the post for the purchase of plate and it was estimated by Thomas Waite, the Under-Secretary for Ireland, that some £500 had been thus expended by the 4th Duke of Bedford, who had been in post from 1757 to 1761.[75] Lord Bristol may have followed suit with this plateau and the other surviving items of 1766–7 engraved with the royal arms or crest (cat. 80–4), though probably not to the extent of £500 which would have equated to 1,200 ounces or so. If so, he behaved with reasonable honour in demarcating the purchases, as possibly had the 2nd Duke of Ormonde at the beginning of the century by engraving several Dublin-made pieces thought to have been his with the arms of Queen Anne.[76] Most other silver commissioned during the tenures of Lords Lieutenant is, in contrast, engraved with personal heraldry, as are the Duke of Bedford's several dozen dinner plates of 1756 by George Methuen.[77] Lord Bristol did make a payment of £81 7s to Frederick Kandler on 7 March 1767 but that falls far short of what would have been needed to cover the relevant surviving items.[78] Either, therefore, the additional cost was charged to the Irish establishment or some of his old plate was turned in to make up the difference, perhaps some of his ambassadorial allocation and hence the royal arms on the replacements.

Having in the past put so much energy into appealing to those with control of patronage for his own advancement and that of his family, Lord Bristol acted in line with the times and ensured that he got as much as he could for the Herveys out of being Lord Lieutenant. He named his brother Augustus as his deputy (Chief Secretary) with a handsome income, secured the Bishopric of Cloyne for Frederick Hervey with the promise of the more lucrative see of Derry upon the death of the aged and sickly incumbent, and obtained an Irish peerage for his brother-in-law Constantine Phipps.[79] Horace Walpole stated that 'all the Herveys in the world are going to Ireland'[80] but in fact only Frederick made it there as events in England intervened. Pitt, having at last secured full control of affairs with a compliant monarch and administration, almost immediately succumbed to the worst and most long-lasting of the string of debilitating bouts of illness that plagued his life. He retreated to Bath and became less and less able to undertake an effective part in government. Without his support Bristol must have been nervous of the merciless approach to British politicians in Ireland; his status as a trusted confidant of Pitt also made his presence in London valued by the King and others, acting as he did as a key conduit for communication with the invalid. There was even a moment in the spring of 1767 when the King suggested to Bristol that he should be one of the Secretaries of State, something he firmly rejected.

Absence from Ireland had the unfortunate consequence of encouraging rumour, much of it vicious and even aimed at innocent family members. As early as November Thomas Waite, the resident Under-Secretary, reported to Sir Robert Wilmot, 1st Bt, English Secretary to the Lord Lieutenant, that the Ladies Emily (1734–1814, fig. 43) and Caroline (1736–1819, fig. 44) Hervey, Lord Bristol's youngest sisters, 'are spoken of here with cast Freedom, as ladies of Easy Virtue; It is reported that they are to come over with His Excy & the Women here are all Furious against them.' One of their supposed crimes was being intimate with 'a Gent whose name is Swan … [who] plays excessively well upon the Guitar' and whom they would foist into some official position or other.[81] Less ill-founded were suggestions that Augustus Hervey was an informant to the opposition Grenville faction, with whom he had always been close, and matters came to a head when it was suggested Lord Bristol was using this closeness as a means to betray Pitt for his own survival.[82] That could not be borne, given the Earl's unswerving loyalty, and Hervey had little choice but to resign, which he did in July 1767. Preparations were renewed for a departure to Ireland[83] but when Pitt finally looked likely to resign in late July, Lord Bristol stepped aside to allow a new administration to be formed with the 4th Viscount Townshend as Lord Lieutenant of Ireland. It was envisaged that he would become Lord Privy Seal in place of Pitt but the great man's departure did not materialise and Lord Bristol was, for the time being, returned to the political wilderness.[84]

Lord Privy Seal and Groom of the Stole

The eventual departure of Pitt in October 1768 cleared the way for the Earl of Bristol to be brought back into the government by the Prime Minister, the 3rd Duke of Grafton, and he was offered the Privy Seal. Before accepting, the Earl sought and obtained Pitt's blessing[85] and his appointment was considered by some as a signal to 'the world that Lord Chatham is not dissatisfied' with the administration.[86] Unlike Pitt, and Lord Hervey forty years previously, Bristol was not to have a seat in the Cabinet, but the lack of any evident concern about that on his part suggests that he had had his fill of active power. At the next governmental upheaval in 1770 the Earl was appointed Groom of the Stole by George III and though this post was nominally considered part of the administration it was, in reality, wholly that of a courtier. With its intimate connection with the monarch, who seems to have been genuinely fond of Bristol, it had sufficient cachet to satisfy his pride, and it also had the potential to lead to that long-cherished Garter.[87]

Lord Bristol did not benefit from the Groom of the Stole's entitlement to 1,000 ounces of perquisite plate as his appointment came just after a change in the rules prompted by some huge accumulations of silver. The most extreme example had been that of the 4th Earl of Sandwich who gained 6,959 ounces as ambassador to the Peace of Aix-la-Chapelle in 1748, the same amount again as ambassador to Spain in April, 1763 and a further 1,000 ounces five months later on becoming Secretary of State.[88] In all, therefore, he had been allocated 14,918 ounces, and several other recipients had received one lot of ambassador's plate plus 1,000 ounces for a previous or subsequent appointment.[89] New Treasury regulations had been approved by the King on 23 January 1767 as follows:

> *My Lords taking into consideration the great expences hitherto incurred by allowces of plate made to the great Officers of State, and to Ministers employed in Foreign Courts are of opinion, that the Publick service does not require that the like expences be continued to their present extent, and that in order to prevent the same, the following Regulations be observed for the future.*
>
> *That no person shall be entitled to receive the same allowance of Plate, a second time, that is to say, That whoever shall by virtue of his Office have rec:d a quantity of Plate from his Majesty's Jewel-Office, shall not again be entitled to the same quantity of Plate upon reappointed to the same Office or appointed to any other in consideration of which an equal allowance of Plate hath hitherto been made.*
>
> *That no person shall be entitled to receive more than 5893 Ounces of White Plate and 1066 Ounces of Gilt Plate in the whole by virtue of any one or more Offices to which he may be appointed.*
>
> *These Regulations not to extend to the Right Honble the Speaker of the House of Commons.*[90]

Thus Lord Bristol, having had an ambassador's quota, was no longer entitled to a grant whether or not the post he filled qualified. It is ironic that the Speaker's entitlement to 4,000 ounces was exempted, as Arthur Onslow had received three grants[91] in the first half of the eighteenth century and Sir John Cust was about to receive his second.[92]

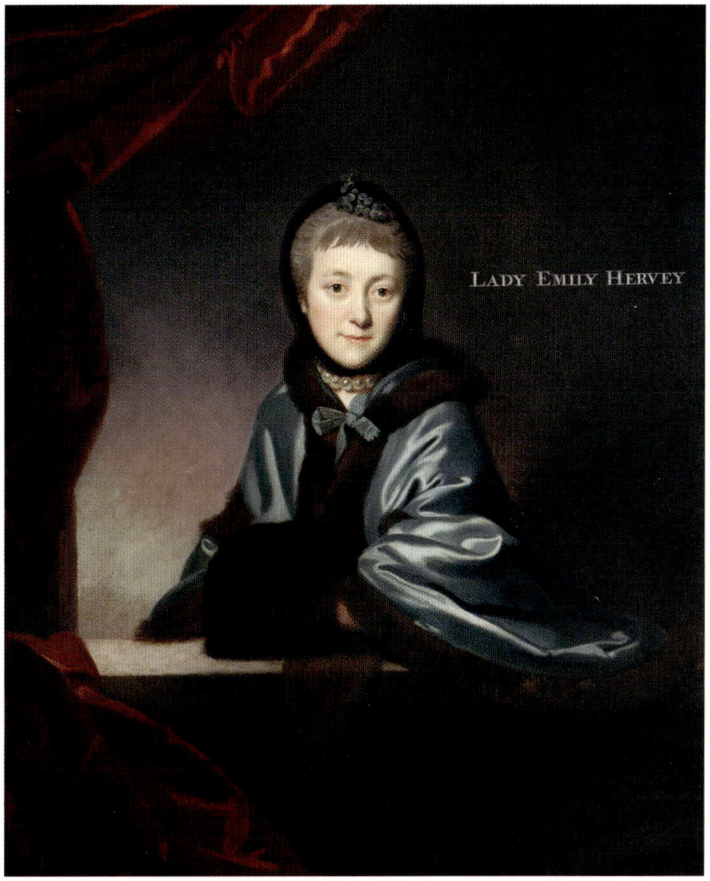

FIG. 43 / *Lady Emily Hervey* attributed to Johann Zofanny, *c.*1765. Oil on canvas: 66 x 51.1 cm (26 x 20⅛ in). National Trust, Ickworth.

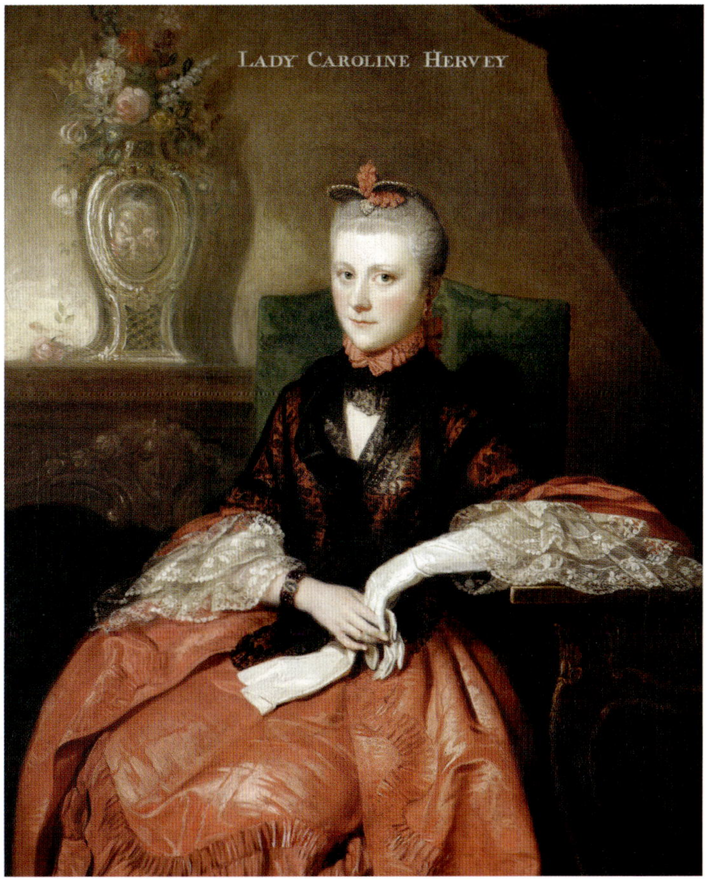

FIG. 44 / *Lady Caroline Hervey* attributed to Johann Zofanny, *c.*1765. Oil on canvas: 66 x 50.8 cm (26 x 20 in). National Trust, Ickworth.

In the 1770s the 2nd Earl of Bristol seems to have settled into a contented mix of pomp, sociability and improvements to his estates. As Groom of the Stole he might be required to head the parade to chapel carrying the Sword of State before the King and Queen,[93] attend theatre with the royal party[94] or deal with such practical issues as the appointment of a new King's Laundress.[95] His position at court also brought such elevated company to St James's Square as the Princes of Mecklenburg-Strelitz, the Queen's brothers,[96] and privately he was regularly to be seen at the salons of some of the older society hostesses, particularly those of the Dowager Marchioness of Blandford which were also attended by Horace Walpole.[97]

When not attending the King the 2nd Earl spent increasing amounts of time at Ickworth (fig. 46) which he seems to have become as fond of as was his grandfather. He had initially intended to build anew in a different location[98] and it was said of Ickworth in the 1750s that 'his Lordship never makes a Stay here as the house is not even fit to receive a private Gentleman.'[99] This was quite clearly an exaggeration, however, as Augustus Hervey records a sociable visit there with the Earl in November 1751[100] and he was, of course, absent from the country anyway for the latter part of the decade. Thereafter his regular presence is attested to by countless surviving letters written from the house plus newspaper reports of him going to and coming from it. At least one good apartment of rooms existed from Flitcroft's work of the early 1740s and the place was not insubstantial.

With the 2nd Earl's prudent approach towards expenditure, which sometimes broke out into blatant parsimony,[101] he no doubt quickly dismissed the idea of a complete rebuild of his country house just as he had declined to have his plate entirely new-made in 1751–2. He did, however, undertake improvements in the last years of his life, payments being made to the architect Henry Holland between 1771 and 1774.[102] As the total sum was nearly £2,000 the works are likely to have been a substantial remodelling[103] and must be what the Reverend Sydenham Hervey attributed in 1894 to the 3rd Earl.[104] This encompassed the heightening of the rooms of the south range which were probably then formed into the suite of anteroom, drawing room, dining room, bedroom (perhaps originally the 2nd Earl's) and library shown on a mid-nineteenth century plan (fig. 45). The battlemented exterior was recorded from memory after the house was again remodelled and reduced in size in the 1830s (fig. 47) and, fortunately, Elizabeth Percy, Duchess of Northumberland, wrote a detailed description of the interior:

> *the present Lord out of many very small has made 2 good and tolerable Room[s] The Eating Room is plain stucco taken off wth columns*[.] *over the chimney is a picture of the present K of Spain* [fig. 41] *and 2 bronzes … the Drawing Room is hung with Blue*[,] *pictures disposed in a particular manner as for example a large one surrounded by small ones of all that persons children*[105][.] *Still in this Room are family portraits, 2 have the name wrote on them … Ickworth Library is small*[.] *Over the Chimney is a half length of the late Princess Caroline*[106] *and over the Bookcases and Doors are heads of the late* [fig. 24] *and present King the Princess Dowager & Dowager of Spain K of Sardinia* [fig. 26] *and Duke and Dutchess of Savoy* [fig. 34 and 35].[107]

It would have been in these rooms that Lord Bristol, sighing after the 'robes and guards' that would have been his had he got to Ireland, 'used to play at drawing-rooms … and ask if the parsons and neighbours loved walking or riding,' according to Horace Walpole. He concluded, 'I do not wonder that people are servile courtiers, when they delight in aping the insipidity of [royal] levées themselves.'[108]

Holland was working at Ickworth in partnership with 'Capability' Brown, to whom payments had commenced a few years earlier in 1768. The introduction to Lord Bristol may well have come from William Pitt, who was a friend of Brown's and employed him at his own estate of Burton Pynsent in Somerset in the 1760s, or from the Duke of Grafton, another Suffolk patron and the Prime Minister under whom the Earl had served as Lord Privy Seal. In total Brown was paid £781 for Ickworth which represented a reasonable commission but not a fully-fledged landscape park, and his interventions may well have been restricted to the wooded pleasure ground immediately adjoining the house, now known as the Albana Walk.[109] Once again, a description survives from the Duchess of Northumberland: 'the House is surrounded by Garden taken off the Park by a sunk fence and consists of grass dotted all over with large trees and a profusion of clumps of Flowers'.[110]

The Bristol plate at the death of the 2nd Earl

In November 1774 Lord Bristol suffered a stroke which initially left him paralysed[111] but by the end of the month he was sufficiently improved to be out in society again.[112] He determined upon a sojourn in Bath to recuperate and left London on the 24 January 1775 with his youngest brother William and his sister, Lady Mary Fitzgerald.[113] After several weeks of being attended daily by his doctor, the fees for which he kept meticulously recorded as was his wont,[114] he was struck down again on the morning of 16 March, seemingly

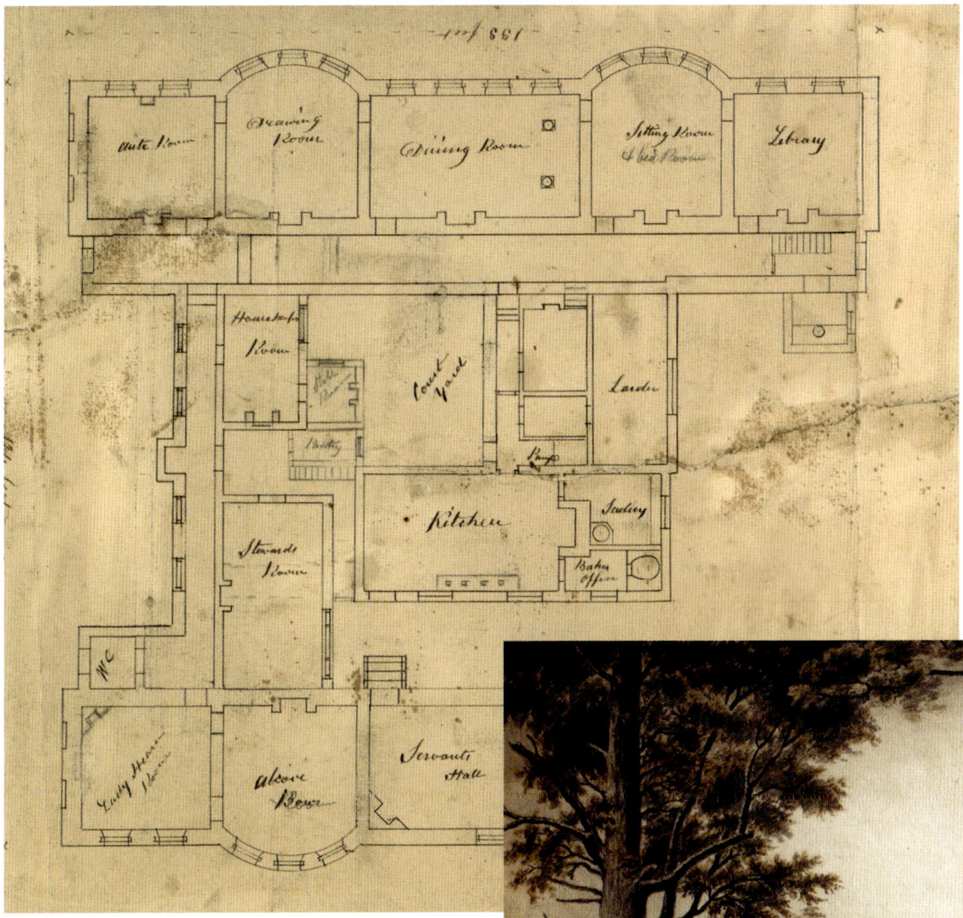

FIG. 45 / Ground plan of Ickworth Lodge as it was prior to remodelling in the 1830s, drawn from memory later in the 19th century, probably by Mrs. George Hervey. The 1st Earl's rooms added by Henry Flitcroft are in the bottom left corner and the 2nd Earl's range by Henry Holland is at the top. Suffolk Record Office, Bury St Edmunds, ref. SRO 941/84/5.

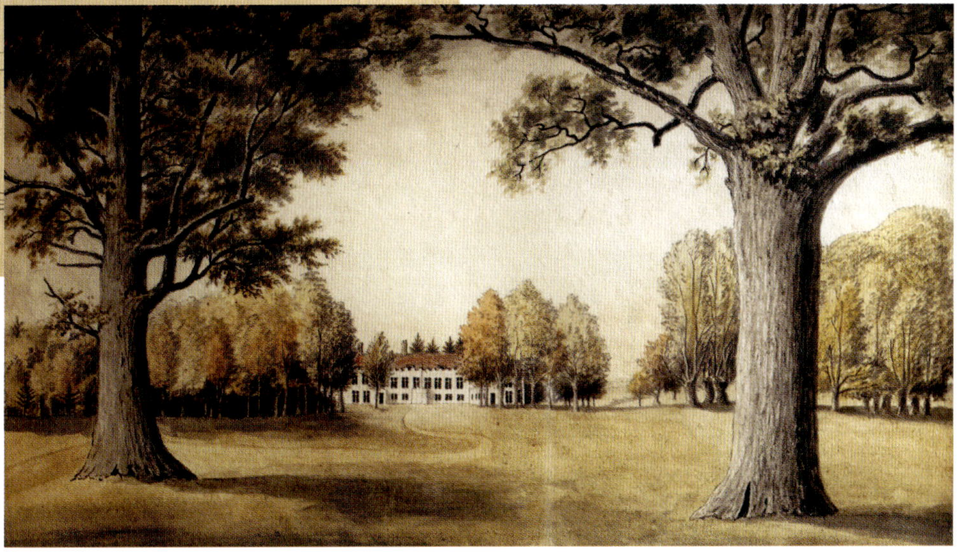

FIG. 46 / *Ickworth Old House* by George Quinton, 1804. The east Entrance Front of the building now known as Ickworth Lodge. Watercolour on paper. National Trust, Ickworth.

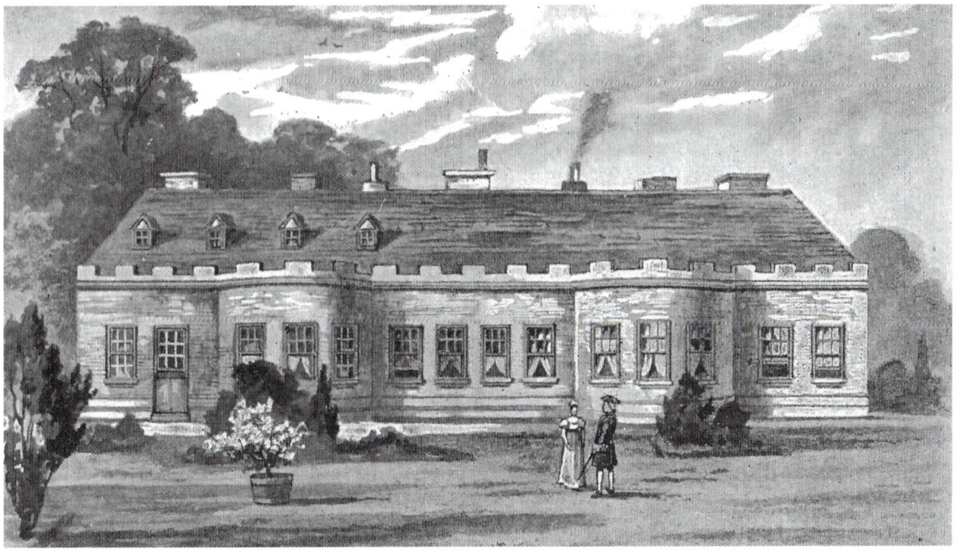

FIG. 47 / The 2nd Earl of Bristol's south range at Ickworth Lodge, as remodelled by Henry Holland, by Mrs. George Hervey, late 19th century. Reproduced in Rev. S.A.H. Hervey, *The Diary of John Hervey, first Earl of Bristol. With Extracts from his Book of Expenses, 1688 to 1742*, Wells, 1894.

recovered but then 'fell into a doze from which he never awaked' and 'without a groan, without a convulsion, died the next morning, Saturday, March 18'.[115] Walpole reported to Sir Horace Mann that the Earl 'was born to the gout from his mother's family, but starved himself to keep it off. This brought on paralytic strokes, which have dispatched him.'[116] George III had been of the same opinion, prophetically pleading with his Groom of the Stole in 1773 to 'change Your Abstemiousness, which if it succeeds in keeping off that horrid complaint [gout] will do it at the expence of Your health, and perhaps be productive of greater evils'.[117]

The Earl died immensely wealthy, having paid off all his grandfather's mortgages and, according to one obituarist, he left 'not a debt of any sort unpaid, not a farm upon any of his estates unrepaired, not a tenant dissatisfied'. His charities, according to the anonymous writer, were 'equal to the great splendor in which he lived. In short the Earl of Bristol died lamented by all the good, by all the virtuous, and all the poor.' Having been a master of hyperbole himself at times, particularly when trying to flatter those who controlled patronage, the Earl would have been rather pleased with that. Although his estate fell short of the £20,000 per annum claimed of it in another obituary, it was nevertheless very considerable at nearly £14,000 and in a far better state than when he inherited, and he did, as reported, bequeath his collection of medals to George III as the final act of obeisance of the latest in a long line of loyal courtiers.[118]

Lord Bristol had lived a remarkable and eventful life but has generally been overlooked since his death because of the surfeit of colourful characters in his family and the rather more titillating escapades of several of them, most notably his parents, his next two brothers and his niece, Lady Elizabeth Foster. He left one indelible legacy, however, and that was his silver, through a study of which his contribution to the family story and to British history can be fully appreciated. In his will he stipulated that 'all the Jewells and plate in my mansion house in St James's Square in the County of Middlesex at the time of my death shall be deemed as Heirs Loom' and thus should pass intact to each successive possessor of the family estates under the entail set up under his grandfather's Will.[119] That plate amounted to 16,700 oz, 11 dwt,[120] which is probably not a great deal more than he inherited in 1751 but in the intervening quarter of a century he had transformed it into what even at the time must have been one of the most impressive dinner services in the country and has been rendered all the more important by surviving largely intact, together with furniture, pictures, porcelain and books that formed its context in the eighteenth century.

---

1. Pijzel-Dommisse 2014, p. 101 and information from the author.
2. I am grateful to Wolf Burchard, Michèle Bimbenet-Privat and Lorenz Seelig for their comments on this subject. Loans of silver were also made later in the century by Catherine the Great to her provincial governors. See Lopato 2015, pp. 16–7.
3. Wickes Ledgers, VAM 6 1756–60, f. 15, 9 April 1756. The total cost of the order was £252 9s 2d. Another significant client was the Portuguese ambassador, M. Carvalho, who purchased 4 dozen plates and 22 dishes amongst other items in 1767, total cost £869 4s 4d, Parker and Wakelin Ledgers, VAM 7 1765–75, f. 186.
4. State Papers Venice, SP 99/64, ff. 13–14, Sir James Gray to Duke of Newcastle, 28 August 1744, The Hague.
5. For information on the history of the Jewel Office see Sitwell 1960 and Lomax 1999.
6. No allocations to Lords Chamberlain were made prior to that of 1766 to the Duke of Portland, Delivery Book 1732–93, f. 228.
7. Jewel Office Warrant Book 1732–62 and Delivery Books 1698–1732 and 1732–93. As with christening plate (see chapter 1, note 91), a variance of a few ounces or so was tolerated, it being near-impossible to get weights precise on handmade objects.
8. Amongst the very few exceptions were some ministers plenipotentiary at peace conferences, such as the Earl of Sandwich at Aix-la-Chapelle in 1748, who were treated as ambassadors and the commissioners sent to the American colonies in 1778–82, though the allocations of 1200 oz to each of the latter were listed separately from indenture plate and do not appear to have been discharged. See Jewel Office Delivery Book 1732–93, ff. 218, 296 and 302. The 4008 oz received by 'Lord King Ld High Chancellor' in 1727–8 was for his brief tenure of the Speaker's chair in 1725; Delivery Book 1698–1732, f. 286. An attempt by Lord Chancellor Apsley (later 2nd Earl Bathurst) to claim plate in 1771 was rebuffed: Wilmot papers, D3155/C4987–8.
9. Jewel Office Warrant Book 1732–62, f. 302.
10. State Papers Spain, SP 94/252, f. 190.
11. Goslings ledgers, 130/27, f. 65.
12. Parker and Wakelin ledgers, VAM 7 1765–75, f. 94
13. Jewel Office Delivery Book 1732–93, f. 248.
14. Jewel Office Plate Book 1728–1767, ff. 166–8. The total amount paid, £2,825 1s 5d, is well within the limit of £2,950 specified in the warrant.
15. They are also accounted for in the half year to Christmas, 1758 in the Jewel Office Warrant Book (see appendix 4).
16. Jewel Office Delivery Book 1732–93, f. 165.
17. Jewel Office Warrant Book 1732–62, ff. 310–11.
18. Letters from Secretaries of State 1755–9, f. 374, 'Fees paid for His Excellency's Plate &c', 11 August 1758 and f. 406, 'Fees paid on passing the Privy Seal for discharge of Plate to the Earl of Bristol', 2 March 1759. The fees and tips payable by the Earl were legion and included £69 17s 6d as the 'Usual Graty. to the Office as Ambr & Plenipoy', June 1758 (f. 320).
19. These are the figures given in the Jewel Office Accounts and Receipts book and are higher than those in the notice of absence and discharge, both of which state 10s and 6s 8d. The total limits differ too, with £2,950 being specified in the initial warrant, which accords with what actually seems to have been paid, whilst £2,500 is intimated by the notice of absence and the discharge. See appendix 4 for all of the documents in which these various figures appear.
20. Lomax 1999, p. 139. The cistern was listed as weighing 2,352 oz but actually weighed just 1,457 oz.
21. Letters from Secretaries of State 1755–9, f. 405, 'An Account of Fees paid at Severall Offices for the Plate &c', 2 March 1759 'To Mr Shackelton, the King's Painter the Usual Gratuity' £4 4s, 'To Mr Stone the Kings Picture Frame Maker' £1 1s. The portrait would have followed the standard pose for later state depictions of George II, such as that painted for the Foundling Museum in 1758.
22. Great Wardrobe Bills 1757–8, nos. 44, 46–8, 52 and 55.
23. Letters from Secretaries of State 1755–9, f.188, Earl of Bristol to Joseph Richardson, 17 October 1758, Madrid.
24. Ibid.
25. Beard and Gilbert 1986, pp. 387–8 and 923–5. There are payments in Lord Bristol's account with Goslings to Hallett in 1750–1, to William Vile from 1752–5, to Vile and Cobb from 1763–4 and thereafter to their successor William France. The family maintained a relationship with France and Co into the nineteenth century, see Strachey 1998, p. 46.
26. Letters from Secretaries of State 1759–61, f. 2, Earl of Bristol's account 18 June–27 July 1759.
27. Beard and Gilbert 1986, p. 652. I am grateful to Lucy Wood for alerting me to the fire and also to the potential link with Samuel Norman that this implies.
28. The portait was still not complete at the end of February, Joseph Richardson writing to Lord Bristol on the 20th 'Mr Shakelton will call upon me tomorrow & let me know the reasons of his delay in not finishing it'. Letters from Secretaries of State 1755–9, f. 401.
29. Parker and Wakelin ledgers, VAM 7 1765–75, ff. 94 and 119.
30. Letters to Admirals, Consuls etc 1759–1761, f. 21–22, Earl of Bristol to Admiral Boscawen at Gibraltar, 8 May 1759, Madrid.
31. TNA, ADM 50/3, Admiral Boscawen's journal, April to September 1759.
32. Letters from admirals, consuls etc 1755–9, ff. 271–274, Burrington Goldsworthy to Earl of Bristol, 16 May 1759, Port St Mary's [El Puerto de Santa María].
33. Ibid., ff. 281–4, Burrington Goldsworthy to Earl of Bristol, 6 June 1759, Port St Mary's.
34. Ibid., ff. 285–8, Burrington Goldsworthy to Earl of Bristol, 13 June 1759, Port St Mary's.
35. Ibid., ff. 293–6, Burrington Goldsworthy to Earl of Bristol, 20 June 1759, Port St Mary's.
36. The first (undated) engraving of the portrait is without the Privy Seal purse or the Groom of the Stole's key and has a slightly different background to either of the surviving versions. It refers to Lord Bristol as ambassador and does not list any of his subsequent appointments. The inventory number of the Ickworth version in oils is 851790.
37. Letters from admirals, consuls etc. 1760–1, ff. 427–30, James Holford to Earl of Bristol, 19 October 1761, Genoa.
38. Simón 2012, pp. 2–5. The palace became an artillery barracks in the late eighteenth century and was the scene of a famous incident in the uprising against the French on 2 May 1808. The entire building was demolished in 1869 to make way for the Plaza Dos de Mayo, with the gate to the outer court preserved as a monument at its centre. Ibid., pp. 13–21.
39. Ibid., p. 4.

40. Lodge 1933, pp. 127, 147, 152–3, 175, 197 and 256.
41. Up to the age of 26 he had drunk 'nothing but water', Hervey 1894b, vol. 3, p. 336.
42. Letters from admirals consuls etc. 1755–9, ff. 103–106 and 237–40, Francis Aiskell to Earl of Bristol, 29 November 1758 and 28 March 1759.
43. Clarke 1763, pp. 342–4.
44. Lodge 1933, pp. 118, 235, 239 and 250.
45. Ibid., pp. 341, 344 and 486.
46. State Papers Spain, SP 94/158, ff. 130–1, Ruvigny de Cosne to William Pitt, 28 August 1758, Madrid. De Cosne had sent gruesomely detailed accounts to Pitt of the Queen's illness over the previous weeks.
47. Ibid. and ff. 223–4, Earl of Bristol to William Pitt, 13 November 1758, Madrid.
48. Ibid., SP 94/159, ff. 353–360, Earl of Bristol to William Pitt, 30 July 1759, Madrid.
49. Leadam 1909, p. 373.
50. Letters from admirals, consuls etc. 1760–1, ff. 117–20 Sir James Gray to the Earl of Bristol, 27 May 1760, Naples.
51. The only country that still routinely insisted on these spectacular events was the Republic of Venice. In 1744 the Duke of Newcastle tried to avoid a public entry there for the Earl of Holderness to save 'trouble and expence to both States' but was unsuccessful. The Venetians valued public entries for supporting 'the dignity of the Republick abroad' and making 'their Government more respected at home,' and they also brought trade into the city through associated 'Masquing & other Publick diversions'. State Papers Venice, SP 99/64, ff. 13–14, Sir James Gray to Duke of Newcastle, 28 August 1744, The Hague.
52. Lodge 1933, pp. 38, 216 and 310.
53. Holderness correspondence, ff. 334–5, Sir James Gray to Earl of Holderness, 3 May 1757, Naples.
54. Chatham papers, ff. 46–7, Earl of Bristol to William Pitt, 26 March 1759, Madrid.
55. Newcastle papers; the correspondence starts with Add MS 32889, ff. 8–9, Earl of Bristol to Duke of Newcastle, 12 March 1759, Madrid and concludes with Add MS 32914, ff. 131–4, Lord Bristol to Newcastle, November 1760 and f. 137, Lord Bristol to George II, 6 November 1760.
56. Chatham papers, f. 50, Earl of Bristol to William Pitt, 25 February 1760, Madrid.
57. State Papers Spain, SP 94/162 and SP 94/163, Earl of Bristol to William Pitt, 16 December 1760 and 5 January 1761. The books are still in the library at Ickworth: Luigi Vanvitelli, *Dichiarazione dei disegni del reale palazzo di Caserta*, Naples, 1756, inventory no. 3108203; O.A. Bayardi and P. Carcani (eds), *Le pitture antiche d'Ercolano e contorni incise con qualche spiegazione*, vols 1–3, Naples 1757–62, inventory no. 3042110. The subsequent five volumes of the latter work, published up to 1792, are also at Ickworth and were probably acquired by the 1st Marquess of Bristol.
58. State Papers Spain, SP 94/164, ff. 200–209 and 213–5, Earl of Bristol to Earl of Egremont, both dated 2 November 1761, 'Apart', Escorial.
59. Ibid, ff. 397–9, Francis Aiskill to Earl of Egremont, 29 December 1761, Malaga. The consul reported that by order of the King of Spain 'the Furnature of my House and all my Effects' had been embargoed along with those of all other British residents in the city.
60. Ibid., f. 314, Earl of Bristol to Earl of Egremont, 25 December 1761, Elvas.
61. Newcastle papers, f. 318, Earl of Egremont to Duke of Newcastle, 24 December 1761, Whitehall, and f. 320, 'Report of Potter, the Messenger's Observations on His Journey to & from Madrid', received 24 December 1761.
62. TNA, ADM 36/6344, 'HMS Portland muster book 1 November 1761–30 June 1762' and ADM 51/3942, 'HMS Portland Captain's Log 1761–2'.
63. State Papers Spain, SP 94/164, f. 401, Earl of Bristol to Earl of Egremont, 28 January 1762, Falmouth. The letter is incorrectly dated 27 February.
64. Newcastle papers, Add MS 32934, f. 322 Earl of Bristol to Duke of Newcastle, 13 February 1762, St James's Square.
65. Ibid., ff. 43–9, Duke of Newcastle to Earl of Egremont and to Earl of Hardwicke, 15 November 1761.
66. *Papers relative to the rupture with Spain In French and English, published by authority* (London, 1762). A copy survives at Ickworth. In the *Public Advertiser*, issue 9677, 6 June 1765, it was stated that Lord Bristol had fulfilled his role 'with so much Dignity to himself, and Advantage to the Public'.
67. Chatham papers, ff. 79–80 and 80, Earl of Bristol to William Pitt, 5 September 1763 and 29 July 1766.
68. *Public Advertiser*, issue 9601, 10 August 1765.
69. Grenville papers, ff. 159–60, Hon. Augustus Hervey to George Grenville, 21 July 1766, Ickworth Lodge.
70. Brown 1978, pp. 323–33.
71. Fortescue 1927, vol. 1, p. 388.
72. Brown 1978, p. 337.
73. Wilmot papers, WH/3470, Thomas Waite to Sir Robert Wilmot, 20 September, 4 October, 14 October and 18 October 1766, Dublin Castle, and 'An Acct. of Money paid to Lord Hertford by Lord Bristol for The State Carriages' etc., 13 November 1766; WH/3471, Thomas Waite to Sir Robert Wilmot, 31 January 1767; C/4323 Earl of Bristol to Sir Robert Wilmot, 14 September 1767.
74. *St James's Chronicle or the British Evening Post*, issue 902, 11–13 December 1766.
75. Wilmot Papers, WH/3459, 'A Rough Estimate of His Excy's [future] Income & Expences as Lord Lieut. of Ireland from 3d. April 1761 to Do. 1763 & from 3d. April 1763 to Do. 1765', drawn up by Thomas Waite, May 1761.
76. Sinsteden 2008, p. 125, n. 6 and Alcorn 2000, cat. 258, pp. 337–9.
77. Sold Christie's, 28 March 1973, lot 121 (12) and Sotheby's, 15 June 1976, lots 145–6 (18).
78. Goslings ledgers, 130/37, f. 84.
79. Holmes 1996, p. 221.
80. Lewis 1937–83, vol. 31, p. 125, Horace Walpole to Lady George Lennox, 8 September 1766.
81. Wilmot papers, WH/3470, Thomas Waite to Sir Robert Wilmot, 8 November 1766, Dublin Castle. Lord Bristol had sent a guitar back to England from Spain in 1759 for Lady Emily Hervey; see Letters from Secretaries of State 1755–9, f. 436 and 1759–61, f. 128.
82. Grenville papers, f. 186, 'Copy of Lord Bristol's Answer to my [Augustus Hervey's] Letter of July 1t. 1767', 1 July 1767, St James's Square.
83. Wilmot papers, WH/3472, Thomas Waite to Sir Robert Wilmot, 9 July 1767, Dublin Castle.
84. Newcastle papers, Add MS 32983, ff. 378–9, Duke of Newcastle to Duke of Portland, 7 August 1767, Claremont, copy.
85. SRO, 941/49/1, Letters of 2nd Earl of Bristol to and from Lord Chatham and to Lord Camden on being offered the Privy Seal, 1768.
86. Newcastle papers, Add MS 32991A, f. 359, Earl of Albemarle to Duke of Newcastle, 30 October 1768, Berkeley Square.
87. In 1769 the King drew up a list of those eligible for the Garter and the 2nd Earl of Bristol was then in eighth place, excluding the royal princes. Fortescue 1927, p. 116.
88. Delivery book 1732–93, ff. 101, 205 and 210.
89. The 3rd Duke of Richmond was the last to benefit from multiple allocations, as ambassador to France in 1765 and, briefly, Southern Secretary in 1766. Delivery book 1732–93, ff. 224 and 238.
90. TNA, LC 5/114, Jewel Office inventories and memoranda 1698–1782, unpaginated.
91. Delivery book 1698–1732, f. 300 and 1732–93, ff. 21 and 40. The third grant, in 1748, was taken as a solid gold cup and cover weighing 124oz.
92. Delivery book 1732–93, ff. 181 and 257. Cust died six months after.
93. *Public Advertiser*, issue 11380, 20 May 1771, issue 11860, 10 April 1773 and issue 12959, 28 February 1774.
94. *Morning Post and Daily Advertiser*, issue 371, 7 January 1774.
95. Fortescue 1927, vol. 3, p. 2, no. 1291, George III to Earl of Bristol, 8 July 1773, Kew.
96. Information from Patricia Ferguson.
97. Lord Bristol's presence is regularly mentioned in the journals of Lady Mary Coke. See for instance Coke 1889–96, vol. 3, pp. 248, 255, 263, 291 and 414. On 29 July 1763 (p. 263) he was part of a large party at Strawberry Hill for 'a great dinner very ill dress'd' after which the unexpected visit of Princess Amelia 'put all in confusion'.
98. Hervey 1894b, vol. 3, p. 356, 1st Earl of Bristol to Lord Hervey, 18 April 1748, Ickworth Park.
99. Strachey 1998, p. 42.
100. Erskine 1953, p. 117.
101. On arrival in Turin he asked the Southern Department clerks 'to cut off the second Leef of the Gazette, when there is no material Article in it, which will make the Pacquet smaller,' in order to reduce the cost. Turin State Papers, SP 92/90, f. 165, Ralph Woodford (Secretary to the Turin embassy) to Mr Payzant (at Whitehall), 1 November 1755, Turin.
102. Goslings ledgers, 130/46, ff. 106–8 and 130/49, ff. 120–2. The payments to Henry Holland totalled £1,974 2s. The 3rd Earl made a single payment to Holland of £279 on 8 July 1776 which, given the two year gap since the last of the 2nd Earl's payments, probably indicates a small amount of additional work. 130/53, f. 133. The 2nd Earl also spent £995 11s on upholstery and furniture in this period with William and Edward France, as recorded in the Goslings ledgers between 1768 and 1775. For the Frances see Beard and Gilbert 1986, pp. 315–7.
103. For comparison, Aston Hall near Oswestry in Shropshire, a middling-sized house new-built to the design of James Wyatt in the early 1790s, cost £5,000 and the substantial remodelling of 16 Grosvenor Square in 1773–5, also to the design of Wyatt, cost £2,989 17s 11d including elaborate decorative schemes. See Robinson 2012, pp. 324 and 336.
104. Hervey 1894a, pp. 279–84.
105. Alastair Laing has suggested that one of these groups could be the van Loo of Lord Hervey (inv. 851778) surrounded by the group of Zoffanys of his children (inv. 851784–5, 851787–9 and 851791).
106. By Jacopo Amigoni, inv. 851698.
107. Archives of the Duke of Northumberland at Alnwick Castle, Duchess of Northumberland's diary *c.*1774, DNP: MS 121/149 p. 24. All of the portraits she lists survive at Ickworth.
108. Lewis 1937–83, vol. 22, p. 549, Horace Walpole to Sir Horace Mann, 18 September 1767 and vol. 33, p. 416, Horace Walpole to Lady Ossory, 9 September 1783.
109. Rutherford 2015, pp. 6–9. Holland and Brown also worked in partnership at Redgrave in north Suffolk.
110. Archives of the Duke of Northumberland at Alnwick Castle, Duchess of Northumberland's diary *c.*1774, DNP: MS 121/149 p. 24.
111. Lewis 1937–83, vol. 24, p. 55, Horace Walpole to Sir Horace Mann, 11 November 1774.
112. Ibid., p. 63, Horace Walpole to Sir Horace Mann, 24 November 1774 and Coke 1889–96, vol. 4, p. 444.
113. Hervey 1906, p. 251.
114. TNA, C 103/174, Hervey-v-Earl of Bristol, account book of the 2nd Earl of Bristol and his executors, 1775.
115. Hervey 1906, p. 251.
116. Lewis 1937–83, vol. 24, p. 86.
117. Fortescue 1927, vol. 3, p. 2, no. 1291, George III to Earl of Bristol, 8 July 1773, Kew.
118. Ickworth House, Geraldine, Marchioness of Bristol's family scrapbook, two undated press cuttings with obituary notices of the 2nd Earl of Bristol. The income from the family estates is given in SRO, 941/50/6, Income and Expenditure of Augustus John, Earl of Bristol's 'Estates in Suffolk, Lincolnshire, and Essex'.
119. SRO, HA 507/5/11, probate copy of the will of George William, 2nd Earl of Bristol, proved 29 March 1775.
120. Bristol plate list, 1811. The 5th Earl (subsequently 1st Marquess) recorded that 'The total quantity of Plate left by George Earl of Bristol was oz: 16700=11.'

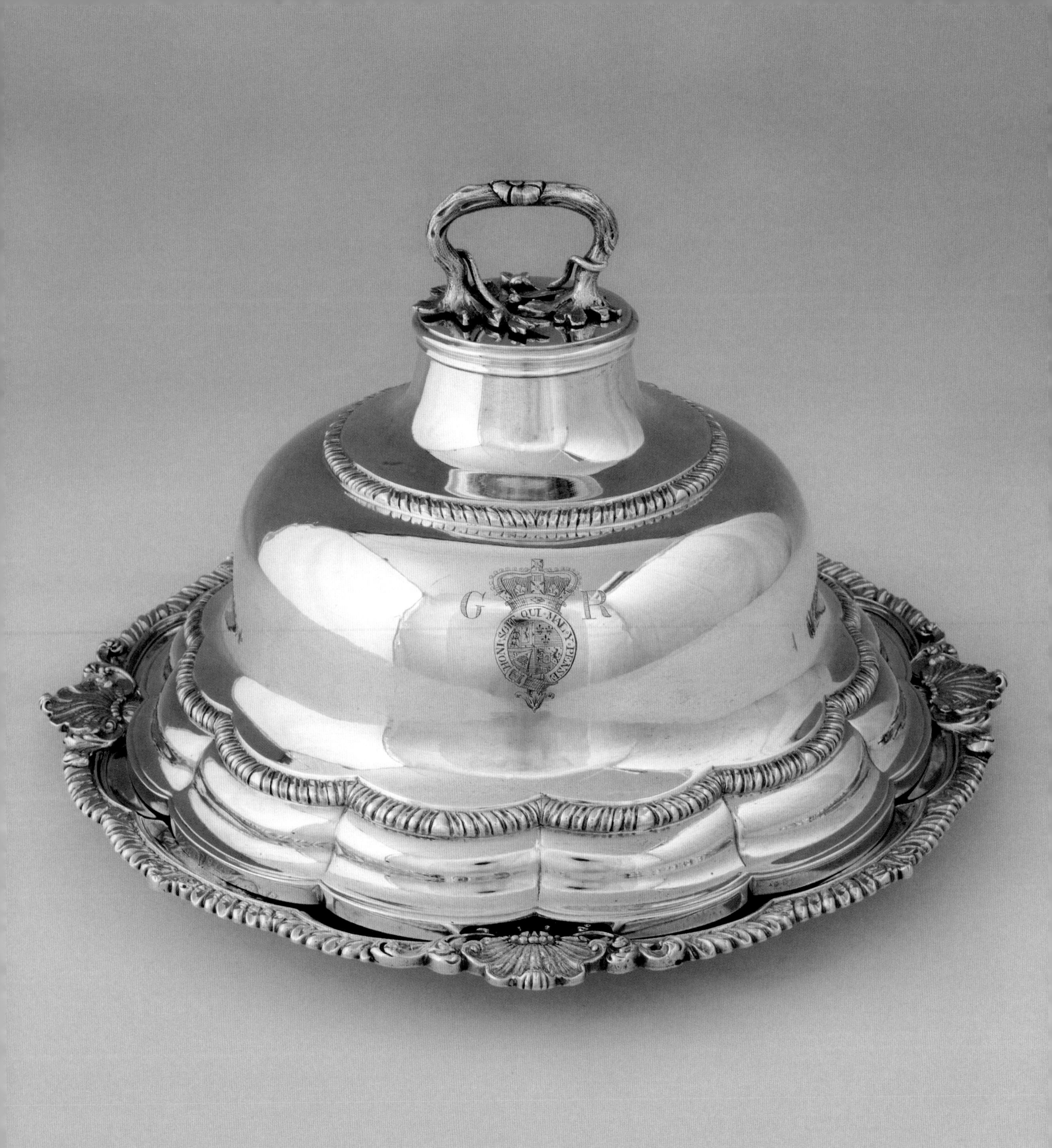

Two dish covers (London, *c.*1758, see cat. 73) on earlier dishes (see cat. 36–7) from the silver of George William Hervey, 2nd Earl of Bristol

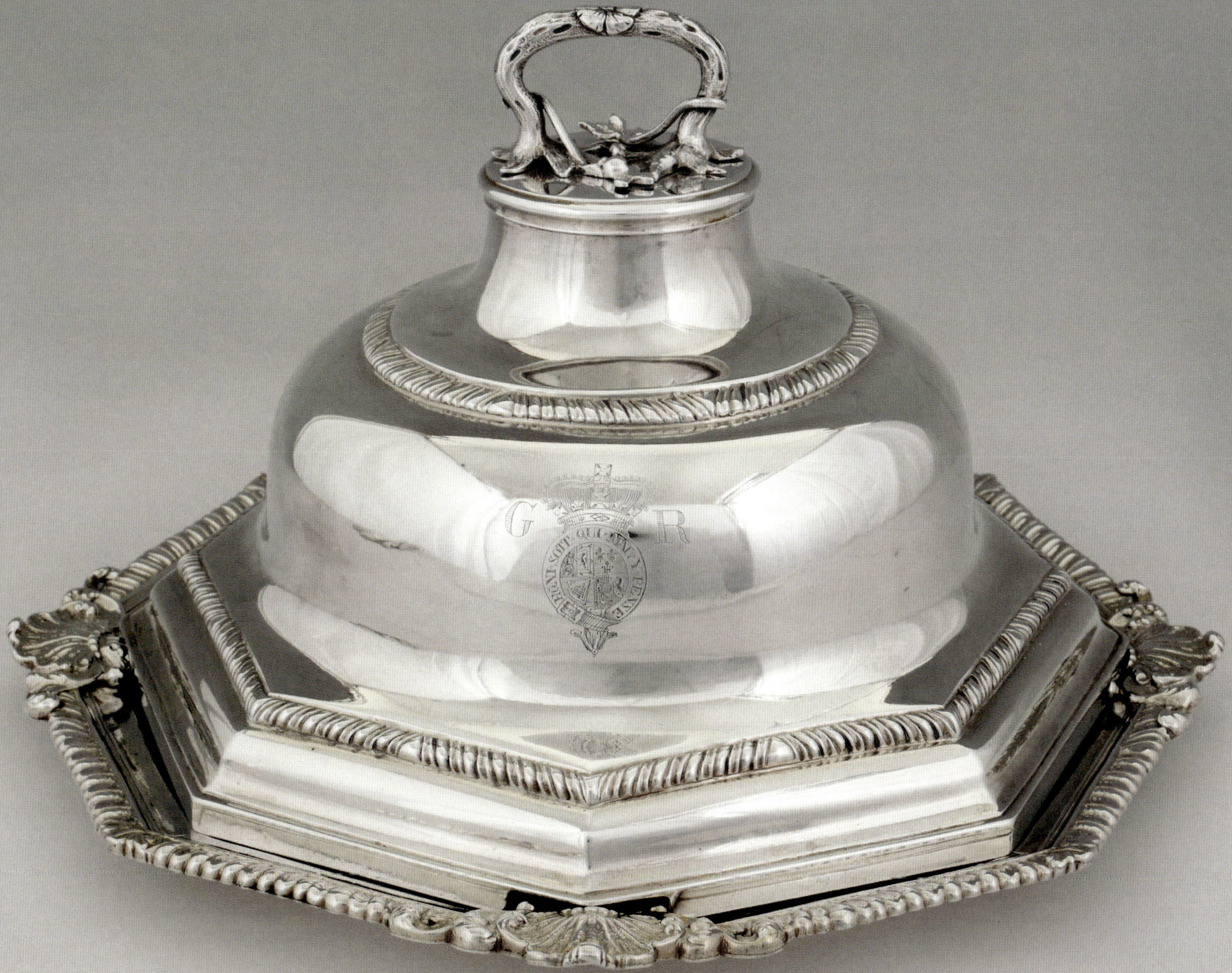
G R

FOUR

SURVIVAL AGAINST THE ODDS
THE ICKWORTH SILVER AFTER 1775

Of the generations that followed the 2nd Earl of Bristol at Ickworth, all had some impact on the collection of silver, whether through denudations, additions or careful guardianship, and all made full use of it too. A number of pieces can quite clearly be made out in a photograph of the family taking breakfast in the library at Ickworth in about 1870 (fig. 48), lists of plate 'in use' survive from later in the century and many of the pieces show clear evidence of long and persistent service. When the 4th Marquess and Marchioness dined at Ickworth or 6 St James's Square in the early 1950s they would have been eating with and from plate that had not only been used by their ancestors back to the reign of William III but that had also been shipped about Europe by the 2nd Earl and been present at dinners and suppers attended by, amongst others, the great Duke of Marlborough and his duchess, Prince Eugene of Savoy, George I and, in the third quarter of the eighteenth century, William Pitt the Elder and other titans then holding sway on the political stage.

In spite of the 2nd Earl's designation of the plate as part of the heirlooms it was certainly not a foregone conclusion that the spectacularly enhanced collection he bequeathed in 1775 would, as it has, survive substantially intact to the present day. His primary concern would have been that the weight was preserved, representing as it did the principal capital wealth of the family after land, and he would have anticipated his heirs keeping up with fashion just as he had done in the early 1750s. Most aristocratic families that maintained their fortunes took that course, and the examples are consequently legion. To name just a few, the 1st Earl Harcourt turned in over 3,000 ounces of old plate to Parker and Wakelin when he acquired a magnificent new dinner service in the French taste in 1768–9,[1] Thomas William Coke of Holkham gave up his great-uncle's Paul de Lamerie silver in favour of the neo-classical in 1775–6[2] and the Onslows of Clandon in Surrey must have swapped copious quantities of eighteenth century perquisite plate for what survives of around 1812 which is by Paul Storr.[3] Even the profoundly conservative 5th and 6th Earls of Stamford turned in over 7,700 ounces of the mighty collection of plate assembled by the 2nd Earl of Warrington, acquiring instead such highly fashionable items as a set of *neo-Grec* candelabra of 1772–3 in the style of Robert-Joseph Auguste.[4]

As it was, the 3rd Earl of Bristol scarcely had time to make an indent on the collection, the 4th Earl was mostly distracted by Ireland, the Continent, art collecting and building, and by the time the 5th Earl inherited the rococo was sufficiently resurgent to render his uncle's ornate and high-quality plate secure from the need to refashion. With the development of an appreciation of the antique as the nineteenth century progressed there was never a risk thereafter of a subsequent owner wishing to change wholly the style of the family silver and nor was there a downturn in the family finances to force dispersal as in the case, for instance, of another great mid-eighteenth-century collection, that of the Ansons at Shugborough in Staffordshire, which was largely sold in 1893.[5]

AUGUSTUS JOHN, 3RD EARL OF BRISTOL

Augustus Hervey (1724–79) (fig. 50) must have been exposed to plenty of silver at the many dinners, balls and other entertainments he attended whilst travelling about the courts of Europe during his active naval career in the 1740s and 50s. It was only during his time in Lisbon, however, that what he saw was sufficiently extraordinary to prompt him to remark upon it in his journal, in between bouts of flirting and being abducted by a rapacious duchess. In October 1753 he went with the French ambassador, the Comte de Baschi to see the

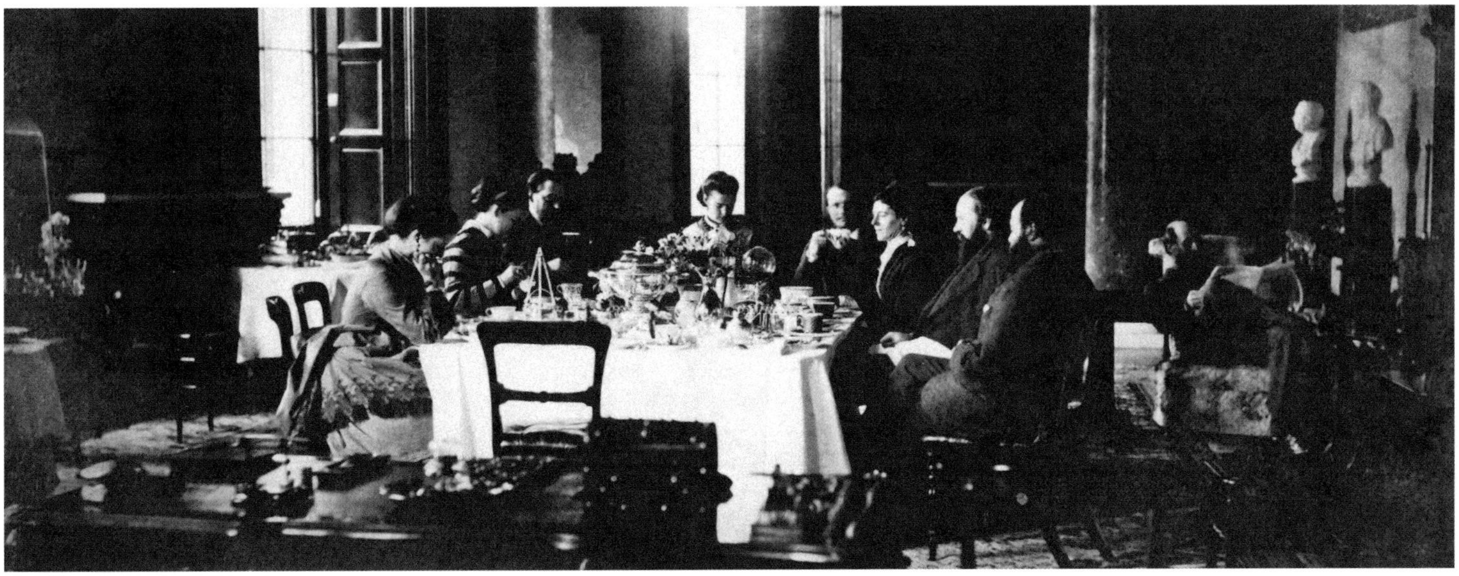

FIG. 48 / Breakfast in the library at Ickworth, *c.*1870. National Trust, Ickworth.

King of Portugal's wardrobe, where he was struck particularly by 'five pairs of very high candlesticks and a cross about seven foot high and very finely wrought indeed,' which were intended for a church, and a gold toilet service 'that was for the present Queen when she married' but which she had never seen let alone used. Shortly beforehand he had been a guest at a 'great dinner' for the Comte on board one of his country's men-of-war, and 'to make it more pompous' the captain had borrowed de Baschi's plate 'and his cooks and indeed fitted his ship very prettily for the purpose'. Sadly Hervey does not record what he did for plate when he reciprocated the next day, nor on the countless other occasions he gave dinners, concerts and even balls on board his ships over the years. He must have had some silver of his own, being a wealthy man by this stage thanks to prizes, and he perhaps hired or borrowed, as had the French captain, when he had the need for more.[6]

By the time he inherited the earldom, town house and family estates, Augustus was not a well man and he would have had little practical need to add to what his brother had left him. Entertaining is likely, for the most part, to have been minimal and his unorthodox family was small, consisting of his mistress, Mary Nesbitt, and an illegitimate son from a previous amour, the younger Augustus Hervey.[7] He was further rendered ineligible for polite society by his long-estranged wife, Elizabeth Chudleigh, now Duchess of Kingston, having finally been accused of bigamy and being tried before the House of Lords, and he absented himself from the country until June 1776. Most of his energies thereafter were devoted to wrangles with the Admiralty, and particularly the Earl of Sandwich, over the state of the Royal Navy.[8]

Though there are no payments to goldsmiths in his account with Goslings bank he does seem to have made at least one purchase of silver whilst Earl of Bristol and that was of a toilet mirror (fig. 51), apparently engraved with his arms and marked by Frederick Kandler for 1777.[9] It must, presumably, have been a present to Mrs Nesbitt with whom he appears to have had an affectionate and settled relationship in the last few years of his life, and, rather touchingly for a couple of relatively advanced years, the arched top has a cast quiver of arrows with a bow in allusion to Cupid.[10] A not dissimilar mirror, though more sinuous in outline, was made by Robert-Joseph Auguste in Paris the same year and it too has quivers of arrows as part of a cresting.[11] As Lord Bristol's was accompanied by a brush in the same style, also engraved with his arms, when it was sold at Sotheby's in 1963 there may well have been a complete toilet service. Whatever it consisted of, it would never have formed part of the Bristol plate, however, and being Mrs Nesbitt's own property it would have been sold with the rest of the contents of her Norwood house following her death in 1825.[12]

The 3rd Earl may have turned in some of his brother's ambassadorial plate to fund the purchase of the mirror and, if so, the most likely candidates are the silver-gilt dessert dishes supplied in 1759 (app. 4). Only one of the twelve round, oval and octagonal dishes survives (cat. 74) and that was given to Ickworth church to serve as an alms dish, probably at the time of the restoration of the building which Lord Bristol had overseen shortly before he died.[13]

THE EARL-BISHOP

Augustus Hervey was succeeded in 1778 by the third of the sons of Lord Hervey to hold the earldom, Frederick (1730–1803) (fig. 49), who had pursued a career in the church. After being ordained in 1754 he had found it hard to gain preferment and having married for love rather than money he did not have the benefit of a substantial dowry either.[14] Though he did possess silver at this stage in his life it was limited to between 100 and 200 ounces as is attested to by the plate tax returns, Hervey paying 5s per annum in 1759 and 1760 whilst he was resident at Horringer on the Ickworth estate.[15]

A rapid change of fortune came following the 2nd Earl's securing for him of an Irish bishopric, quickly upgraded to that of Derry which was the richest in Ireland, with an estimated income of £20,000.[16] He spent lavishly, collecting sculpture and paintings on ever-longer and more frequent Continental tours and from 1775 building a great house at Downhill on the north Ulster coast. As well as filling this with his fast-accumulating treasures, the Earl-Bishop, as he was dubbed by Horace Walpole, also entertained liberally and in 1785 he described to his eldest daughter, Mary, Lady Erne, how 'we commonly sit down to table from 20 to 25. We have cold Suppers and a bottle of Champaign at each end of the table.'[17] He acquired the necessary silver to serve such numbers, having at least seven dozen dinner plates and two dozen of soup, all of them of the same shaped circular pattern as those surviving at Ickworth and all engraved with the arms of the See of Derry impaling those of Hervey. They were made in London rather than Dublin and are marked for 1776, by John Rowe and Andrew Fogelberg, apart from twelve of the dinner plates which are of 1784 by Fogelberg and Stephen Gilbert and were presumably an augmentation.[18] The Earl-Bishop does not appear as a client of Parker and Wakelin and the acquisition may well have been made through Frederick Kandler, given the long family association with him, or Pickett and Rundell who, as Rundell, Bridge & Rundell, were to be the favoured goldsmiths of the 5th Earl. The Earl-Bishop did buy some silver in Ireland, his arms also being engraved on an elaborate oval bread basket of 1773 by John Lloyd of Dublin with chased dolphins supporting the swing handle and a shell and gadroon shaped border.[19]

The 4th Earl bequeathed his Irish estates and personal property to his cousin, Henry Bruce, rather than to his son, and Downhill and the silver it contained passed away from the Herveys on his death in 1803.[20] Because of this and the lack of need to add to the plate in England, which was plenteous enough already, there is only a handful of items of silver at Ickworth today that may relate to the Earl-Bishop, a set of dessert knives of 1790 (cat. 90) and four chamber sticks of 1791 (cat. 91) by John Scofield. They could have been acquired for St James's Square during a rare period of residence in London in the summer of 1792. On a previous, longer English sojourn Lord Bristol had had a plate chest transported to the Bull Inn at Bishopsgate, then a principal collecting point for goods bound for East Anglia and the north.[21] This happened in October 1781 and is likely to have been in anticipation of a year during which the 'Episcopal Earl of Bristol lived at Ickworth both summer and winter,' according to the great eighteenth-century agriculturalist and economist Arthur Young. He and a group of like-minded academics and antiquarians dined every Thursday with the Earl and as Lady Bristol and various of his now numerous family were also residing, the silver brought up would have been put to plentiful use. It may well have stayed at the house thereafter too, Lady Bristol making Ickworth her permanent residence after a final falling-out with her impossible husband in the latter part of 1782. They had gone for a drive together in the course of which something unrecorded was said 'and they came home and never spoke to each other again'.[22]

With his Continental visits being so drawn out the Earl is likely to have travelled with at least some silver, and it is tempting to envisage this including the pair of small tureens from the 1758 Jewel Office allocation which had certainly disappeared from the collection by 1811 (see appendix 4 and 5). If so, one of them could have been at the heart of perhaps the most obnoxious of Lord Bristol's many eccentric acts. According to the contemporary Scottish writer, Pryse Lockhart Gordon, the Earl was annoyed whilst dining in Siena by the tinkling of bells accompanying a procession of the Host beneath his windows, 'seized a tureen of *pasta*, and the sash being open, threw the contents in the midst of the holy groupe!' The justly outraged citizens besieged the house and the miscreant prelate had to escape out the back, concealing himself until nightfall and then fleeing the country. He was, reputedly, banned for ever from Tuscany by the Grand Duke 'under pain of the galleys'. Gordon also relates that whilst subsequently imprisoned by the French the Earl was required to 'furnish daily a dinner of six covers for the maintenance of a guard which was placed over him' and that he himself 'lived like a prince … entertaining very

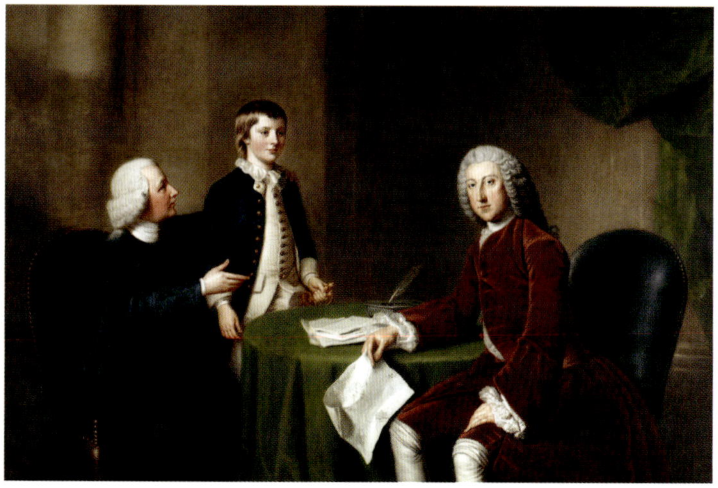

FIG. 49 / *Frederick Hervey, 4th Earl of Bristol and Bishop of Derry, presenting his son John Augustus to William Pitt, 1st Earl of Chatham* by William Hoare of Bath RA, 1771. A silver inkstand is depicted on the table. Oil on canvas: 167.6 x 233.7 cm (66 x 92 in). National Trust, Ickworth.

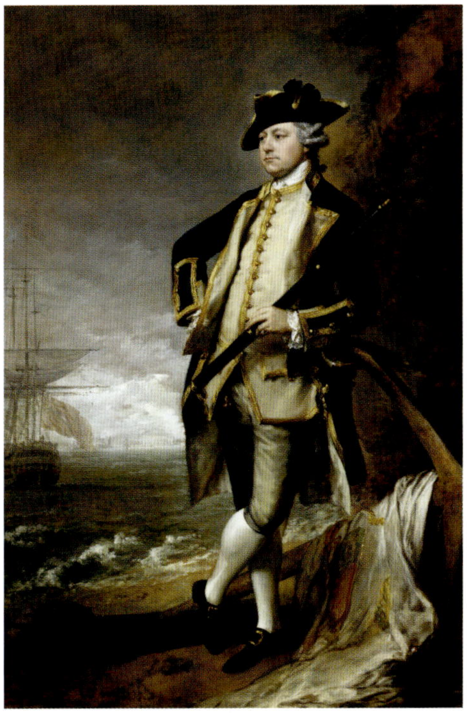

FIG. 50 / *Augustus John Hervey, 3rd Earl of Bristol* by Thomas Gainsborough, 1767. Oil on canvas: 232 x 152.5 cm (91½ x 60 in). National Trust. Ickworth.

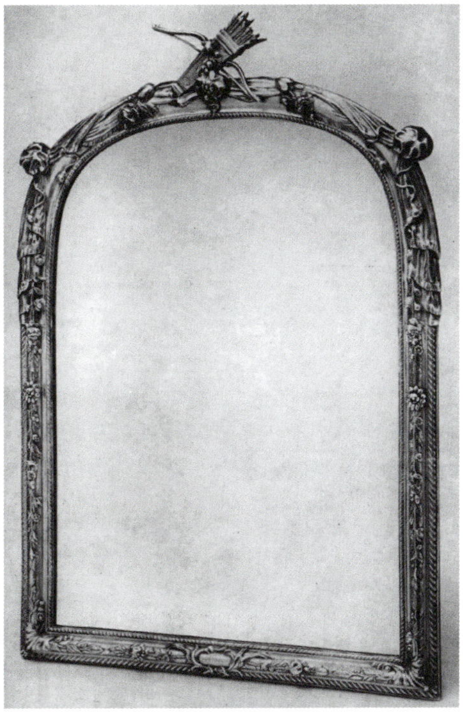

FIG. 51 / Toilet mirror, by Frederick Kandler, 1777. Silver: h. 27½ in. Sotheby's.

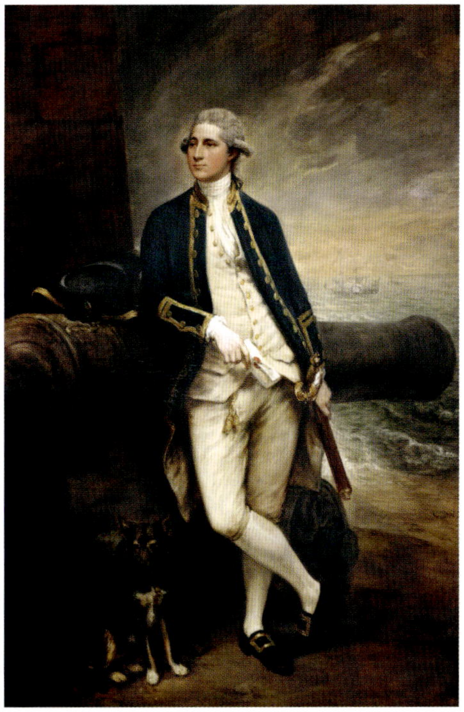

FIG. 52 / *John Augustus, Lord Hervey* by Thomas Gainsborough, *c.*1779. Oil on canvas: 221 x 149.9 cm (87 x 59 in). National Trust, Ickworth.

frequently the commandant and other officers of rank'.[23] Whether or not it was present at these extraordinary escapades, if the Earl-Bishop had had any silver with him in Italy in these chaotic last years of his life it would have been most unlikely to have made it back to England, and that could, in part at least, explain the loss of over 1,000 ounces of Hervey heirloom plate by the early nineteenth century.

Little better than the Earl-Bishop's behaviour was that of his eldest son, John Augustus, Lord Hervey (1757–96) (fig. 52), who was recalled from his post as British Minister in Florence in 1793 after calling the Grand Duke a fool and his chief minister a knave.[24] Hervey had held the post since 1787 and as his country's representative permanently resident in a city so popular with Grand Tourists he would have been required to entertain on a large scale and thus to have a sizeable store of silver, just as Sir Horace Mann had before him (see chapter 2). Whether he took anything from the plate room at St James's Square is not known but it would seem probable, and he also commissioned additional pieces, there surviving at Ickworth a coffee pot (cat. 92) and a set of dessert flatware (cat. 93) which are both of 1788 and engraved with the Hervey crest beneath a baron's coronet. To soften the blow of his dismissal William Pitt the Younger allowed Lord Hervey's younger brother, Frederick, to travel to Florence to deliver the news and it was probably left to him to organise the return of the baggage, including any silver.[25] Three years later John Augustus died at sea 'of a chill' and Frederick succeeded as Lord Hervey, inheriting the earldom and English estates on his father's death in 1803.

Regency restitution

Frederick William Hervey, 5th Earl and later 1st Marquess of Bristol (1769–1859) (fig. 53), had the steely determination typical of his family but combined with the gentle good nature of his mother, and he appears to have been an altogether more likeable character than his father and elder brother. Having fended off the Earl-Bishop's attempts to marry him to the illegitimate daughter of the King of Prussia[26] he had a long and apparently happy union with the Hon. Elizabeth Albana Upton, the couple producing six sons and three daughters and living a settled and conventional life between Ickworth and St James's Square. The Bristol estates in 1803 were not, however, in the same sound state they had been on the death of the 2nd Earl, being encumbered with 'heavy burdens' according to the new Earl's brother-in-law, Lord Liverpool, and there was also the problem of the vast and eccentric palace of a house that the Earl-Bishop had commenced at Ickworth in 1795, to the design of Mario Asprucci the Younger and Francis Sandys. It had been dubbed 'a stupendous monument of folly' by the late Countess and though the central rotunda had been roofed it was unfinished internally and little more than the foundations had been completed of the wings and connecting galleries which extended the overall length of the house to a breathtaking 600 feet.[27]

Work was brought to a halt, with the family continuing to use the old house when in Suffolk; their prudent existence, in place of runaway extravagance, eventually turned the situation around so that from 1819, gradually and out of income, the St James's Square house was able to be rebuilt and the new Ickworth House completed (fig. 54). The highest-quality fittings and furnishings were employed, Lord Bristol using Banting and France who were the inheritors of the business of the 2nd Earl's cabinetmakers and upholsterers, Vile and Cobb. Before turning his attention to furnishings and buildings, however, the Earl had faced up to a glaring deficit in the family plate. As he noted at the end of a list of the collection drawn up in 1811 (appendix 5), 'The total quantity of Plate left by George [2nd] Earl of Bristol was oz: 16700=11' but it now stood at 15,302oz 1dwt and therefore 'oz 1398=10 are wanting to make up the quantity entailed.' He determined to put this right and had, in fact, begun as soon as he had inherited, with the purchase of an enormous service of table knives and flatware (see cat. 102) plus substantial additions to his brother's dessert service (cat. 100). This may well indicate that the depredations under the 3rd and 4th Earls had been particularly severe in this category of plate. The 5th Earl's other early acquisitions were practical and simple in style and included new forms of dishes for the dinner table (cat. 98–9) which were needed to accommodate the changes that had occurred in culinary fashions since the 1770s. The financial situation must have improved significantly by the second decade of the nineteenth century when more showy additions were made, which would have had a substantial charge for fashion. Chief amongst these were a fine set of cast rococo candlesticks (cat. 103) and the magnificent tea urns and first course dishes by Paul Storr (cat. 104–5) but there were also more chamber sticks (cat. 110) and inkstands (cat. 109) and a new chalice for Ickworth church (cat. 106).

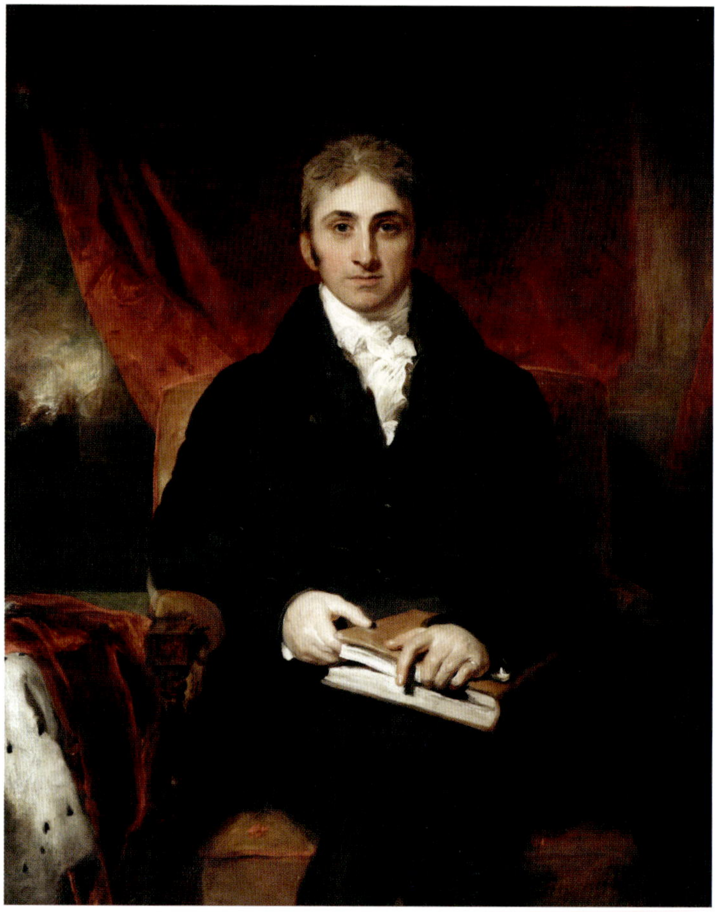

FIG. 53 / *Frederick William Hervey, 5th Earl and 1st Marquess of Bristol* by Sir Thomas Lawrence PRA, *c.*1810. Oil on canvas: 124.5 x 99.1 cm (49 x 39 in). National Trust, Ickworth.

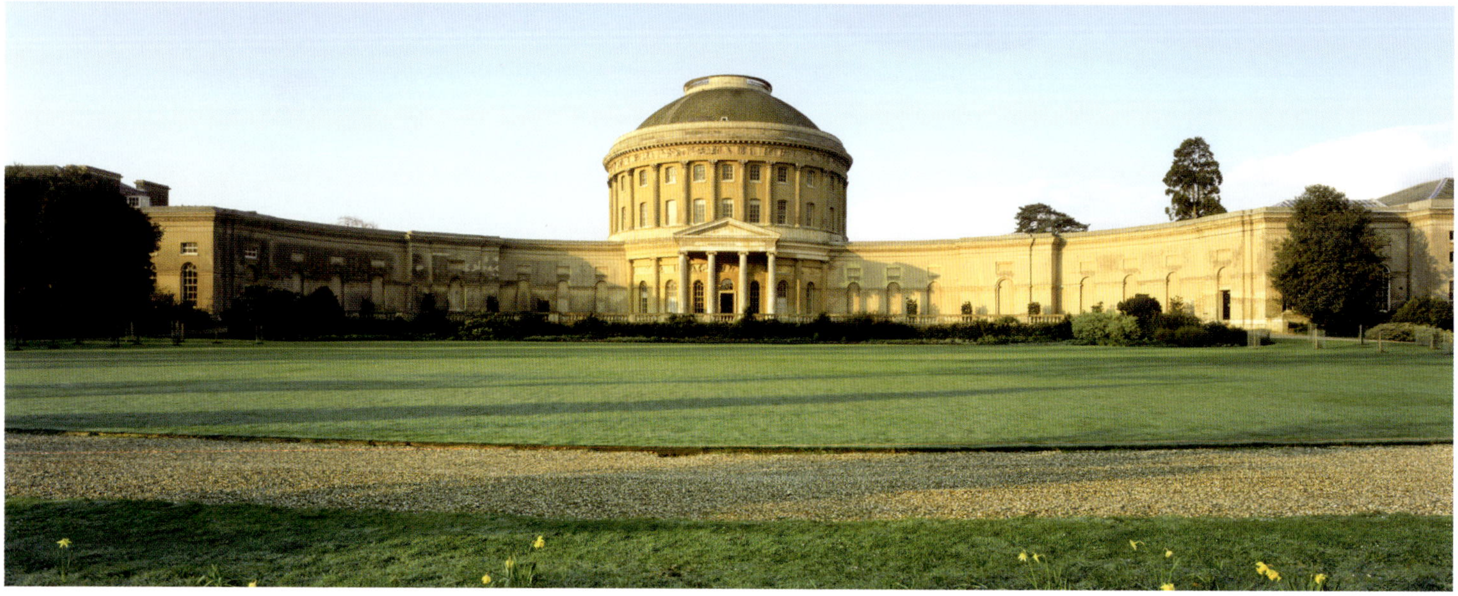

FIG. 54 / The North Front of Ickworth showing the central rotunda and curved galleries as completed by the 1st Marquess of Bristol in the 1820s.

Two more dessert services followed in 1823 (cat. 113–4) and in 1826 there were also additions to the 1758 service (cat. 119), meaning that Lord Bristol had four separate sets available. This probably reflected another of his key aims in purchasing silver, as well as reaching the quantity entailed, which was to provide for all of his residences. As Ickworth and St James's Square were where the principal entertaining was undertaken the great bulk was split between them but there were smaller allocations of more practical plate at Bristol House on Putney Heath and the Earl's Brighton house in Sussex Square. This was a marked change from the eighteenth century when almost the entirety of the plate was in London with very little permanently at Ickworth and none at all at the 2nd Earl's house in Lincolnshire, Leasingham Hall. The early-nineteenth-century division is not precisely recorded but there is a list of those items at Putney Heath in 1826 not deemed 'Family Plate' and they included a bread basket, a tea pot, salvers and candlesticks plus a few plated pieces.[28] No cutlery or flatware is listed, probably because that was recorded with the family plate, whatever its location.

On 27 May 1826 Lord Bristol once more calculated the combined weight of his plate and at 16,349 oz, 16 dwt, it was just 350 ounces short of the target (see appendix 5). Rather satisfyingly for him it was as a consequence of his own generosity in reducing rents at times of great agricultural distress that full restitution was achieved, and indeed, surpassed. First of all his Lincolnshire tenants presented the Earl with a candelabrum weighing just over 298 ounces in 1826 (cat. 118) and fourteen years later, by which time he had been created a marquess, the Suffolk tenants followed suit, their testimonial being a prodigious 482 ounces (cat. 121). Lord Bristol triumphantly recorded that the heirloom plate now stood at 17,130 ounces 19 pennyweight and 12 grains, over 400 ounces more than in 1775.

The 5th Earl and 1st Marquess of Bristol died in 1859 in his ninetieth year and was genuinely mourned by his family and tenants and the people of Bury St Edmunds. Thousands came to see him lying in state in the library at Ickworth which was prepared for the purpose, as described in the local paper:

> *To avoid disturbance to the books in the apartment, a room was built inside the library, and the whole was lined with black cloth, elegantly fluted. A barrier was erected round the coffin, also covered with the same material … The coffin was partially covered with a very rich velvet pall, edged with white satin. Upon this was placed a cushion, surmounted by the deceased Marquis's coronet. An elegant plume was placed at the head of the coffin, and immediately behind, affixed to the wall was the family escutcheon. The apartment was lighted with wax candles, and on either side of the coffin, within the barrier, were placed four massive silver candle-sticks, of the plainest possible pattern, each supporting enormous wax candles.*[29]

Preservation

None of the succeeding holders of the estate made significant additions to the Hervey plate, though the wife of the 3rd Marquess, Geraldine Anson (1843–1927) (fig. 55), did gather together the collection of nineteenth-century articulated silver fish (fig. 56) which were made as scent bottles and vinaigrettes. The primary contribution of these later generations of the

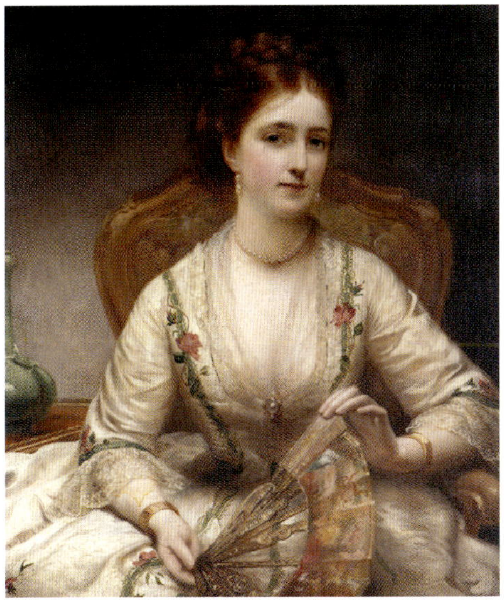

FIG. 55 / *Geraldine Anson, Marchioness of Bristol* by the Hon. Henry Graves, 1870. Oil on canvas: 87.6 x 68.6 cm (34½ x 27 in). National Trust, Ickworth.

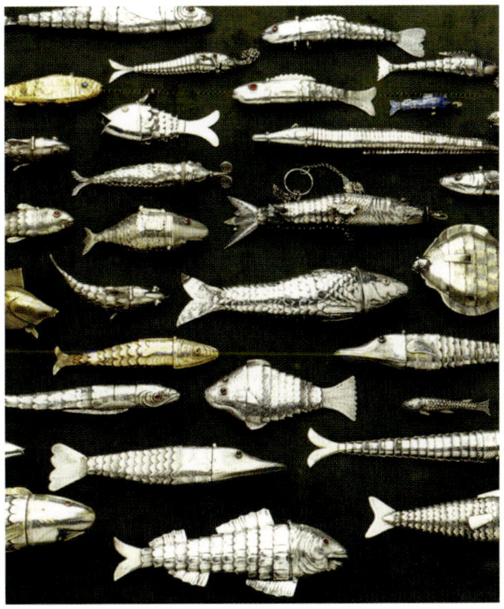

FIG. 56 / Some of the articulated silver fish collected by Geraldine, Lady Bristol in the late 19th century. National Trust, Ickworth.

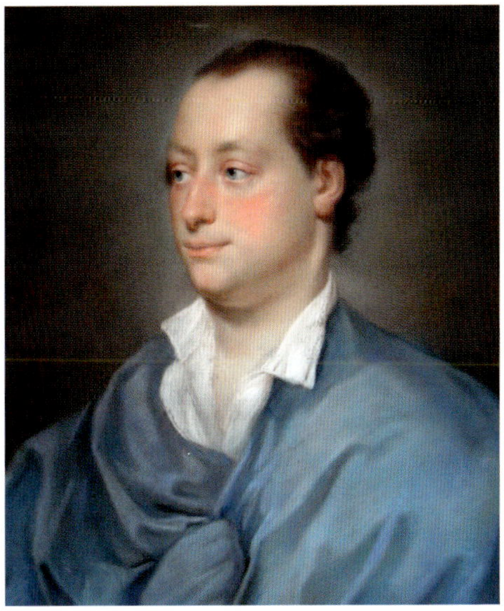

FIG. 57 / *George William Hervey, 2nd Earl of Bristol* by Anton Raphael Mengs, *c.*1761. Pastel on paper or vellum: 54 x 41.5 cm (21¼ x 16⅓ in). National Trust, Ickworth.

family was, rather, their careful guardianship of the Ickworth treasures, including the silver, which ensured that they survived unscathed and appreciated into the late twentieth century. The two successive châtelaines, Geraldine Anson and Theodora Wythes (1875–1957), took an enlightened curatorial approach to everything at Ickworth, recording what was known about the Herveys, the house and the collections, and initiating the purchasing of items of family importance that came onto the market. This was particularly concentrated on pictures, including the portrait by Anton Raphael Mengs of the 2nd Earl of Bristol (fig. 57) which was bought in Rome in 1868, but there were also other items including significant ceramics and books.

Silver did not go unnoticed either and it is probable that Lady Hervey's French tumbler (cat. 24) was retrieved by Theodora, Marchioness of Bristol. In 1932 the Marchioness attempted to secure some representative pieces from the plate commissioned by the Earl-Bishop in the 1770s and 1780s for his house at Downhill. Eighty-four dinner plates and twenty-four soup plates were sold at Christie's in London on 27 July 1932 and Lady Bristol wrote immediately to enquire whether the purchaser, the prominent silver dealer Walter H. Willson, would let her have two of them. His response, of 29 July, was understandable but not generous, indicating that 'it would detract considerably from its value to have ten odd plates because it is at present an even number of dozens.' Should he have to split the service, however, he promised to reserve two for Lady Bristol 'out of the last dozen'. That was not to be and the Marchioness noted against a press cutting about the sale that an American buyer had been found for the whole. Willson had paid £563 5s 1d at the auction which equated to 6s 1d per ounce, considerably less than the 4th Earl would have been charged in the eighteenth century, and he sold the service on for 10s per ounce, a handsome profit.[30] Lady Bristol had also made note of a Dublin-made bread basket of 1773 a few years earlier but that went for the then substantial sum of 46s per ounce and if she tried for it she must have been outbid.[31] There remains no representation of the Earl-Bishop's silver from his Irish houses at Ickworth.

The enlightened tenure of the 4th Marquess and Marchioness also saw the Ickworth plate being brought to public attention for the first time at the loan exhibition held at Seaford House, Belgrave Square in aid of Queen Charlotte's Hospital in May and June 1929. This was a spectacular display of silver made prior to 1740 which was gathered together before many of the great private collections represented were dispersed, or at least depleted, as heavy taxation took its toll during the course of the twentieth century. Lord and Lady Bristol lent the 1680 wine cistern (cat. 1), the 1708 candlesticks by Pierre Platel (cat. 7), the Rollos ice pails (cat. 18) and all the pieces by that darling of twentieth-century collectors and curators, Paul de Lamerie (cat. 11–13 and 19).[32] Some sense of the scale of the displays is given by a photograph of 'Room B' in the elegant catalogue, the Ickworth cistern being partly visible on the far right-hand side (fig. 59).

Public exposure must have helped in negotiations following the death of Lord Bristol in 1951 when a huge tax bill had to be met and there were also concerns about the impact of the next but one in the line of succession, Victor Hervey (subsequently 6th Marquess), who before the Second World War had been involved with jewel theft and arms dealing as well as being sentenced to three months' penal servitude for another scrape.[33] The Marchioness was determined to ensure that the collection, including the silver, would not have to be broken up, and put her own money forward as the endowment.[34] Although land and buildings had been able to be transferred in lieu of tax for some time, contents were only permitted to be considered from 1953[35] and Ickworth and Petworth were effectively the test cases. Negotiations proved especially complex and protracted over Petworth because of the enormous values involved[36] and both cases suffered from the rather haughty advice of the National Gallery over pictures.[37] Initially it looked as if the silver would throw up even greater difficulties for Ickworth with a preliminary report by H.D. Molesworth, Keeper of Woodwork at the Victoria and Albert Museum, suggesting that the choicest pieces only should be acquired, and for transfer to his museum rather than being left in situ. The National Trust, he suggested, could instead furnish the dining table with Sheffield plate which would be 'quite as effective, a tithe of the responsibility, and less temptation to burglars'.[38] A subsequent visit to Ickworth, however, resulted in a startling volte-face. Molesworth was utterly beguiled by the place, describing the house and grounds as 'superb' and identifying the silver as the most important element of the chattels. Having damned the pictures and furnishings with faint praise, as a 'very adequate filling for the house', he continued:

> *all this plate … really is of exceptional quality and interest as a collection, and were it to be properly displayed, quantity added to this quality would make a really splendid effect. On occasion, no doubt, for special purposes or propaganda, complete services might be set out in the dining-room. In any event, there can be little doubt that with such a display the public would visit Ickworth for the house, the grounds and the plate, and be well rewarded for their trouble … against my initial feelings, I think there is perhaps reason and justification for accepting this large quantity of material for the very impression it affords of the grand scale of life in the grand manner in the 18th century.*

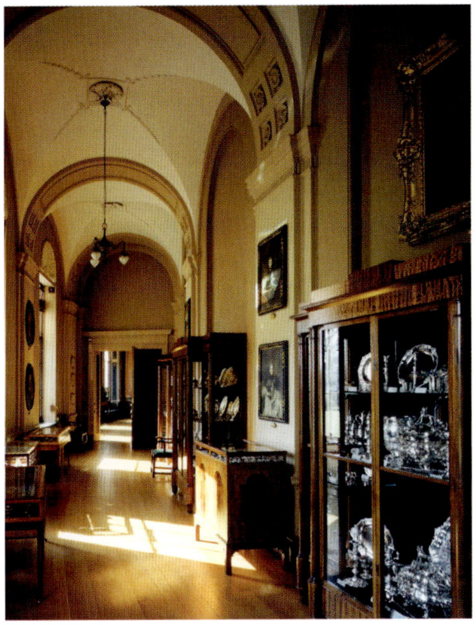

FIG. 58 / The West Corridor at Ickworth, *c.*1970.

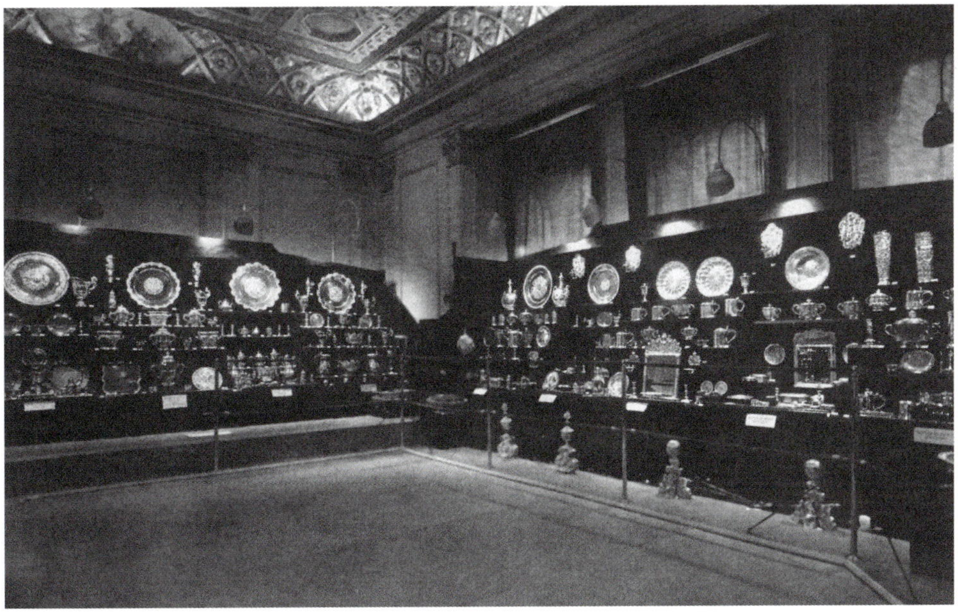

FIG. 59 / Room B of the Seaford House exhibition in aid of Queen Charlotte's Hospital, 1929. Photograph from the catalogue.

He further concluded that the values attributed to the silver had been 'so modestly assessed … I do not feel that anybody could question that in normal trade terms the nation has done a good piece of business'.[39] Thus when the house, park and principal contents passed to the Inland Revenue, and then onto the National Trust, in August, 1956, the great bulk of the silver was included.[40] The family, who continued to occupy the East Wing until 1998, retained only what they needed for late-twentieth century aristocratic living, namely some salvers, candlesticks, coffee and tea pots, sauce boats (see cat. 29–30) and, most significantly, much of the early-nineteenth century flatware and cutlery. In total this probably accounted for less than five per cent of what had been listed as heirloom plate in 1811–40 (appendix 5). It was dispersed in part in the late 1990s by the 7th Marquess and, after his death, by his executors.[41]

The National Trust

As well as being the first example of a great store of plate accepted in lieu of tax, the Ickworth silver also represented by some margin the National Trust's most important collection and that remained the case until 1976 when, with the bequest of Dunham Massey in Cheshire, it was matched in calibre by the superb plate of the 2nd Earl of Warrington.[42] The Ickworth acquisition was announced to the art world through two articles by Norman Penzer in *Apollo* in February and April 1957, and because of its quality a significant representation was regularly on exhibition, across England and also in Italy, Germany and the United States.[43] In 1985–6 two items, a Kandler tureen of 1752 (cat. 43) and one of the Le Sage candelabra of 1758 (cat. 72), were included in the celebrated *Treasure Houses of Britain* exhibition at the National Gallery of Art, Washington.

There was initially nowhere to show the silver safely which meant that it was not on display in 1957, the first open season, but the National Trust was determined that it would be there for Easter of the following year and made promises to that effect.[44] The decision was taken to use the West Corridor and designs for cases were obtained from the distinguished post-war classical architect, Raymond Erith, who was then based in Ipswich. He reflected the bold Regency detail and rich mahogany fittings of the interiors of the house and incorporated a slight concave curve to fit the north wall of the corridor. Approval came from the Trust's Historic Buildings Committee in October and the commission was undertaken by Frederick Sage & Co of Gray's Inn Road, a distinguished firm of shopfitters who had been responsible for refitting the House of Commons after the Second World War.[45] The corridor was painted 'celadon green' in readiness and a picture hang was devised incorporating the series of Zoffanys of the 2nd Earl of Bristol's siblings. As the cases arrived on 31 March, just four days before Easter,[46] it proved impossible to arrange them in time so the final unveiling to the public did not happen until the summer. Photographs from the period (fig. 58) record the effect, which was impressive with a dense array of silver and other showcases, all packed with treasures of the highest order. When H.D. Molesworth of the V&A carried out the first official inspection on behalf of the Treasury in December 1958 he was pleased to find the house 'most beautifully kept' by the curator-brothers, Angus and Douglas Davidson, and the silver, 'one of the most important features of the collections', 'in mint condition and admirably displayed'.[47]

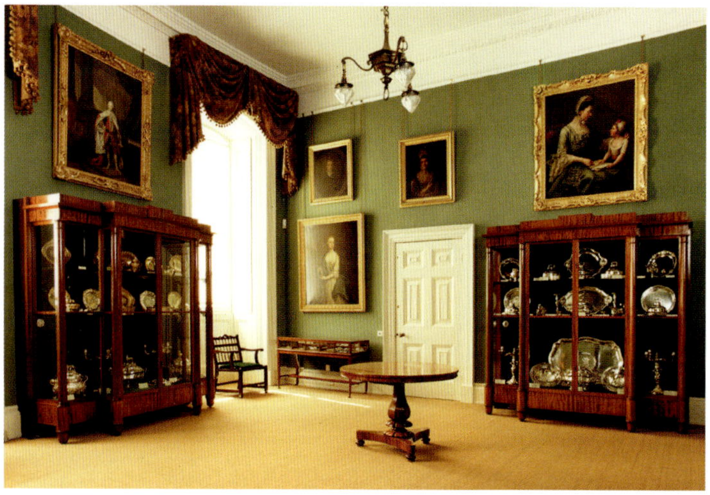

FIG. 60 / The silver display in the Museum Room at Ickworth, 1999

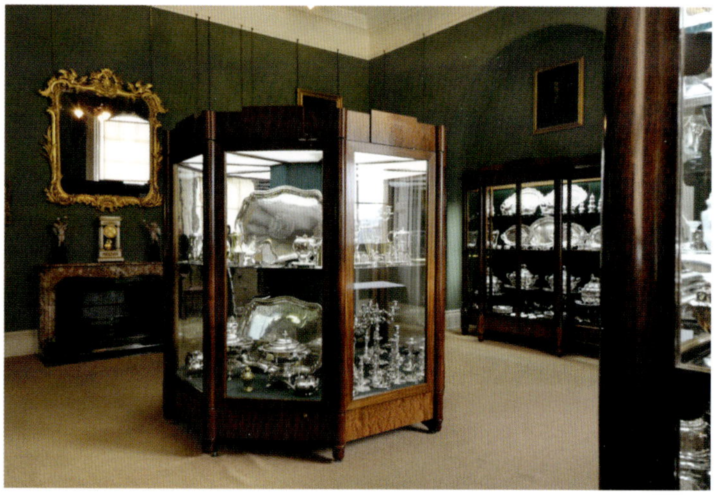

FIG. 61 / The new silver case and rearranged display, 2015.

The silver display remained in the West Corridor until the 1990s when a comprehensive review of the presentation of the whole house resulted in the decision to open additional rooms on the first floor, one of which was allocated to the silver, miniatures and *objets de vertu*.[48] As it was a dedicated space and not a corridor leading to another room, it was more conducive to the museum displays required and has proved very successful. The Erith cases were retained, being of significance in their own right as pieces of twentieth-century furniture, highly effective in their intended task and as well suited to the lofty first-floor former bedroom as they had been to the West Corridor. Their gently curved form is sufficiently subtle as not to be obviously discernible. The walls were painted a soft green to harmonise with the velveteen used to line the cases in the 1950s and the portrait of the 2nd Earl attributed to Zoffany (fig. 37) was put in prime position between the windows, presiding over his spectacular accumulation of plate. John Cornforth wrote up the redisplay of the house for *Country Life* in 1999 and was full of admiration for the new museum room (fig. 60) which, he stated, would remind visitors that 'Ickworth was always intended to be a gallery of art as well as a family seat.' He did, however, feel that the display of the silver was not entirely resolved and that what had been achieved should only be considered a 'reasonable interim measure'.[49] Large quantities remained in store and there had never been a detailed study of the collection to inform the choice and arrangement of the exhibits.

Successive National Trust curators were of the same mind but a lack of money prevented any progress being made until 2010 when, highly appropriately, a donation came in memory of John Cornforth, who had died six years earlier.[50] This was bolstered by a contribution from Royal Oak, the American organisation which exists to fundraise for the Trust,[51] and in 2013 a large new central case, inspired by those existing, was produced to the design of the exhibition specialist, Ian Drake.[52] With the benefit of a thorough analysis of the entire collection a comprehensive redisplay was effected (fig. 61) and almost everything was able to be incorporated. For the first time in its history the Ickworth silver was fully on view to the public, its intricacies understood and its makers, both English and Turinese, either verified or newly identified. It was through this process that the astonishing significance of the collection became widely appreciated and the National Trust consequently committed to the publication of this catalogue.

1. Parker and Wakelin Ledgers, VAM 7 1765–75, f. 119 and Sotheby's, 10 June 1993, 'The Harcourt Collection'.
2. Mortlock 1997, p. 553 and Hartop 2010, pp. 41–5, ill.
3. A pair of sauce tureens is all that is now at Clandon, inv. 1441577, but much else has been in the market. See, for instance, Bonhams, New York, 24 September 2012, lot 5065, a set of twelve plates by Paul Storr, London, 1812, and Christie's New York, 23 May 2013, lot 126, a bread basket, and lots 128–9, three dozen plates, all by Paul Storr, 1812.
4. Lomax and Rothwell 2006, pp. 124–6 and cat. 76, pp. 147–8.
5. Much of it was by Paul de Lamerie and several pieces are now in public collections. See, for instance, the pair of waiters in the Ashmolean Museum, Schroder 2009, cat. 93, pp. 256–9. Two other waiters of 1747 (inv. 1271250) and a meat dish of 1746 (inv. 1271293), all by de Lamerie, remain at Shugborough.
6. Erskine 1953, pp. 149–50.
7. Holmes 1996, p. 262–5. Young Augustus was anyway at school at Loughborough House, Lambeth, where the aristocratic pupils are said to have eaten off silver.
8. Ibid., pp. 269 and 281–3.
9. Sotheby's, 14 November 1963, lot 104 and 16 July 1970, lot 120.
10. This does seem rather an unlikely gift after nine years together and at their age. It could, alternatively, be associated with John Augustus, Lord Hervey, and his wife Elizabeth Drummond who married in 1779. Should it ever come to light again it would be possible to examine the arms in order to confirm one way or the other. They are not visible in the Sotheby's photograph.
11. Dennis 1960, vol. 1, pp. 38–40, figs. 17 and 17c.
12. Holmes 1996, p. 291.
13. Yates 2013, pp. 8–10.
14. Fothergill 1974, pp. 19–20.
15. Plate tax list 1757–62, p. 813.
16. Fothergill 1974, p. 25.
17. Ibid., p. 42.
18. Christie's, 27 July 1932, lot 85.
19. Sotheby's, 18 July 1929, lot 53.
20. The contents of Downhill were dispersed in the early twentieth century and the house is a ruin, though it and its demesne are, like Ickworth, in the care of the National Trust.
21. Goslings ledgers, 130/65, f. 183; the payment was made on 26 October and amounted to 6s 6d. In 1731 the London bookseller John Brindley sent the antiquarian Cambridge clergyman Zachary Grey a parcel containing 'the six additional volumes of the Byzantine historians' via the Bull Inn, Bishopsgate and *c.*1780 the same inn was used for another parcel of books, being sent to London 'by the Cheshunt coach'. See Nichols 1822, pp. 262 and 551.
22. Fothergill 1974, pp. 83–90.
23. Gordon 1830, vol. 1, pp. 173–6.
24. Fothergill 1974, pp. 155–7.
25. Ibid.
26. Ibid., pp. 189–96.
27. Ibid., pp. 173–4 and Strachey 1998, pp. 45–6 and 53.
28. SRO, 941/75/2, 'A List of Plate at Putney Heath not included in the List of Family Plate and not Belonging to it', 4 April 1826.
29. SRO, 941/80/13, obituary leaflet of the 1st Marquess of Bristol, extracted from the Bury St Edmunds Free Press. The candlesticks referred to do not accord to anything that has ever been known to have been at Ickworth and were probably hired in for the lying in state.
30. SRO, 941/12/60a–c, cuttings and correspondence relating to Earl Bishop's dinner service, 1932. Christie's, 27 July 1932, lot 85 'A dinner service, comprising eighty-four shaped circular dinner-plates with gadrooned borders, engraved with the arms of the See of Derry impaling the arms of Bristol – forty-eight by John Rowe, 1776, twenty-four by Andrew Fogelberg, 1776, twelve by Andrew Fogelberg and Stephen Gilbert, 1784; and Twenty-four Soup-plates, similar – by Andrew Fogelberg, 1776. 1851[oz] 16[dwt]'.
31. SRO, 941/12/61b, extract from Sotheby's sale catalogue for 18 July 1929, lot 53, 'An oval cake basket, pierced with trellis work of different patterns in panels divided by wheat ears and leaves, the shaped border with gadroon and shell decoration, on oval foot with trellis work and gadroon edge, the swing handle supported by finely chased dolphins, 15in. wide. By John Lloyd, Dublin, 1773. Weight, 39oz. 10dwt.'
32. Watts and Shirley 1929, pp. 39, 57, 67 and 68, cat. 327A, 485, 573, 577, 581 and 584–5. There were also 'examples of present day work'.
33. Waterson 1994, pp. 136–7 and TNA, T 227/1244, f. 26, Treasury memorandum from Sir Alexander Johnston to Mr Couzens, 28 June 1955. The family, according to the latter document, were desperate for matters to be settled 'before Lord Jermyn [as Victor Hervey then was] is in a position to influence matters at all'. I am grateful to David Adshead for alerting me to the Land Fund files amongst the Treasury papers.
34. The sum eventually settled upon for the endowment was £185,000. TNA, T 227/1243, ff. 70–1, J.F.W. Rathbone (NT Secretary) to O.C. Thorley (Treasury), 31 January 1955.
35. Under Section 30 of the Finance Act, 1953.
36. Waterson 1994, pp. 142–4. Ickworth's chattels were settled at £80,000 whereas Petworth's were finally agreed at more than £500,000.
37. The initial advice relating to Ickworth was to reject certain pictures, including those of the Sardinian royal family presented to the 2nd Earl of Bristol, but the National Trust successfully appealed against this. TNA, T 227/1245, ff. 8 and 22, J.F.W. Rathbone (NT) to Sir Alexander Johnston (Treasury), 10 and 19 April 1956.
38. TNA, T 227/1244, ff. 68–9, preliminary report on Ickworth chattels by H.D. Molesworth, Keeper of Woodwork, V&A, 10 October 1955.
39. Ibid, ff. 75–6, report on the Ickworth chattels by H.D. Molesworth, 15 October 1955.
40. TNA, T 227/1245, f. 119, Secretary's Office (Taxes), Inland Revenue to The Secretary, HM Treasury, 2 August 1956. The transfers happened that day and represented the first successful case under the 1953 provision. Those items then valued at more than £1000 were initially retained in government ownership and placed on loan, being fully transferred subsequently. Amongst the silver these were the bottle cistern (cat. 1), the Rollos ice pails (cat. 18) and the Le Sage candelabra (cat. 72). Ibid, ff. 64–5, 'Objects at Ickworth House which are to be loaned to the National Trust', May 1956. In addition to the silver there were eleven paintings and a 'Chippendale' writing desk (NT inv. no. 850058).
41. Sotheby's Suffolk, 11–12 June 1996, 'The East Wing, Ickworth, Suffolk', lots 320–79 and Sotheby's Summers Place, 14–16 September 1999, lots 1174–211. Some of these lots had probably been purchased by the 6th and 7th Marquesses. There must also have been private sales (see cat. 41 and 52).
42. See Lomax and Rothwell 2006.
43. See individual catalogue entries for details of loans to exhibitions.
44. Ickworth House, archive files, Nicholas de Bazille Corbin (NT Regional Agent) to Gordon Watts (Raymond Erith's office), 9 January 1958, copy letter.
45. Ibid., Robin Fedden (NT Secretary of Historic Buildings Committee) to Raymond Erith, 10 October 1957, copy letter, and Gordon Watts to Nicholas de Bazille Corbin, 24 January 1958, copy; Abel 1960, pp. 38–9.
46. Ibid., Douglas Davidson (NT, Ickworth curator) to Mr Scoggins, 2 February 1958, copy, and Douglas Hawes (Frederick Sage & Co) to Douglas Davidson, 19 March 1958.
47. TNA, T 227/1245, ff. 219–22, H.D. Molesworth (V&A) to A.J.D. Winnifrith (Treasury), plus report, 11 December 1958.
48. The work was carried out under the direction of Jeremy Musson and the Hon. Nino Strachey, successive Assistant Historic Buildings Representatives for the National Trust.
49. Cornforth 1999, pp. 43–4.
50. Approximately £14,000, coming from the John Cornforth Memorial Fund, raised through a series of lectures given by distinguished speakers.
51. Royal Oak contributed $25,000.
52. The National Trust curator who directed the project was Jan Summerfield, with guidance from the author as Adviser on Silver. The re-display of the silver coincided with the distinguished contemporary silversmith, Miriam Hanid, having a residency in the house sponsored by the Goldsmiths' Company. She created a silver beaker inspired by Ickworth which was the subject of a raffle.

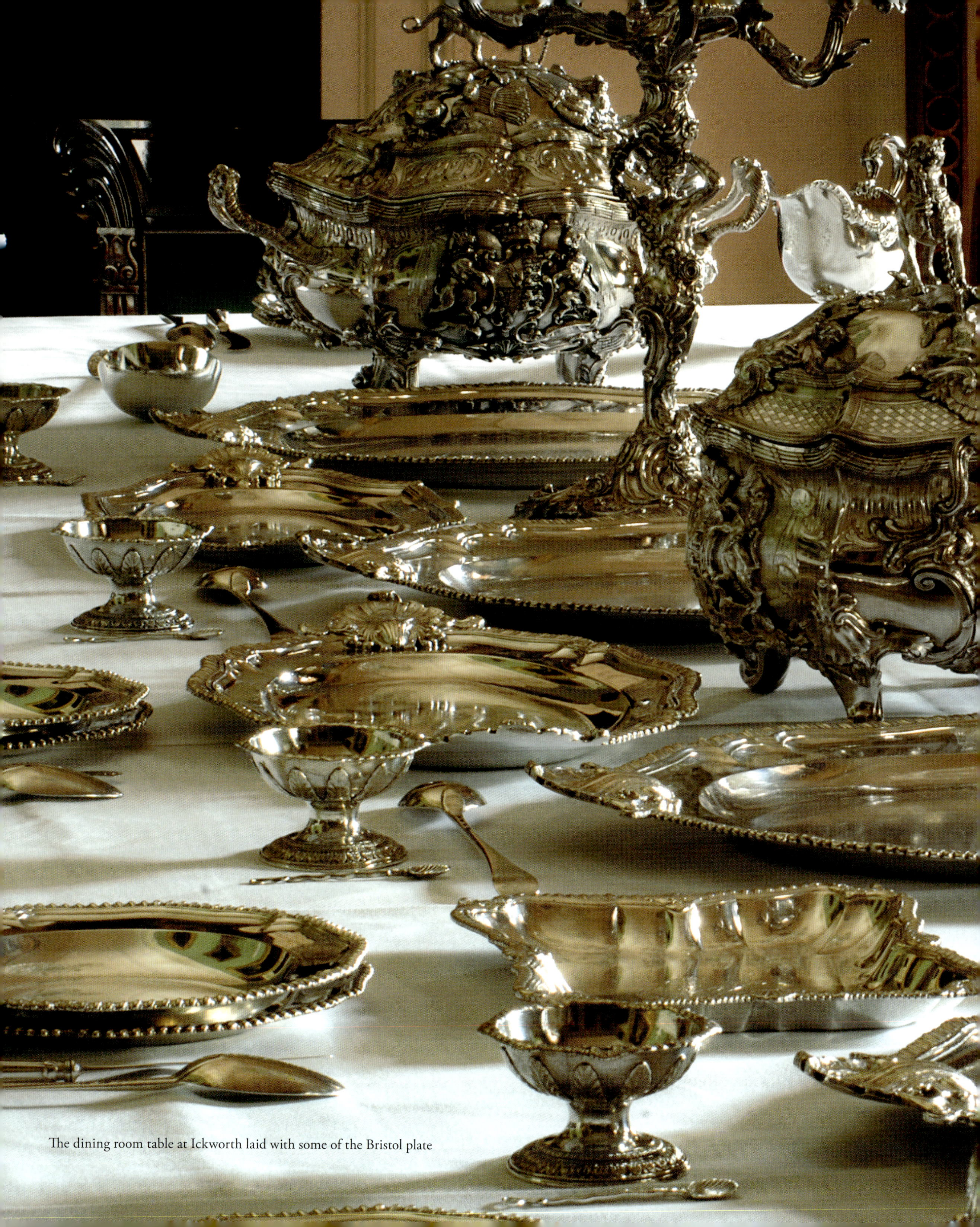
The dining room table at Ickworth laid with some of the Bristol plate

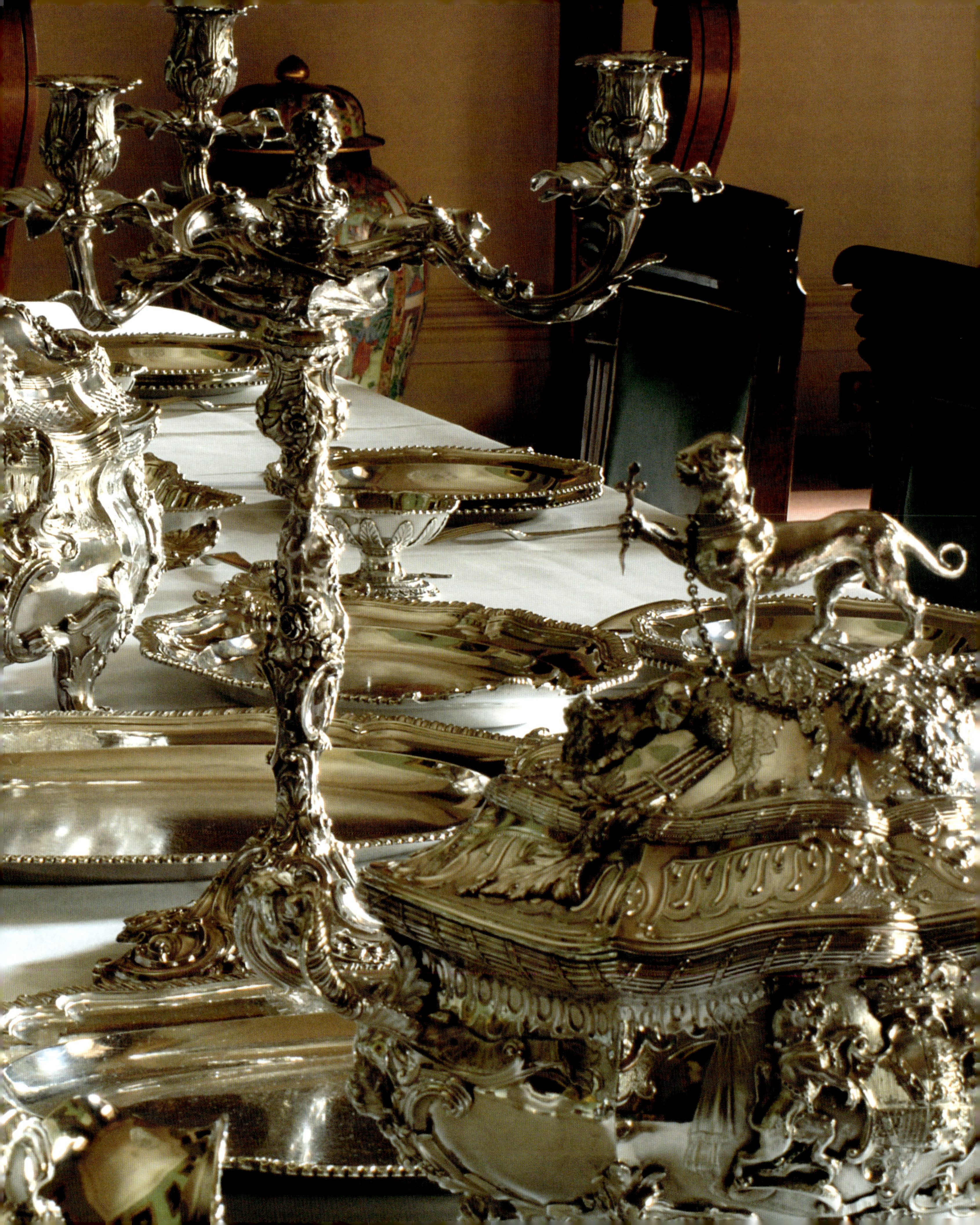

THE CATALOGUE

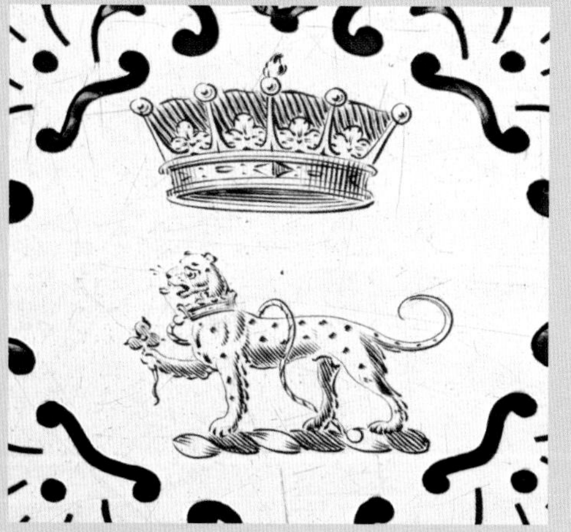

FIG. 62 / The Hervey crest beneath an earl's coronet on one of the mazarines by Frederick Kandler, 1751 (cat. 33).

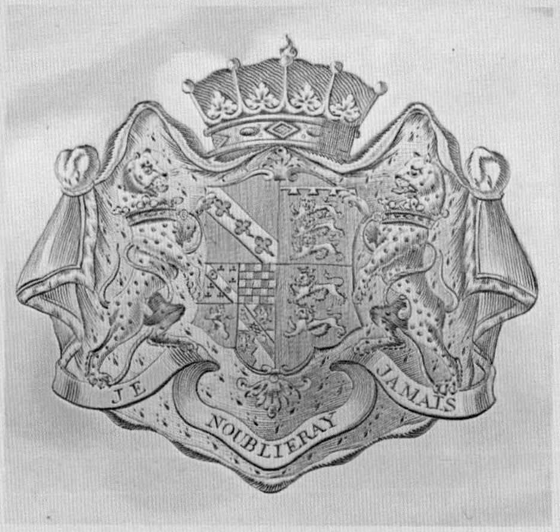

FIG. 63 / The heraldic bearings of the 2nd Earl of Bristol, as engraved on the bread baskets by John Robinson, 1754 (cat. 50).

A NOTE ON PROVENANCE

The great majority of the silver at Ickworth was collected by four successive generations of the Hervey family: John, 1st Earl of Bristol (1665–1751); John, Lord Hervey (1696–1743) and his wife, Mary Lepel, Lady Hervey (1706–68); George William, 2nd Earl of Bristol (1721–75); and Frederick Hervey, 5th Earl and 1st Marquess of Bristol (1769–1859). The accumulated collection passed by descent to Frederick William, 4th Marquess of Bristol (1863–1951) and in 1956 it was accepted by the Treasury in lieu of death duties and handed over to the National Trust. Some additional items have been re-acquired in recent years from amongst the small number reserved from the 1956 transfer for family use or previously alienated by gift or bequest.

HALLMARKS

These are described in the order in which they are stamped on individual objects. In the case of multiples one example is followed.

DATE LETTERS

Up to 1974 the date letters stamped on English silver changed on 19 May, the Feast Day of the patron saint of goldsmiths, St Dunstan. Thus a mark spans two years. In the heading to each catalogue entry the date letter is interpreted in its full form, e.g. 1724/5. Thereafter, and in all references to pieces outside the collection, the calendar year of the introduction of the date letter is generally used, e.g. 1724.

WEIGHTS

Scratchweights (in Troy ounces and pennyweight) are given where they occur and are on the underside of an object unless described to the contrary. Where there are no scratchweights actual weights have been taken, or reference is made to the 1811 plate list.

HERALDRY

The Hervey crest (fig. 62) is engraved on much of the silver surviving at Ickworth: an ounce passant sable besantée (black snow leopard with gold spots), ducally collared and chain reflexed over the back or, holding in the dexter paw a trefoil slipped vert. The motto of the family, where referred to, is 'Je n'oublieray jamais' which means 'I shall never forget'.

Where, in the catalogue, references are made to the quarterings of the 2nd Earl and the 5th Earl/1st Marquess they are engraved as follows unless otherwise specified.[1]

GEORGE WILLIAM HERVEY,
2ND EARL OF BRISTOL (fig. 63):
1st quarter: gules, on a bend argent three trefoils slipped vert (HERVEY).
2nd quarter: gules, three lions passant guardant or, a label of three points argent (PLANTAGENET, as borne by Thomas of Brotherton, son of Edward I).
3rd quarter: quarterly, 1st gules a bend between six cross crosslets fitchée argent, on the bend an escutcheon or, charged with a demi-lion rampant pierced through the mouth with an arrow, within a double tressure flory counter-flory gules for Howard, 2nd chequy or and azure for Warren, 3rd gules a lion rampant argent for Mowbray and 4th quarterly per pale indented or and azure on a bend of the second between two eagles displayed gold a fret between two martlets of the last for Audley of Walden (HOWARD, Earl of Suffolk and Lord Howard de Walden).
4th quarter: gules two lions passant in pale ermine ducally crowned or (FELTON).[2]

FIG. 64 / The heraldic bearings of the 5th Earl (subsequently 1st Marquess) of Bristol, as engraved on the first-course dishes by Paul Storr, 1809 (cat. 105).

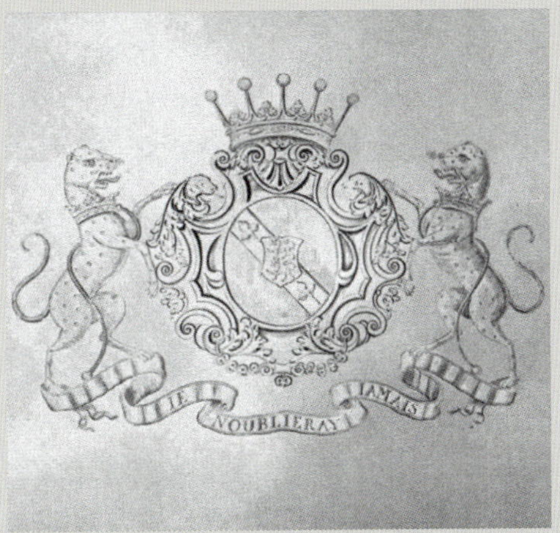

FIG. 65 / The only surviving example of the engraved arms of John Hervey as 1st Earl of Bristol, engraved on a waiter by Robert Cooper, 1712.

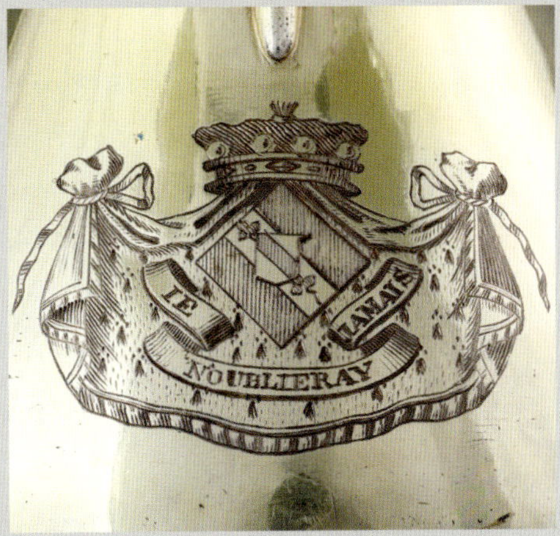

FIG. 66 / Mary, Lady Hervey's arms, as engraved on the silver-gilt coffee pot of 1762 by Frederick Kandler (cat. 22).

FREDERICK WILLIAM HERVEY, 5TH EARL AND 1ST MARQUESS OF BRISTOL (fig. 64):
1st to 4th quarters: as the 2nd Earl.
5th quarter: quarterly 1st and 4th argent on a bend gules three martlets or for Davers, 2nd and 3rd sable a crescent between two mullets in pale argent for Jermyn quartering sable a fess between three roses or for Rushbrooke (DAVERS).
6th quarter: gules on a chevron or, three estoiles sable (CARR).[3]

The 2nd Earl, not being married, did not have reason to impale his arms with those of a spouse. There is no silver at Ickworth relating to the 3rd Earl but he would not have done so either, not being publically acknowledged to be married. The few pieces acquired by the 4th Earl (cat. 90 and 91) only bear the family crest but he is known to have impaled his arms with those of the See of Derry rather than those of his wife (see chapter 4). The 5th Earl/1st Marquess, though married, seems, from the evidence of the plate surviving at Ickworth, to have chosen not to impale his arms, the only exception being the candelabra presented to him by his tenants in 1826 (cat. 121).

Only two pieces of the silver associated with the 1st Earl are known to have survived both melting and being re-engraved: the chocolate pot of 1704 at Ickworth (cat. 5) which has Hervey impaling Felton, and the waiter which passed away from the direct line in the eighteenth century (Sotheby's, London, 4 March 1965, lot 169, ill.; fig. 65) which has Hervey with Felton in pretence, both for his second wife, Elizabeth, daughter of Sir Thomas Felton, 4th Bt.

No examples of the engraved arms of the 1st Earl's two eldest sons, Carr and John, successively Lords Hervey, are known to survive. John's wife, Mary Lepel, as a widow engraved her silver with a lozenge bearing the arms of Hervey with Lepel (argent, a bend gules)[4] in pretence (fig. 66). The only silver at Ickworth certainly associated with the 4th Earl's eldest son, John Augustus, Lord Hervey, the coffee pot and flatware of 1788 (cat. 92–4), is engraved with the Hervey crest beneath a baron's coronet.

---

1. All these descriptions are taken from Burke 1884.
2. Though the 2nd Earl was entitled to the second and third quarters as heir general of the 3rd Earl of Suffolk, the arms of Thomas of Brotherton should not have been detached from those of the Howards. This was done purely to accentuate his royal lineage, albeit very distant, through his grandmother, Elizabeth Felton.
3. Though the 1st Marquess had inherited the remnants of the Carr estates in Lincolnshire he was not entitled to quarter the arms, being descended from the 1st Earl's second wife, Elizabeth Felton and not his first, Isabella Carr.
4. This is the coat of arms of the German von Lepel family, from whom Lady Hervey was probably descended, and is not registered in the College of Arms.

PART ONE

SILVER OF JOHN HERVEY, 1ST EARL OF BRISTOL (1665–1751)

1. **Bottle cistern**

Sterling silver / **Robert Cooper, London** / **1680/1**

MARKS: Fully marked on the underside with maker's mark 'RC' in dotted circle[1] (Pickford 1989, p. 137), leopard's head crowned, lion passant, date letter 'c'.

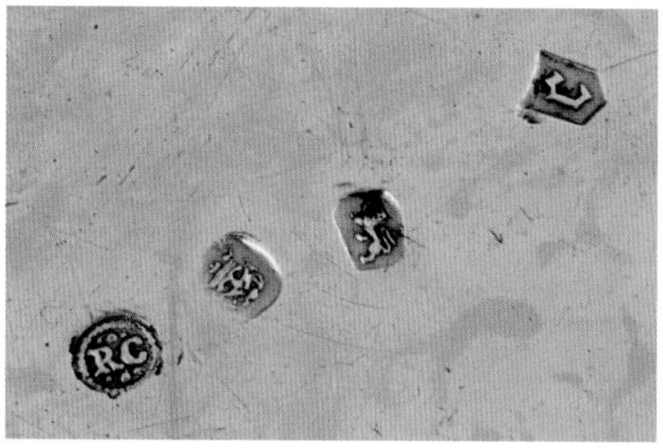

SCRATCHWEIGHT: '314=15'

MEASUREMENTS: h. 24.1 cm (9½ in); w. 69.5 cm (27⅜ in); d. 60 cm (23⅝ in).

INVENTORY: 852068

PROVENANCE: Baptist May; bought from his executors by John Hervey (subsequently Lord Hervey and 1st Earl of Bristol) 7 May 1697; by descent to the 4th Marquess of Bristol.

LITERATURE: Penzer 1957a, I, pp. 40-1, fig. IV; Penzer 1957b, p. 42, fig. VI; Banister 1980, p. 792, fig. 1.

EXHIBITED: *Queen Charlotte's Loan Exhibition of Old Silver*, Seaford House, London, 1929, cat. no. 327A; *Treasures from National Trust Houses*, London 1958, cat. no. 151; Society of the Four Arts, Palm Beach, 1959; *The Age of Charles II: Winter Exhibition 1960–61*, Royal Academy of Arts, London, 1960–1; *British Week*, Milan and Frankfurt, 1965; *Silver from National Trust Houses*, Treasurer's House, York Festival, 1969, cat. 7; *Treasures from Country Houses of the National Trust and National Trust for Scotland, Europalia 1973*, Brussels, cat. 109.

DESCRIPTION: The large oval body is raised from a single sheet of silver, the bulbous lower part being chased to form broad, outward-facing flutes with flat, matted borders and separated from each other by thin, vertical concave flutes. In the upper interstices are chased acanthus leaves and forming the neck of the cistern is a broad band of trailing foliage with flowers and grapes carried by four putti, chased to be read on the interior. Further floral bands with matted grounds, divided into four by classical female masks, are chased into the flat rim which is bounded by a heavy reed and tie moulding soldered and riveted to the outer edge. Cast lion masks are set at either, narrow end of the exterior and hold in their mouths the pivot pins of the C-shaped swing handles, also cast, each of which has a winged cherub's face with foliage above and pairs of outward facing scrolls designed to stop the handles against the lion masks when the cistern is carried. The cistern is raised on four scroll and dolphin feet, each cast in two parts with a beaded foliage strip soldered down the front to disguise the joint.

HERALDRY: The floor of the cistern has been re-engraved *c.* 1751 with the quartered shield, supporters and motto of the 2nd Earl of Bristol in an ermine mantling and beneath an earl's coronet.

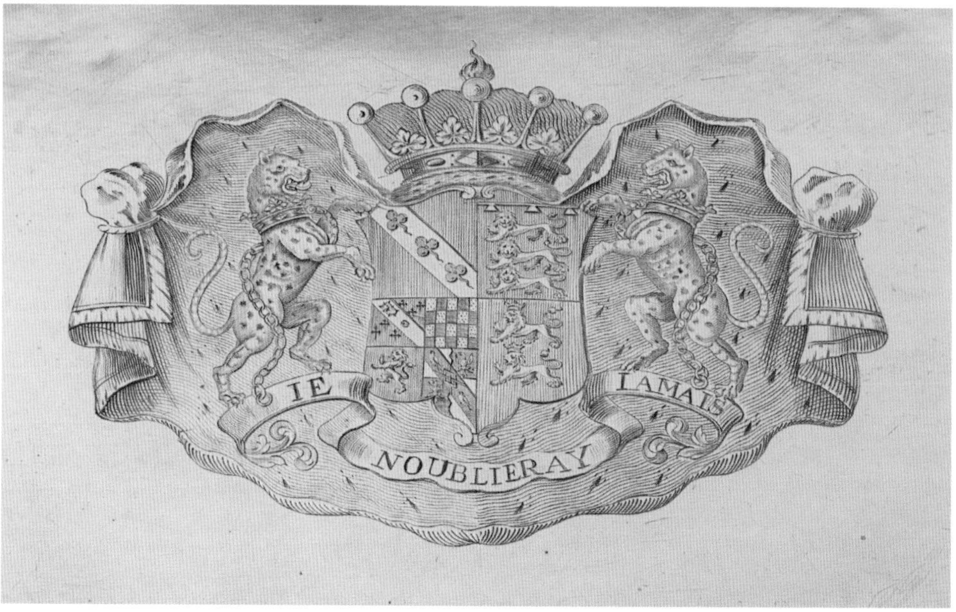

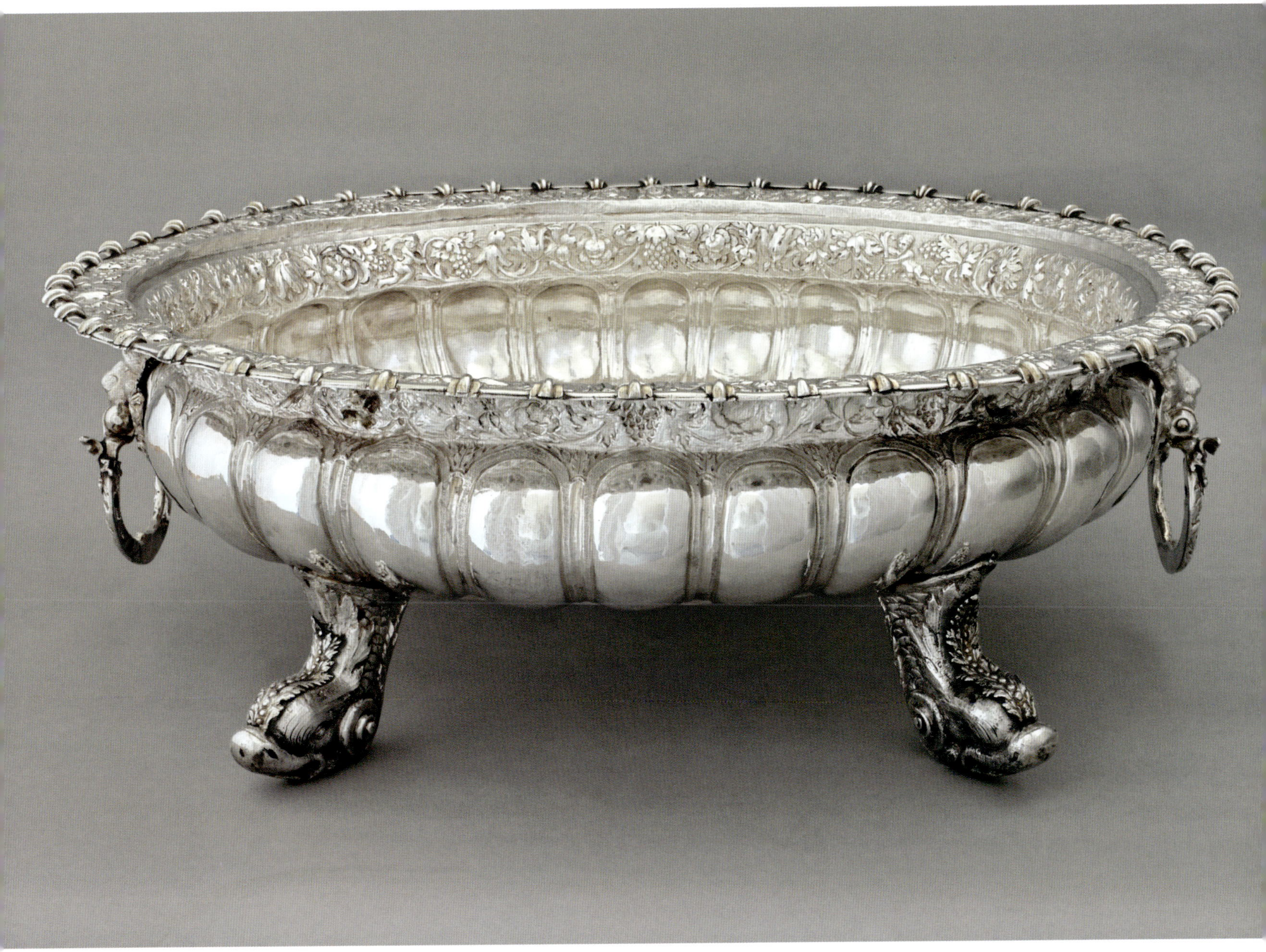

Cisterns associated with the service of wine at a meal have been in existence in Europe since at least the fourteenth century and have been made of marble, pewter, copper and brass as well as silver.[2] None in silver from England is known to survive from before the Restoration but there was then a comparative surge in their production and there are at least sixteen surviving which were made up to the end of William III's reign.[3] Of these nine are of a comparable scale and weight to that at Ickworth and three are around fifty per cent bigger, and quadruple the weight. The larger cisterns were undoubtedly intended to rest on the floor and to act as coolers for bottles, being filled with water for the purpose. A number of paintings from the seventeenth and early eighteenth centuries show them in use in this way, including Jan Baptist van Meunincxhove's 1671 depiction of the guild banquet given to Charles II and the Duke of Gloucester in Bruges on the 2 October 1656 (fig. 67). This shows a lobed silver-gilt vessel of broadly the same pattern as the Ickworth cistern, filled with water and containing what are probably a silver wine bottle and a gilt water ewer.[4]

Six of the smaller cisterns from the period have contemporary silver water fountains associated with them and were intended to be used 'to wash glasses in', as stated to be the case in the eighteenth-century inventory reference to the Rollos cistern of 1701 at Dunham Massey.[5] As such they would have been raised above the floor and placed directly beneath the tap of the fountain, putting them at eye level to those sitting at the dining table. The Ickworth cistern, however, with its elaborately decorated neck being chased to be viewed on the inside, must have been intended to be seen from above and thus to have been placed on or just above the floor. It is therefore likely to have been designed primarily as a 'bottle cistern', the term used for the larger of the Dunham Massey duo, and the same must be the case for the similarly scaled and decorated cistern of 1694 by George Garthorne in the collection of the Bank of England (fig. 68).[6] It is quite understandable that silversmiths supplied smaller versions of the monsters required by such princes of the aristocracy as the 1st Duke of Rutland, whose bottle cistern of 1681, also by Robert Cooper and of the same basic model as those at Ickworth and the Bank of England, weighs just under 2,000 ounces.[7] That supplied in 1687 to the future 1st Duke of Devonshire, which does not survive, was perhaps the greatest of all in the late seventeenth century, weighing 3,496 ounces and costing £1,223 12s.[8] Lesser noblemen, the gentry and merchants would not have had the wealth to support such purchases and nor would their scale of dining have required anything so grandiose.

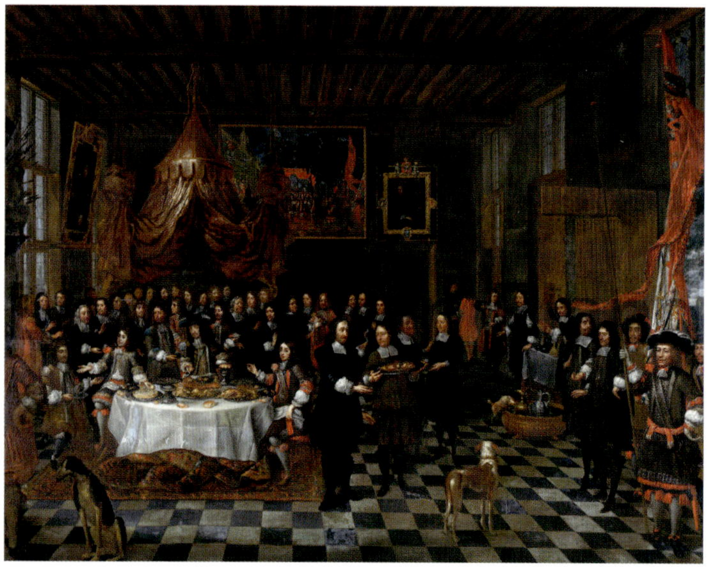

FIG. 67 / *Reception of Charles II and the Duke of Gloucester by the Bruges Guild of St Barbara on the 2nd October, 1656* by Jan Baptist van Meunincxhove. Oil on canvas: 249 x 199 cm (98 x 78¼ in).

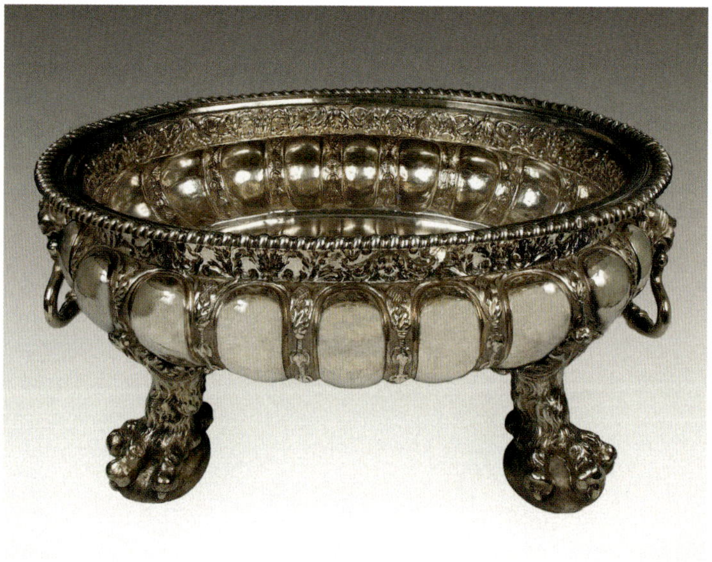

FIG. 68 / Cistern by George Garthorne, London, 1694. Silver: 33.1 x 84.1 cm (13 x 30½ in); weight 19,167 g (616 oz, 5 dwt). Bank of England.

The original owner of the Ickworth cistern was Baptist May (1628–1697) (fig. 69), a prominent Restoration courtier whose sister Isabella, Lady Hervey, was the mother of the 1st Earl of Bristol. May's father, Sir Humphrey, had been Vice-Chamberlain to the Household of Charles I and Baptist told Gilbert Burnet that he had been 'bred about the king [Charles II] since he was a child'. In 1662 he became one of the Duke of York's grooms of the bedchamber and in 1665 he was elevated to Keeper of the Privy Purse to Charles II. Thereafter he was one of the King's most trusted courtiers in spite of being a staunch Protestant and demonstrating an aptitude for tactlessness, most famously when he welcomed the effects of the Great Fire of London. Bishop Burnet summed up his contribution as follows:

he had the greatest and longest share in the king's secret confidence of any man in that time; for it was never broke off, though often shaken, he being in his notions against every thing that the king was for, both France, popery, and arbitrary government: but a particular sympathy of temper, and his serving the king in his vices, created a confidence much envied, and often attempted to be broke, but never with any success beyond a short coldness.

On the accession of James II May was dismissed from the keepership but retained his other office, Ranger of Windsor Great Park, and resided in the official residence, the Great Lodge (subsequently Cumberland Lodge) until his death on 2 March 1697.[9]

John Hervey (the future Earl of Bristol) made a note in his diary of his uncle's death and subsequent burial in St George's Chapel, Windsor,[10] and within two months he had acquired a large quantity of silver from May's estate, as recorded in his accounts:

May 7 [1697]
Paid Mr Duncombe & Mr Pigeon (as Execs: of Mr Bapt May) for a large silver Cystern, 2 Dozen of nurld plates, 1 large Cup & Cover, 1 Bason, 1 Chamber pott, 1 Ladle & 1 Skimer, all weighing – 1128 ounces 15 peny weight which at 5s:4d p ounce came to 301 £[11]

His motive for doing so was not family loyalty but sound economics, for he thereby made a considerable saving on commissioning new pieces and he was actually paying less than the worth of the raw material which he could be sure would hold its value as it was inextricably linked to the coin of the realm. The cistern would, according to the evidence of that by Robert Cooper at Belvoir, have cost Hervey 6s 2d per ounce if made new, or £98, and, at 5s 4d, he paid just £83 4s 5d.[12] Furthermore, though no longer at the cutting edge of fashion it was by no means outdated, as is shown by the commissioning just three years earlier of the remarkably similar Garthorne cistern, now in the Bank of England. There is no evidence from his accounts that Lord Bristol ever purchased either a water fountain or a 'washer' in silver; these items – to make up the trio for the service of wine – would have become increasingly necessary as his social position and involvement in politics progressed in the first decades of the eighteenth century. It is possible that he had inherited suitable items from his father on his death in 1694 but if not he may only ever have had the two missing components in silvered or japanned brass or copper.[13]

Robert Cooper, who gained his freedom in 1670 and seems to have been working independently from about 1675, was one of the most prominent of native-born silversmiths in the latter half of Charles II's reign. He created major pieces of plate for significant courtiers, including the cisterns for May and the 8th Earl (subsequently 1st Duke) of Rutland, and amongst commissions from the goldsmith-banker Richard Hoare was the alteration and refurbishment in 1685 of several items for Samuel Pepys.[14] Other fine display pieces followed, including a pair of gadrooned sideboard dishes of 1687 in the Ashmolean Museum and a ewer and basin of 1691 and 1693 in the National Museum of Wales.[15] No more cisterns by him are known, however, and the lack of stylistic flair in a ewer of 1702 suggests that he did not manage to keep pace with his increasingly successful and well-established Huguenot rivals.[16] Amongst his later commissions is a substantial oblong salver of 1712, subsequently engraved with the arms of the 1st Earl of Bristol but no longer in the collection (fig. 14).

1. This mark has been convincingly attributed to Cooper. See Wees 1997, p. 100, note 1 and Schroder 2009, p. 229.
2. Penzer 1957b, part 1, p. 3 and Jourdain 1926, p. 853.
3. Murdoch 2010 contains the most up to date list of surviving English silver cisterns made prior to 1730. Thirteen made prior to 1700 are listed but the whereabouts of one is unknown.
4. The painting is in the Groeningemuseum, Bruges, inv. no. 1378 32.
5. Murdoch 2010, Cornforth 1996, pp. 128–30, ill., Glanville 1992, pp. 152–4, ill., and Lomax and Rothwell 2006, cat. 12, pp. 58–60, ill. The cisterns with associated contemporary fountains are that of 1670 by 'IC' bearing the arms of the 2nd Earl of Chesterfield (private collection), the pair by Ralph Leake of 1698 from Kedleston (now V&A and Goldsmiths' Company; one of the fountains at the Goldsmiths' Company, the other at the Getty Museum, California), the pair by David Willaume of 1700 at Boughton House, Northamptonshire and that by Pierre Harache of 1700 at Althorp, Northamptonshire. The fountain which goes with the Rollos cistern of 1701 at Dunham Massey was not supplied until 1729.
6. Lomax and Rothwell 2006, cat. 14, pp. 62–4.
7. Murdoch 2010.
8. Hayward 1959, p. 76.

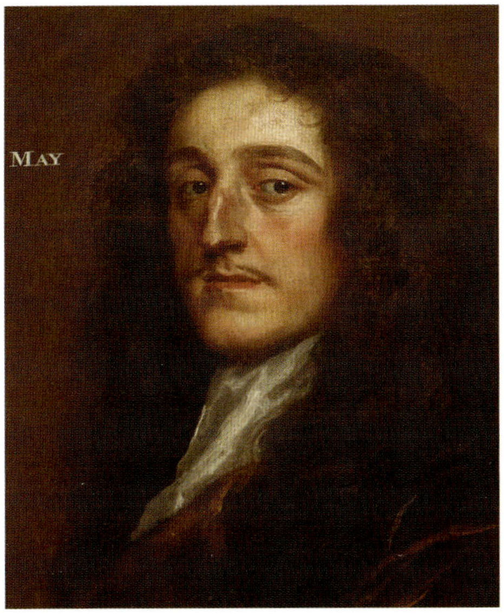

FIG. 69 / *Baptist May* [detail] by John Greenhill, 1662. Oil on canvas: 66 x 51.4 cm (26 x 20¼ in). National Trust, Ickworth

9. Andrew Barclay, 'May, Baptist (*bap.* 1628, d. 1697)', ODNP; online edn, Jan 2008, http://www.oxforddnb.com/view article/18418 (accessed 16 Oct 2015).
10. Hervey 1894a, p. 26.
11. SRO, 941/46/13, 1st Earl of Bristol's expenses and diary 1688–1742.
12. Belvoir Castle *c.* 1990, pp. 16–17, ill.
13. There is a fine japanned copper cistern bought in 1699 at Chatsworth. See Jourdain 1926, p. 854, ill.
14. Grimwade 1990, p. 472.
15. Schroder 2009, cat. 83, pp. 229–231; National Museum of Wales accession no. NMW A 50305–6.
16. Brett 1986, p. 153, no. 582, ill.

2. Snuff, subsequently nutmeg grater

Silver, gilt inside / probably London / *c.* 1695

MARKS: Unmarked.

SCRATCHWEIGHT: '3=3'

MEASUREMENTS: h. 1.9 cm (¾ in); w. 12.7 cm (5 in); d. 3.2 cm (1¼ in).

INVENTORY: 852795

PROVENANCE: John Hervey (subsequently Lord Hervey and 1st Earl of Bristol); by descent to the 4th Marquess.

DESCRIPTION: The raised, bow-shaped base is of semicircular section and is divided internally into two uneven compartments both of which are gilded, the larger having a roughly perforated silver (?) grating plate. A silver divider between the compartments, soldered in place, has a semicircular opening at the base. The flat lids with raised, right-angled lips open from a shared nine-part pinned hinge, with bands of baroque engraving to either side. Two lugs of silver are soldered at the wider end as finger holds.

HERALDRY: The larger of the lids has been re-engraved later, probably *c.* 1751, with the Hervey crest and an earl's coronet.

Double compartmented boxes of this period with graters are exceptionally rare survivors and are thought to have been intended either for nutmeg or for snuff, the latter commonly being provided in a solid form as well as ready powdered in the late seventeenth and early eighteenth centuries.[1] The 1811 plate list (see appendix 5) prepared for the 5th Earl (subsequently 1st Marquess) of Bristol specifies that this and the other grater in the collection (cat. 17) were then for nutmeg, which was at the height of its popularity as part of the late Georgian craze for toddy-drinking.[2] By then too, personal snuff grating appears to have completely ceased, certainly amongst the wealthy classes.[3] There are, however, no references to nutmeg boxes or graters in the 1st Earl's accounts whereas both he and Lady Bristol, plus their children once in adulthood, were enthusiastic consumers of snuff. Further support for snuff is given in the case of this grater by its large size (unusual for nutmeg graters), its gilded interior (common in snuff boxes) and by a comparably shaped and dated grater in the Victoria and Albert Museum which is considered to have been for snuff.[4] Other snuff graters of a similarly elongated form are also to be found in ivory and boxwood, again well demonstrated by examples in the V&A.[5]

A conveniently sized block of solid tobacco would be grated to produce powdered snuff which could pass from the large to the small compartment and from there be dispensed. The small compartment also acted as a store for the block of tobacco which, in that form, would retain freshness and flavour. Although snuff taking may have been introduced to the French court as early as the late sixteenth century, Catherine de' Medici supposedly using it as a cure for persistent headaches, the habit took hold under Louis XIV in spite of that monarch's disapproval. From France

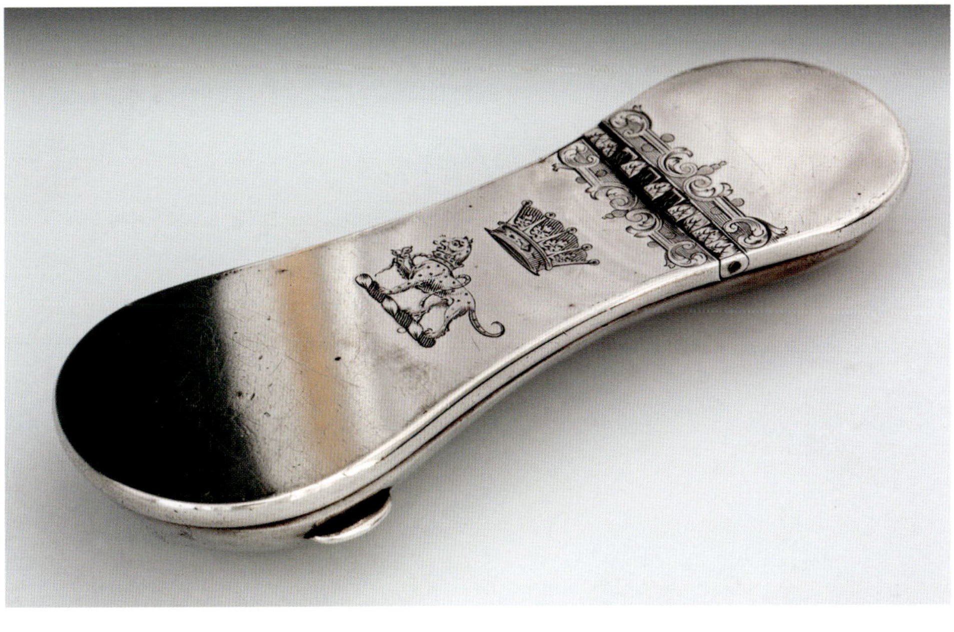

it spread to England at the Restoration and was widespread amongst the aristocracy by the last decade of the seventeenth century.[6]

Early boxes of a small size are hard to date because of their lack of hallmarks, at most having a maker's mark and in this case lacking even that. The style of the engraving around the hinge on this example, however, suggests that it was made in the very late seventeenth century or early eighteenth century and it could be the silver snuff box for which John Hervey (the future 1st Earl) paid £1 10s on the 30th January, 1690. The sum is about right for the weight and intricate workmanship required for such a precisely engineered object. Furthermore, graters and snuff boxes were carried about as a pair by partakers at this time and a few days earlier, on 24 January, Hervey recorded that he 'Paid then for a Gold Snuff box, which be it here remembered, ye Goldsmith Mr Howerd of whom I bought it, is obliged whenever I return it, to allow me for it again six pounds, & a Crown' (5 shillings less than Hervey paid; see appendix 1). Sadly no early gold snuff boxes survive at Ickworth. Hervey went on to buy another silver snuff box, along with other items, in 1695, from Charles Mather 'ye Cane-man in ffleet Street', perhaps for his second wife, Elizabeth Felton, whom he married that year. In 1713 she was the recipient of a gold snuff box from her husband, bought for £20, and he acquired two more, for himself and his eldest son, Carr Hervey, in 1714, for £22 6s and £19 14s 6d respectively. Finally, on 21 October 1726, what must have been a silver snuff box was purchased for £1 10s and given to a Mrs Saint Hayes (see appendix 1 for all these payments).

1. Pickford 1998, p. 134.
2. Hughes 1957, p. 58.
3. *Edinburgh Review or Critical Journal for January … May 1828*, p. 500. The text suggests that snuff graters had been almost entirely forgotten about by 1828.
4. V&A museum number 1348-1902. For a further example of a bow-shaped silver grater, then thought to be for nutmeg, see Smith 1907, p. 173, plate H.
5. For instance V&A museum nos. CIRC. 489-1923 and 1417-1902.
6. For a detailed analysis of the history of snuff taking see Billings 1875, pp. 218–258. An illustration of a two-compartmented grater is given on p. 220.

3. Four candlesticks

Sterling silver / John Laughton I, London / 1695/6

MARKS: Fully marked on the underside of each with maker's mark 'IL' with mullet below and coronet above (Pickford 1989, p. 135, where attributed to John Laughton), lion passant, date letter 'S' and leopard's head crowned.

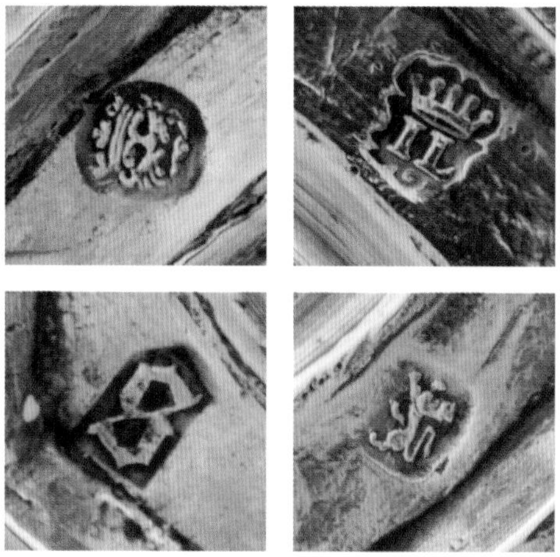

SCRATCHWEIGHT: 1. 'Nº 15 [/] 14=9' and '~~15=9~~'; 2. 'Nº 16 [/] 14=6' and '~~15=8~~'; 3. 'Nº 17 [/] 14=10' and '~~15=14~~'; 4. 'Nº 18 [/] 14=17' and '~~15-14~~'.

MEASUREMENTS: h. 17.5 cm (6⅞ in); w. and d. (of base) 11.7 cm (4⅝ in).

INVENTORY: 852076

PROVENANCE: Probably acquired by John Hervey (subsequently Lord Hervey and 1st Earl of Bristol); by descent to the 4th Marquess.

LITERATURE: Penzer 1957a, II, p. 133; Banister 1980, p. 792.

EXHIBITED: *Treasures from National Trust Houses*, Christie's, London, 1957–8, cat. 158 (two); Society of the Four Arts, Palm Beach, Florida, 1959; *Ideal Home Exhibition*, London, 1960 (2 of 4); *Silver from National Trust Houses*, Treasurer's House, York Festival, 1969.

DESCRIPTION: The stepped, square bases with cut corners are cast. They have a bold gadrooned border and a dished centre within a circular moulding. The circular baluster stems, also cast, are partly fluted and formed of a compressed knop and a vase rising to a spool-shaped socket.

HERALDRY: The dish of each base has been re-engraved (probably in the 1750s) with the Hervey crest beneath an earl's coronet.

These candlesticks follow the pattern of the earliest cast baluster examples, which appeared in England with the Huguenots (and thus from France) in the 1680s.[1] The maker's mark they bear is found on candlesticks from 1678, suggesting a specialist in the field.[2] The attribution to John Laughton by Ian Pickford is supported by similarities to his son's Britannia marks registered in 1699[3] which appear on numerous comparable sticks from around 1700.[4]

This set was probably acquired by the 1st Earl of Bristol from his goldsmith-banker, James Chambers, to whom he made a payment of £115 for what must have been a large quantity of plate, unfortunately unspecified, on 6 May, 1696 (see appendix 1). The original scratch-weights, crossed through, suggest that there may at some point have been nozzles, or the sticks could have lost silver from their bases on being refurbished in the 1750s for the 2nd Earl of Bristol. All the small table candlesticks were re-weighed, probably at that time, and they were then numbered in one sequence, up to at least thirty. Twenty-six survived in 1811 (see appendix 5), when it is clear this particular set was not more numerous, and by 1874 they had declined to the fourteen still at Ickworth today.[5] The quantity of candles, both superior beeswax and tallow, consumed by the Herveys in the eighteenth century was prodigious, as indicated in the 1st Earl's accounts. In the mid-1710s he was paying the wax chandler about £12 a year and the tallow chandler £44, equating to quantities of at least 500 and 6,500 candles respectively.[6]

1. See, for instance, a plain pair by Pierre Harache, 1685 sold Christie's, 29–30 November 2006, lot 711. A pair marked for Grenoble *c.*1680 with fluting to the stem was sold at Christie's Monaco, 3 March 1989, lot 98. A slight variant to the Ickworth set, *c.*1695, bearing the same mark, was sold Christie's, 27 February 1985, lot 230.
2. Pickford 1989, p. 135. A pair of plain baluster sticks of 1686 with the same maker's mark was sold Christie's 14 December 1966, lot 82.
3. Grimwade 1990, p. 140, nos. 1898–90
4. See, for example, Christie's, 23 October 1968, lot 150 and 6 July 1966, lot 106. A gadrooned stem stand and snuffers with Laughton's mark was sold at Sotheby's, 17 November 1937, lot 50.
5. Bristol plate list 1874b.
6. 1st Earl of Bristol's accounts 1688–1742. On 6 July 1717 the wax chandler John Pigou was paid £50 for a period of just over four years. The tallow chandler, Bartholomew Wimberly, was paid £66 13s for 18 months of supply on 24 May 1717. The quantities of candles have been estimated upon costs given in Temple Newsam 1992, p. 6, assuming six candles per pound of weight.

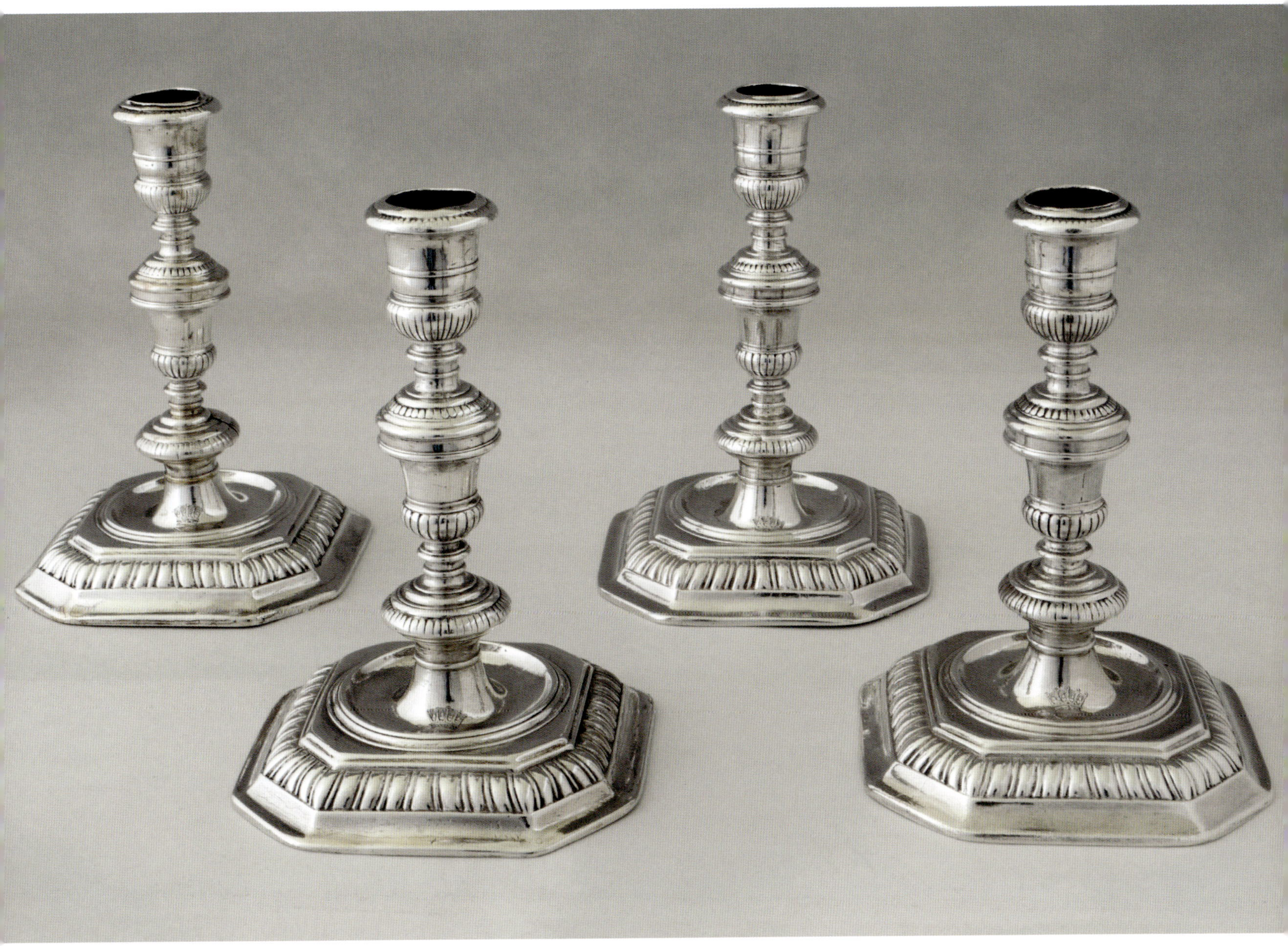

4. Four candlesticks

Britannia silver / Pierre Harache I or II, London / 1701/2 (altered?)

MARKS: On outer edge of foot rim (all partial and rubbed), stem and socket. 1. Rim, edge only of maker's mark with no initials visible, edges only of other three marks; 2. Rim, maker's mark 'HA' (probably Grimwade 1990, no. 937) struck twice, Britannia, lion's head erased, date letter 'f'. On socket and inverted vase of stem, two lion's heads erased; 3. Lion's head erased, Britannia, date letter 'f'. On socket and inverted vase, two lion's heads erased; 4. As 3, except no lion's head erased on inverted vase.

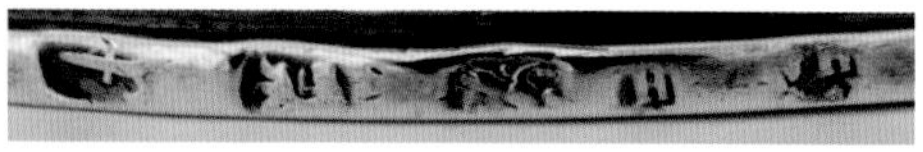

SCRATCHWEIGHT: 1. 'No 9 [/] 16=16' and '~~14°:13~~'; 2. 'No 10 [/] 17=10' and '~~15°:07~~'; 3. 'No 11 [/] 17=6' and '~~15~~'; 4. 'No 11 [/] 17=6' and '~~15~~'.

MEASUREMENTS: h. 23.2 cm (9⅛ in); diam. of base 12.1 cm (4¾ in).

INVENTORY: 852059

PROVENANCE: Probably acquired by John, 1st Lord Hervey (subsequently 1st Earl of Bristol); by descent to the 4th Marquess of Bristol.

LITERATURE: Penzer 1957a, II, p. 133; Banister 1980, p. 792.

EXHIBITED: *Treasures from National Trust Houses*, Christie's, London, 1957–8, cat. 162 (two).

DESCRIPTION: The circular cast base of each candlestick has a chased palm-leaf border and a dished centre which rises to a reeded and ribbon-tied compressed knop. The rest of the circular baluster, also cast, comprises a fluted and banded tapering stem with a row of incised stops below a lobed shoulder and an inverted, banded vase with chased palm leaves. The sockets are vase-shaped, banded and with chased palm leaves. The circular nozzles with moulded borders are fixed.

HERALDRY: The dish of each base has been re-engraved *c.*1751 with the Hervey crest beneath an earl's coronet.

The pattern for these candlesticks, excluding the inverted vase above the shoulder, was established among London makers by the turn of the eighteenth century. A set of four by David Willaume I is dated 1700, though with octagonal shoulders and without ribbon tying to the knops. They are seven inches high which is standard for the period, whereas the Ickworth set exceeds nine. Given that the revised scratchweights suggest an increase of about two ounces per stick it is probable that the inverted vase above the lobed shoulder is an addition, thus explaining the extra height. If so, the work may have been undertaken comparatively soon afterwards as the lion's head erased of the Britannia standard is stamped on two of the inverted vases. It is even possible that the alteration was carried out to stock items for the Earl, whose other candlesticks suggest he had a preference for those taller than the norm (see cat. 7–9). If so then the payment to James Chambers on 17 November 1707 (see appendix 1) of £20 10s 'for ye two new Pair of Candlesticks, & for a dressing weight for dear wife' may relate to the Harache sticks. There are no other likely candidates surviving at Ickworth.

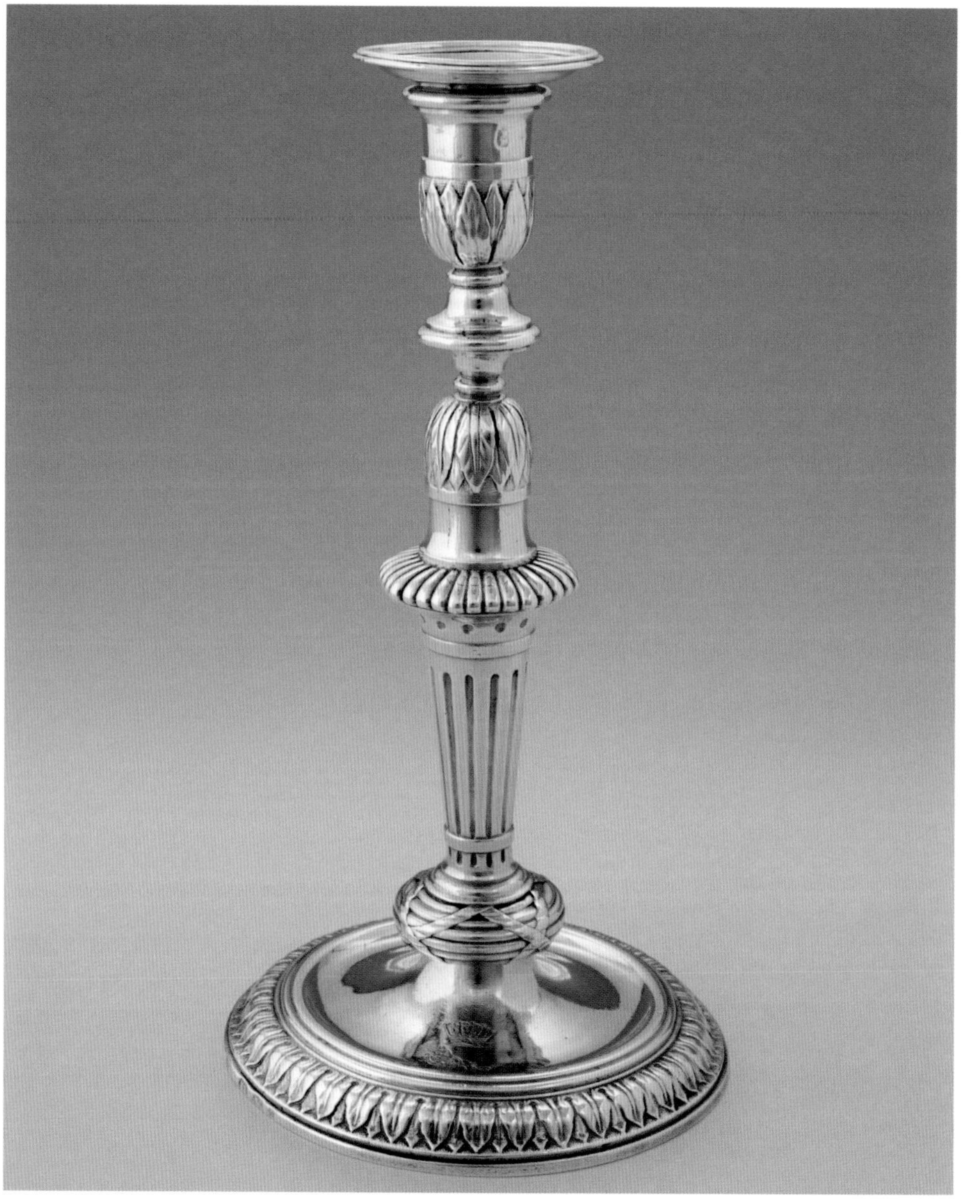

1. Sotheby's, 20 June 1974, lot 109.

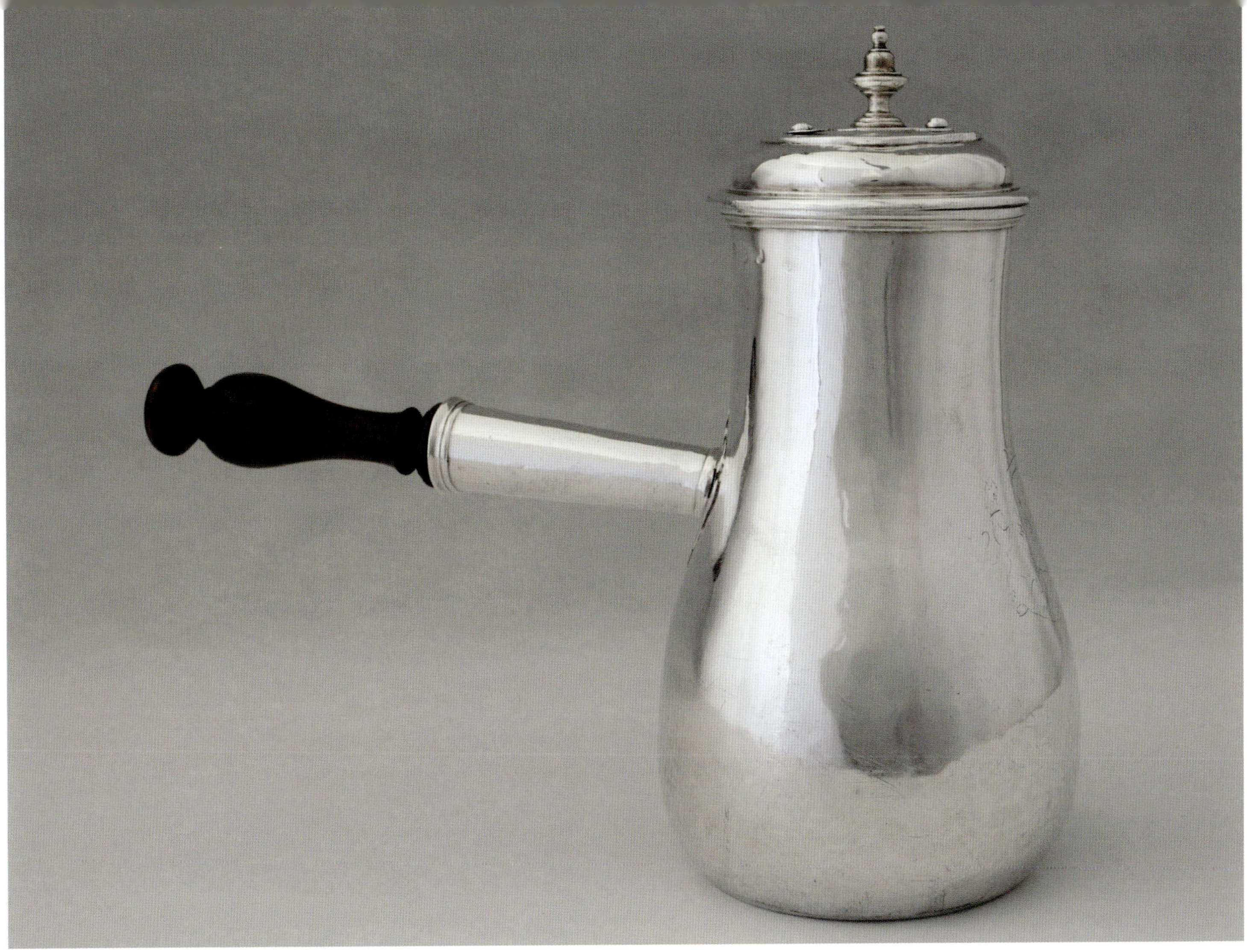

5. Chocolate pot

Britannia silver / Pierre Platel, London / 1704/5 (?)

MARKS: At top of body, beneath rim (very rubbed), maker's mark 'PL' beneath a star and a crown and above a fleur-de-lis (Grimwade 1990, no. 2200), Britannia, lion's head erased, date letter 'J' (?). On neck of lid, maker's mark as above, twice (partial).

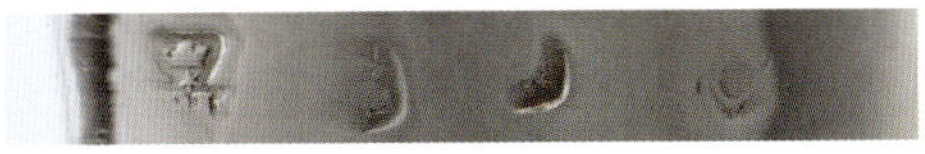

SCRATCHWEIGHT: None;
Actual weight: (incl. handle) 833 g (26 oz, 16 dwt.)

MEASUREMENTS: h. 24.8 cm (9¾ in); w. including handle 28.9 cm (11⅜ in); diam. at widest point 12.1 cm (4¾ in).

INVENTORY: 852070

PROVENANCE: Possibly Sir Thomas Felton, 4th Bt (d. 1709); John, 1st Lord Hervey (subsequently 1st Earl of Bristol); by descent to the 4th Marquess.

LITERATURE: Hernmarck 1977, vol. 1, p. 156; Banister 1980, p. 792.

EXHIBITED: Society of the Four Arts, Palm Beach, Florida, 1959; *Silver from National Trust Houses*, Treasurer's House, York Festival, 1969.

DESCRIPTION: The elongated pear-shaped or 'bellied'[1] body is raised and has an applied, stepped moulding at the lip. There is no spout. A tapering, seamed stem is soldered to the side of the pot, the joint disguised by cut-card work. It terminates in an applied stepped moulding and acts as a socket for the turned fruitwood handle. The detachable domed and stepped lid is raised and has an applied lip moulding and a seamed bezel. A hole is cut in the centre of the top for the insertion of a mill or stirring rod (sometimes also called a molinet)[2] and is covered by a simple flat, shaped plate rotating on a fixed staple riveted through the lid. The plate, to which is soldered a cast baluster finial, has an incision forming a hook which closes over a second riveted staple.

HERALDRY: Engraved on the body of the pot, opposite the handle, is a shield bearing the impaled arms of Hervey and Felton with the Hervey supporters and motto and a baron's coronet for John Hervey, 1st Baron Hervey (cr. 1703, subsequently 1st Earl of Bristol). This is the only surviving example of the 1st Earl's engraved arms as Lord Hervey, all other pieces having been re-engraved by the 2nd Earl.

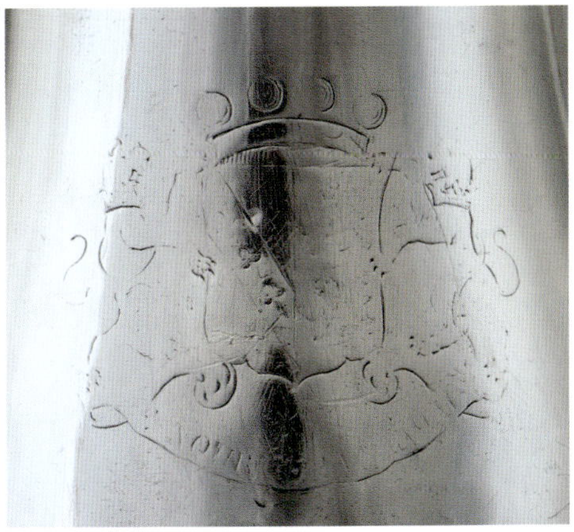

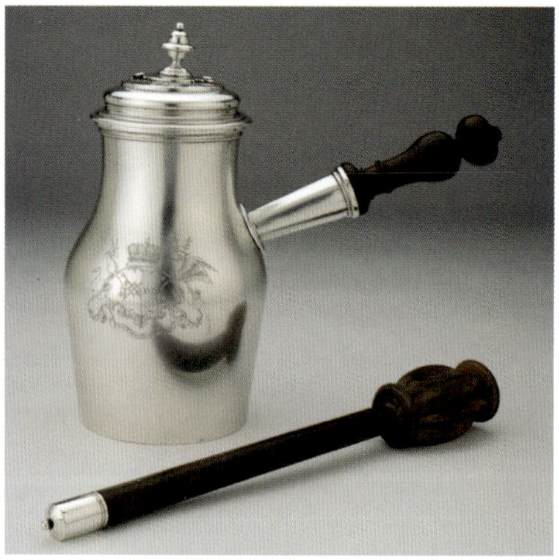

FIG. 70 / Chocolate pot by Paul Crespin, London, 1738. Silver: h. 25 cm (9⅞ in), weight 1263g (40 oz) 10 dwt. The stirring rod is probably later. Ashmolean Museum.

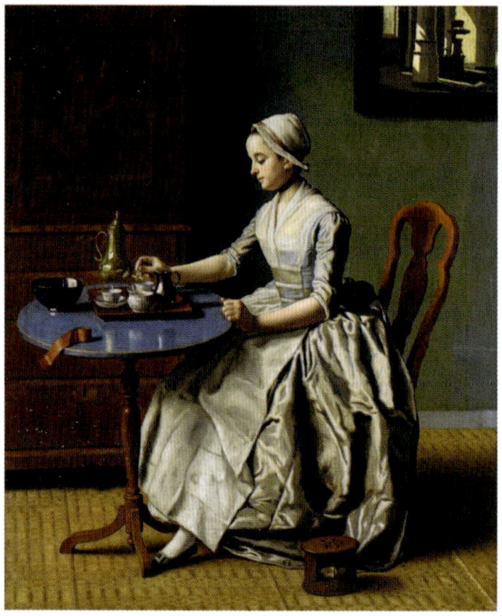

FIG. 71 / *A Dutch girl at breakfast* by Jean Etienne Liotard, *c.*1744. Oil on canvas. Courtesy of Lowell Libson Ltd.

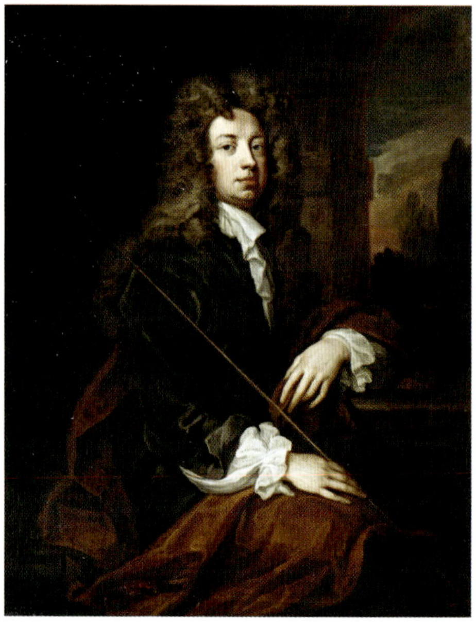

FIG. 72 / *Sir Thomas Felton, 4th Bt* by Sir Godfrey Kneller, 1699. Oil on canvas: 127 x 101.6 cm (50 x 40 in). National Trust, Ickworth

This is an object which bears manifest signs of intensive use and it is quite clear from his correspondence and account books that John Hervey, 1st Earl of Bristol, had a great fondness for drinking chocolate. The first mention in the accounts of the expensive and highly desirable comestible is made on 16 May 1711 when he paid £12 10s to 'Mrs Hyde for 50 Pounds of Chocolate' and just a few months later, on 21 August 1711, 'Mrs Ryff ye Dutch woman' supplied another 20 pounds or so.[3] Consumption, which initially settled to about 50 pounds a year, rose to 100 or more in the early 1720s and Lord and Lady Bristol are revealed as habitually taking it with breakfast in letters to each other of the time. Writing on 6 September, 1721, Lord Bristol railed against his 'ungovernable' servants at Ickworth and wrote of hounds causing chaos in the kitchen and the bread being 'left all night in the oven and utterly spoyld, and not so much as a toaste left for me to eat with my chocolate'. Lady Bristol, two years later and on her way to Bath, wrote on the morning of 12 September 'tis 8 a clock, & I am just going to drink your dear health in chocolate, and then set out.'[4] The Earl continued to partake for the rest of his life. In July 1746 his daughter-in-law Lady Hervey brought chocolate with her from London when she visited him at Ickworth and on 5 January 1751, just two weeks before his death at the age of 85, he paid Mrs Mary Pitts £4 19s 'for 11 pounds of Vanillo Chocolate at 5s p[er] pound & 11 pounds of plain Do at 4s p[er] pound'.[5]

Instructions for making chocolate varied but the no-nonsense recipe recorded in *The experienced English house-keeper* of 1769 by Mrs Raffald, who had served at Arley Hall in Cheshire, could well have been followed in the 1st Earl's still room:

Scrape four Ounces of Chocolate and pour a Quart of boiling Water upon it, mill it well with a Chocolate Mill, and sweeten it to your Taste, give it a boil and let it stand all Night, then mill it again very well, boil it two Minutes, then mill it 'till it will leave a Froth upon the Top of your Cups.[6]

The chocolate would have been supplied in solid blocks and as the cocoa butter was not extracted stirring, or milling, was a key part of preparation to prevent coagulation, and continued to be required during serving, thus the need for the hole in the cover. As evidenced by Lord Bristol's 1751 purchase, chocolate could also be acquired ready flavoured and, in addition to vanilla, cinnamon was also added.[7] Although it was primarily drunk, chocolate was also used sparingly for flavour and colour in dessert dishes such as chocolate puffs which were a form of meringue.[8]

The very unusual form of the Ickworth chocolate pot, without either feet, hinged lid or pouring spout and being of a larger capacity than the norm, suggests that it was used in the initial preparation of the drink in the still room, as well as in serving. There is only one comparator in silver currently known to survive and that is the Dysart pot of 1738 by Paul Crespin (fig. 70) now in the Ashmolean Museum.[9] Timothy Schroder ponders whether such a model might have been intended to replenish a smaller, more conventional chocolate pot and although there is no evidence of a second pot having existed at Ickworth, the 1st Duke of Chandos does seem to have had such an arrangement at Cannons. In addition to the chocolate pot recorded with tea and coffee silver in the Drawing Room there was amongst the plate in the pantry '1 New Chocolate pott 40 [oz]. 14 [dwt] + 1 trivett 4 [oz]. 6 [dwt]', trivet being used by the inventory maker to mean the frame of a lamp.[10] It may have been employed in the manner shown in Jean-Étienne Liotard's *A Dutch girl at breakfast* where a lamp in a circular frame is on the floor by the side of the young woman (fig. 71).

There is no specific reference to this pot in the 1st Earl's accounts, nor are there any purchases of chocolate prior to 1711.[11] It may therefore be that the piece was not acquired new and that it reached the Herveys around 1711, either in response to their enthusiasm for the drink or as the spur to it. If the latter it could well have been amongst the 115 ounces of plate acquired from the estate of the Earl's father-in-law, Sir Thomas Felton, 4th Baronet (fig. 72), on 6 October 1709 (see appendix 1). It must have been with Lord Bristol at Ickworth in his later years, probably in use right up to his death, given the purchase of chocolate in January 1751, and it may never have left thereafter, thus escaping the comprehensive re-engraving of arms carried out by the 2nd Earl in the 1750s.

1. This was the eighteenth-century name for the pear shape, as used in the Wickes Ledgers and elsewhere.
2. Davis 1976, p. 84.
3. Bristol accounts 1688–1742. The payment to Mrs Ryff was made exactly a month later, on 21 September 1711.
4. Hervey 1894b, vol. 2, pp. 184 and 327.
5. Ibid. and Bristol accounts 1742–51.
6. Raffald 1769, p. 295.
7. Lady Mary Booth 1730, pp. 208–9.
8. Ibid., p. 254.
9. Schroder 2009, cat. 279, pp. 254–7.
10. Jenkins 2005, pp. 121 and 145.
11. Though chocolate was certainly being consumed by the future Countess of Bristol in the late seventeenth century. On 5 April 1698 she wrote to her husband of drinking his and the Duke of St Albans' 'health in chocolate' with the Duchess that morning. Hervey 1894b, vol. 1, p. 125.

6. **Communion flagon**

Britannia silver, gilt / **John Jackson I and John Fawdery I, London** / **1705/6**

MARKS: Fully marked on the side of the body and the underside of the lid with maker's mark 'Ia' above a cross (Grimwade 1990, no. 1092), Britannia, lion's head erased and date letter 'k' for 1705. The lion's head erased only is repeated on the underside of the flagon. The handle bears the maker's mark 'FA' for John Fawdery I (Grimwade 1990, no. 662).

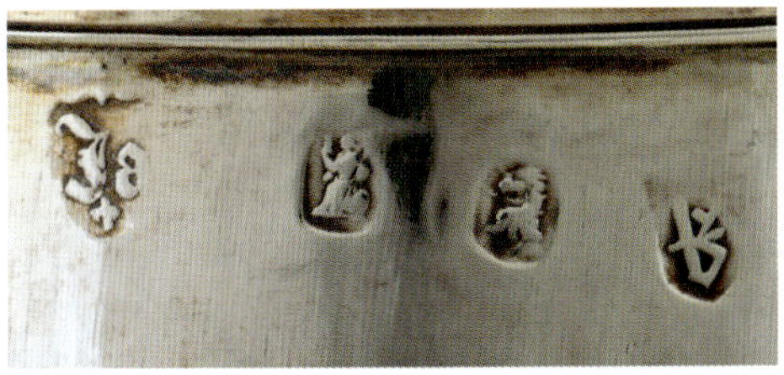

SCRATCHWEIGHT: none.
Actual weight: 1026 g (33 oz).

MEASUREMENTS: h. 26 cm (10¼ in); w. incl. handle 20.3 cm (8 in); diam. of foot 16.5 cm (6½ in)

INVENTORY: 852903

PROVENANCE: John, 1st Lord Hervey (subsequently 1st Earl of Bristol); given by him to the church of St Mary, Ickworth; transferred to the church of St Leonard, Horringer in 1984; on loan to the National Trust at Ickworth House.

DESCRIPTION: The skirted and stepped foot is raised and has a moulded wire concealing the joint with the circular, slightly tapering body above, which is seamed and has an inset base and an applied moulding at the lip. The front is engraved with the sacred monogram, cross and nails within a sunburst or glory. The stepped and domed lid is raised and has an applied, seemed bezel. It is engraved with the 'Eye of God' – an eye in a sunburst. The tapering scroll handle is of D section and formed of a raised concave inner piece soldered to a flat cover strip. It has a curved shield-shaped heel plate soldered to the lower end. A cast three-part pin hinge is soldered to the top of the handle and has an arched connector to the lid, conforming to the curve of the handle, and a scroll thumb piece.

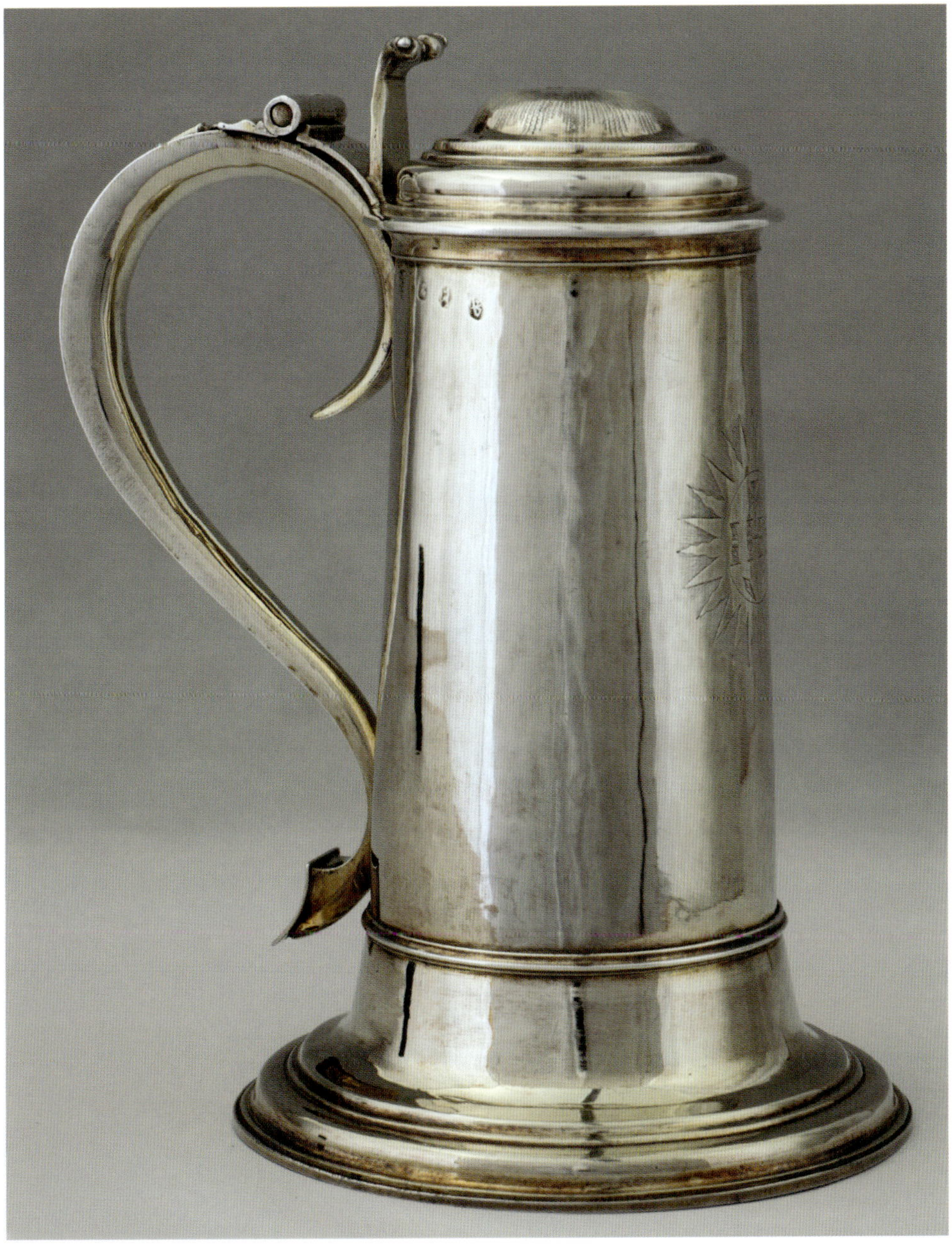

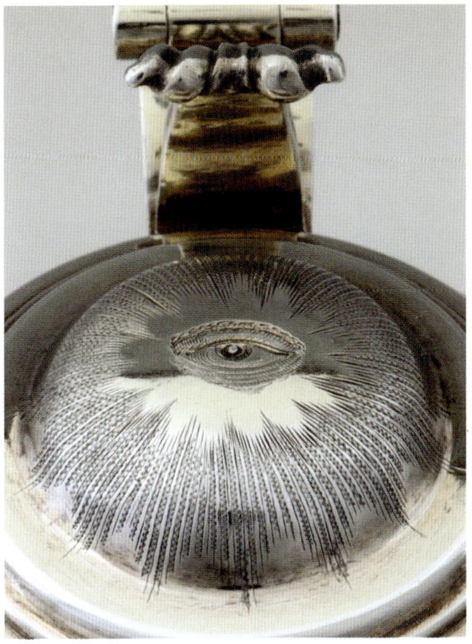

Silver by John Jackson is now comparatively rarely found but he seems to have been one of the more successful indigenous makers of the early eighteenth century. A pair of sconces of 1707 by him in the Museum of Fine Arts, Boston, formerly at Belton House in Lincolnshire, probably originated in the royal collection[1] and he supplied silver to the banker-goldsmith James Chambers over a number of years, as is evidenced by pieces with his mark at Ickworth. Plates and dishes destined for the newly ennobled Lord Hervey (later Earl of Bristol) were provided in 1703 (see cat. 35) and he went on to receive this flagon from Chambers in 1706, the entry in his accounts being as follows: 'July ye 5 Paid Chambers in full of his Bill for Ick: Church ffagon &c [£]19'.

The fact that the handle bears John Fawdery i's mark and that Jackson appears to have stamped his over another's on the lid implies that Fawdery was actually the maker of the flagon, and supplied it to Jackson. Further evidence of collaboration between the two exists in the form of a kettle of 1708 bearing Jackson's mark while its undated stand has Fawdery's.[2] Fawdery, who was also indigenous and had been apprenticed to Anthony Nelme,[3] has rather more work surviving than Jackson and is revealed by it to have been an accomplished silversmith. He produced other sacred pieces, including a chalice and paten cover of 1714 also in the Museum of Fine Arts, Boston,[4] and such high-quality domestic pieces as the chocolate pot of 1698 in the collection of the Salters' Company.[5]

Flagons 'to fetch wine to serve the Lord's table, reserved and kept clean to that use only, being no tavern pots,' are a post-Reformation vessel and were being recommended for use in Anglican churches by the end of the sixteenth century.[6] Thereafter they were either made with a bulbous, pear-shaped body or as a plain, slightly tapering cylinder. The latter form was almost exclusively followed in the first quarter of the eighteenth century and the only significant reflection of changing fashions could be found in the style of engraving.

The church for which this flagon was acquired, dedicated to St Mary (fig. 73), lies at the heart of the park of Ickworth House, adjacent to the site of the mediaeval manor house and presumably in the vicinity of the lost village. Its chancel is of the thirteenth century, the tower was rebuilt by the 3rd Earl in 1778 and major refurbishments and alterations were carried out in the 1830s and in 1909–10, the latter being overseen by Arthur Blomfield who also worked on the house.[7] Having been declared redundant in 1984 and falling into disrepair thereafter, the building was vested in a charitable trust by the present, 8th Marquess of Bristol in 2006 and has recently emerged from a triumphant restoration. The interior is dominated by the memorial stones to the Herveys who are buried in the vault beneath the family pew in the south aisle. Amongst them is that of the 1st Earl of Bristol, who gave the flagon.

For the other items of plate from Ickworth church, all given by the Herveys, see cat. nos 74, 106 and 107.

1. Alcorn 2000, cat. 19, pp. 70–1.
2. Schroder 2009, p. 764.
3. Ibid., p. 1242.
4. Alcorn 2000, cat. 27, pp. 80–1.
5. Hughes 2000, p. 105, ill.
6. Lee and Ryrie 2008, pp. 34–5. The quote is from Archbishop Whitgift's 1597 articles for the Deanery of Shoreham.
7. Yates 2013, pp. 4–5.

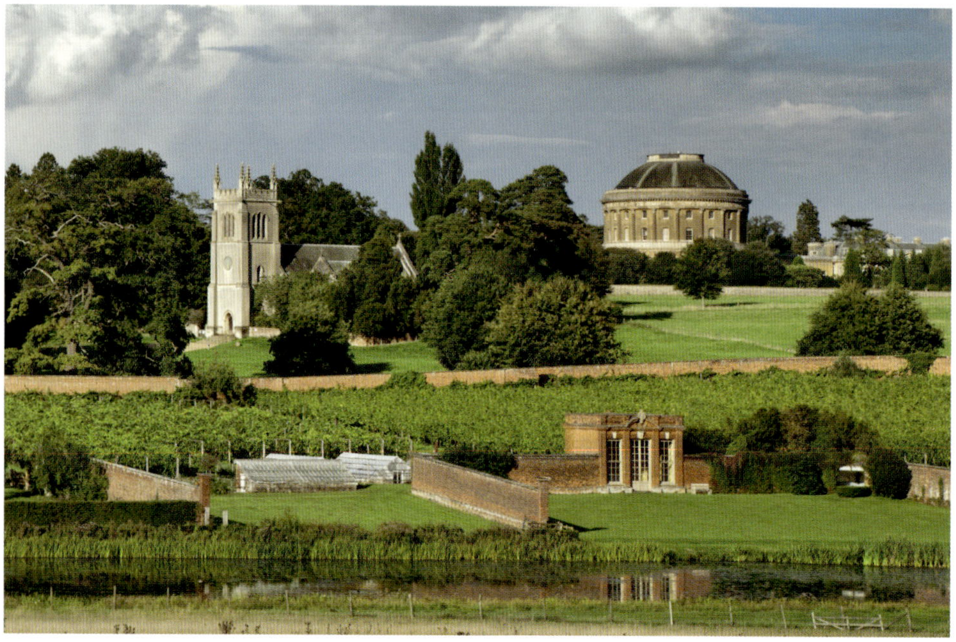

FIG. 73 / St Mary's church, Ickworth, with the Rotunda in the background.

7. Pair of candlesticks

Britannia silver
Pierre Platel, London / 1708/9
the nozzles probably sterling, *c.*1751

MARKS: Both fully marked on the underside, Britannia, lion's head erased, date letter 'N', maker's mark 'PL' with crown and star above, fleur-de-lis below (Grimwade 1990, no. 2200).

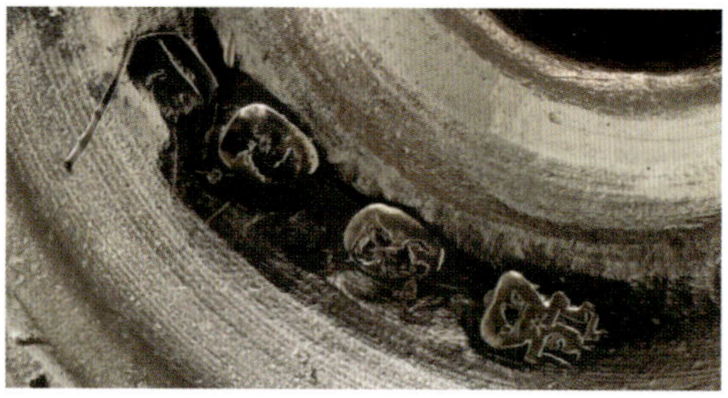

SCRATCHWEIGHTS: 1. 'Nº 13 [/] 14=8'; 2. 'Nº 14 [/] 15=0' and [former weight] '13 – 9'.

MEASUREMENTS: h. 21 cm (8¼ in); w. 11.4 cm (4½ in).

INVENTORY: 852112

PROVENANCE: Possibly Sir Thomas Felton, 4th Bt (d.1709); John, 1st Lord Hervey (subsequently 1st Earl of Bristol); by descent to the 4th Marquess.

LITERATURE: Penzer 1957a, II, p. 133; Hernmarck 1977, p. 263; Banister 1980, p. 792.

EXHIBITED: *Queen Charlotte's Loan Exhibition of Old Silver*, Seaford House, London, 1929, cat. no. 485; *Treasures from National Trust Houses*, Christie's, London, 1957–8, cat. 39; Society of the Four Arts, Palm Beach, Florida, 1959; *Silver from National Trust Houses*, Treasurer's House, York Festival, 1969.

DESCRIPTION: The circular feet with dished centres are cast and chased with borders of shells, scrolls and foliage. The cast and chased baluster stems rise from the dished centres to compressed circular knops decorated with a band of guilloche and rosettes above which are stepped octagonal bases. The stem is then wasted before swelling as an inverted octagonal tear-drop, decorated with four vertical panels comprising medallions of classical heads above ribbon-tied floral pendants, all on matted grounds. Between the panels are shallow flutes with matted grounds. The stems terminate in a pair of small knops chased with shells and C-scrolls on matted ground below and ovoid strapwork on foliate matted ground above. The cast and chased vase-shaped sockets each have a calyx of formal stiff palm leaves at the base. The plain, circular nozzles have seamed necks and raised, flaring wax pans.

Comparable French candlesticks with polygonal stems and classical medallions exist from the 1690s but the most direct design source seems to be Daniel Marot's *Nouveau livre d'orfèvrerie* of 1703 in which a similar candlestick is illustrated.[1] The earliest English example appears to be the set of twelve at Welbeck Abbey of 1702 on which the maker's mark is illegible,[2] and a near-identical foursome by David Willaume, probably of 1706.[3] The pattern, with slight variations, had great resilience over the next thirty years, its ornamentation particularly suiting the *Régence* love of crisp, intricate patterning and classical detail. The Ickworth pair departs from the other early examples in having an additional double knop detail immediately below the socket but this appears to be original and must have been Platel's own inventive and possibly unique interpretation. The addition of the fixed nozzles, probably in the 1750s, is likely to explain the change in scratchweight.

Frustratingly, as with so many of the surviving early pieces of silver in the Ickworth collection, these candlesticks cannot be directly linked with a payment in the 1st Earl of Bristol's accounts. They and the following two pairs could, however, have formed part of the unspecified plate of Sir Thomas Felton, 4th Bt, purchased by Lord Bristol in October 1709 along with the chocolate pot (cat. 5), or that of Sir Thomas's sister, Lady Howard of Effingham, bought on 23 April 1727 (see appendix 1 for details of these purchases). Both siblings may well have had fashionable plate from the early eighteenth century, though Sir Thomas is the more likely candidate given that he was at the heart of court affairs from 1689, as Master of the Household to William and Mary, and had been elevated to Comptroller by Queen Anne in 1708. Sir Thomas may well have seen Sir Robert Harley's set of candlesticks of the same pattern (those now at Welbeck), issued to him by the Jewel Office on becoming Speaker of the House of Commons.[4] Had such candlesticks been amongst Felton's plate Lord Bristol's proven eye for a bargain suggests he would have been unlikely to have missed the opportunity to acquire items at the height of fashion for less than the residual value of the metal. He paid 5s 1d per ounce.

1. For a comprehensive assessment of the pattern see Lomax and Rothwell 2006, p. 121. The Marot engraving is illustrated on p. 159, fig. 56.
2. Jones 1935, p. 60.
3. Christie's, 23 April 1966, lot 37
4. Jewel Office Delivery Book 1698–1732, f. 65.

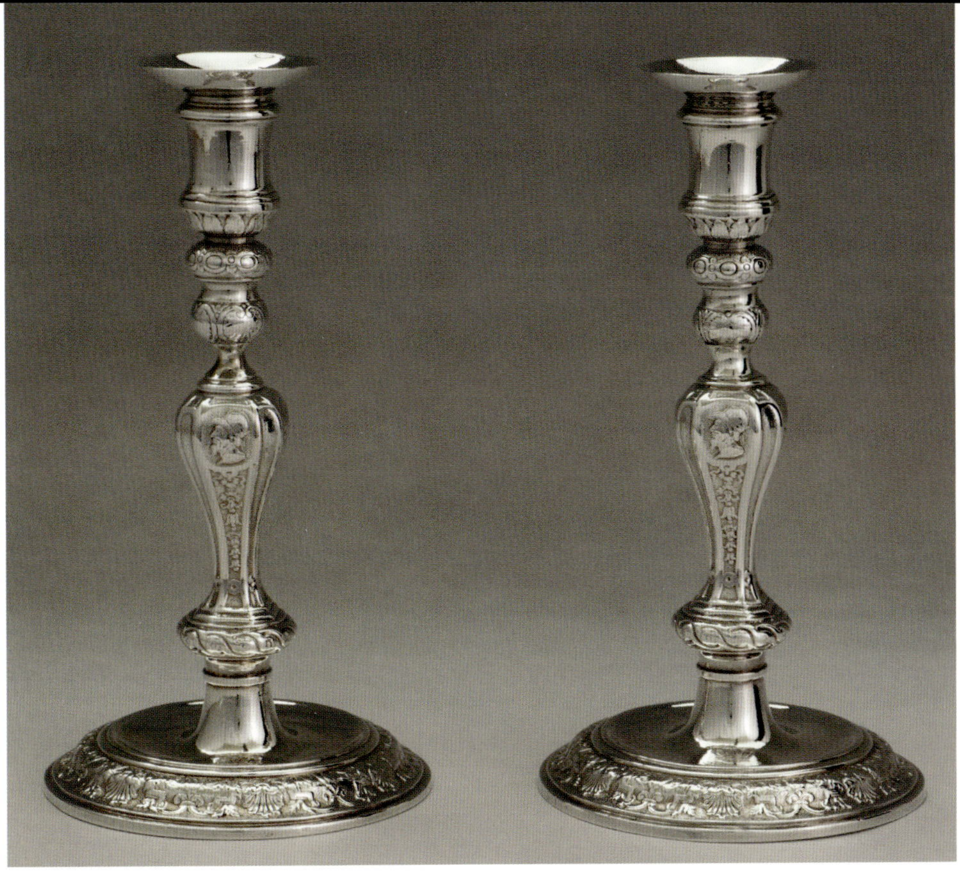

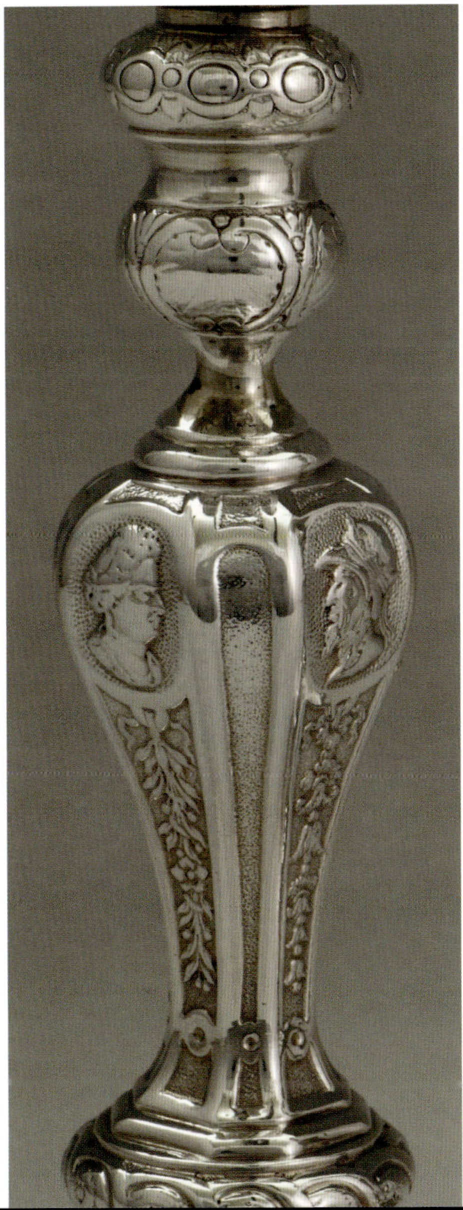

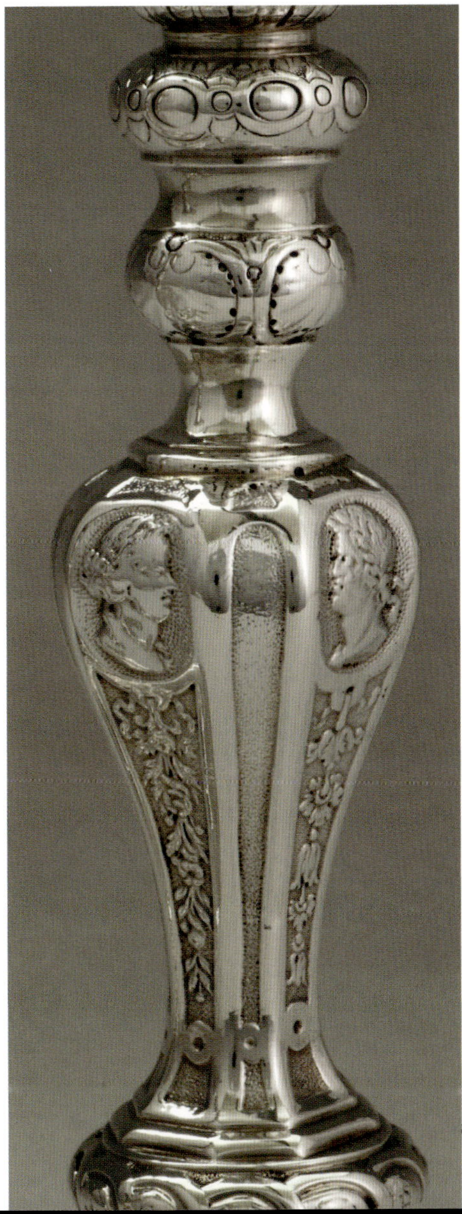

8. Pair of candlesticks

Britannia silver / Louis Mettayer / 1708/9 / altered *c.*1751

MARKS: Both fully marked on underside with maker's mark 'ME' beneath two sickles and a sheaf of corn (Grimwade 1990, no. 2018), Britannia, lion's head erased and date letter 'N'.

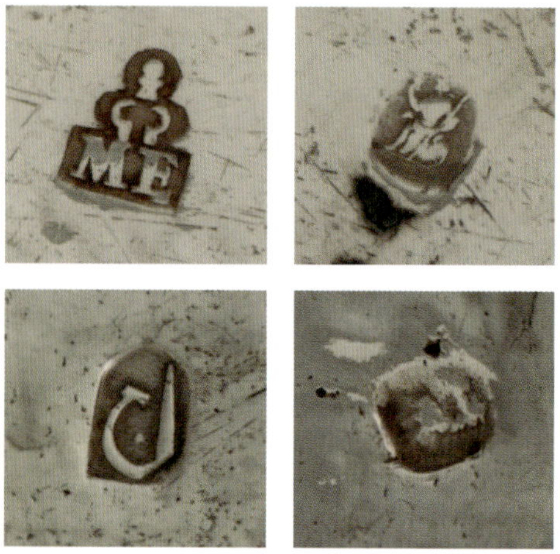

SCRATCHWEIGHTS: 'No 29 14·14'; 'N 30 15·17'

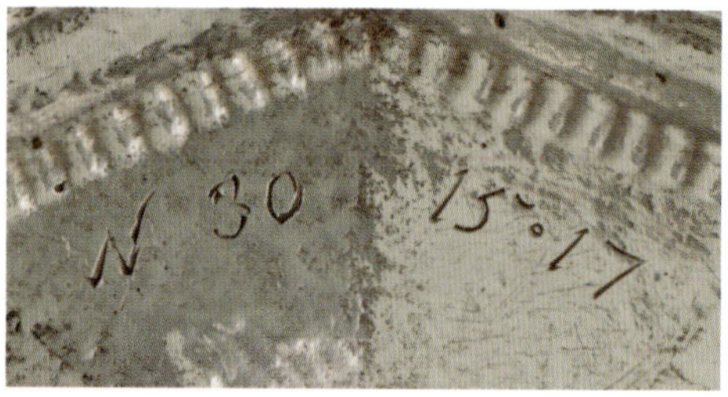

MEASUREMENTS: h. 20.3 cm (8 in); w. 11.4 cm (4½ in).

INVENTORY: 852114

PROVENANCE: Possibly Sir Thomas Felton, 4th Bt (d.1709); John, 1st Lord Hervey (subsequently 1st Earl of Bristol); by descent to the 4th Marquess.

LITERATURE: Penzer 1957a, II, p. 133; Banister 1980, p. 792.

DESCRIPTION: The octagonal cast feet have chased *rocaille* decoration (later) around the base of the stem and on the border moulding. The cast baluster stems, which are tapering, banded, knopped and shouldered, have been similarly chased as have the cast vase-shaped and banded sockets. The circular nozzles (later), which are removable, have seemed necks and raised, dished drip pans chased with *rocaille* work.

HERALDRY: Re-engraved on the flat of the foot, probably around 1751, with the Hervey crest beneath an earl's coronet. The necks of the nozzles are similarly engraved.

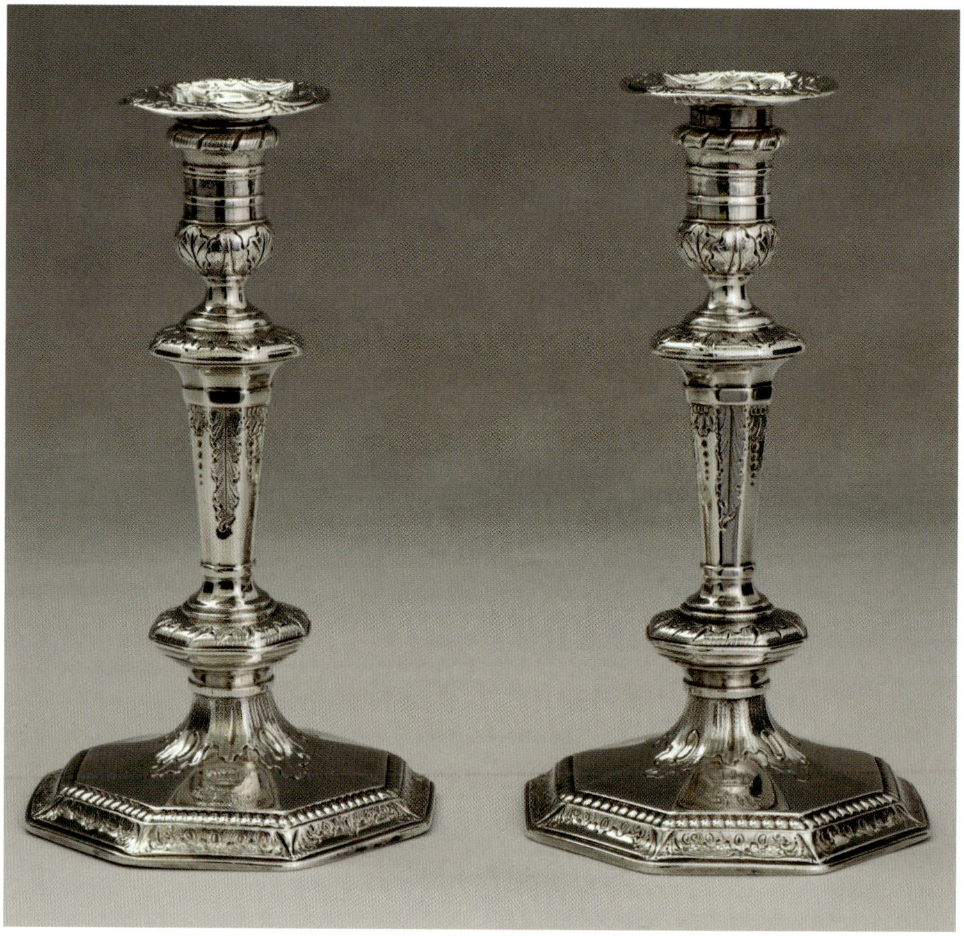

The *rocaille* chasing of these candlesticks and the addition of drip pans are likely to have been carried out *c.*1751 for the 2nd Earl of Bristol when he was overhauling his recently inherited plate. Their previous, starkly plain appearance, relying for effect entirely on fine proportions and geometry, which was such a feature of Queen Anne silver, would not have been sufficient for the fashionable mid-eighteenth century nobleman who aspired to the exuberance of the rococo. This model appeared in the early years of the eighteenth century, particularly amongst the wares of Huguenot makers, and the intended effect can be seen in a fine set of four by Simon Pantin of 1710, without later embellishment (fig. 74), sold at Christie's, 14 December 1966, lot 81. Having broken away from the late-seventeenth century dished centres they have a greater lightness of effect than many of their contemporaries.

As with the previous catalogue entries, these candlesticks may well have formed part of the plate purchased by the future 1st Earl of Bristol from the estate of his father-in-law, Sir Thomas Felton, 4th Bt, in 1709 (see cat. 4 and 5).

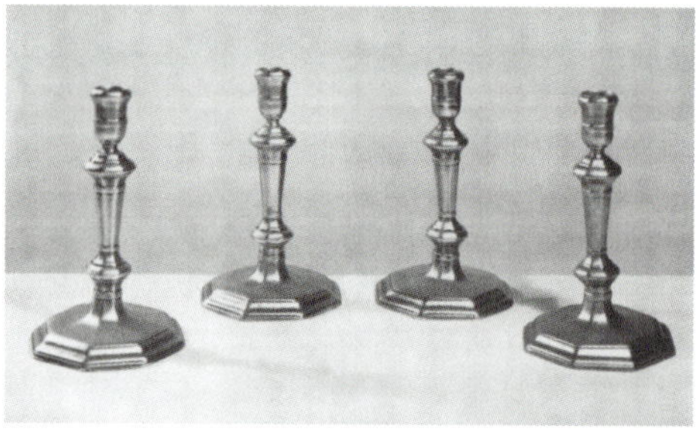

FIG. 74 / Four candlesticks by Simon Pantin, London, 1710. Silver: h. 19.1 cm (7½ in); weight 1711 g (55 oz). Christie's.

9. **Pair of candlesticks**

Britannia silver / **Louis Mettayer** / **1708/9** / **altered *c.* 1751**

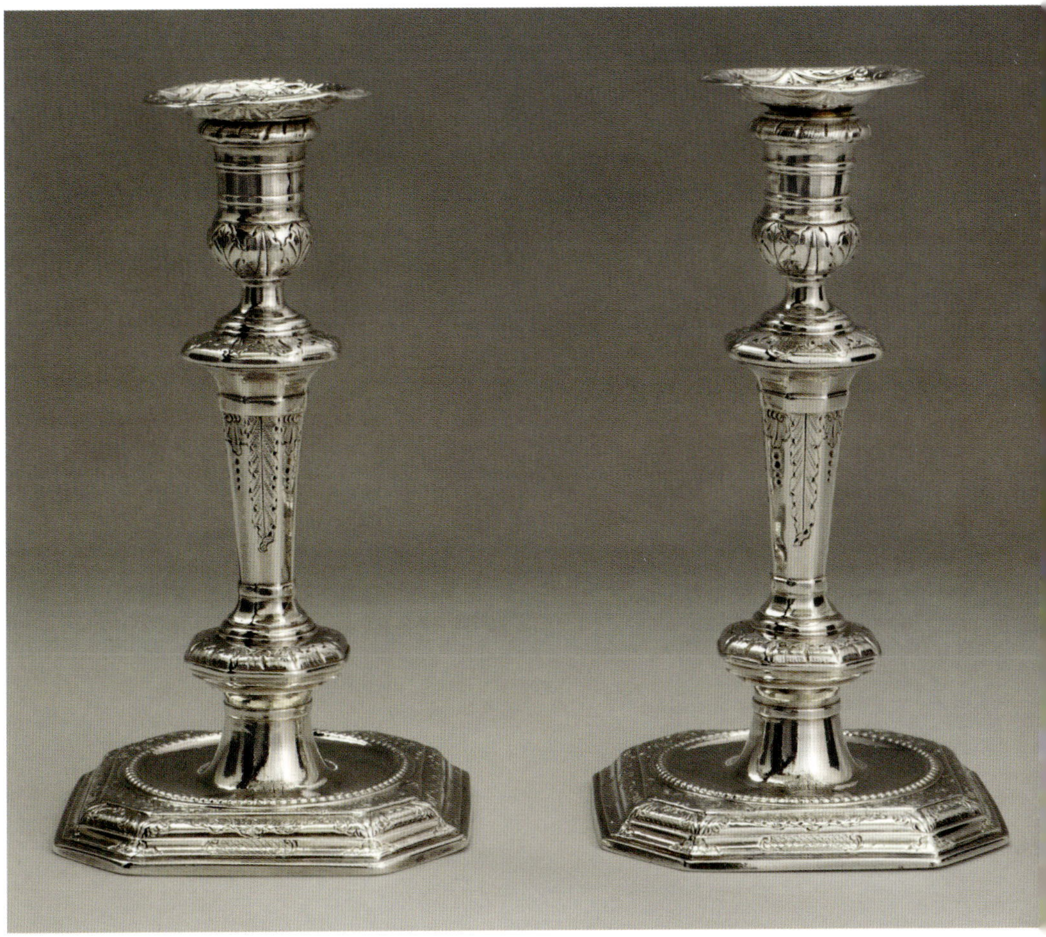

MARKS: Fully marked on underside with maker's mark 'ME' beneath two sickles and a sheaf of corn (Grimwade 1990, no. 2018), Britannia, lion's head erased and date letter 'N'.

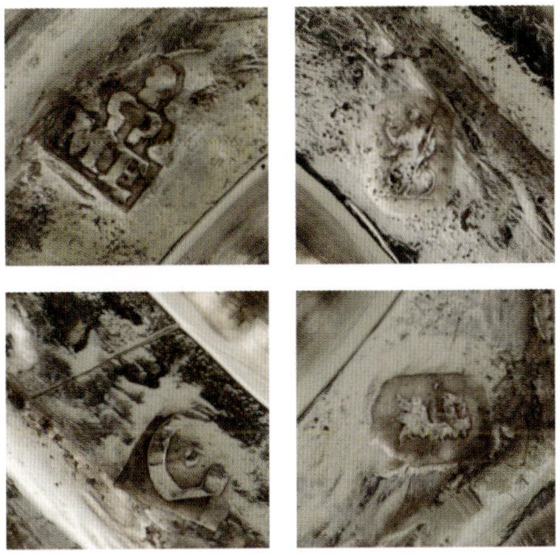

SCRATCHWEIGHT: 1. 'N° 21 [/] 15=15' and [old] '15·5'; 2. 'N° 22 [/] 16=2' and [old] '15·5'.

MEASUREMENTS: h. 19.7 cm (7¾ in); w. 10.8 cm (4¼ in).

INVENTORY: 852113

PROVENANCE: Possibly Sir Thomas Felton, 4th Bt (d.1709); John, 1st Lord Hervey (subsequently 1st Earl of Bristol); by descent to the 4th Marquess.

LITERATURE: Penzer 1957a, II, p. 133; Banister 1980, p. 792.

HERALDRY: Re-engraved within the dish of the foot, probably around 1751, with the Hervey crest beneath an earl's coronet. The necks of the nozzles are similarly engraved.

These are identical in form to the other pair by Mettayer (cat. 8) except for their cast feet which are square with cut corners and dished centres. The *rocaille* chasing also matches.

10. Preserving basin

Britannia silver
Simon Pantin, London / 1716/7

MARKS: Fully marked beneath lip. date letter 'A', Britannia, maker's mark 'PA' beneath tree (Grimwade 1990, no. 2124), lion's head erased.

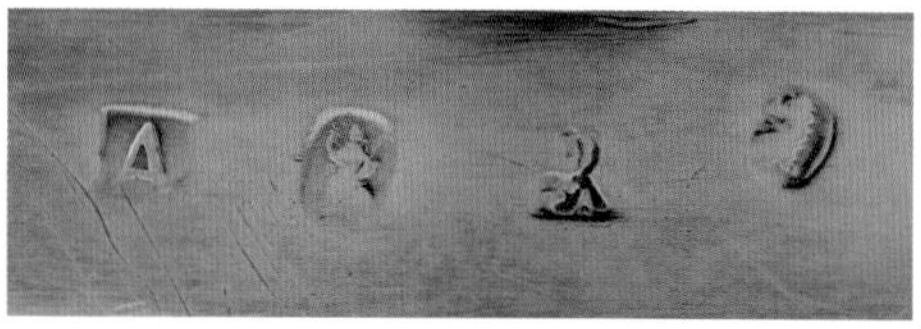

SCRATCHWEIGHT: '57 18 [/] 11'

MEASUREMENTS: (including handles) h. 19.5 cm (7⅔ in); diam: 34.6 cm (13⅝ in).

INVENTORY: 852083

PROVENANCE: Possibly Susan Felton, Lady Howard of Effingham (d. 1726); 1st Earl of Bristol; by descent to the 4th Marquess.

LITERATURE: Penzer 1957a, I, p. 40; Banister 1980, p. 792, fig. 2.

EXHIBITED: Society of the Four Arts. Palm Beach, Florida, 1959; *Silver from National Trust Houses*, Treasurer's House, York Festival, 1969.

DESCRIPTION: The simple, circular basin, raised into a deep, steep-sided bowl with an applied lip moulding, has two thick wires curved to form handles which are flattened at the ends and soldered to the body.

HERALDRY: On one side of the basin has been engraved, possibly *c.*1727, the Hervey crest beneath an earl's coronet.

This piece bears the date-letter for 1716 and on 29 August that year Lord Bristol paid his banker-goldsmith James Chambers 'for a silver stew-pan'. As a consequence, the two were generally conflated in the twentieth century.[1] The weight of the stew-pan at 67 oz, 14 dwt, is, however, so far apart from that scratched on the surviving piece – 57 oz, 18 dwt – that this cannot be the case. Wear and tear would not have removed so much silver and there is no evidence of alteration or even the loss of a lid, convention including such associated parts in the scratchweight. Stew pans seem in fact to have been large saucepans with single, turned-wood handles as was that supplied to the Duke of Devonshire by George Wickes in 1738.[2] It would also appear, from the well-recorded equivalent of 1728 by Isaac Liger at Dunham Massey in Cheshire (fig. 75), that this sort of bowl-like, two-handled vessel was known as a preserving basin, which the Ickworth piece was recorded as in the 1811 inventory (see appendix 5).[3] This is corroborated by Sir Robert Walpole's 'Preserving Pann' and Sir Henry Harpur's 'preserving dish', supplied by George Wickes in 1738 and 1743 respectively, as neither included a wooden handle. They weighed 40 oz, 9 dwt, and 28 oz and were charged at 6s 5d per ounce and 6s 4d.[4] There is no other specific entry in Lord Bristol's accounts that could relate to the basin so it is likely to have been another of his purchases of second hand plate, perhaps being amongst the items from the estate of the Countess's aunt, Susan Felton, Lady Howard of Effingham, paid for on 23 April 1727 (see appendix 1).

Silver was used in the kitchen and still room because of its excellent conductivity, which assisted sensitive cooking, and for use with acidic ingredients where copper, brass and iron may have been vulnerable and have risked tainting or even, in the case of copper, poisoning. Ingredients high in acid, notably fruit, can result in the formation of copper acetates, or verdigris, which when consumed is potentially fatal. This danger was well understood in the eighteenth century and an anonymous pamphleteer writing in 1755 noted the particular risk associated with the preparation in untinned copper of 'preserved fruits and sweetmeats of every kind. Of these sweetmeats children of almost every rank and age, even infants, eat in abundance; but people of quality most of all, as they scarce ever dine without a desert.'[5] Tinning or silvering could be applied but that was not permanent or fail-safe and solid silver was the ideal for those who could afford it.[6]

The sort of concoction for which a silver cooking vessel might have been used is indicated in the published and manuscript recipe books of the period. Hannah Glasse in *The art of cookery made plain and easy* of 1747 recommended silver in preparing, amongst other things, a dish called 'Lemon Cream', and for simply melting butter,[7] and numerous of Lady Mary Booth of Dunham Massey's recipes, recorded in 1730, are likely to have employed the surviving basin there. For the preserving of 'Goosberries in Jelly before they are ripe', requiring countless rounds of boiling and resting and aiming at a jelly 'as clear as Rock water', Lady Mary unconditionally specified a 'Silver Bason'.[8]

1. See for instance Penzer 1957a, I, p. 40.
2. Wickes Ledgers, VAM 1 1735–40, f. 162.
3. Christie's 12 June 2007, lot 55. This item was purchased by the National Trust but subsequent to the publication of the catalogue.
4. Wickes Ledgers, VAM 1 1735–40, f. 137 and VAM 2 1740–8, f. 73.
5. Copper pamphlet 1755, p. 22
6. Mason 1787, pp. 120 and 475–6.
7. Glasse 1747, pp. 5 and 281. Jonathan Swift recommended the same, to avoid tainting the butter – see Swift 1745, p. 42.
8. Lady Mary Booth 1730, pp. 143–5. I am grateful to Nicola Whyton for transcribing these and other entries for me.

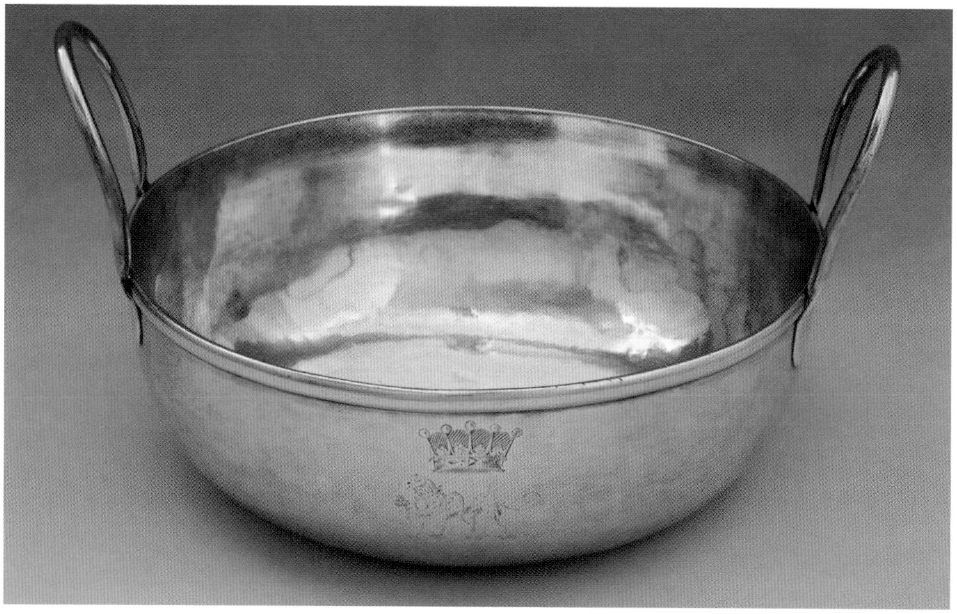

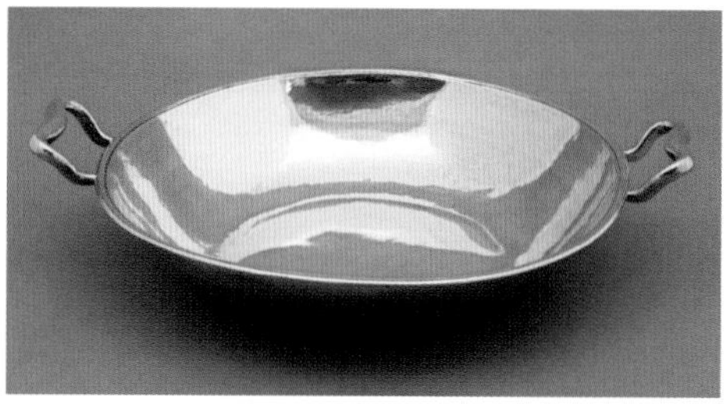

FIG. 75 / Preserving basin by Isaac Liger, London, 1728. Silver: w. 46 cm (18⅛ in); scratchweight 60 oz 10 dwt. National Trust, Dunham Massey.

11. **Six casters from an epergne**

Britannia silver / Paul de Lamerie, London / 1723/4

MARKS: Each fully marked on the underside with maker's mark 'LA' star and closed crown above fleur-de-lis below (third mark, unregistered),[1] Britannia, lion's head erased, date letter 'H'. No. 6 has the maker's mark struck twice, partly obscured by the other marks.

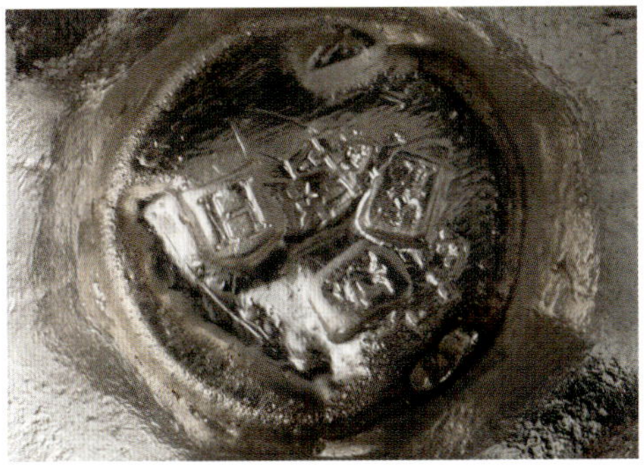

SCRATCHWEIGHTS: 'N° 1 [/] 14=8'; 'N° 2 [/] 12=15'; 'No 3 [/] 24=16'; 'N° 4 [/] 12=6'; 'N° 5 [/] 12=12'; 'N° 6 [/] 23=0'.

MEASUREMENTS: Large (2): h. 21.6 cm (8½ in); w&d. 8.6 cm (3⅜ in). Small (4): h. 16.2 cm (6⅜ in); w&d. 6.7 cm (2⅝ in).

INVENTORY: 852084

PROVENANCE: Nicholas Leke, 4th Earl of Scarsdale (d.1736); 1st Earl of Bristol (bought, as part of an epergne, 1737, at the Scarsdale sale); by descent to the 4th Marquess.

LITERATURE: Phillips 1935, p. 79, plates XXIV and XXV; Penzer 1957a, II, pp. 133–4, fig. 11; Banister 1980, pp. 792-3, fig. 4.

EXHIBITED: *Queen Charlotte's Loan Exhibition of Old Silver*, Seaford House, London, 1929, cat. 581 and 585; *Treasures from National Trust Houses*, Christie's, London, 1957–8, cat. 166 (one set); Society of the Four Arts, Palm Beach, Florida, 1959 (one set); *British Week*, Milan and Frankfurt, 1965; *Silver from National Trust Houses*, Treasurer's House, York Festival, 1969, cat. 28 (one set); *Treasures from Country Houses of the National Trust and National Trust for Scotland, Europalia 1973*, Brussels, cat. 117 (one set).

DESCRIPTION: The baluster-shaped casters are entirely octagonal in plan, the sides alternately incurved and straight from the foot through to the piercings of the covers. The upper part of the covers is also octagonal but without any incurving. The spreading feet are cast in one piece and the bodies in two vertical halves, with chased gadrooning on the foot and at the waist. The high-domed covers have seamed bezels and cast rims with chased gadroon borders. Above on each are eight panels soldered together, pierced and engraved with alternating designs of foliate strapwork and trelliswork with C-scroll oval bust medallions. The busts represent classical deities, one bearing the crescent of Diana and another in armour and a helmet probably being Mars. The covers culminate in cast and chased gadroon caps and baluster finials.

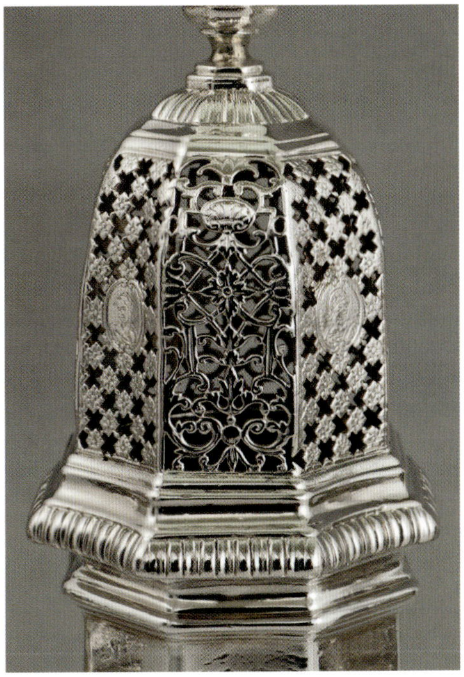

HERALDRY: Each caster has been re-engraved *c.*1751 on one of the flat sides above the waist with the quartered shield of the 2nd Earl of Bristol in an ermine mantling and beneath an earl's coronet.

THE SCARSDALE EPERGNE

On 1 April 1737 Lord Bristol noted in his accounts that he 'Paid Christopher Cock ye Auctioneer in full for a silver Epargne weight 497 ounces, 12d weight at 6s.08½d pr ounce, bought at Ld Scarsdales sale [£]166:17[s]' (see appendix 1). These six casters, two cruet frames (cat. 12) and an oval dish (cat. 13) are what remain of that epergne and all are by Paul de Lamerie. It is possible, in addition, that the four waiters bearing the mark of Lewis Mettayer and re-shaped in the 1750s by Kandler (cat. 51) might also have been part of it. The original appearance of the whole is suggested by the two surviving intact epergnes of this sort, that for the Williams family of 1730 predominantly by Edward Feline and George Wickes (fig. 76) and now in the collection of the National Museum, Wales[2] and the other of 1731 by David Willaume and Anne Tanqueray (fig. 77) from Kirkleatham in Yorkshire. Relating to the latter, James Lomax has given a comprehensive assessment of the evolution and use of these monumental centrepieces in his catalogue of the silver at Temple Newsam where it now resides.[3]

Nicholas Leke, 4th Earl of Scarsdale (*c.*1682–1736) had succeeded to the title and to Sutton Scarsdale in Derbyshire on the death of his uncle, a prominent Jacobite, in 1707. As a staunch Tory himself and a close associate of Robert Harley, 1st Earl of Oxford, he rose to some prominence in the second half of Queen Anne's reign. In 1710 Scarsdale was appointed Lord Lieutenant of Derbyshire in place of his principal Whig rival in the county, the 2nd Duke of Devonshire,[4] and in 1712 he was named Envoy to the Holy Roman Emperor, though his departure for Vienna was to be delayed until the outcome of the Utrecht negotiations was known. He never in fact went, but remained in favour and in July 1713 he was the peer designated to receive the French ambassador, the Duc d'Aumont, at his public entry into London. On the death of Queen Anne he was dismissed from the Lord Lieutenancy, Devonshire returning to the post, and implication in the Jacobite rising led to him being taken 'under a strong guard' to the Tower of London in October 1715.[5] He was not bailed until the following May and after a few years of keeping a low profile he began in 1724 to rebuild the family seat (fig. 78) in a grandiose manner. His architect was Francis Smith of Warwick and the interior was lavishly finished, the exuberant stuccowork being by the Italians, Alberto Artari and Francesco Vassalli.[6]

At the same time as Lord Scarsdale was erecting his splendid new house he was also embellishing his store of plate by the purchase of at least two pieces from Paul de Lamerie. The first was the epergne subsequently acquired by Lord Bristol and although the Leke family papers are not known to survive, Scarsdale fortuitously banked with the forerunners of Goslings and their ledgers from 1718 are still in existence in the Barclays Bank archive. On 26 August 1725 the Earl is recorded as having paid £150 to 'Paul Delamiere' (see appendix 3) and that is very likely to have been a part payment for the epergne, given the dates of manufacture of the surviving pieces (1723 and 1724). The remainder

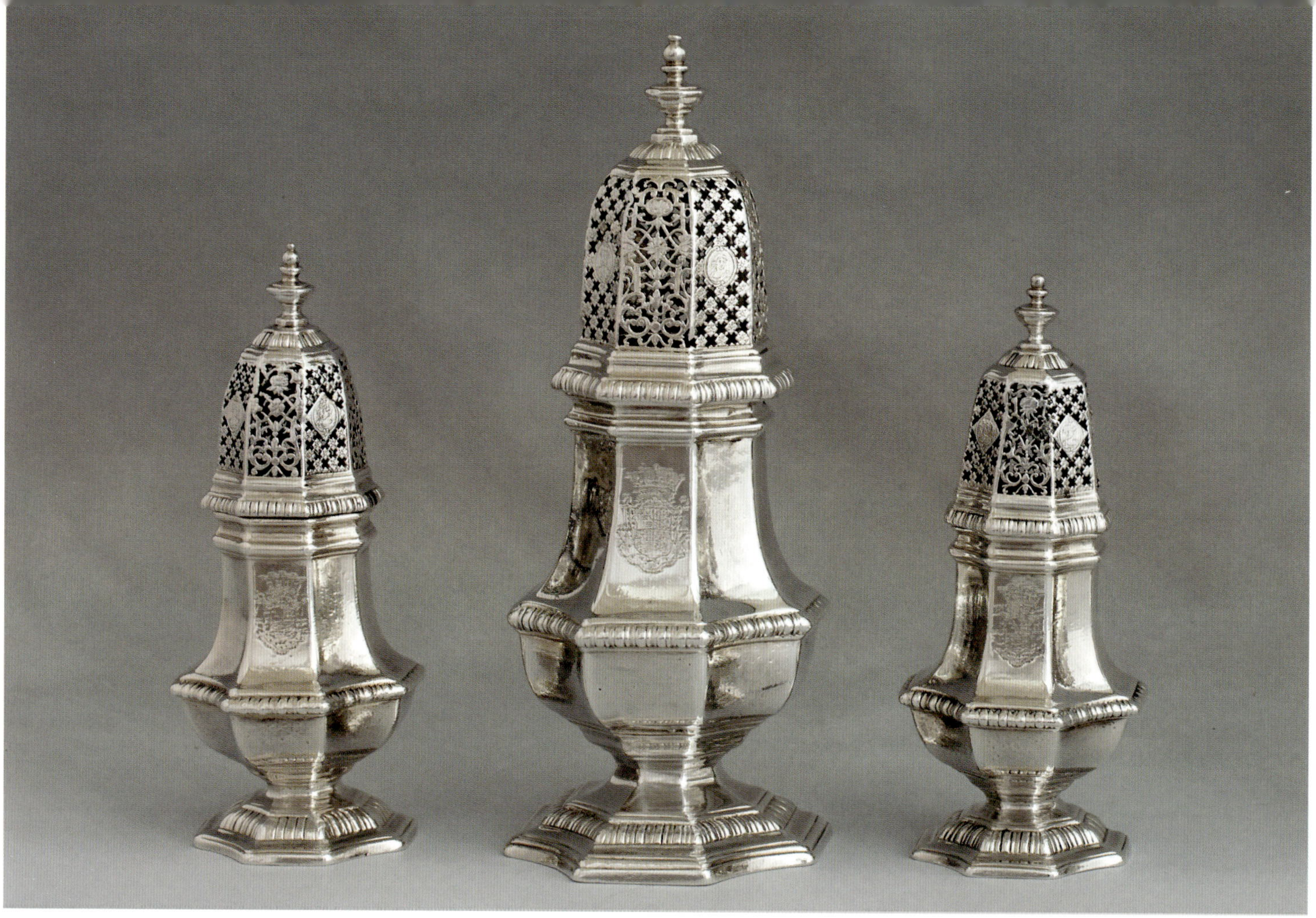

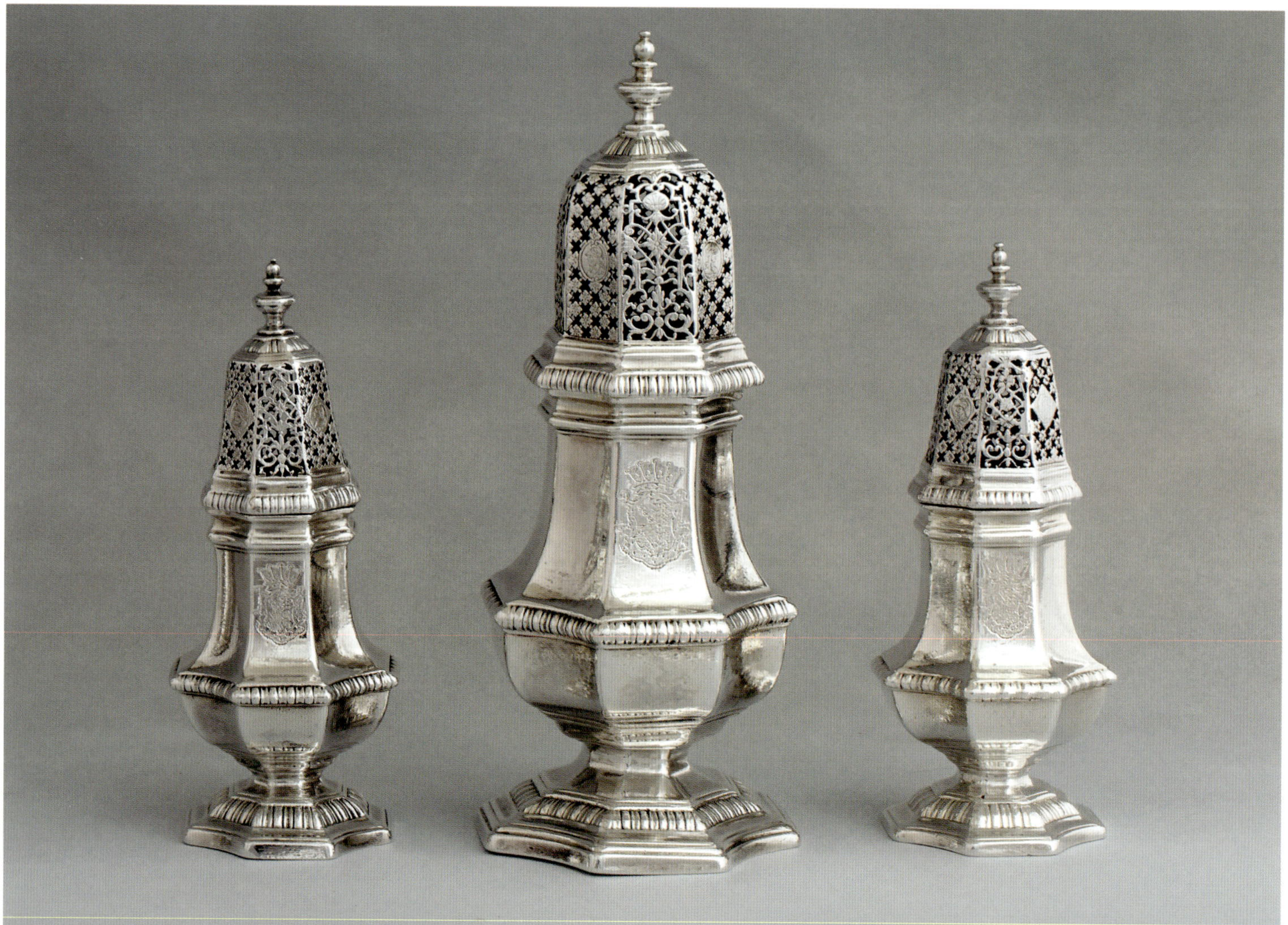

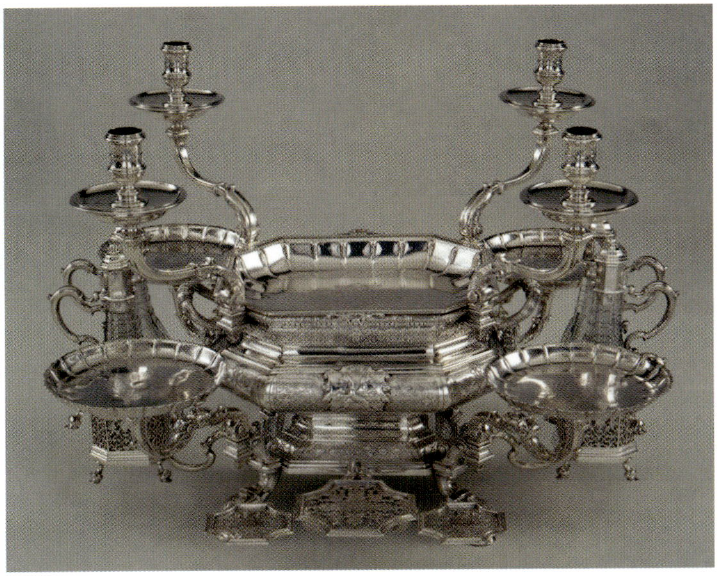

FIG. 76 / The Williams epergne by Edward Feline, London, 1730. The casters, by George Wickes, were in separate ownership when this photograph was taken but have since been secured. Silver: 40.6 x 58 x 49 cm (16 x 22½ x 19¼ in); weight (without casters) 12,174 g (391 oz) 8 dwt. National Museum, Wales.

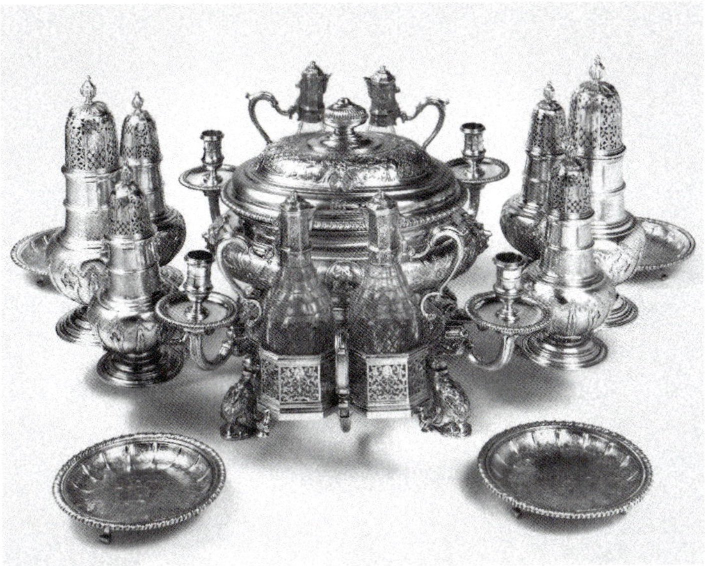

FIG. 77 / The Kirkleatham epergne by David Willaume and Anne Tanqueray, London, 1731. Silver: h. 28.5 cm (11¼ in), w. 55.9 cm (22 in); weight 13,649 g (438 oz) 18 dwt. Temple Newsam, Leeds.

is probably the £100 to 'Mr. Lemerie' which followed on 4 March 1726 as the total price would have been £250 10s, or thereabouts. This figure, equating to at least £35,000 today,[7] is based on the 1718 charges per ounce of 5s 8d for the silver and 3s 6d for fashion, plus £10 for engraving, of Lamerie's epergne for Thomas Coke of Holkham, added to which is the 6d per ounce duty payable from 1720.[8]

The epergne must have been spectacular enough but the Earl of Scarsdale's other principal purchase from de Lamerie is one of the most monumental and striking objects in silver to survive from the first quarter of the eighteenth century: a massive cast and chased silver cistern of 1726 (fig. 79) with winged female masks representing plenty, extravagantly modelled armorial assemblages (the Scarsdale arms subsequently covered over) and weighty scroll and female term handles.[9] At 2,646 ounces this piece would have cost well over £1,000, which is symptomatic of Lord Scarsdale's reckless spending in the last fifteen years of his life.

Both epergne and cistern would undoubtedly have been on display at the 'Grand entertainments' he gave, such as that on 29 May 1729 'to divers of the Nobility and Gentry, at his House in Duke-street Westminster', and may also have been amongst his baggage when he progressed from London to Sutton Scarsdale 'with a great Retinue' in September, 1731.[10]

By the time of his death six years later he had run up enormous debts and both Sutton Scarsdale and the silver had to go to meet them.[11] Lord Bristol bought the epergne and the cistern ended up in the collection of the Empress Anna of Russia's favourite, Ernst Johann von Biron, Duke of Courland, and is now in the Hermitage.[12] Even if Bristol had not attended any of the 'grand entertainments' in Duke Street, within a few hundred yards of his own house in St James's Square, he is likely to have heard reports of the magnificence of its furnishing and as an avid buyer of second-hand plate he would have been alert to the opportunities offered by the sale. Only three full-scale epergnes, comprising a central tureen, casters, cruet frames, saucers and candle arms, were supplied by George Wickes between 1738 and 1743 and they were charged at 9s 7d, 9s and 9s 2d per ounce plus additional costs for elements such as the cut-glass bottles, silver mounts and a case.[13] The second-hand purchase, at 6s 8½d, therefore saved the Earl of Bristol at least £55 and possibly up to £70.

The Scarsdale epergne was only a little over a decade old in 1737 and would have more than held its own on the dinner table. Though the rococo was beginning to take hold, decoration up to the mid-1730s continued to be mostly *Régence* in its inspiration and the surviving centrepiece from a 1734 epergne by de Lamerie in the Metropolitan Museum in New York has the same female masks, classical busts, diaperwork, shell motifs and tied reeding seen on the Scarsdale cistern and probably also present on the lost elements of the epergne.[14] The oval dish of the 1734 model, as well, is very close in form and decoration to the Ickworth one, and cruet

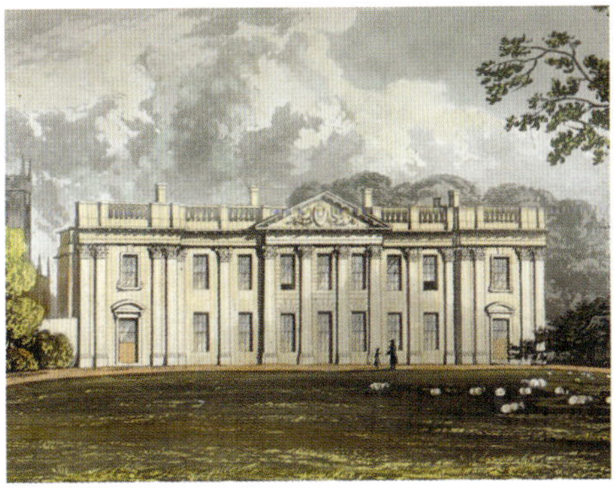

FIG. 78 / Sutton Scarsdale Hall, Derbyshire, *c.*1820. Engraving from Frederic Shoberl (ed.), *The Repository of arts, literature, commerce, manufactures, fashions and politics*, 1827. British Library.

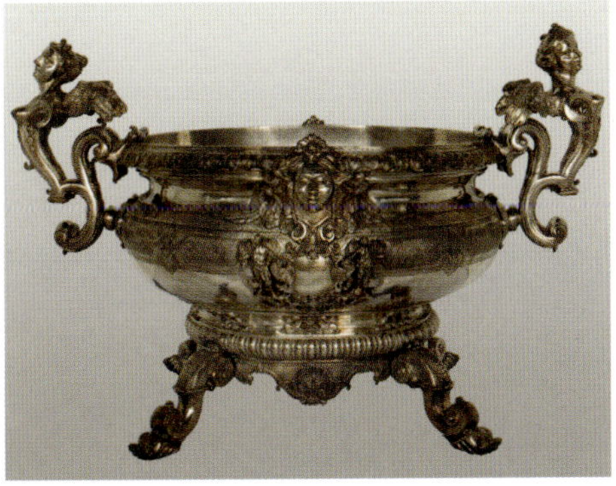

FIG. 79 / Wine cistern by Paul de Lamerie, London, 1726. Silver: 89 x 134.5 x 85 cm (35 x 53 x 33½ in); weight 82,300 g (2646 oz). The Hermitage Museum, St Petersburg.

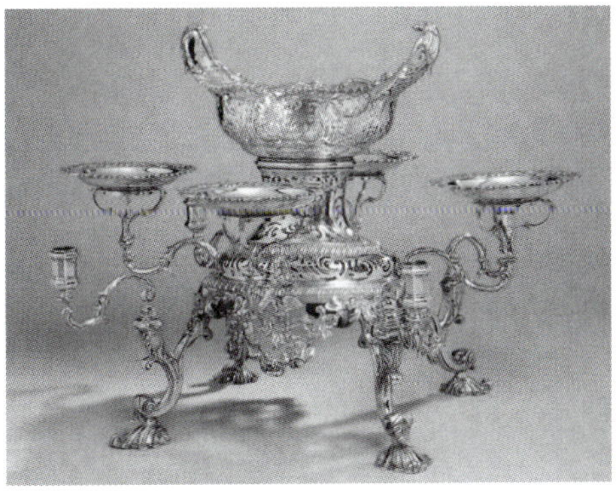

FIG. 80 / Epergne by William Cripps, London, 1757. Silver: h. 36 cm (14¼ in); weight 4833 g (157 oz). Christie's.

frames continued to be made to an almost identical model into the 1740s.[15] Casters, including de Lamerie's, were mostly round by the 1730s, as on the Kirkleatham epergne, but still sometimes supplied as octagonal.

However good a deal the epergne was in 1737 its life thereafter was to prove short, as by the time the 2nd Earl of Bristol inherited in 1751 such ponderous multi-purpose concoctions were being replaced with lighter affairs, restricted to a central basket, surrounding saucers and occasionally also candle arms, and associated primarily with dessert. These 'epargnes with 4 saucers & a basket', as George Wickes frequently termed them, had been around for many years, previously often described as 'machines', but from the late 1740s they were the subject of a positive craze and swept aside their mighty predecessors, most of which ended up being turned in to be melted. This must have been the fate of the Scarsdale epergne though, as in many other cases, the central dish, saucers, casters and cruets, which were all demountable and were designed to work visually as separate units as well as with the whole, were retained though not necessarily for their intended uses.

The 2nd Earl received a new epergne in 1759 as part of his perquisite plate when Ambassador to Spain. It weighed just 157 oz, 10 dwt, and was no doubt spidery and lace-like with an inverted trumpet stem and a boat-shaped central basket, as was the fashion by then.[16] Contemporary examples from the period include two by William Cripps of 1757 and 1758. The former (fig. 80) weighs almost exactly the same as did Lord Bristol's whereas the latter, of the same form but without candle arms, is considerably lighter.[17] There was no epergne surviving amongst the Bristol plate by the time the 5th Earl (future 1st Marquess) recorded his collection in 1811 and it is likely that it had been taken by his father, the Earl-Bishop, either ending up at Downhill, County Londonderry or, if it was amongst the plate he travelled with in Europe, being seized along with his accumulated artworks by the Napoleonic army in Italy in 1798.

THE CASTERS

Whilst part of the complete ensemble these casters would have rested on projecting platforms as seen on the Williams and Kirkleatham epergnes. Sets of three casters were produced in substantial numbers from the end of the seventeenth century, the larger one being for sugar and the smaller pair for pepper and mustard. This allocation is clearly articulated in Lord Warrington of Dunham Massey's manuscript plate list of 1750/4.[18] The cover of the caster for mustard was either supplied with a liner or left blind (unpierced) as the condiment was served dry in the eighteenth century to preserve its flavour. There are frequent mentions in the Wickes ledgers of mustard and sometimes pepper glasses – presumably liners for the casters – and there were also accompanying silver mustard spoons which must have projected into the covers. Eight glasses (spares always seem to have been provided) and two spoons, for instance, accompanied Everard Fawkener's surtout in 1735, and the following year Colonel Cornwell received six glasses and 'a large Mustard Spoon' with his set of casters.[19] None of the Ickworth casters appears to have been blind, so it is probable that those for mustard were fitted with liners.

Casters from the last decades of the seventeenth century are generally of the straight-sided cylindrical type such as those supplied to the 2nd Earl of Warrington *c.*1695 by Daniel Garnier.[20] The circular baluster is seen in a design for a parcel-gilt *sucrier* for Louis XIV of *c.*1700,[21] and at around the same time the form was established in England, as in the particularly magnificent set of three gilt casters, probably by Philip Rollos I, supplied to Lord Raby in 1705 on his appointment as ambassador to the King of Prussia.[22]

By 1720 the octagonal baluster held sway and continued to do so up to the early 1730s when the round form began to dominate again. Casters of the 1720s were for the most part devoid of decoration apart from moulded wires and the piercing of their covers. That was not the case for those supplied with Lord Scarsdale's epergne, however. Not only is their piercing particularly impressive and intricate, as well as being enhanced by engraving, but they are also gadrooned and demonstrate a variation on the standard planform, with alternately incurving sections to the octagon. These run right through the caster from foot to top of cover, giving greater movement and interest and being perhaps the earliest surviving example of an extremely rare feature. Other known representations are on the gilt casters of 1727 by Paul Crespin supplied to the Earl of Chesterfield for his embassy to The Hague and a small pair of 1730 without maker's marks engraved with a 'G' monogram beneath an earl's coronet.[23] All of these casters share very similar or identical patterns of piercing to their covers, as do others of the period including the set of three of 1725 by de Lamerie in the Museum of Fine Arts, Boston.[24] The same specialist subcontractor may well have been involved with the whole group.

Having survived the melting of the body of the epergne, the casters continued in regular use right up to the death of the 4th Marquess of Bristol in 1951, hence their considerable wear. Latterly the bases had been used on their own as mustard pots and the covers lay forgotten in an attic, though fortunately not discarded.[25]

1. Hare 1990, p. 29.
2. National Museum Wales, nos. NMW A 51194 and 51709–12, on display at Bodelwyddan Castle. Last sold at Sotheby's New York, 19 October 1995, Lot 454.
3. Lomax 1992, cat. 81, pp. 87–91.
4. https://en.wikipedia.org/wiki/Lord_Lieutenant_of_Derbyshire, accessed on 31 October 2015.
5. *Post Boy*, 2–4 October 1712, issue 377; *British Mercury*, 5 November 1712, issue 383; *London Gazette*, 30 June–4 July 1713, issue 5134; *Flying Post*, 11–13 October 1715, issue 3709 and 26–9 May 1716, issue 3807.
6. Craven and Stanley 2004, pp. 216–7.
7. Calculated using the converter on https://www.measuringworth.com.
8. Mortlock 1997, p. 556 and Dove 2007, p. 105.
9. Lopato 2015, cat. 26, pp. 85–90, ill. As discussed by Lopato there is a possibility that a pair of chandeliers by de Lamerie of 1724 in the Kremlin may also have been Scarsdale's.
10. *Daily Journal*, 30 May 1729, issue 2619 and *Daily Advertiser*, 6 September 1731, issue 185. Other entertainments given by Lord Scarsdale were reported in the *London Journal*, 21–28 May 1720, issue 44, commemorating his release from the Tower, and in the *London Evening Post*, 7–9 Nov 1728, issue 144, marking his birthday.
11. Craven and Stanley 2004, p. 217.
12. Lopato 2015, p. 90.
13. Wickes Ledgers, VAM 1 1735–40, f. 193, 1740, Viscount Duncannon, f. 182, 15 February 1739, Earl of Macclesfield and VAM 2, f. 69, 16 August 1742, Joseph Ledson.
14. Metropolitan Museum, accession no. 58.7.2 a–j.
15. See for instance the cruet frame and bottles of 1742 by George Wickes sold at Sotheby's, 21 February 1980, lot 163, also illustrated in Barr 1980, p. 74, fig. 37.
16. Jewel Office Delivery Book 1732–93, f. 165.
17. Christie's, 23 May 1990, lot 167 and 13 June 2001, lot 112.
18. Lomax and Rothwell 2006, pp. 128 and 175. By 1750 Lord Warrington had an epergne with six casters, a cruet frame with three and an independent set of four, the latter being specified for sugar (the two large), pepper and mustard (the two small).
19. Wickes Ledgers, VAM 1 1735–40, ff. 38 and 69.
20. Bonhams, 12 November 2014, lot 115. This set of three casters, one large and two small, with superbly patterned piercing to the lids, had been relegated to the servants' table by 1750. See Lomax and Rothwell 2006, p. 170.
21. Versailles 1993, p. 128, ill., and Wees 1997, cat. 125, pp. 212–3.
22. Lomax 2014, pp. 68 and 75.
23. Hartop 1996, cat. 10, pp. 108–9. The 1730 pair were sold by Wax Antiques, 49 Camden Passage, London N1 8EA (http://www.waxantiques.com/antique-silver/d/pair-of-george-ii-silver-casters/170730).
24. MFA, Boston, acc. no. 2001.47. See also Hartop 1996, cat. 24, pp. 158–61.
25. Penzer 1957a, II, p. 134.

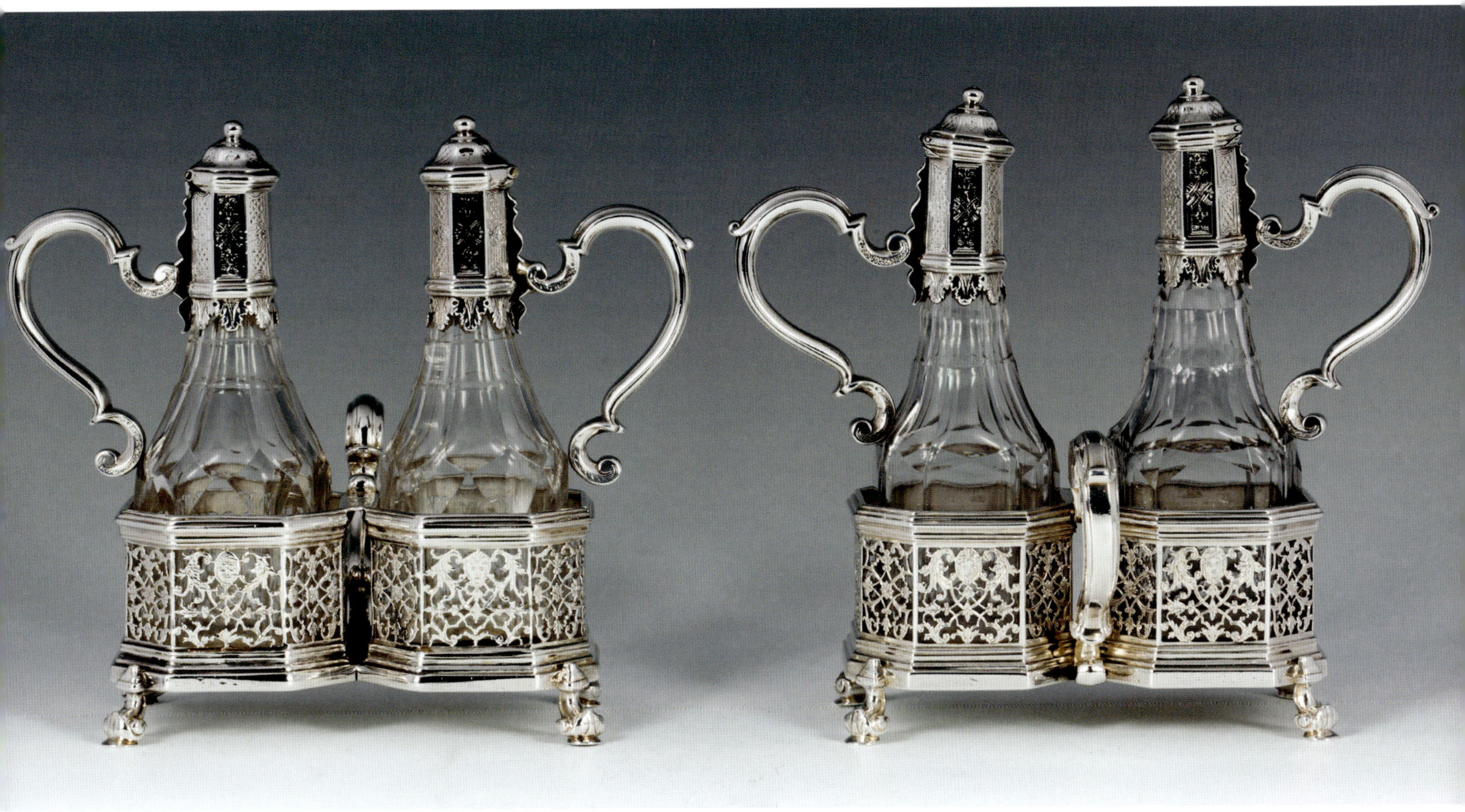

12. **Pair of cruet frames with bottles from an epergne**

Britannia silver / **Paul de Lamerie, London** / **1723/4**

MARKS: Fully marked on underside of both frames, maker's mark 'LA' star and closed crown above fleur-de-lis below (third mark, unregistered),[1] date letter 'H', Britannia and lion's head erased. Bottle mounts unmarked.

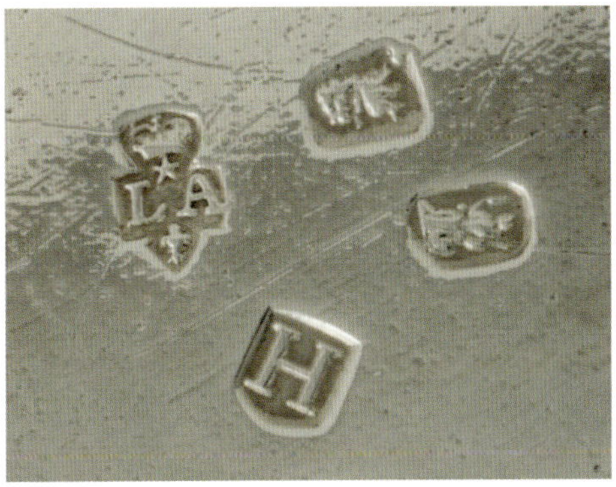

SCRATCHWEIGHTS: On undersides of frames, 'Nº 1 [/] 20=11' and 'Nº 2 [/] 20=13'

MEASUREMENTS: Frames: h. 10.2 cm (4 in); w. 15.9 cm (6¼ in); d. 7.9 cm (3⅛ in). Bottles: h. 18.1 cm (7⅛ in) and 17.1 cm (6¾ in). Combined heights: 20.6 cm (8⅛ in) and 19.7 cm (7 ¾ in).

INVENTORY: 852085

PROVENANCE: Nicholas Leke, 4th Earl of Scarsdale (d. 1736); 1st Earl of Bristol (bought, as part of an epergne, 1737, at the Scarsdale sale); by descent to the 4th Marquess.

LITERATURE: Phillips 1935, p. 79, plate XXIII; Penzer 1957a, II, p. 134; Banister 1980, pp. 792–3, fig. 4.

EXHIBITED: *Queen Charlotte's Loan Exhibition of Old Silver*, Seaford House, London, 1929, cat. no. 577; *Treasures from National Trust Houses*, Christie's, London, 1957–8, cat. 167 (one set); Society of the Four Arts, Palm Beach, Florida, 1959; *British Week*, Milan and Frankfurt, 1965; *Silver from National Trust Houses*, Treasurer's House, York Festival, 1969 (one set).

DESCRIPTION: The frames are each formed as two irregular octagons on four cast scroll and pad feet. The upper and lower mouldings are cast in two halves and the sides are pierced and engraved with foliate scrolls and female masks. The cast scroll handles, which are ribbed and capped and have trelliswork on matted grounds on the outer edges at their extremities, are soldered to the frames at the joint between the two octagons. Bridging the horizontal upper gap between the octagons is a slip of sheet silver engraved with a C-scroll cartouche between leaves and on a matted panel with incurving ends. The facet-cut colourless glass bottles conform to the frames in their lower halves, rising to true octagons. They are surmounted by silver octagonal neck mounts engraved in *Régence* fashion, alternately with double incurved panels of trelliswork around stylised flowers and interlocking foliate strapwork. The mounts have chased leaf skirts and hinged domed octagonal covers engraved to match. There are plain ball finials and no spouts. Applied to the rear panels of the mounts are wavy crestings to which are soldered the tops of the scroll handles, the bottoms resting against the glass bottles. The pairs of bottles are not of the same height, suggesting that one or other is a replacement.

HERALDRY: Within the cartouche of the bridge between the octagons of each frame the Hervey crest beneath an earl's coronet has been engraved *c.* 1737.

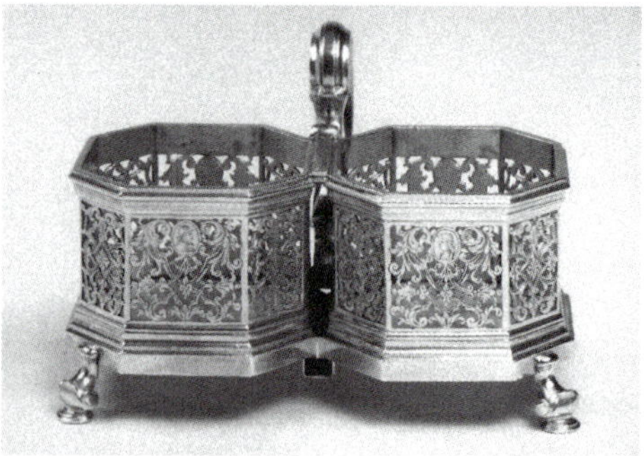

FIG. 81 / Cruet frame from the Kirkleatham epergne, Anne Tanqueray and David Willaume II, 1731. Silver. Temple Newsam, Leeds.

For general comments on the Scarsdale epergne see cat. 11. The glass bottles were for oil and vinegar which would have been used as condiments in much the same way as they are now. Many such bottles were supplied in frames and mounts similar to these which are amongst the earliest English survivors, the only older examples so far recorded being two of 1722, one by de Lamerie and the other by Benjamin Pyne.[2] The form originated in late-seventeenth century France and can be seen on a surviving cruet of 1697 probably by Claude Charpentier and constructed of two conjoined circles.[3] Other comparable frames to those at Ickworth in public collections include that of 1727 by de Lamerie at the Ashmolean Museum, with a more open, strapwork gallery, and one of 1723 by Paul Crespin in the Museum of Fine Arts, Boston.[4] The latter, probably having always been gilded, survives in pristine condition with crisp engraving and piercing and allows a full appreciation of the superb craftsmanship which has been somewhat blurred on the Ickworth frames by their extensive wear.

The piercings of the Ickworth, Williams and Kirkleatham (fig. 81) frames are near identical, suggesting shared design sources amongst the three goldsmiths and the likely use of the same highly skilled subcontractor. The cruet frames would have been fitted beneath with square sockets enabling them to be held aloft on brackets connected to the body of the epergne. These have been removed but they survive on many other frames from the period which must originally have been part of epergnes, and they are, of course, also present on the Williams and Kirkleatham examples where they continue to perform their intended purpose.[5]

1. Hare 1990, p. 29.
2. Christie's, 26 April 1966, lot 138.
3. Dennis 1960, vol. 1, p. 88, fig. 90. See also the drawing of one belonging to the Duc d'Aumont *c.*1700, Hernmarck 1977, vol. 2, fig. 437.
4. Schroder 2009, cat. 134, pp. 352–4 and Hartop 1996, cat. 22, pp. 154–5.
5. For other examples of surviving sockets on frames no longer part of epergnes see Sotheby's 20 April 1972, lot 148 (Paul de Lamerie, 1733), Christie's 27 November 1991, lot 99 (Paul de Lamerie, 1723) and Christie's 25 November 2008 (Peter Archambo, 1733, from Althorp).

13. Dish from an epergne, subsequently dessert dish

Britannia silver, subsequently gilded / Paul de Lamerie, London / 1724/5

MARKS: Lion's head erased, Britannia, maker's mark 'LA' star and closed crown above fleur-de-lis below (third mark, unregistered),[1] date letter 'I'.

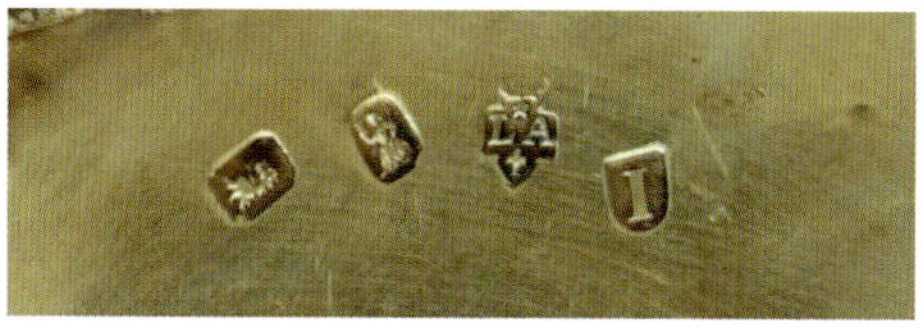

SCRATCHWEIGHT: 'N1 [/] 31=7'

MEASUREMENTS: h. 2.5 cm (2 in); w. 33.7 cm (13¼ in); d. 29.6 cm (11⅔ in).

INVENTORY: 852064.1

PROVENANCE: Nicholas Leke, 4th Earl of Scarsdale (d.1736); 1st Earl of Bristol (bought, as part of an epergne, 1737, at the Scarsdale sale); by descent to the 4th Marquess.

LITERATURE: Phillips 1935, p. 82, plate XXXVIII; Penzer 1957a, I, pp. 41-2, fig. 4; Banister 1980, p. 793, fig. 6; Schroder 1988, p. 151, ill.; Hare 1990, cat. 66, p. 110. Penzer, Banister and Hare wrongly recorded the date of the dish as 1734.

EXHIBITED: *Queen Charlotte's Loan Exhibition of Old Silver*, Seaford House, London, 1929, cat. no. 573; *Treasures from National Trust Houses*, Christie's, London, 1957–8, cat. 168; Society of the Four Arts, Palm Beach, Florida, 1959; *British Week*, Milan and Frankfurt, 1965; *Silver from National Trust Houses*, Treasurer's House, York Festival, 1969, cat. 28; *Treasures from Country Houses of the National Trust and National Trust for Scotland, Europalia 1973*, Brussels, cat. 118; *Paul de Lamerie, At the Sign of the Golden Ball*, Goldsmiths' Hall, London, 1990, cat. no. 66.

DESCRIPTION: The oval dish is raised and has a series of narrow ribs around the perimeter, the compartments thereby created being flat-chased and engraved with foliate strapwork panels, alternately decorated with stylised leaves on matted grounds and trelliswork. There is a cast gadrooned rim and four cast triangular handles, each with a three-dimensional classical bust against an irregular shell and scrolling foliage, the backgrounds matted. The base of the dish is fitted with a seamed bezel and four scroll feet.

HERALDRY: The centre of the dish has been re-engraved *c.*1751 with the quartered shield, supporters and motto of the 2nd Earl of Bristol in an ermine mantling and beneath an earl's coronet.

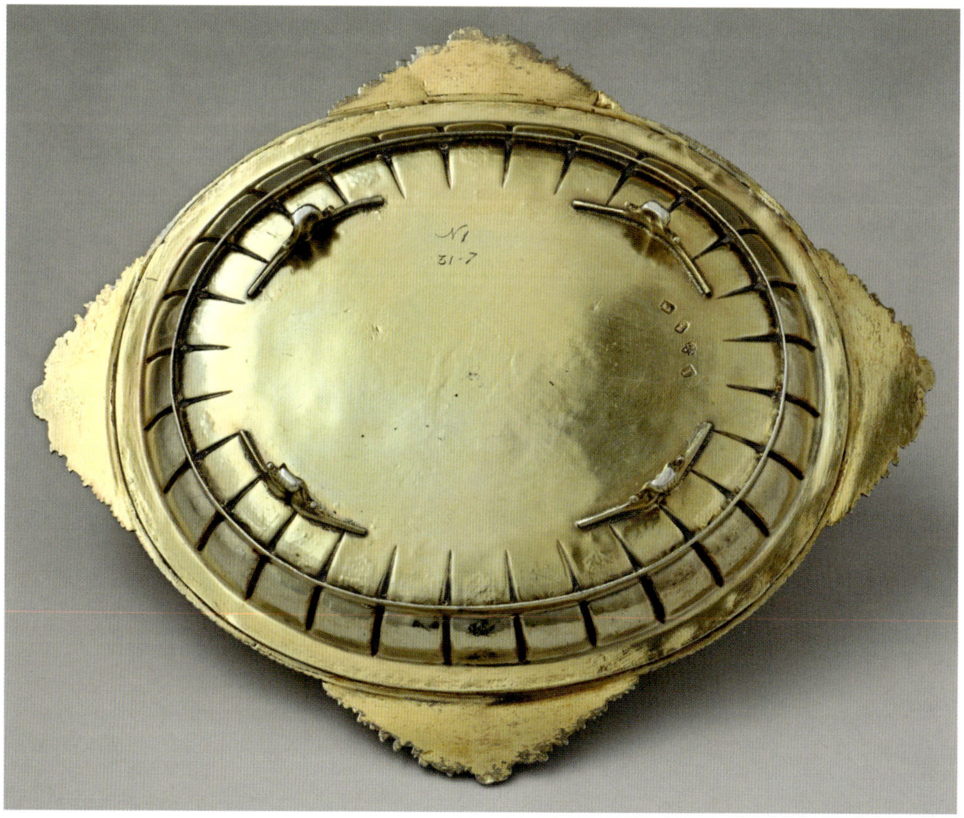

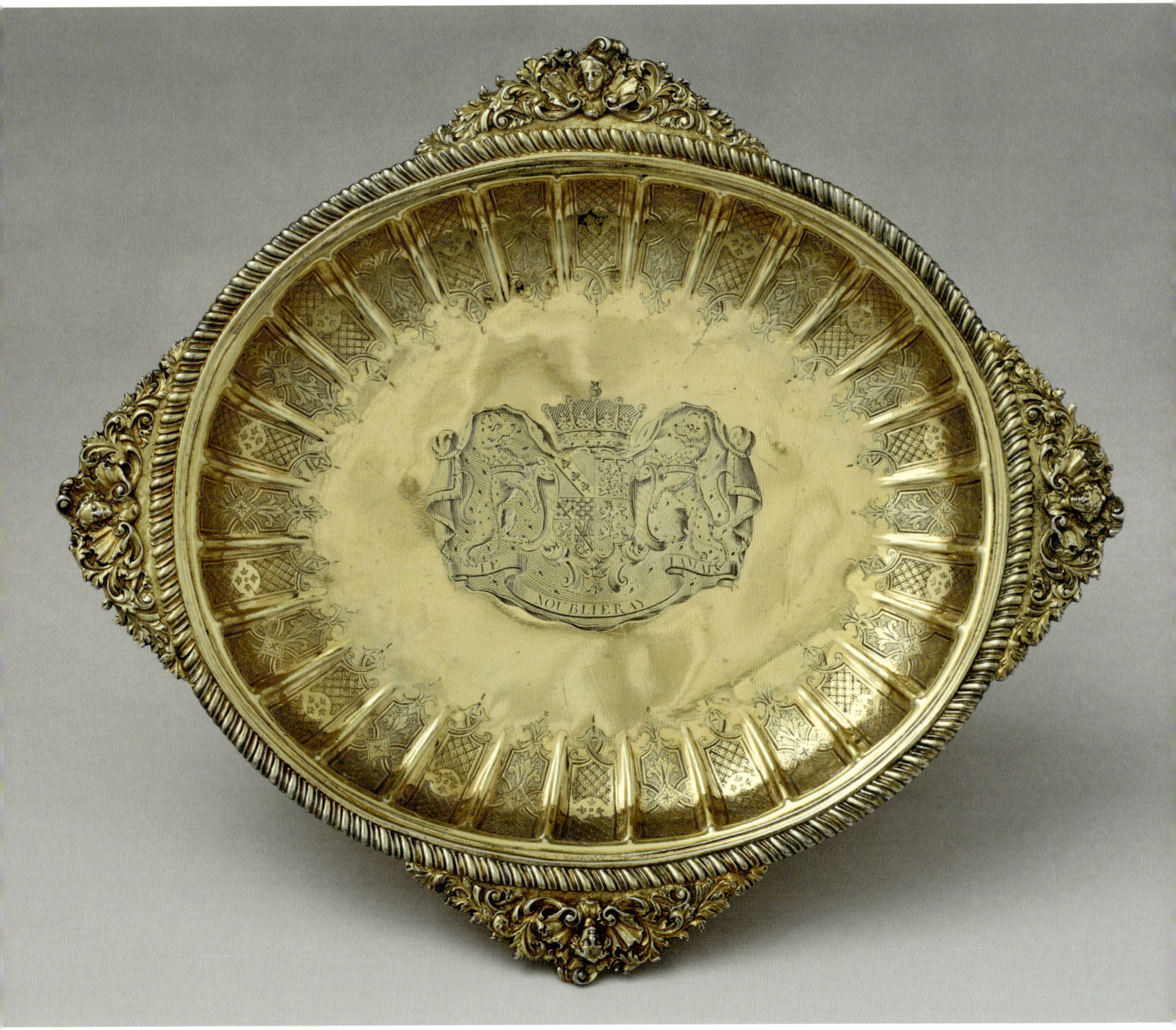
NOUBLIERAY

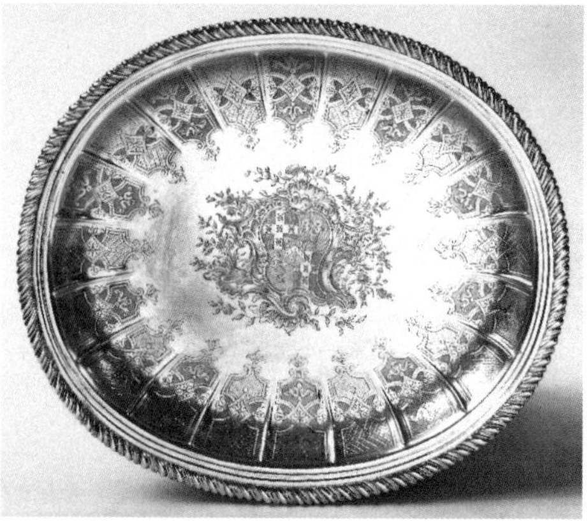

FIG. 82 / Kirkleatham epergne dish, Anne Tanqueray, London, 1731. Silver. Temple Newsam, Leeds.

This dish would have fitted into the top of the epergne tureen as an alternative to the cover, in the same way as does the dish of the intact Kirkleatham epergne (fig. 82).[2] Its fluted form suggests the circular salad dishes of the early eighteenth century which were also used for dessert and thus sometimes called strawberry dishes.[3] It would have been put in place once the initial courses of the meal had been completed, and been mounded with fruit or sweetmeats along with the vanished epergne saucers which would have projected on arms and been decorated to match. Glass liners were often provided for such dishes and saucers, protecting the silver and its intricate *Régence* decoration from the acidic fruit. These liners accompanied all of George Wickes' epergnes of the 1730s and 40s, Viscount Duncannon being provided with '8 cutt saucers' at 16s in 1740 whilst the ill-fated Admiral Byng received '2 ovell & 8 round Glass Saucers' with his 'Epargne with 4 branches' in 1749.[4] It is to be hoped that at some point examples of these glass liners will be identified.

An alternative dish shape was the extended octagon, as on the Williams epergne, but oval seems to have been more popular and to have persisted longer, outlasting even the inclusion of tureens in epergnes. A fine example with a frothily rococo cast border and wavy fluting is, for instance, found as late as 1753 on an epergne by Eliza Godfrey.[5] Paul de Lamerie seems only ever to have used the oval form and on at least one other epergne dish, that made for the 6th Earl of Mountrath in 1737 (fig. 83), he combined it again with the prominent cast handles employed for Lord Scarsdale thirteen years earlier.[6] These handles, in quadruplicate, are also to be found on an inkstand of 1732 by de Lamerie[7] and it is possible that the same moulds were employed when the Scarsdale dish was duplicated for the 2nd Earl of Bristol by Frederick Kandler in 1751 (cat. 28) and again in 1766 when another pair was added (cat. 85). The whole set was then gilded to serve as dessert dishes and this use resulted in the miscomprehension in the twentieth century, starting with P.A.S. Phillips in his 1935 work on Paul de Lamerie, that the piece had been intended for that purpose from the beginning.[8] The same mistake has previously been made in relation to a number of other remnant dishes from epergnes, such as that of 1734 by de Lamerie in the Ashmolean Museum which still has its six accompanying saucers.[9] Some, like that at Ickworth, retain the bezel which allowed the dish to fit securely onto the tureen.[10]

1. Hare 1990, p. 29.
2. Lomax 1992, pp. 88–9, ill.
3. See Schroder 2009, cat. 86, pp. 240–2 for a clear summary of the current understanding of fluted salad dishes.
4. Wickes Ledgers, VAM 1 1735–40, f. 193 and VAM 3 1747–50, f. 83.
5. Christie's 15 June 1977, lot 116.
6. Christie's 17 December 1986, lot 240 and Hare 1990, cat. 87, pp. 134–5, ill.
7. Jackson 1911, p. 904, fig. 1181.
8. Phillips 1935, p. 82.
9. Schroder 2009, cat. 103, pp. 279–81. Schroder has identified the set as being from an epergne but notes that they were previously described as dessert dishes.
10. See, for example, that of 1742 by John Hugh Le Sage supplied to the 4th Marquess of Tweeddale as Secretary of State for Scotland by the Jewel Office as part of a surtout, sold at Christie's, 23 March 1966, lot 23.

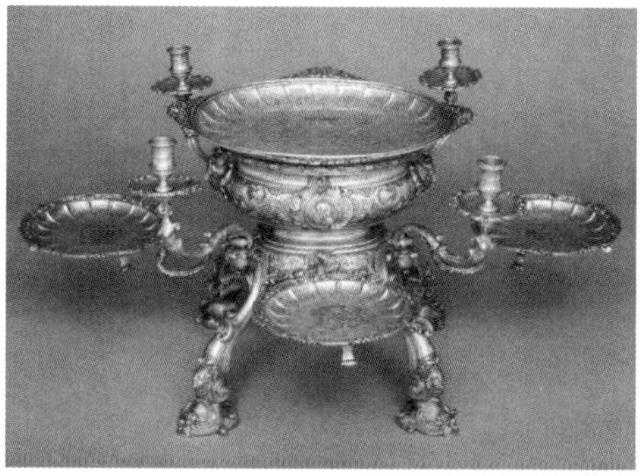

FIG. 83 / The Mountrath epergne by Paul de Lamerie, London, 1737. Silver: h. 36.3 cm (14¼ in); width of the main dish 35 cm (13¾ in); weight 9362 g (301 oz). Christie's.

14. **Tea kettle and lamp**

Sterling silver / **Pierre Le Cheaube, London** / **1726/7**

MARKS: Kettle and lamp fully marked on underside with maker's mark 'PC' between club and five-pointed star in extended octagon (Grimwade 1990, no. 2145), sterling lion, leopard's head, date letter 'L'. Lamp frame not marked.

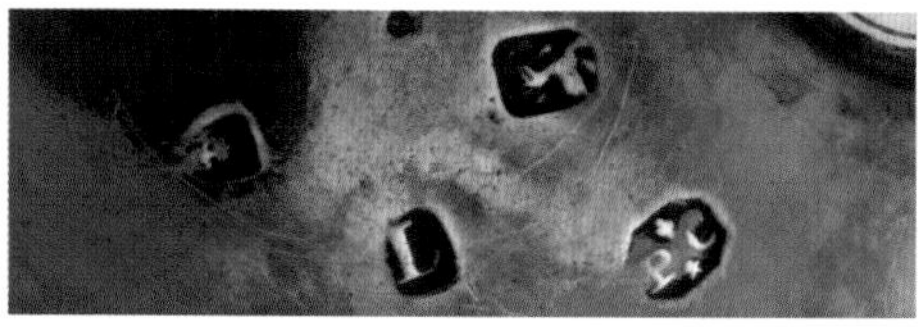

SCRATCHWEIGHT: On underside of kettle '52=6'

MEASUREMENTS: h. of kettle and lamp-frame combined 29.2 cm (11½ in). Kettle h. (including handle) 22.9 cm (9 in); w. 23.5 cm (9¼ in); d. 16.8 cm (6⅝ in). Frame h. 8.6 cm (3⅜ in); w & d. 15.9 cm (6¼ in). Lamp h. 3.5 cm (1⅜ in); w & d. 7.6 cm (3 in).

INVENTORY: 852071.1-3

PROVENANCE: probably 1st Earl of Bristol; by descent to the 4th Marquess.

LITERATURE: Penzer 1957a, II, p. 134 (erroneously attributed to Paul Crespin).

EXHIBITED: *Treasures from National Trust Houses*, Christie's, London, 1957–8, no. 52; Society of the Four Arts, Palm Beach, Florida, 1959; *Silver from National Trust Houses*, Treasurer's House, York Festival, 1969.

DESCRIPTION: The plain kettle, which is raised, is of compressed spherical form with an applied, seamed foot ring. The flush circular lid, with a crudely pierced later steam hole and a cast baluster finial with ivory knop, has a flush five-part pin hinge. The S-shaped spout is cast in two pieces and has a C-scroll moulding at the lip. The bases to the button hinges of the plain bail handle are cast and soldered to the body of the kettle. The wickering of the upper part of the handle may be original. The frame on which the kettle sits has three cast cabriole legs terminating in claw-and-ball feet and rising to a flaring cast and pierced ring, conforming internally to the base of the kettle. Three flattened and curved wire brackets connect the legs to a moulded and seamed ring which holds the raised semi-spherical lamp. The lamp has a flattened base, an applied moulded wire which supports it in the ring and a cast dished cover, the wick fitting of which is absent.

HERALDRY: On the side of the kettle, with the spout to the left, have been re-engraved *c.*1751 the quartered shield, supporters and motto of the 2nd Earl of Bristol in an ermine mantling and beneath an earl's coronet. The side of the lamp is engraved with the Hervey crest beneath an earl's coronet.

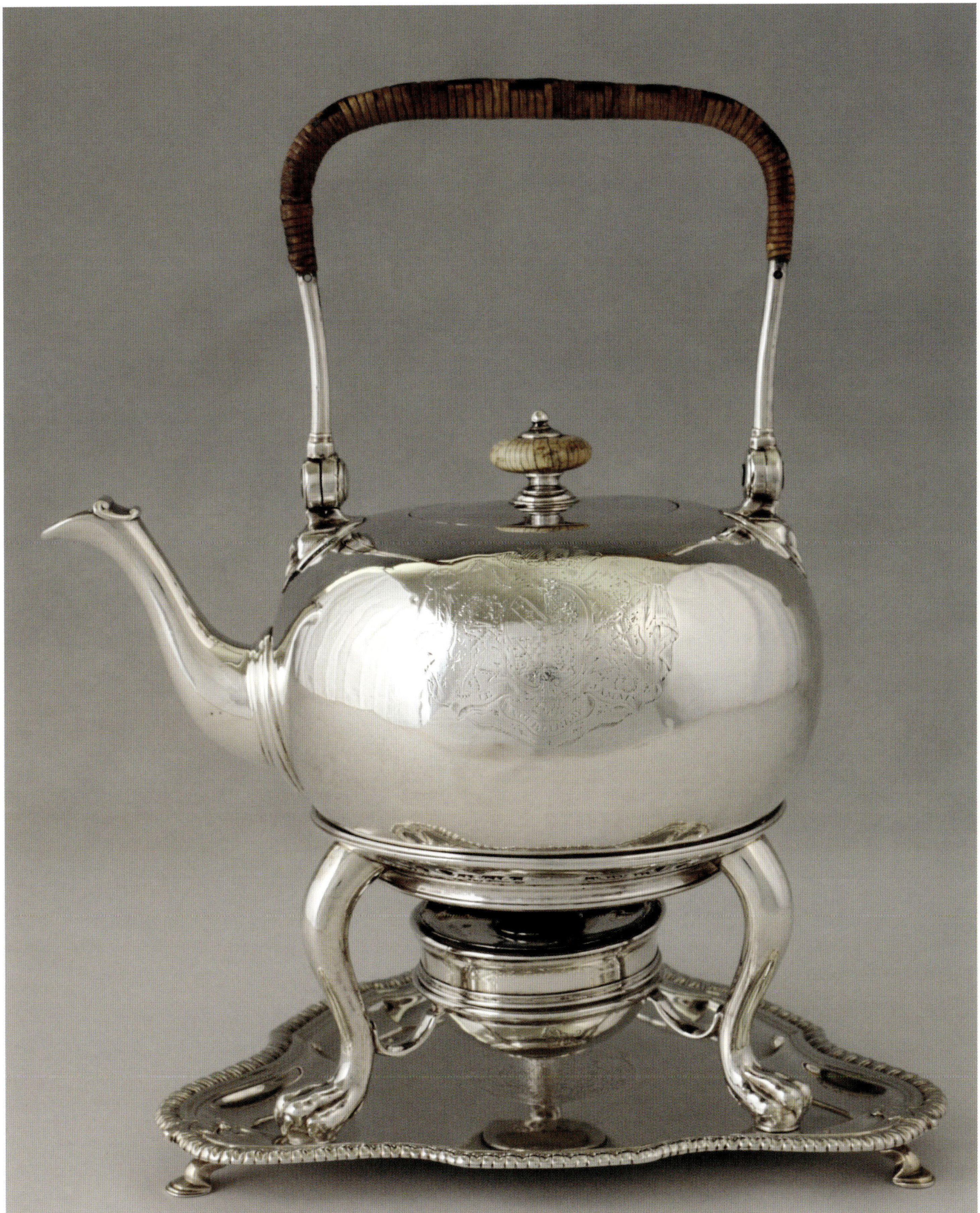

cat. 14 on cat. 25

The 1st Earl of Bristol became convinced that excessive tea drinking was bad for the health of his sons, even potentially fatal, and a number of rants against it are included in his later letters. On 27 December 1735, for instance, he wrote to John, Lord Hervey:

Your constitution would never have deserved half the hard words you have given it, had not you ruind it by forceing on it so many tuns of that detestable infusion of tea, by the constant use wherof, tho' not for near so long a time nor to so strong a degree as you have done, your brother Felton hath already destroyd the strongest stamina that ever any man was blessd ...[1]

In spite of such vociferous outbursts, and a personal preference for chocolate (see cat. 5), Lord Bristol does not seem to have banned 'that poysonous plant tea'[2] from his house. To do so would, anyway, have been socially unacceptable, so intertwined was it with the rituals of aristocratic life, and there are numerous references to items associated with the service of tea in the Earl's accounts. In 1689 he bought 'a white Teapot & bason' for his first wife, adding 'a Tea=Table & 2 pair of China Cupps' the following year. The tea pot is likely to have been Chinese porcelain, perhaps with silver or silver-gilt mounts, and the table to have been carved and gilt and one of the large number imported from China and Japan at the end of the seventeenth century. Good examples survive of both at Ham House in Surrey where they would have been used in the Duchess's private closet.[3]

On 7 December 1698 the future 1st Earl paid his goldsmith-banker, James Chambers, 'for a Tea-Kettle & Lampe wt. 90 ou, 11 dwtt at 6s. 2d.' Kettles were then something of a novelty and this one, which was of a prodigious weight, is likely to have been of the flattened pear or loaf form as is the earliest surviving English example, that of 1694 in the Norwich Castle Museum (fig. 84). The shape persisted for the first two decades of the eighteenth century. There is no mention of the 1698 kettle being turned in subsequently and it may well have been relegated to Suffolk when in 1726 Lord Bristol acquired a new kettle, not long before Lord Hervey suffered the severe bout of fever that may have sparked his father's fear of the effects of tea.[4] The entry in the Earl's accounts is dated 6 April 1726 which is too early for the commencement of the 1726/7 date letter and as no weight is given it is impossible to be certain that it relates to the surviving kettle. The probability is, however, that it does and that Lord Bristol either paid in advance (which seems unlikely) or that he got the date wrong when he transferred his individual notes of payments into the account book. The simple, restrained form of the kettle is common for the period and likely to have been the preference of the Earl, particularly given his antipathy to the associated drink. Had it been the acquisition of his son and daughter-in-law it would most probably have had some at least of the *Régence* embellishment seen on their ice pails and bread basket (cat. 18 and 19). An example of 1726 by de Lamerie with such decoration around the lid is in the Clarke Art Institute at Williamstown, Massachusetts.[5]

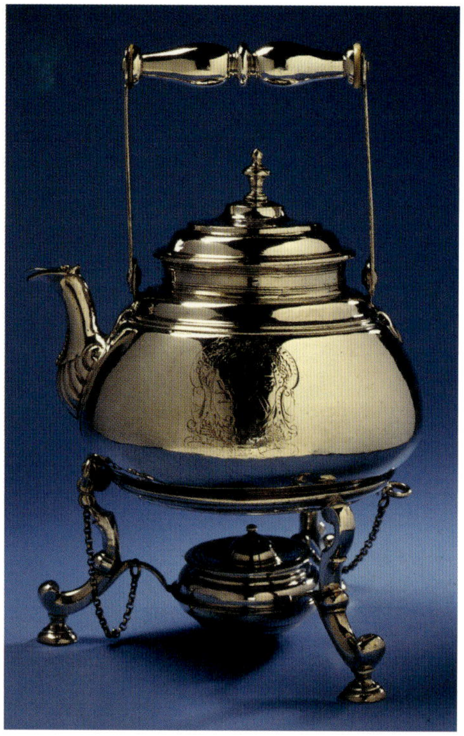

FIG. 84 / Kettle, London, 1694. Silver: h. 19.5 cm (7⅝ in). Norwich Castle Museum.

Further corroboration is given to the 1st Earl having been the purchaser by the maker being Pierre Le Cheaube (anglicised to Peter Le Chouabe in the register entry for 1726), not Paul Crespin as previously attributed. Crespin was patronised by Lord Hervey (see cat. 18) whereas Lord Bristol by this time was acquiring all his new silver through David Willaume I. Le Cheaube was from Metz, as was Willaume, and was apprenticed to him in 1700. When he entered his first mark in 1707 he gave his address as Pall Mall and was probably thus still employed by Willaume, who was at that point based there. Arthur Grimwade has suggested that the rarity of his mark is likely to be the result of his continuing to be employed by Willaume for much of his career, and his late adoption of a sterling mark supports that. Of those few pieces by him that are known, a covered tankard also bears the date letter for 1726 while an orange strainer possibly by him is marked for 1735.[6] As he entered his second, sterling mark on 27 June 1726, giving as his address Glasshouse Street in Soho, he may have left Willaume's workshop that year and thereafter practised independently.[7]

See cat. 25 for the associated waiter.

1. Hervey 1894b, vol. 3, p. 147. See also pp. 48, 68 and 152 for similarly vociferous condemnations in letters of 7 July 1729, 5 August 1731 and 8 May 1736. Lord Bristol was not alone in his beliefs – see Emmerson 1992, pp. 9 and 13.
2. Ibid., p. 48.
3. Pettigrew 2001, pp. 22–3 and 30, ills. NT inv. nos. 1139006 and 1140034.
4. This occurred in March 1728. See Halsband 1973, p. 76.
5. Wees 1997, cat. 247, pp. 355–7.
6. The tankard was with Wax Antiques, 49 Camden Passage, Islington, London N1 8EA and the orange strainer (identified as a lemon strainer) was sold at Martel Maides, Guernsey, 27 November 2014, lot 438.
7. Grimwade 1990, pp. 578 and 703–4.

15. Coffee pot

Probably sterling silver
Thomas Cooke II and Richard Gurney
***c.*1735**

MARKS: Marked on underside with maker's mark 'R G' and 'T C' as a cross with a pellet between (Grimwade 1990, no. 2324), and transposed sterling lion and lion's head erased, both pre-1697. The Gurney and Cooke marks are stamped over the previous maker's mark and date letter, the latter possibly 'l' for 1688.

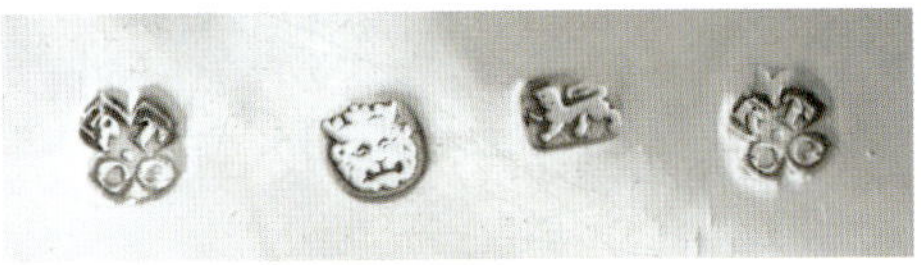

SCRATCHWEIGHT: '17:10'

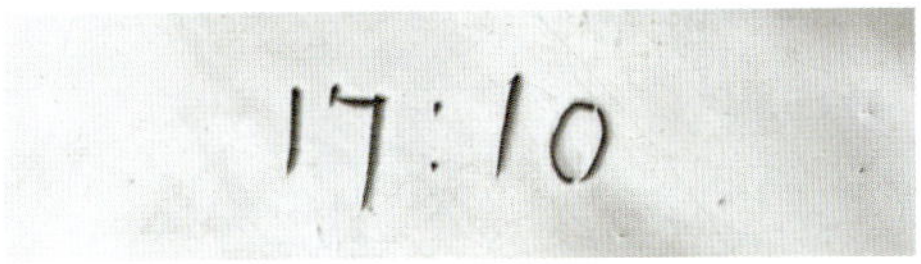

MEASUREMENTS: h. 18.1 cm (7⅛ in); w. 19.1 cm (7½ in); diam. (at base) 13.7 cm (3⅞ in).

INVENTORY: 852108

PROVENANCE: 1st Earl of Bristol; by descent to the 4th Marquess.

LITERATURE: Penzer 1957a, I, p. 42; Banister 1980, p. 792.

DESCRIPTION: The plain, tapering cylindrical pot is made of sheet seamed behind the handle. The moulded base and lip are applied and the swan-neck spout is cast in two vertical halves. The scrolling handle brackets are cast and secured to the double-scroll wooden handle by silver pins. The lid is raised to form a flattened dome and has an applied lip and bezel and a cast baluster finial. It is attached to the upper handle bracket by a five-part pin hinge.

HERALDRY: On the side of the pot, with the spout to the right, have been re-engraved *c.*1751 the quartered shield, supporters and motto of the 2nd Earl of Bristol in an ermine mantling and beneath an earl's coronet. The engraving is very worn.

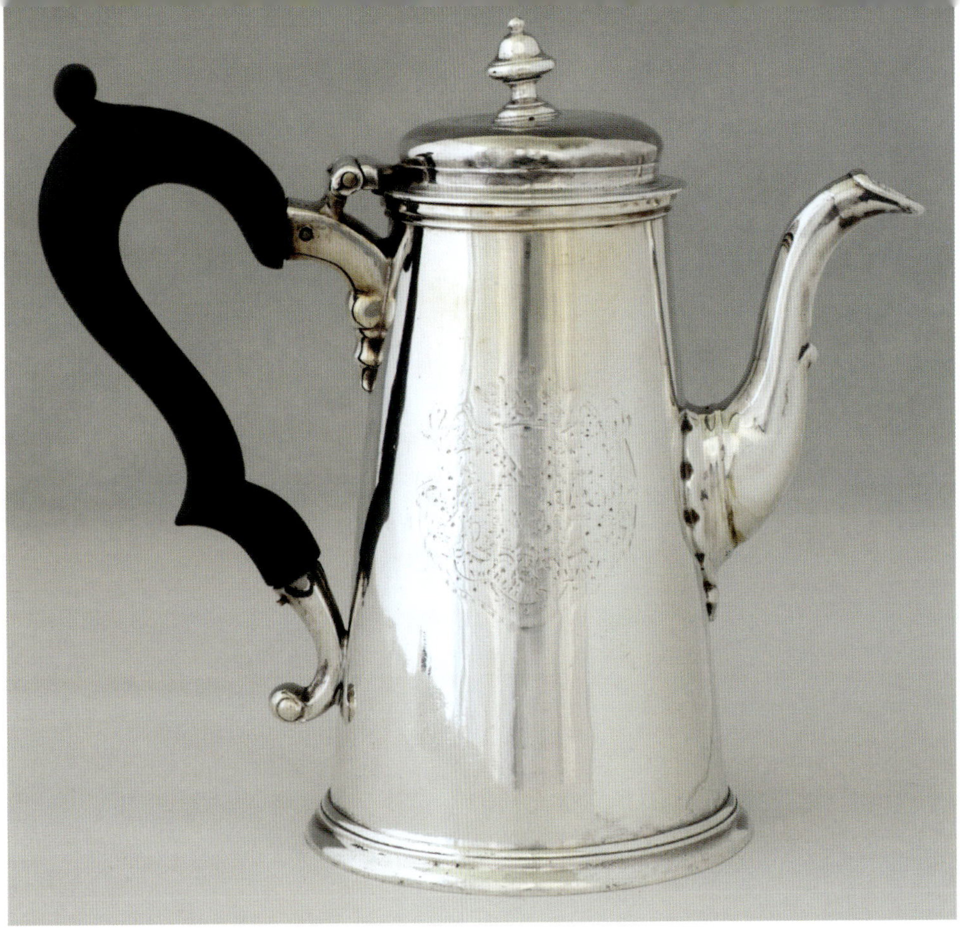

The 1st Earl's accounts reveal that he bought coffee pots in 1696, 1733 and 1735 (see appendix 1). The first one was acquired from Edward Waldegrave, a retail goldsmith at the sign of the Anchor in Russell Street, Covent Garden who was active between 1690 and 1720.[1] It was part of a substantial purchase, amounting to 802 ounces and charged at 5s 3¼d per ounce, which indicates that the whole lot was second-hand. In 1733 Lord Bristol must have decided that his old pot was so out of date or battered that it needed replacing and one was supplied at 5s 9d per ounce by George Wickes & John Craig. As it cost £11 18s it must have weighed 38 oz, 8 dwt, and the charge per ounce indicates that it too was second-hand.[2] This pot is likely to have been for his St James's Square house as only two years later he bought another, lighter and no doubt smaller coffee pot for £6 18s from Peter Rogers, a retail silversmith in Bury St Edmunds. This is the one still surviving and its scratchweight of 17 oz, 10 dwt, indicates a rate per ounce of 6s 11d. At last Lord Bristol had bought new, and yet the pot is not straightforward. The makers, Richard Gurney and Thomas Cooke II, had dodged the duty of 6d per ounce by inserting an old disc of silver in the base with late-seventeenth-century sterling marks, their own device stamped twice to conceal the original date letter and maker. They had quite clearly not passed on the saving to Lord Bristol which would suggest that he did not pay close attention to hallmarks. It would be interesting to know if Gurney and Cooke sent duty dodgers to the provinces routinely, perhaps relying upon the distance from London for safety from detection. Did their names also, both having East Anglian resonance if not actual connections, help them to obtain commissions in the region?

This coffee pot is of the standard plain, tapering form of the late 1720s and 1730s. Gurney and Cooke marked a wide range of plate in the middle decades of the eighteenth century including a good number of coffee pots. In February, 1741 Lord Bristol made a direct purchase from Richard Gurney and Company, acquiring 'four Gaudroned silver Dishes weighing 155 ounces 7 d weight at 7s.6d pr oz, ingraving at 5s. each' for £59 5s 3d (see appendix 1).

Though Lord Bristol seems to have favoured chocolate (see cat. 5), others preferred coffee and in 1724 one candidate for the vacant post of housekeeper revealed that she had left a previous employer because 'she must have coffee every morning, and could not but at her own expence'. Lord Bristol was not inclined, however, 'to add that article, where necessary ones already … exceed my income,' so presumably her application was not successful.[3]

1. Heal 1935, p. 51.
2. In the later 1730s Wickes was charging between 5s 6d and 5s 10d per ounce for old plate. See Wickes Ledgers, VAM I 1735–40, ff. 87 (Mr Gash, 2 January 1737/8), 100 (Duchess Dowager of Norfolk, 23 October 1736) and 140 (Captain Duncombe Backwell).
3. Hervey 1894b, vol. 2, p. 373.

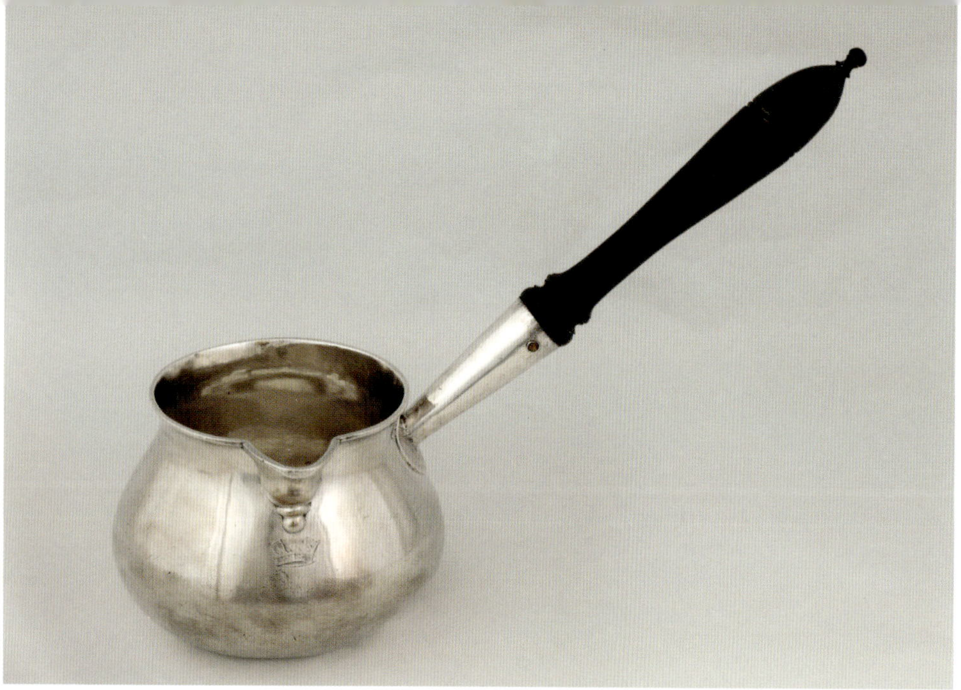

16. Saucepan

Sterling silver / **London** / **1745/6**

MARKS: Very worn marks on underside, lion's head erased, sterling lion, date letter 'K', maker's mark indecipherable.

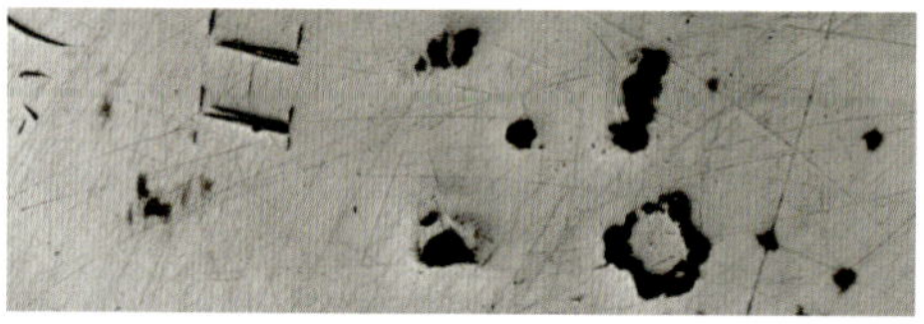

SCRATCHWEIGHT: 'N1 [/] [36] [/] 11'. Almost worn away but confirmed as being 36 oz by the 1811 plate list.
Actual weight: (incl. handle) 1068 g (34 oz, 7 dwt).

MEASUREMENTS: (including handle) h. 29.5 cm (11⅝ in); w. 38.1 cm (15 in); d. 15.6 cm (6⅛ in).

INVENTORY: 852092

PROVENANCE: 1st Earl of Bristol; by descent to the 4th Marquess.

DESCRIPTION: The bulbous circular body is raised, flattened on the base and drawn in at the neck. The cast and applied beak-shaped pouring lip has a double drop beneath and is at right angles to the turned wooden baluster handle which is fixed to the body via a seamed, tapering tubular silver bracket, the junction with the body concealed by a ring of sheet silver.

HERALDRY: On the front of the saucepan, beneath the spout, is engraved the Hervey crest beneath an earl's coronet. This is probably contemporary and is very worn.

This saucepan is of the standard form for the eighteenth century. Its condition suggests that it was used intensively and when Lord Bristol bought it in 1746 he paid for it in part through the exchange of an old pan, presumably itself worn out through use. He paid Peter Rogers of Bury, retail silversmith, £5 8s 4d on 15 March 1746 (see appendix 1) and as the saucepan would have been charged at something like 6s 8d an ounce, based on those supplied to the Duke of Devonshire by George Wickes in 1738,[1] the old pan, which would probably have been credited at 5s 6d, must have weighed just under 24 oz.

1. Wickes Ledgers, VAM 1 1735–40, f. 162.

PART TWO

SILVER OF JOHN, LORD HERVEY (1696–1743) AND MARY LEPEL, LADY HERVEY (1706–68)

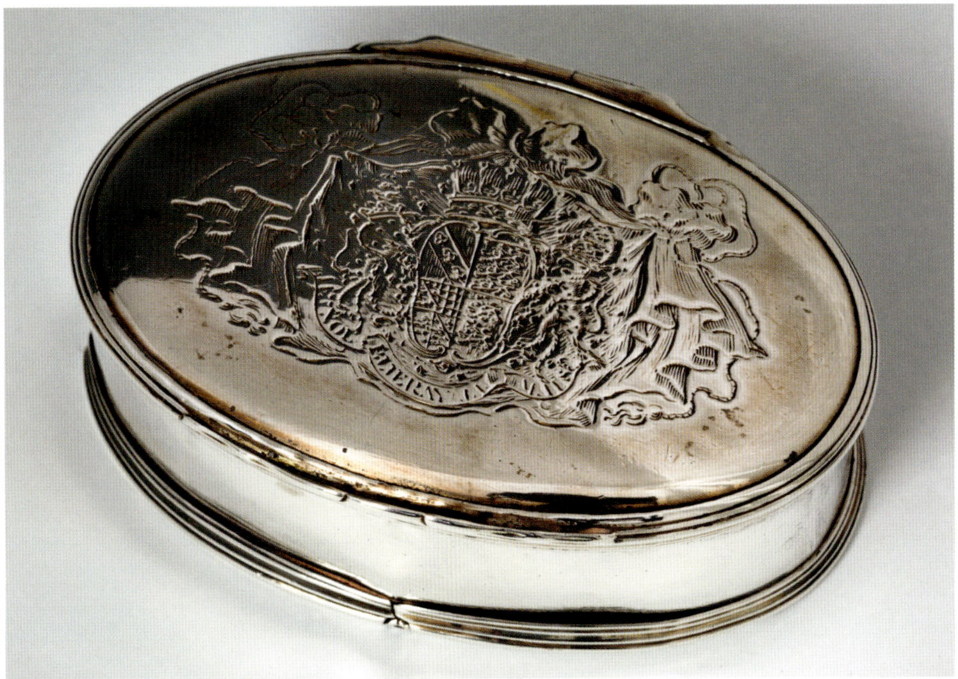

17. **Double snuff box and grater, subsequently nutmeg grater**

Silver / *c.*1730

MARKS: None

SCRATCHWEIGHT: (on the inside of one of the base lids) '2 17'

MEASUREMENTS: h. 2.9 cm (1⅛ in); w. 7.9 cm (3⅛ in); d. 5.4 cm (2⅛ in).

INVENTORY: 852796

PROVENANCE: Probably John, Lord Hervey; by descent to the 4th Marquess of Bristol.

DESCRIPTION: The sides of the oval box are formed from seamed sheet. The top has a protruding five-part pin hinge and a slightly domed, raised cover with an applied moulded lip. The cover opens to reveal a silver (?) grater, domed to conform. Beneath the grater the box is divided by a horizontal strip of silver into two even compartments, these being accessed from the underside through lids opening centrally from a shared flush hinge engraved with a band of stylised flower-heads. The lid and side of one compartment have been cut through at a later date to allow the contents to be dispensed, probably when the box was turned over from use for snuff to nutmeg.

HERALDRY: The cover has been re-engraved *c.*1751 with the quartered shield, supporters and motto of the 2nd Earl of Bristol beneath an earl's coronet, all in an ermine mantling. The engraving is very worn.

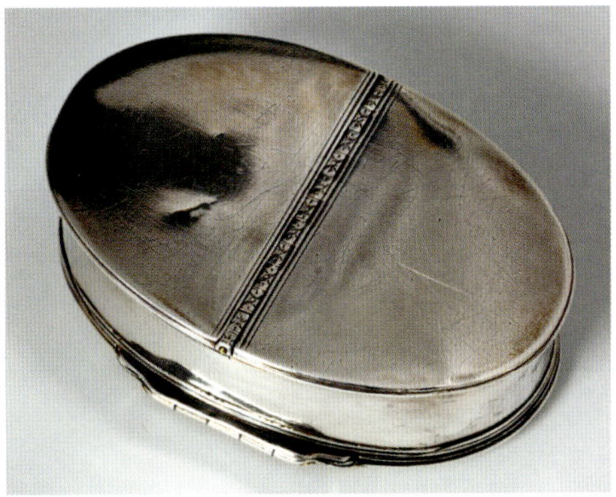

See cat. 2 for a discussion of the evolution in use of this and the other Ickworth snuff/nutmeg grater. When made this box was probably for snuff with the compartmentation allowing two types to be grated.[1] It was intended for both grating and partaking, being turned over to allow access to the two compartments from which pinches could be taken. By 1811 (see appendix 5) the box, which was probably initially acquired by Lord Hervey, was described as being for nutmeg.

1. A very similar snuff box, undated and without its grater, is described in Hughes 1957, p. 183. Several examples of double snuff boxes are in the Lion Collection, though none with a grater as well. See Culme 2015, pp. 120, 123, 150, 166 and 193.

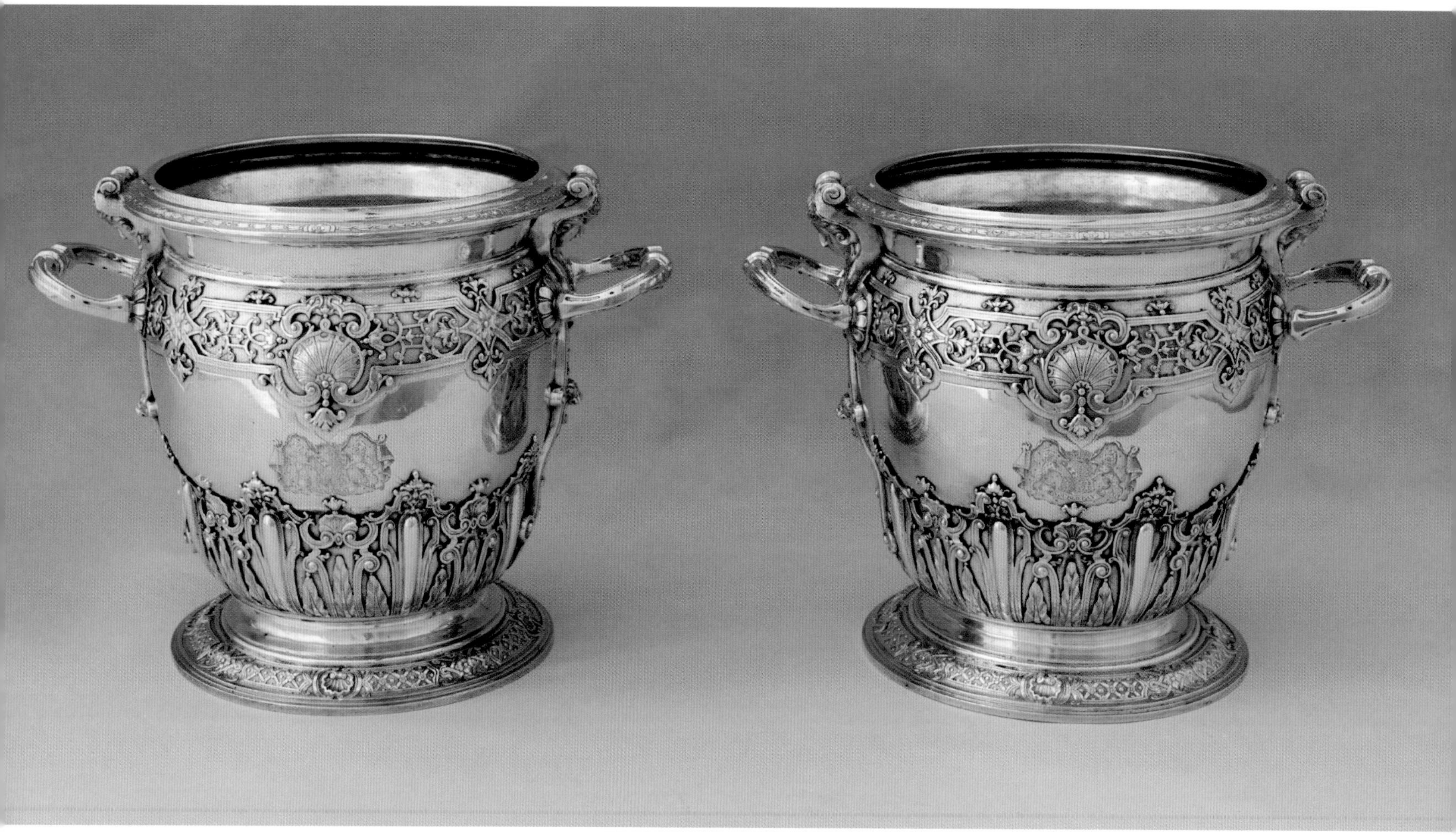

18. **Pair of ice pails**

Probably Britannia silver / **Philip Rollos II, London** / ***c.*1730**

MARKS: Maker's mark 'RO' either side of an anchor in a shield, struck on the underside of each, four times on one and five on the other. This is an unregistered version of Philip Rollos II's first, Britannia mark entered in 1705 (Grimwade 1990, no. 2392), in a shield-shaped rather than octagonal punch.

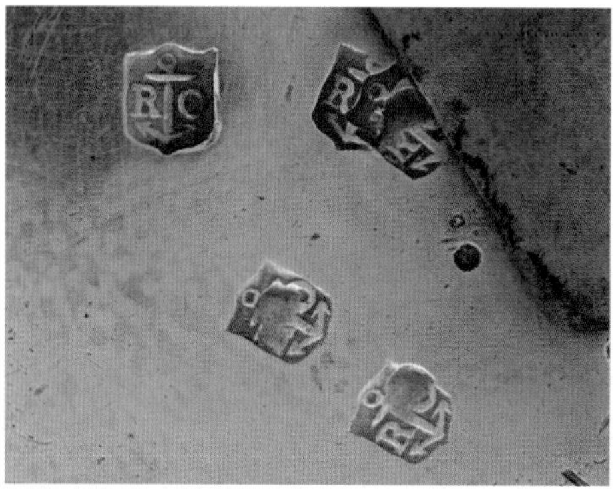

SCRATCHWEIGHTS: '168' and '168=18'

MEASUREMENTS: h. 26.7 cm (10½ in); w. (incl. handles) 34.6 cm (13⅝ in); diam. (at rim) 24 cm (9½ in).

INVENTORY: 852069.1–2

PROVENANCE: Probably John, Lord Hervey; by descent to the 4th Marquess of Bristol.

LITERATURE: Penzer 1957a, II, p. 133, fig. 1; Hernmarck 1977, vol. 1, pp. 140–1; Banister 1980, pp. 792–3, fig. 3; Clayton 1971, p. 328, plate 48.

EXHIBITED: *Queen Charlotte's Loan Exhibition of Old Silver*, Seaford House, London, 1929, cat. 602; *Treasures from National Trust Houses*, Christie's, London, 1957–8, cat. 164 (one); British Council Exhibition of English Silver, 1957–8 (one); Society of the Four Arts, Palm Beach, Florida, 1959 (one); *British Week*, Milan and Frankfurt, 1965; *Silver from National Trust Houses*, Treasurer's House, York Festival, 1969; *Treasures from Country Houses of the National Trust and National Trust for Scotland, Europalia 1973*, Brussels, cat. 116.

DESCRIPTION: The bodies of the ice pails are raised and of circular *bombé* form, the lower part matted and applied with nine-pin ribs and elaborate cast and chased strapwork, shells and lanceolate palm leaves. The pails are pinched-in beneath the rim, the undecorated, everting neck being a separate, seamed piece with the soldered joint disguised by a plain wire. Below the wire is another, broad band of rich strapwork on a matted ground with central shell cartouches on either side. The cast and faceted baluster handles with foliate roses are fixed onto plain strips of silver over the upper strapwork band. Thick lateral straps with lion masks are applied to either side and rise from the foot through the handles to the rim, terminating with classical masks against inward-facing volutes. The rim, which steps in, is cast and chased with bands of husks between rosette medallions. The lower part of the spreading foot is cast and chased with panels of floral trelliswork, strapwork and four sculpted shells in C-scroll cartouches. Both pails are in excellent condition.

HERALDRY: On one side of each pail, between the bands of strapwork, have been re-engraved *c.*1751 the quartered shield, supporters and motto of the 2nd Earl of Bristol in an ermine mantling and beneath an earl's coronet.

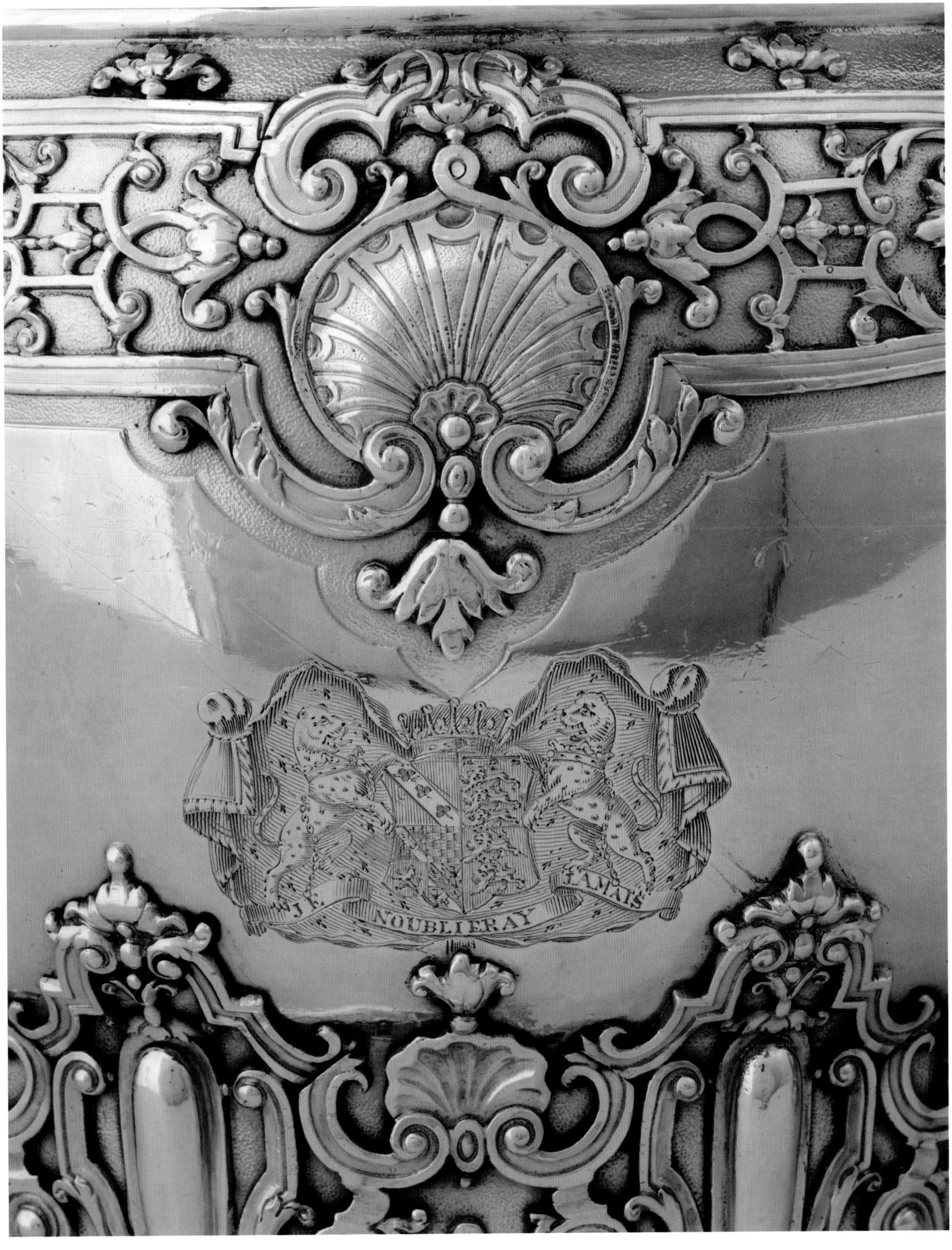
JE
NOUBLIERAY
JAMAIS

These magnificent objects, amongst the finest ice pails to survive from the eighteenth century, are superbly designed and crafted. They were intended for individual bottles of wine and would have been placed on the table after dessert, or in the event of a men's drinking party (fig. 85). From the Jewel Office records it is clear that they were made throughout the eighteenth century, two forming part of the Earl (subsequently Duke) of Marlborough's perquisite plate as Ambassador to the States General in 1701 and a further thirty-nine pairs being supplied to ambassadors, secretaries of state, senior royal dignitaries and Commons speakers up to Lord Macartney's embassy to China in 1792.[1] An average of a pair every two years was being issued in the first three decades of the century and there was then a lull with subsequent peaks of enthusiasm from 1746 to 1763 and from 1782 onwards. In 1750 Benjamin Keene took no less than four to Spain and that became the norm thereafter, with gilding adopted for some from the 1780s.

Ice pails, the name commonly given to these bottle coolers throughout the eighteenth century, scarcely get a mention in the surviving ledgers of George Wickes, an exception being the four in 'Brass Silver'd' for the 1st Lord Montfort in March, 1751.[2] They can never have been universal in the first half of the century even among the highest echelons of the nobility, the 2nd Duke of Montagu, for instance, not possessing any at Montagu House in 1733 or 1746.[3] They were probably most *de rigeur* for those at the heart of politics where lengthy discussions after dinner or in the evening, accompanied by wine, were an essential part of business. The Hervey town house in St James's Square served as a venue for such meetings in the tense months following the dismissal of Marlborough in early 1712, the great Duke being there with Prince Eugene of Savoy in late January and on 2 April closeting himself with the Hanoverian envoy, Count Bothmar, 'and some others of the foreign ministers' following an entertainment given by Lady Hervey.[4] Wine would no doubt have been provided on both occasions though it is not known if the 1st Earl of Bristol had silver or other ice pails.

Given the lack of references to such major pieces of plate in the 1st Earl's accounts and their sophistication of design, it is likely that the Rollos pails at Ickworth were acquired by John, Lord Hervey. They were made when he was entering the inner circle of government as a close associate of Sir Robert Walpole who had his own pair of octagonal pails by William Lukin of 1716.[5] Hervey would have seen these in Walpole's dining parlour, which he frequented, and he would also have known the circular pair by Lewis Mettayer granted to his father's cousin and close friend, Sir Thomas Hanmer, 4th Bt, as Speaker of the House of Commons in 1714.[6] These were the principal models of the first two decades of the century and the shape of the Ickworth pails is an evolution of the circular variety, the first known appearance of which was in a pair by David Willaume of 1700 (fig. 86).[7] By being pinched in more at the base and neck and with their *bombé* curves Rollos created something more sinuous, light and lively. The richness of the bands of cast ornamentation is, as well, given balance and contrast by the smooth, polished midriff. It is a considerably more successful construct than that of the Bute pails of 1728 and 1729 marked by Paul Crespin.[8] These have a pronounced pulvination beneath the neck which makes them look ungainly and squat.

There are clear signs of a connection between the Ickworth pails and the works of Crespin and de Lamerie from around 1730. Most noticeably, the foot, lateral straps and handle roses are of the same pattern as those on the Chesterfield pails of 1727, made by de Lamerie and overstruck by Crespin, who presumably supplied them.[9] The upper band of Rollos's strapwork, in addition, follows the basic form of the engraved borders much employed by de Lamerie in the 1720s and inspired by the published designs of Jean Berain.[10] The close collaboration between de Lamerie and Crespin, who overstruck each other's work,[11] suggests that Rollos worked with one or both of them which may be why there are so few pieces bearing his mark. As to who acted as retailer for the pails, sadly none of Hervey's personal financial papers survive and his account with Hoare's Bank is frustratingly lacking in detail. However, amongst the plate altered by the 2nd Earl of Bristol in the 1750s there are significant numbers of pieces bearing Crespin's mark (see cat. 35-6, 38 and 40) so the probability is that Hervey was supplied by him. The same may well be the case for the 1731 basket (cat. 19).

For the later liners see cat. 108.

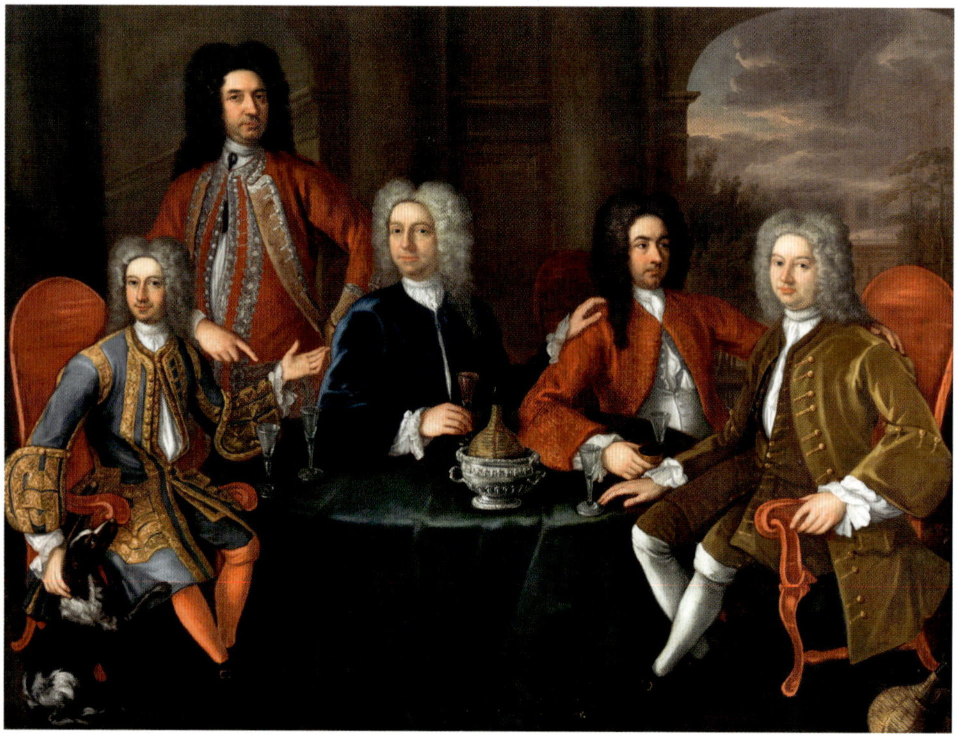

FIG. 85 / *A meeting of the Hell Fire Club, Dublin* by James Worsdale. Oil on canvas: 210 x 275 cm (82⅔ x 108¼ in). National Gallery of Ireland.

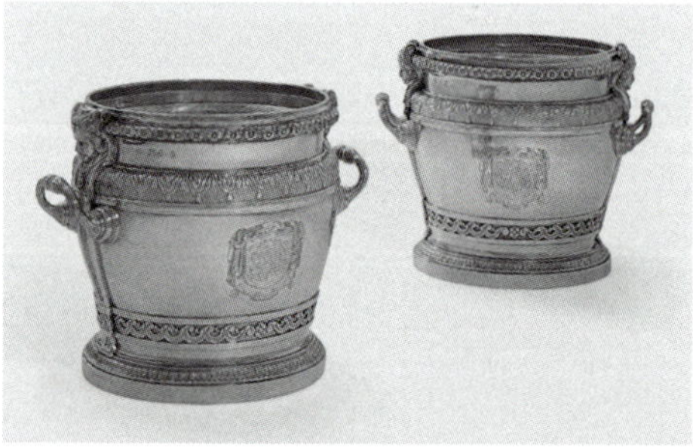

FIG. 86 / Pair of wine coolers by David Willaume I, 1700. Silver: h. 23.2 cm (9⅛ in); weight 7,824 g (251 oz) 12 dwt. Christie's.

1. Jewel Office Delivery Book 1698–1732, ff. 58, 144, 171, 173, 184, 185, 202, 210, 224, 242, 258, 264, 286, 297 and 319; 1732–93, ff. 101, 108, 111, 151, 170, 178, 205, 307, 317, 321, 323 and 341.
2. Unpublished analysis of object types in the first two Wickes ledgers by Elaine Barr, drawn to my attention by Philippa Glanville. For the reference to the silvered pails see Wickes Ledgers, VAM 5 1750–4, f. 12. They cost £16 16s, plus £3 for engraving '8 Coats & supporters in Mantlings'.
3. Murdoch 2006, pp. 44 and 108–9.
4. Hervey 1894b, vol. I, pp. 316 and 321.
5. Metropolitan Museum of Art, acc. no. 68.141.128–9. See Hackenbroch 1963, cat. 43, p. 28, plates 50–51.
6. Jewel Office Day Book 1698–1732, f. 185. Now in the Eton College collection, see Jones 1938, p. 15, plate XI. These are identical to the second pair supplied by the Jewel Office in 1714, to Lord Bingley as Ambassador to Spain, except for the lateral strap on the Bingley pails. Sold Christie's, 7 July 2011, lot 49.
7. Christie's, 3 June 2014, lot 369.
8. Christie's, 3 July 1996, lot 100.
9. V&A, museum no. M.1 to B-1990. See Hare 1990, cat. 49, pp. 90–1.
10. Hartop 1996, pp. 344–5.
11. Hare 1990, p. 90.

19. Bread basket, subsequently dessert basket

Britannia silver, subsequently gilded / Paul de Lamerie, London / 1731/2

MARKS: Fully marked on the underside with maker's mark 'LA' star and closed crown above fleur-de-lis below (third mark, unregistered),[1] lion's head erased, Britannia and date letter 'Q'.

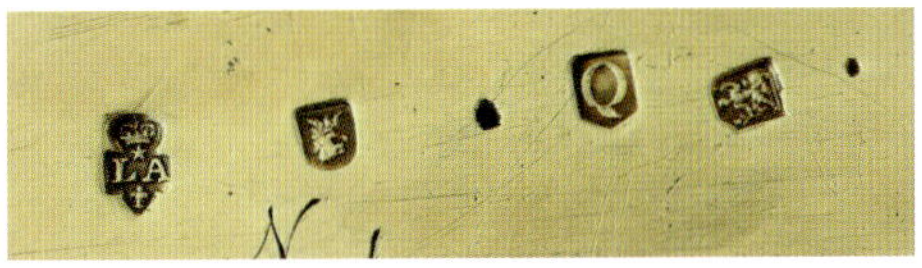

SCRATCHWEIGHT: 'N1 43=13'

MEASUREMENTS: h. 8 cm (3⅜ in); w. (incl. handles) 13¾; d. 27 cm (10⅝ in).

INVENTORY: 852063.1

PROVENANCE: Probably John, Lord Hervey; by descent to the 4th Marquess of Bristol.

LITERATURE: Phillips, 1935, p. 92, plate LXXV; Penzer 1957a, I, pp. 40 and 42, fig. III; Banister, 1980, pp. 792–3, fig. 5; Schroder 1988a, p. 198.

EXHIBITED: *Queen Charlotte's Loan Exhibition of Old Silver*, Seaford House, London, 1929, cat. 584; *Treasures from National Trust Houses*, Christie's, London, 1957–8, cat. 169); Society of the Four Arts, Palm Beach, 1959; *British Week*, Milan and Frankfurt, 1965; *Silver from National Trust Houses*, Treasurer's House, York Festival, 1969, cat. 42; *Treasures from Country Houses of the National Trust and National Trust for Scotland, Europalia 1973*, Brussels, cat. 119.

DESCRIPTION: The body of the basket has been raised from a single sheet to form an oval with a flat base, slightly angled sides and flared rim. The sides and rim are pierced in a graded diaper pattern and chased inside and out to resemble plaited willow-cane basketwork. A corded wire is soldered to the outer edge of the rim. At the angle between the rim and the sides, on the inside face, is a reed-and-tie moulding surmounted by a narrow corded wire. These are soldered against a plain, unpierced band of the body, presumably left to provide strength. The rising loop handles are constructed of three thick wires twisted together with narrow corded wires and terminating in the form of tendrils soldered to the body of the basket at the narrow ends. The rim foot is made up of a seamed strip pierced with open ovals and bounded by reed-and-tie mouldings. The floor of the basket is engraved in a late *Régence* style with trelliswork, shells, scrolls and straps, the outer band being hatched to imply shading.

HERALDRY: The centre of the floor of the basket was re-engraved *c.*1752 with the quartered shield, supporters and motto of the 2nd Earl of Bristol within an ermine mantling and beneath an earl's coronet.

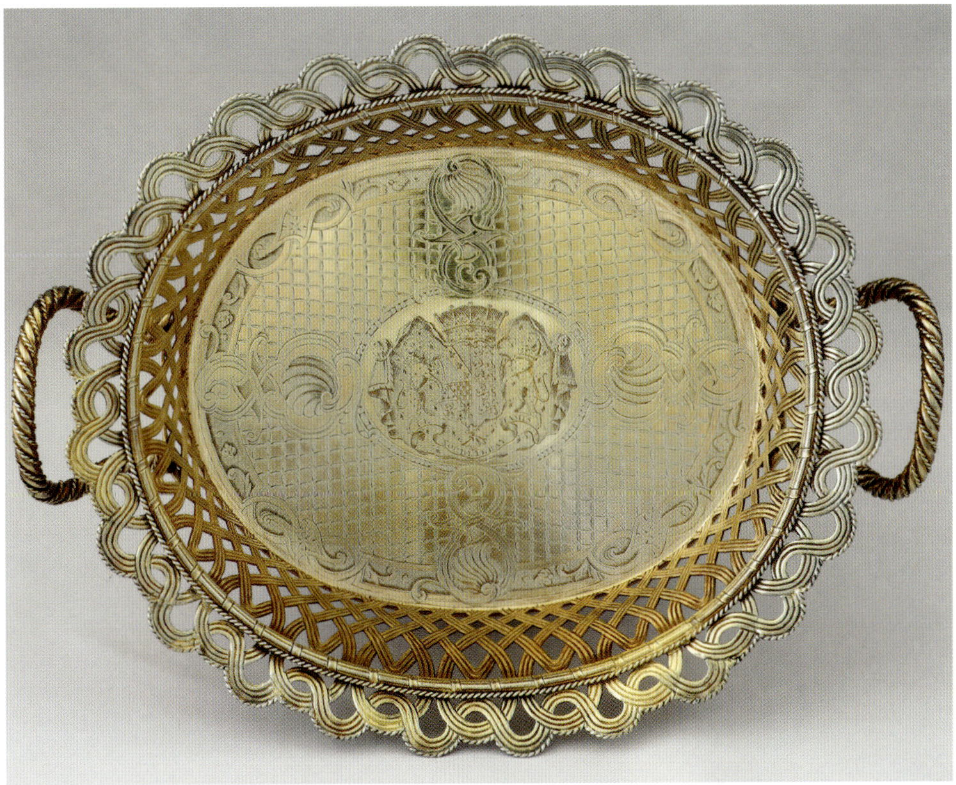

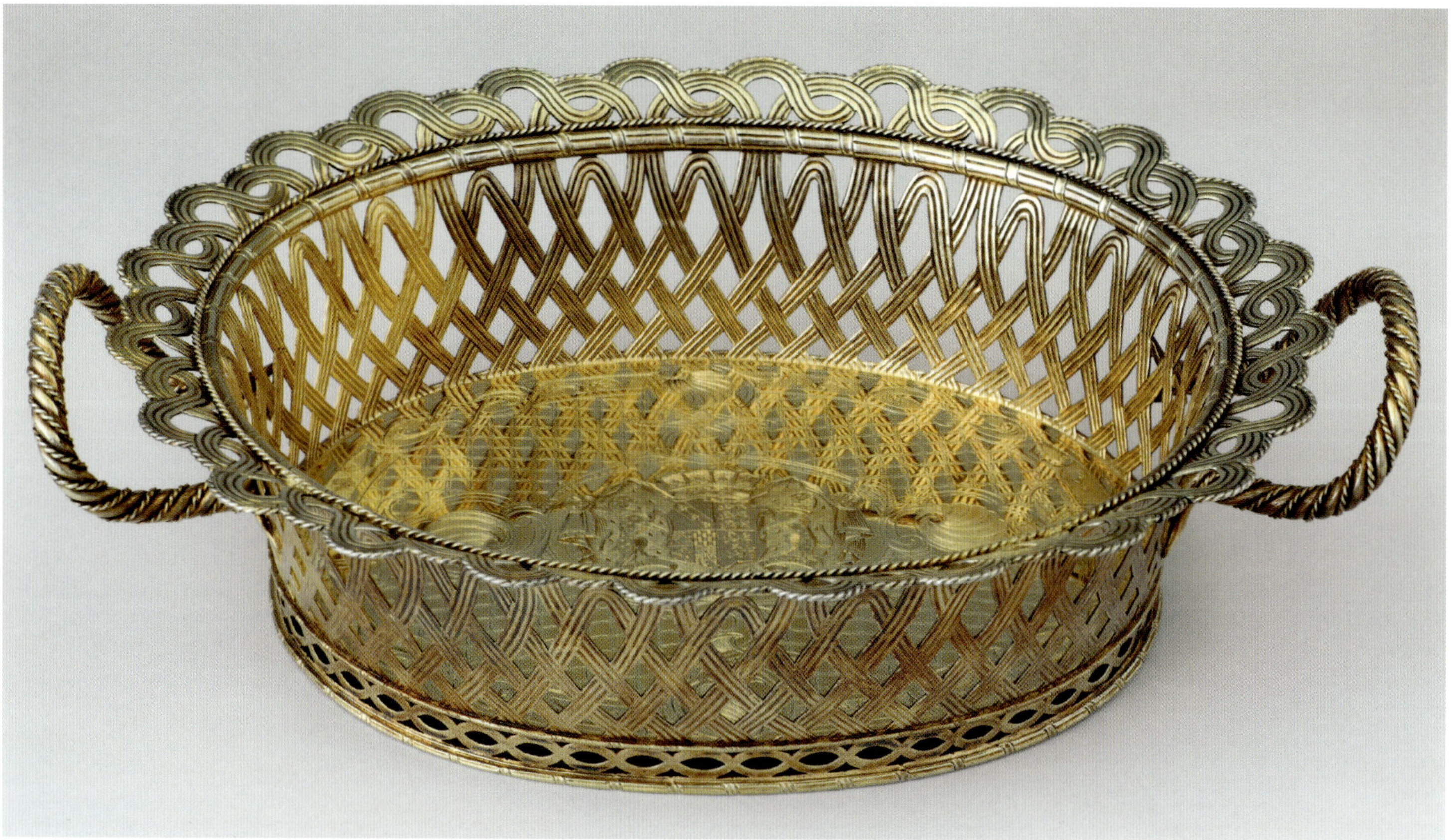

Baskets for the service of bread would have resided on the sideboard and been brought to the table by a footman, the handles allowing the contents to be offered with stability and elegance, as well as with ease of access for the diners. An analysis of the Jewel Office records suggests that they began to be fashionable in silver from the early 1720s, being issued both in pairs and individually.[2] The earliest of these was a pair granted in 1723 as part of his perquisite plate (for an explanation of perquisite plate see chapter 3) to the Hon. Spencer Compton, Speaker of the House of Commons. With a combined weight of just over 204 ounces, each of the Compton baskets would have been around 100 ounces, and as the other four supplied up to 1732 were in the same league the group may well have been of a broadly standard form.[3] Fortunately one at least is known to survive: that granted to the 1st Duke of Dorset as Lord Steward of the Household in 1725.[4] It is by Thomas Farren and is circular with diaper piercing, a chased, spreading foot, a flared rim and a cast and fixed pail handle. This form appears to be an adaptation of the earliest English silver baskets of a comparable size to survive, those of 1597 and 1641 which both bear London marks.[5] They lack carrying handles and are thought to have been intended for fruit which had become fashionable as part of the dessert.[6] The transition of silver baskets from fruit to bread is strikingly illustrated by the plate lists of the Dukes of Montagu. In 1706 two baskets for lemons and one for fruit are recorded, lemons and fruit are again specified in 1709 but in 1733 the only one of the three remaining is described as a 'Bread or Lemon Basket'.[7] Furthermore, the reference to fruit may only have been retained in this instance because of previous recordings and the distinct form of the piece, and all other examples of a comparable scale in the Jewel Office records and the Wickes ledgers, up to the mid-century, are described as bread baskets.[8]

The upright, circular form of the Farren and Elizabethan examples was not exclusive and the Ickworth basket derives from the other principal strain in which natural willow basket-work was accurately mimicked in the pierced and chased sides. This went to the extent of replicating the three canes of willow gathered together in each strap, as still commonly practised today in basketwork.[9] The earliest English examples known to survive are two baskets by John Eckford of 1703 (fig. 86a) and they in turn are comparable to a pair made in Paris in 1657, perhaps suggesting that the form derives from mid-seventeenth-century France, though the paucity of survivals prevents any definitive conclusions being drawn.[10] David Willaume I produced a circular version in 1723 with somewhat clumsy basketwork, and the following year saw a more accomplished rendering, also circular, by Paul de Lamerie.[11] There were numerous subsequent versions, almost exclusively oval, by different makers over the next thirty years, but the pronounced peak occurred in 1731 and the great majority of those produced that year, including the Ickworth basket, bear Lamerie's mark. Even amongst these there are variances: some, for instance, have single, pail handles, others pairs of twisted wire handles, and the basketwork is either rigidly laid out in a perfect diaper or follows a more relaxed, naturalistic pattern with graduated and attenuated lozenges. The latter, which more effectively sustains the illusion, must have been especially difficult to achieve and is the pattern adopted for both the Ickworth basket and its closest comparator from that year, which bears the arms of Sir Robert Walpole and is now in the Gilbert Collection at the V&A.[12] It, though, is half an inch higher and considerably heavier, at 57 oz, 6 dwt.

Unlike the baskets of the mid-1720s, which have plain, polished bases around central armorials, Lamerie's baskets, and those of some other makers, exhibit lavish late-*Régence*

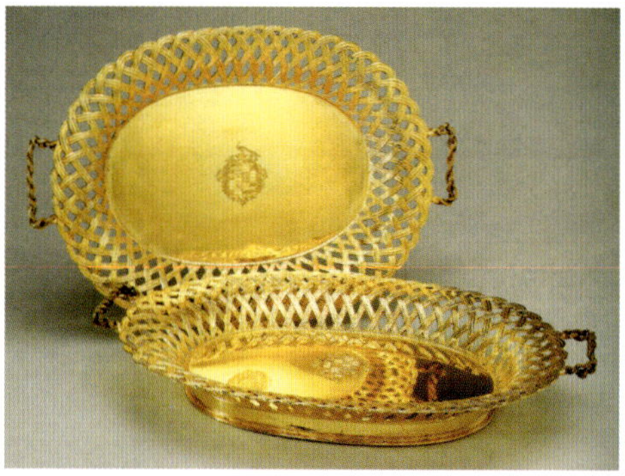

FIG. 86a / Pair of baskets by John Eckford, London, 1703. Silver-gilt: w. 41.2 cm (16¼ in). Sotheby's.

detail, veering towards the rococo, which almost completely fills the field: space is just left for the owner's arms. The Ickworth and Walpole models are, once again, near-identical and given that Lord Hervey was becoming increasingly intimate with Walpole at this time, having thrown in his lot with the administration in 1730 and been appointed Vice-Chamberlain of the Royal Household, it is tempting to see a link. Hervey certainly dined with the First Lord of the Treasury at this time and could well have been inspired by the sight of the new and superbly crafted basket.[13] It is evident anyway from the number of baskets of a comparable form produced in such a short period that the fashion for them spread very rapidly, and being seen at the table of the most powerful subject in the country could only have helped. Much attention has been given to the hand of Lamerie's engraver, who exhibits particular prowess, and both William Hogarth and his master, Ellis Gamble, have previously been suggested. It has now been convincingly argued by Timothy Schroder, however, that it was neither. He has identified a group of engraved plate, including several of these baskets, which has evidence of the same authorship and, in the absence of a name, he has dubbed him the 'Hasell engraver' after the family who acquired a number of the pieces.[14]

The evidence of contemporary plate lists, the Wickes ledgers and the Jewel Office records, together with the fact that silver for the main courses of dinner was almost without exception white, make it highly probable that the Ickworth basket was ungilded when it was acquired. Given its date the first owner could have been either the 1st Earl of Bristol or Lord Hervey, but such a highly fashionable acquisition would seem more likely for the son than the father, particularly given Hervey's intimate connection with both the Court and the Walpole administration. The original armorials do not survive and nor do Lord Hervey's accounts but his father's are more comprehensive (see appendix 1) and they corroborate that he was not the purchaser. Lord Hervey had been accumulating a dinner service over the previous decade and with his additional income of £600 as Vice-Chamberlain he would have been in a good position to continue doing so into the 1730s.

Assuming the basket was Lord Hervey's it would have been inherited on his death in 1743 by his eldest son, George. Following his succession as 2nd Earl in 1751 it would have been sent with the bulk of the family plate to Frederick Kandler to be refashioned and 'done up as new', as George Wickes termed a comprehensive overhaul of old pieces that were to be retained. Given that the basket was of a form still being produced and was intricately decorated, the fact that it was not at the cutting edge of fashion must have been outweighed in Lord Bristol's mind by the considerable monetary saving. A wholly new piece would have cost at least 3 shillings an ounce for fashion, amounting to over £6, whereas 'doing up' might have been as little as 10 shillings, if needed at all.[15] The Earl's ambition was such, however, that he required a prodigious dinner service, and though a single bread basket might have been adequate in a great household in his grandfather's day, it was so no longer. Lord Bristol thus commissioned a copy from Kandler, which bears the date letter for 1752 (cat. 45). It too would have been supplied without gilding and the pair probably stayed in that state for another sixteen years. The addition of two more bread baskets in 1754 (cat. 50), marked by John Robinson and in an entirely different and quite simple fashion, may well have been for everyday use, but in 1768 a further pair of copies of the Lamerie basket was commissioned from Kandler and it was probably at this point that the complete set of four was gilded and turned over to use as dessert baskets.[16]

1. Hare 1990, p. 29.
2. Jewel Office delivery book, 1698–1732.
3. Ibid., fos. 218, 264, 271, 286 & 300. The Compton pair weighed 182 oz, 10 dwt, to which 21 oz, 18 dwt, were added, perhaps in the form of handles. Three of the others were around 94 oz and the fourth was 77 oz.
4. Hartop 1996, cat. 7, pp. 94–7. It passed by descent with Knole in Kent until being sold at Christie's, London, 20 May 1987, lot 172.
5. The 1597 basket was sold at Christie's, London, 25 November 2008, lot 53. The 1641 basket is in the Metropolitan Museum, New York, acc. no. 68.141.60.
6. Glanville 1990, p. 220; Bimbenet-Privat and Mitchell 2003, pp. 50–51
7. NRO Montagu Papers MH2, 'An Acct. of the Plate', 21 November 1706, and MH6, 'His Grace the late Duke of Montague's Plate Weighed and Valued by Geo. Lewis', 28 March 1709. The 1733 inventory of Montagu House, including plate, is included in Murdoch 2006, pp. 27–48. As the 1709 plate list indicates that of the two baskets then present the one for lemons was 'Old Sterling' and that for fruit 'New', or Britannia, the latter must be that by George Lewis, *c.*1700, now in the Clark Art Institute, Williamstown (see Wees 1997, cat. 99, pp. 179–81) and have been the sole survivor in 1733.
8. Jewel Office delivery books, 1698–1732 and 1732–93. Wickes Ledgers 1735–51
9. See for instance the products of The Bengal Basket Company, http://www.bengalbasket.co.in/willow-basket-2586440.html.
10. John Eckford baskets: Sotheby's, London 10 July 1990, lot 399 and Christie's 12 June 2002, lot 112. These are silver-gilt but are not likely to have been gilded when supplied. French baskets, 1657: Christie's, Geneva, 13 May 1981, lot 159.
11. David Willaume basket: Christie's, London, 6 March 1991, lot 136. Lamerie 1724 baskets: one of the pair, Christie's, New York, 22 April 1998, lot 6, the other, Minneapolis Institute of Art, Acc. no. 68.16.1.
12. Schroder 1988b, cat. no. 49, pp. 200–3 and Hartop 2013, pp. 40–41.
13. Halsband 1973, pp. 94–7.
14. Schroder 2009, pp. 216–7 and 666–9.
15. Wickes Ledgers 1735–54. The new baskets recorded up to 1740 range from 9s. to 10s. per oz, excepting that for the Prince of Wales billed on 1 May 1736 at just under 11s 5d per ounce. The metal was being charged at between 5s 6d and 6s per ounce, thus fashion was at least 3s.
16. Sir Benjamin Keene, Lord Bristol's predecessor as ambassador at Madrid, made a distinction between his wrought plate for dining in state and that of plain form 'for every day's use.' Lodge 1933, p. 240.

20. Pair of tea canisters

Silver-gilt
Christian Hillan, London / Sterling, 1738/9

MARKS: Both fully marked on the underside with date letter 'C', leopard's head, lion passant and maker's mark 'CH' with a pellet below and a leaf above (Grimwade 1990, no. 326).

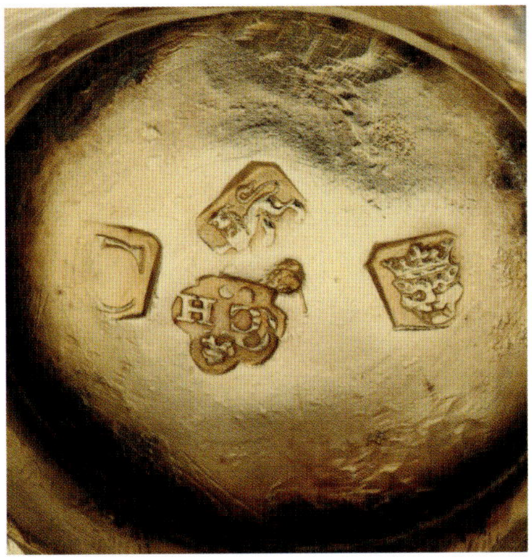

SCRATCHWEIGHTS: None.
Actual weights: 329 g (10 oz, 12 dwt); 335 g (10 oz, 15 dwt)

MEASUREMENTS: h. 15.9 cm (6¼ in); diam. 9.2 cm (3⅝ in).

INVENTORY: 852066

PROVENANCE: Probably John, Lord Hervey; by descent to the 4th Marquess.

LITERATURE: Penzer 1957b, I, p. 43, fig. IX; Banister 1980, p. 793.

EXHIBITED: Society of the Four Arts, Palm Beach, Florida, 1959; *Ideal Home Exhibition*, London, 1960; *Silver from National Trust Houses*, Treasurer's House, York Festival, 1969.

DESCRIPTION: The inverted pear-shaped bodies are raised and have cast floral swags hung from bearded and behatted masks on matted grounds with chased additional foliage, shells and husks. Below are swirling flutes and attenuated palm leaves, alternating, and above is ruffling, all being chased. The raised and applied domed shoulders are chased with grotesque masks breathing fire and the necks, over which the lids fit, are seamed and applied. The plain sleeve necks of the lids are seamed, and capped by raised domes with foliate chasing perhaps intended to represent steam. The knop finials are cast and chased on top with a stylised flower. Bands of chased shells and foliate strapwork on matted grounds decorate the cast feet.

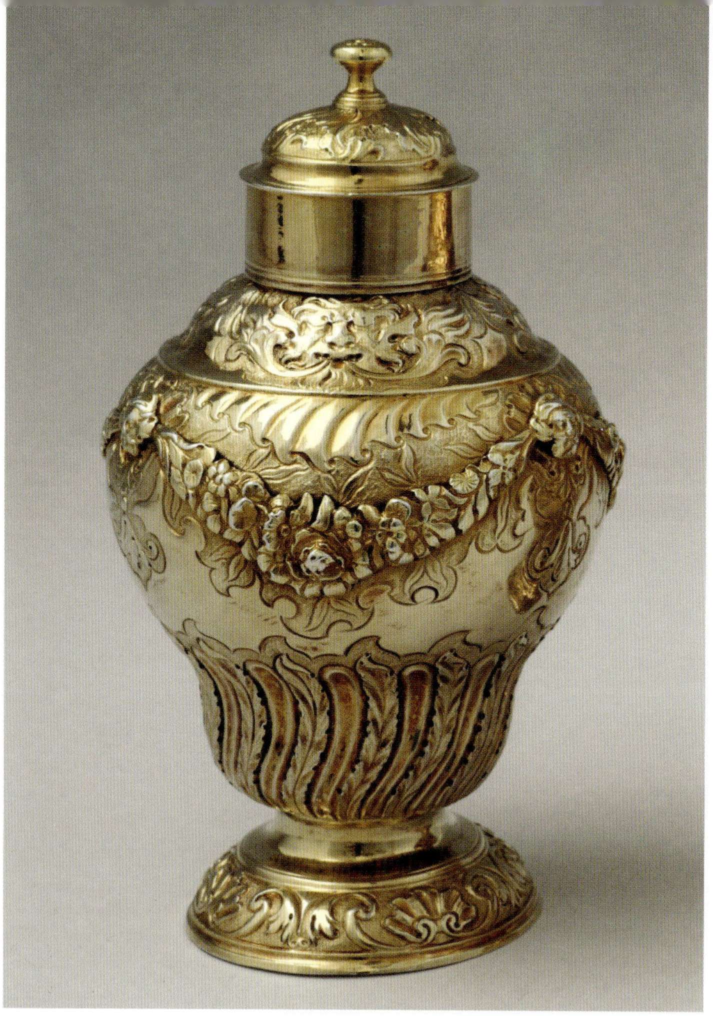

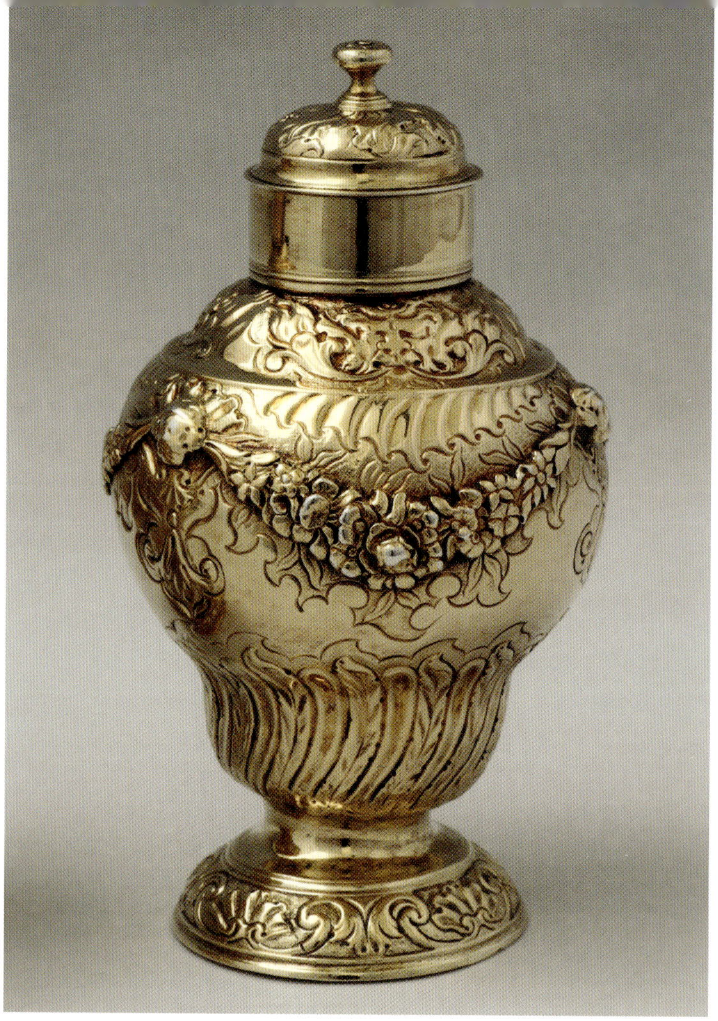

In spite of being active for less than a decade after entering his first mark in 1736, Christian Hillan produced a relatively wide range of wares and seems to have had a significant output. It is, however, his fantastical decorative style, particularly on tea silver, that marks him out; quite unlike anything being produced at the time and in some elements almost reminiscent of the Renaissance. In addition to being a highly skilled chaser, he clearly had a vivid imagination and a wide range of sources and although he produced many tea canisters of the same basic form as these, no two pairs are exactly the same.[1] His distinctiveness could be the result of a Scandinavian origin, suggested by Arthur Grimwade.[2] Though joyous, his schemes of decoration are not always entirely coherent, but in the case of these canisters he has produced something very successful, and also playful, with the allusion to boiling water in the splendid fire-breathing grotesque masks chased beneath the necks. Others of his works in public collections, similarly exuberant in their decoration, include a covered jug, also of 1738, in the Museum of Fine Arts, Boston and a cream boat in the Ashmolean Museum, the purpose of the latter alluded by the cow and calf in its chased decoration.[3]

Pairs of tea canisters were often sold with covered sugar boxes and contained in an exotic wood casket with silver mounts.[4] Most of the other elements of the tea equipage could also be provided in silver – tea spoons, sugar tongs, strainer spoons, slop basins, tea pots plus waiters to place them on, tea kettles, cream ewers and, to contain the whole ensemble other than the kettle, large salvers or tables. All these pieces appear in the ledgers of George Wickes, provided individually or in groups such as that supplied to Mrs Fellowes in March, 1736:

To a tea pott & waiter Carved 19[oz]-9[dwt]
[at] 8[s]/ £7-16
To Handle & graving £0-10-0
To six TeaSpoons Tongs & Strainer
3[oz]-4[dwt] £2
To a fluted Cream boat 5[oz]-8[dwt] £2-16
To a Slop Bason 11[oz]-3[dwt] [at] 7/6 £4-3
To a Sugardish & cover 11[oz]-2[dwt]
[at] 7/6 £4-3
To graving 4 Coats [of arms] £0-10-0[5]

It seems, however, that silver did not dominate at Ickworth and St James's Square in the eighteenth century, beyond the tea kettle (cat. 14), tea tables (cat. 58) and tea spoons. In the time of the 1st Earl all the other items may well have been in Oriental porcelain, numerous purchases being recorded in his accounts in the decades around 1700. The 2nd Earl added substantial quantities of Meissen, Chelsea and Sèvres including tea pots and stands, sugar dishes, slop basins and cream and milk pots.[6] As no porcelain canisters are listed those by Hillan must have been used alongside such pieces as the Sèvres tea cups and saucers 'Elegantly Enamelled with flowers and richly finish'd in burnish'd Gold'.[7] In that context it makes sense that the canisters are not plain silver, though the current gilding is later as there is significant wear beneath its surface. The canisters were, for some reason, omitted from the 1811 plate list but that must have been a mistake as they appear in the next reckoning, drawn up on 15 April 1826, and are not noted as being additions.

1. See, for instance the pairs sold at Sotheby's, 26 February 1981, lot 179 and 14 March 1996, lot 147. They and the Ickworth pair share the cast swags hung from masks but the chasing varies significantly.
2. Grimwade 1990, p. 546.
3. Hartop 1996, cat. 73, pp. 304–5 and Schroder 2009, cat. 148, pp. 384–5.
4. See for instance that in the Ashmolean Museum, Schroder 2009, cat. 305, pp. 794–5. The caskets might also contain other elements of the equipage such as tea spoons and slop basins.
5. Wickes Ledgers, VAM 1 1735–40, f. 19, 20 March 1736. Mrs Fellows was probably Mary Martin, widow of the enormously wealthy merchant, William Fellowes of Eggesford in Devon.
6. Bristol accounts 1688–1742 and TNA, C 103/174 Hervey – v – Bristol 1762–79, 'An Inventory of the Rt. Honble the Earl of Bristol's China taken in St. James's Square ye eighteenth July 1765'. See Ferguson 2011 for a comprehensive analysis of the evidence for Lord Bristol's porcelain.
7. TNA, C 103/174 Hervey – v – Bristol 1762–79, 'An Inventory of China belonging to the Earl of Bristol – taken the 5th day of May 1775'.

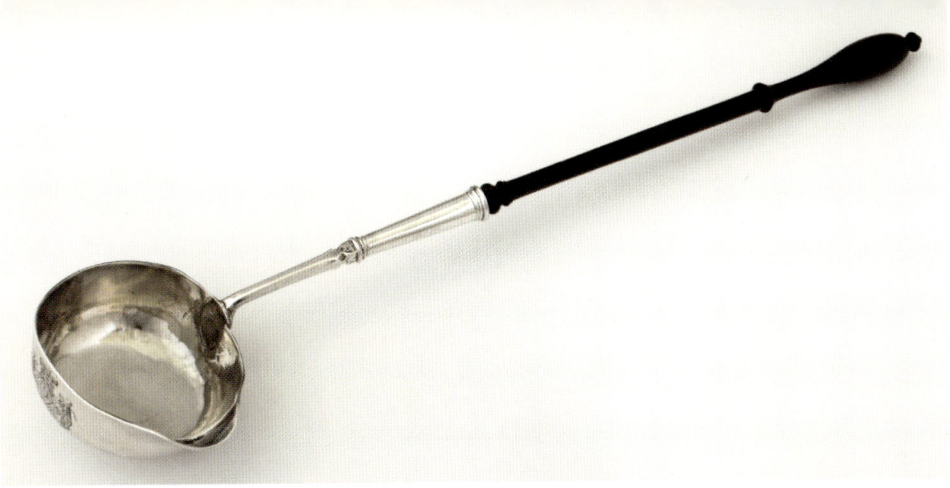

21. Punch ladle

Sterling silver / Louis Laroche, London / 1738/9 / Wooden handle

MARKS: On underside of bowl, date letter 'C', leopard's head, lion passant and maker's mark 'LL' with lion below and crown above (Grimwade 1990, no. 1941).

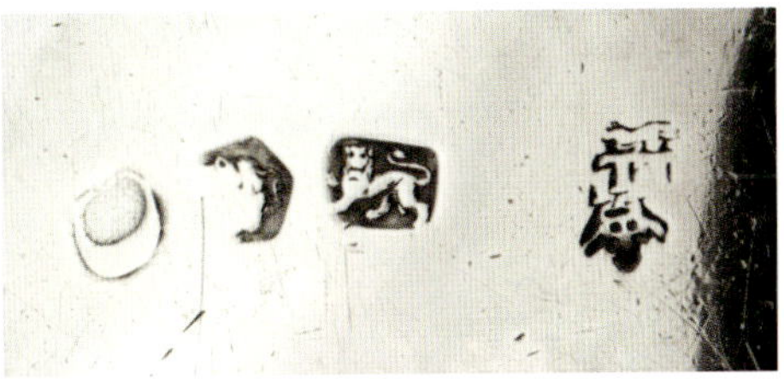

SCRATCHWEIGHT: none. Not weighed because of the handle.

MEASUREMENTS: h. (of bowl) 2.9 cm (1⅛ in); w. (with lip) 7.6 cm (3 in); l. (incl. handle) 35.2 cm (13⅞ in).

INVENTORY: 852192

PROVENANCE: Mary Lepel, Lady Hervey; by descent to the 4th Marquess.

DESCRIPTION: The ovoid bowl is raised and has a shaped pouring lip to one side. A silver, faceted stem is soldered to the bowl at right angles to the lip and at its other end joined to a seamed tube with cast, moulded terminals. The turned wooden handle is fitted into the tube of the stem. The bowl is distorted and slightly split at the junction with the stem.

HERALDRY: The front of the bowl has been engraved *c.*1744 with the lozenge of arms and motto of Mary Lepel, Lady Hervey as a widow in an ermine mantling and beneath a baron's coronet.

Early-eighteenth-century punch ladles, which are marked out by their plain bowls, single pouring lips and turned wooden handles, are comparatively rare survivals.[1] This one could have been associated with either a silver or a ceramic bowl (fig. 87), there being no evidence either way. The 1st Earl of Bristol is known to have purchased 'a large china punch-bowl', paying £3 5s for it 'with a large jarr & two white cupps for dear wife' on 1 March 1690.[2] Lady Hervey probably acquired the ladle second-hand following Lord Hervey's death, when the family plate, including that bought by her husband, went to their eldest son along with the St James's Square house. On her death in 1768 it would have passed, with the rest of her plate, to the 2nd Earl.[3]

1. Pickford 1983, p. 188.
2. Hervey 1894a, p. 139.
3. SRO, HA 507 May 10, Probate copy of the Will of Mary, Lady Hervey. Written 28 May 1768; codicil 28 May 1768; proven 15 September 1768.

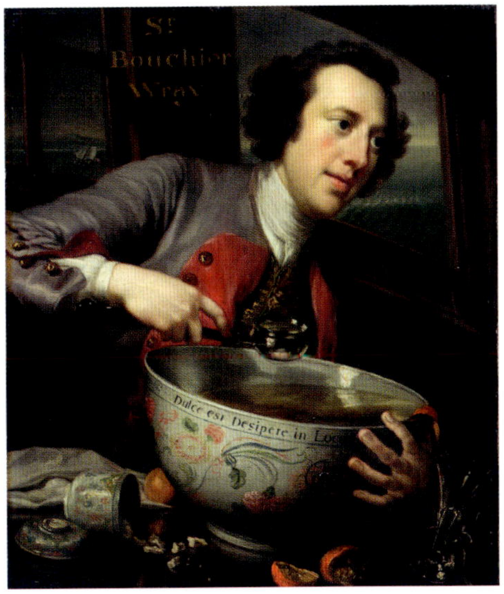

FIG. 87 / *Sir Bourchier Wrey, 6th Bt* by George Knapton, 1744. Oil on canvas: 73 x 61 cm (29 x 24 in). Society of Dilettanti, London.

22. Coffee pot

Sterling silver, gilt
Frederick Kandler, London / 1762/3

MARKS: Fully marked on the underside with maker's mark 'FK' in italics beneath a fleur-de-lis (Grimwade 1990, no. 691), lion passant, date letter 'G'. The bezel of the lid is marked with the lion passant only.

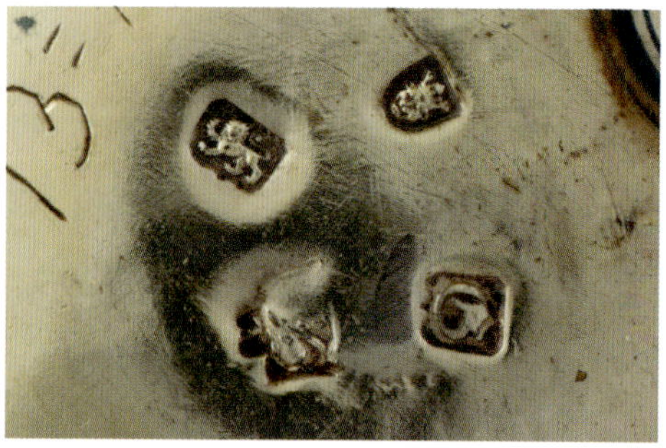

SCRATCHWEIGHT: '13=11'

MEASUREMENTS: h. 24.4 cm (9⅝ in); w. (incl. handle) 13.3 cm (5¼ in); diam. 11.4 cm (4½ in).

INVENTORY: 852072

PROVENANCE: Mary Lepel, Lady Hervey; 2nd Earl of Bristol; by descent to the 4th Marquess.

EXHIBITED: Society of the Four Arts, Palm Beach, Florida, 1959; *Ideal Home Exhibition*, London, 1960.

DESCRIPTION: The elongated pear-shaped body, which is raised, splays towards the rim and has an applied, beak-shaped spout, also raised. The flattened base has an applied and seamed foot ring and the handle is formed of a curved strip of sheet silver, wickered. A five-part pin hinge is fixed to the handle. The domed cover is raised and has a cast and chased gadroon rim, a seamed bezel and a cast baluster finial.

HERALDRY: The contemporary engraving on the front of pot, beneath the spout, shows the motto and arms in a lozenge of Lady Hervey as a widow in an ermine mantling beneath a baron's coronet.

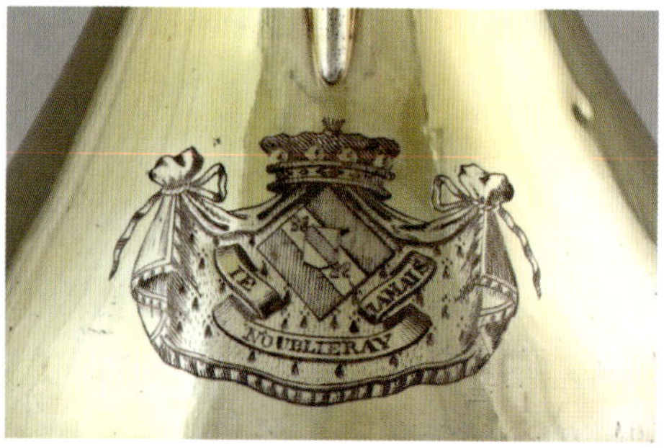

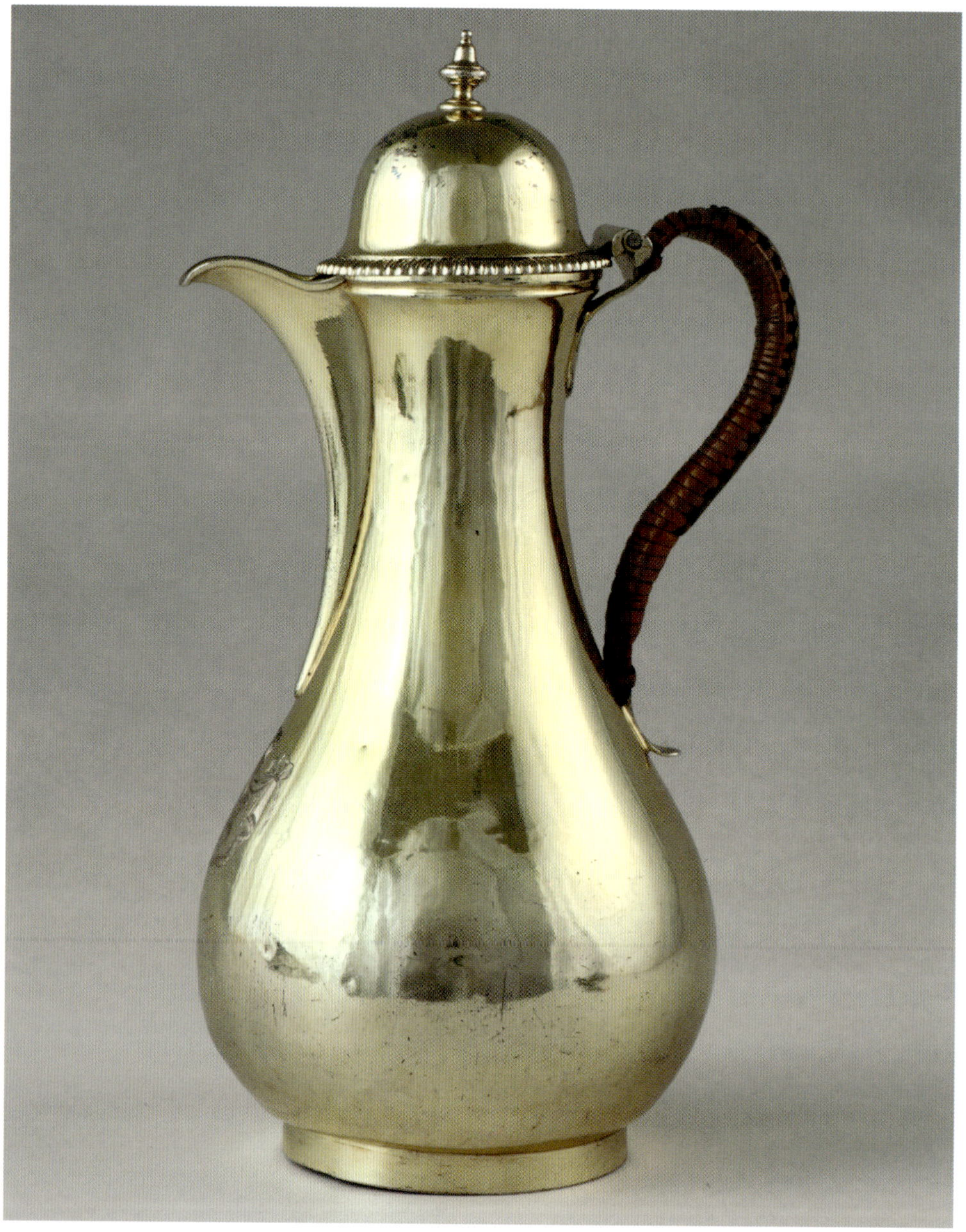

Jugs for hot water are rarely if ever mentioned in the Wickes ledgers, apart from those associated with shaving, and they are also absent from the 1811 Bristol plate list. There are not even examples, again excepting shaving ewers, amongst the prodigious collections of the 2nd Earl of Warrington at Dunham Massey and the 1st Duke of Chandos at Cannons, between which most silver objects in domestic use are represented.[1] Many of the vessels identified as hot-water jugs in recent years, including this one, are likely to have been coffee pots, which this is recorded as in 1874.[2]

The pear-shaped body reflects the French form of the late seventeenth century which had persisted on the Continent but was rarely employed in England again until the 1750s. It may well have appealed to Lady Hervey as an avowed Francophile. The coffee pot was either bought with cash or it was from stock and formed part of Lady Hervey's last order to Frederick Kandler, whom she had been patronising since the early 1750s. Her bank account with Goslings reveals that there were no payments to Kandler in the mid-1760s but that she paid him £34 on 9 July 1768, just under two months before her death.[3] That would have been enough for about 90 ounces of silver at 7s 8d, or less if many of the pieces were gilt, as is the coffee pot.

This is probably the gilt coffee pot listed in the 1811 plate list (appendix 5) as weighing 12 ounces, an allowance having been made for the handle. It is recorded with its scratchweight in the 1874 plate list.[4]

1. See Lomax and Rothwell 2006, pp. 167–183 and Jenkins 2005, pp. 121, 125 and 140–8 for the 1750/54 and 1725 plate lists of Dunham Massey and Cannons.
2. Bristol plate list 1874.
3. Goslings ledgers, 130/41, f. 404.
4. Bristol plate list 1874.

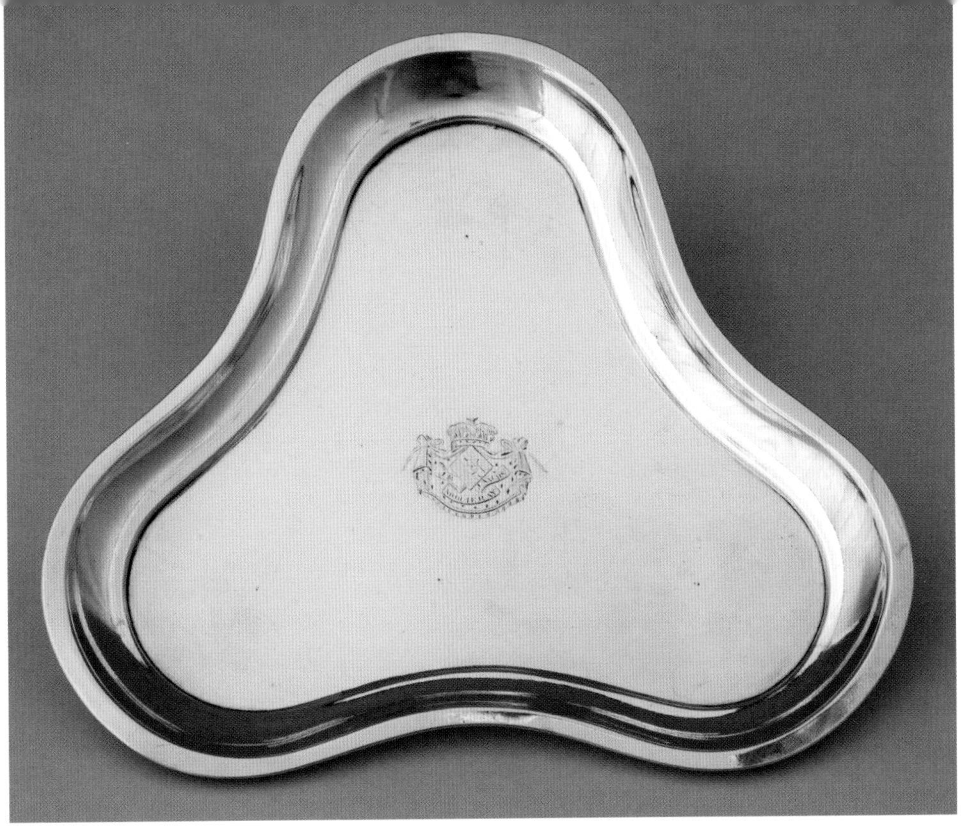

23. **Kettle waiter**

Sterling silver / Frederick Kandler, London / 1764/5

MARKS: Fully marked on the underside with maker's mark 'FK' in italics beneath a fleur-de-lis (Grimwade 1990, no. 691), date letter 'J', lion passant and leopard's head.

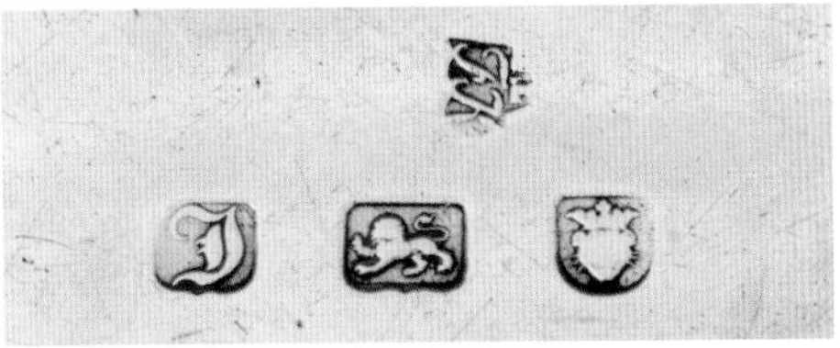

SCRATCHWEIGHT: none.
Actual weight: 184 g (5 oz, 18 dwt)

MEASUREMENTS: w. 18.5 cm (7¼ in); h. 1.3 cm (½ in).

INVENTORY: 2900049

PROVENANCE: Mary Lepel, Lady Hervey; 2nd Earl of Bristol by whom probably gifted to another member of the family; Koopman Rare Art; purchased 2012 by the National Trust through Christopher Hartop for £5,500 with funds from gifts and bequests and a substantial contribution from the Chelmsford National Trust Centre.

DESCRIPTION: The trefoil-shaped waiter is raised and has a plain, concave rim with a flat lip. There are abrasions in each lobe of the stand, caused by the feet of the frame of a kettle.

HERALDRY: The contemporary engraving in the centre of the waiter shows the arms in a lozenge and motto of Lady Hervey as a widow in an ermine mantling beneath a baron's coronet.

The unusual trefoil shape is an evolution from the triangular kettle waiters popular from the 1730s to the 1750s (see cat. 25).[1] The associated tea kettle and lamp are not known to survive nor is whether they pre-existed or were supplied at the same time. The waiter may have been from stock and formed part of Lady Hervey's final purchase from Frederick Kandler (see cat. 22).

1. A kettle waiter of a more attenuated trefoil form, by William Peaston, 1755, was sold at Christie's, 5/7/2005, lot 481.

24. Tumbler

Silver / Henry Allain (?), Paris / 1755/6

MARKS: Marked under base with a crowned 'A' between palm and laurel branches for Paris, warden's mark of a crowned 'P' for 1755/6 and a mis-struck maker's mark, possibly that of Henry Allain (Nocq 1926–31, vol. 1, p. 7), a fleur-de-lis crowned, two grains, the letters 'HA' and an orb.

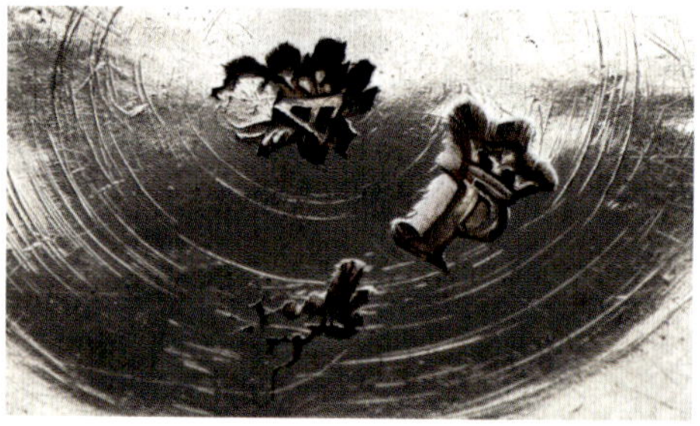

SCRATCHWEIGHT: '1=18'

MEASUREMENTS: h. 5.4 cm (2⅛ in); diam. (at rim) 6.7 cm (2⅝ in).

INVENTORY: 852089

PROVENANCE: Mary Lepel, Lady Hervey; probably by descent to the 4th Earl of Bristol and removed by him to Ireland, thereby passing to the Bruce family; probably reacquired by Theodora, Marchioness of Bristol.

EXHIBITED: *Treasures from National Trust Houses*, Christie's, London, 1957–8, cat. 174.

DESCRIPTION: The raised tumbler is of more upright form than the norm and has a dimpled base. Two parallel lines are engraved beneath the slightly flaring rim which has an applied moulding.

HERALDRY: The contemporary engraving on the side of the tumbler shows the motto and arms in a lozenge of Lady Hervey as a widow, in an ermine mantling and beneath a baron's coronet.

Tumblers were primarily used for spirits such as brandy and were often part of the travelling equipment of the wealthy in the eighteenth century.[1] As such they were for personal use and this one would have accompanied Lady Hervey during the latter part of her active and sociable widowhood. She was an enthusiastic Francophile and resided in Paris for long periods in the first half of the 1750s. It must have been during the last of these sojourns, which began in mid-May 1755, that Lady Hervey commissioned, or was given, this tumbler.[2] The engraving of the arms is noticeably more assured than that on her English pieces though the foreign hand of the craftsmen is revealed by his depiction of the finial of the coronet's velvet cap as a ball rather than a tuft. The tumbler does not appear in any of the nineteenth-century plate lists and is likely to have been among the substantial quantity of family objects retrieved by Theodora, Marchioness of Bristol, many of them from the Bruces of Downhill in County Londonderry who had inherited from the 4th Earl.

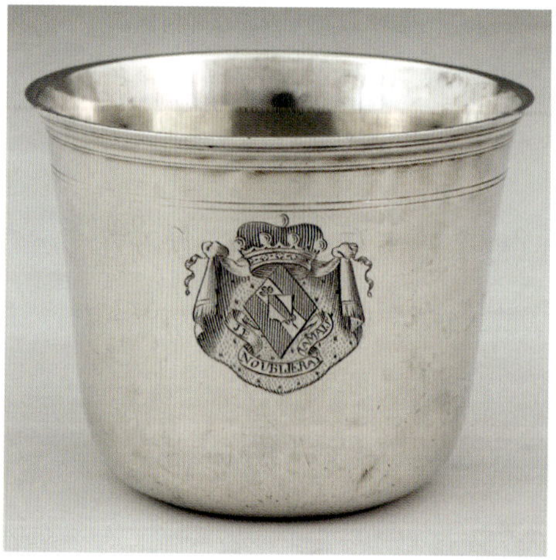

1. Schroder 2009, p. 64 and Hughes 1957, p. 115.
2. Croker 1821, p. 211.

PART THREE

SILVER OF GEORGE WILLIAM HERVEY, 2ND EARL OF BRISTOL (1721–75)

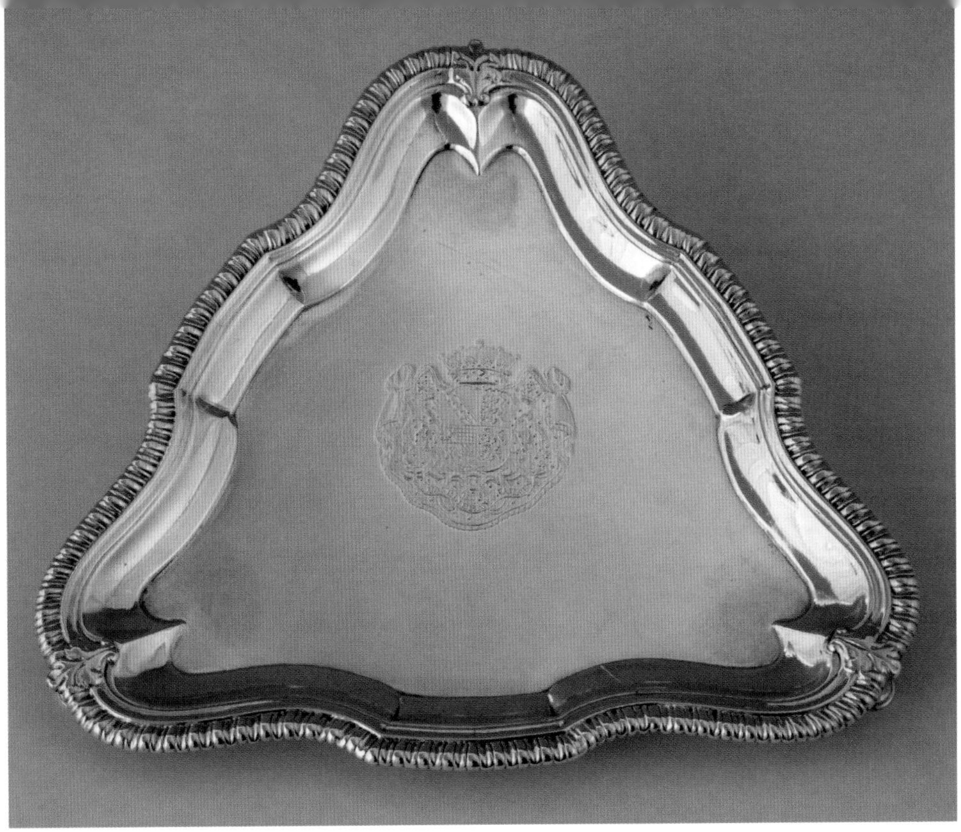

25. **Kettle waiter**

Sterling silver / Frederick Kandler, London / 1745/6

MARKS: Fully marked on the underside with maker's mark 'FK' in italics beneath a fleur-de-lis (Grimwade 1990, no. 691), lion passant, leopard's head and date letter 'k'.

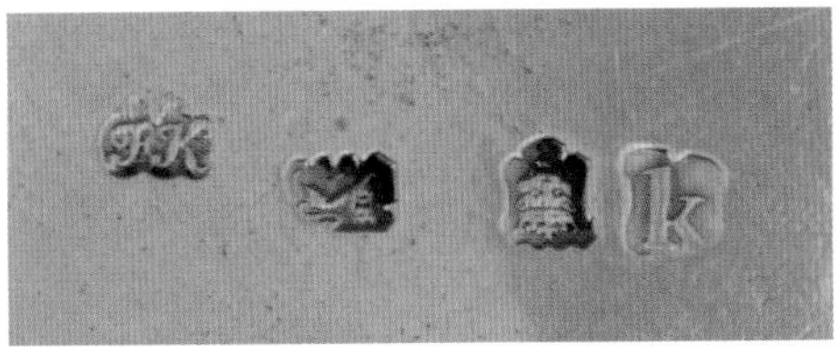

SCRATCHWEIGHT: '13=18'

MEASUREMENTS: h. 1.9 cm (¾ in); w. 22.9 cm (9 in).

INVENTORY: 852071.4

PROVENANCE: Probably acquired by the 2nd Earl of Bristol; by descent to the 4th Marquess.

LITERATURE: Penzer 1957a, II, p. 134.

EXHIBITED: Society of the Four Arts, Palm Beach, Florida, 1959; *Silver from National Trust Houses*, Treasurer's House, York Festival, 1969.

DESCRIPTION: The shaped triangular waiter with incurved corners is raised with a cast gadroon border enriched by leaves at the terminal points of the triangle. It has three cast hoof feet.

This waiter, which is associated with the 1726 kettle and lamp by Pierre Le Cheaube (cat. 14), was probably part of the large order given to Frederick Kandler by the 2nd Earl of Bristol in 1751. Although the piece was made in 1745 the arms do not seem to have been re-engraved so must date from the Earl's accession six years later.

Triangular waiters for kettles became fashionable in the 1730s, with large numbers appearing in the early ledgers of George Wickes.[1] They were perfectly suited to the three-legged kettle stands of the period and the shaped gadroon border of this one conformed to the dishes and plates of the Earl's dinner service. Waiters were often provided for vessels associated with hot water, presumably with the practical intention of containing drips and reducing the risk of overturning. The borders are usually deeper than those intended to be used by a footman to serve, as when delivering wine glasses to the table during dinner (see cat. 51). The survival of some pairs and groups of triangle waiters suggests that they were not just employed for kettles. Three from the fine silver of the Lords King, two by John White of 1734 and a third by Robert Abercromby of 1740, have elaborate flat-chased borders which cannot have been intended to be interrupted by the feet of a lamp frame.[2]

1. Wickes Ledgers, VAM 1–3 1735–50.
2. Christie's, 12 May 1993, lots 148–9. Another pair, by Richard Rugg, 1754, was sold at Sotheby's Olympia, 6 June 2002, lot 129.

26. **Table spoon**

Sterling silver / **Dru Drury I, London** / **1745/6**

MARKS: Fully marked on the stem with maker's mark 'DD' (Grimwade 1990, no. 455), lion passant, leopard's head and date letter 'k'.

SCRATCHWEIGHT: none.
Actual weight: 58 g (1 oz, 17 dwt)

MEASUREMENTS: l. 20 cm (7⅞ in).

INVENTORY: 852099.1

PROVENANCE: 2nd Earl of Bristol; by descent to the 4th Marquess.

DESCRIPTION: The spoon is forged from a single piece of silver. It is of the Hanoverian single-drop pattern with raised egg-shaped bowl, plain, tapering stem and single drop at the junction with the bowl. The terminal is upturned on the bowl side with a slight rib.

HERALDRY: The head of the stem is engraved with the Hervey crest beneath an earl's coronet.

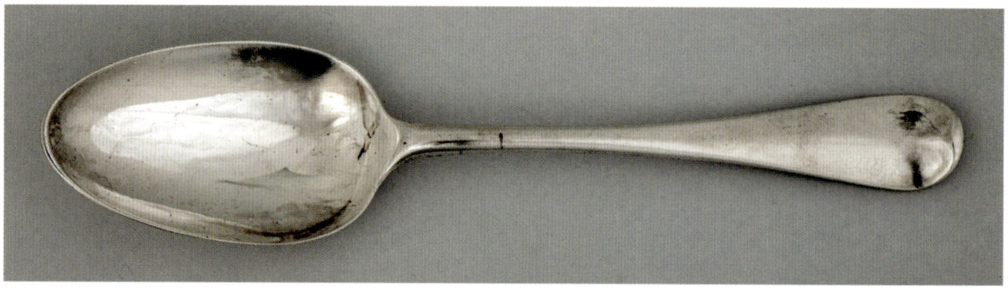

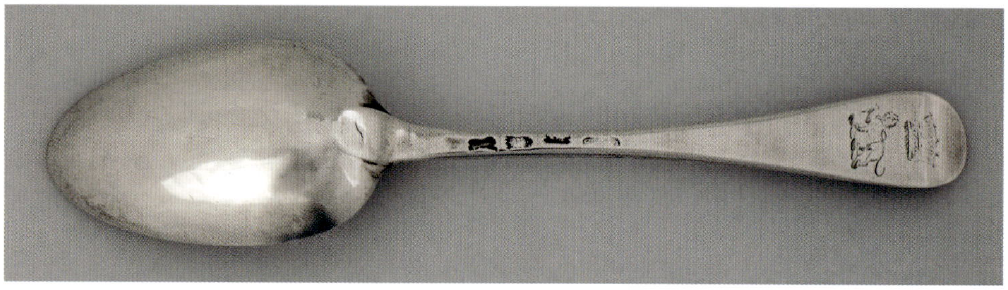

This is the only survivor at Ickworth of a service of spoons and forks that probably extended to seven dozen to match the quantity of plates commissioned *c.*1751. Whether some had been acquired in the mid-1740s or they were merely from stock and formed part of the 1751–2 order from Frederick Kandler is not known. For the other spoons see cat. 69 and 83.

27. **Inkstand**

Sterling silver / **Edward Feline, London** / **1746/7**

MARKS: Fully marked on the underside of the stand and each of the three pots with date letter 'l', leopard's head, maker's mark 'EF' in italics beneath a pellet (Grimwade 1990, no. 587) and lion passant. The seal pot and pounce pot are also marked on the underside of their lids with the maker's mark and lion passant.

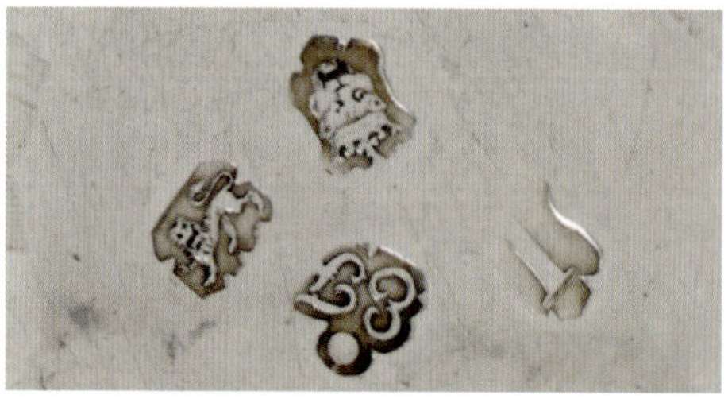

SCRATCHWEIGHT: '65=4'

MEASUREMENTS: h. 10.2 cm (4 in); w. 32.1 cm (12⅝ in); d. 25.7 cm (10⅛ in).

INVENTORY: 852075

PROVENANCE: Probably acquired by the 2nd Earl of Bristol; by descent to the 4th Marquess.

LITERATURE: Penzer 1957a, II, p. 136.

EXHIBITED: *Treasures from National Trust Houses*, Christie's, London, 1957–8, no. 64; Society of the Four Arts, Palm Beach, Florida, 1959; *Silver from National Trust Houses*, Treasurer's House, York Festival, 1969.

DESCRIPTION: The rectangular stand is of sheet silver with a cast and chased shell-and-scroll border. The two pen wells, which are raised and soldered in place, have cast and chased shell-and-scroll borders. The hemi-spherical, convex stays for the pots are also raised and applied and the scroll and lion's paw feet are cast and chased. Each of the three circular pots is seamed, the ink and pounce pots embossed to produce the bulbous part of the upper body and the seal pot having a moulded wire at the top. All three have a moulded wire at the base and are flat-chased with shell and scrollwork, the middle only left plain. The lids are cast and have chased running bands of open ovals on their rims. The lid of the ink pot, which retains a clear-glass cylindrical liner, has a large central hole and three smaller surrounding holes for the pen. The pounce pot lid is pierced in a trellis pattern surrounded by scrolls.

HERALDRY: The stand is twice engraved, off-centre behind the pen trays, with the Hervey crest beneath an earl's coronet. Each of the pots is engraved once with the same.

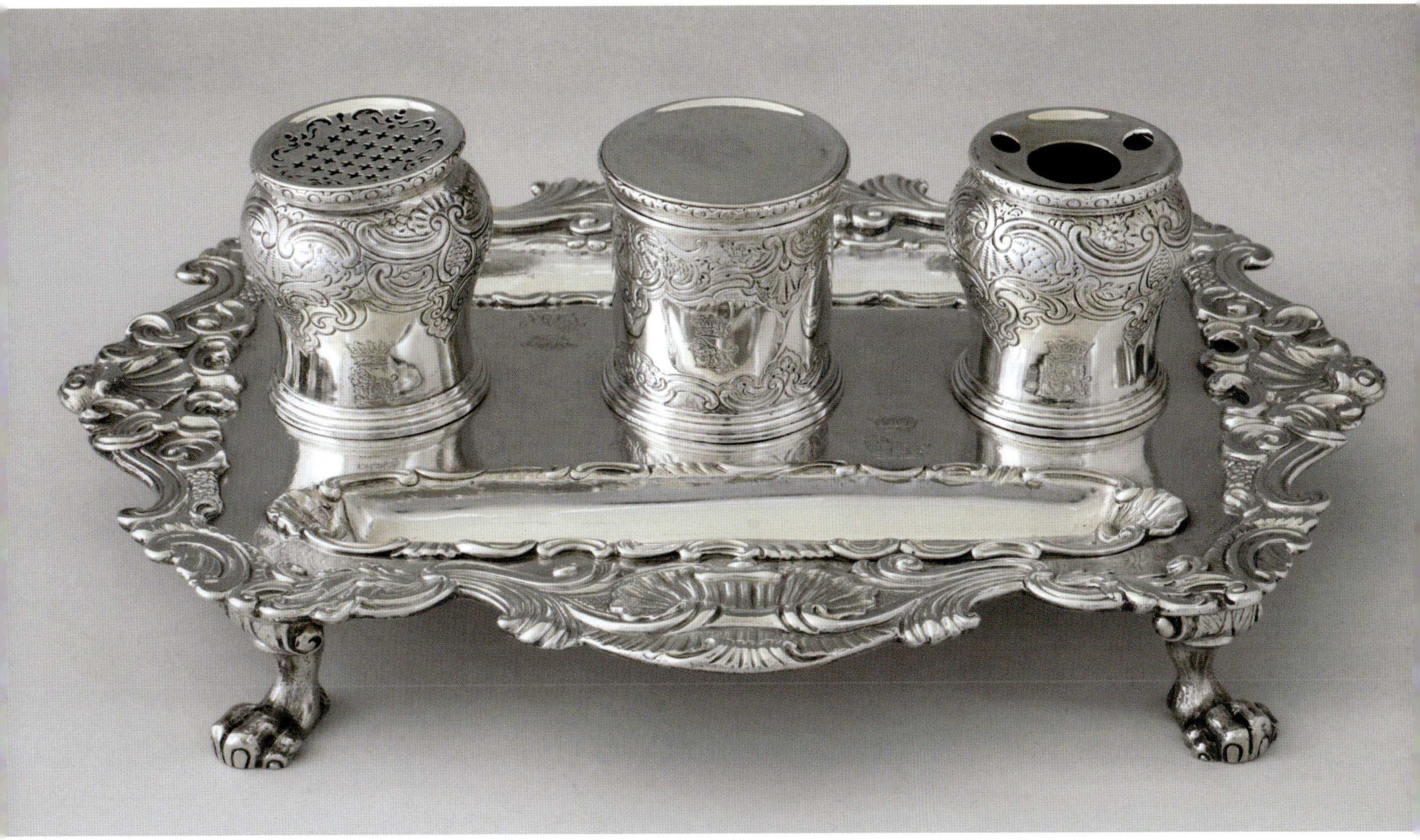

This is probably the inkstand which the 2nd Earl had with him at Turin and Madrid and it would also have been used in his subsequent political career. His many surviving letters would thus have been written from it. In the absence of evidence of any earlier purchases of plate or of re-engraving of the crest and coronet it is probable that it, like the kettle waiter (cat. 25), formed part of his first recorded commission from Kandler in 1751 (see appendix 3).

The great majority of inkstands were much plainer in appearance than Lord Bristol's, writing generally being undertaken in the privacy of the chamber or closet and not therefore requiring overt display. The Earl might, therefore, have had his intended diplomatic career in mind when ordering this more florid example, conscious of the need to closet himself on a regular basis with the envoys of other states and the ministers of the court to which he had been assigned.

Early eighteenth-century inkstands, where not of the casket type, tended to be in the form of deep trays, like that of 1716 by Isaac Liger surviving at Dunham Massey.[1] Though this style persisted well into the century the more fashionable models gradually flattened out until they scarcely had a raised outer edge at all, as on this example. From the late 1730s several makers fully embraced the rococo and produced wildly naturalistic forms, such as that at Chatsworth by Paul Crespin of 1739 with pots masquerading as conch shells, a coral as a pen rest and divers other shells piled up to form the tray.[2] Such creations were, of course, exceptional but the rectilinearity of earlier stands was often now broken by at least a shaped outline and in some cases the addition of elaborate cast borders. The Ickworth stand has particularly extensive cast ornament, the broadly triangular flanges packed full of shells and C-scrolls, the pen trays being embellished to match and the whole being supported on bold, clenched lion claw feet suitable to the substantial weight. A precedent for the flanged form, which is rare, exists in an inkstand of 1732 by Paul de Lamerie,[3] though in that case the detail of the casting is *Régence*, being a reuse of the moulds for the handles of his 1724 Scarsdale epergne dish (cat. 13).

The flanking pots of the Ickworth inkstand would have been for ink and for sand or powder (also known as pounce) for preparing unsized paper and for blotting after writing. The central seal pot would have contained wafers which were an alternative to wax for sealing.

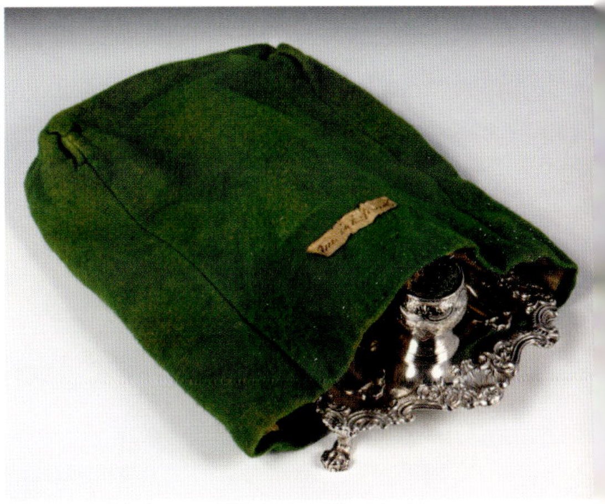

FIG. 88 / The mid-18th century bag for the inkstand. Baize with cotton lining and cotton tape draw-string; 11.4 x 25.4 x 35.6 cm (4½ x 10 x 14 in). Cotton tape label inscribed 'One Inkstand'. National Trust, Ickworth.

One of a handful of what are probably mid-eighteenth-century baize bags, lined with soft cotton and with a cotton tape drawstring, survives for this piece, together with its linen label inscribed 'One Inkstand' (fig. 88).

1. Lomax and Rothwell 2006, cat. 43, pp. 101–2.
2. Grimwade 1974, p. 58 and plate 85. For other examples see also plates 84 and 86a and b.
3. Jackson 1911, p. 904, fig. 1181.

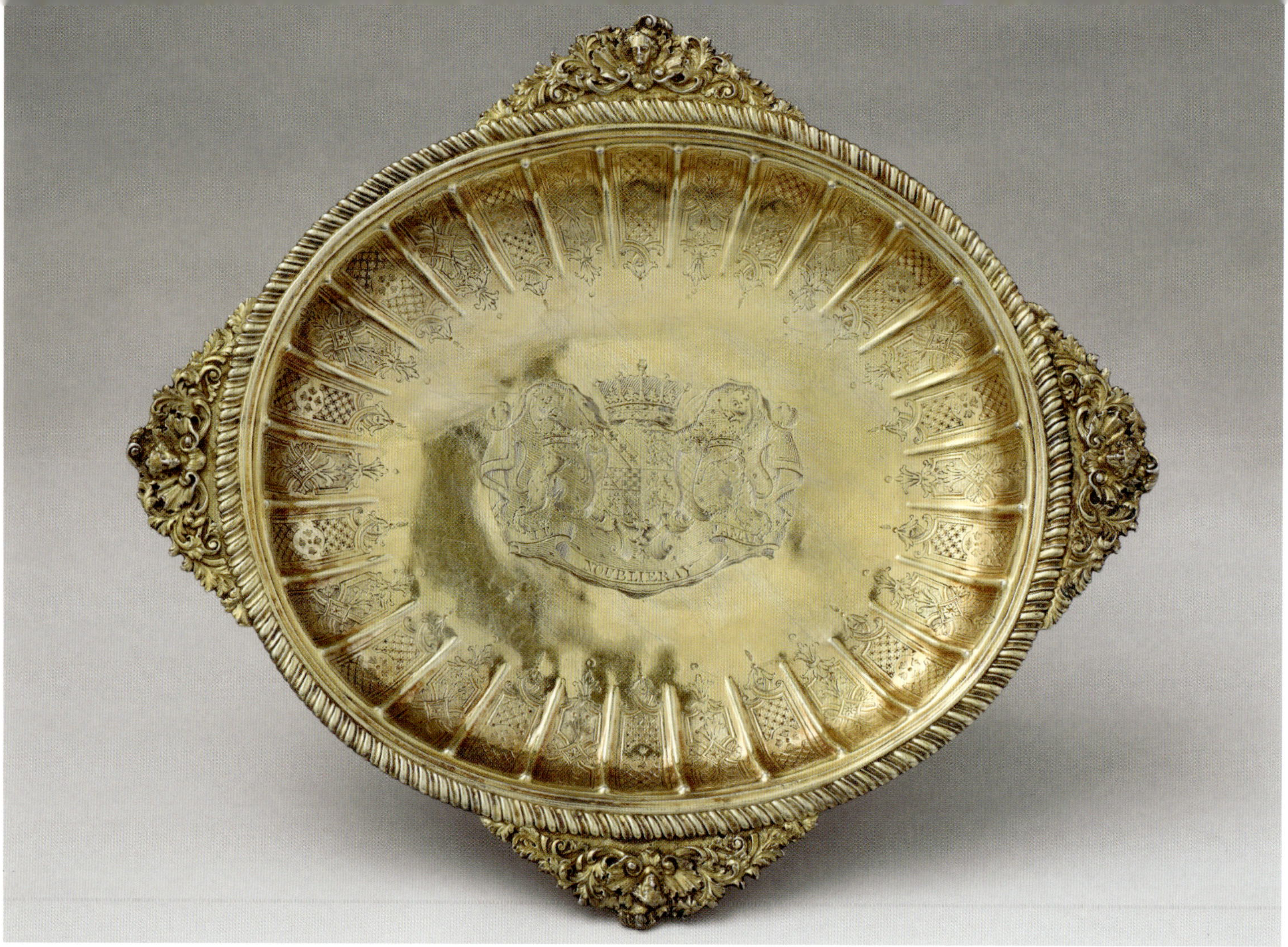

28. **Salad, subsequently dessert dish**

Sterling silver, subsequently gilded / Frederick Kandler / 1751/2

MARKS: Fully marked on the underside with date letter 'q', lion passant, maker's mark 'FK' in italics beneath a fleur-de-lis (Grimwade 1990, no. 691) and leopard's head.

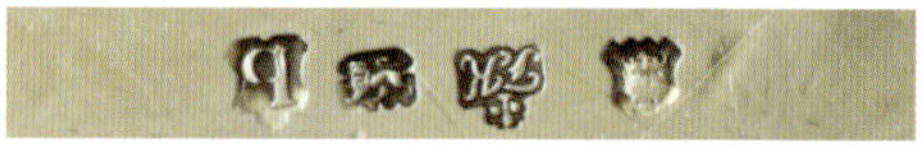

SCRATCHWEIGHT: 'N 2 [/] 32=3'

MEASUREMENTS: h. 4.4 cm (1¾ in); w. 33.7 cm (13¼ in); d. 30.2 cm (11⅞ in).

INVENTORY: 852064.2

PROVENANCE: 2nd Earl of Bristol; by descent to 4th Marquess.

LITERATURE: Penzer 1957a, I, pp. 41–2, fig. v; Banister 1980, p. 793.

EXHIBITED: Society of the Four Arts, Palm Beach, Florida, 1959; *British Week*, Milan and Frankfurt, 1965; *Silver from National Trust Houses*, Treasurer's House, York Festival, 1969; *Treasures from Country Houses of the National Trust and National Trust for Scotland, Europalia 1973*, Brussels.

DESCRIPTION: A near-exact copy of the dish by Paul de Lamerie of 1724; see cat. 13.

HERALDRY: The centre of the dish is engraved with the quartered shield, supporters and motto of the 2nd Earl of Bristol in an ermine mantling and beneath an earl's coronet.

This copy of the dish for the Scarsdale epergne (see cat. 13) is a superb piece of craftsmanship and is barely distinguishable from the original, being within an ounce of the same weight and even having a bezel which would have been redundant if not in use with the tureen of the epergne. Only on very close inspection can the slightest of variances be detected such as in the execution of the engraved border and in the form of the panel and scroll feet. The four cast handles are precisely the same size which would suggest that Kandler had access to Lamerie's moulds. Had he needed to take new ones from the original dish the copies thus produced would be expected to be fractionally smaller.

It is possible that the epergne was not melted at this stage, and as it would have had a cover for the central tureen as well as the dish the latter would have been available for alternative use. This is typical of the 2nd Earl's thrifty and measured approach to the augmentation of his plate as he thereby gained two dishes for the fashion cost of one. The gilding penetrates the engraved lines on both this dish and its Lamerie pair, suggesting that they were initially left white, perhaps until 1766 when two more were added (cat. 85). Thus they could have been intended to form part of the plate for the first courses of the meal, acting as salad dishes which, with their ribbing, they resemble. They may even have still been laid on the table with the epergne, perhaps flanking it, up to its demise *c.* 1754.

29. **Sauce boat**

Sterling silver / **Edward Feline, London** / **1751/2**

MARKS: Fully marked on the underside with lion passant, date letter 'q', maker's mark 'EF' in italics beneath a pellet (Grimwade 1990, no. 587) and leopard's head.

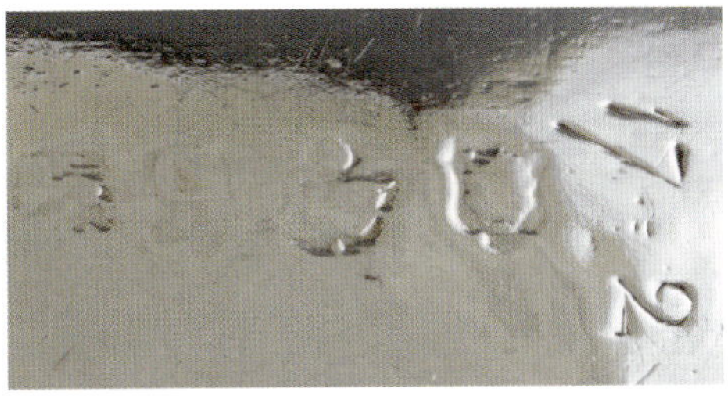

SCRATCHWEIGHT: 'No 1 [/] 17=2'

MEASUREMENTS: h. 10.8 cm (4¼ in); w. 20.6 cm (8⅛ in); d. 10.2 cm (4 in).

INVENTORY: 852081

PROVENANCE: 2nd Earl of Bristol; by descent to the 4th Marquess.

LITERATURE: Penzer 1957a, II, p. 137; Banister 1980, p. 793.

EXHIBITED: Society of the Four Arts, Palm Beach, Florida, 1959.

DESCRIPTION: The oval sauce boat is raised with a cast gadrooned and shaped border and four cast lion's paw and acanthus leaf feet. A cast Neptune mask is applied beneath the lip and the scroll handle, which is cast in two equal parts, is in the form of a stylised dolphin, its head resting on a cast leaf-and-scroll fitment applied to the body of the boat. The condition is poor, the sauce boat having evidently been the subject of regular use.

HERALDRY: Both sides are engraved with the quartered shield, supporters and motto of the 2nd Earl of Bristol in an ermine mantling and beneath an earl's coronet. The engraving is very worn.

The 1811 plate list (appendix 5) reveals that this and the other two types of sauce boat in the collection (cat. 30 and 65) were each in sets of four, giving a total of twelve available for the dinner table. This was quite a prodigious quantity for the mid-eighteenth century, the same as found at Dunham Massey in 1750/54 and two more than in the great Leinster dinner service of 1747.[1] In contrast the decidedly conservative 2nd Duke of Montagu had just four at Montagu House in 1746.[2] The Wickes ledgers and Jewel Office records corroborate a general increase in numbers for the tables of grandees as the century progressed. This is particularly clearly expressed by the case of Henry Bromley, 1st Baron Montfort, of whom Lady Hervey wrote on his unexpected suicide in 1755 that he had 'a great taste for pleasure and an ample fortune to gratify it'.[3] In February 1743 he turned in eight sauce boats to George Wickes and replaced them with ten and in 1751 the number was upped to twelve.[4]

Sauces were critical to fine cuisine in the mid-eighteenth century and Vincent La Chapelle in *The modern cook*, first published in 1733, explains the preparation of over thirty different varieties.[5] They had become increasingly elaborate and extravagant, rumour having it that the Duke of Newcastle's French chef, Clouet, used

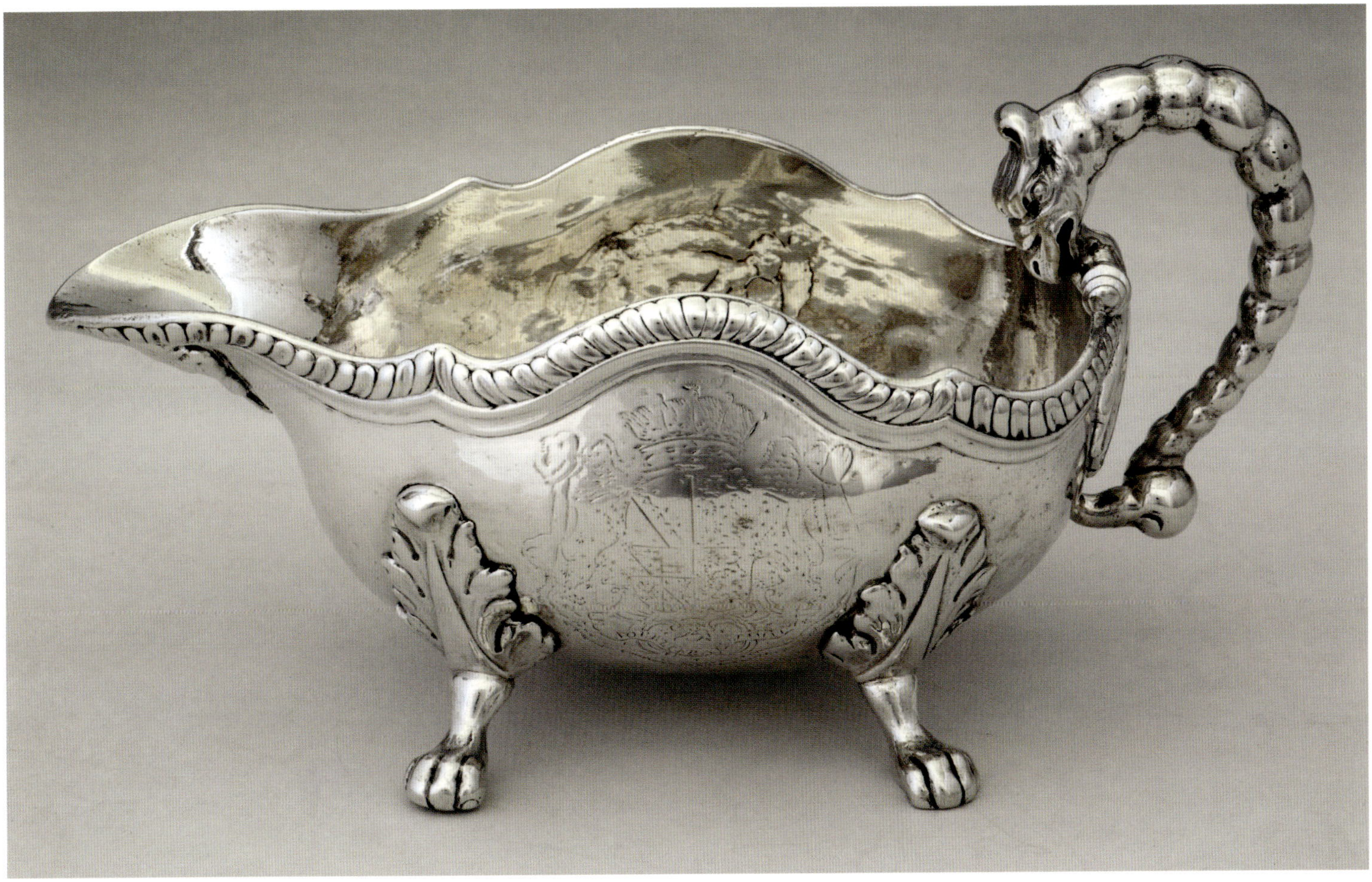

a whole ham to make a sauce and twenty-two partridges to produce gravy for a mere brace.[6] William Verral, who had worked with Clouet at Claremont and defended his master against such accusations, included a few more straightforward sauces specifically for sending up in boats in his 1759 publication *A complete system of cookery*. Amongst these is his (and thus, presumably Clouet's) version of *Sauce Robert*:

To a ladle of cullis [stock] put a glass of your best white wine, a spoonful of mustard, pepper, salt, shallots and parsley, with plenty of such sorts of herbs as you best approve on; let all stew a minute or two, squeeze in plenty of juice [lemon/orange], and send it up hot in a boat … The reason why the Sauce Robert *should not boil long, is, because mustard in boiling grows bitter, and of a nauseous taste.*[7]

Of the set of four associated with the Feline sauce boat at Ickworth, one is noted as having been 'lost' in the copy plate list of 1874[8] and the other two were retained by the family before being sold by the 7th Marquess in 1996.[9] One of those is also by Feline whilst the second bears marks for John Jacob and 1738, suggesting that there were originally pairs by each. The Jacob boats are likely to have been supplied to Lord Hervey by Paul Crespin (see cat. 18) and the dolphin handle and Neptune mask are consistent with the 1730s and with plate from the de Lamerie/Crespin circle. The knuckled dolphin handle is of seventeenth-century auricular inspiration and was, with its allusion to water, particularly appropriate for vessels intended for liquids.[10] It is thus far first recorded in 1719 on a cream ewer by David Willaume I,[11] which also exhibits a cast mask beneath the lip, and it has a strong association thereafter with de Lamerie. Examples are found by him on several pairs and groups of sauce boats with conch-shell bodies made between 1729 and 1738, many also with Neptune masks.[12] The Jacob sauce boat and pairs by Aymé Videau and Paul Crespin, both of 1735,[13] suggest that the mould was being used by several silversmiths and it was very probably still available for Feline in 1751.[14]

If the shaped, gadrooned rim on the Jacob sauce boat is contemporary then it is an exceptionally early example.[15] It could be, however, that Feline re-shaped a simple, wavy rim, which would have been more typical for the time, and applied the gadrooning before copying that adapted form to create the set of four. Why Lord Bristol chose not to have all eight in the same pattern, and added yet another type in 1758, is an interesting question. It is probably partly answered by his desire to concentrate the cost of fashion where it would really count and in this and many of the other elements of his dinner service the Earl does not seem to have minded a harlequin effect, provided there were even sets that could be placed symmetrically. Indeed the variety thereby created may even have been seen as a positive advantage in the age of riotous movement and distortion that was the rococo.

1. Lomax and Rothwell 2006, pp. 53 and 167 and Barr 1980, p. 198.
2. Murdoch 2006, p. 109.
3. Croker 1821, pp. 206–7
4. Wickes Ledgers, VAM 2 1740–8, f. 86 and VAM 5 1750–4, f. 12.
5. La Chapelle 1736, pp. 94–104.
6. Wheaton 1983, pp. 166 and 204–5.
7. Verral 1759, pp. xxx–i and 233–4.
8. Bristol plate list 1874b.
9. They were offered first by Sotheby's, 9 November 1995, lot 299, but must have failed to sell as they were offered again at Sotheby's Suffolk, 11–12 June 1996, East Wing Ickworth, lot 344b (not in catalogue) when they sold for £2,500.
10. For a discussion of the Van Vianen source of this feature and its use by different silversmiths see Hartop 1996, cat. 30, pp. 175–7, Alcorn 2006, cat. 18, pp. 71–2 and Schroder 2009, cat. 153, pp. 396–7.
11. Wees 1997, cat. 253, pp. 365–6
12. Sotheby's, 11 November 1993, lot 462 (1729), Alcorn 2006, cat. 18, pp. 71–2 (1730), Christie's, 16 June 1965, lot 36 (1734) and Hartop 1996, p. 176, ill. (1738).
13. Sotheby's, 27 June 1963 and Hartop 1996, cat. 32, pp. 182–3.
14. Timothy Schroder has pointed out that two not quite identical moulds were in use amongst silversmiths in the 1730s and 1740s. See Schroder 2009, pp. 396–7.
15. The first mention of a 'knurl'd' or gadrooned sauce boat in the Wickes ledgers is in 1744, VAM 2 1740–8, f. 53, Sir John Chapman, 15 December 1744, and one of the earliest surviving examples, with a shaped rim, is found on a pair of double-lipped sauceboats of 1741 by Peter Archambo in the Museum of Fine Arts, Boston. See Hartop 1996, cat. 41, pp. 206–7.

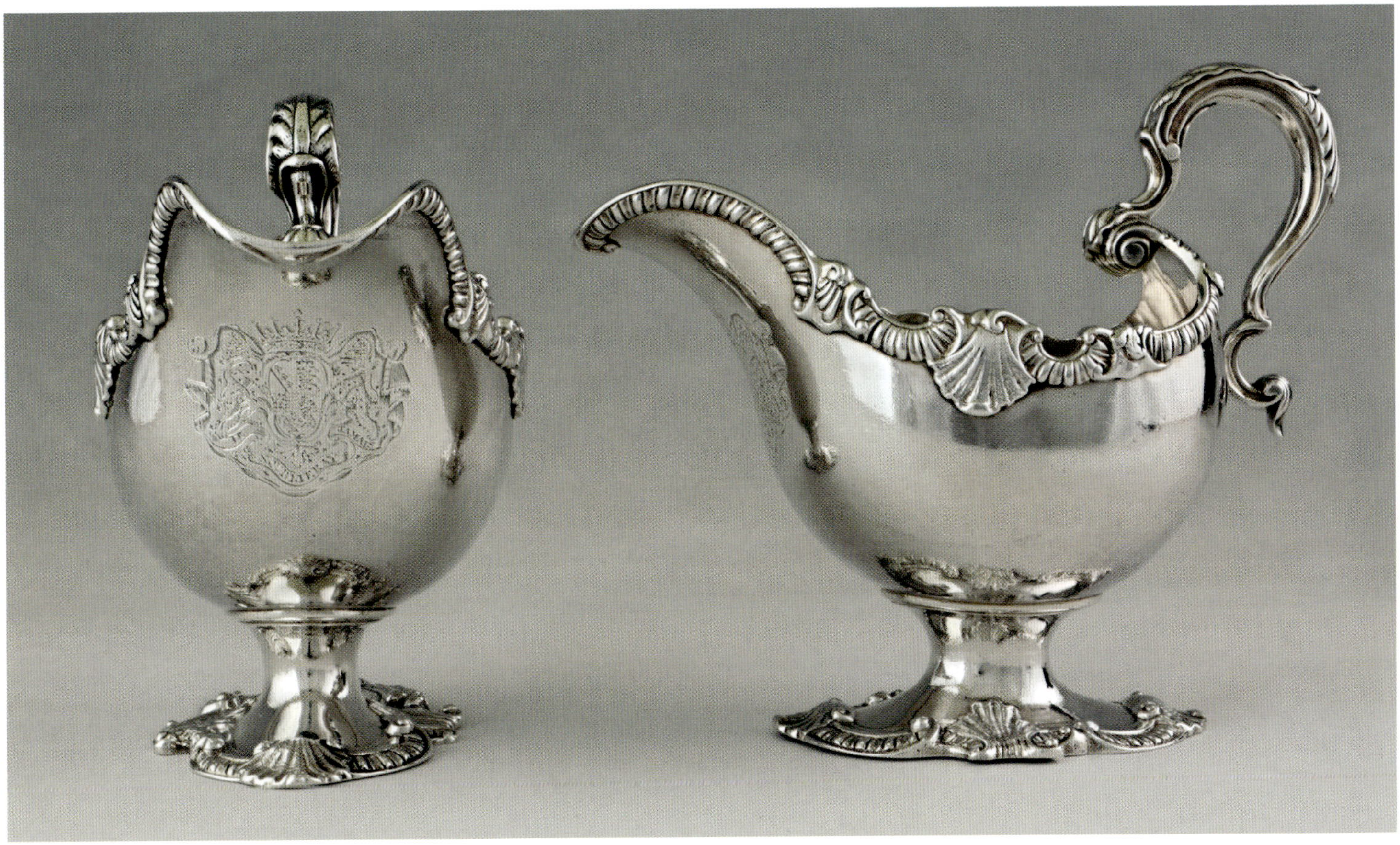

30. Two sauce boats

Sterling silver / **Daniel Piers, London** / **1751/2**

MARKS: Both are fully marked on the underside with maker's mark 'DP' beneath a pellet (Grimwade 1990, no. 493), lion passant, date letter 'q' and leopard's head.

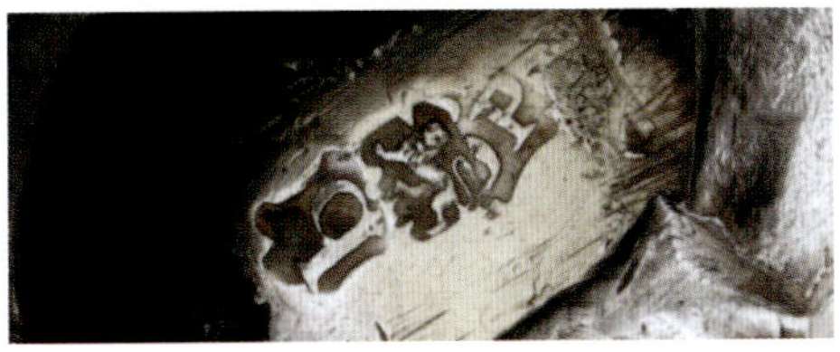

SCRATCHWEIGHTS: '23=2 [/] N1' and '23=3' [/] N2'

MEASUREMENTS: h. 17.5 cm (6⅞ in); w. 20.3 cm (8 in); d. 10.8 cm (4¼ in).

INVENTORY: 852082

PROVENANCE: 2nd Earl of Bristol; by descent to the 4th Marquess.

LITERATURE: Penzer 1957a, II, p. 137.

EXHIBITED: Society of the Four Arts, Palm Beach, Florida, 1959; *Ideal Home Exhibition*, London, 1960; *Silver from National Trust Houses*, Treasurer's House, York Festival, 1969.

DESCRIPTION: The raised oval, helmet-shaped body of each boat rests on a shaped oval foot with cast and chased shells, C-scrolls and gadrooning. The same decoration augments the cast and chased rim which rises to a broad pouring lip and an inward curving scroll upon which rests the double-scroll and leaf-capped handle.

HERALDRY: On the front beneath the lip of each is engraved the quartered shield, supporters and motto of the 2nd Earl of Bristol in an ermine mantling and beneath an earl's coronet.

Mono-footed sauce boats were popular from the late 1720s and the elaborate profile of the rim seen on these examples first appeared around 1740.[1] It seems to have been Frederick Kandler who put the elements together with shells and gadrooning, as exhibited on sauce boats by him of 1744 (fig. 89),[2] and Christopher Hartop has identified that the inspiration is likely to have come from a design published in Nuremburg *c.*1740.[3] Given Kandler's German origins, close connection to the Meissen porcelain manufactory and extraordinarily sculptural *oeuvre* he is certainly

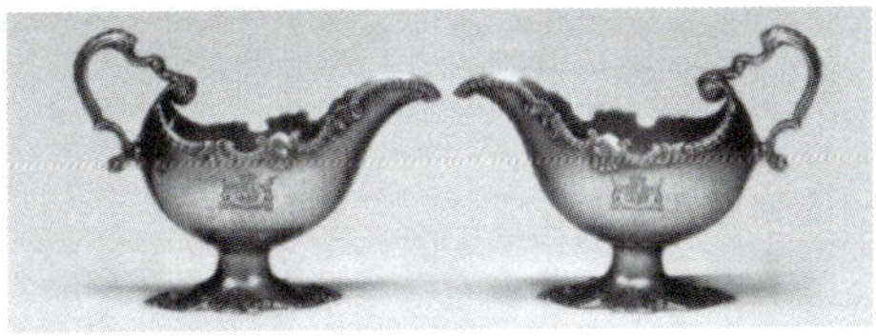

FIG. 89 / Two from a set of four sauce boats by Frederick Kandler, 1744. Silver: 2799 g (90 oz). Christie's.

the most plausible candidate to have made the introduction. As Daniel Piers was supplying Kandler he would no doubt have had access to his designs, or would even have been instructed to follow them, but he does not appear to have been using the same moulds as employed in 1744. His handling of the model is, if anything, rather superior to that of its originator with bolder detail, a more upright form and better proportioned handles. All four of this set of sauce boats survive but only two passed to the National Trust in 1956.

1. See for instance the pair by David Willaume II, 1738, sold at Christie's, 14 December 1966, lot 72.
2. Christie's, 21 November 1973, lot 70.
3. Hartop 1996, cat. 42, pp. 208–11.

31. Four circular salad dishes

Sterling silver / Frederick Kandler, London / 1751/2

MARKS: All fully marked on the underside with leopard's head, date letter 'q', maker's mark 'FK' in italics beneath a fleur-de-lis (Grimwade 1990, no. 691) and lion passant.

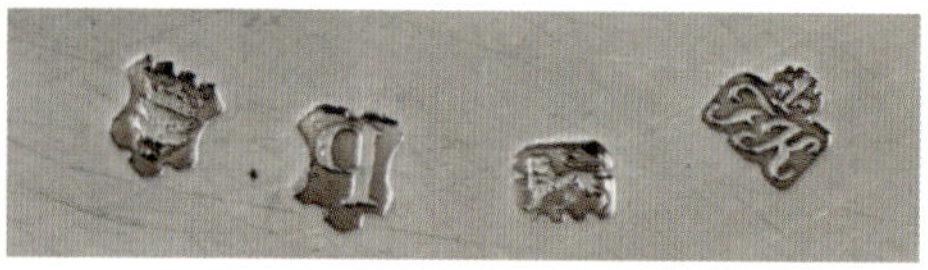

SCRATCHWEIGHTS: 'N1 [/] 25=11', 'N2 [/] 26=11', 'N3 [/] 26=17' and 'N4 [/] 26=18'

MEASUREMENTS: h. 3.8 cm (1½ in); diam. 27.9 cm (11 in).

INVENTORY: 852062

PROVENANCE: 2nd Earl of Bristol; by descent to the 4th Marquess.

LITERATURE: Penzer 1957a, II, p. 137.

DESCRIPTION: The dishes are raised with chased spiral ribs commencing on the outer edges of the base and rising up the sides. The shaped rims have cast and chased shell, leaf and gadroon borders.

HERALDRY: In the centre of the dishes are engraved the quartered shield, supporters and motto of the 2nd Earl of Bristol in an ermine mantling and beneath an earl's coronet.

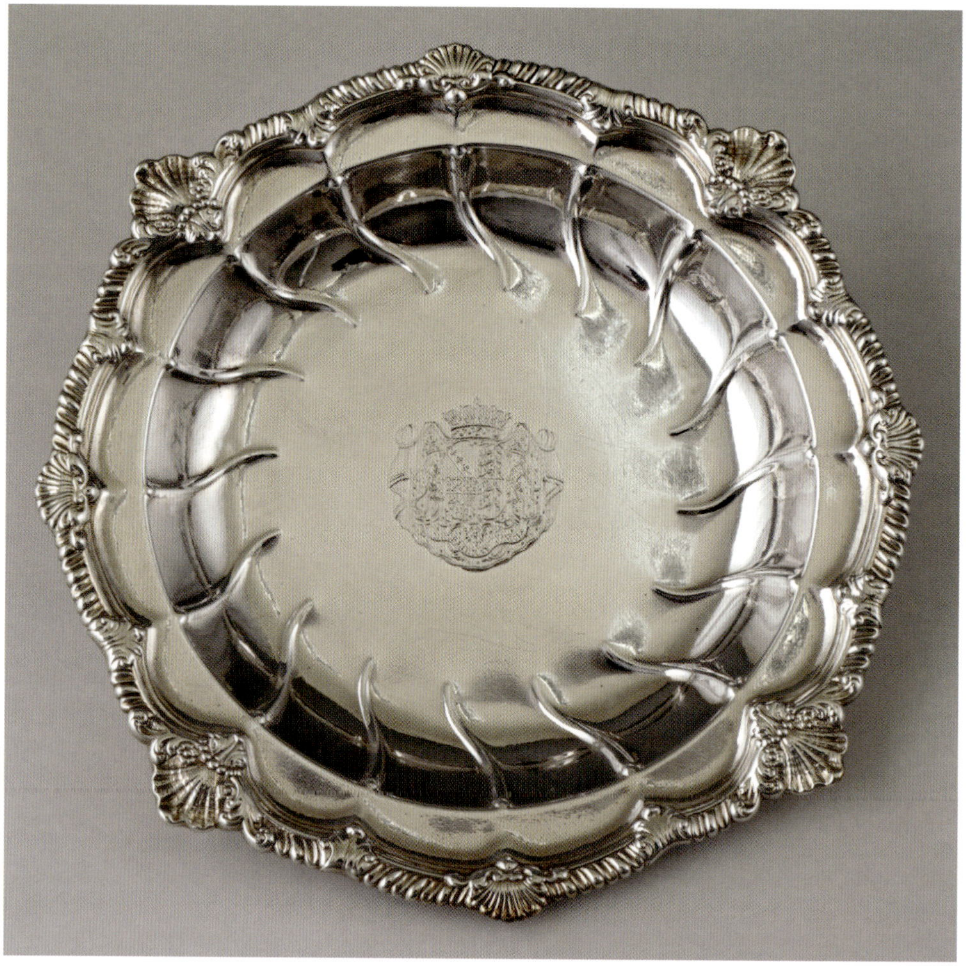

These are recorded in the 1811 plate list as 'Sallad Dishes' which was the term applied throughout the eighteenth century to such ribbed vessels.[1] They were used for both cooked vegetables and what we now know as salads,[2] the ribs presumably allowing water to drain from the leaves. As such they would have accompanied the second course of dinner or supper.[3] Fruit may well also have been served in them, some of those of apparently the same form provided by the Jewel Office being specified as 'fruit dishes' early in the century.[4] It was probably the subsequent, often exclusive adoption of this type of vessel as part of the dessert service that resulted in them becoming known as 'strawberry dishes', by which name they are still regularly catalogued today. That term never took hold with the Herveys but the pieces certainly became associated with dessert as they were, perhaps uniquely, described as 'jelly dishes' in the 1874 plate list.[5]

In some cases, by the mid-eighteenth century, salad dishes were having feet added but this was by no means exclusive as is proved by these examples and many others surviving without.[6] From their inception in the 1690s salad dishes had tended to have scalloped sides and no horizontal rims, making them particularly distinct from the other tableware with its generally simple outlines, but that changed with the advent of shaped plates and dishes in the late 1730s (see cat. 32 and 35), and a good early example of the new form is seen in a pair by Paul de Lamerie of 1742 sold by Sotheby's in 1987.[7] The cast gadroon borders on the Ickworth salad dishes are further enriched with shells, this pattern having been introduced in the early 1740s and being seen on sauce boats by Kandler of 1744 (see cat. 30) and a set of plates by Paul de Lamerie of 1745.[8] Shells large and small were successfully employed throughout the Earl of Bristol's dinner service to unify new and old pieces and varying forms.

Salad dishes tended to be supplied in pairs, fours and eights and by the mid-century larger sets were sometimes provided in a combination of round and oval shape, George Wickes supplying Admiral Byng with '4 Round & 4 Ovell Sallett Dishes' in May 1749 and the Dowager Duchess of Somerset with two of each in the same month.[9] Thus Lord Bristol's adoption of the epergne dish and its new pair (cat. 28) for salad dishes would have been quite in keeping with the trends of the time and would have provided him with a respectable total of six for his table.

1. There are constant references to salad, or 'Sallett', dishes in the Wickes Ledgers and the Jewel Office records.
2. Hartop 1996, p. 168.
3. La Chapelle 1736, plate VII.
4. Jewel Office Delivery Book 1698–1732, f. 253, 6 June 1721, christening present to Viscount Howe of 'four Gilt Scollopt fruite Dishes' weighing 120 oz.
5. Bristol Plate List 1874b.
6. For example, a pair also by Kandler of 1749 sold at Christie's, 24 March 1965, lot 79.
7. Sotheby's, 26 April 1987, lot 187.
8. Christie's, 14 December 1962, lot 140.
9. Wickes Ledgers, VAM 3 1747–50, ff. 83 and 86.

32. Pair of large oval dishes

Sterling silver / Frederick Kandler, London / 1751/2

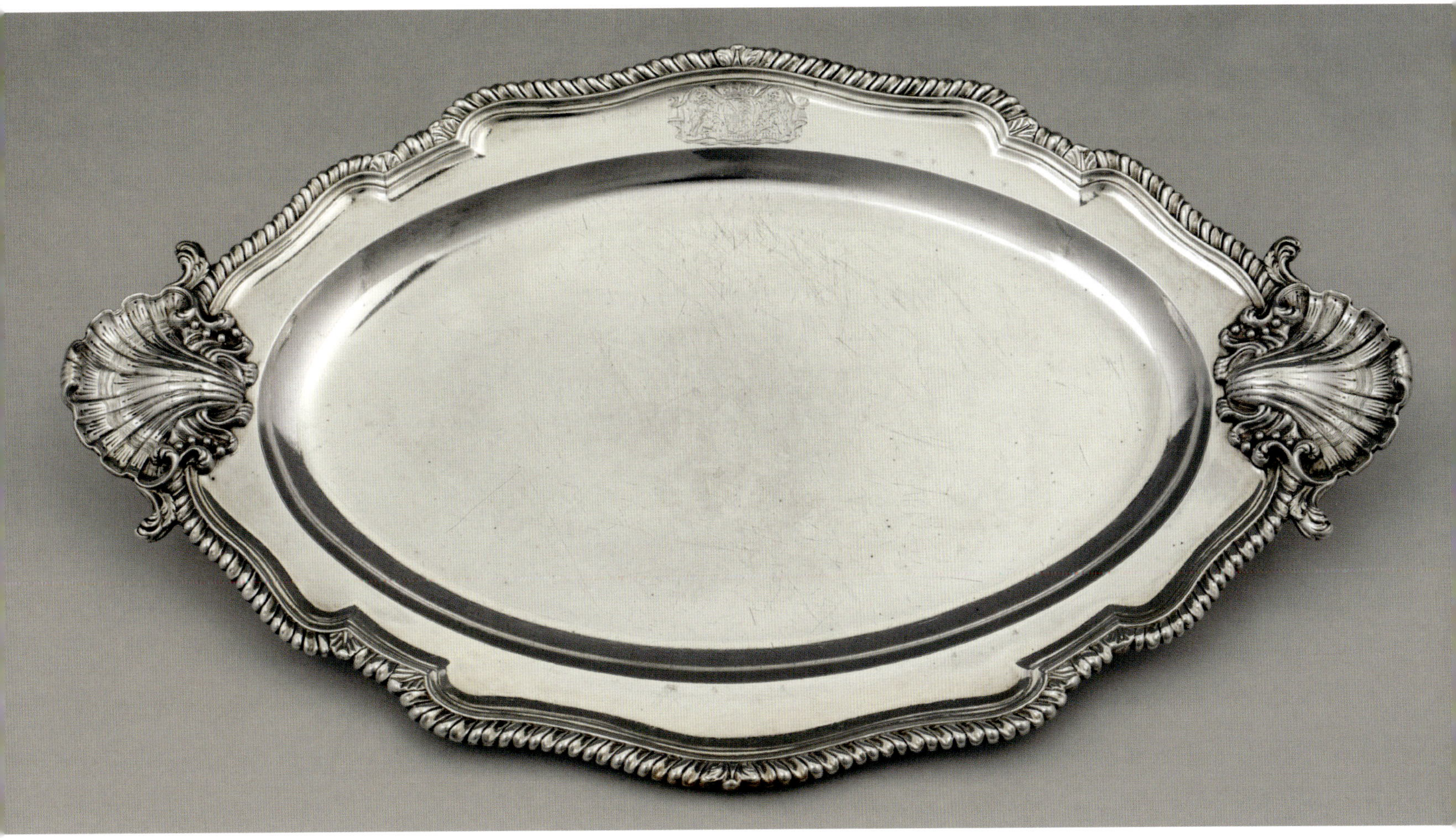

MARKS: Both fully marked on the underside of the rim with maker's mark 'FK' in italics beneath a fleur-de-lis (Grimwade 1990, no. 691), date letter 'q', leopard's head and lion passant.

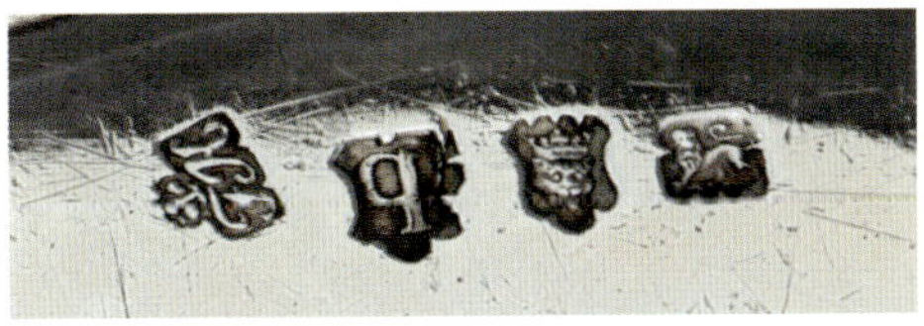

SCRATCHWEIGHT: 'N1 [/] 92=15' and 'N2 [/] 93=10'

MEASUREMENTS: h. 5.1 cm (2 in); w. 59.4 cm (23⅜ in); d. 36.5 cm (14⅜ in).

INVENTORY: 852080.1 and 3

PROVENANCE: 2nd Earl of Bristol; by descent to the 4th Marquess.

LITERATURE: Penzer 1957a, II, pp. 136–7, fig. VII; Banister 1980, p. 794, fig. 8.

EXHIBITED: Society of the Four Arts, Palm Beach, Florida, 1959; *Silver from National Trust Houses*, Treasurer's House, York Festival, 1969.

DESCRIPTION: The dishes are raised and have flat oval wells and broad rims with shaped borders applied with cast and chased gadrooning. Two large cast and chased shells are applied to each as handles.

HERALDRY: Engraved on the rim are the quartered shield, supporters and motto of the 2nd Earl of Bristol in an ermine mantling and beneath an earl's coronet.

For *service à la française*, which held sway until the mid-nineteenth century, dishes were supplied in gradated sizes and arranged on the table for diners to help themselves to the food thereon. In the decades around 1700 the dishes were generally of circular shape as is made abundantly clear by surviving examples[1] and also by the table layouts given by François Massialot in his *Nouveau cuisinier royal et bourgeois*, first published in 1691 and translated into English as *The court and country cook* in 1702.[2] Oval dishes were not unknown[3] but they seem to have been rare and it was only in the 1730s that significant numbers began to appear in England.[4] They were shown in the plates of Vincent La Chapelle's highly influential *The modern cook* of 1733, some with shaped borders,[5] and by 1740 they were becoming commonplace, often augmented by gadrooning as seen on the Ickworth examples.

An exceptionally early group of oval-shaped dishes, with elaborate *Régence* decoration, is that of 1731 made by Charles Kandler for the 9th Duke of Norfolk.[6] They exhibit diminutive cast shells protruding at either end, presumably there in part to assist with lifting the dishes as were the flanges of 1720s epergne dishes (see cat. 13). It could thus have been from the Kandler workshop that the idea emanated of more prominent shell handles as seen on the Ickworth dishes, though they were more probably directly inspired by Continental *ecuelles*[7] and their English equivalents, porringers. A good example of the latter with prominent shell handles is a pair by David Willaume marked for 1721 at Winterthur.[8]

The earliest dishes extant of the Ickworth type are all of 1741, a large batch (some circular) by Paul de Lamerie (fig. 90) and a pair by George Wickes.[9] The shell handles on these are very similar but not identical, that employed by Wickes being more symmetrically arranged and having lateral fronds projecting beyond the border plus trios of pearl-like balls. It is the Wickes model that was used by Edward Wakelin in 1748 for Admiral Byng's dinner service[10] and by Kandler from 1751 onwards for all of Lord Bristol's larger dishes. Thus the two most prominent retailers of the mid-century were either sourcing from the same outworkers or sharing moulds, and a third option might even be that Kandler had simply taken a cast from a Wickes dish. The feature was to prove a resilient one, being further copied in the early nineteenth century by Rundell, Bridge & Rundell for the dinner service provided to William IV,[11] and in that case the inspiration is very likely to have been the Bristol plate (see cat. 105) to which Rundells had had access.

It is evident from wear and tear that the Ickworth dishes were not exclusively used with the fish plates or mazarines with which they were supplied (cat. 33) but the need to ensure that they fitted when thus employed is probably why, unlike the other eight oval dishes of *c.* 1751 (cat. 39–40), these ones were new-made. As the largest of all the sizes of dish they would have contained the principal focus of the first and second courses, other than the soups. When being used for fish they might, for instance, have contained a turbot and a salmon to replace the two principal soup tureens as part of the first course. For the second they could take the same place, Vincent La Chapelle suggesting Savoy Cake and 'a Cake of mille Feuilles'. Alternatively, if used for meat, they might contain a quarter of veal or a roasted ham.[12]

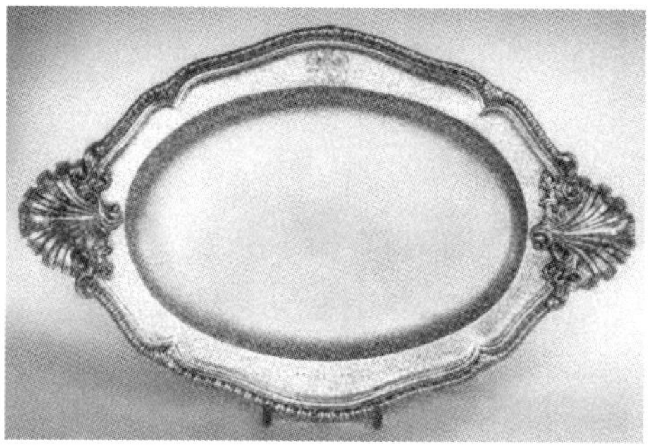

FIG. 90 / Meat dish with shell handles by Paul de Lamerie, London, 1741. Silver: w. 48.3 cm (17¼ in); weight 1213 g (39 oz). Christie's.

1. See for instance Sir Rowland Winn, 3rd Bt's dinner service of 1716 by David Willaume I, with three sizes of dish, sold at Christie's, 3 November 1999, lots 86–9.
2. Massialot 1702, illustrative plates, not paginated. See particularly 'The Model of a Table for fourteen or fifteen Persons' which shows three gradations of circular dishes plus plates in use for service as well.
3. See for instance that of 1684 illustrated in Clayton 1971, p. 111, no. 235. The Earl of Strafford received four oval dishes in 1713/4 as part of his ambassadorial allocation of plate on going to Utrecht; see Jewel Office Delivery Book 1698–1732, f. 171.
4. Initially these were primarily oval wells within a polygonal surround, or a rectangle with lobed ends. See Clayton 1971, p. 111, no. 234 for a polygonal set by David Willaume I, 1725 and Lomax and Rothwell 2006, cat. 25, pp. 73–5 for rectangular lobed examples by Peter Archambo 1731.
5. La Chapelle 1733, unpaginated plates showing table layouts at the beginning of volume I.
6. Sotheby's New York, 22 October 2002, lot 589.
7. For an example of 1735 by Antoine Plot of Paris see Dennis 1960, p. 188, fig. 280.
8. Fennimore and Halfpenny 2000, cat. 9, pp. 24–5.
9. For the de Lamerie dishes see Christie's, 19 June 1957, lot 24, and 29 June 1977, lot 88, and Sotheby's 24 March 1960, lot 6 plus a gradated set of seven in the Metropolitan Museum, New York, acc. nos. 58.7.23–9. The Wickes pair, which had been supplied to Sir Henry Harpur, 5th Bt, was sold at Christie's New York, 28 October 1986, lot 34. See also Barr 1980, p. 23, figs 6a–d.
10. This service was delivered in March 1749; Wickes Ledgers, VAM 3 1747–50, f. 83. Four dishes from it by Edward Wakelin, 1748 were sold at Sotheby's New York, 23 October 2006, lots 287–8.
11. A dish with shell handles from this service was sold at Christie's, 10 June 2010, lot 483.
12. La Chapelle 1736, plate VII.

33. Pair of mazarines

Sterling silver
Frederick Kandler, London / 1751/2

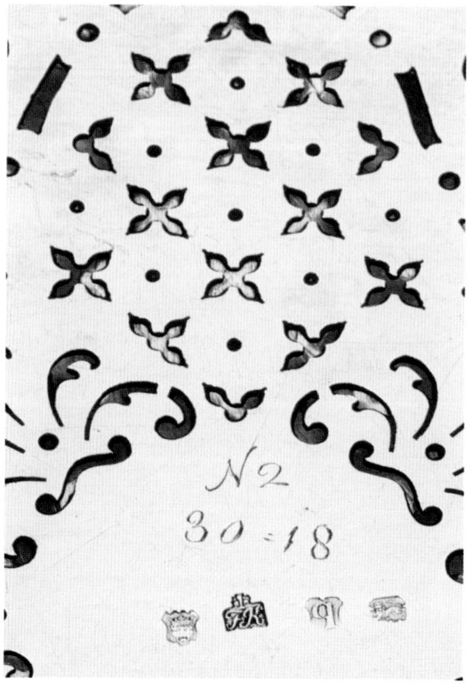

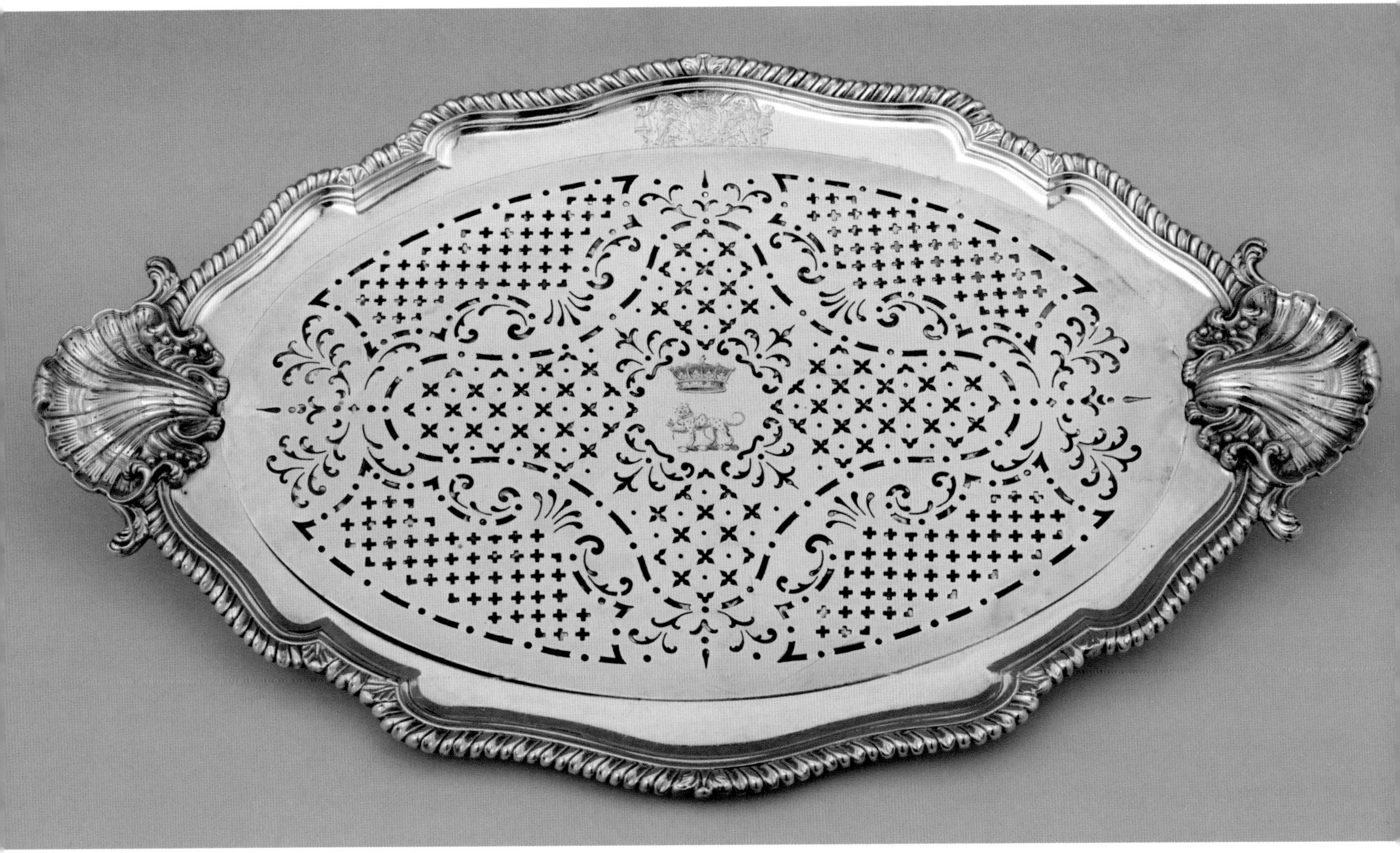

MARKS: Fully marked on the underside with leopard's head, maker's mark 'FK' in italics beneath a fleur-de-lis (Grimwade 1990, no. 691), date letter 'q' and lion passant.

SCRATCHWEIGHTS: 'N1 [/] 28=11' and 'N2 [/] 30=18'

MEASUREMENTS: w. 43.5 cm (17⅛ in); d. 27.3 cm (10¾ in).

INVENTORY: 852080.2 and 4

PROVENANCE: 2nd Earl of Bristol; by descent to the 4th Marquess.

LITERATURE: Penzer 1957a, II, pp. 136–7, fig. VII; Banister 1980, p. 794, fig. 8.

EXHIBITED: *Silver from National Trust Houses*, Treasurer's House, York Festival, 1969.

DESCRIPTION: A flat oval sheet of silver pierced with a symmetrical pattern of foliate scrolls and diaperwork.

HERALDRY: The centre of each mazarine is engraved with the Hervey crest beneath an earl's coronet.

Pierced strainers for fish emerged as a feature of the Georgian dinner service around the year 1730 and two names coexisted for them, 'fish plate' and 'mazarine'. George Wickes exclusively used the former whereas the Jewel Office favoured the latter. In 1708 mazarines were defined in John Kersey's *Dictionarium Anglo-Britannicum* as 'little Dishes to be set in the Middle of a larger Dish, for the setting out of Ragoos, or Fricassies'[1] and that is clearly what the Earl (later Duke) of Marlborough was receiving from the Jewel Office in 1702. Amongst his plate as Captain General of the Forces in Holland he had thirty-two gilt 'mazarines' which were listed after the large dishes upon which they would presumably have been placed.[2] No more of this type are mentioned after 1705, when sixteen formed part of Lord Raby's ambassadorial plate,[3] and they can never have been common, but the fact that they rested upon another dish has been plausibly suggested by Susan Hare as the reason for the term subsequently being applied to fish strainers.[4] That is what must have been meant when in 1728 the 4th Earl of Chesterfield received 'Three Mazareens' weighing 58 oz, 6 dwt, as part of his allowance on going to the States General as ambassador[5] and those granted to the 2nd Lord Tyrawley and the 4th Earl of Holderness in 1744 are specified as 'pierced'.[6]

Large numbers of fish mazarines were produced in the eighteenth century, every significant household having at least one, yet hardly any survive today and even fewer are on public display. Ickworth is particularly fortunate to have the full complement of two mazarines with their associated dishes (cat. 32). Amongst the handful of earlier examples still in existence are four by Paul de Lamerie; a pair of 1743 from his extensive dinner service for the 7th Earl of Thanet and individuals of 1744 and 1745, the latter from the plate of the Parkers, Earls of Morley.[7]

1. Kersey 1708, under the entry for 'Mazarines' (not paginated).
2. Jewel Office Delivery Book 1698–1732, f. 74. Substantial quantities of this sort of mazarine had been recorded in the royal scullery in 1698 and William III took 56 with him to Holland in 1700, in three different sizes, see ff. 11 and 47.
3. Ibid., f. 112.
4. Hare 1990, p. 167.
5. Jewel Office Delivery Book 1698–1732, f. 297.
6. Jewel Office Delivery Book 1732–98, f. 92
7. Sold Sotheby's 22 November 1984 (1743) and 24 April 1969, lot 242 (1744) and Christie's New York, 22 April 1993, lot 58 (1745).

34. Eighteen soup plates

Sterling silver / Frederick Kandler, London / 1751/2

MARKS: All fully marked on the underside with leopard's head, maker's mark 'FK' in italics beneath a fleur-de-lis (Grimwade 1990, no. 691), date letter 'q' and lion passant.

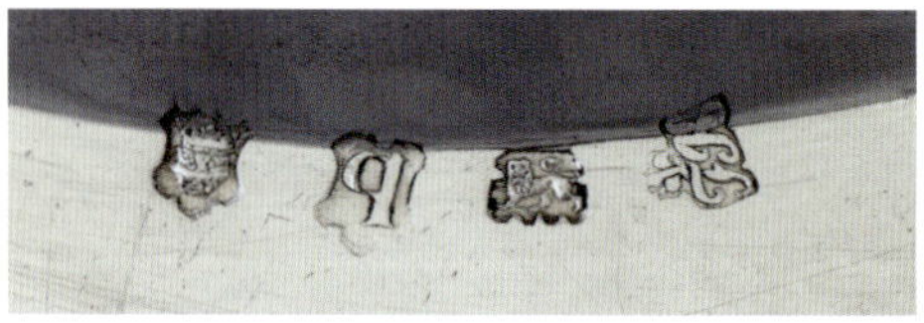

SCRATCHWEIGHTS: 'Nº=127 [/] ~~N 90~~ [/] 20 =4'; 'Nº=128 [/] ~~N 89~~ [/] 20=18'; 'Nº=129 [/] ~~N 88~~ [/] 20=12'; 'Nº=130 [/] ~~N 87~~ [/] 20=4'; 'Nº=131 [/] ~~N 86~~ [/] 20=14'; 'Nº-132 [/] ~~N 85~~ [/] 20=2'; 'Nº=133 [/] ~~N 84~~ [/] 20=12'; 'Nº 134 [/] ~~N 83~~ [/] 20=14'; 'Nº=135 [/] ~~N 82~~ [/] 20=19'; 'Nº=136 [/] ~~N 81~~ [/] 20=15'; 'Nº 137 [/] ~~N 80~~ [/] 20=19'; 'Nº 138 [/] ~~N 79~~ [/] 21=5'; 'Nº=139 [/] ~~N 78~~ [/] 20=19'; 'Nº=140 [/] ~~N 77~~ [/] 20=6'; 'Nº=141 [/] ~~N 76~~ [/] 21=5= ~~¼~~'; 'Nº=142 [/] ~~N 75~~ [/] 20=11'; 'Nº=143 [/] ~~N 74~~ [/] 20=3'; 'Nº 144 [/] ~~N 73~~ [/] 20=10'.

MEASUREMENTS: h. 2.9 cm (1⅛ in); diam. 24.8 cm (9¾ in).

INVENTORY: 852126.1–18

PROVENANCE: 2nd Earl of Bristol; by descent to the 4th Marquess.

LITERATURE: Penzer 1957a, II, pp. 134 and 136, fig. v; Banister 1980, p. 793.

DESCRIPTION: The deep, circular plates are raised and have a broad rim with an applied cast and chased shaped border of gadrooning.

HERALDRY: Each plate is engraved on its rim with the quartered shield, supporters and motto of the 2nd Earl of Bristol in an ermine mantling and beneath an earl's coronet.

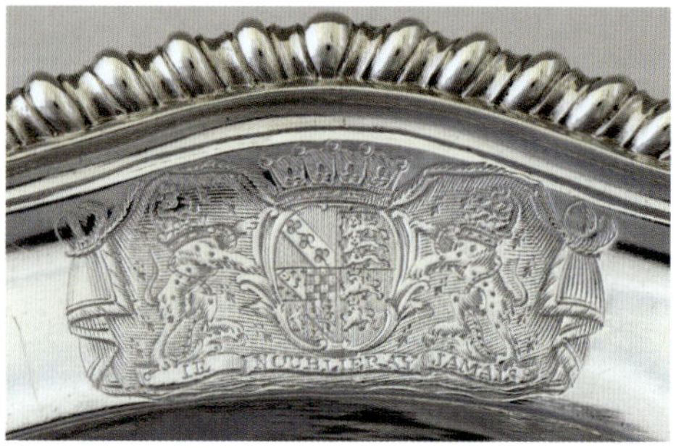

These plates have clearly been altered since first being made, the hallmarks on many of them being distorted by the crease between the bowl and the rim. It is likely that they were intended to be dinner plates and were deepened at some point to serve for soup. Given that they do not seem to have been re-engraved this could have occurred very quickly and before they left Kandler's workshop. Their original numbering followed on from the seventy-two dinner plates (cat. 35) and this was maintained when additional soup and dinner plates were procured in Turin later in the 1750s (cat. 57 and 56 respectively). As a consequence the soup plates were numbered between the two sets of dinner plates and this inconsistency probably remained until after Lord Bristol's return from the Continent in 1762, judging by what looks to be English renumbering. Within the original numbering of soup plates there is a gap of twelve between the end of the surviving English run and the commencement of the Turinese. It is therefore likely that the Earl had additional soup plates and as they were almost invariably supplied in dozens there must have been six more of this set, giving two dozen, and six from Turin, a further dozen. Those that are missing may well have been lost in the mêlée surrounding the hasty departure from Madrid following Britain's declaration of war against Spain in the last days of 1761.

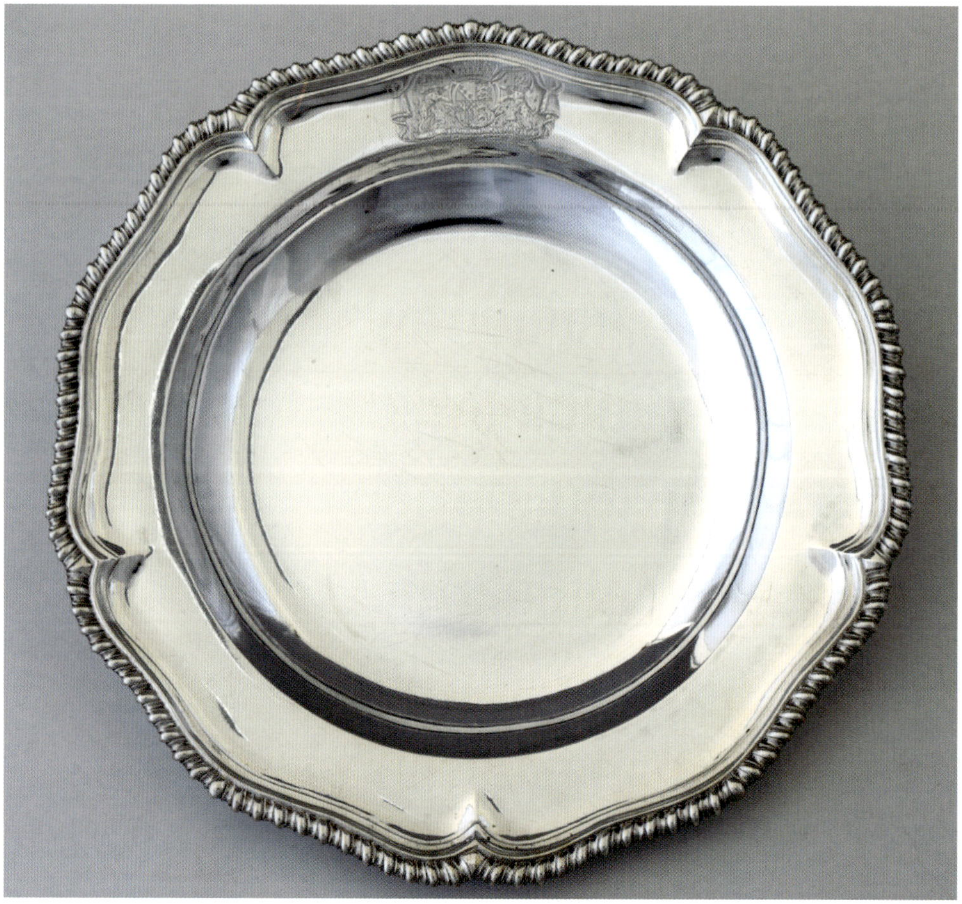

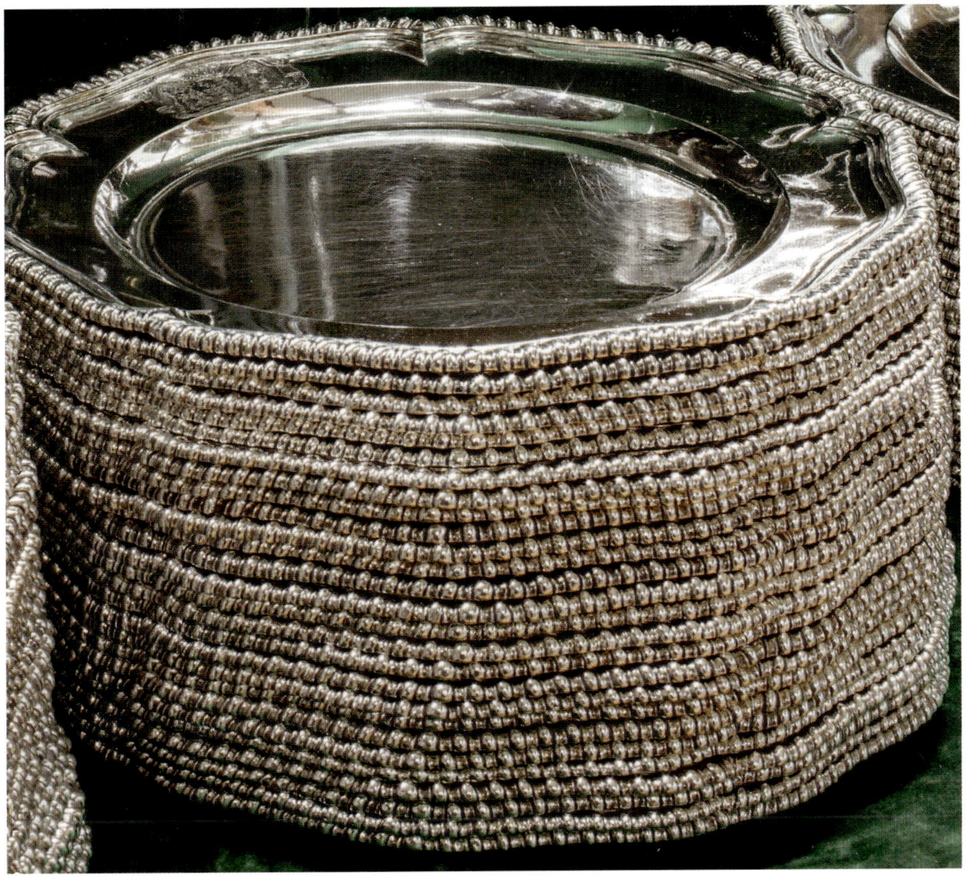

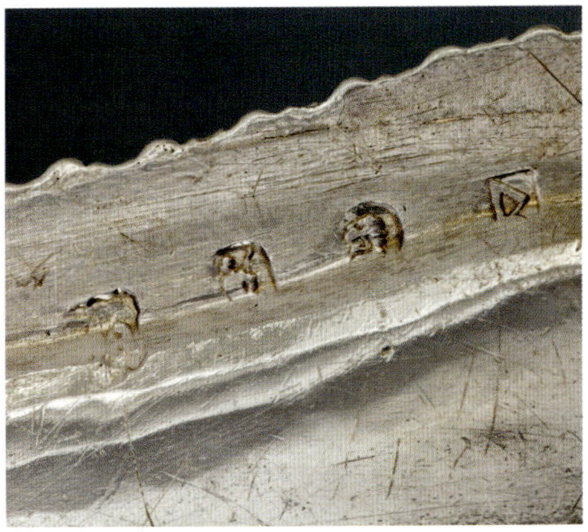

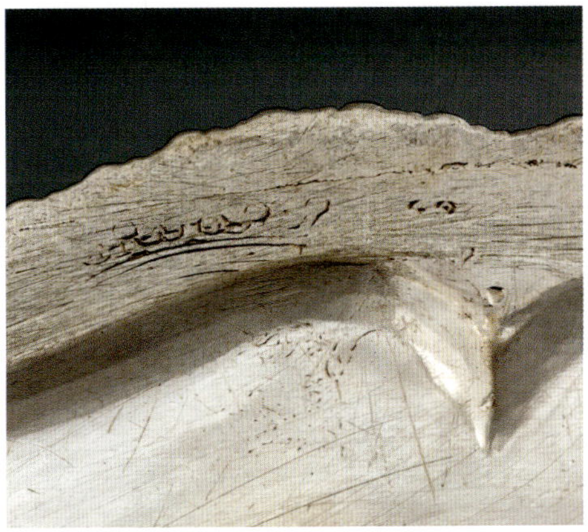

35. Seventy-two dinner plates

Silver / probably Frederick Kandler, London / *c.*1751

MARKS: Only one plate, no. 60, bears a mark from the date of manufacture, the maker's mark 'FK' in italics beneath a fleur-de-lis (Grimwade 1990, no. 691) for Frederick Kandler. Many of the remainder, however, have vestiges of those of former pieces. Twenty-six (nos. 5, 7, 12, 18, 22–5, 30, 32–3, 35 , 41, 46, 51, 54–59, 61, 63–4, 68 and 72) bear remnants of the sequence of maker's mark 'Ia' in Gothic script above a cross (Grimwade 1990, no. 1092) for John Jackson I, Britannia, lion's head erased and date letter 'h' for 1703. Seven more (nos. 19, 28, 31, 36, 38, 39 and 71) have Jackson's mark and/or the date letter 'g' for 1702 and two (nos. 47 and 52) have the same for Anthony Nelme (Grimwade 1990, no. 68) and 1701. Paul Crespin (Grimwade 1990, no. 2143a), 1726 appears on nos. 20 and 65 whilst Simon Pantin (Grimwade 1990, no. 2124), 1725 is on no. 66. No. 70 is marked for 1718, no. 42 for 1720 or 21 and no. 67 for 1725. Finally, no. 53 has the lion's head erased only and no. 69, the Britannia mark, lion's head erased and, very feint and separate, Frederick Kandler's maker's mark (Grimwade 1990, no. 691).

SCRATCHWEIGHTS: 'No 1 [/] 17=6'; 'No 2 [/] 17=5'; 'No 3 [/] 17=18'; 'No 4 [/] 16=5'; 'No 5 [/] 18=0'; 'N 6 [/] 16=17'; 'N 7 [/] 18=4'; 'N 8 [/] 17=14'; 'N 9 [/] 18=2'; 'N 10 [/] 18=8'; 'N 11 [/] 18=15'; 'N 12 [/] 17=19'; 'N 13 [/] 18=13'; 'N 14 [/] 17=0'; 'N 15 [/] 16=18'; 'N 16 [/] 16=11'; 'N 17 [/] 18=11'; 'N 18 [/] 18=17'; 'N 19 [/] 17=14'; 'N 20 [/] 18=9'; 'N 21 [/] 18=9'; 'N 22 [/] 17=17'; N 23 [/] 17=12'; 'N 24 [/] 18=6'; 'N 25 [/] 17=11'; 'N 26 [/] 18=11' plus old scratchweight 'N° 10 [/] 19–15'; 'N 27 [/] 19=0; 'N 28 [/] 19=9'; 'N 29 [/] 18=12'; 'N 30 [/] 18=3'; 'N 31 [/] 18=1'; 'N 32 [/] 18=1'; 'N 33 [/] 17=16'; 'N 34 [/] 17=9'; 'N 35 [/] 17=16'; 'N 36 [/] 17=18'; 'N 37 [/] 16:3'; 'N 38 [/] 18=13'; 'N 39 [/] 17=12'; 'N 40 [/] 18=18'; 'N 41 [/] 16=19'; 'N 42 [/] 19=6'; 'N 43 [/] 18=2'; 'N 44 [/] 18=14'; 'N 45 [/] 18=6'; 'N 46 [/] 17=17; 'N 47 [/] 17=1', plus old scratchweight 'N° 23 [/] 17–18', 'N 48 [/] 16=13'; 'N 49 [/] 18=6'; 'N 50 [/] 16=7'; 'N 51 [/] 17=17'; 'N 52 [/] 19=3'; 'N 53 [/] 19=4', 'N 54 [/] 18=0'; 'N 55 [/] 17=10'; 'N 56 [/] 17=13'; 'N 57 [/] 18=4'; 'N 58 [/] 18=4'; 'N 59 [/] 17=16'; 'N 60 [/] 18=10'; 'N 61 [/] 17=19'; 'N 62 [/] 17=3'; 'N 63 [/] 17=15'; 'N 64 [/] 17=7'; 'N 65 [/] 18=4'; 'N 66 [/] 17=6'; 'N 67 [/] 18=8'; plus vestige of old scratchweight '.. – 19'; 'N 68 [/] 18=5'; 'N 69 [/] 19=4'; 'N 70 [/] 18=11'; 'N 71 [/] 18=3'; 'N 72 [/] 17=13'.

MEASUREMENTS: h. 1.6 cm (⅝ in); diam. 24.8 cm (9¾ in).

INVENTORY: 852124.1–72

PROVENANCE: 2nd Earl of Bristol; by descent to the 4th Marquess.

LITERATURE: Penzer 1957a, II, pp. 136-8, fig. VI; Banister 1980, p. 793.

EXHIBITED: *British Week*, Milan and Frankfurt, 1965 (eight).

DESCRIPTION: Each plate is raised and has a shallow circular well, a broad rim and shaped and moulded cinquefoil borders with applied gadrooning. Their borders are of the same pattern as the soup plates (cat. 34).

HERALDRY: The rim of each plate is engraved with the quartered shield, supporters and motto of the 2nd Earl of Bristol in an ermine mantling and beneath an earl's coronet. On the reverse of many of the plates are vestiges of the engraved arms of the 1st Earl of Bristol, as executed in 1703 and altered in May 1721 when the baron's coronets were replaced with those of an earl (see appendix 1). Plate nos. 9, 12, 23, 32 and 33 have particularly clear remnants and the combined evidence of all the plates shows that when turned in they bore the arms of Hervey impaling Felton with the Hervey supporters and motto as survive only on the 1704 chocolate pot (cat. 5).

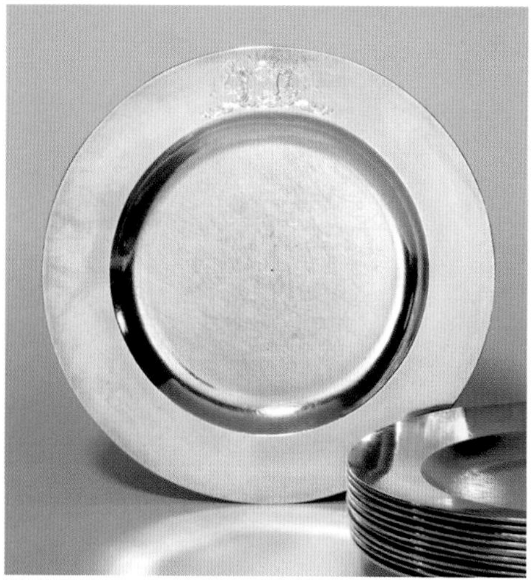

FIG. 91 / Dinner plates by Peter Archambo, London, 1728 Silver: diam. 24.7 cm (9¾ in). National Trust, Dunham Massey.

John Hervey (the future 1st Earl of Bristol) bought three dozen plates in 1696 and a further two dozen 'nurld' (gadrooned) the following year (see appendix 1).[1] In 1703 some of these may have been amongst the 1,236 ounces of old plate sent to the banker-goldsmith James Chambers in part exchange for '22 new Dishes & 3 Doz: of Plates weighed in all 1668 ou: 05 dwtt at 10d ffashion'. As no knurls are mentioned it is likely that these plates conformed to the simplicity which was then predominant and at most they would have had a moulded rim. Large numbers of this severe form survive, including those of 1728 by Peter Archambo at Dunham Massey (fig. 91).[2]

In France, under the influence of the *Régence*, the borders of dinner plates began to be given a wavy or lobed shape in the 1720s, thereby achieving a greater richness of effect as can be seen in a fine hexafoil example of 1725 by Paul Solaine of Paris and a set of six with cinquefoil borders of 1727 by an unknown Parisian maker (fig. 92).[3] It was these two variants on the same theme that eventually triumphed across Europe and remained in favour for 150 years. Their progress in England was slow, however, and the simple circular form, occasionally gadrooned, remained standard until the late 1730s.[4] What finally tipped the scales is not known but it may have been the impression made by the tables of the more Francophile amongst the nobility, such as the 4th Earl of Chesterfield, or those of foreign diplomats, aided by the illustrations in the oft-reprinted cookery book of Lord Chesterfield's erstwhile chef, Vincent La Chapelle.[5]

A flood of plates in the new style appeared in the years around 1740, either new-made or altered to suit, and the ledgers of George Wickes bear witness to the fashion taking hold. The four dozen plates and twenty-two dishes of the dinner service provided to Everard Fawkener in late 1735 must, at 6s 3½d per ounce, have been simple and circular whereas Sir Jacob Bouverie, 3rd Bt's five dozen plates accompanying '18 Shape Dishes' at 7s 2d an ounce in February 1738 are very likely to have been of the new form.[6] Over the next fifteen years large numbers of plates and dishes were sent in to be altered, 1743 being especially busy. Lord Montfort was billed for nine dozen plates and thirty-three dishes in February, George Brown for five dozen and fourteen in March and Lord Tyrawley for six dozen and eighteen in May. That was a total of 240 plates in four months, all charged at 1s 2d per ounce fashion plus duty on the knurls at 2s to 2s 8½d per plate.[7]

Other refashionings were prompted by inheritance, as was the case with the 6th Earl of Coventry in 1751 and the 4th Earl of Scarborough in 1752, the rate for making the alterations remaining the same.[8] Both those earls, who were young and fashionable, sent their plate to be upgraded within months of inheriting the family estates and the same was to be the case with George William Hervey, 2nd Earl of Bristol. His grandfather died on 20 January 1751 and his first tranche of new and altered silver was paid for on 29 July 1752, costing £263 13s 5d (see appendix 3). That is very likely to have included the dinner plates, as the Wickes ledgers reveal that they and the dishes were almost invariably the first elements to be dealt with, such major pieces as tureens following on later. Frederick Kandler, to whom the Earl turned to undertake the work, was faced with the dilemma of many of the plates having hallmarks on their fronts, as had been the practice at the beginning of the century, and he was compelled to essentially turn them inside out. He is very likely to have charged the same 1s 2d for fashion as George Wickes but whether he also billed Lord Bristol for the duty on the knurls is not known. If he did he may not have passed it on to the Treasury, his careful preservation of so many of the old hallmarks in spite of substantial reworking raising strong suspicions that he was duty dodging. Analysis of a selection of the plates carried out at the London Assay Office has confirmed that the bodies are of the Britannia standard and the borders sterling, so the pieces should have been re-marked as the latter.[9] At least, however, he did not use silver significantly below the sterling standard, as had Paul Crespin a decade earlier on Lord Hervey's dishes (see cat. 38 and 40).

The preservation of old hallmarks is fortunate for historians, provided that the trap is avoided of assuming they give the date of manufacture of the extant pieces. What they can tell us is something about the items that had been turned in to be transformed, helped in the case of the Bristol silver by the detailed accounts of the 1st Earl. Thus some twenty-nine of the thirty-six

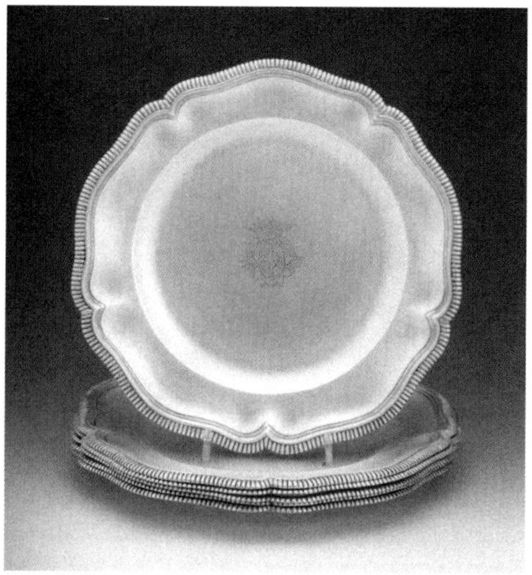

FIG. 92 / Dinner plates, Paris, 1727. Silver: diam. 25.5 cm (10 in). Christie's.

plates supplied by James Chambers in 1703 can be identified through hallmarks and vestiges of engraving as can the fact that they were made by John Jackson I. Furthermore, the dishes supplied at the same time are also represented amongst these plates and they too were by Jackson, hallmarked for 1702. Several pieces of Lord Hervey's silver are also present, including plate no. 42, bearing the date letter for 1720, which is likely to have been acquired with the 300 Guineas given to him by his father in October of that year 'to buy him silver Plates & Dishes when he went to Housekeeping' following his marriage to Mary Lepel. There are also two plates (nos. 20 and 65) with marks for Paul Crespin and 1725 which may well be connected to Lord Bristol's payment of £78 on 26 February 1726 to 'Mr David Willaume ye silver-smith in full for ye dozen of silver plates I gave my son Lord Hervey'. If that connection is correct then it suggests that Crespin was supplying Willaume at this early stage in his career.

1. Only two dozen plates are specified in the accounts for 1696, on 18 May and 7 November, but the first of these payments was for 'an other Dozen' so the £115 worth, unspecified, noted on 6 May must have included an initial purchase of plates.
2. Lomax and Rothwell 2006, cat. 24, pp. 72–3.
3. Dennis 1960, vol. II, p. 211, fig. 313 and Christie's Monte Carlo, 3 December 1989, lot 86.
4. The English seem to have been more comfortable with true polygons, such as the richly engraved hexagonal plates by Charles Kandler of 1730 sold at Christie's, 27–8 April 1983 and a full octagonal service of 1728–42 by Benjamin and Eliza Godfrey, Sotheby's 19 October 1961, lot 129. Even such breaks from the pure circle as these, however, were exceptionally rare.
5. Lomax 1992, p. 94, ill.
6. Wickes Ledgers, VAM I 1735–40, ff. 38 and 142.
7. Ibid, VAM 2 1740–8, ff. 86, 105 and 106.
8. Ibid, VAM 4 1747–60, ff. 65, 69 and 114. There was almost indecent haste in both cases, Lord Coventry's father dying in March and his account with Wickes and Netherton dated June whilst Lord Scarborough inherited in March and was being billed in November.
9. X-ray fluorescence (XRF) analysis carried out March 2015. Plates 20, 23, 47, 50 and 60 were analysed. For a discussion of plate duty and its avoidance see Barr 1980, pp. 191–6 and Dove 2007.

36. **Four round dishes**

Silver
probably Frederick Kandler, London
***c.*1751**

MARKS: There are no marks on these dishes contemporary with their making. Two are unmarked and two retain the marks on their undersides of the old pieces that were altered *c.*1751. Dish no. 1 has the maker's mark 'BO' beneath a mitre and above a cross (Grimwade 1990, no. 201) for John Bodington, lion's head erased, Britannia and date letter 'R' for 1712. Dish no. 2 has, distorted by the re-working, the maker's mark 'CR' beneath a pair of mullets and above a fleur-de-lis (Grimwade 1990, no. 406) for Paul Crespin.

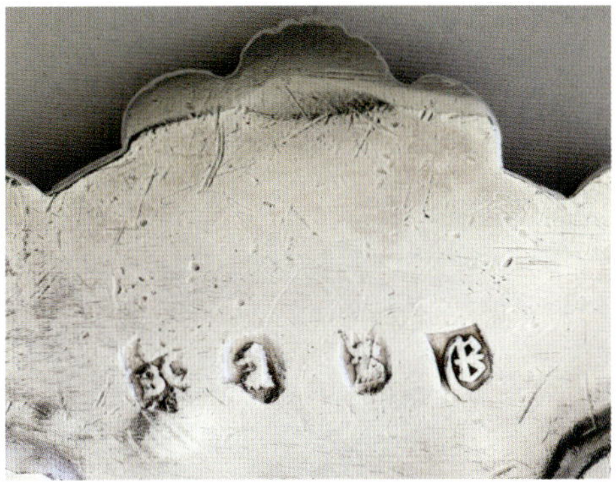

SCRATCHWEIGHTS: 'N 1 [/] 32=19'; 'N 2 [/] 34=2'; 'N° 3 = 34=14'; 'N° 4 [/] 34=15'.

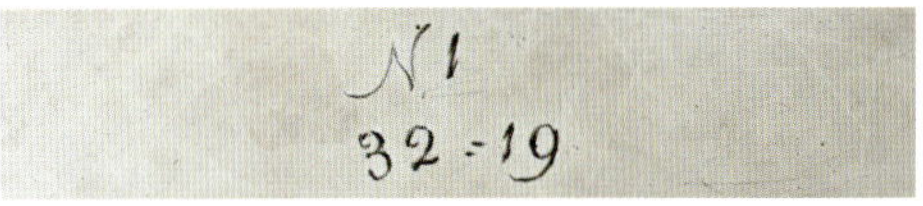

MEASUREMENTS: h. 2.2 cm (⅞ in); diam. 32.4 cm (12¾ in).

INVENTORY: 852121.3.1–4

PROVENANCE: 2nd Earl of Bristol; by descent to the 4th Marquess.

EXHIBITED: *British Week*, Milan and Frankfurt, 1965 (nos. 3 and 4).

DESCRIPTION: The dishes are raised with shallow circular wells, broad rims and cast shaped borders with twelve gadrooned lobes each having a central acanthus leaf. At four of the intersections between the lobes are cast scallop shells with pearl bands and flanking foliate scrolls.

HERALDRY: The rims of the dishes are engraved with the quartered shield, supporters and motto of the 2nd Earl of Bristol in an ermine mantling and beneath an earl's coronet. The reverse of dish no. 1 also has the wreath of a crest from the old vessel turned in.

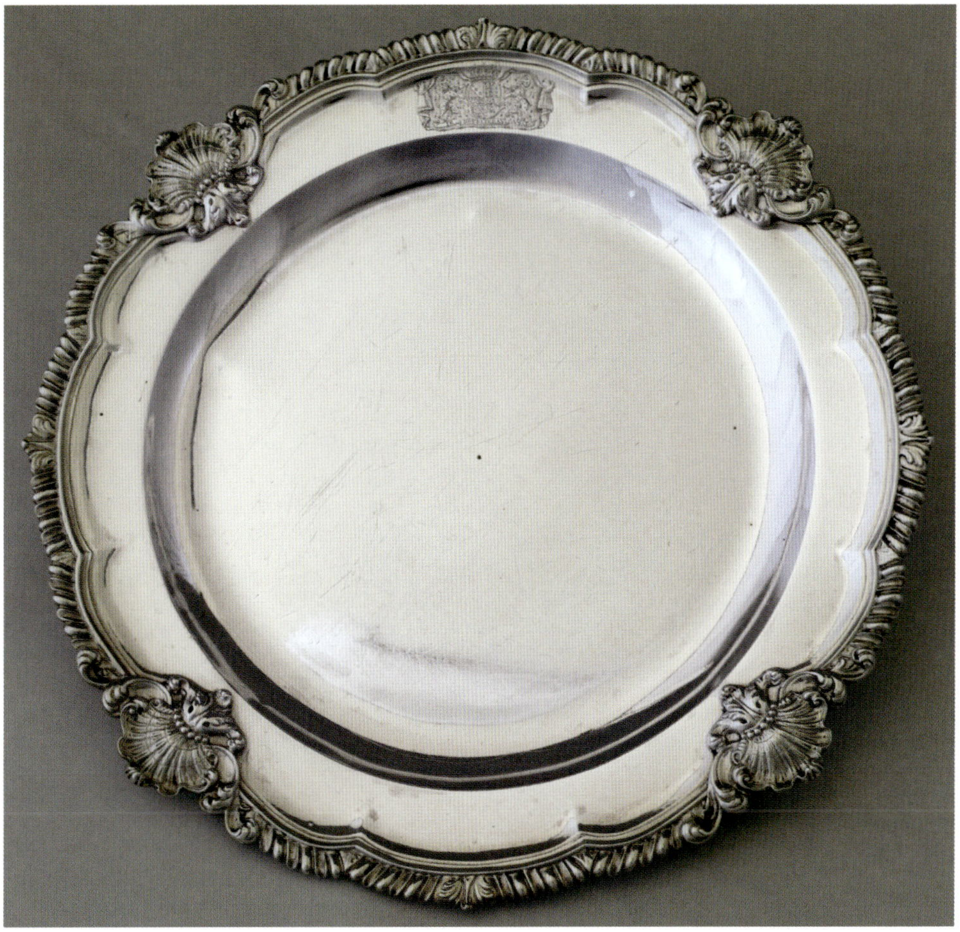

As with the large oval dishes (cat. 32), sauce boats (cat. 30) and salad dishes (cat. 31), these pieces have cast shells to unite them with the rest of the service. The borders, which are particularly finely modelled, derive from those which emerged in the mid-1740s and were most spectacularly employed on the Leinster dinner service supplied by George Wickes in 1747, though in that case combined with reeding rather than gadrooning.[1]

From the evidence of the hallmarks (two without any and two with those of former pieces) and scratchweights, plus slight differences in the engraving of the arms, these four dishes represent the combination of two separate sets, so there may well have been eight originally, supplied in two batches. Although often referred to as 'second course dishes' such a term seems only rarely to have been applied in the mid-eighteenth century[2] and they would have been able to be used with the first, second or third courses, all of which needed subsidiary dishes, or *hors d'oeuvres*, on the table around the principal fare.[3] *Hors d'oeuvres* were described by Louis Liger in his 1711 publication, *Les ménage des champs et le jardinier françois* as being served 'aux trois premiers services'[4] and examples given by Vincent La Chapelle in 1736 for 'a Supper of 15 or 16 Covers' included 'Mutton-Cutlets glaz'd with Endive', 'Larks the *Moscovite* way' and 'Fillets of Soles with Champain'.[5]

As with the plates (cat. 35), scientific analysis has confirmed that the body of the dish sampled (no. 1) is Britannia standard and the border sterling.[6] This piece also has an old setting-out mark well off the current centre which suggests a previous existence as a much larger dish.

The 1st Earl does not record any silver purchases in 1712–13, the date of the hallmark, but that year does coincide with both Carr Hervey's return from three years abroad and his coming of age, so the dish could have been his. Alternatively it could have formed part of the plate acquired from the estate of Lady Howard of Effingham in 1727 (appendix 1), as might the surviving salver by Robert Cooper (fig. 14), made the same year and subsequently owned by the Hon. Felton Hervey.[7]

For the later covers associated with these dishes see cat. 73.

1. Barr 1980, pp. 197–205, ill.
2. Three dishes of 1759 at Temple Newsam by William Reynolds or Reynoldson have been inscribed '2nd course' on their undersides, probably contemporaneously. See Lomax 1992, cat. 85, pp. 94–5. I am grateful to the author for alerting me to this example.
3. Wheaton 1983, p. 140.
4. Noël-Waldteuffel 1993, p. 76.
5. La Chapelle 1736, vol. 1, plate VII.
6. X-ray fluorescence (XRF) analysis carried out March 2015 on dish no. 1. The body is 96.94% silver and the border 95.71%.
7. Sotheby's, 4 March 1965, lot 169.

37. **Four octagonal dishes**

Silver / probably Frederick Kandler, London / *c.*1751

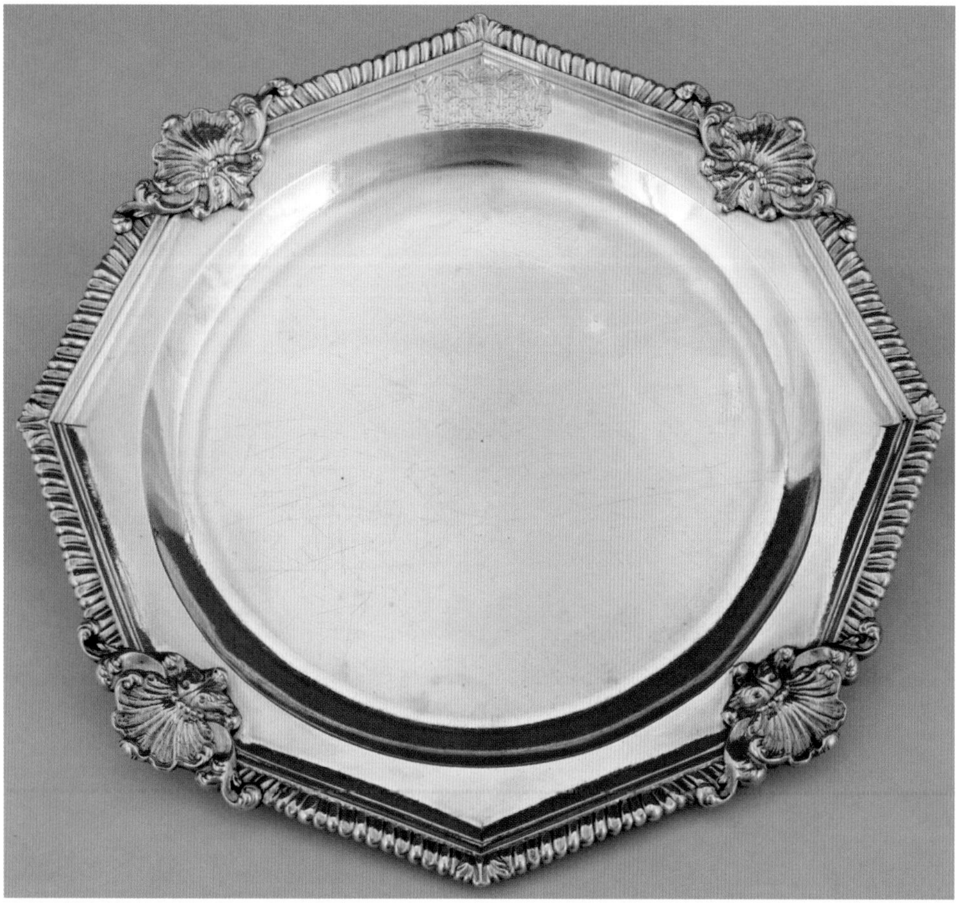

MARKS: No hallmarks on any of the dishes.

SCRATCHWEIGHTS: 'N1 [/] 33=10'; 'N2 [/] 34=16'; 'N3 [/] 34=14'; 'N4 [/] 35=9'.

MEASUREMENTS: h. 2.9 cm (1⅛ in); w. 32.4 cm (12¾ in).

INVENTORY: 852115.1.2, 2.2, 3.2 and 4.2.

PROVENANCE: 2nd Earl of Bristol; by descent to the 4th Marquess.

EXHIBITED: Society of the Four Arts, Palm Beach, Florida, 1959 (one); *British Week*, Milan and Frankfurt, 1965 (two).

DESCRIPTION: The dishes are raised with shallow circular wells, broad rims and cast octagonal gadrooned borders with palm leaves at four of the angles and cast scallop shells with pearl bands and flanking foliate scrolls at the other four.

HERALDRY: The rims of the dishes are engraved with the quartered shield, supporters and motto of the 2nd Earl of Bristol in an ermine mantling and beneath an earl's coronet.

These are an octagonal version of the round dishes (cat. 36) and would have been used in the same way. Polygonal shapes had been present in English silver throughout the eighteenth century, and mixing circles, octagons and shaped ovals, as could Lord Bristol, would have greatly suited the rococo table. Three of the four dishes (nos. 1–3) have old setting-out marks well off-centre and thus are likely to have been made from significantly larger dishes turned in by the Earl. No attempt has been made here to disguise the fact that hallmarking has not occurred.

For the later covers associated with these dishes see cat. 73.

38. **Four dishes with lobed ends**

Silver / probably Frederick Kandler, London / *c.*1751

MARKS: No marks contemporary with the pieces as they now are. Nos. 1 and 2 have redundant hallmarks on the underside of their rims, leopard's head, lion passant, date letter 'F' for 1721 and maker's mark 'P.C' beneath a shell and above a mullet (Grimwade 1990, no. 2143a) for Paul Crespin. Nos. 3 and 4 are marked on the underside of the rim with the redundant date letter 'e' for 1740, leopard's head, lion passant and maker's mark 'PC' in italics (Grimwade 1990, no. 2149) for Paul Crespin (1739 registration).

SCRATCHWEIGHTS: 'N 1 [/] 38=14' and [old] 'N^{O} 2 = ~~33~~ = ~~11~~ [/] 33–'; 'N 2 [/] 39=9' and [old] 'N^{O} 1 = ~~34~~ = ~~4~~ [/] 33–17'; 'N 3 [/] 40=7' and [old] '34=10'; 'N 4 [/] 41=3' and [old] '35=14'.

MEASUREMENTS: h. 4.4 cm (1¾ in); w. 42.2 cm (16⅝ in); d. 25.4 cm (10 in).

INVENTORY: 852110.1.1, 2.1, 3.1 and 4.1.

PROVENANCE: 2nd Earl of Bristol; by descent to the 4th Marquess.

DESCRIPTION: The dishes are raised and have oval wells with broad rims, straight sides and indented, lobed ends. The cast gadroon borders with palm leaves are applied as are the cast and chased shell handles which cover the indents.

HERALDRY: The rims of the dishes are engraved with the quartered shield, supporters and motto of the 2nd Earl of Bristol in an ermine mantling and beneath an earl's coronet.

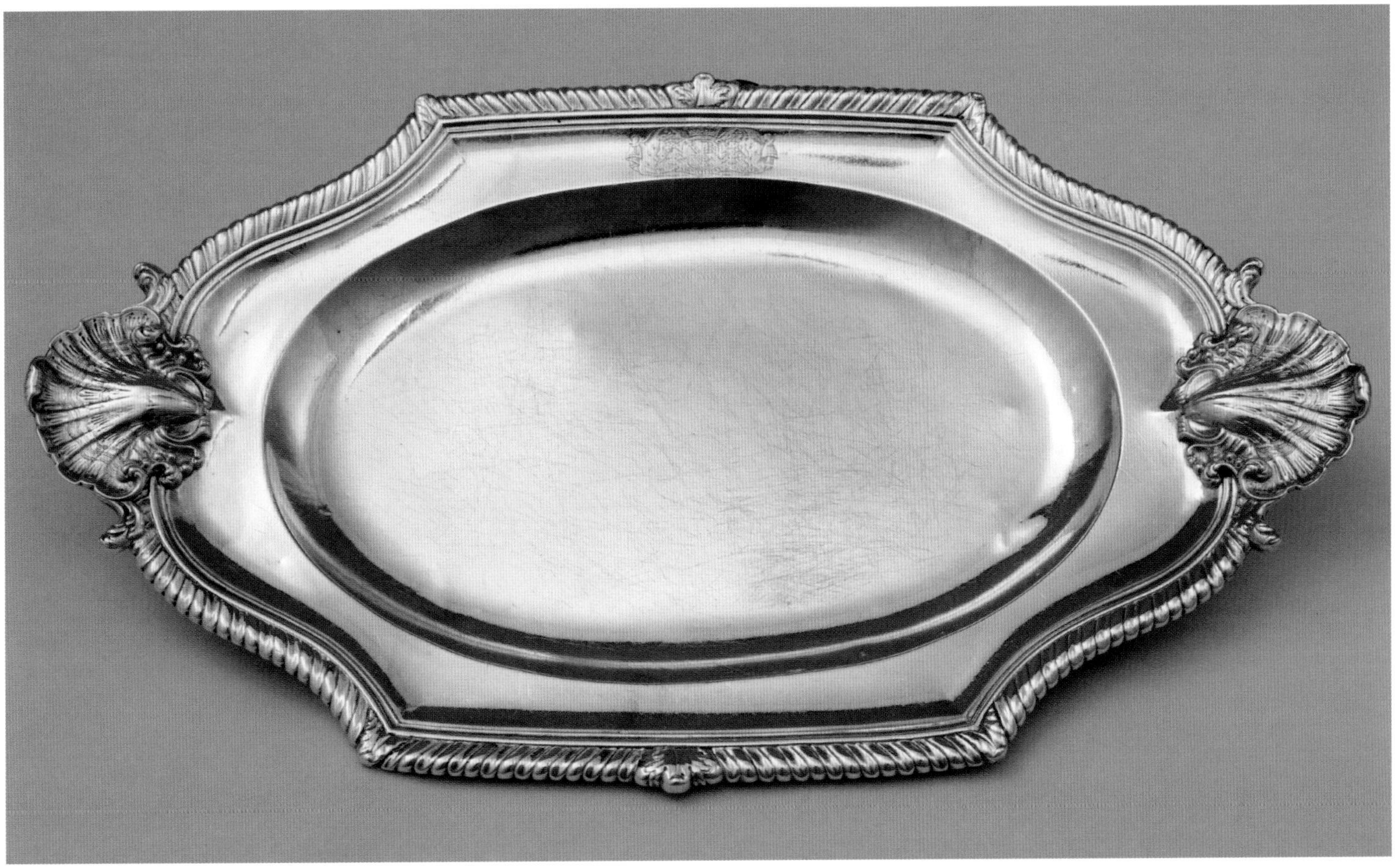

With the exception of the shell handles, which are accounted for in the additional five ounces of the altered scratchweights, these dishes survive exactly as they would have been when inherited from John, Lord Hervey on his death in 1743. The 2nd Earl of Bristol's pragmatic and prudent approach to the transformation of his old plate is once again demonstrated, the addition of the shells proving highly effective and at considerably less expense than making anew. These pieces were thus rendered suitable to take their place alongside the other dishes of the dinner service, for use in the same manner as those of smaller size (see cat. 36).

The dishes do, however, have greater complexity in their early history than is at first apparent, with those marked for 1721 clearly having been reshaped to some extent, the maker's mark on one being distorted. This work probably took place in 1740 when the other two were made and is likely to have been mostly restricted to the addition of gadrooning which by that time would have been more *de rigueur*. Curiously the later dishes, one of which has been scientifically analysed, have bodies of Britannia standard, so they too must have been transformed from earlier pieces yet presumably to such an extent that Crespin felt obliged to have them hallmarked. He took quite a risk as it turns out, for the borders contain nearly ten per cent copper and are thus considerably below sterling, which the dishes are marked for.[1] The shape of the dishes, before the addition of the shell handles, is one of those illustrated in the 1736 edition of Vincent La Chapelle's *The modern cook*.[2]

For the later covers associated with these dishes see cat. 88.

1. Analysis carried out March–April 2015 at the London Assay Office by XRF and Inductively Coupled Plasma Optical Emission Spectroscopy (ICP-OES). The border of dish no. 3 contains 0.219% gold, 0.048% bismuth, 0.143% lead, 9.919% copper, 0.004% tin and 0.003% antimony.
2. Lomax 1992, p. 94, ill.

39. **Four small oval dishes**

Silver / probably Frederick Kandler, London / *c.*1751

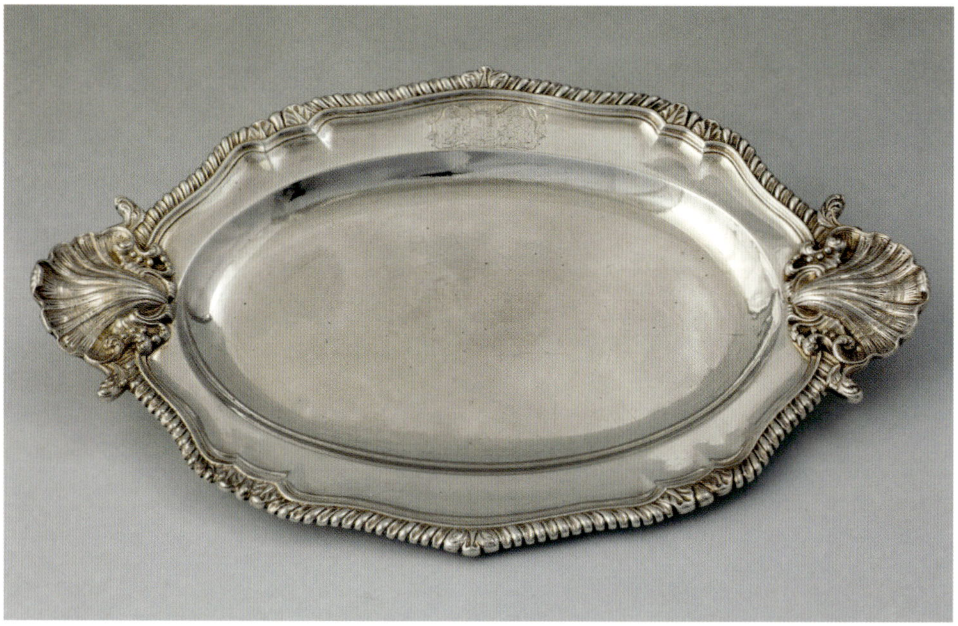

MARKS: No marks contemporary with the pieces as they now are. No. 1 has old marks on the underside of the right hand shell, makers mark obscured by reworking, lion's head erased, date letter 'L' for 1726 and Britannia. No. 2 (image below) has a transposed set of marks introduced on the underside of the right-hand shell of which only two are legible, the lion's head erased and the date letter 'g' for 1702. No. 3 has a transposed set of marks on the underside of the left shell, one mark not legible, lion's head erased and date letter 'L' for 1726. No. 4 has old marks, not transposed, on the underside of the left shell, maker's mark 'SA' with crown and cup above and pellet below (Grimwade 1990, no. 2469) for John Hugh Le Sage, Britannia, lion's head erased and date letter F for 1721.

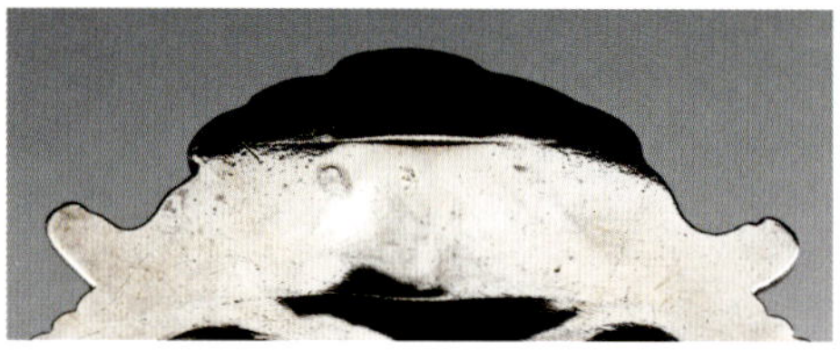

SCRATCHWEIGHTS: 'N1 [/] 34=6'; 'N2 [/] 34=7'; 'N3 [/] 34=13'; 'N4 [/] 34=19'.

MEASUREMENTS: 1. h. 3.5 cm (1⅜ in), w. 37.1 cm (14⅝ in), d. 24.4 cm (9⅝ in); 2. h. 3.5 cm (1⅜ in), w. 37.1 cm (14⅝ in), d. 24.8 cm (9¾ in); 3. h. 3.5 cm (1⅜ in), w. 37.5 cm (14¾ in), d. 24.4 cm (9⅝ in). 4. h. 3.2 cm (1¼ in), w. 37.5 cm (14¾ in), d. 24.4 cm (9⅝ in).

INVENTORY: 852096

PROVENANCE: 2nd Earl of Bristol; by descent to the 4th Marquess.

DESCRIPTION: The oval dishes, which are raised, have shallow wells and broad rims with shaped, gadrooned borders and cast and chased shell handles.

HERALDRY: The rims of the dishes are engraved with the quartered shield, supporters and motto of the 2nd Earl of Bristol in an ermine mantling and beneath an earl's coronet.

For general comments on this form of oval, shell-handled dish see cat. 32. These four are equivalent in size to the circular, octagonal and lobed dishes (cat. 36–8) and would have been used in the same fashion during the meal, around the main focus of the soup, roasts and fish. They might have been particularly reserved for fare that was to be removed at the end of the first or second course, given the manipulability provided by the handles, and also have proved suitable for such elongated *hors d'oeuvres* as Vincent La Chapelle's 'Eels glaz'd with an *Italian* sauce'.[1]

As with the round dishes predominant in the early eighteenth century, these oval versions were provided in several sizes of which this was the smallest (see cat. 32 and 87 for the large and 40 for the middle sizes). Three were made from significantly larger old dishes, as proved by former setting-out punchmarks which are substantially off-centre.[2] The redundant hallmarks, both preserved and transposed, are clearly intended to deceive and thus to avoid duty. They are likely to be from the plate of Lord Hervey, as given to him by his father in 1720 and from his own subsequent purchases (see cat. 35).

1. La Chapelle 1736, plate VII.
2. Analysis of dish no. 1 by XRF carried out March, 2015 confirmed that the body is of Britannia standard at 97.72% and the border is sterling at 94.44%.

40. **Four medium oval dishes**

Silver / probably Frederick Kandler, London / *c.*1751

MARKS: No marks contemporary with the pieces as they now are. Nos. 1 and 2 are marked on the underside of the rim with the redundant date letter 'S' for 1733, leopard's head, lion passant and maker's mark 'P.C' beneath a shell and above a mullet (Grimwade 1990, no. 2143a) for Paul Crespin.

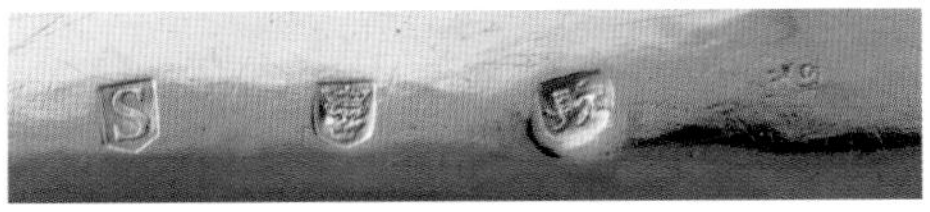

Nos. 3 and 4 are marked on the underside of the rim with the redundant date letter 'e' for 1740, leopard's head, lion passant and maker's mark 'PC' in italics (Grimwade 1990, no. 2149) for Paul Crespin (1739 registration).

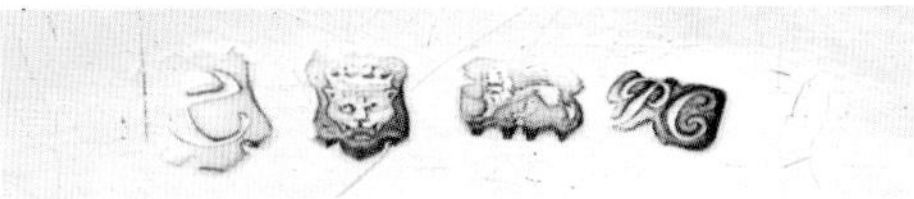

SCRATCHWEIGHTS: 'N 1 [/] 43=9' and [old] 'Nº 2 [/] ~~37=1~~ [/] 36'; 'N 2 [/] 46=0 and [old] 'Nº 1 ~~39=0~~ [/] 38=7'; N3 [/] 49=12 and [old] ~~42=5~~'; 'N 4 [/] 50=2 and opposite [old] '42=18'.

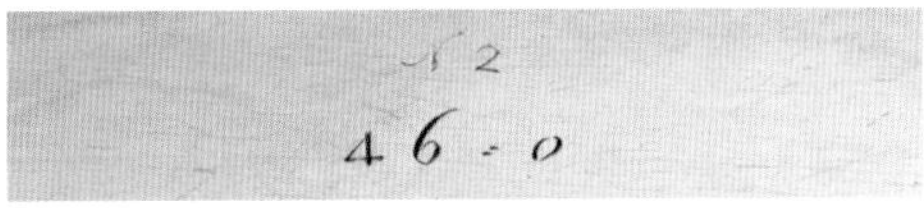

MEASUREMENTS: 1. h. 4.1 cm (1⅝ in), w. 47 cm (18½ in), d. 30.2 cm (11⅞ in). 2. h. 5.1 cm (2 in), w. 46.4 cm (18¼ in), d. 30.1 cm (11⅞ in). 3. h. 4.4 cm (1¾ in), w. 46.4 cm (18¼ in), d. 30.5 cm (12 in). 4. h. 2.5 cm (1 in), w. 46 cm (18⅛ in), d. 30.5 cm (12 in).

INVENTORY: 852095.1–2 and 7–8

PROVENANCE: 2nd Earl of Bristol; by descent to the 4th Marquess.

DESCRIPTION: The oval dishes, which are raised, have shallow wells and broad rims with shaped, gadrooned borders and cast and chased shell handles.

HERALDRY: The rims of the dishes are engraved with the quartered shield, supporters and motto of the 2nd Earl of Bristol in an ermine mantling and beneath an earl's coronet.

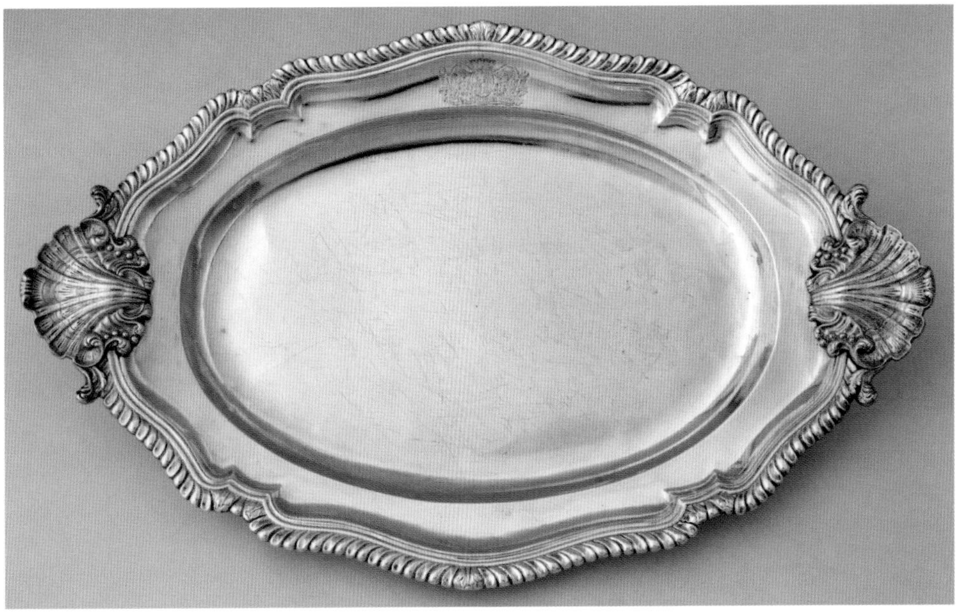

The difference of about 7½ oz between the new and old scratchweights is accounted for by the addition of the shells. They are some 2 oz heavier than the shells on the lobe-ended dishes (cat. 38) and constitute the middle of three sizes of shell handle employed on the Bristol dinner service, according to the scale of the overall piece. These dishes, being of the middling size, would probably have been used for the entrées of the first course, such as La Chapelle's 'Partridges the Spanish Way' and 'young Ducks with Orange-Juice', and for the 'Dishes of roast Fowl' that might have come with the second course.[1]

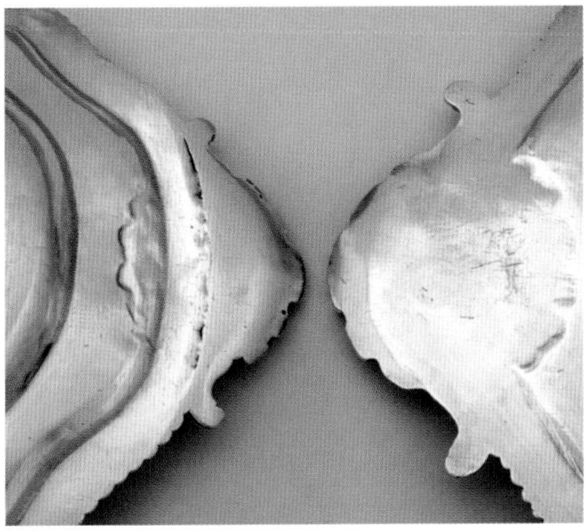

As with the lobe-ended dishes, these four are in the same form, apart from the shells, as when inherited by the 2nd Earl from his father in 1743. They are somewhat less complex in their earlier history as none appears to have been reshaped since the dates of their hallmarks. Analysis of dish no. 2, however, does show that, once again, the body is of Britannia standard and the border well below sterling. Crespin was presumably, therefore, using old pieces but substantially re-forming them. The physical evidence of the addition of the shell handles *c.* 1751 is clear when compared with the 1768 dishes on which they were part of the original design (see image; cat. 87 on the right).

1. La Chapelle 1736, plate VII.

41. **Kitchen spoon**

Silver / probably London / *c.*1751 / repaired in Madrid by Carlos Gomis de Fornas, 1760

MARKS: Fully marked on the front of the stem with the castle mark of Madrid, maker's mark 'CARLS [/] GOMIS' in a plain rectangular stamp for Carlos Gomis de Fornas and the assay mark of '60·[/]MEL[/]CON' for Eugenio Melcón, 1760.[1]

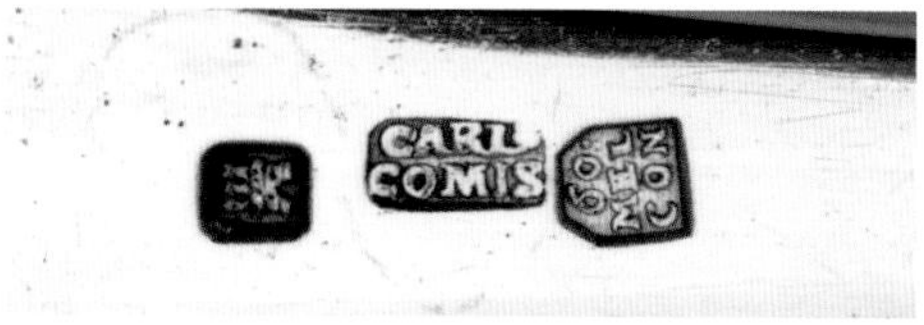

SCRATCHWEIGHT: None.
Actual weight: 302 g (9 oz, 15 dwt).

MEASUREMENTS: l. 38.7 cm (15¼ in).

INVENTORY: 852909

PROVENANCE: Probably the 2nd Earl of Bristol; by descent to the 7th Marquess and probably sold privately by him; Perry T. Foster, San Francisco; given by him to the National Trust for Ickworth, 2008.

LITERATURE: Rowell 2009, p. 33.

DESCRIPTION: The plain spoon has a raised oval bowl and a narrow stem with a downturned end.

HERALDRY: The front of the top of the stem is engraved with the Hervey crest beneath an earl's coronet.

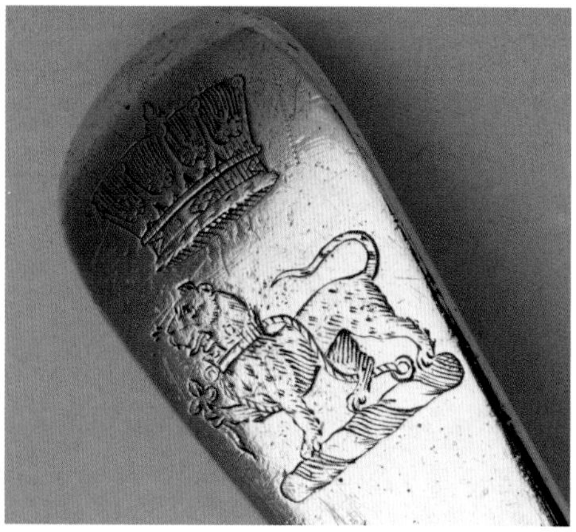

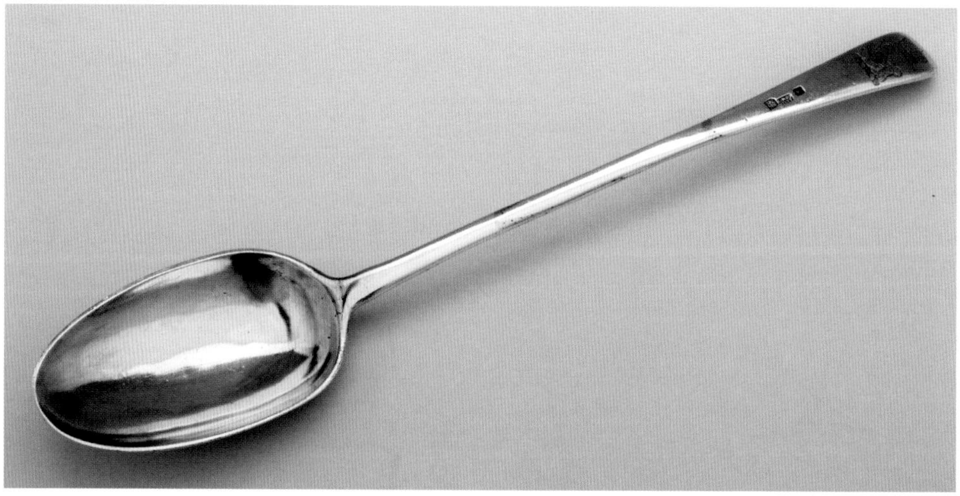

Judging by the style of its engraving the spoon was almost certainly made in England and scientific analysis has confirmed that its handle is of sterling standard and the bowl slightly below that.[2] Breaks in the stem are clearly evident and it may have been snapped more than once. On the last occasion that it was repaired, in Madrid, the work was done by the Valencian-born silversmith, Carlos Gomis de Fornas, who was active in the 1750s. A censer and incense boat marked by him survive in the parish church at La Puebla de Montalbán, Toledo.[3] He made sure to strengthen the stem by splicing in a thickened central section. Survivals of Spanish domestic plate from the eighteenth century are exceptionally rare.

The damage to what must have been a robust spoon and the strengthening deemed necessary when it was repaired suggest that it was intensely used by the chef in the kitchen of the Earl of Bristol's Madrid palace, who would no doubt have been French like the famous M. Clouet who served the Duke of Newcastle. Clouet is shown holding a large spoon, probably made of silver, in a contemporary engraving (fig. 93). Jonathan Swift's satirical *Directions to servants* of 1745 shows that rough use was one of his bugbears as he sarcastically recommended the cook to 'Scrape the Bottoms of your Pots and Kettles with a Silver Spoon.'[4] All the principal recipe books of the eighteenth century make reference to the need for silver spoons in cooking and a number of 'kitchen spoons' were supplied by George Wickes. For example, against the account of Mr Mann for 9 April 1736 is 'a Kitchen Spoon & Graving 3[oz]-19[dwt]' at £1 7s 6d whilst that of Coulson Fellowes of Eggesford in Devon has 'a Kitchen Spoon and Crest', weight 4 oz, 12 dwt, at £1 11s on 28 February 1737.[5] As with saucepans (see cat. 16), they would have been used where

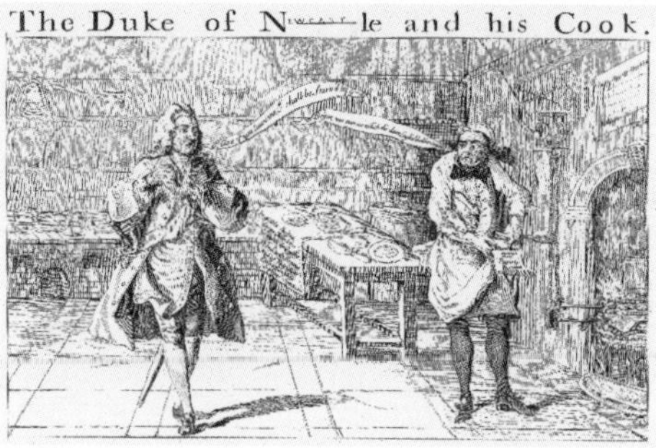

FIG. 93 / *The Duke of N[ewcast]le and his [French] Cook*, English, 1745. Print: 19.1 x 28.6 cm (7½ x 11¼ in). British Museum.

there was a need for greater sensitivity or with delicate foods that might otherwise taint. The smoothness of finish was probably why Mrs Raffald advised a silver spoon for drawing threads of sugar in *The experienced English house-keeper* of 1769.[6]

There is a payment of 1s in the 1st Earl's bank account on 26 March 1726 for 'Engraving a Large Spoon wth Crest' which could relate to this piece, but it could equally well have been acquired by the 2nd Earl in the 1750s. The spoon must be that recorded in the 1874 plate list as plain and 'Extra Large' and weighing 9½ oz.[7] It was retained by the family in 1956 and sold at some point thereafter.

1. I am grateful to José Manuel Cruz Valdovinos for identifying these marks.
2. Analysis carried out March–April 2015 at the London Assay Office by XRF and Inductively Coupled Plasma Optical Emission Spectroscopy (ICP-OES). The bowl has 8.429% copper, the middle section of the handle 7.217% and the terminal 6.137%.
3. Information from José Manuel Cruz Valdovinos, via Christopher Rowell.
4. Swift 1745, p. 42.
5. Wickes Ledgers, VAM I 1735–40, ff. 51 and 66.
6. Raffald 1769, p. 225.
7. Bristol Plate List 1874b.

42. **Pair of carving knives**

Silver handles / probably London / *c.*1751 / Steel blades, early twentieth century

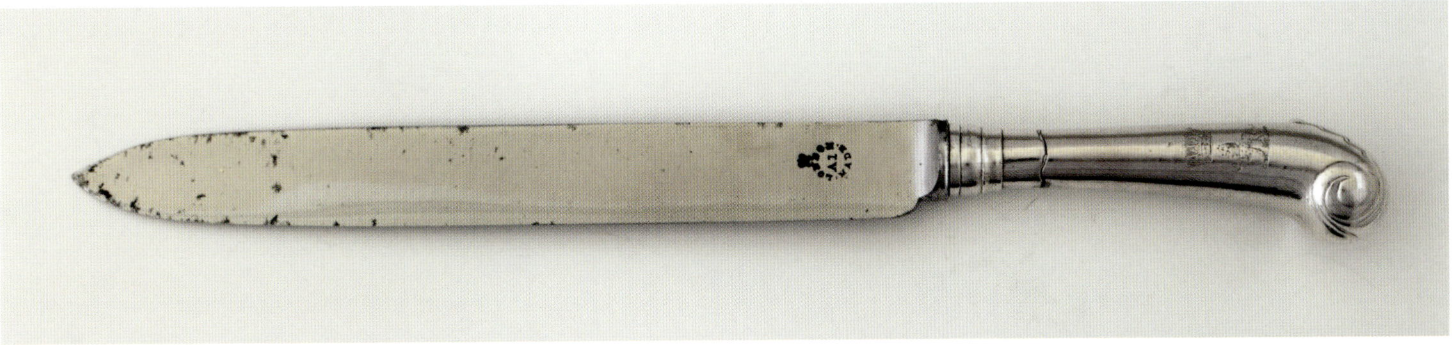

MARKS: No marks on the handles. The blades are stamped with a crown above 'LONDON MADE' in a circle around 'A1'.

MEASUREMENTS: l. of handle 11.4 cm (4½ in); l. of knife (overall) 34.9 cm (13¾ in).

INVENTORY: 852205

PROVENANCE: Probably 2nd Earl of Bristol; by descent to the 4th Marquess.

DESCRIPTION: The cast pistol handles have scroll ends and chased wavy lines on the stem. The straight steel blades with pointed ends are probably early twentieth century.

HERALDRY: The handle is engraved with the Hervey crest beneath an earl's coronet.

Joints of meat would have been carved at the table and hence the need for fine implements to undertake the task. John Trusler explained the protocol in his *The honours of the table* of 1788:

When there are several dishes at table, the mistress of the house carves that which is before her, and desires her husband, or the person at the bottom of the table, to carve the joint or bird, before him.[1]

As the 2nd Earl of Bristol was unmarried it would have been one of his sisters, or whoever else was acting as hostess when company was mixed, who would have taken on the role with him.

The art of carving was considered an essential part of the training of a gentleman, Lord Chesterfield stating 'that to carve well … is useful twice every day [dinner and supper], and the doing of it ill is not only troublesome to ourselves, but renders us disagreeable and ridiculous to others.'[2] Trusler's work is subtitled *The art of carving* and seventy pages are devoted to explaining how to tackle all manner of beasts, birds and fish, with detailed descriptions, accompanying illustrations, and guidance on the choicest parts. Carving was to be executed from a seated position, the carver was also expected to add gravy and he or she should either distribute the meat evenly, ask what part was preferred or give the best 'to those of superior rank, in preference to those of inferior'.[3] Trusler's instructions for a young hare, as an example (fig. 94), were as follows:

The genteelest, best and readiest way, is … to put in the point of the knife at g, *and cut it through all the way down the rump, on one side the back-bone, in the line* g h. *This done, cut it similarly on the other side … You have now an opportunity of cutting the back through the spine or back-bone, into several small pieces, more or less in the lines* i k, *the back being by far the tenderest part, fullest of gravy, and the greatest delicate. With a part of the back should be given a spoonful of pudding, with which the belly is stuffed, below the letters* k … *The legs are the part next in estimation … The shoulders or wings are to be cut off in the circular lines* e f g … [*they*] *are generally bloody; but many like the blood … Some like the head, brains and bloody part of the neck … cut off the ears at the roots, which if roasted crisp, many are fond of, and may be asked if they please to have one.*[4]

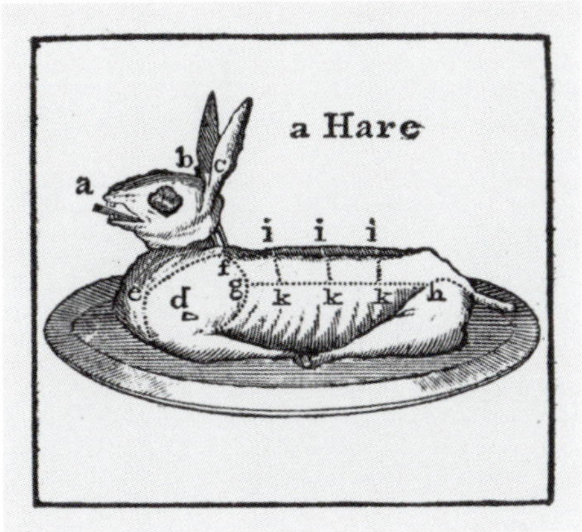

FIG. 94 / Illustration of carving lines on a hare from John Trusler, *The Honours of the Table, or, Rules for Behaviour during Meals with the whole Art of Carving illustrated by a variety of cuts*, London, 1788, p. 63. Library of Congress.

The forks that would have accompanied these knives do not survive. They were present in 1811 (appendix 5) but had gone by 1874, presumably worn out by use and discarded.[5]

1. Trusler 1788, p. 7.
2. Ibid., frontispiece.
3. Ibid., pp. 25–6.
4. Ibid., pp. 63–5.
5. Bristol plate list 1874b.

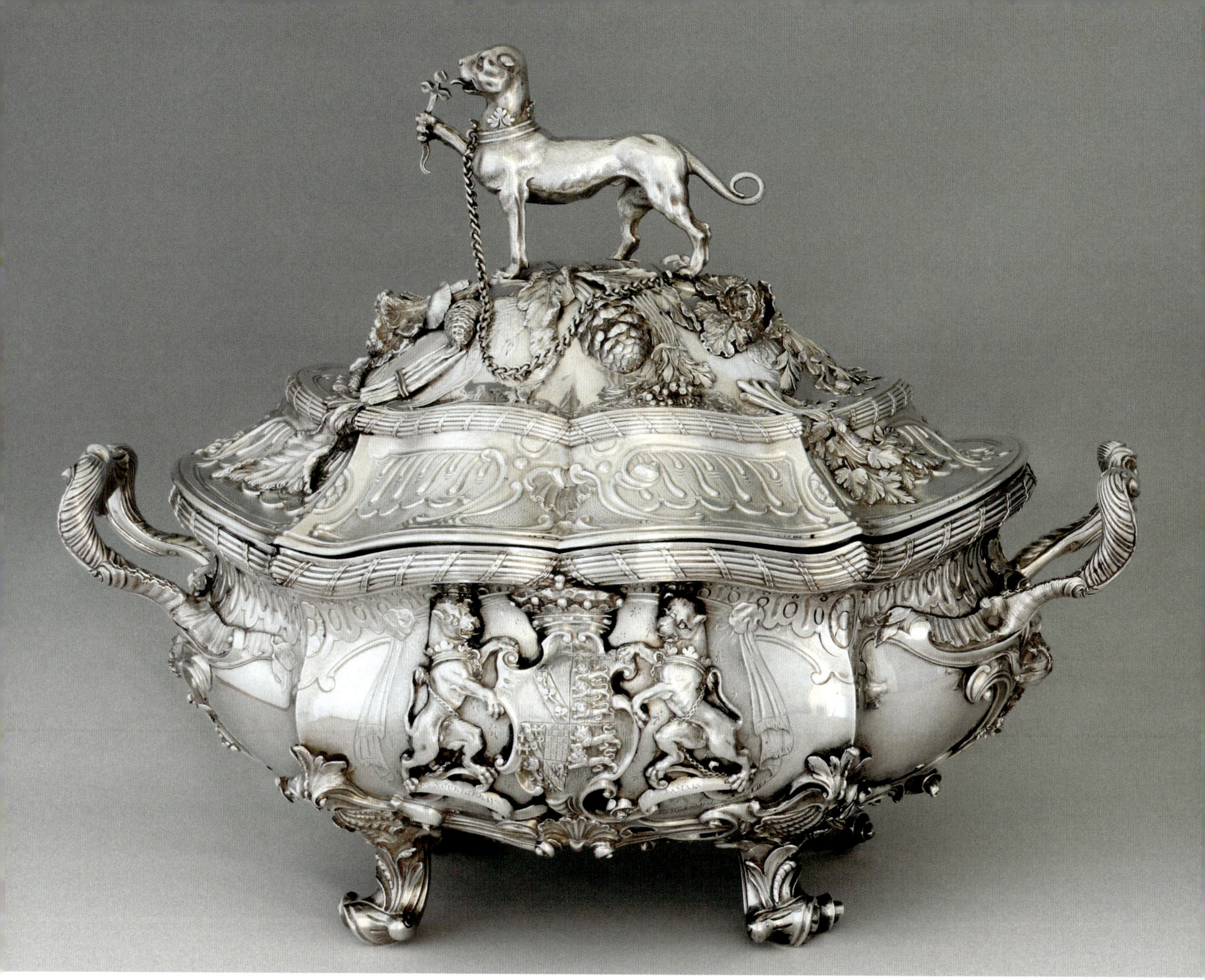

43. Pair of oval tureens

Sterling silver / **Frederick Kandler, London** / **1752/3**

MARKS: Each tureen base is fully marked on the outside below the handles with leopard's head, date letter 'r', lion passant and maker's mark 'FK' in italics beneath a fleur-de-lis (Grimwade 1990, no. 691). The same set of marks appears on the bases of the liners and on the bezels of the covers.

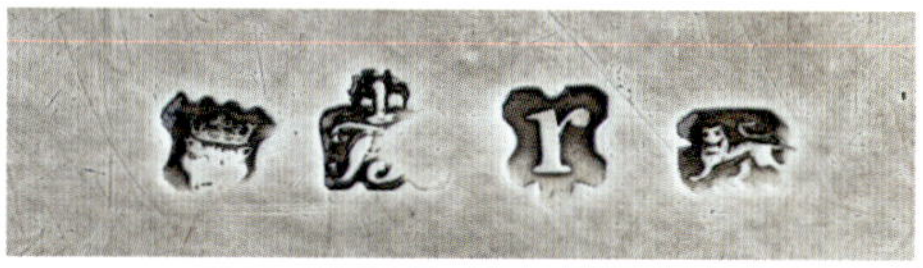

SCRATCHWEIGHTS AND INSCRIPTIONS: 1. 'N1 [/] 231=15' on the base of the liner plus 'B' on inside face beneath a handle and on the inside face of the base; 2. 'N2 [/] 236=5' on the base of the liner plus '„' on inner face by handle, 'A' at opposite end beneath the handle and 'A' on the inside face of the base.

MEASUREMENTS: 1. h. 35.6 cm (14 in), w. 44.5 cm (17½ in), d. (handles) 27 cm (10⅝ in); 2. h. 36.2 cm (14¼ in), w. 44.5 cm (17½ in); d. (handles) 27.9 cm (11 in).

INVENTORY: 852127

PROVENANCE: 2nd Earl of Bristol; by descent to the 4th Marquess.

LITERATURE: Penzer 1957a, II, pp. 134–5, fig. IV; Clayton 1971, p. 267; Hernmarck 1977, vol. 1, p. 187, vol. 2, p. 163, fig. 418; Banister 1980, pp. 793–4, fig. 7.

EXHIBITED: *Treasures from National Trust Houses*, Christie's, London, 1957–8, cat. 172 (one); Society of the Four Arts, Palm Beach, Florida, 1959 (one); *British Week*, Milan and Frankfurt, 1965; *Silver from National Trust Houses*, Treasurer's House, York Festival, 1969, cat. 36 (one); *Treasures from Country Houses of the National Trust and National Trust for*

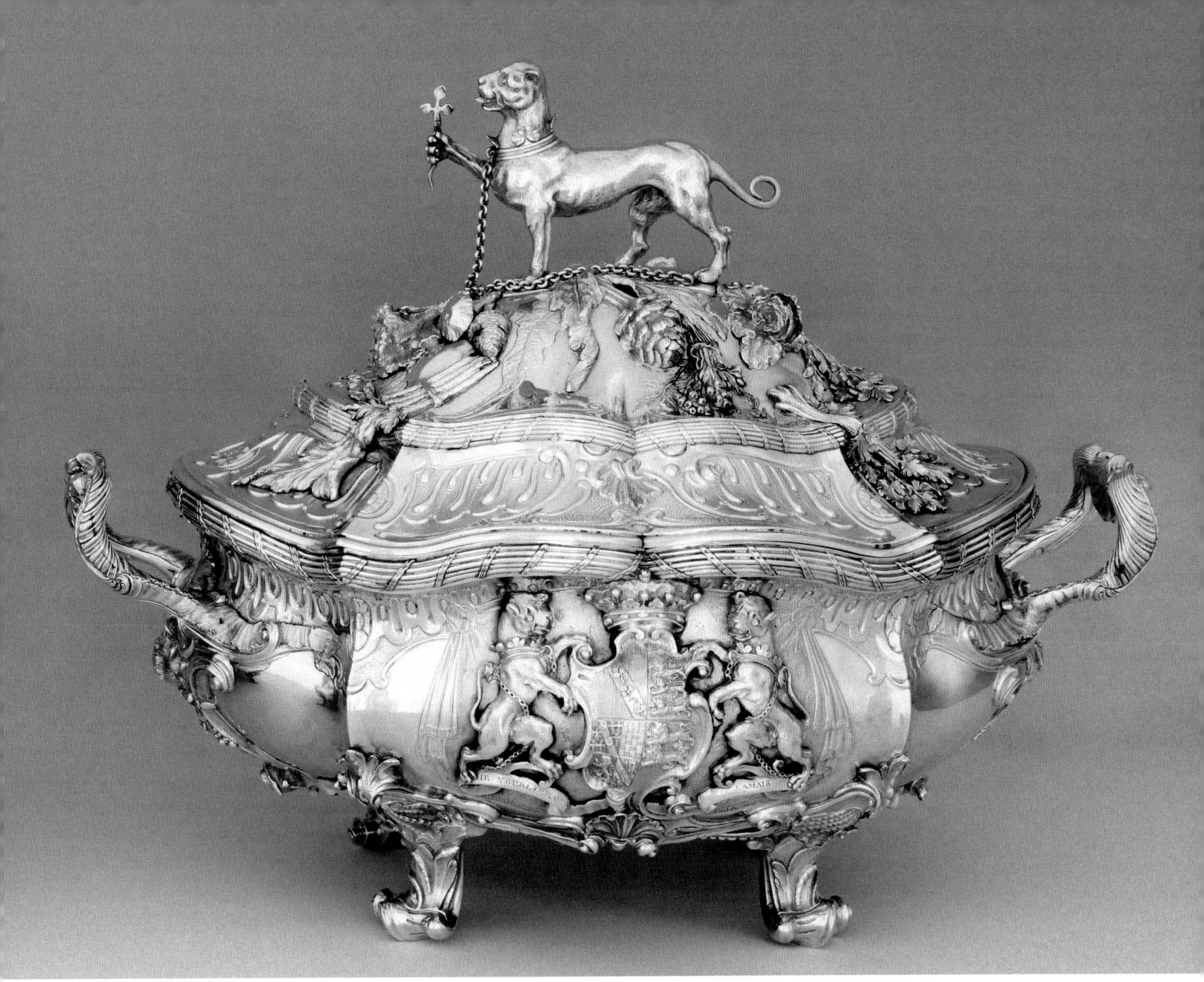

Scotland, Europalia 1973, Brussels, cat. 120 (one); *The Treasure Houses of Britain*, National Gallery of Art, Washington, 1985–6, cat. 454.

DESCRIPTION: The shaped oval *bombé* bases of the tureens each rest on four cast and applied foliate scroll feet, the foliage continuing around the lower edge of the body, intertwining at either end with scroll and rocaille-work that rises around root vegetables to the shell and leaf handles. All this detail is cast and applied as are the coats of arms on either side with asymmetrical shields which rise above shells and have chased mantled backgrounds. Also chased is the lambrequin fringe with repeating ovals and flutes and corner floral medallions below a cast and chased reed-and-tie rim. The underside has been cut out of the tureen base around the peripheral scrollwork.

The domed cover is shaped to conform to the base with a seamed bezel. Above a simple moulded rim is a chased band of scrollwork around a ribbed lambrequin fringe and with floral medallions at the corners. Another cast reed-and-tie band divides off the tops of the domes which are liberally applied with cast and chased vegetables including artichokes, cabbage, celery, mushrooms, broccoli, cauliflower, parsnips, carrots, bound asparagus, swede and beetroot. The cast handles are in the form of ounces, or snow leopards, ducally collared and chained, each holding a trefoil.

The plain oval liners are raised and have rims shaped to fit the bases, applied moulded borders and two cast and applied swan-neck-and-ball handles fixed horizontally.

HERALDRY: On either side of each tureen is the cast, chased and engraved quartered shield, supporters and motto of the 2nd Earl of Bristol beneath an earl's coronet and against a chased ermine mantling. The finial handles of the covers are in the form of the Hervey crest.

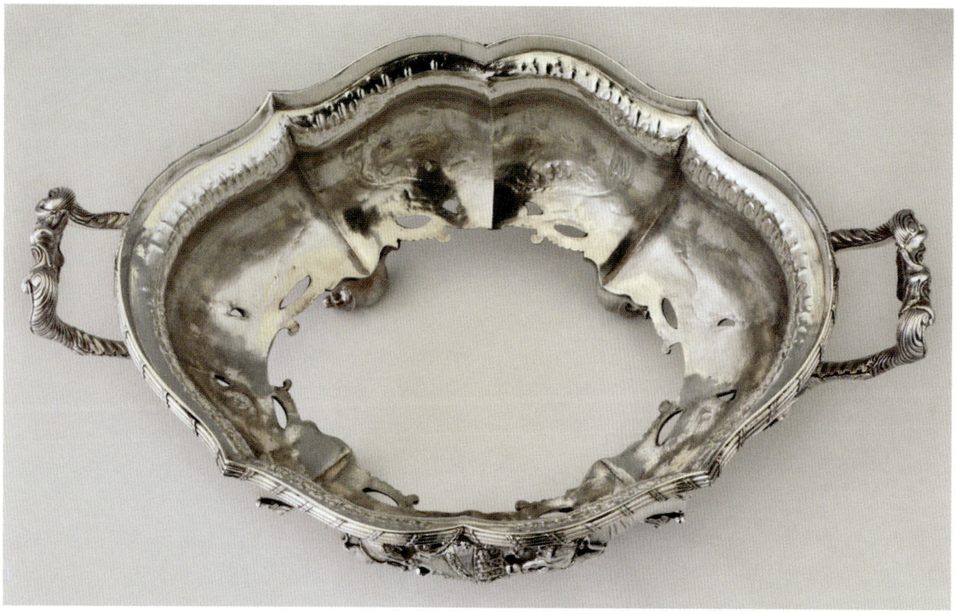

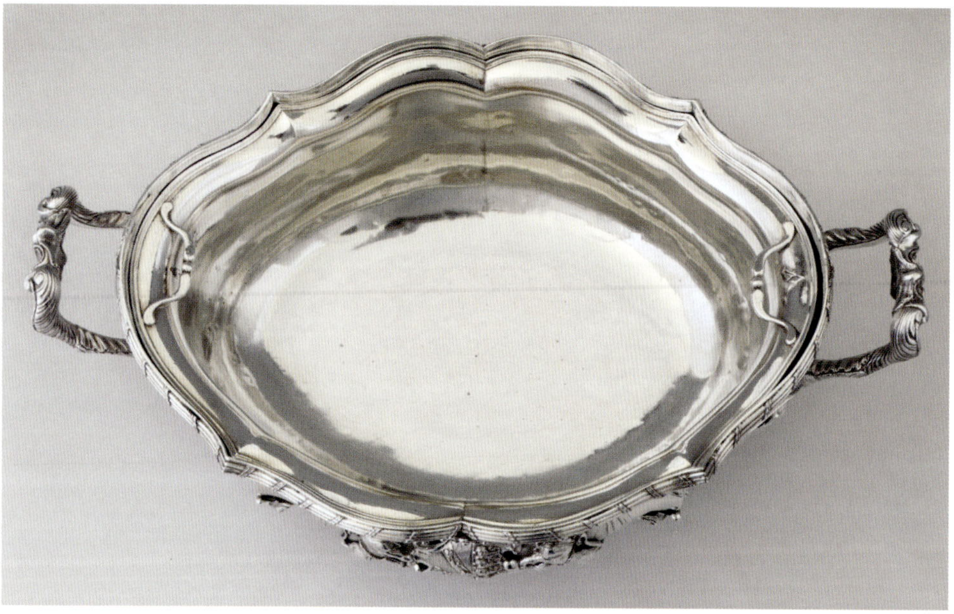

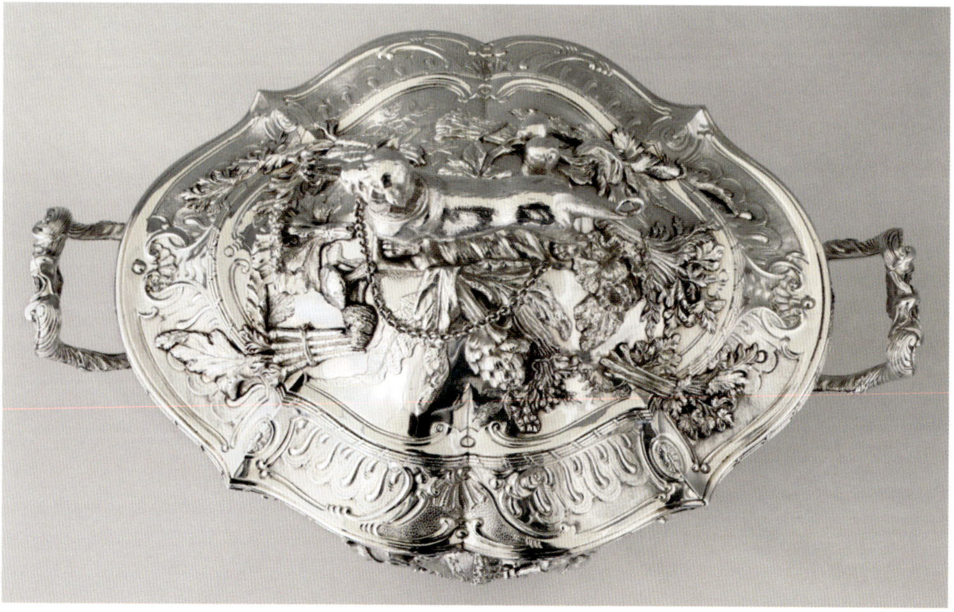

It is reputed that it was Louis xiv's love of the Spanish stew called *oille* that resulted in the appearance of a new and prominent vessel in silver on the late-seventeenth-century French dining table, known as a *pot-à-oille*.[1] The fashion for soup-like stews spread to England and the Jewel Office issued soup dishes in 1702 and 1703 which must have been reasonably substantial as they weighed 85 oz, 10 dwt, and 73 oz, 15 dwt, respectively.[2] In 1704 the Duchess of Marlborough as Groom of the Stole to Queen Anne received a 'Toureene' weighing 143 oz and there was clearly a distinction between the two vessels which was not just about scale, as three years later the Earl of Sunderland received both a 'Toureene pott & cover' of 76 oz, 5 dwt, and two 'soupe Dishes' with a combined weight of 206 oz, 5 dwt.[3] Perhaps early examples of the latter were merely dishes to serve from whereas the former could also be cooked in, although if so that did not continue to be the case. The word tureen, which was favoured over *pot-à-oille* in England, is thought to derive from '*terrine*', the French word which John Kersey in his 1708 dictionary interpreted as 'an Earthen Pan: In Cookery, a Mess made of a Breast of Mutton, with Quails, Pigeons, &c. stew'd in a Pan.'[4]

No very early examples of tureens are thought to survive and though Sir Charles Jackson does refer to one of 1703 by Anthony Nelme being exhibited in 1862, it has since disappeared so its veracity cannot be checked, there being a suspicion that it was a duty dodger with transposed marks.[5] The tureen of 1723 by Paul de Lamerie in the collection of the Duke of Bedford currently stands as the oldest known and it is of the oval, bellied form that was favoured in England up to the late eighteenth century.[6] Another survival from a few years later, of the more German-baroque fluted and sharp-ribbed variety, is by Charles Kandler and bears the mark for 1728.[7] The elder Kandler went on to produce, in 1732, a more fluid and heavily decorated version with a stepped, domed cover for the 2nd Earl of Rockingham (fig. 95).[8] In it can be seen the essence of the Ickworth tureens, mixed up with the spectacular forms coming out of France in the 1730s and 1740s.

Numerous aspects of the designs of the Parisian masters of the rococo, notably Thomas Germain and Jacques Roëttier, emerge in Frederick Kandler's magnificent creations for the Earl of Bristol. The bands of fluted and ribbed lambrequins, vegetables piled on top, foliate scroll feet and handles, lavish cast ornament around the base, reed and tie borders and the shaped, *bombé* form all derive from France and are more wholly embraced in the Ickworth tureens than in most other examples of the period. The features can be seen in the engraved designs published by Pierre Germain in his *Éléments d'orfèvrerie* of 1748 which include the works of Roëttier

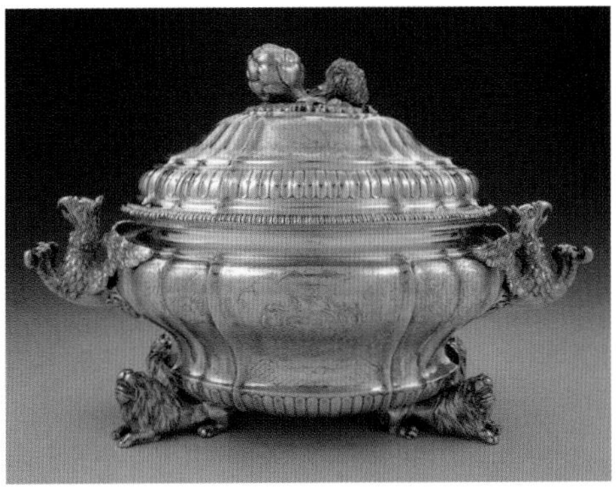

FIG. 95 / Tureen by Charles Kandler, London, 1732. Silver: 27.8 x 42.7 x 25 cm (11 x 16¾ x 9¾ in); weight 4564.4 g (146 oz, 15 dwt). Museum of Fine Arts, Boston.

for the Dauphin.[9] There was quite clearly a familiarity in England well before that too, a related design by Nicholas Sprimont of the early 1740s surviving in the Victoria and Albert Museum[10] and the frontispiece to Vincent La Chapelle's *The modern cook* of 1733 showing a similarly embellished circular tureen, probably based on those of the Francophile 4th Earl of Chesterfield whom La Chapelle had served as chef at The Hague. Lord Chesterfield's liberal table would have been there to inspire other courtiers and their goldsmiths and in 1736 Paul de Lamerie produced a pair almost exactly matching those illustrated by La Chapelle, one of which is now in the Metropolitan Museum, New York.[11] The 4th Earl of Berkeley was amongst those who went further and ordered directly from France, obtaining a full dinner service from Roëttier which is marked for 1735–8 and includes pairs of oval and circular tureens.[12]

One element for which French sources were not strong was prominent heraldic display and that was a frequent requirement of British patrons, being a reflection of the greater power of the aristocracy compared with that of absolutist France. Charles Kandler's 1732 tureen, referred to above, has the lion and griffin supporters of the patron, the Earl of Rockingham, as its feet and handles,[13] one of 1744 by James Shruder has multiple castings of the Legh crest of a ram's head[14] and the pair of tureens of the same year made by George Wickes to a design by William Kent for the 1st Lord Montfort reflect the supporters of his arms in the horses' heads holding the drop handles.[15] Many further examples exist on tureens as well as on other significant display items such as epergnes, ewers and basins, fountains and cisterns and even on less prominent tableware. For the Earl of Bristol Kandler did as George Wickes had on a pair of tureens for the Earl of Malton in 1737,[16] casting and applying the arms to make them the centre of attention and forming the handle out of the family crest. His careful integration of these signs of dynastic distinction with the most fashionable of rococo forms resulted in a highly successful end product which must have served its purpose at the increasingly grand gatherings associated with Lord Bristol's burgeoning career.

Of all Lord Bristol's initial purchases of silver these tureens would have been the most costly, their prominent role as the focus of attention at the commencement of the meal undoubtedly being the spur for such investment. Although only the overall cash payments to Kandler are known, it is likely that the cost per ounce would have been similar to the 13s 7d charged by George Wickes to the Earl of Kildare in 1747 for his tureens and the 13s 6d to the Marquess of Granby for '2 Fine Tureens & Covers & Lynings' in 1750.[17] In the latter case this represented a fashion charge of 8s per ounce, which was about as high as Wickes ever got, and would have been justified by the large amount of one-off casting work required. If such a charge was applied to the Ickworth tureens then the total cost to Lord Bristol, on a combined weight of 468 ounces, would have been £315 18s, a prodigious sum and the equivalent today to at least £42,000.[18]

The tureens would have been placed at either end of the table with the two soups that they contained being the first part of the meal to be consumed. Vincent La Chapelle devoted some eighty pages to bisques, pottages, broths and *ollios* in *The Modern Cook*, a rather gruesome one to our modern sensibilities being 'Pottage of a Lamb's Head' which was prepared as follows:

Having scalded your Lamb's Head and Feet, boil them with the Livers and some midling Bacon in a pot of good Broth; then soak your Crusts, as usual, and place the Heads on them in the soop-dish, garnish it handsomely with Livers and Feet, fry the Brains with the Yolk of an Egg and some crums of Bread, and let them take a fine colour, then put them in their place, and upon the whole throw a white Cullis well tasted, and serve it hot. [19]

The 1st Viscount Jocelyn, Lord Chancellor of Ireland, kept a record of dinners that he gave from 1740 to 1751 and on 1 July 1747 (fig. 96), with twelve at table, he served a 'Crawfish Soop' and a 'Soop Loraine'. When done with, these were removed and replaced with a 'Haunch of Vennison Roast' and a 'Chine of Beef' which would have been served on the largest of the dishes (see cat. 32 and 87) and carved at the table. A central dish of 'Broild Mackrall' made way at the same time for a turkey pie but the sixteen subsidiary dishes remained until the conclusion of the first course.[20] The need to remove the tureens during the progress of the meal probably accounts, along with reducing cost, for the cutting away of unseen silver from the bases of the Ickworth pair. Even so they are unusually heavy because of all the cast work, and would probably have been set on the table before the meal, the liners full of soup being placed in afterwards, immediately before the company entered.

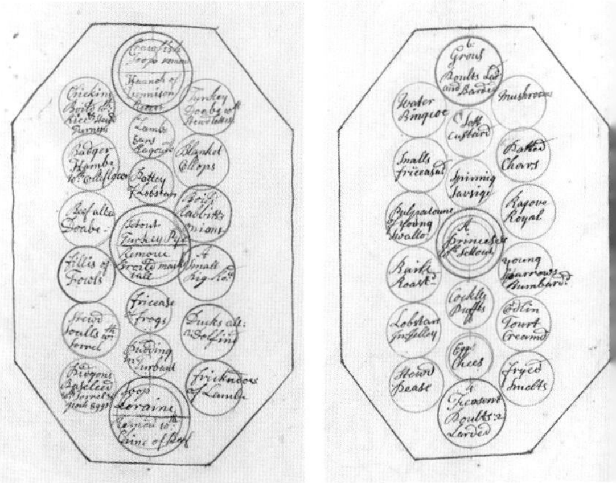

FIG. 96 / First and second courses of the dinner given on the 1st July 1747, from the Dinner Book of the 1st Viscount Jocelyn, October 1740 to November 1755, ff. 215–6. Ink on paper. Winterthur Library, Delaware.

For the contemporary ladles associated with these tureens see cat. 44. Dishes to serve as stands were made in Turin in the mid-1750s (cat. 55), as were complementary circular tureens (cat. 53).

1. Noël-Waldteuffel 1993, p. 80, note 11 and Wees 1997, p. 120.
2. Jewel Office Delivery Book 1698–1732, ff. 65 and 95.
3. Ibid., ff. 95 and 116.
4. Kersey 1708, unpaginated.
5. Jackson 1911, p. 816 and Clayton 1971, p. 267.
6. Clayton 1971, p. 275, plate 43.
7. Cincinnati Art Museum, acc. no. 1982.187.
8. Alcorn 2000, cat. 74, pp. 130–2.
9. Germain 1748, notably plates 51 and 76–83.
10. V&A Museum no. E.2606-1917. The design is undated but is thought to be *c.*1744–5.
11. Metropolitan Museum acc. no. 49.7.99a–d. The pair was sold from the Ortiz-Patiño Collection at Sotheby's, 4 June 1998, lot 223.
12. Sold Sotheby's, 16 June 1960 as a single lot.
13. Alcorn 2000, pp. 130–1, ill.
14. Christie's, 23 November 1999, lot 241.
15. Sotheby's, 10 November 1994, lot 174.
16. Davis 1976, cat. 123, pp. 123–4.
17. Wickes Ledgers, VAM 3 1747–50, f. 166.
18. Calculated using the converter on https://www.measuringworth.com.
19. La Chapelle, 1736, vol. 1, p. 33.
20. Jocelyn Dinner Book, f. 215.

44. Pair of soup ladles

Sterling silver / Frederick Kandler, London / 1752/3

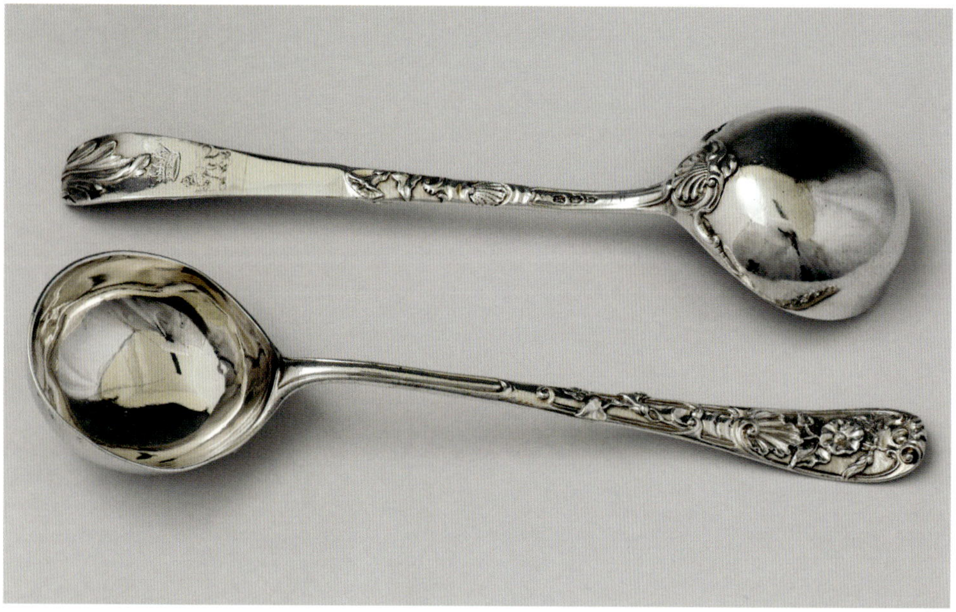

MARKS: One is fully marked on the underside of the stem with the date letter 'r', leopard's head, lion passant and the maker's mark 'FK' in italics beneath a fleur-de-lis (Grimwade 1990, no. 691). The other has the first three the same but no maker's mark.

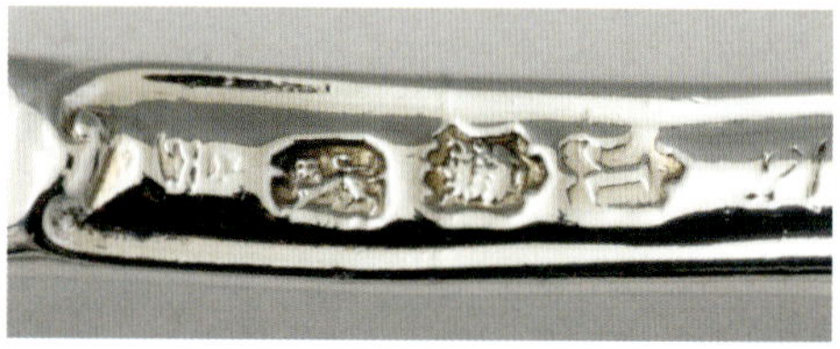

SCRATCHWEIGHTS: '11:15' and '11:16'.

MEASUREMENTS: l. 36.5 cm (14⅜ in).

INVENTORY: 852078.1–2

PROVENANCE: 2nd Earl of Bristol; by descent to the 4th Marquess.

EXHIBITED: Society of the Four Arts, Palm Beach, Florida, 1959 (one); *British Week*, Milan and Frankfurt, October, 1965.

DESCRIPTION: The ladles have deep, almost hemispherical raised bowls soldered to the stems which are cast and chased on both sides with trailing convolvulus, shells, scrollwork and reeding on matted grounds. Beneath the junction of the stems with the bowls are cast and applied shells in scrollwork cartouches.

HERALDRY: Each of the ladles is engraved on the underside of the upper part of the stem with the Hervey crest beneath an earl's coronet.

As is evident from the Wickes ledgers tureens were often supplied with ladles but surviving pairings are now comparatively rare, as are such extravagantly cast stems as these exhibit.[1] The engraved crest and coronet being on the reverse of the stem might suggest that the ladles were to be placed face-down when the table was set, along with all the soup and serving spoons. The engraving of the scratchweights on the same side indicates the opposite, however, and the armorials may just have been forced to the reverse by the lack of space amidst the profuse sculpted decoration of the front. Most other ladles of the period seem to have been designed to be placed face-up, this being more stable and more practicable for the elegant manipulation of such heavy and unwieldy objects.[2]

1. Another good example is the pair of ladles by Paul de Lamerie of 1747 in the Gilbert Collection at the V&A, accompanying two earlier tureens altered *c.*1747. See Schroder 1988b, cat. 41, pp. 169–74.
2. See for instance those supplied with the tureens of the Earls of Thanet and Milltown in 1743 by Paul de Lamerie and George Wickes respectively, sold Christie's 5 July 2000, lot 10 and 25 November 2008, lot 39; those of the Leinster (George Wickes, 1747) and Exeter (Edward Wakelin, 1755) dinner services, Barr 1980, pp. 203–4, figs. 122 and 123; and those of the Bute service (1758), sold Christie's 3 July 1996, lot 82. All survive with their contemporary tureens.

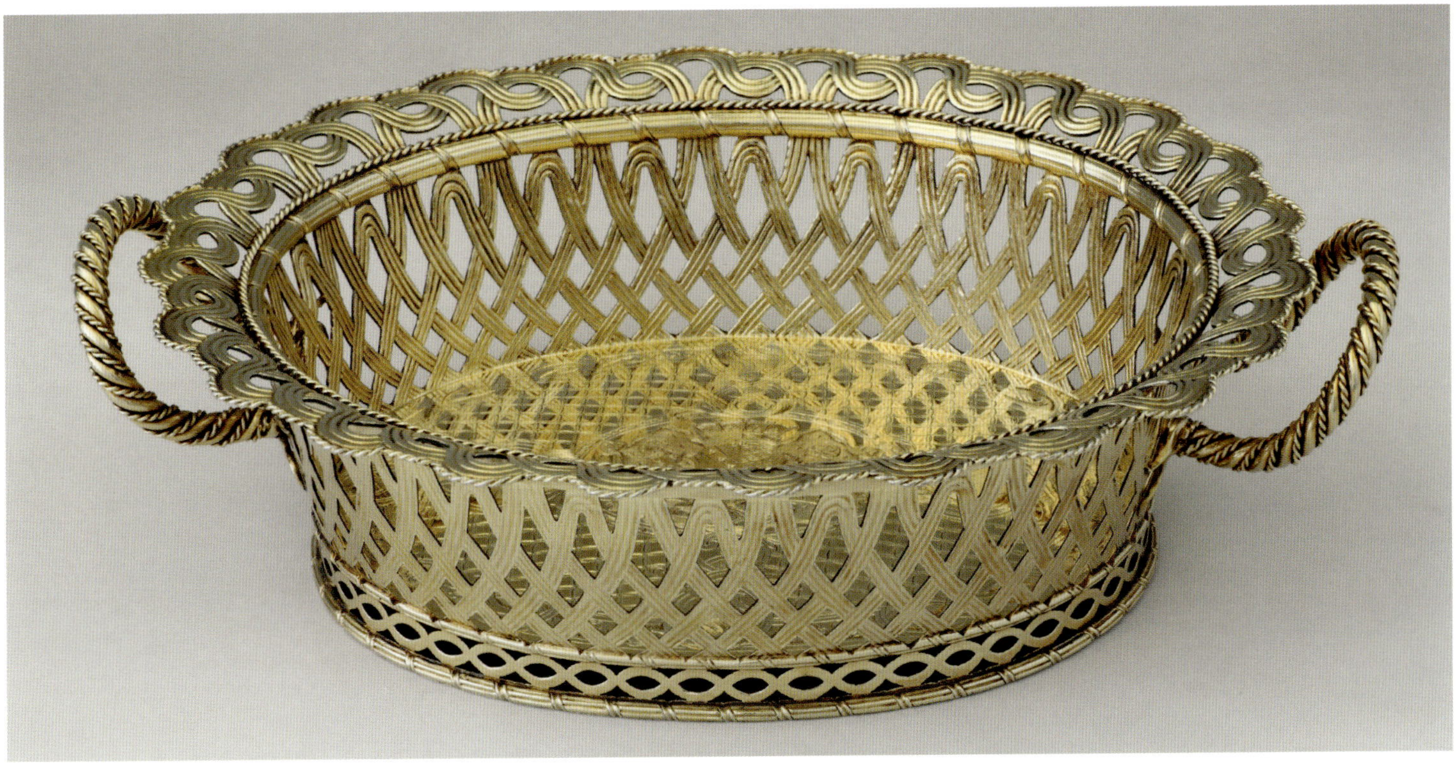

45. Bread basket, subsequently dessert basket

Sterling silver / Frederick Kandler, London / 1752/3 / subsequently gilded

MARKS: Fully marked on the underside with maker's mark 'FK' in italics beneath a fleur-de-lis (Grimwade 1990, no. 691), leopard's head, lion passant and date letter 'r'.

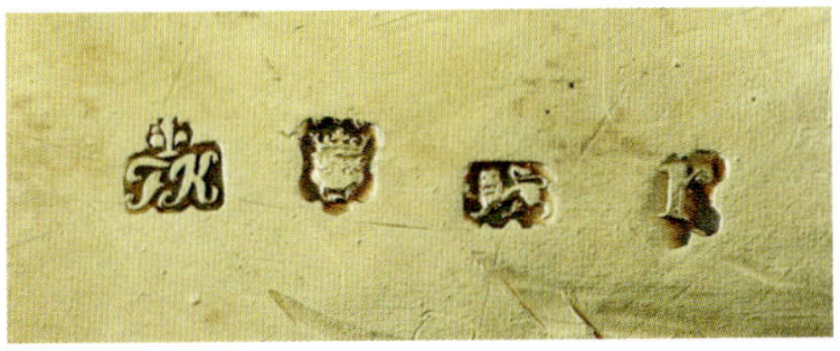

SCRATCHWEIGHT: 'N2 [/] 43=17'

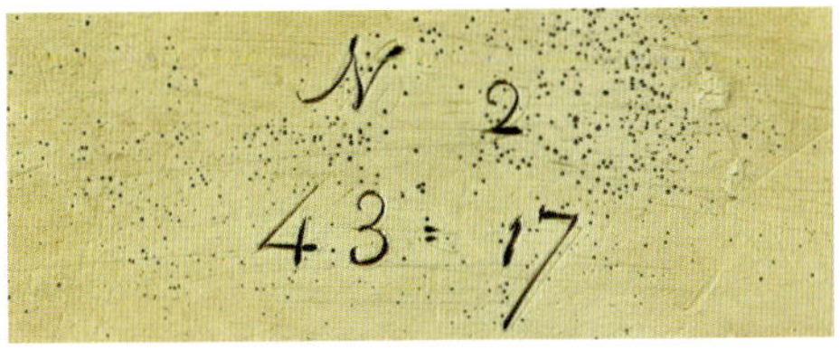

MEASUREMENTS: h. 9.2 cm (3⅝ in); w. 35.2 cm (13⅞ in); d. 27.3 cm (10¾ in).

INVENTORY: 852063.2

PROVENANCE: 2nd Earl of Bristol; by descent to the 4th Marquess.

LITERATURE: Penzer 1957a, I, p. 42; Banister, pp. 791–2.

EXHIBITED: Society of the Four Arts, Palm Beach, Florida, 1959; *British Week*, Milan and Frankfurt, 1965; *Silver from National Trust Houses*, Treasurer's House, York Festival, 1969.

DESCRIPTION: As the basket by Paul de Lamerie of 1731, see cat. 19.

HERALDRY: The centre of the floor of the basket is engraved with the quartered shield, supporters and motto of the 2nd Earl of Bristol within an ermine mantling and beneath an earl's coronet.

Although bread baskets continued to be supplied individually the social and political ambitions of the 2nd Earl of Bristol required a pair, and he had the one by de Lamerie (cat. 19; left in the picture below) which had been supplied to his father in 1731–2 precisely copied by Frederick Kandler. The names of those who executed the raising, piercing, chasing and engraving are not known but they were clearly highly skilled, attaining an almost exact match to the earlier work. It is only in the minute detail of execution that differences can be discerned. The fine and profuse nature of the late *Régence* decoration, coupled with the suitability of feigned basketwork for the rococo, must have persuaded Lord Bristol to keep the earlier basket and copy it rather than commissioning a new pair. He would thus have made a saving on fashion as on so many other of his pieces. The baskets were probably not gilded until the supply of another pair in 1768 (cat. 86) when the whole set was turned over for use as part of the dessert service.

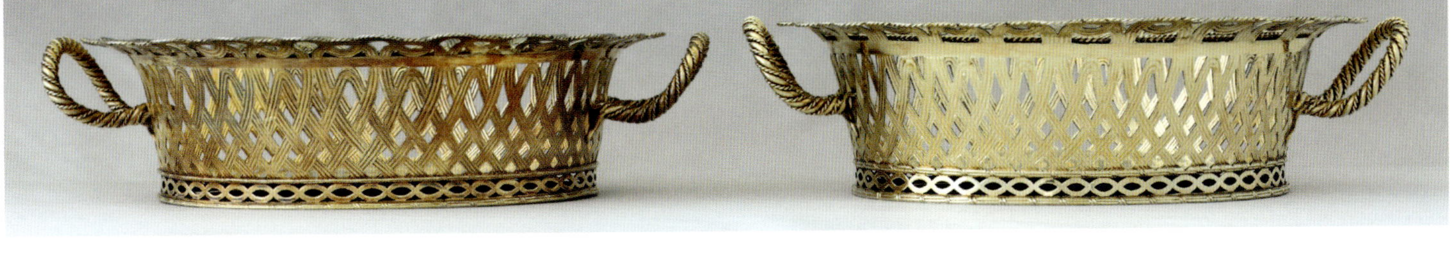

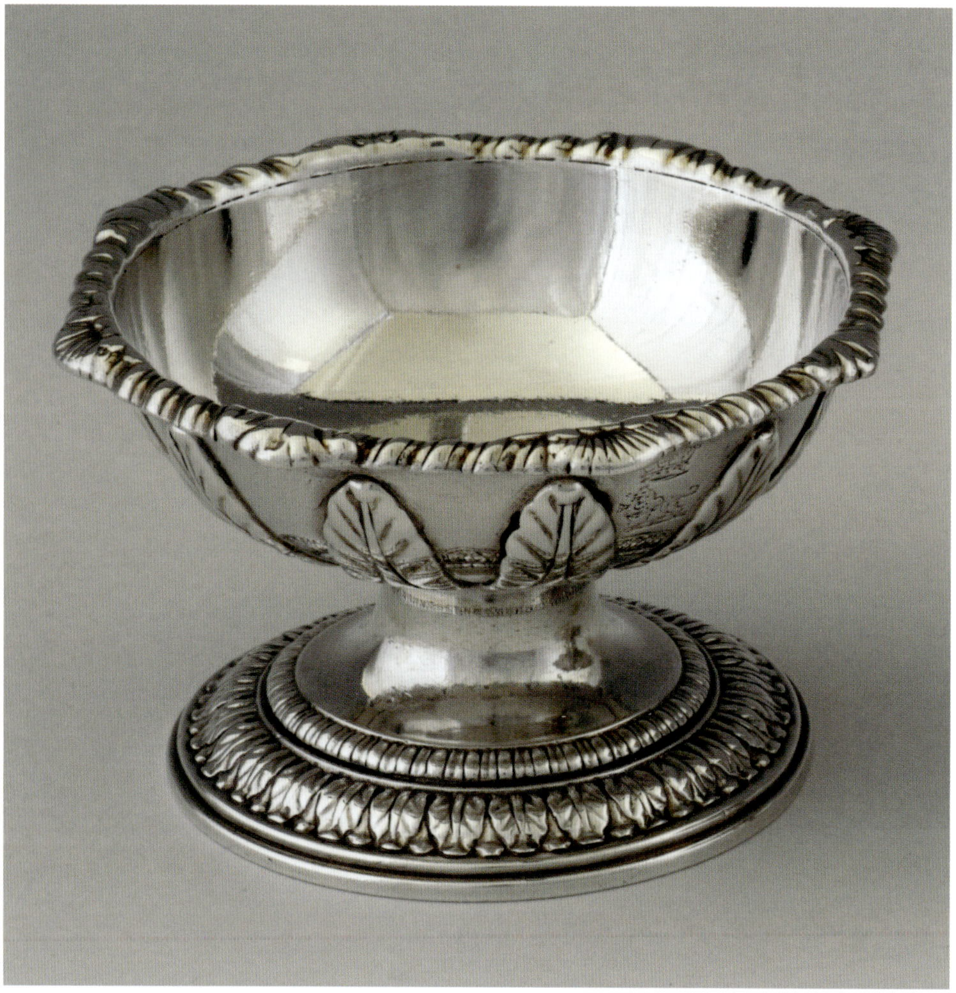

46. **Eight salts**

Sterling silver / **Frederick Kandler, London** / **1752/3**

MARKS: No. 6 is fully marked on the outside of the foot rim with the lion passant, date letter 'r', leopard's head and maker's mark 'FK' in italics beneath a fleur-de-lis (Grimwade 1990, no. 691). Nos. 1–5 and 7–8 have the lion passant, date letter 'r' and leopard's head but either lack a maker's mark or it is only partial and mostly indecipherable.

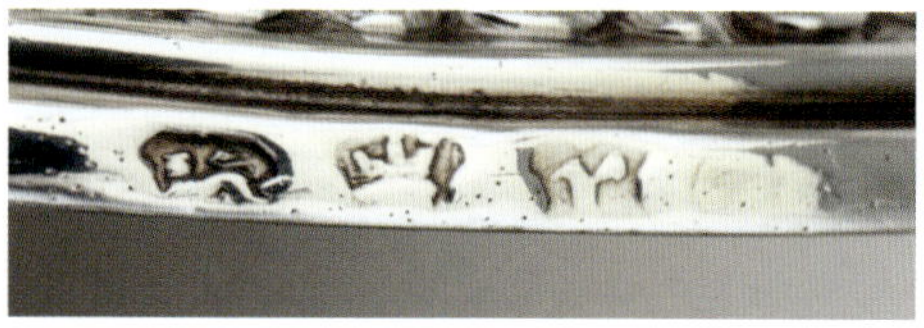

SCRATCHWEIGHTS: '1 [/] 9=5'; '2 [/] 9=16'; '3 [/] 10=3'; '4 [/] 10=5'; '5 [/] 10=5'; '6 [/] 9=18'; '7 [/] 10=1'; 'N° 8 [/] 10=2'

MEASUREMENTS: h. 6.4 cm (2½ in); diam. 10.5 cm (4⅛ in).

INVENTORY: 852086

PROVENANCE: 2nd Earl of Bristol; by descent to the 4th Marquess.

LITERATURE: Penzer 1957a, II, pp. 134–5, fig. 111; Banister 1980, p. 794.

EXHIBITED: Society of the Four Arts, Palm Beach, Florida, 1959 (four); *British Week*, Milan and Frankfurt, 1965 (four).

DESCRIPTION: Each of the circular bowls is cast and has an applied calyx of eleven cast and chased stiff leaves. The octagonal gadroon border with shells and leaves alternating at the corners is cast and applied. The circular, stepped foot, which is cast in vertical halves and chased, has an outer band of overlapping leaves and an inner band of gadrooning. The trumpet-shaped stem is raised.

HERALDRY: Between two of the stiff leaves of the body of each salt is engraved the Hervey crest beneath an earl's coronet.

This form of salt appears to have been developed by the Huguenot silversmiths in London without a French precedent and the earliest examples, from the late 1720s, bear the maker's marks of Anne Tanqueray and her brother-in-law David Willaume II.[1] It remained popular into the 1760s, being referred to by George Wickes as the 'leaf salt'.[2] Kandler's version for Lord Bristol differs from the basic model in having a plain, trumpet stem and an octagonal gadroon and shell rim, the latter allowing it to blend with the rest of the Earl's dinner service. The full set extends to twelve, the other four having been stolen *c.* 2000. If Lord Bristol had been entertaining twenty-four to dinner the salts would have been placed between each pair of covers.

It was not the usual practice to gild the inside of salts in the mid-eighteenth century to protect from corrosion and the Wickes Ledgers reveal that most sets were instead supplied with glass liners. The Earl of Kildare acquired '16 salt glasses' for eight salts in 1747 at a cost of £1 12s and the Marquess of Granby, three years later, had the same quantity for his ten new salts at the considerably lower cost of 12s, presumably reflecting a less complex form.[3] It was common for the number of liners to exceed the salts, allowing for breakages which must have been frequent given the absence of surviving examples.

For the associated salt spoons see cat. 47.

1. Schroder 2009, p. 314 and Lomax 1992, p. 87.
2. Wickes Ledgers, VAM 5 1750–4, f. 130. Colonel Sotherby received '6 Leave Salts' on 18 October 1752, charged at £14 13s for the silver and £3 3s for making.
3. Wickes Ledgers, VAM 3 1747–50, ff. 1 and 164. An early instance of internal gilding is that of the '6 Boat Salts' supplied to Sir Ralph Milbanke, 5th Bt, in 1765. See Parker and Wakelin Ledgers, VAM 7 1765–75, f. 22.

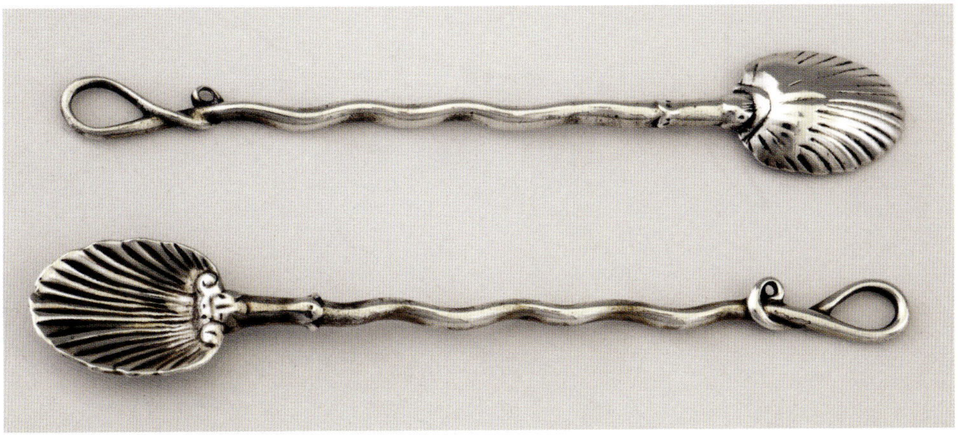

47. Twelve salt spoons

Silver (x 8) / **probably Frederick Kandler, London** / ***c.*1752** (above, front and reverse)
Sterling silver (x 4) / **Leslie Durbin, London** / **1968** (below)

MARKS: None on the eighteenth-century spoons. The four twentieth-century spoons are marked on the reverse of the stem with maker's mark 'LGD' in a rectangular punch with curved ends, date letter 'n', leopard's head and lion passant.

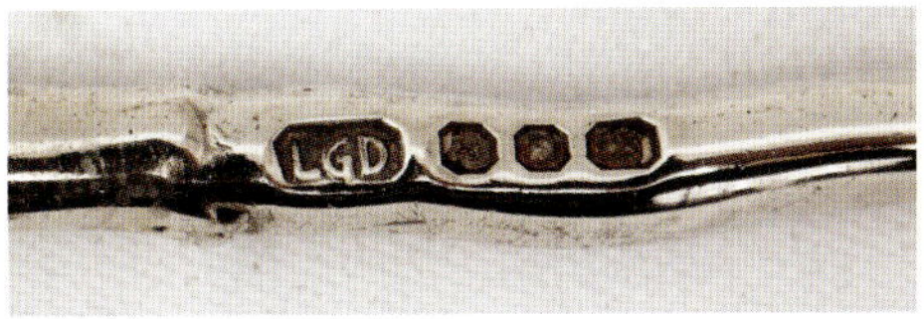

SCRATCHWEIGHTS: None. A combined weight for twelve of 3 oz, 19 dwt, is given in the 1811 plate list, giving an average of 6½ dwt. This tallies with the weights of the surviving eighteenth-century spoons, which range between 8 and 11 grams. The Durbin spoons are slightly heavier at 12–13 grams.

MEASUREMENTS: l. 10.5 cm (4⅛ in).

INVENTORY: 852074.1–12

PROVENANCE: 8. 2nd Earl of Bristol; by descent to the 4th Marquess. 4. commissioned by the National Trust from Leslie Durbin, 1968.

LITERATURE: Penzer 1957a, II, pp. 134–5, fig. III.

EXHIBITED: *British Week*, Milan and Frankfurt, 1965 (four).

DESCRIPTION: The spoons have cast shallow shell bowls and wavy stems and a forged whip end, bent over and coiled around the stem. One of the bowls is a plain, later replacement.

HERALDRY: None

These whip-ended spoons have always been associated with the Kandler salts (cat. 46). The pattern was developed in the early rococo period and is seen on a set of teaspoons forming part of a tea equipage now at Temple Newsam, other items of which are marked by Paul de Lamerie and for 1735.[1] It is closely related to a drawing in the Victoria and Albert Museum, now attributed to Nicholas Sprimont[2] and is presumably what was being supplied to Lady Anne Cavendish by George Wickes in 1739 when she received '2 Twisted Salt Spoons'.[3] Such small, fragile items as salt spoons were exempted from hallmarking under the Plate (Offences) Act of 1738[4] and their general vulnerability was demonstrated when four were lost whilst on exhibition in Italy and Germany in 1965.[5] The National Trust, after considering acquiring antique replacements, decided to commission copies and these were produced by the renowned twentieth-century silversmith Leslie Durbin, best known for his work on the contrastingly massive Stalingrad Sword of Honour.[6] The initial idea was that the replacement spoons would be of Durbin's own design but ultimately it was decided to copy the remaining originals.[7] Durbin's estimate, dated 20 June, 1968 totalled £43 7s.[8] The spoons were delivered in early July and James Tudor-Craig, then resident curator at Ickworth, forwarded the bill to the regional agent at Blickling, Nicholas de Bazille Corbin. The final cost came to £48 15s 8d but as the insurance payment had amounted to £97 10s, Tudor-Craig noted with some glee, 'we are thus some £47 up on the deal'.[9]

1. Lomax 1992, cat. 125, pp. 122–7.
2. V&A museum number 2592. I am grateful to James Lomax for bringing this to my attention.
3. Wickes Ledgers, VAM I 1735–40, f. 121.
4. Schroder 2009, p. 314.
5. Ickworth House, archive files, copy letter from James Tudor-Craig to T.B. Burr, 17 February 1966.
6. *Guardian*, 1 March 2005, obituary of Leslie Durbin.
7. Ickworth House, archive files, copy letters from James Tudor-Craig to Leslie Durbin, 22 March 1966 and 15 May 1968.
8. Ibid., letter from Leslie Durbin to James Tudor-Craig, 20 June 1968. The detail of Durbin's estimate was as follows: mould charge £10 10s; 4 spoons at £6 each £24; 8.75% Purchase Tax £2 2s; rail fares to Bury from London to collect the original for copying £1 10 and expenses £5 5s.
9. Ibid., copy of memorandum from J. Tudor-Craig to N. de B. Corbin, 19 July 1968.

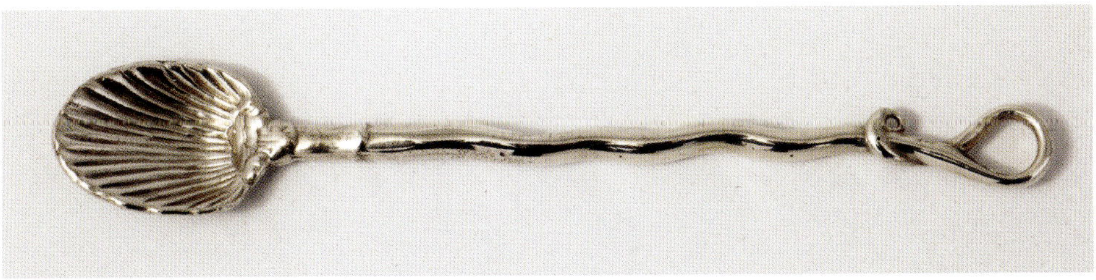

48. **Four oblong salad dishes**

Sterling silver / Frederick Kandler, London / 1753/4

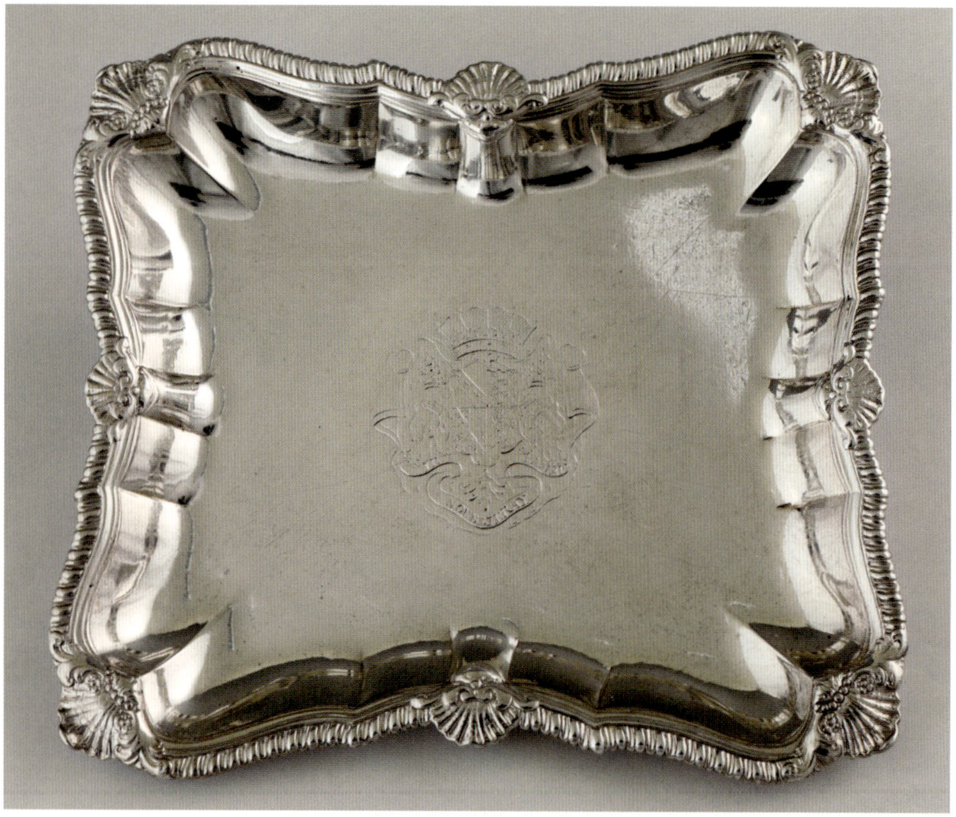

MARKS: Each dish is fully marked on the underside with the leopard's head, date letter 's', lion passant and maker's mark 'FK' in italics beneath a fleur-de-lis (Grimwade 1990, no. 691).

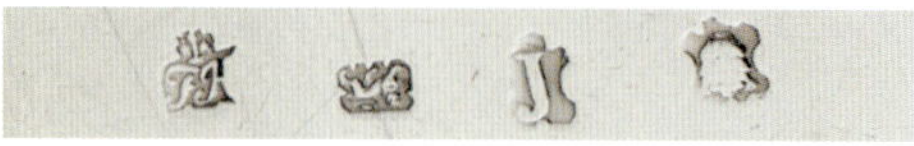

SCRATCHWEIGHTS: 'N° 1 [/] 28"o', 'N° 2 [/] 28"6', 'N° 3 [/] 29 6' and 'N° 4 [/] 29"18'

MEASUREMENTS: h. 2.9 cm (1⅛ in); w. 31.4 cm (12⅜ in); d. 23.2 cm (9⅛ in).

INVENTORY: 852094

PROVENANCE: 2nd Earl of Bristol; by descent to the 4th Marquess.

DESCRIPTION: Each indented rectangular dish is raised and has multiple creases to the deep sides following the applied shaped rim with inverted corners which is cast and consists of bands of moulding and gadrooning between shells. There is a shell at the centre of each side and at the corners are four larger shells with upturned ends, flanked by rosettes and bound by a line of pearls.

HERALDRY: The centre of each dish is engraved with the quartered shield, supporters and motto of the 2nd Earl of Bristol within an ermine mantling and beneath an earl's coronet.

Deep dishes of this general shape – with indented sides and creased, inverted corners – were usually known from the 1760s as 'pin-cushion dishes'. Thus they are referred to from the mid-1760s in the Jewel Office records and in the Parker and Wakelin Ledgers,[1] as well as in the 1811 Bristol plate list (see appendix 5). When made, however, it is probable that they were intended as salad dishes and would have been known as such, to be used alongside the circular versions already in existence (cat. 31). There would thus have been eight available for use on the 2nd Earl's table and that accords with the norm for the time, the 9th Earl of Exeter, for instance, receiving '4 square sallets & 4 round ditto' from George Wickes and Samuel Netherton in 1756.[2] Further evidence for their intended use is provided by Sir Ralph Milbanke, 5th Bt's receipt in 1765 from Wickes and Netherton's successors, John Parker and Edward Wakelin, of '4 Nurl'd heart Corner'd Sallad Dishes', weighing 83 oz, 2 dwt, and costing £31 3s 4d.[3]

Dishes of the 'pincushion' form seem to have made their first appearance in England around 1750, perhaps the earliest surviving being four of 1751 by Thomas Heming.[4] These are of the more common and simpler design, without shaped rims and intermediate folds (see cat. 77). The source was probably France, as usual, and a plain pincushion shape is included amongst dish outlines on plate 51 of Pierre Germain's *Éléments d'orfèvrerie* published in Paris in 1748 (fig. 97). The enriched, Ickworth version may have been Kandler's own invention, seeming to hark back to the Germanic baroque forms of Charles Kandler, and relating also to his own multi-faceted tureens (see cat. 43).[5] The square dishes by Edward Wakelin of 1762 made to augment the Leinster dinner service, and presumably supplied through Parker and Wakelin, are a rather less successful attempt at the same thing with their intermediary folds arranged outwards and appearing as creases.[6]

The early nineteenth century baize bag, probably supplied by Rundell, Bridge & Rundell, survives and is entitled '4 O[B]LONG DISHES'.

1. Jewel Office Delivery Book, 1732–93, f. 216, 29 October 1765, Thomas Pelham as Comptroller of the King's Household received 4 gadrooned pincushion dishes weighing 100 oz, 12 dwt; Parker and Wakelin Ledgers, VAM 7 1765–75, f. 66, 6 October 1766, the 4th Viscount Howe acquired '4 Hatt [probably triangular] & 4 Pincushion Comport Dishes'.
2. Wickes Ledgers, VAM 6 1756–60, f. 1.
3. Parker and Wakelin Ledgers, VAM 7 1765–75, f. 22.
4. Christie's, 27 March 1968, lot 173.
5. He continued to produce dishes in this form, as those of 1766 sold Sotheby's, 22 March 1979, lot 122.
6. Sotheby's, 23 May 1985, lot 92.

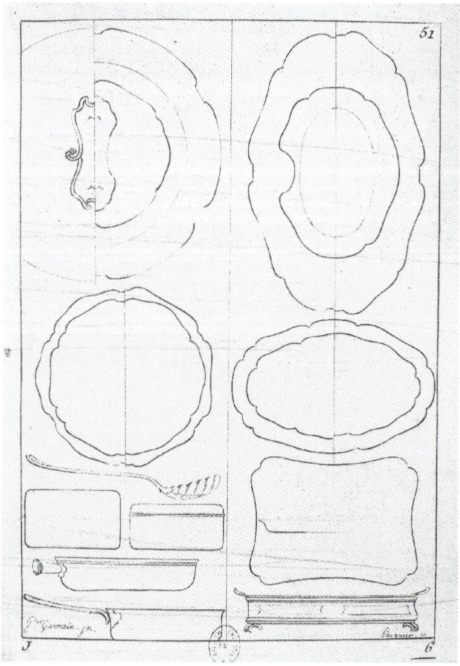

FIG. 97 / Shapes of dishes and other items, plate 51 from Pierre Germain's *Elements d'orfevrerie*, Paris, 1748. British Library.

49. Four small round dishes

Sterling silver / Frederick Kandler, London / 1754/5

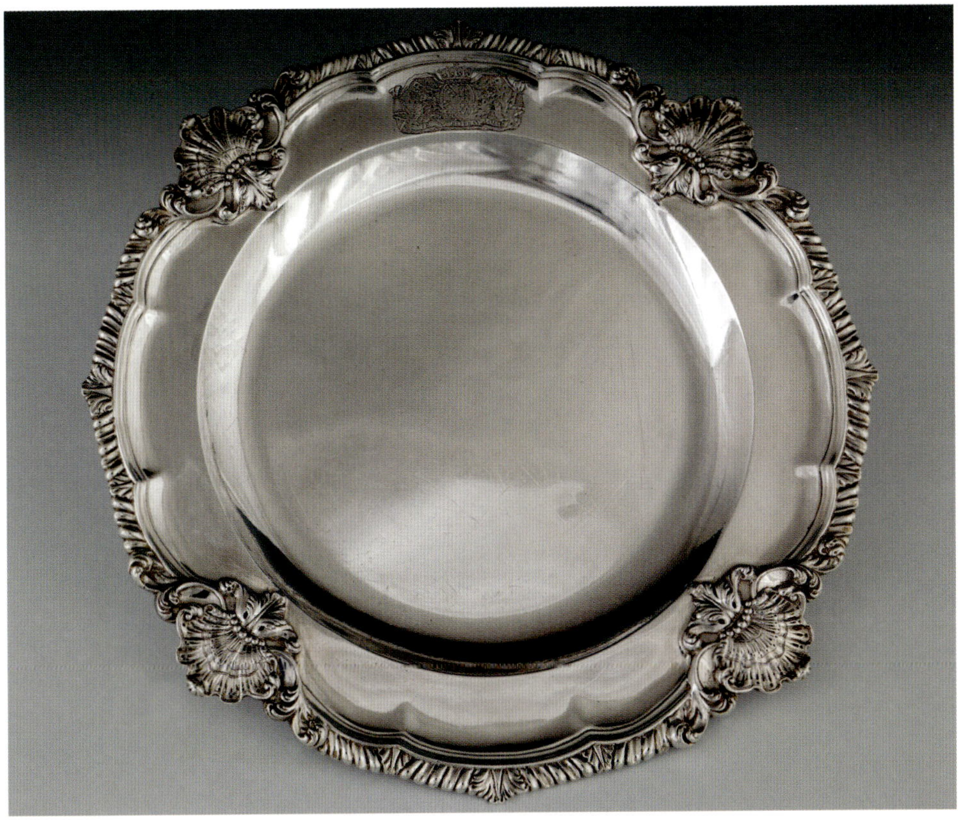

MARKS: The dishes are fully marked on the underside of their rims with the lion passant, date letter 't', maker's mark 'FK' in italics beneath a fleur-de-lis (Grimwade 1990, no. 691) and leopard's head.

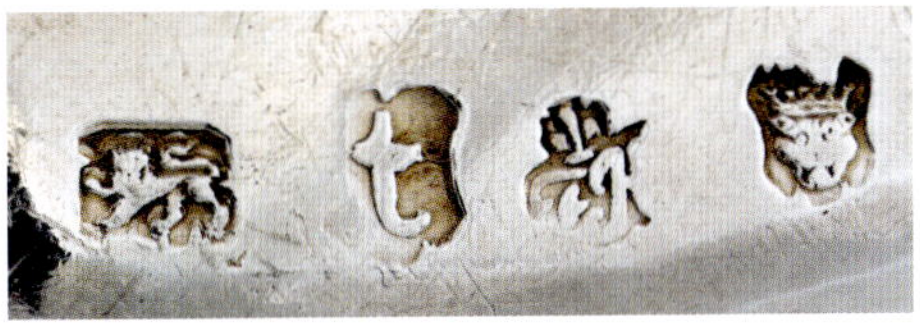

SCRATCHWEIGHTS: 'No=1 [/] 23=13'; 'No=2 [/] 24=3'; 'No=3 [/] 24=5'; 'No=4 [/] 24=10'.

MEASUREMENTS: h. 2.5 cm (1 in); diam. 27.3 cm (10¾ in).

INVENTORY: 852121.2.1-4

PROVENANCE: 2nd Earl of Bristol; by descent to the 4th Marquess.

DESCRIPTION: These are a smaller version of cat. 36.

HERALDRY: Each dish is engraved on its rim with the quartered shield, supporters and motto of the 2nd Earl of Bristol within an ermine mantling and beneath an earl's coronet.

Unlike the handles on the oval dishes, the prominent shells on the borders of these have not been scaled down from the larger set (cat. 36) though the gadrooning has been. They are the smallest of all the dishes and might have been used for *hors d'oeuvres* or for some of the light *entremets*[1] placed instead of salads and sauces for the third course. On Vincent La Chapelle's 'Bill of Fare for a Supper of 15 or 16 Covers' these included cock's combs, green peas, duck's tongues and eggs with gravy.[2] The dishes are much worn and were evidently heavily used by the Herveys up to 1951.

1. *Entremets* from old French means 'between courses'. See Visser 1991, pp. 200–1.
2. La Chapelle, 1736, plate. VII.

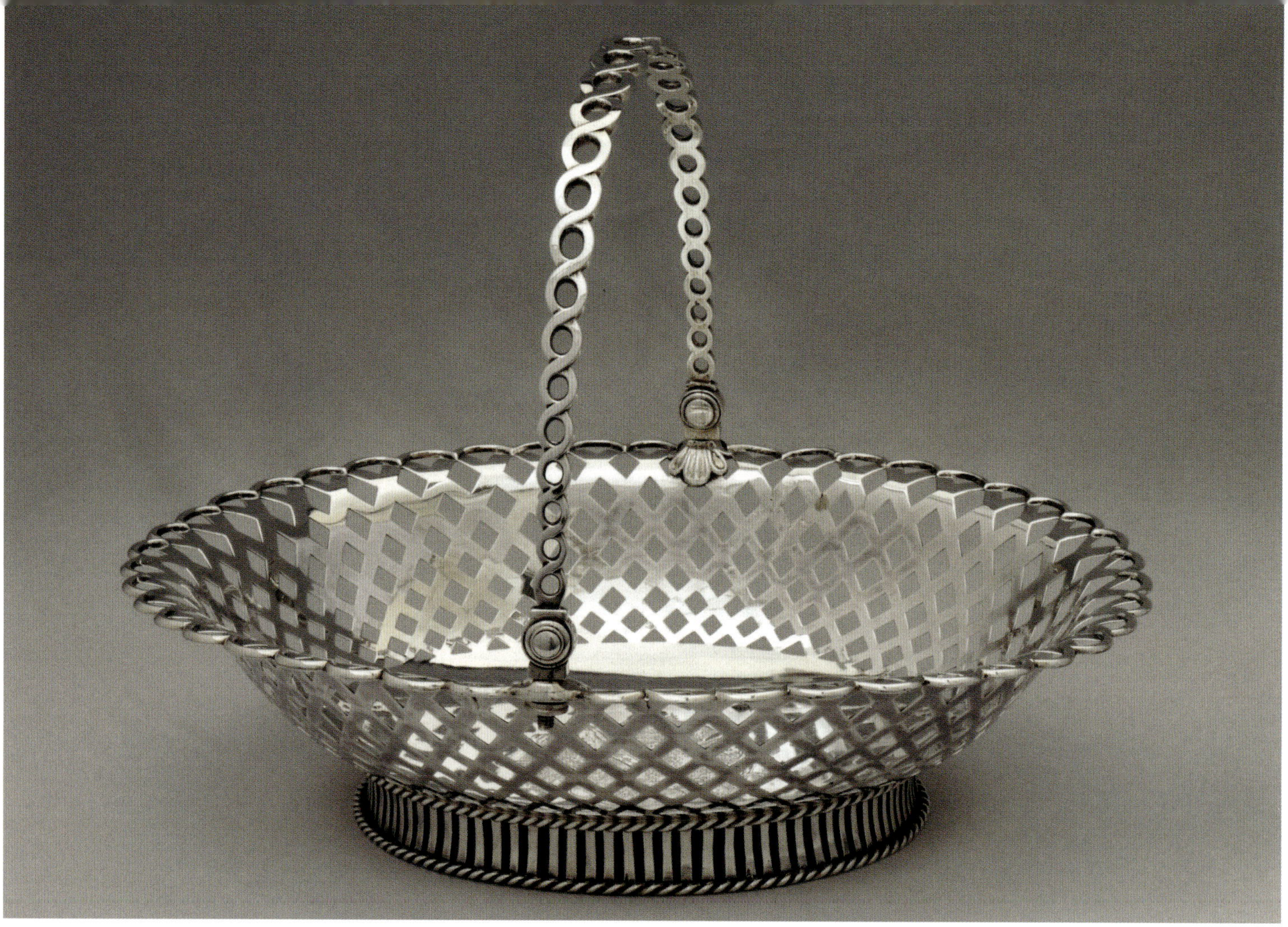

50. **Pair of bread baskets**

Sterling silver / **John Robinson, London** / **1754/5**

MARKS: Both are fully marked on their undersides with maker's mark 'JR' in italics beneath an eight-pointed star (Grimwade 1990, no. 1630), date letter 't', lion passant and leopard's head. The handles have the maker's mark and lion passant only.

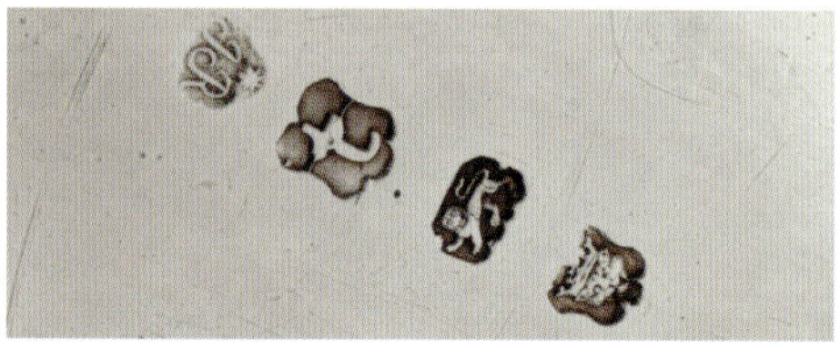

SCRATCHWEIGHTS: 'N. 1 [/] 42"16' and 'N°. 2 [/] 42"0'.

MEASUREMENTS: h. 29.2 cm (11½ in); w. 37.5 cm (14¾ in); d. 29.5 cm (11⅝ in).

INVENTORY: 852109

PROVENANCE: 2nd Earl of Bristol; by descent to the 4th Marquess.

LITERATURE: Penzer 1957a, II, p. 136.

DESCRIPTION: The splayed oval baskets with concave bases are raised and diaper-pierced with a flaring rim terminating in a scalloped edge with an applied moulded wire. The pierced and seamed gallery rim feet are bounded top and bottom by corded wires and the curved open guilloche handles are cast, terminating in button hinges with cast leaf attachments soldered to the inside face of the top of the basket.

HERALDRY: In the centre of each basket is engraved the quartered shield, supporters and motto of the 2nd Earl of Bristol within an ermine mantling and beneath an earl's coronet.

This model, which evolved from the flat-bottomed and more naturalistic baskets of earlier in the century (see cat. 19), was at the height of its popularity in the 1750s. With minor variations it was produced by a number of different goldsmiths including Benjamin Cartwright, Edward Aldridge, Samuel Herbert and Co. and John Robinson.[1] The relative plainness of the baskets and the fact that they do not match those by de Lamerie and Kandler (cat. 19 and 45) may indicate that they were intended for Lord Bristol's 'every day' service of silver.[2] Once the other baskets had been augmented and gilded for dessert in 1768 (see cat. 86), however, these would have been the only ones available to the 2nd Earl and his successors. Their simplicity of form and lightness in appearance would have suited the burgeoning neoclassicism of the late eighteenth century and rendered them fitter for the grandest of dinner tables.

1. Christie's 13 June 2000, lot 204 (Benjamin Cartwright, 1751); Sotheby's 15 June 1978, lot 41 (Edward Aldridge, 1751); Sotheby's 19 July 1982, lot 124 (Samuel Herbert & Co., 1753).
2. See cat. 19, footnote 16.

51. **Six waiters**

Sterling silver (x 2) / Frederick Kandler / London, 1754/5
Silver (x 4) / probably Frederick Kandler / London, *c.*1754 / duty dodgers

MARKS: Nos. 5 and 6 are fully marked on the underside with the leopard's head, date letter 't', lion passant and maker's mark 'FK' in italics beneath a fleur-de-lis (Grimwade 1990, no. 691). Nos. 1–4, which are duty dodgers, have on their undersides the partly distorted marks of the old pieces reworked by Kandler: maker's mark 'ME' beneath two sickles and a sheath of corn (Grimwade 1990, no. 2018) for Lewis Mettayer, Britannia, lion's head erased and date letter 'Q' for 1711.

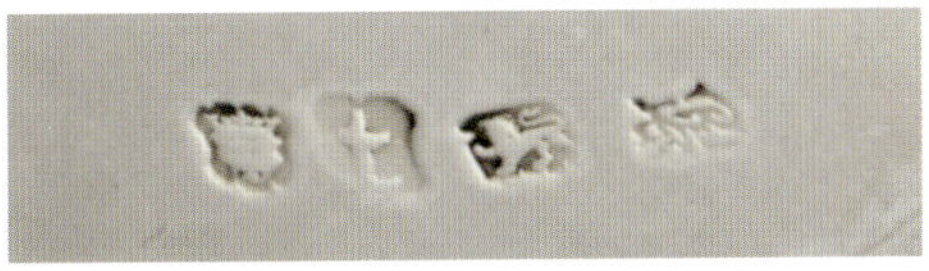

SCRATCHWEIGHTS: 'N1 [/] 9=7'; 'N2 [/] 9=12'; 'N3 [/] 8=19'; 'N4 [/] 9=5'; 'N^{o}: 5 [/] 9=2'; 'N^{o}: 6 9=7'.

MEASUREMENTS: h. 2.5 cm (1 in); diam. 18.1 cm (7⅛ in).

INVENTORY: 852097

PROVENANCE: 2nd Earl of Bristol; by descent to the 4th Marquess.

LITERATURE: Penzer 1957a, II, p. 134.

DESCRIPTION: The circular waiters are raised with shallow rims and cast and applied shaped, gadrooned borders. Each has three shell and scroll feet, those on the pair marked by Kandler being soldered whilst on the others (pictured below) they are riveted.

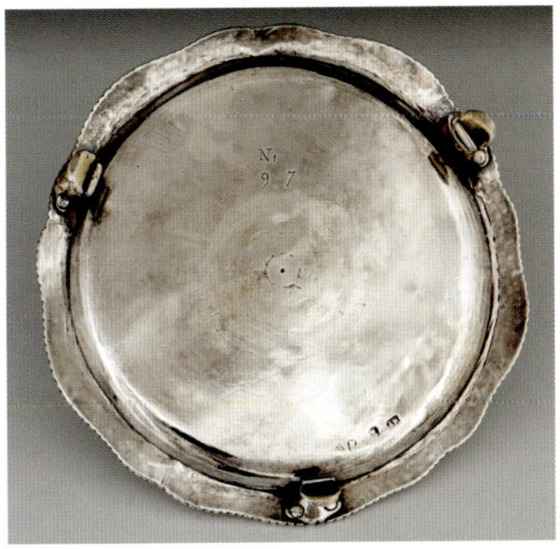

HERALDRY: The centre of each waiter is engraved with the quartered shield, supporters and motto of the 2nd Earl of Bristol within an ermine mantling and beneath an earl's coronet.

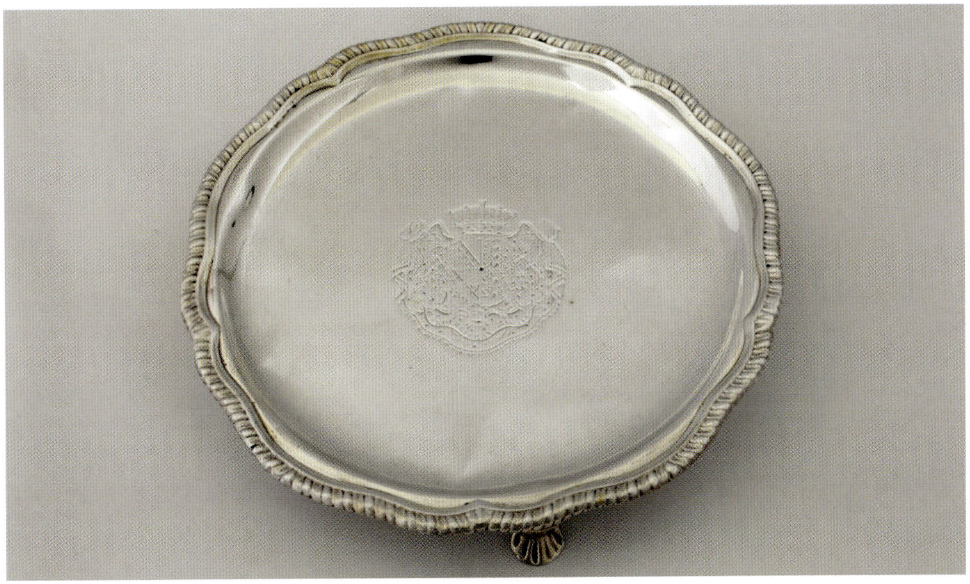

Small waiters with shallow rims such as these were intended for the service of wine and other drinks at meals. The equivalents amongst the 2nd Earl of Warrington's plate, also six in number, were recorded by him in 1750 as 'small Waiters … to give drink on'.[1] Their three feet kept them stable and raised them up sufficiently for the footman to easily insert his fingers when lifting from the table[2] whilst their shallow rims allowed him to clamp the glass by placing his thumb on its base. Once at the table the thumb would be released and the diner could take the proffered glass direct from the silver waiter without making physical contact with the servant. This process would have been constant during dinner as, although by the middle of the century it was becoming fashionable to leave glasses on the table rather than immediately draining their contents in a toast, it was still not considered acceptable to refill a glass without first rinsing and buffing it at the sideboard.[3] Jonathan Swift, in his satirical *Directions to servants* of 1745 gives some sense of how wine should be served by describing how it should not:

When you carry a Glass of Liquor to any Person who hath called for it, do not bob him on the Shoulder, or cry, Sir, or Madam, here's the Glass; that would be unmannerly, as if you had a Mind to force it down one's Throat; but stand at the Person's Right Shoulder and wait his Time; and if he strikes it down with his Elbow by Forgetfulness, that was his Fault and not yours.[4]

Kandler was quite clearly dodging the plate duty of 6d per ounce by refashioning old pieces of Lord Bristol's plate for four of the waiters, carefully preserving the 1711 Mettayer hallmarks (bottom left) in the process. Interestingly, there is evidence on the undersides of a former fitting which was probably to allow for screwing onto an epergne or surtout arm. If this was the case then these waiters could previously have been the saucers on the de Lamerie epergne, and would thus have been reused by him from an earlier set perhaps sent in for exchange by the Earl of Scarsdale (see cat. 11 for a general note on the epergne). The Wickes ledgers contain evidence of a similar reuse of old saucers on the epergne provided to the 2nd Earl of Macclesfield in February 1739.[5] Potentially, therefore, these four waiters are a case of double duty dodging.

Waiters were commonly in two or three sizes, such as the set supplied by Kandler to John Chute of The Vyne in Hampshire in 1769. That consisted of one very large waiter, weighing 80 oz, 16 dwt, two medium-sized with a combined weight of 97 oz, 4 dwt, and a diameter of 15¼ in, and three small at 28 oz, 3 dwt, which would have been for the service of wine.[6] There must have been a similar gradation amongst the Bristol plate but by 1811 only these six small waiters survived plus a later, footless set of four with a diameter of 13½ inches (cat. 82).

1. Lomax and Rothwell 2006, cat. 16, p. 66.
2. Ibid.
3. Trusler 1775, p. 65 and 1788, p. 13.
4. Swift 1745, p. 53.
5. Wickes Ledgers, VAM I 1735–40, f. 182. Lord Macclesfield's epergne was entirely new apart from its four saucers for which the only charge was 10 shillings for the addition of silver.
6. Hampshire Record Office, Winchester, ref. 31M57/638, receipt from Frederick Kandler for plate, 2 March 1774. I am grateful to Vanessa Brett who transcribed the receipt and gave me a copy.

52. **Four ragout spoons**

Sterling silver / Ebenezer Coker, London / 2 x 1751/2 and 2 x 1754/5

MARKS: Each is fully marked on the underside of the stem with maker's mark 'EC' italics in a shaped punch (Grimwade 1990, no. 556), lion passant, leopard's head crowned and date letters 'q' and 't'.

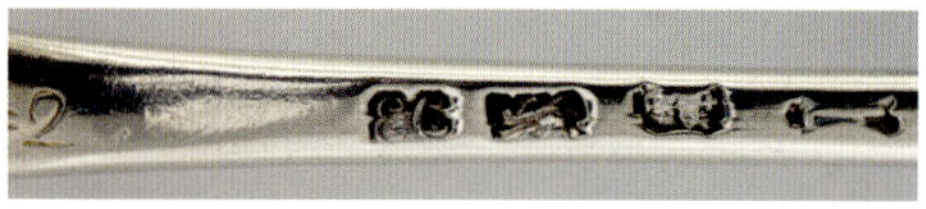

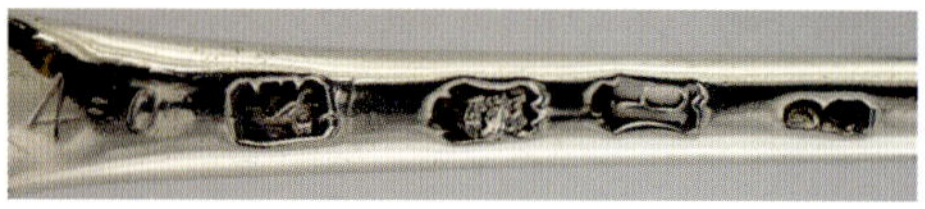

SCRATCHWEIGHTS: '4=1', '4=2', '4=0' and '4=1'.

MEASUREMENTS: l. 28.6 cm (11¼ in).

INVENTORY: 852099.53–6

PROVENANCE: 2nd Earl of Bristol; by descent to the 7th Marquess and probably sold by him privately; Robert P. Eaton; Christie's New York, 23 October 2013, lot 116; purchased by the National Trust via Christopher Hartop for $3,800 ($4,750 inclusive of premium).

DESCRIPTION: These spoons, which are forged from single pieces of silver, are of the Hanoverian single-drop pattern[1] with raised egg-shaped bowls, plain, tapering stems and single drops at the junction with the bowl. The terminals are upturned on the bowl side with slight ribs.

HERALDRY: Each terminal is engraved on the opposite side to the bowl with the Hervey crest beneath an earl's coronet.

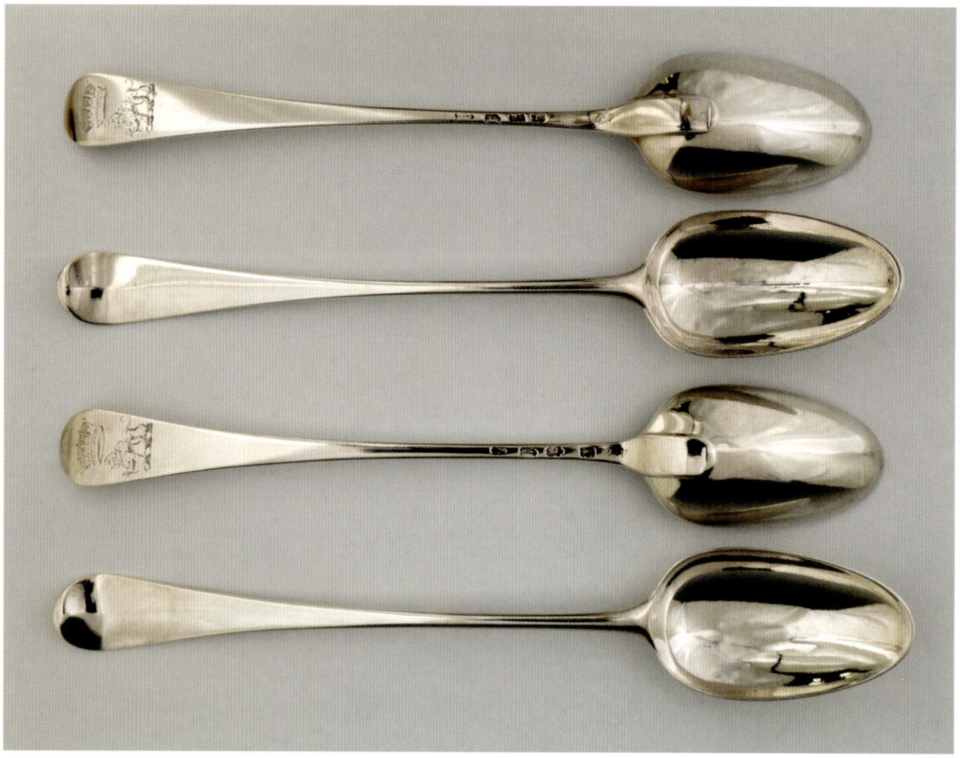

These spoons are of the standard pattern for the mid-eighteenth century, as was the rest of Lord Bristol's flatware apart from the set for dessert acquired in 1758 (cat. 71). Although they may have been supplied in two batches it is probably more likely that all four came in 1754–5 and that two were from stock. Ragouts were rich, sauced dishes of meat, game, fish or vegetables probably first developed in early seventeenth-century France and increasingly popular on both sides of the Channel over the first half of the eighteenth century.[2] As they were of a sloppy consistency and might be at some distance from the diner they required long-handled spoons to serve them. Such spoons, which would also have been used for fricassees (thickened using egg yolks and cream rather than a roux),[3] had been part of the necessary equipment for the dining table since the beginning of the century. The 1st Earl of Bristol's accounts include a payment of £15 15s on 7 July 1700 to 'Williams ye french silversmith [David Willaume I] for 2 pottage & 4 ragow spoons' (see appendix 1) and it may have been these that the 2nd Earl exchanged in 1754 to get an updated set. An additional two, matching, were acquired whilst he was in Turin (private collection)[4] and the total was brought up to twelve in 1758 with his ambassadorial plate (see cat. 64). Whilst abroad, and particularly in Madrid, he would have had regular need to dine in state, with three courses before dessert all of which would have included ragouts or fricassees, so the full dozen might well have been made use of at a single meal.

There has been much debate about the respective work of Ebenezer Coker and Elias Cachart, their marks being very similar. These spoons clearly bear Coker's mark and Ian Pickford has shown that though he has been assumed to have been a maker primarily of candlesticks and salvers he was actually also a significant spoon-maker, with several others prominent in the field having been his apprentices, including Thomas Chawner and John Lambe.[5]

1. Pickford 1983, pp. 84–5, fig. 90.
2. Pinkard 2009, pp. 107–9 and 124.
3. Ibid., p. 140.
4. I am grateful to the owner for drawing them to my attention and allowing me to make an inspection. They bear the Turin mint mark of a Savoy cross surmounted by another couped cross in a shield beneath a crown enclosing a trefoil (see Bargoni 1963, p. 15, no. 79, ill.) and the counter assay mark of Bartolomeo Pagliani (in office 1753–75), *BP* in a dotted oval (see Fina and Mana 2012, p. 248, ill.). The terminals are engraved with the Hervey crest beneath an earl's coronet, executed by an Italian hand. The scratchweights are '3-6/8' and '3=4/8-½'.
5. Pickford 1983, pp. 31–2.

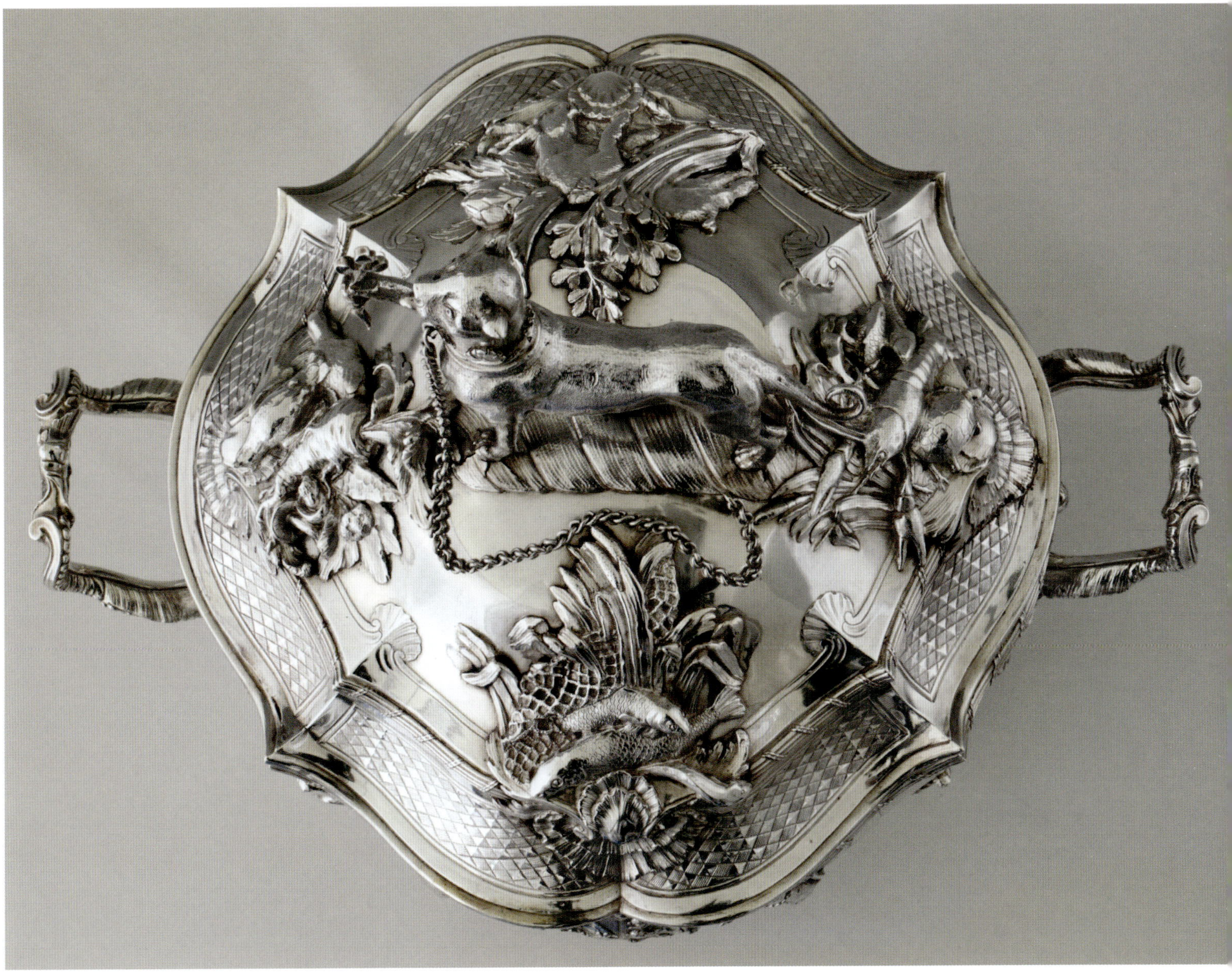

53. Pair of round tureens

Silver / probably Andrea Boucheron and Paolo Antonio Paroletto, Turin / *c.*1756

MARKS: Each of the bases is stamped on the inside face with the assay mark of Giovan Battista Carron (in office 1753–78), the Savoy cross in a shield flanked by 'GB' with 'C' beneath and a closed crown above.[1]

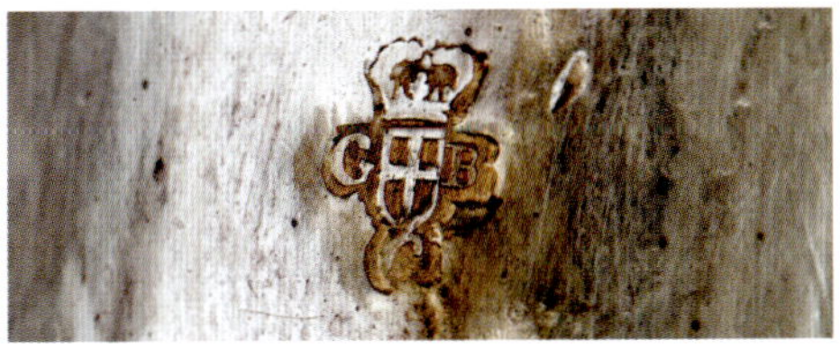

SCRATCHWEIGHTS AND INSCRIPTIONS: On the underside of the covers: 'A d [/] oz [/] ~~202=6~~ [/] 199=7' and 'B d [/] oz [/] ~~196 = 21~~ [/] 194=2'. The liners and the bases have either A or B scratched on them to identify the correct components of each tureen.

MEASUREMENTS: A. h. 34.6 cm (13⅝ in), w. (incl. handles) 36.2 cm (14¼ in), d. 28.6 cm (11¼ in); B. h. 34.7 cm (13⅔ in), w. 37 cm (14⅝ in), d. 28.6 cm (11¼ in).

INVENTORY: 852128

PROVENANCE: 2nd Earl of Bristol; by descent to the 4th Marquess.

LITERATURE: Penzer 1957a, II, pp. 134–5, fig. IV; Banister 1980, p. 793.

EXHIBITED: *Treasures from National Trust Houses*, Christie's, London, 1957–8, cat. 173 (one); *Ideal Home Exhibition*, London, 1960 (one).

DESCRIPTION: The shaped circular *bombé* bases of the tureens each rest on four cast and applied foliate scroll feet, the foliage continuing around the lower edge of the body, intertwining at either end with scroll and rocaille-work that rises around root vegetables to the shell-and-leaf upturned handles. All this detail is cast and applied as are the coats of arms on either side with frilled shields contained within C- and S-scrolls. Behind are chased ermine mantles and a chased lambrequin band with flutes and ovals sits below a cast and chased reed-and-tie moulding applied to the lip. The undersides have been cut out of the tureen bases around the peripheral scrollwork.

The domed covers are shaped to conform to the bases and have seamed bezels. Above a simple moulded rim are chased horizontal panels of diaper-work and then another cast reed-and-tie moulding. At the corners above this moulding are chased shells and spanning it at all four centres are large cast shells and scrolls which support four distinct cast and chased trophies. Those above the coats of arms have fish and an eel in front of bullrushes and a net, and a rabbit or hare against celery and an artichoke, whilst above the handles there is a group of a turtle, lobster and fish and, finally, game birds with a turnip and cauliflower against a net with water plants and root vegetables. The cast handles are in the form of ounces, or snow leopards, ducally collared and chained, each holding a trefoil.

Both covers have had their bezels crudely manipulated to try to get them to fit the bases properly. The plain oval liners are raised and have rims shaped to fit the bases, applied moulded borders and two cast and applied swan-neck-and-ball handles fixed horizontally and secured by rivets.

HERALDRY: On either side of each tureen is the cast, chased and engraved quartered shield, supporters and motto of the 2nd Earl of Bristol beneath an earl's coronet and against a chased ermine mantling. The finial handles of the covers are in the form of the Hervey crest.

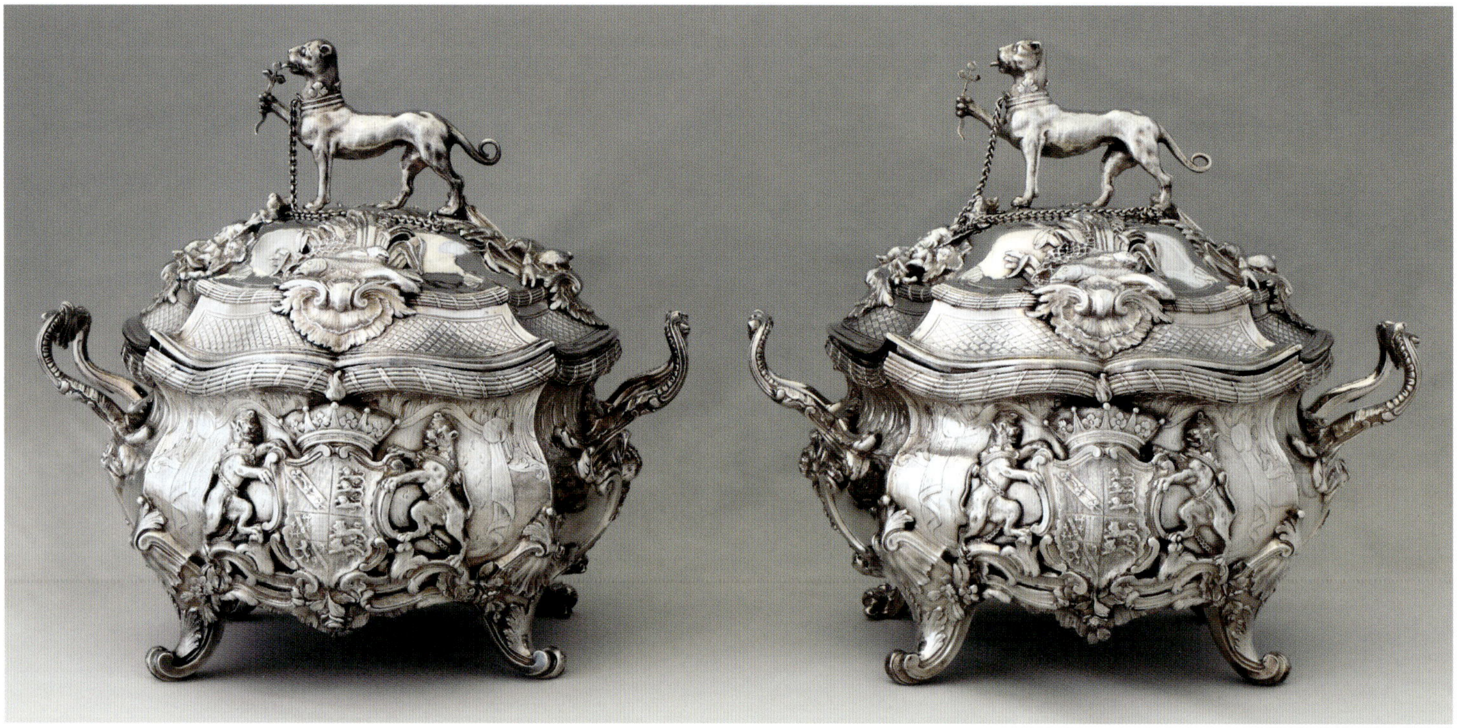

These tureens are almost certainly by either Andrea Boucheron or Paulo Antonio Paroletto, or them both working together. Although their maker's marks are lacking here they are present on many of Lord Bristol's other Turin commissions and as the most prestigious and talented goldsmiths then working in the city it seems highly unlikely that the premier pieces made for the English envoy would not have been executed by them, or at least to their design.

Lord Bristol must have discovered quite quickly after his arrival in Turin that although his oval tureens (cat. 43) were magnificent and sufficiently fashionable, it was *de rigeur* at the grand tables of the city, as in other Continental capitals that followed French fashions more closely than the English, to have sets of four tureens – two oval and two round, the latter to flank a dish or epergne in the centre of the table. Such an arrangement had been shown by Vincent La Chapelle in his 1742 *Le cuisinier moderne* (fig. 98), the first French edition of *The modern cook*, and the tureens he was depicting were probably those of the 4th Earl of Chesterfield so they would have been known in London. So too would the four provided to the 4th Earl of Berkeley by Jacques Roëttier, bearing Paris marks for 1736 and 1737,[2] but the norm in Britain remained a pair or a trio with an additional, larger tureen for the centre of the table. Lord Warrington had three at Dunham Massey in 1750 as did the 2nd Duke of Montagu at Montagu House in 1733 and 1746,[3] but even the magnificent and lavish dinner services supplied by George Wickes to the future 1st Duke of Leinster in 1747 and the Marquess of Granby in 1750 had just two tureens.[4] One of the first instances of a set of four appearing in the Jewel Office records amongst perquisite plate is that issued to Benjamin Keene as ambassador to Spain in 1750. He was a man who was fully conversant with the more purely French fashions of the continent, having spent most of the last thirty years resident in Madrid and Lisbon. His two oval and two circular tureens were not, he wrote shortly after their arrival, 'for every day' but he had the opportunity to make full use of them when the King of Spain's Secretary of State, the Marquis de la Ensenada, dined with him on 30 July 1750. As Ensenada had 'taste and magnificence, I thought no occasion so proper to lose the maidenhead of my plate as in his presence.'[5]

In creating the required round tureens for Lord Bristol the Turin goldsmiths followed the spirit if not the fine detail of the oval pair by Kandler and a comparison is instructive. Their bases have broadly the same elements as Kandler's but the *bombé* form is more accentuated and the corners are uplifted at the rim resulting in a tighter, more upright appearance. The feet are less recessed and curved, bringing them in line with the body and giving better visual support, the handles slimmer and less distracting and the chased and cast elements more effectively integrated. Particularly improved is the handling of the coats of arms, somewhat ponderous and detached on the oval tureens but fully integrated and better proportioned in their individual elements on the Turin pair. Thus the quarterings are rendered clearer by being in a symmetrical shield, the earl's coronet is larger and more firmly balanced, the ounce supporters stand on scrolls linking to the feet and the chased mantling has more life and movement. Generally the chasing is far superior as in the lambrequin band beneath the reed-and-tie rim, which is much more confident and subtle, abandoning the corner rosettes and with more intense surface treatment. Boucheron created a similar effect on an *ecuelle* (*paiola* in Italian) of *c.*1750.[6]

The covers are of the same domed form as Kandler employed but they do not follow his scheme of decoration beyond the reed-and-tie band and the handle in the form of the ounce crest of the Herveys. They are more compartmented with their panels of diaper-work and four distinct trophies of fish, game and vegetables and that helps give space to the ounces as finials but is less charmingly naturalistic than Kandler's loosely scattered vegetables spilling down beyond the reed-and-tie.

The liners are of a thinner gauge of metal than those of the English tureens and they have consequently suffered more from two hundred years of use. Generally, Kandler's tureens are more practically successful with the component parts fitting together more precisely and the side handles and the ounces being more comfortable in the hold.

For the associated dishes made as stands for these tureens see cat. 55.

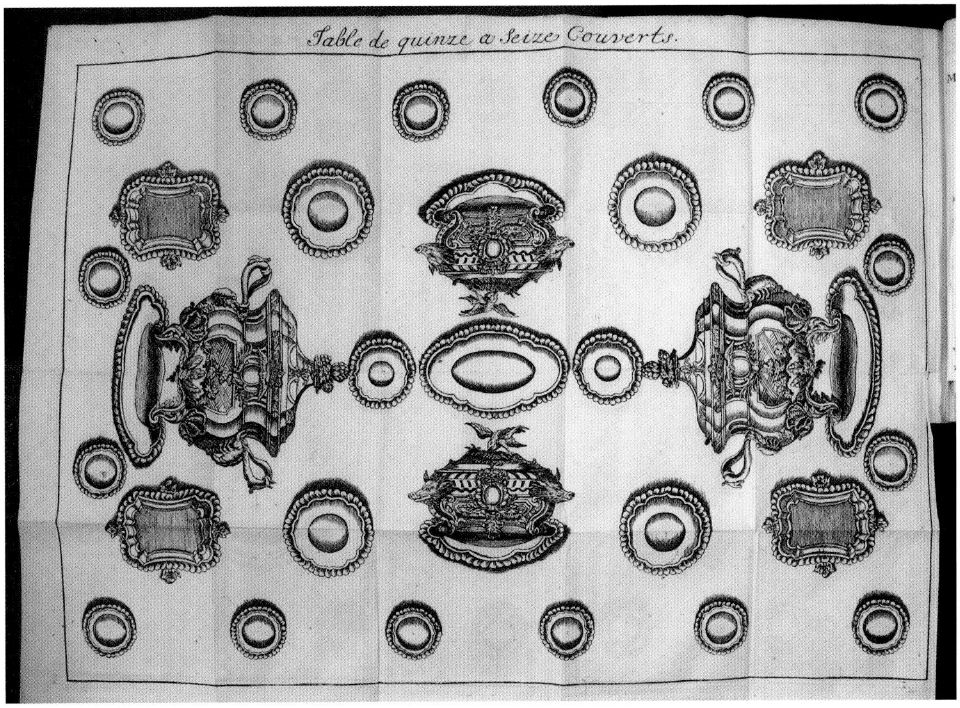

FIG. 98 / *Table de quinze ou seize Couverts* [table of 15 or 16 covers], from Vincent La Chapelle, *Le Cuisinier moderne*, Paris, 1742. Queen's College Library, Oxford.

1. Fina and Mana 2012, p. 248.
2. Sotheby's, 16 June 1960, '*The Berkeley Castle Service (to be sold as one lot)*'.
3. Lomax and Rothwell 2006, p. 76 and Murdoch 2006, pp. 44 and 108.
4. Wickes Ledgers, VAM 3 1747–50, ff. 1 and 166.
5. Lodge 1933, pp. 239–40, Benjamin Keene to Abraham Castres, Madrid, 31 July 1750.
6. Fina and Mana 2012, p. 117, fig. 108.

54. **Pair of soup ladles**

Silver / **Turin** / ***c.*1756**

MARKS: Each has the Turin mint mark of the Savoy cross surmounted by another cross couped in a shield beneath a crown enclosing a trefoil.[1]

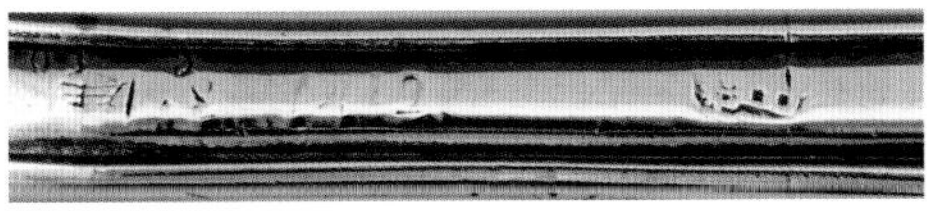

SCRATCHWEIGHTS: '~~14.18~~ 14=12' and 'oz d [/] ~~14~~.8 14=2'.

MEASUREMENTS: l. 32.4 cm (12¾ in).

INVENTORY: 852078.3–4

PROVENANCE: 2nd Earl of Bristol; by descent to the 4th Marquess.

DESCRIPTION: The ladles have deep, almost hemispherical raised bowls soldered to the stems which are cast and chased on both sides with trailing convolvulus, shells, scrollwork and reeding on matted grounds. Beneath the junction of the stems with the bowls are cast and applied shells in scrollwork cartouches.

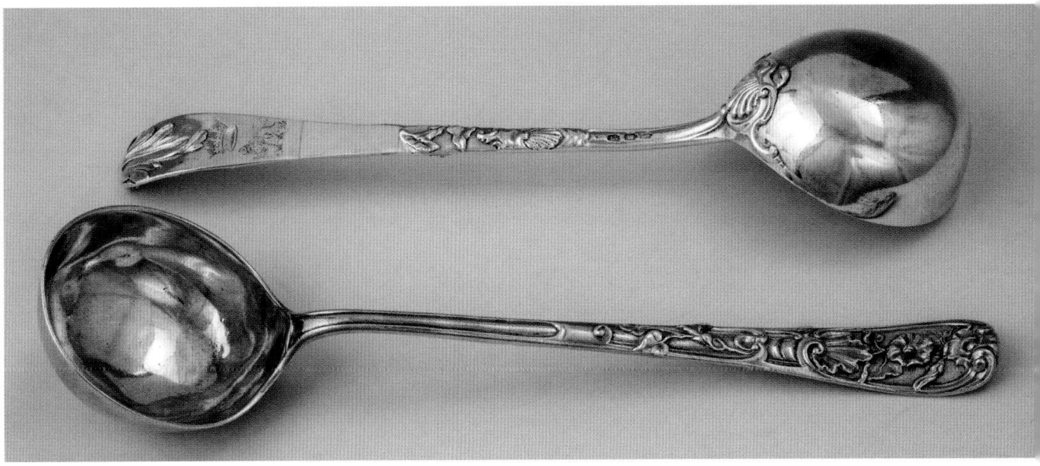

HERALDRY: Each of the ladles is engraved on the underside of the stem terminal with the Hervey crest beneath an earl's coronet.

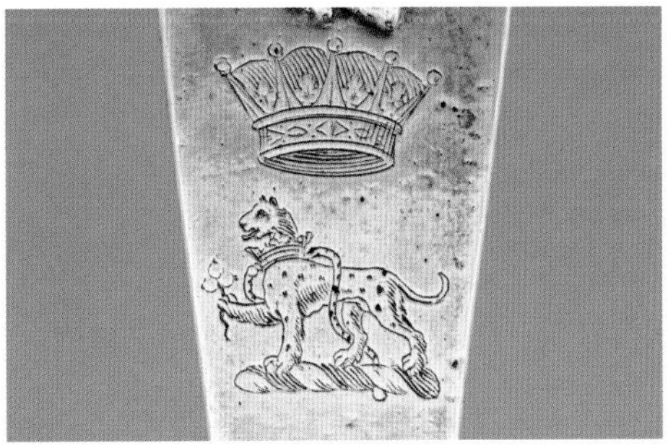

These ladles are near identical to the pair made for the Kandler tureens in 1752 (cat. 44), the only significant difference being the execution of some small, subsidiary leaves on the fronts of the terminals in cast-work rather than chasing and the slightly shorter length of the handles. The engraved crests and coronets are of a high quality but are marked out as being done by an Italian rather than an English hand by the angularity of the stems to the balls.

1. Bargoni 1963, p. 15, no. 79, ill.

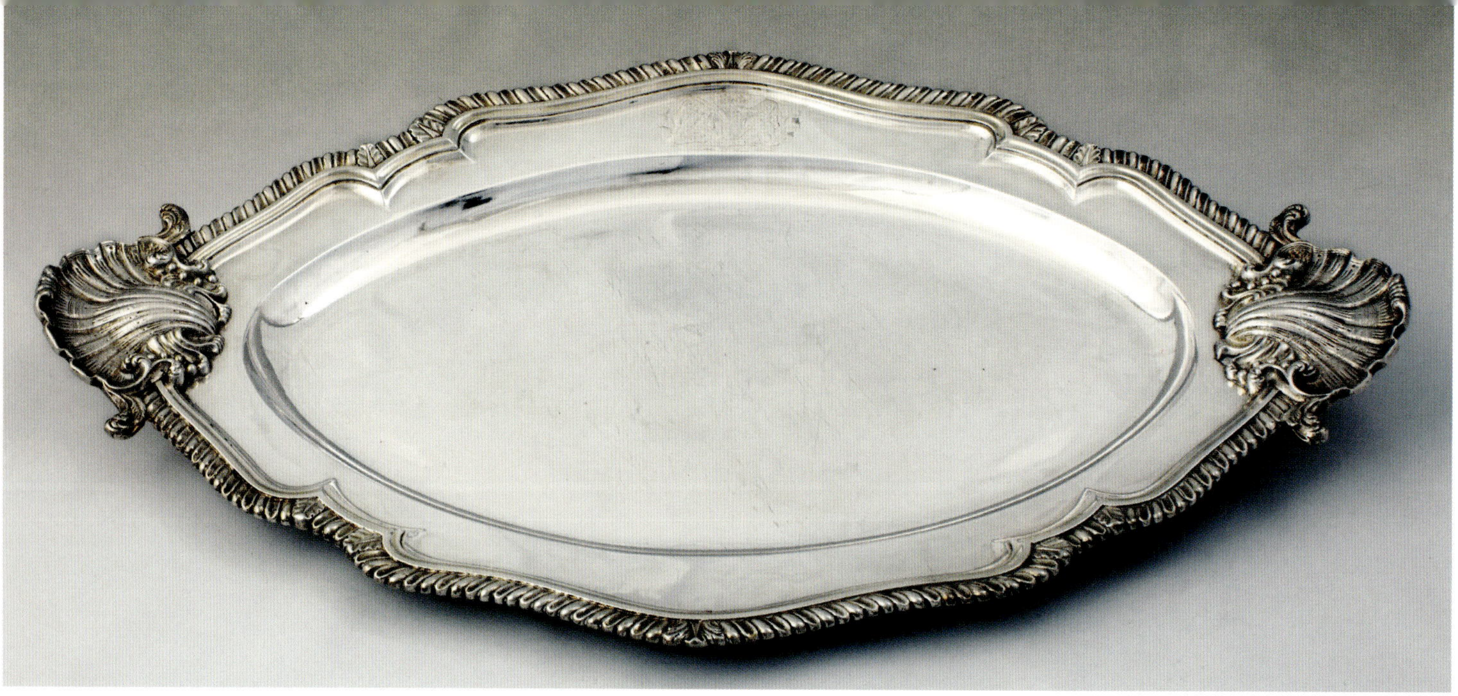

55. Two round and two oval tureen dishes

Silver / **Turin** / ***c.*1756**

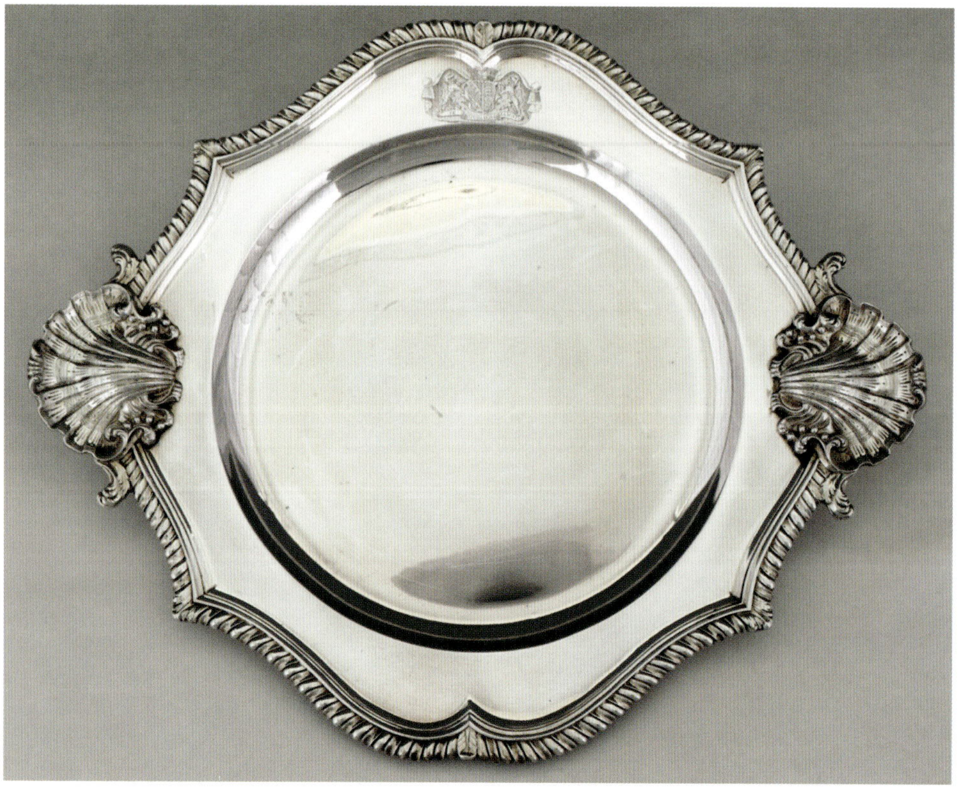

MARKS: The underside of each round dish is struck with the assay mark of Giovan Battista Carron (in office 1753–78), the Savoy cross in a shield flanked by 'GB' with 'C' beneath and a closed crown above. Dish A also has the counter-assay mark of Bartolomeo Pagliani (in office 1753–75), 'BP' in a dotted oval. The underside of each oval dish is struck with the assay mark of Bartolomeo Pagliani, the Savoy cross in a shield flanked by 'BP' with a closed crown above.[1]

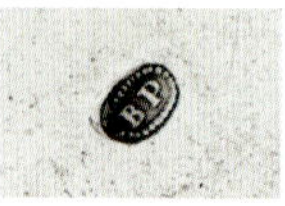

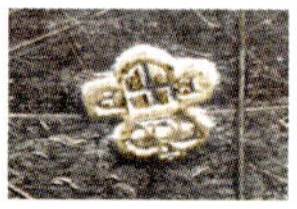

SCRATCHWEIGHTS: Round dishes: 'A oz d [/] ~~68~~. ~~12~~ [/] 67=7' and 'B oz d [/] ~~69~~. ~~12~~ [/] 68=7'. Oval dishes: 'A oz d [/] ~~74~~ ∆ ~~18~~ [/] 73=15' and 'B oz d [/] ~~74~~ ∆ ~~15~~ [/] 73=11'.

MEASUREMENTS: Round dishes: h. 4.4 cm (1¾ in), w. 47.6 cm (18¾ in), d. 40.3 cm (3¼ in). Oval dishes: h. 4.8 cm (1⅞ in); w. 57.5 cm (22⅝ in); d. 36.5 cm (14⅜ in).

INVENTORY: 852105 (round dishes) and 852080.5–6 (oval dishes)

PROVENANCE: 2nd Earl of Bristol; by descent to the 4th Marquess.

DESCRIPTION: The dishes are raised and have flat wells and broad rims with shaped borders applied with cast and chased gadrooning. Two large cast and chased shells are applied to each as handles.

HERALDRY: Engraved on the rim of each dish are the quartered shield, supporters and motto of the 2nd Earl of Bristol in an ermine mantling and beneath an earl's coronet. The engraving is Italian (see cat. 54).

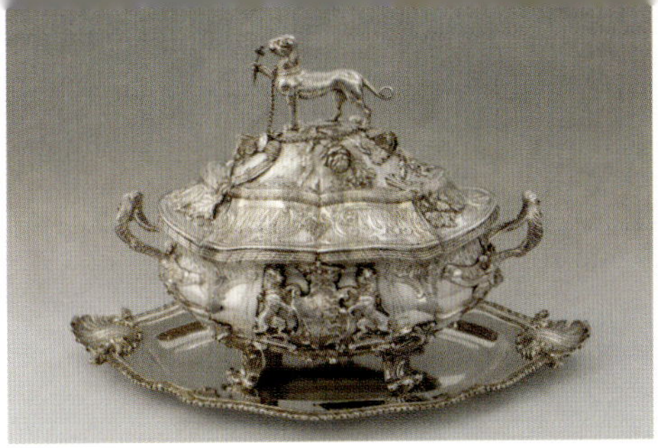

Cat. 43 on an oval tureen dish

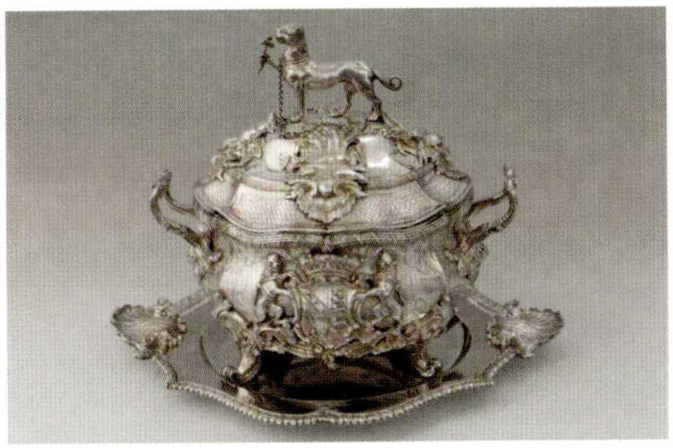

Cat. 53 on a round tureen dish

Not only did Lord Bristol discover that he needed additional tureens when he came to Turin (cat. 53) but he must also have realised that he could not present them or their oval equivalents at table without dishes beneath them as stands. These were not uncommon in Britain and had been regularly supplied by the Jewel Office and George Wickes since the 1720s but they were by no means universal in use, even in the most elevated and fashionable of households. Thus, although the future 1st Duke of Leinster was in advance of his times in having matching dishes for his tureens in 1747, the Marquis of Granby did not have them for the 'Fine Tureens' of his dinner service of 1750.[2] French examples were by this time often ornamented specifically to suit the tureens that were to stand on them, as that made by Étienne-Jacques Marcq in 1755 now in the Musée des Arts Décoratifs, Paris.[3] This meant that they had no other practical use which, combined with the large amount of workmanship and their consequent cost, probably militated against Lord Bristol commissioning anything on such lines. His tureen dishes therefore matched exactly the dishes he had already commissioned from Frederick Kandler (cat. 32) and as a consequence their intended primary purpose was soon forgotten. Tureen stands never became universal in Britain and the 2nd Earl's successors had ceased to record these ones as such by 1811, when the future 1st Marquess's plate was listed (appendix 5). Fortunately, however, the round dishes were noted as being for the Turin tureens on the death of the 4th Marquess[4] and an inspection of the oval pair revealed they had been marked by the feet of the Kandler tureens.

1. Fina and Mana 2012, p. 248.
2. Wickes Ledgers, VAM 3 1747–50, ff. 1 and 166.
3. Frégnac 1965, p. 160, ill.
4. Death Duties List *c.*1951, p. 9.

56. Forty-eight dinner plates

Silver / Andrea Boucheron and Paolo Antonio Paroletto, Turin / *c.*1756

MARKS: All the plates are marked on their undersides.

NOS. 73–8 and 80–3 have the Turin mint mark of a cross of Savoy surmounted by another couped cross in a shield beneath a crown enclosing a trefoil[1] plus the maker's mark of 'VA' in monogram beneath a crown for Andrea Boucheron (1693–1760).[2]

NOS. 79 and 84 have the same plus the assay mark of Giovan Battista Carron (in office 1753–78), the Savoy cross in a shield flanked by 'GB' with 'C' beneath and a closed crown above.[3]

NOS. 85–96 have the assay mark of Giovan Battista Carron (as above), the counter-assay mark of Bartolomeo Pagliani (in office 1753–75), 'BP' in a dotted oval,[4] and the maker's mark of St Francis Xavier in the form of a pilgrim above the letters 'PPA' for Paolo Antonio Paroletto (*c.*1715–after 1759).[5]

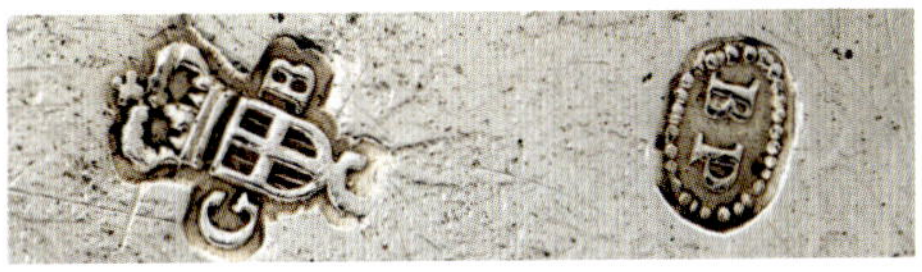

NO. 97 has only the assay mark of Bartolomeo Pagliani, the Savoy cross in a shield flanked by the letters 'BP' and beneath a closed crown.

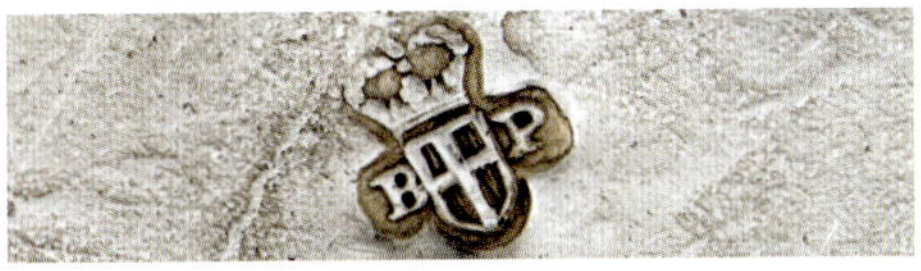

NOS. 98–102 have the assay mark of Bartolomeo Pagliani (as above) plus the maker's mark of Paolo Antonio Paroletto (as above) and an unidentified maker's mark, a monogram incorporating 'V' and 'C' under a stylized crown.[6]

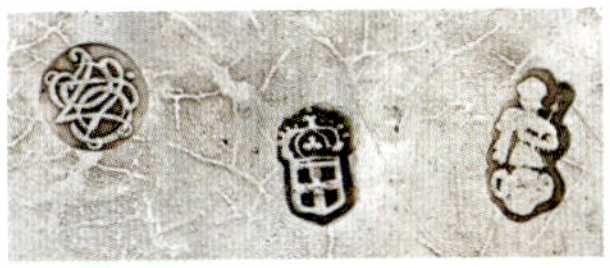

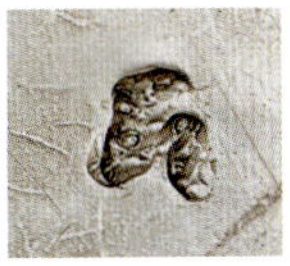

NO. 101 has the same unidentified monogram as above, the maker's mark of Paolo Antonio Paroletto and the Turin mint mark (all as above) plus the multiple over-stamping of a maker's mark, possibly that of a saint flanked by the letters 'FP' which is unidentified.[7]

NOS. 103–8 and 115–20 have the assay mark of Giovan Battista Carron plus the maker's mark of Paolo Antonio Paroletto (both as above).

NOS. 109–14 have the Turin mint mark, Bartolomeo Pagliani's counter-assay mark and Paolo Antonio Paroletto's maker's mark (all as above).

SCRATCHWEIGHTS: 'Nº 73 [/] on. 16 . 20 [/] 16=11'; 'Nº 74 [/] on. 16 . 7 [/] 16=1'; 'Nº 75 [/] on. 17 . 1 [/] 16=15'; 'Nº 76 [/] on. 16 . 14 [/] 16=7'; 'Nº 77 [/] on. 16 . 8 [/] 16=1'; 'Nº 78[/] on. 17 . 9 [/] 16=14'; 'Nº 79[/] on. 16 . 8 [/] 16=1'; 'Nº 80 [/] on. 16 . 7[/] 16=1'; 'Nº 81 [/] on 16 . 4 [/] 15=18'; 'Nº 82 [/] on 16 . 18 [/] 16=7'; 'Nº 83 [/] on 16 . 1 [/] 15=15'; 'Nº 84 [/] on 16 . 1 [/] 15=15'; 'Nº. . 85 . [/] o. 17 : 11 [/] 17=2'; 'Nº . 86 . [/] o. 17 : 12 [/] 17=4'; 'Nº. 87. [/] o. 17 : 6 [/] 16=18'; 'Nº. 88 . [/] o. 17 : 3 [/] 16=16'; 'Nº. 89 . [/] o. 17 : 20 [/] 17=10'; 'Nº. 90 [/] o. 17 : 6 [/] 16=19'; 'Nº. 91 [/] o. 17 : 13 [/] 17=5'; 'Nº. 92 [/] o: 17 : 19 [/] 17=10'; 'Nº 93. [/] o. 17 : 10 [/] 17=9'; 'Nº. 94 [/] o: 17 : 15 [/] 17=7'; 'Nº. 95 [/] o: 17 : 1 [/] 16=16'; 'Nº. 96 [/] o 17 : 14 [/] 17=6'; 'N.97 : on : 17 . 2/8 [/] 16=16'; 'N.98. on 16 : 12 [/] 16=4'; 'N.99 : on. 17 : 15 [/] 17=5'; 'N=100. on. 17 : 21 [/] 17=10'; 'N=101. on. 16 : 4 [/] 15=16'; 'N=102= on. 15 : 23 [/] 15=13'; 'Nº=103 [/] ~~Nº 138~~ [/] 19 : 3/d [/] 18=17'; 'Nº.=104 [/] Nº ~~139~~ [/] 18 : 23/d [/] 18=12'; 'Nº.=105 [/] Nº ~~137~~ [/] 18^3/d[/] 17=17'; 'Nº=106 [/] Nº ~~136~~ [/]18^3/d [/] 17=16'; 'Nº.=107 [/] ~~Nº 144~~ [/] 18^8/d [/] 17=19'; 'Nº=108 [/] Nº 143 [not struck through] [/] 18^14/d [/] 18=4'; 'N 109 [/] 17^21 [/] 17=11'; 'N 110 [/] 16^18 [/] 16=10'; 'N 111 [/] 18^5 [/] 17=18'; 'N 112 [/] 17^19[/] 17=11'; 'N 113 [/] 18^17 [/] 18=9'; 'N 114 [/] 18^2 [/] 17=15'; 'Nº.=115 [/] Nº 142 [not struck through] [/] 17^21/d [/] 17=9'; 'Nº.=116 [/] ~~Nº 141~~ [/] 18^1/d [/] 17=14'; 'Nº. 117 [/] ~~Nº 140~~ [/] 18^1/d [/] 17=13'; 'Nº. -118 [/] ~~Nº 135~~ [/] 19^7/d [/] 19=0'; 'Nº.=119 [/] ~~Nº 134~~ [/] 18^3/d [/] 17=15'; 'Nº=120 [/] ~~Nº 133~~ [/] 18^3/d [/] 17=17'

MEASUREMENTS: h. 1.7 cm (⅔ in); diam. 24.8 cm (9¾ in).

INVENTORY: 852124.73–120

PROVENANCE: 2nd Earl of Bristol; by descent to the 4th Marquess.

LITERATURE: Penzer 1957a, II, p. 136.

DESCRIPTION: Each plate is raised and has a shallow circular well, a broad rim and shaped and moulded cinquefoil borders with applied gadrooning.

HERALDRY: The rim of each plate is engraved with the quartered shield, supporters and motto of the 2nd Earl of Bristol in an ermine mantling and beneath an earl's coronet. The style of engraving is Italian (see cat. 54).

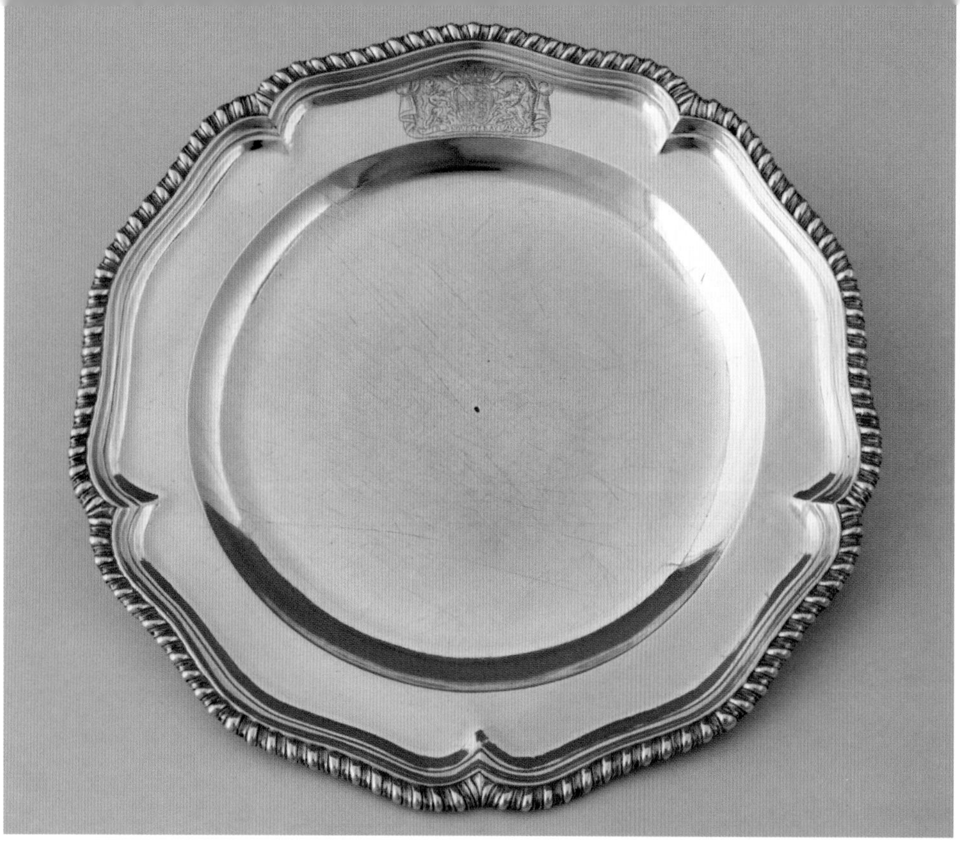

Twelve of the plates are marked by Andrea Boucheron and the other three dozen by Paolo Antonio Paroletto (see cat. 53), Lord Bristol's commission presumably being split between them to produce the large quantity required as quickly as possible. Such collaboration reflects what is known of working relationships between goldsmiths in London (see cat. 18). With which of the eminent pair the Earl dealt is not known but Andrea Boucheron is most likely, given that he was Royal Goldsmith, the introduction probably being made by the King of Sardinia's chief minister, Giuseppe Osorio. Other goldsmiths appear to have been involved in the manufacture of the plates as well, with two unidentified makers' marks appearing on some. One, having a monogram incorporating a V under a stylised crown, may perhaps be connected to Boucheron and the other, with the figure of a saint and the initials FP, could be that of a member of the Paroletto family.

Lord Bristol was not wanting to embrace Turinese or French styles but merely to augment the plates he already had so as to accommodate larger numbers of guests (see chapter 2). The Turinese craftsmen showed their high level of skill in achieving more-or-less exact copies of those produced by Kandler *c.* 1751 (cat. 35), the only appreciable, slight difference being the style of the engraving. Even the weight range is comparable to the earlier plates at between fifteen and twenty ounces though the scratch-weights applied in Turin have had to be amended down subsequently by between one and fifteen pennyweight. There was clearly not a complete grasp of British weights and measures, with some of the pennyweight figures being given in excess of twenty, but the fact that the scratchweights on these plates and the other Turin pieces are all higher than those applied back in England, and not at a consistent percentage either, does tend to imply that the intention was to overcharge Lord Bristol. All in all the difference in weight was 45 oz, 6 dwt, and at London prices that would have represented an excessive payment of about £18.[8]

Scientific analysis of one of these plates (no. 98) has indicated that the body is of Britannia standard and that the gadrooned border falls well below sterling standard.[9] This suggests that Lord Bristol exchanged at least some old plates that had not succumbed to his campaign of refashioning in the early 1750s. Perhaps these had been retained in their plain, early-eighteenth-century form for the Earl's day-to-day use.

1. Bargoni 1963, p. 15, no. 79, ill.
2. Fina and Mana 2012, p. 222, fig. 8.
3. Ibid., p. 248, ill.
4. Ibid.
5. Ibid., p. 235–6, fig. 43. Fina and Mana give his death as being after 1750 but it must have been after 1759, as some of his works are assayed by Carlo Micha who did not take up post until that year.
6. This mark does not appear in any of the major works on Turin silver.
7. Fina and Mana 2012, p. 238, fig. 48.
8. Assuming an average charge of 8s per ounce to include silver and fashion.
9. Analysis carried out March–April 2015 at the London Assay Office by XRF and Inductively Coupled Plasma Optical Emission Spectroscopy (ICP-OES). The centre of the plate is 96.62% silver and the gadrooning 89.88% silver.

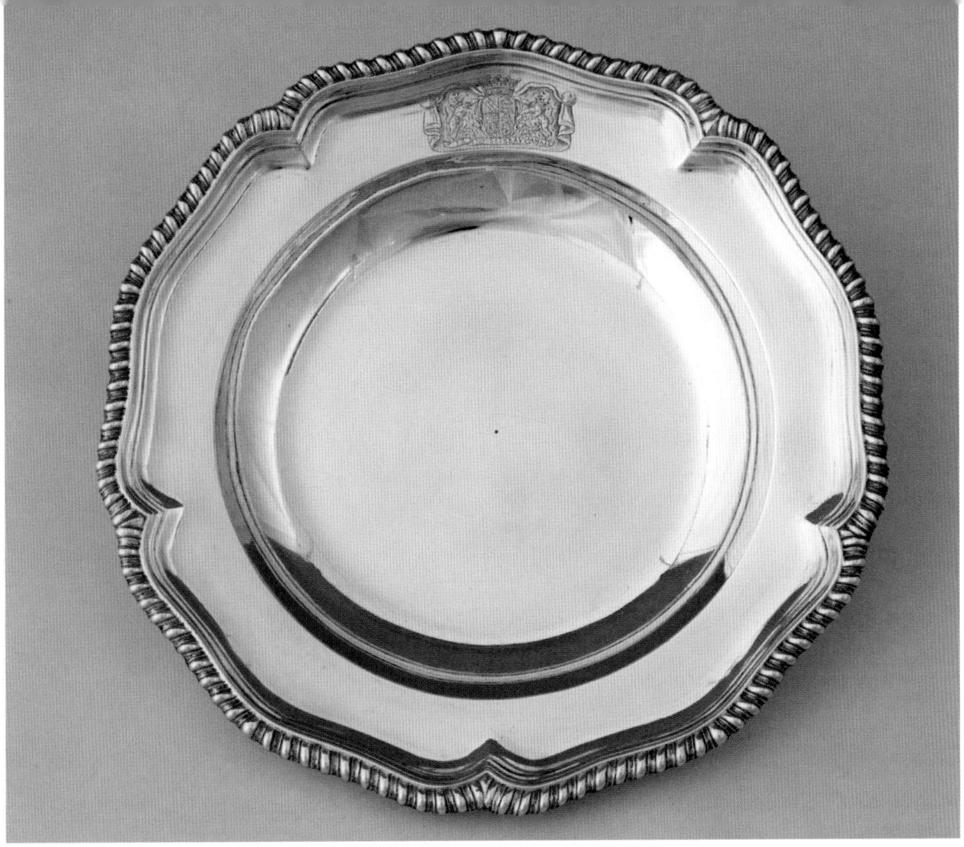

57. Six soup plates

Silver / Paolo Antonio Paroletto, Turin / *c.*1756

MARKS: All the plates are marked on their undersides.

NO. 121 has the Turin mint mark of a cross of Savoy with a couped cross on top in a shield below a crown enclosing a trefoil[1] and the maker's mark of St Francis Xavier in the form of a pilgrim above the letters PPA for Paolo Antonio Paroletto (*c.*1715–after 1759).[2]

NOS. 123–4 and 126 have the Turin mint mark and Paolo Antonio Paroletto's maker's mark (both as above) plus the counter-assay mark of Bartolomeo Pagliani (in office 1753–75), BP in a dotted oval.[3]

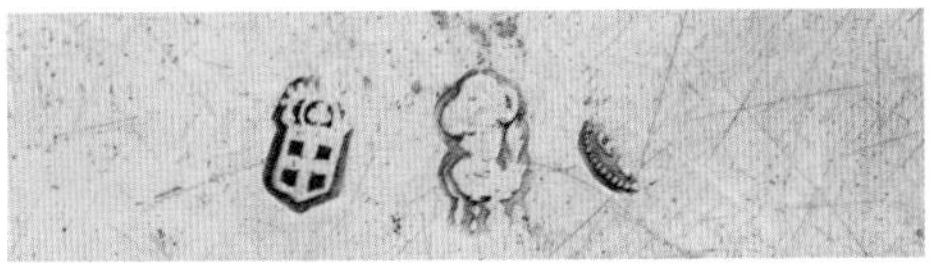

NOS. 122 and 125 have the maker's mark of Paolo Antonio Paraletto and the counter-assay mark of Bartolomeo Pagliani (both as above) plus the assay mark of Giovan Battista Carron (in office 1753–78), the Savoy cross in a shield flanked by GB with C beneath and a closed crown above.[4]

SCRATCHWEIGHTS: 'Nº· 121 [/] ~~N 108~~ [/] ~~20~~∧~~6~~ [/] 19=17'; 'Nº· 122 [/] ~~N 107~~ [/] ~~20~~ [/] 19=12'; 'Nº·=123 [/] ~~N 106~~ [/] ~~21~~∧~~6~~ [/] 21=1'; 'N. 124 [over '104'] [/] ~~19~~∧~~10~~ [/] 19=1'; 'N. 125 [over '105'] [/] ~~21~~∧~~15~~ [/] 21=5'; 'Nº· 126 [/] ~~N 103~~ [/] ~~21~~∧~~15~~ [/] 21=7'.

MEASUREMENTS: h. 2.9 cm (1⅛ in); diam. 25.1 cm (9⅞ in).

INVENTORY: 852126.19–24

PROVENANCE: 2nd Earl of Bristol; by descent to the 4th Marquess.

LITERATURE: Penzer 1957a, II, p. 134.

DESCRIPTION: The deep, circular plates are raised and have a broad rim with an applied cast and chased shaped border of gadrooning.

HERALDRY: Each plate is engraved on its rim with the quartered shield, supporters and motto of the 2nd Earl of Bristol in an ermine mantling and beneath an earl's coronet. The style of engraving is Italian (see cat. 54).

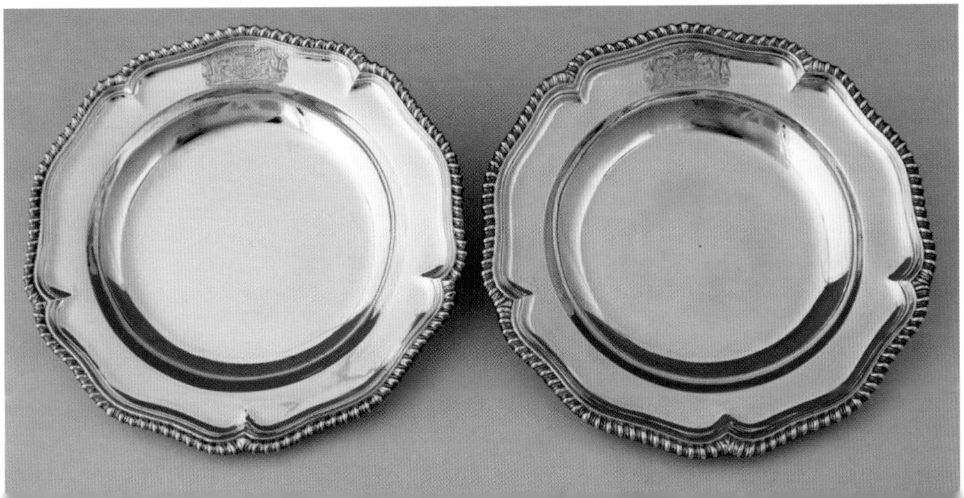

An analysis of the cancelled numbers on these and other plates suggests that they are from a set of twelve and that Lord Bristol had three dozen in this pattern, including those by Kandler of 1752. The others were probably lost in the departure from Spain in 1762. See cat. 34 (pictured here on the far left with cat. 57) for a general discussion of the soup plates.

1. Bargoni 1963, p. 15, no. 79, ill.
2. Fina and Mana 2012, pp. 235–6, fig. 43.
3. Ibid., p. 248, ill.
4. Ibid.

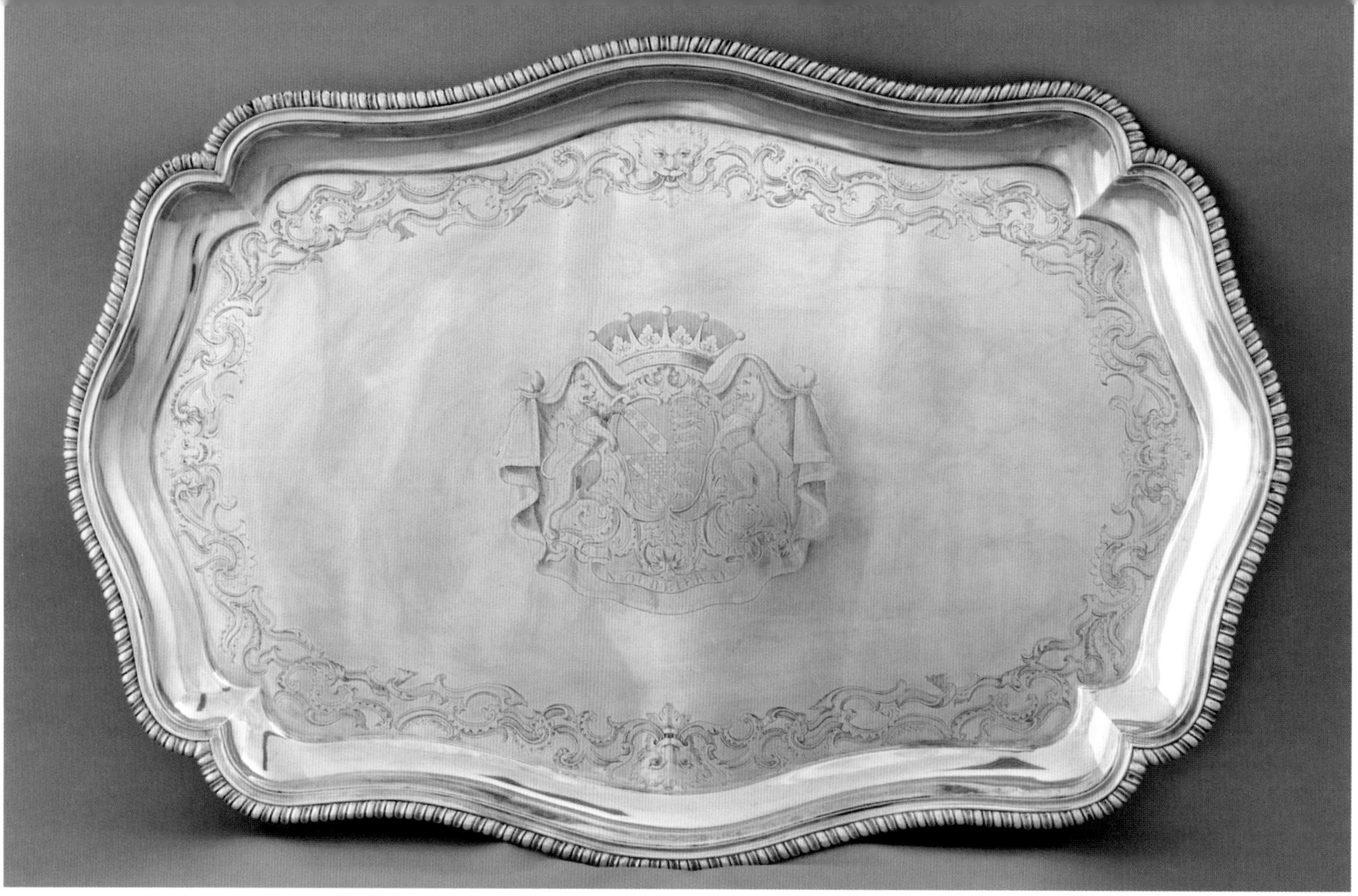

58. **Two tea tables**

Silver / Paolo Antonio Paroletto, Turin / *c.*1756

MARKS: Each is marked on the underside with the Turin mint mark of a cross of Savoy with a couped cross on top in a shield below a crown enclosing a trefoil[1] and the maker's mark of Paolo Antonio Paraletto (*c.*1715–after 1759), St Francis Xavier in the form of a pilgrim above the letters 'PPA'.[2]

SCRATCHWEIGHTS: 'N^1 on^~~237 22/d~~i [/] 235=0' and 'N^2 on^~~238 6~~/di [/] 235=6'

MEASUREMENTS: 1. h. 3.8 cm (1½ in), w. 84.1 cm (33⅛ in), d. 58.1 cm (22⅞ in); 2. h. 3.5 cm (1⅜ in), w. 84.8 cm (33⅜ in), d. 57.8 cm (22¾ in).

INVENTORY: 852116

PROVENANCE: 2nd Earl of Bristol; by descent to the 4th Marquess.

LITERATURE: Penzer 1957a, II, p. 134.

DESCRIPTION: The oblong tables are raised with pulvinating, shaped rims and indented corners and a cast and applied gadroon border. Around the edge of the well of each table is an engraved band of scrollwork emanating from four grotesque masks, one at the centre of each side.

HERALDRY: The centre of each table is engraved with the quartered shield, supporters and motto of the 2nd Earl of Bristol in an ermine mantling and beneath an earl's coronet. The style of engraving is Italian (see cat. 54).

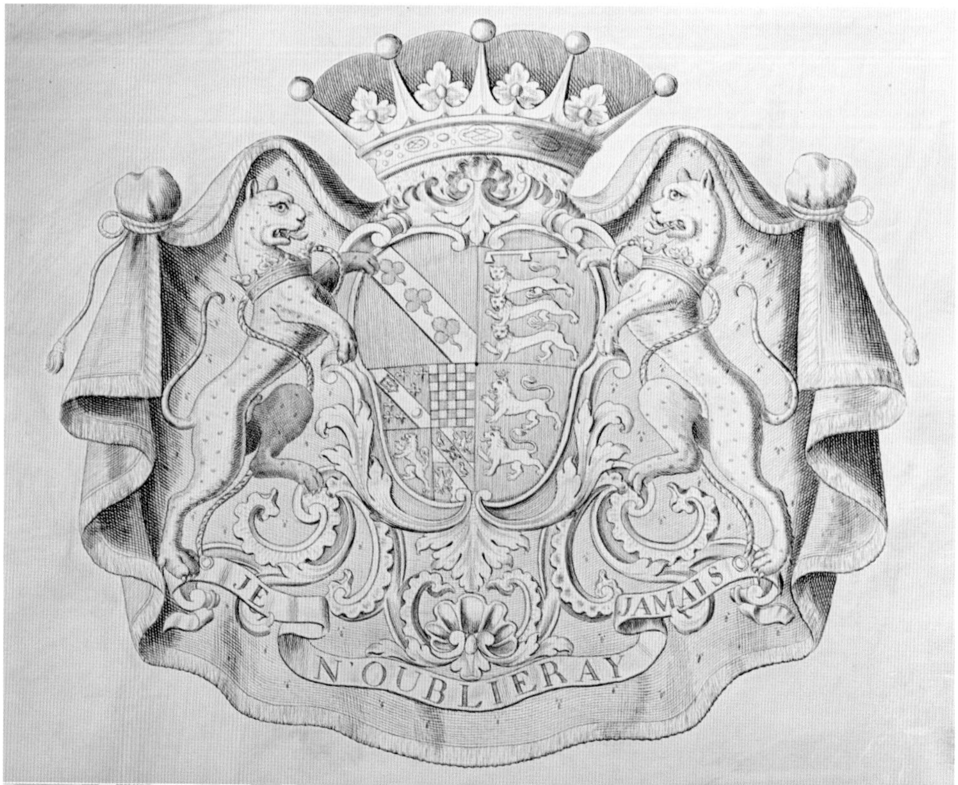

These enormous pieces would have been intended for the service of tea, coffee and chocolate and are larger than most others of the period for the same purpose, suggesting the scale of entertainment that the 2nd Earl of Bristol found himself committed to in Turin. They are marked out as Italian by the superb band of rococo engraving on each which has a freedom and lightness of effect rarely achieved in England. The high quality extends to the coat of arms in the centre, which shows a brilliant handling of light and shade and is closely modelled on that in cast form on the round tureens (cat. 53). The engraver has omitted the tassel finial which should emanate from the velvet cap of the earl's coronet, and though this could be out of ignorance of British forms it is not absent on any of the other Turin pieces and is likely to be a conscious decision in order to preserve the balance of clear space around the arms. They are perfectly placed and scaled.

The shape of the tables is essentially an enlarged, rectangular form of the plates and dishes of Lord Bristol's dinner service and had come into fashion in England alongside the more typical round and plain oblong varieties *c.*1750. Two magnificent examples made by Edward Wakelin in 1749 and 1754 are illustrated by Elaine Barr in her study of George Wickes, but they are smaller dimensionally by several inches than Paroletto's, which are amongst the biggest made in the mid-eighteenth century.[3] The Earl must have known exactly what he wanted, and as it was a wholly English form he would have had to describe it to the Turin goldsmith, or to have sketched it out for him. There would presumably also have been designs presented for approval. Other than the canisters of 1738 by Christian Hillan (cat. 20) and the kettle of 1726 by Peter Le Chouabe (cat. 14) no other contemporary tea silver survives at Ickworth and none is listed in the 1811 plate list, where these are described as 'tea trays' (see appendix 5). There would, of course, have been tea spoons which must have been lost or alienated in the late eighteenth century but much of the rest of the tea equipage may well have been porcelain (see cat. 20) given Lord Bristol's fine collection recorded in a series of inventories surviving in the National Archives.[4] Having a pair of such tables was rare but not unheard of, Lord Warrington's tea and coffee tables still being part of the collection at Dunham Massey with their purpose-made mahogany tripod stands.[5]

1. Bargoni 1963, p. 15, no. 79, ill.
2. Fina and Mana 2012, pp. 235–6, fig. 43.
3. Barr 1980, p. 117, figs. 71 and 72. The 1754 table was sold at Sotheby's, 5 March 1998, lot 231. It weighs slightly more than the Ickworth pair because of the additional cast decoration.
4. TNA, C 103/174 Hervey – v – Bristol 1762–79 and Ferguson 2011, pp. 72–85.
5. Lomax and Rothwell 2006, cat. 37 and 38, pp. 88–93.

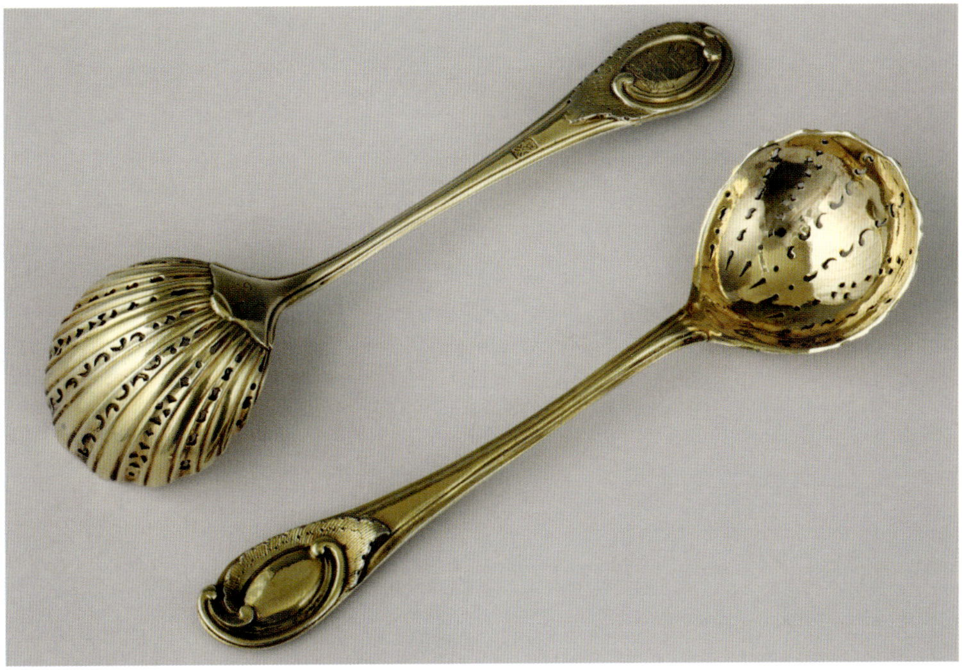

59. Four sugar ladles

Silver-gilt / Andrea Boucheron, Turin / *c.*1756

MARKS: All four are marked on the underside of the stem with the maker's mark of Andrea Boucheron (1693–1760), 'VA' in monogram beneath a crown.[1]

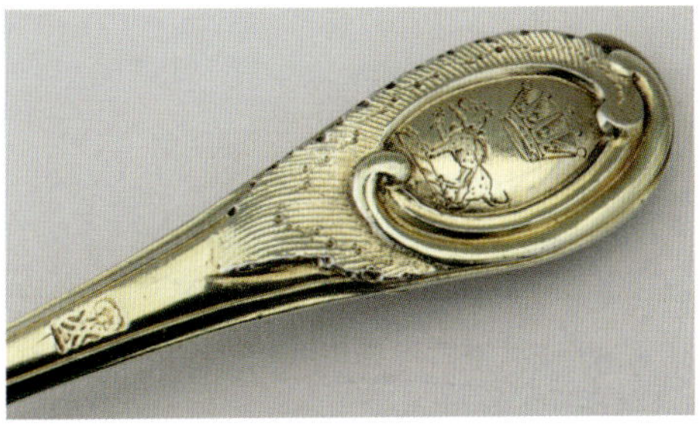

SCRATCHWEIGHTS: '1 [/] 2:5'; '2 [/] 2:5'; '3 [/] 2:9'; '4 [/] 2:4'.

MEASUREMENTS: l. 17.5 cm (6⅞ in).

INVENTORY: 852065.1.4, 2.4, 3.4 and 4.4.

PROVENANCE: 2nd Earl of Bristol; by descent to the 4th Marquess.

DESCRIPTION: The ladles are cast, chased and pierced with reeded stems, C-scroll and rocaille cartouches on both sides of the terminals and bowls modelled as shells on the exterior and pierced in diverging lines of droplets.

HERALDRY: The terminal cartouches on the undersides of the sifters are each engraved with the Hervey crest beneath an earl's coronet. The style of engraving is Italian (see cat. 54).

With ever-increasing quantities of sugar being consumed as the eighteenth century progressed, casters were no longer adequate to service dessert, and multiple basins began to be provided instead (see cat. 75). As Lord Bristol's surviving basins were not supplied until 1758 these sifters must initially have been used with some old pieces of silver improvised for the purpose, or perhaps with ceramic or glass vessels. Sugar pots are listed amongst his Dresden dessert porcelain in 1765.[2]

Of all Lord Bristol's Turin commissions these are the most obviously Italian, not needing to copy or ape London styles as the Earl would never have had such objects before, nor have been particularly familiar with them. The rococo of their terminal cartouches is typical of the forms then being produced in the city. The engraved crests do not, however, do justice to the fine quality of the ladles, being very badly executed and appearing more like indifferent dogs than majestic cats.

1. Fina and Mana 2012, p. 222, fig. 8.
2. Ferguson 2011, p. 84.

60. Tumbler

Silver / Paolo Antonio Paroletto, Turin / *c.*1756

MARKS: Marked on the underside with the assay mark of Bartolomeo Pagliani (in office 1753–75), the Savoy cross in a shield flanked by 'BP' with a closed crown above, and the maker's mark of Paolo Antonio Paraletto (*c.*1715–after 1759), St Francis Xavier in the form of a pilgrim above the letters 'PPA'.[1]

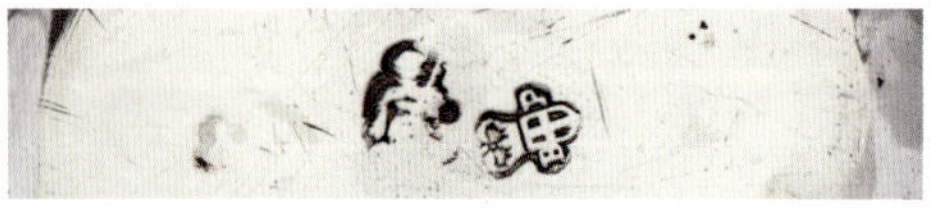

SCRATCHWEIGHT: None.
Actual weight: 145 g (4 oz, 13 dwt).

MEASUREMENTS: h. 8.6 cm (3⅜ in); diam. (at lip) 8.6 cm (3⅜ in).

INVENTORY: 852090

PROVENANCE: 2nd Earl of Bristol; by descent to the 4th Earl of Bristol and probably removed by him to Ireland, thereby passing to the Hervey-Bruce family; probably reacquired by Theodora, Marchioness of Bristol.

EXHIBITED: *Treasures from National Trust Houses*, Christie's, London, 1957–8, cat. 175.

DESCRIPTION: The trumpet-shaped tumbler is raised and has a flared, thickened lip below which are engraved three pairs of concentric lines.

HERALDRY: The front is engraved with the quartered shield, supporters and motto of the 2nd Earl of Bristol in an ermine mantling and beneath an earl's coronet. The style of engraving is Italian (see cat. 54).

For general comments on tumblers see cat. 24. Lord Bristol would presumably have kept this with him on his regular forays to court in Turin and Madrid, on the arduous journey to Spain in 1758 and on his rushed exit in the first days of 1762. This tumbler, like that of Lady Hervey (cat. 24), is not recorded in any of the nineteenth-century plate lists. It is likely therefore, that it was removed to Ireland by the Earl-Bishop – and may even have been used by him during his travels on the Continent – and reacquired for Ickworth by Theodora, Marchioness of Bristol in the early twentieth century.

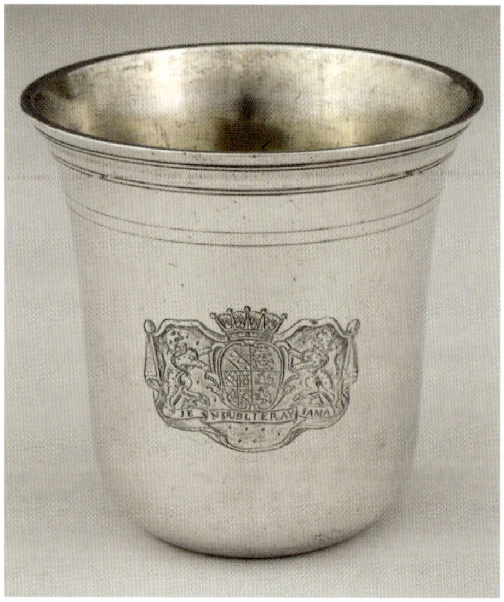

1. Fina and Mana, p. 248, ill., and pp. 235–6, fig. 43.

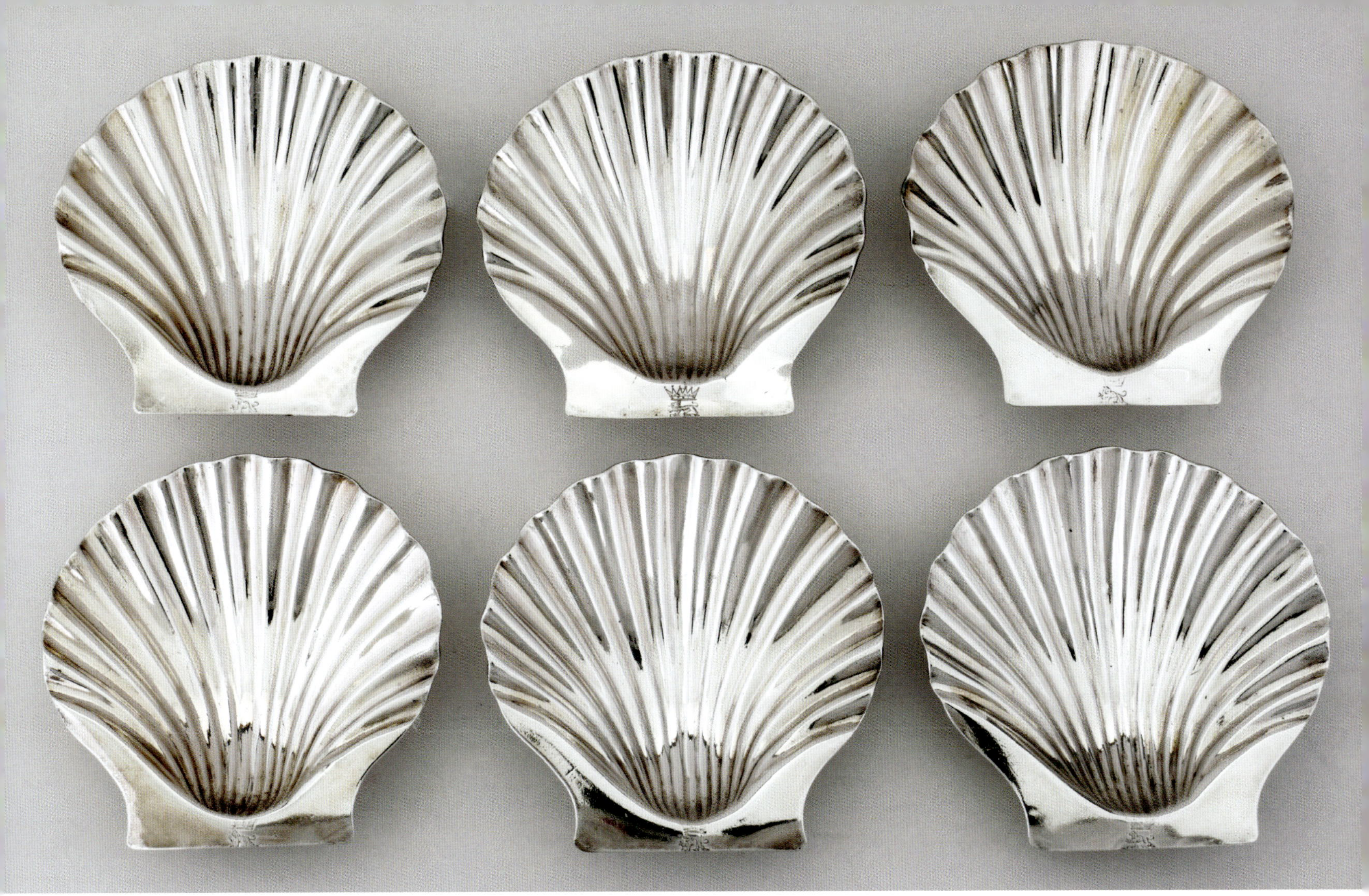

61. **Six scallop shells**

Silver / probably Turin / *c.*1756

MARKS: None.

SCRATCHWEIGHTS: 'N1 5=9'; 'N2 4=8'; 'N3 4=0'; 'N4 3=7'; 'N5 4=[2]' (according to the 1811 plate list); 'N6 4=0'

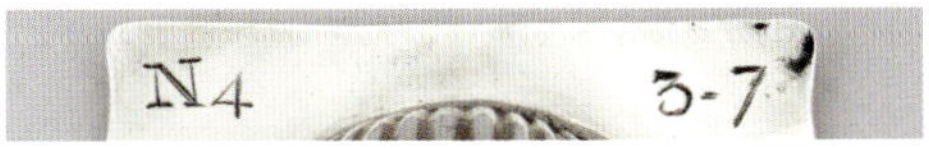

MEASUREMENTS: h. 1.9 cm (¾ in); w. 11.4 cm (4½ in); d. 11.4 cm (4½ in).

INVENTORY: 852186

PROVENANCE: 2nd Earl of Bristol; by descent to the 4th Marquess.

DESCRIPTION: The shell-shaped dishes with flat end grips are raised and have chased, fanning flutes.

HERALDRY: Each of the dishes is engraved on the end grip with the Hervey crest beneath an earl's coronet.

Sets of silver scallop shells had been made since at least the Restoration and there are significant survivals from as early as 1675.[1] Many have additional, chased surface treatment to give an even more naturalistic appearance and the provision of winkle or other feet had become commonplace by the mid-eighteenth century to stabilise them on the table. The Ickworth shells are, however, of the simplest form, without feet or surface treatment, and the style of engraving and of the scratchweights suggests they were made in Turin. The rendering of the Hervey crests and earl's coronets is, to say the least, rudimentary, and is comparable to that on Boucheron's sugar ladles (cat. 59). Scientific analysis has confirmed that the metal used was of sterling standard, the silver content being 94.3%.[2]

Such shells were probably most often used for oyster recipes, which would have been cooked and served in them, as is still the case with natural shells in French cuisine today. An example is to be found in Elizabeth Moxon's *English housewifry*, first published in 1741:

Take half a Dozen small Scallop Shells, lay in the bottom of every Shell a Lump of Butter, a few Bread-crumbs, and then your Oysters; lying over them again a few more Bread-crumbs, a little butter, and a little Pepper, so set them to crisp, either in the Oven or before the Fire, and serve them up. They are proper for either a side Dish or middle Dish.[3]

A similar recipe of 1723 specified the shells to be of silver[4] as did Vincent La Chapelle for his 'Pigeons in Scollop Shells'. In that recipe, once the pigeons had been stewed with bacon, lemon 'and a Glass of white Wine', and ragout sauces had been prepared, the cook was instructed to:

Then take six Shells, there are some of Silver, which are very like the natural ones, in which you make a small Border of Paste [pastry] round it as neat as you can; rub it over with Egg, and let it be baked in the Oven; then order your Shells in the Dish. Take your Pigeons out of their Seasoning … put one of them into each Shell, and order the whole as neat as you can, and serve it up hot for Entry [entrée]; and let it be pleasing to the Eye.[5]

1. A set of ten by Samuel Hood, 1675, were sold at Christie's 12 June 2002.
2. X-ray fluorescence (XRF) analysis carried out by the London Assay Office, March, 2015.
3. Moxon 1753, p. 115.
4. Cited in Glanville 1996, p. 43.
5. La Chapelle 1736, vol. 1, p. 247.

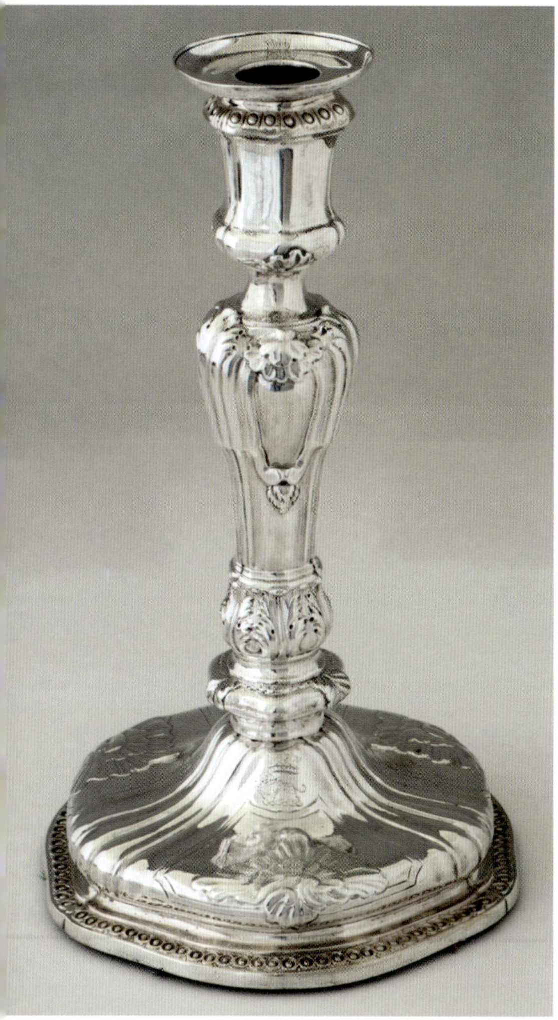

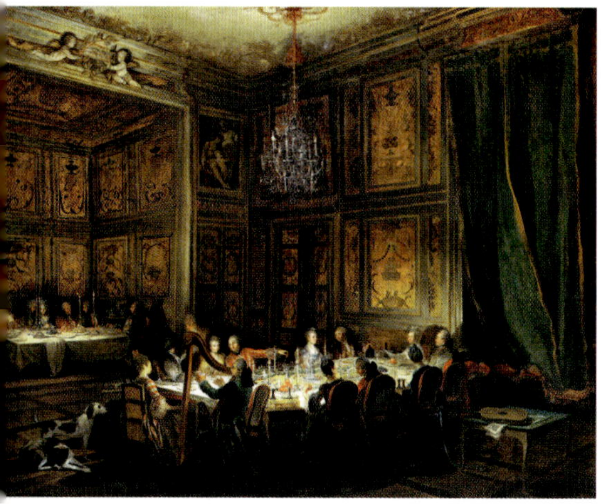

FIG. 99 / *A supper party of the Prince de Conti at The Temple*, 1766 by Michel-Barthélemy Ollivier. Oil on canvas: 56 x 71 cm (22 x 28 in). Musée national des châteaux de Versailles et de Trianon.

62. Twelve candlesticks

Silver, weighted with pitch / possibly Turin / *c.*1756

MARKS: At least three of the nozzles[1] have on their bases the maker's mark of 'NS' in italics beneath a mullet (Grimwade 1990, no. 2102) (fig. 11) for Nicholas Sprimont. There are no other marks visible on the candlesticks.

SCRATCHWEIGHTS: None. As these are weighted it is not possible to establish the quantity of silver.

MEASUREMENTS: h. 27.3 cm (10¾ in); diam. (of base) 16 cm (6⅓ in).

INVENTORY: 852104

PROVENANCE: Possibly 2nd Earl of Bristol; by descent to the 4th Marquess.

DESCRIPTION: The stepped, rounded hexagonal bases are raised and chased, each having a beaded guilloche outer band and being divided above by fluted lines into three sections with chased shells in triangular panels with concave cut corners. The baluster stems are raised and seamed and have compressed hexagonal knops above which are ogee swellings with palm leaves. The stems swell again up to the shoulders which are decorated with ovoid cartouches and scrolls, shells and leaves. The spool-shaped sockets have chased leaves on their undersides and a beaded band around the rim. The circular nozzles are seamed and have plain, raised drip pans, each with a chased line at the lip.

HERALDRY: The bases and drip pans are engraved with the Hervey crest beneath an earl's coronet.

These candlesticks are a conundrum. They are of an extremely thin gauge of silver which necessitated weighting with pitch and strengthening with a metal armature; they are far from the quality of any of the 2nd Earl's other silver and their country of origin is not immediately obvious. Further confusion is added to the mix by Nicholas Sprimont's mark on several of the nozzles (fig. 11). The stems are close in detail to a silver candlestick by Louis Leroy of Paris marked for 1752[2] but the shallow-domed feet are definitely not French in form. A set of candlesticks of the same model in ormolu, but of a finer finish, is in a French private collection and they are thought to be Italian.[3] Most probably they are a Turinese interpretation incorporating French details and would have been purchased whilst the 2nd Earl was envoy, perhaps prompted by the fashion for suppers which would have required a significant run of matching sticks, as seen in the 1766 painting of the Prince de Conti's supper at the Temple by Michele-Barthélemy Ollivier (fig. 99). They might also have been used individually on card tables, cards being an extremely popular evening entertainment and one that Lord Bristol was very fond of.[4] Candlesticks can be seen in such use in the background of the second painting of Hogarth's *Marriage A-la-mode* in the National Gallery.

The nozzles with Sprimont's mark, or at least their sleeves, may represent all that survives of the 'two Pair of Silver Candlesticks' purchased from him by the 1st Earl of Bristol on 14 July 1743 for £25 4s 4d (see appendix 1). If so then his grandson is likely, tragically, to have turned them in to meet all or part of the cost of this extensive, if flimsy set. Scientific analysis of one of the sticks shows that it is of sterling standard, coming out as 94.97% silver. A nozzle sleeve with Sprimont's mark is Britannia, at 95.84%, but the drip pans are sterling, at 94.6%.[5]

The candlesticks do not appear in either the 1811 or 1826 silver lists, probably because, with their lack of marks, they were assumed to be plated. They are thus recorded in 1874.[6] The engraving of the Hervey crests and earls' coronets looks mid-eighteenth century and is consistent with that on other of the 2nd Earl's acquisitions, such as the Edward Feline inkstand (cat. 27).

1. Two are stuck fast and cannot be examined.
2. Sotheby's, Monaco, 23–4 June 1976, lot 228.
3. Information from Christopher Hartop and Catherine Arminjon.
4. He is regularly described playing cards later in life by Lady Mary Coke. See, for instance, Coke 1889–96, vol. 3, p. 87.
5. X-ray fluorescence (XRF) analysis carried out by the London Assay Office, March 2015.
6. Bristol Plate List 1874b.

63. Pair of soup ladles

Sterling silver / Paul Callard, London / 1758/9

MARKS: Each is fully marked under the stem with the maker's mark 'PC' beneath two mullets and above a fleur-de-lis (Grimwade 1990, no. 2150), lion passant, leopard's head and date letter 'C'.

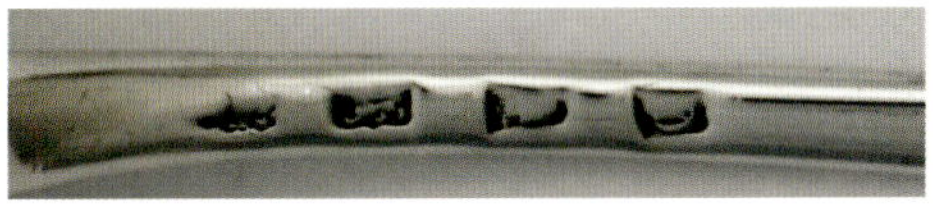

SCRATCHWEIGHTS: 'Nº 1 [/] 8∧4' and 'Nº 2 [/] 8∧12'.

MEASUREMENTS: l. 34.7 cm (13⅔ in).

INVENTORY: 852099.51–52

PROVENANCE: Jewel Office; allocated to the 2nd Earl of Bristol as Ambassador to Madrid 1758; discharged to Lord Bristol 9 April 1759 (see appendix 4); by descent to the 4th Marquess.

LITERATURE: Penzer 1957a, II, p. 136.

DESCRIPTION: The almost hemispherical bowls are raised and soldered to the tapering stems which are of the Hanoverian pattern with an upturned terminal and a single drop at the junction with the bowl.

HERALDRY: The underside of each terminal is engraved with the quartered arms of the Hanoverian monarchs (pre-1801) within the Garter and beneath an imperial crown flanked by the initials GR.

The simplicity of these ladles suggests that the tureens they accompanied, which have not survived, were also quite plain. They were certainly comparatively light at around 100 oz – less than half the weight of the Kandler tureens. As Lord Bristol had already acquired such lavish plate in London and Turin it would appear that he decided to use part of his ambassadorial allowance to equip himself with a service for everyday use. Sir Benjamin Keene, the Earl's predecessor, had had the same. As he wrote to Abraham Castres, the British Envoy in Lisbon, 'I have plain plate of my own for 12 covers' for daily use.[1]

1. Lodge 1933, p. 240.

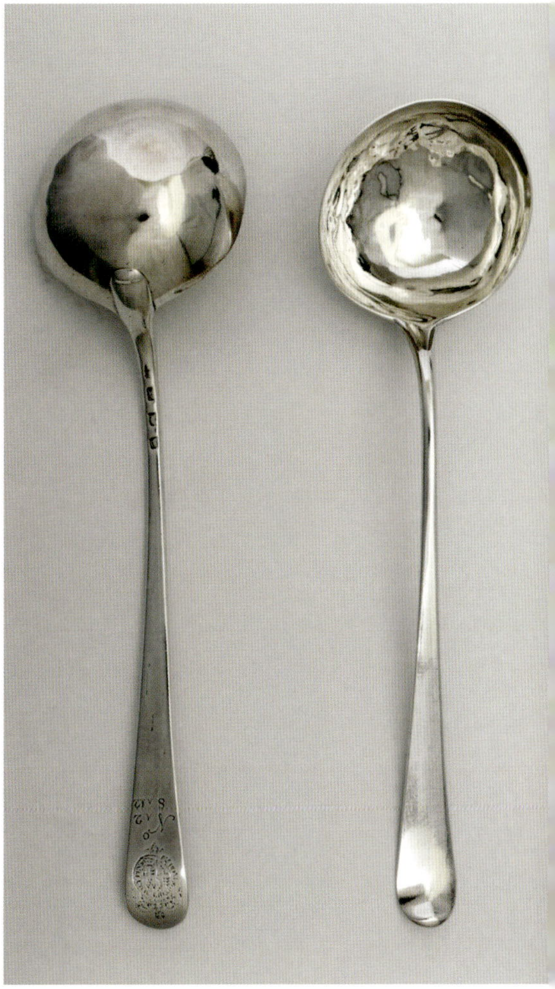

64. Six ragout spoons

Sterling silver / Paul Callard, London 1757/8 (x 2), 1758/9 (x 4)

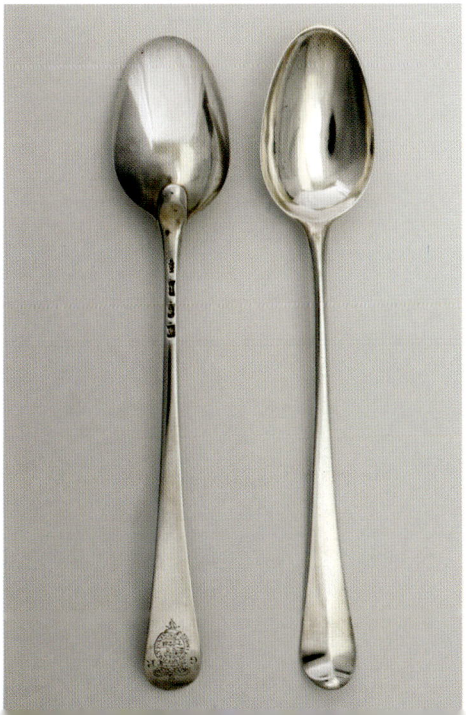

MARKS: Each is fully marked on the back of the stem with the maker's mark 'PC' beneath two mullets and above a fleur-de-lis (Grimwade 1990, no. 2150), lion passant, leopard's head and date letters 'B' (2) and 'C' (4).

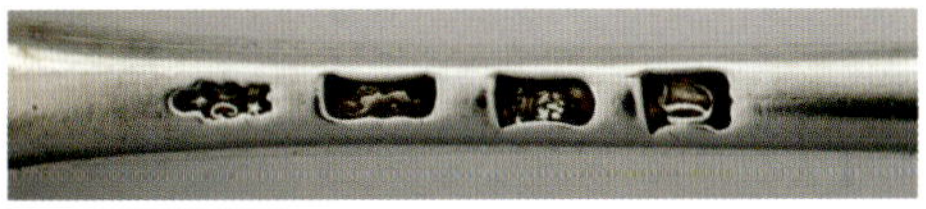

SCRATCHWEIGHTS: None.
Actual weight: (combined) 692 g (22 oz, 5 dwt).

MEASUREMENTS: l. 28.6 cm (11¼ in).

INVENTORY: 852099.45–50

PROVENANCE: Jewel Office; allocated to the 2nd Earl of Bristol as Ambassador to Madrid 1758 (see appendix 4); discharged to Lord Bristol 9 April 1759 (see appendix 4); by descent to the 4th Marquess.

LITERATURE: Penzer 1957a, II, p. 136.

DESCRIPTION: These spoons, which are forged from single pieces of silver, are of the Hanoverian single-drop pattern[1] with raised egg-shaped bowls, plain, tapering stems and single drops at the junction with the bowl. The terminals are upturned on the bowl side with slight ribs.

HERALDRY: The underside of each terminal is engraved with the quartered arms of the Hanoverian monarchs (pre-1801) within the Garter and beneath an imperial crown flanked by the initials GR.

These ragout spoons are identical to those acquired by Lord Bristol in 1754 (cat. 52). See that entry for a discussion of the whole set.

1. Pickford 1983, pp. 84–5, fig. 90.

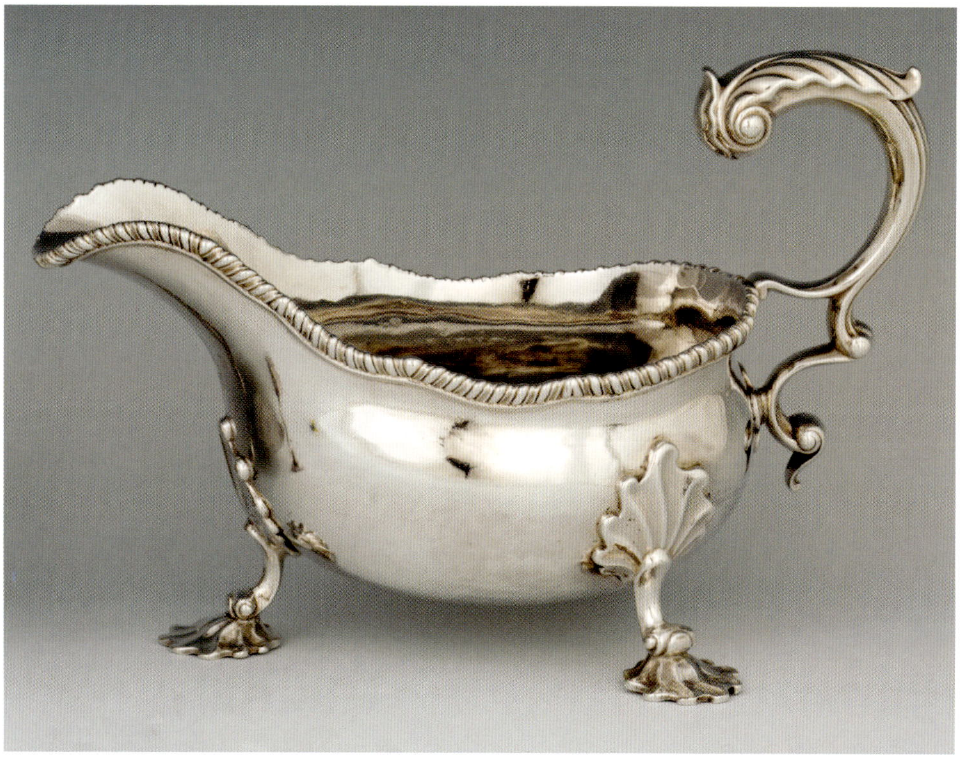

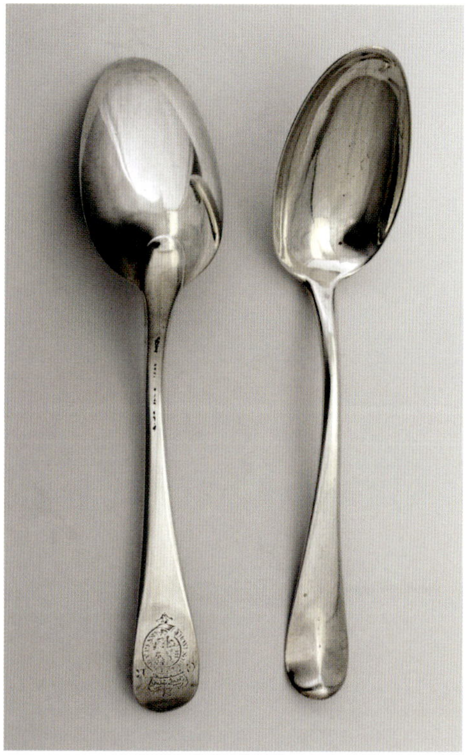

65. Four sauce boats

Sterling silver / Simon Le Sage, London / 1758/9

MARKS: All fully marked on their undersides with date letter 'C', leopard's head, lion passant and maker's mark 'S·L' in italics with a cup above and mullet below (Grimwade 1990, no. 2576). The marks are all very worn.

SCRATCHWEIGHTS: 'Nº 1 [/] 18=^6'; 'Nº 2 [/] 18^3'; 'Nº 3 [/] 18^4'; 'Nº 4 [/] 18=10'.

MEASUREMENTS: h. 14.9 cm (5⅞ in); w. 23.2 cm (9⅛ in); d. 11.4 cm (4½ in).

INVENTORY: 852122

PROVENANCE: Jewel Office; allocated to the 2nd Earl of Bristol as Ambassador to Madrid 1758; discharged to Lord Bristol 9 April 1759 (see appendix 4); by descent to the 4th Marquess.

LITERATURE: Penzer 1957a, II, p. 137

EXHIBITION: *British Week*, Milan and Frankfurt, 1965.

DESCRIPTION: The oval bodies are raised and have broad, beak-shaped pouring lips and shaped rims with applied cast gadrooning. Each boat rests on three cast scroll and wavy-shell feet with wavy-shell terminals against the body. The open double-scroll handles with leaf capping are cast.

HERALDRY: Beneath the pouring lip of each boat are engraved the quartered arms of the Hanoverian monarchs (pre-1801) within the Garter and beneath an imperial crown flanked by the initials GR.

This was one of the most popular models for sauceboats in the 1750s and was produced by numerous different goldsmiths. These ones are rendered superior to many by their finely modelled feet and handles and their well-considered composition. Nos. 1 and 3 have been exposed to greater wear than the others and are dented and worn. For general comments on the 2nd Earl's sauce boats see cat. 29.

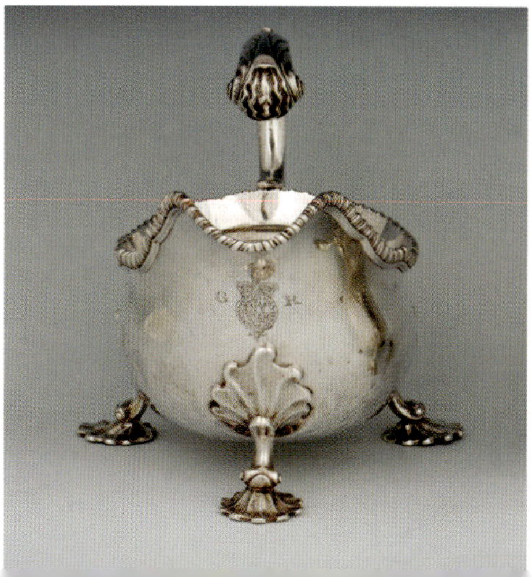

66. Four sauce spoons

Silver / Paul Callard / probably 1758/9

MARKS: Each spoon is stamped four times on the reverse of the stem with the maker's mark 'PC' beneath two mullets and above a fleur-de-lis (Grimwade 1990, no. 2150).

SCRATCHWEIGHTS: None.
Actual weight: (combined) 294 g (9 oz, 9 dwt).

MEASUREMENTS: l. 20.3 cm (8 in).

INVENTORY: 852099.30–34

PROVENANCE: Jewel Office; allocated to the 2nd Earl of Bristol as Ambassador to Madrid 1758; discharged to Lord Bristol 9 April 1759 (see appendix 4); by descent to the 4th Marquess.

LITERATURE: Penzer 1957a, II, p. 136.

DESCRIPTION: The spoons are forged from single pieces of silver. They are of the Hanoverian single-drop pattern[1] with raised egg-shaped bowls, plain, tapering and curved stems and single drops at the junction with the bowl. The terminals are upturned on the bowl side with slight ribs.

HERALDRY: The underside of each terminal is engraved with the quartered arms of the Hanoverian monarchs (pre-1801) within the Garter and beneath an imperial crown flanked by the initials GR.

These spoons have curved stems in order to rest comfortably in the Le Sage sauce boats (cat. 65) with which they were delivered as part of Lord Bristol's ambassadorial allocation of plate (see appendix 4). Specific flatware for serving sauces seems from an analysis of the Wickes ledgers and Jewel Office records to have emerged in the 1740s, amongst the earliest references being the receipt by Lord Tyrawley and the 4th Earl of Holderness of sauce spoons with their boats on becoming ambassadors in 1744.[2] George Wickes supplied ten spoons with the future 1st Duke of Leinster's ten sauce boats in 1747[3] and equal numbers of boats and spoons were the norm, the Dowager Duchess of Somerset receiving four of each in 1749.[4] Ladles were also an option, the Earl of Albemarle receiving four on going to Paris in 1749, and they gradually began to supplant spoons.[5] Whereas in 1758 and in 1760 both Lord Bristol and the 9th Earl of Kinnoull, the latter as ambassador to Portugal, chose sauce spoons, in 1762 the 2nd Earl of Egremont as Secretary of State, Sir John Cust as Speaker and the 2nd Earl of Buckinghamshire as ambassador to Russia all had ladles rather than spoons with their sauce boats.[6] Because such spoons can easily become detached from their boats, and even be straightened, it is rare to find a recorded pairing such as that at Ickworth surviving intact. There must, presumably, have been sauce spoons for Lord Bristol's other eight sauce boats but they have not survived.

1. Pickford 1983, pp. 84–5, fig. 90.
2. Jewel Office Delivery Book 1732–93, f. 92. In 1719 Lord Cartaret had received 'Eight Sauce Spoones' on going to Sweden as ambassador but their combined weight of 59 oz, 7 dwt, suggests they were ragout spoons rather than for use with sauce boats: Jewel Office Delivery Book 1698–1732, f. 232. There are ladles of *c.*1740 by Paul de Lamerie associated with a pair of earlier sauce boats in the Gilbert Collection, see Schroder 1988b, cat. 53, pp. 214–7.
3. Wickes Ledgers, VAM 3 1747–50, f. 1.
4. Ibid., f. 86.
5. Jewel Office Delivery Book 1732–93, f. 108.
6. Ibid, ff. 165, 181 and 196.

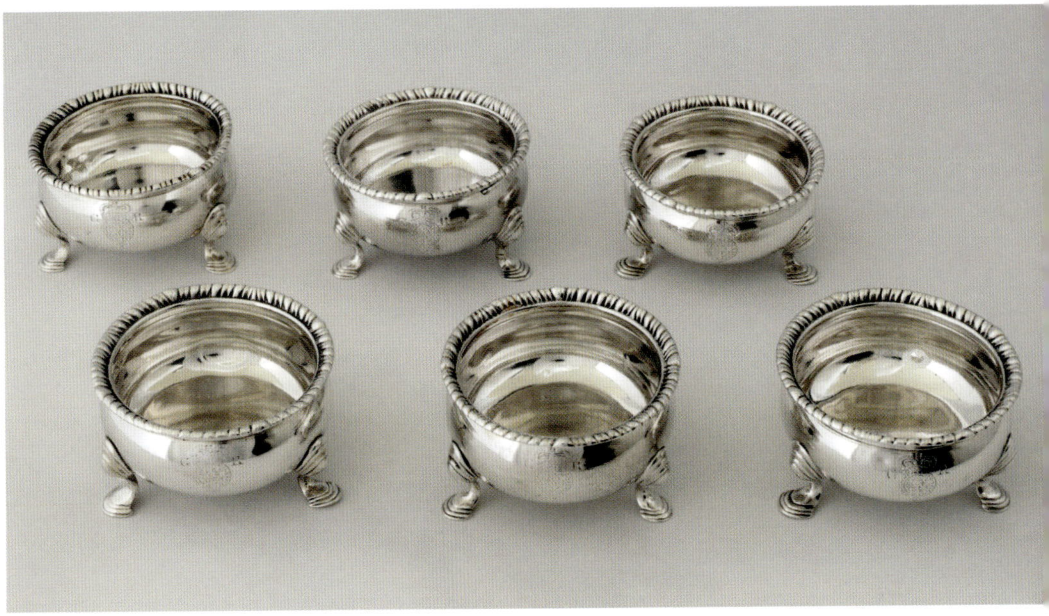

67. Six salts

Sterling silver (x 2) / **Lewis Hamon, London** / **1736/7**
Sterling silver (x 4) / **David Hennell I, London** / **1758/9**

MARKS: All are fully marked on their undersides.

NOS. 2 and 6 have the maker's mark 'LH' beneath a dove of peace (Grimwade 1990, no. 1925), leopard's head, lion passant and date letter 'a'.

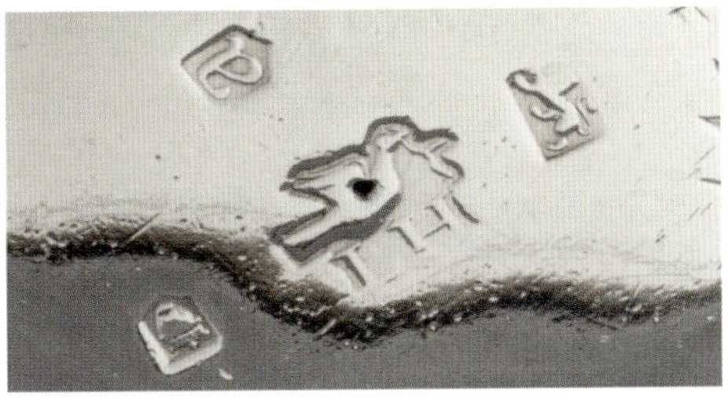

NOS. 1 and 3–5 have maker's mark 'D·H' (Pickford 1989, p. 206),[1] leopard's head, lion passant and date letter 'C'.

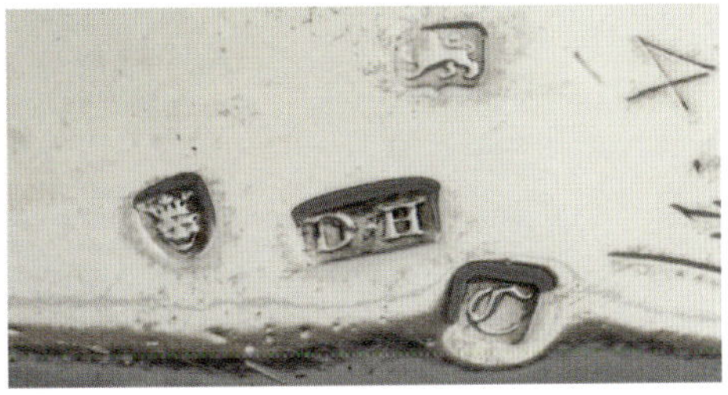

SCRATCHWEIGHTS: 'Nº 1 [/] 4=14½'; 'Nº 2 [/] 4=17'; 'Nº 3 [/] 4=14 ½'; 'Nº 4 [/] 4=17'; 'Nº 5 [/] 4=16' ; 'Nº 6 [/] 4=12'.

MEASUREMENTS: h. 4.4 cm (1¾ in); diam. 7.9 cm (3⅛ in).

INVENTORY: 852073

PROVENANCE: Jewel Office; allocated to the 2nd Earl of Bristol as Ambassador to Madrid 1758; discharged to Lord Bristol 9 April 1759 (see appendix 4); by descent to the 4th Marquess.

LITERATURE: Penzer 1957a, II, p. 136.

EXHIBITED: Society of the Four Arts, Palm Beach, Florida, 1959 (Hamon pair).

DESCRIPTION: The circular-bellied body of each salt is raised and has a cast gadroon rim and three cast concertina pad and scroll feet.

HERALDRY: The front of each salt is engraved with the quartered arms of the Hanoverian monarchs (pre-1801) within the Garter and beneath an imperial crown flanked by the initials GR.

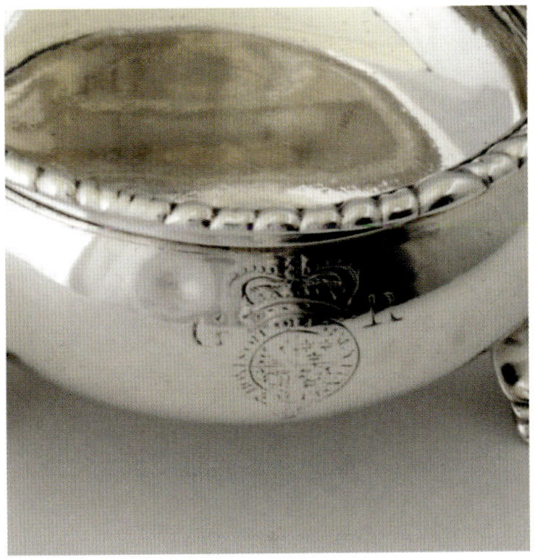

This form of salt, sometimes called 'cauldron', appeared in the mid-1720s[2] but is uncommon before the date of the pair by Lewis Hamon at Ickworth. Little of Hamon's work survives and these are amongst the even rarer pieces by him bearing a full set of hallmarks.[3] They had presumably been turned in to David Hennell I who is much better known for salts than Hamon and had produced the same model himself since at least 1737.[4] Their extreme simplicity and diminutive size make it unlikely that they would have been on the table at the same time as the magnificent and extensive set of salts by Kandler (cat. 46) and, like the ambassadorial soup ladles (cat. 63), they were probably part of Lord Bristol's everyday service.

The salts would have been provided with glass liners which were sometimes blown directly into them and often had a star cut into the base. Surviving examples are extremely rare but one from a salt of this model is illustrated by Percy Hennell in *The Hennell Salt Cellars*.[5]

1. This is more likely to be Hennell's second mark, probably of 1739 but not in the register, rather than that given by Arthur Grimwade (1990, no. 471). The form seen on the Ickworth salts appears on other examples of 1757 and 1758 illustrated in Hennell 1986, pp. 43 and 48, figs. 20b and 25b.
2. Hughes 1957, p. 95.
3. Information from Peter Cameron.
4. Hennell 1986, p. 30, fig. 4.
5. Ibid., p. 56, fig. 33.

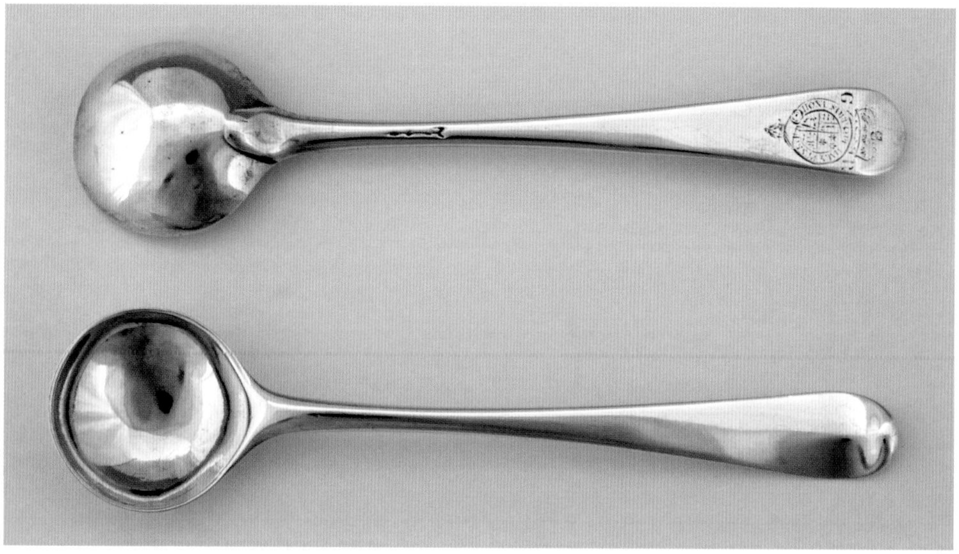

68. **Four salt spoons**

Silver / Paul Callard / probably 1758/9

MARKS: On the back of each stem is the maker's mark 'PC' beneath two mullets and above a fleur-de-lis (Grimwade 1990, no. 2150).

SCRATCHWEIGHT: None.
Actual weight: (combined) 28g (0 oz, 18 dwt).

MEASUREMENTS: l. 8.9 cm (3½ in).

INVENTORY: 852074.13–16

PROVENANCE: Jewel Office; allocated to the 2nd Earl of Bristol as Ambassador to Madrid 1758; discharged to Lord Bristol 9 April 1759 (see appendix 4); by descent to the 4th Marquess.

DESCRIPTION: The spoons are forged out of individual pieces of silver and have almost hemispherical raised bowls and tapering stems which are of the Hanoverian pattern with an upturned terminal end and a single drop at the junction with the bowl.

HERALDRY: The underside of each terminal is engraved with the quartered arms of the Hanoverian monarchs (pre-1801) within the Garter and beneath an imperial crown flanked by the initials GR.

These survive from the set of six salt spoons delivered with the Hamon and Hennell salts (cat. 67). They are miniature versions of Callard's soup ladles (cat. 63).

69. **Table service of knives, forks and spoons**

Silver handled knives (x 6)
probably London / *c.*1758

Sterling silver forks (x 9)
Paul Callard, London / 1758/9

Sterling silver spoons (x 5)
Ebenezer Coker, London / 1751/2

Sterling silver spoons (x 12)
Paul Callard, London / 1758/9

MARKS: The knives have traces of a maker's mark on the front of the handles but they are too worn to identify. The steel blades are stamped 'GR' either side of an imperial crown above 'GILBERT'.

Each fork is fully marked on the reverse of the stem with the maker's mark 'PC' beneath two mullets and above a fleur-de-lis (Grimwade 1990, no. 2150), lion passant, leopard's head and date letter 'C'.

All the spoons are fully marked on the underside of the stem. Five have the maker's mark 'EC' italics in a shaped punch (Grimwade 1990, no. 556) for Ebenezer Coker, date letter 'q', leopard's head and lion passant. Twelve have the date letter 'C', leopard's head, lion passant and maker's mark 'PC' beneath two mullets and above a fleur-de-lis (Grimwade 1990, no. 2150) for Paul Callard.

SCRATCHWEIGHTS: None. Estimated combined weights for four dozen knives and forks and three dozen spoons are given in the 1811 plate list as 73 oz, 120 oz and 88 oz respectively.

MEASUREMENTS: Knives (l. of handles) 9.5 cm (3¾ in), l. (overall) 25.7 cm (10⅛ in). Forks l. 19 cm (7½ in). Spoons l. 20.3 cm (8 in).

INVENTORY: Knives 852203.5–10. Forks 852099.36–44. Spoons 852099.2–18

PROVENANCE: Jewel Office; allocated to the 2nd Earl of Bristol as Ambassador to Madrid 1758; discharged to Lord Bristol 9 April 1759 (see appendix 4); by descent to the 4th Marquess.

LITERATURE: Penzer 1957a, II, p. 136 (forks and spoons).

EXHIBITED: *British Week*, Milan and Frankfurt, 1965.

DESCRIPTION: The cast, pistol-shaped handles of the knives are plain apart from round-moulded cappings. They are very worn. The early-nineteenth-century steel blades are scimitar-shaped. The forks and spoons are forged from single pieces of silver and are of the Hanoverian pattern with a single drop to the base of the bowl of the egg-shaped spoons and four tines to the forks. The stems are plain and tapered, the upturned terminals having slight ribs.

HERALDRY: The left sides of the knife handles and the rear terminals of the spoons and forks are engraved with the quartered arms of the Hanoverian monarchs (pre-1801) within the Garter and beneath an imperial crown flanked by the initials GR.

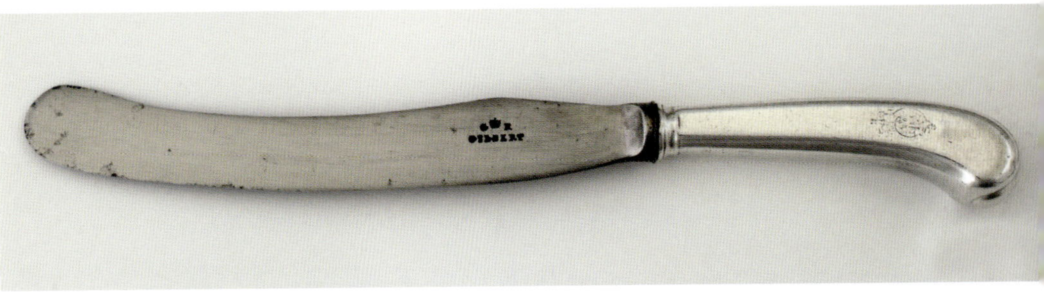

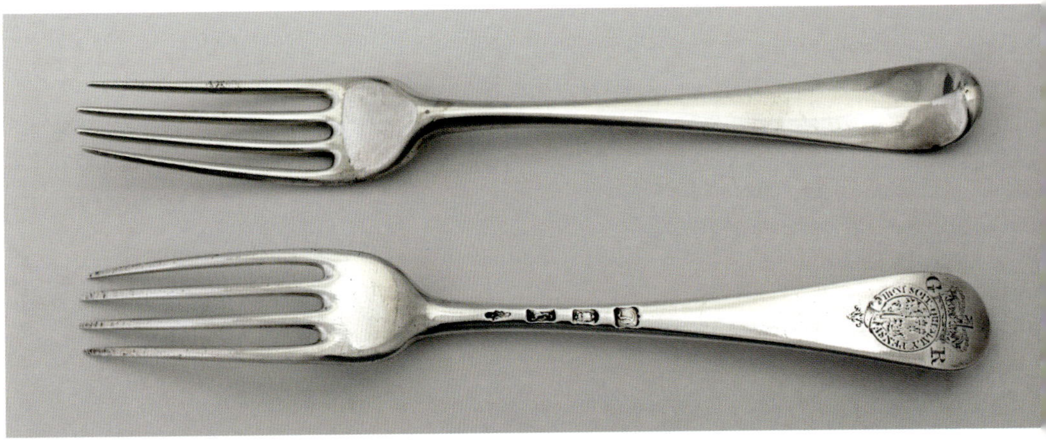

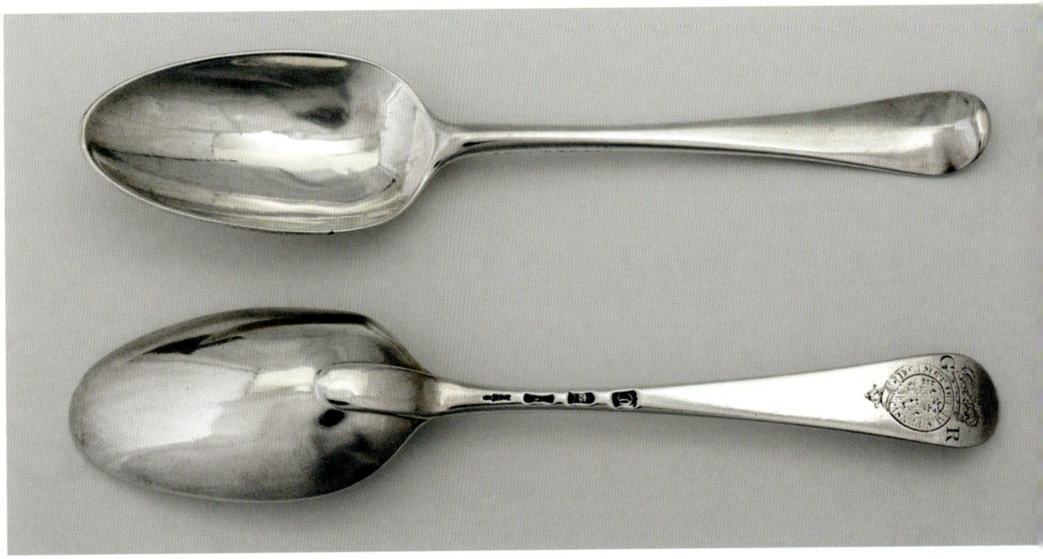

Three dozen of these table knives, forks and spoons came to Lord Bristol in 1758 (see appendix 4) and they probably matched another seven dozen already in his possession (see cat. 26). He would have needed that number as the English custom was to change them each time a plate was removed,[1] and he had ten dozen plates. For his cutlery and flatware the Earl did not expend any more than he needed to on fashion, sticking to the simplest of forms. With his shrewd assessment of where display would count he must have decided that the diner's eye would not be sufficiently resting on the implements they were using and would be drawn more by the dishes and tureens containing the fine food they were feasting upon. It was, anyway, very unusual for more decoration to be applied to knives and flatware at this time in England, an exception being the early 1740s table service of the 4th Earl of Chesterfield, made partly in Paris and partly by Paul Crespin in London.[2]

By 1811 there were forty-eight of this pattern of knife and fork remaining, and thirty-six spoons. They had diminished to twenty-four, nine and twenty-seven by 1951, including the earlier and later spoons (cat. 26 and 83).[3] All the surviving forks and spoons and six of the knives came to the National Trust in 1956. The steel blades of the knives are early-nineteenth-century replacements.

1. Muyden 1902, p. 222.
2. Hartop 1996, p. 101, ill.
3. Death Duties List *c.*1951, pp. 6 and 16.

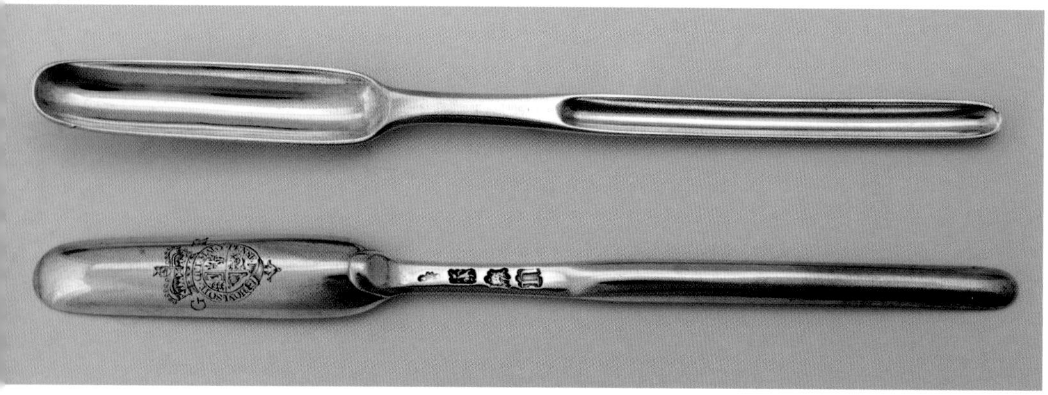

70. **Two marrow spoons**

Sterling silver / Paul Callard, London / 1755/6

MARKS: Each is marked on the reverse of the stem with the date letter 'u', leopard's head, lion passant and maker's mark 'PC' beneath two mullets and above a fleur-de-lis (Grimwade 1990, no. 2150).

SCRATCHWEIGHTS: None.
Actual weight: (combined) 101 g (3 oz, 5 dwt).

MEASUREMENTS: l. 21.6 cm (8½ in).

INVENTORY: 852099.34–35

PROVENANCE: Jewel Office; allocated to the 2nd Earl of Bristol as Ambassador to Madrid 1758; discharged to Lord Bristol 9 April 1759 (see appendix 4); by descent to the 4th Marquess.

LITERATURE: Penzer 1957a, II, p. 136.

DESCRIPTION: The spoons are forged from a single rod of silver and are double-ended with two concave recessions, one long and thin and the other wider and shorter. They have no ornamentation apart from single drops at the junctions of the stems with the backs of the large scoops.

HERALDRY: On the back of each of the large scoops are engraved the quartered arms of the Hanoverian monarchs (pre-1801) within the Garter and beneath an imperial crown flanked by the initials GR.

Silver marrow spoons, as these implements were commonly known until the mid-nineteenth century and at Ickworth even beyond that,[1] probably came into being in the late seventeenth century. They were used to extract the marrow from the inside of bones, which was considered a delicacy and continued to be widely valued until the early twentieth century.[2] Lord Bristol acquired three with his ambassadorial plate but only two of them remained amongst the future 1st Marquess's silver in 1826.[3] The other one probably found its way to Ireland with the Earl-Bishop and passed with his property there. The spoons would have been laid on the table by dishes containing meat on the bone, with the carving knives and forks. Given their date they must have been taken from stock in 1758. Paul Callard made most of Lord Bristol's ambassadorial flatware (see cat. 69 and 71) and seems to have had a brief spell as a rival to Ebenezer Coker in the second half of the 1750s.

1. Death Duties List *c.*1951, pp. 6 and 16.
2. Hughes 1957, pp. 199–200.
3. Bristol Plate List 1826, f. 3.

71. **Dessert service of knives, forks and spoons**

Silver knives (x 6)
probably London / *c.*1758.

Sterling silver forks and spoons (x 23 of each)
Paul Callard, London / 1758/9.

MARKS: Knives: none. Forks and spoons: all are fully marked on the rear of the stem with maker's mark 'PC' beneath two mullets and above a fleur-de-lis (Grimwade 1990, no. 2150), lion passant, leopard's head and date letter 'C'.

SCRATCHWEIGHTS: None. Combined weights for two dozen knives, forks and spoons are given in the 1811 plate list (appendix 5) as 59 oz, 12 dwt; 39 oz, 8 dwt; and 38 oz, 13 dwt, respectively.

MEASUREMENTS: Knives l. (overall) 20.3 cm (8 in); l. (of handle) 8.3 cm (3¼ in). Forks l. 17.1 cm (6¾ in). Spoons 17.8 cm (7 in).

INVENTORY: Knives 852204. Forks and spoons 852098.

PROVENANCE: Jewel Office; allocated to the 2nd Earl of Bristol as Ambassador to Madrid 1758; discharged to Lord Bristol 9 April 1759 (see appendix 4); by descent to the 4th Marquess.

DESCRIPTION: The enriched pistol-shaped handles of the knives are cast and have scroll ends, turned back cappings, reeded stems and stylised leaf calyces by the junction with the scimitar-shaped silver blades. The spoons and four-tined forks are of the Hanoverian pattern with reeding to the handles front and back and substantial single drops on the backs at the tine and bowl ends.

HERALDRY: The upper edge of the knives and the rear of the terminals of the forks and spoons are engraved with the quartered arms of the Hanoverian monarchs (pre-1801) within the Garter and beneath an imperial crown flanked by the initials GR.

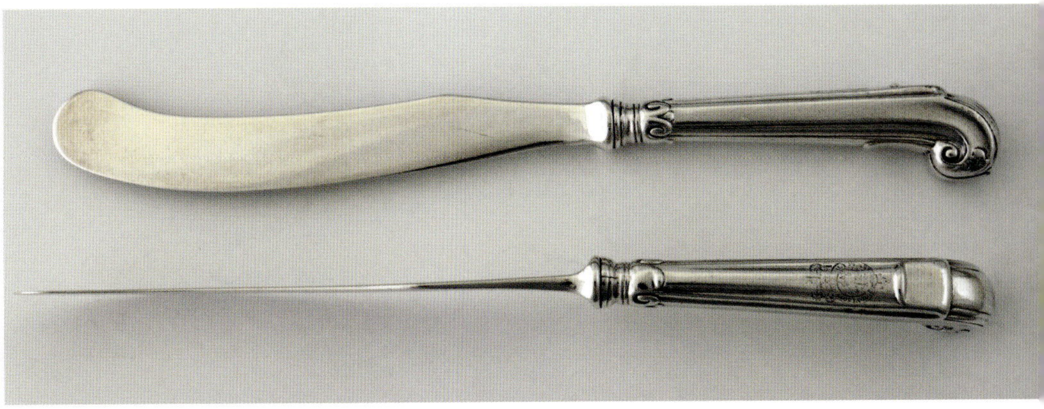

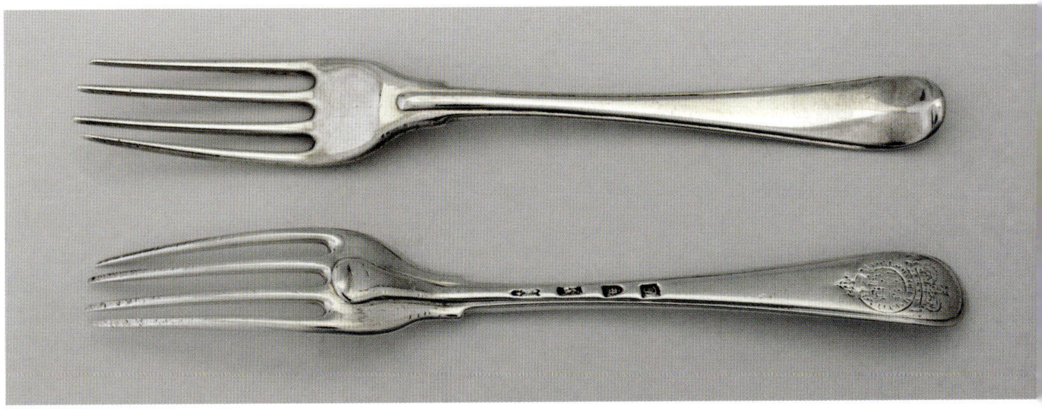

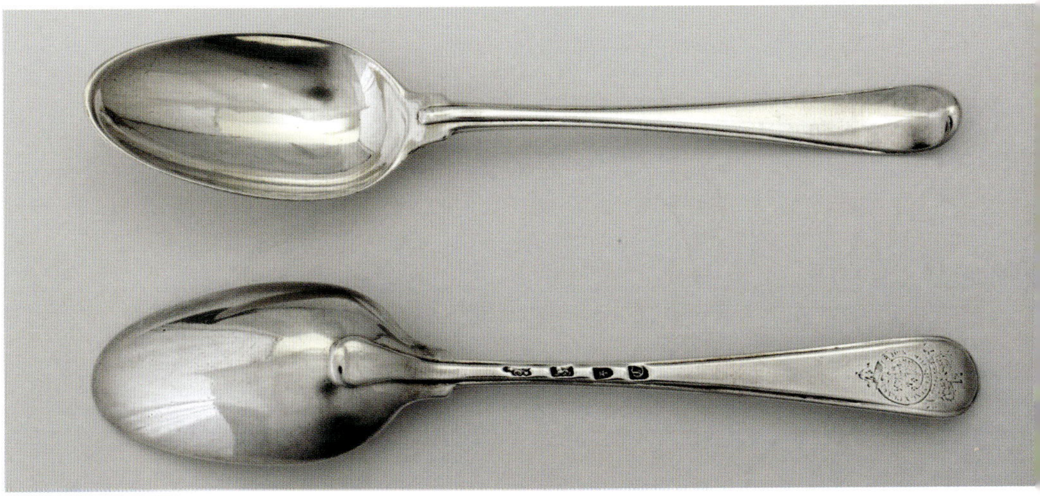

Lord Bristol received two dozen dessert knives, forks and spoons in 1758. As this quantity would only have sustained a party of twenty-four and Lord Bristol had adequate silver for thirty-six for the earlier courses, it is likely that he already owned either a larger set of a different pattern or at least a dozen more matching these. If so, however, none survives. The knives in particular are considerably more ornamental than those of the table service (cat. 69) and are a rare survival. The arms being engraved on the top edge suggests that they may have been laid on the table upon the knife edge, the flat base of the scroll end holding them steady.

Silver blades were employed because they looked more impressive than steel and also because it was not necessary to maintain such a sharp cutting edge as for the earlier courses. Furthermore, silver would have resisted better the acids of fruit consumed during dessert. It was typical, but not universal, in the mid-eighteenth century for dessert flatware and cutlery not to be gilded, even when being used with silver-gilt plates as were these.[1] By 1800 gilding was much more common as on the extensive dessert service of the future 1st Marquess of Bristol (cat. 100).

A comparable but even more elaborate contemporary service, albeit without silver blades to the knives, was supplied by Frederick Kandler to a Dutch client in the early 1750s and is now in the Museum of Fine Arts, Boston.[2] That also consisted of two dozen of each implement (subsequently augmented by Dutch copies) and has two silver-mounted cases, one for the knives and the other for the spoons and forks. 'Half round cases', as they were called by George Wickes, might cost £1 4s, as did those of the 6th Earl of Coventry's new dessert service in 1757.[3] Though Lord Bristol would undoubtedly have had his service cased too, all the more so because of the need to transport it safely to Madrid, his thrifty temperament is more likely to have led to the choice of the more prosaic 'wainscot boxes lined with bays' used for the Marquess of Granby's knives, forks and spoons in 1750 and costing him just four shillings each.[4]

All two dozen of the knives survived in 1951 but only six passed to the National Trust together with the twenty-three each of forks and spoons remaining.[5]

1. The 6th Earl of Coventry's 1757 service was supplied gilded, at a cost of 3s per implement, £10 18s in total.
2. Hartop 1996, cat. 48, pp. 226–9. A service with silver blades and with elaborately chased handles, of *c.*1730, is in the Ashmolean Museum, Schroder 2009, cat. 395, pp. 920–2.
3. Wickes Ledgers, VAM 5 1750–4, f. 69.
4. Ibid., VAM 3 1747–50, f. 166.
5. Death Duties List *c.*1951, pp. 6 and 17.

72. Twelve candlesticks with four-light branches

Sterling silver / Simon Le Sage and James Peltro, London / 1758/9

MARKS: All the branches except those of no. 3, which have been altered, are fully marked on their pintles with the date letter 'C', leopard's head, lion passant and maker's mark 'S·L' in italics, cup above and mullet below (Grimwade 1990, no. 2576) for Simon Le Sage.

The candlesticks are all marked on their undersides. Nos. 6, 7 and 9–12 have the same marks as the branches as do no. 1 except for the lion passant and no. 5 except for the lion passant and leopard's head. No. 2 is fully marked but Le Sage's punch has been struck twice, once over another's. No. 8 also has Le Sage's mark and another struck out plus the lion passant and leopard's head but no date letter. Nos. 3 and 4 are fully marked and struck with both Le Sage's mark and maker's mark 'IP' beneath a pellet (Grimwade 1990, no. 1575) for James Peltro.

All the component parts, including the nozzles, are scratched with the number of the candlestick to which they belong, either with arabic or roman numerals. Not all the nozzles are still with the correct sticks.

SCRATCHWEIGHTS: On the underside of the candlesticks: '1 oz [/] 147 [/] No 1'; '2 oz [/] 145 [/] No 2'; '3 [/] 147oz [/] No 3'; '4 [/] 146 oz [/] No 4'; '5 oz [/] 149.5 [/] No 5'; '6 [/] 148 [/] No 6'; 'oz [/]153.10 [/] N 7'; 'oz [/] 151.15 [/] No 8'; '9 [/] 154 [/] No. 8'; '156oz 10 [/] No 10'; 'oz [/] 159 10 [/] N.11'; '153oz [/] No 12'.

MEASUREMENTS: h. (of stick) 32.4 cm (12¾ in); h. (with three-light branches) 46.4 cm (18¼ in); h. (with fourth light fitted) 57.8 cm (22¾ in); w. (of base) 21.3 cm (8⅜ in); w. (of branches) 36.2 cm (14¼ in).

INVENTORY: 852077

PROVENANCE: Jewel Office; allocated to the 2nd Earl of Bristol as Ambassador to Madrid 1758; discharged to Lord Bristol 9 April 1759 (see appendix 4); by descent to the 4th Marquess.

LITERATURE: Hernmarck 1977, vol. 1, p. 265, vol. 2, p. 286, fig. 753; Banister 1980, p. 794, fig. 9; Schroder 1988a, pp.210–11, ill.

EXHIBITED: *Treasures from National Trust Houses*, Christie's, London, 1957–8, cat. 178; Society of the Four Arts, Palm Beach, Florida, 1959 (two); *Ideal Home Exhibition*, London, 1960 (one); *British Week*, Milan and Frankfurt, 1965 (six); *Silver from National Trust Houses*, Treasurer's House, York Festival, 1969 (two), cat. 37; *Treasures from Country Houses of the National Trust and National Trust for Scotland, Europalia 1973*, Brussels (two), cat. 121; *The Treasure Houses of Britain*, National Gallery of Art, Washington, 1985–6 (one), cat. 453.

DESCRIPTION: The candlesticks are cast and chased and consist of irregular triform, domed bases of scrolls and flowers with stems formed as female terms rising out of further scrolls and entwined in floral swags. Each term holds a hand up to a vase-shaped scrollwork and floral socket which is also supported by the continuation of the floral swag. The branches fit into the socket and consist of three spiralling and twisting reeded branches embellished with applied cast and chased leaves and terminating in horizontal calyces of further leaves which form the drip pans. Above are foliate, vase-shaped sockets, the leaves bent over at the top to form a serrated, horizontal lip and the seamed, open-bottomed nozzles having rims shaped to conform. An additional, central socket can either be fitted with a shell and flower finial[1] or with a fourth arm which spirals well above the other three and has the same form of socket and nozzle. All of the fourth arms have been drilled for electricity and one stick (no. 3) has had a bolt applied to hold the stick and branches together with the finial in place.

HERALDRY: On the underside of each candlestick and on the pintle of the branches (except no. 3 which has been altered) are engraved the quartered arms of the Hanoverian monarchs (pre-1801) within the Garter and beneath an imperial crown flanked by the initials GR.

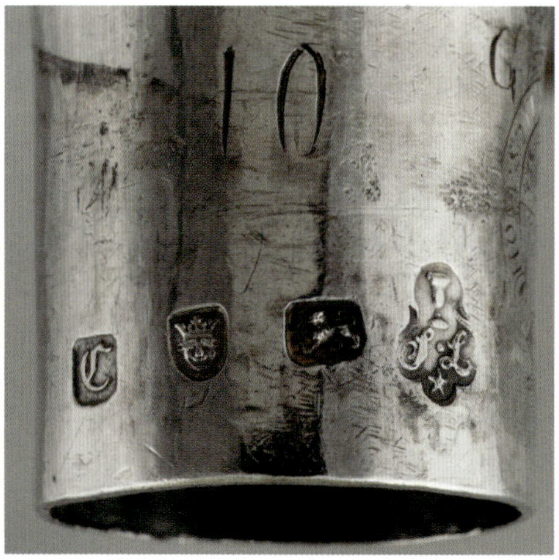

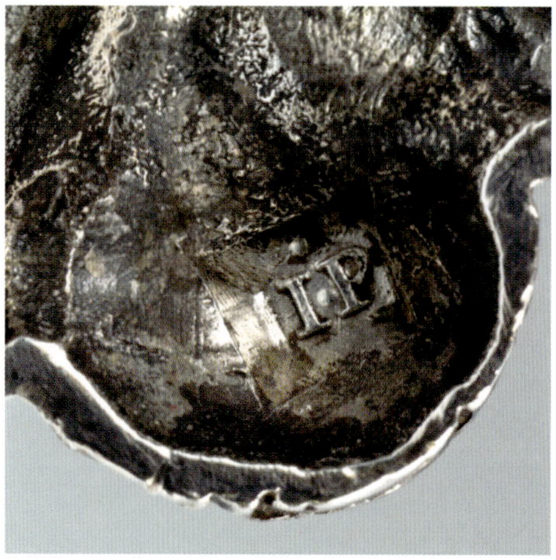

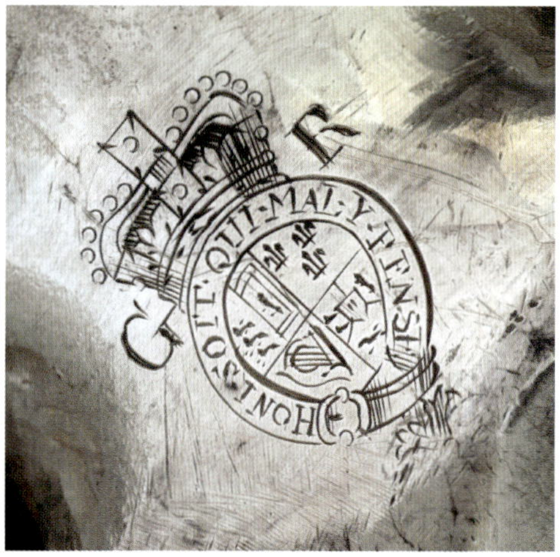

The sources and evolution of this most rococo of candlestick forms have been carefully analysed by a number of writers in recent years, most notably by Timothy Schroder in his catalogue of the Ashmolean collection.[2] There was a vogue for figural candlesticks in the mid to late seventeenth century[3] and Meissonier and Thomas Germain brought them into high fashion again in Paris around 1730. It may have been in Paul de Lamerie's workshop that the form evolved successfully in London and he produced a set of candlesticks with bearded terms in 1746, the swirling triform bases of which are close to those of the Ickworth sticks.

From two years later are his paired male and female terms (fig. 100) now in the Ashmolean Museum and the Virginia Museum of Fine Arts.[4] More of the same form were produced in 1752 (the year after de Lamerie's death), this time struck with the marks of Frederick Kandler (Ashmolean Museum)[5] and Robert Tyrill (Museum of Fine Arts, Houston).[6] Schroder's careful comparison shows that the Kandler set appears to be from the same moulds and to have been chased by the same sophisticated hand as those by de Lamerie.

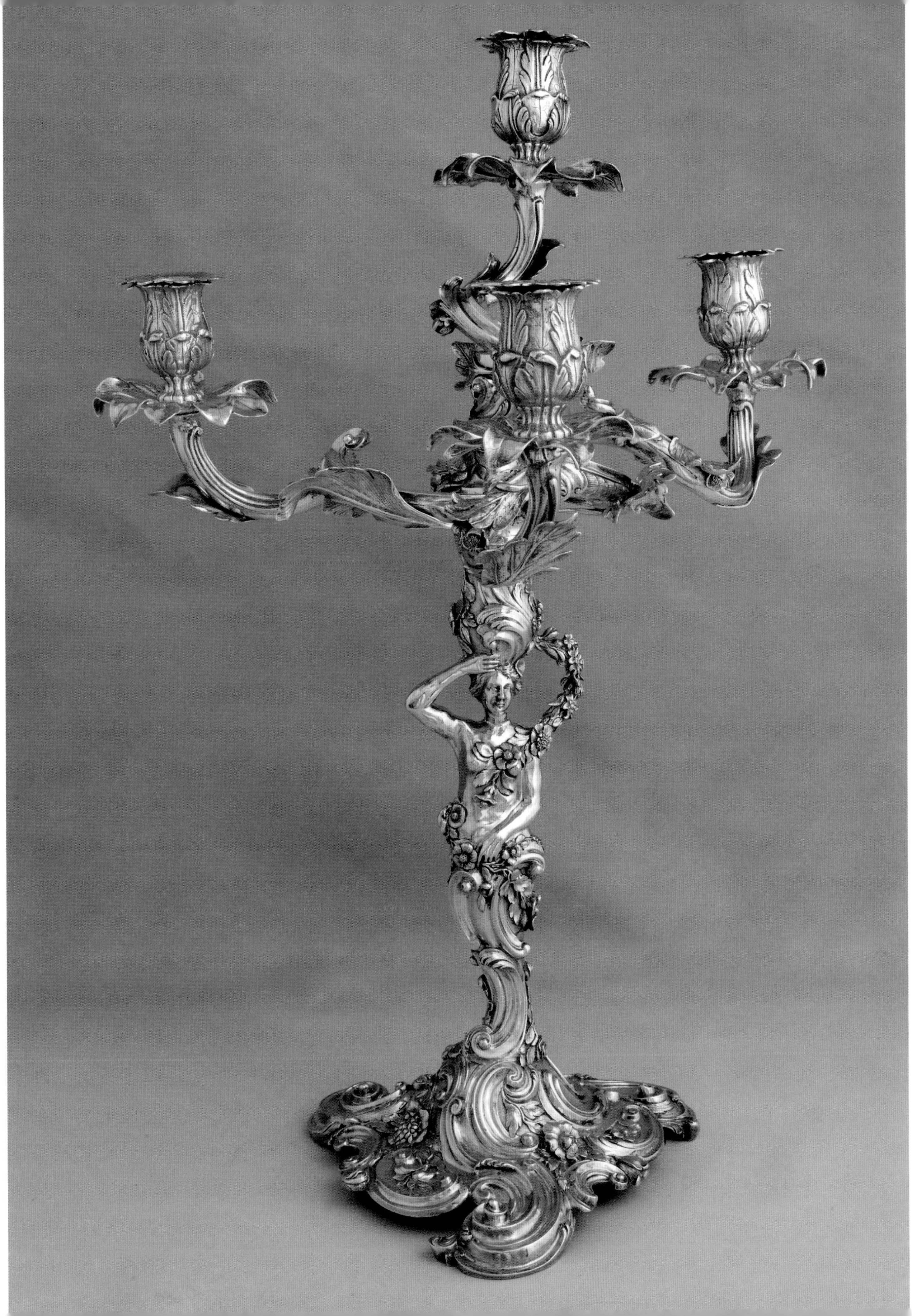

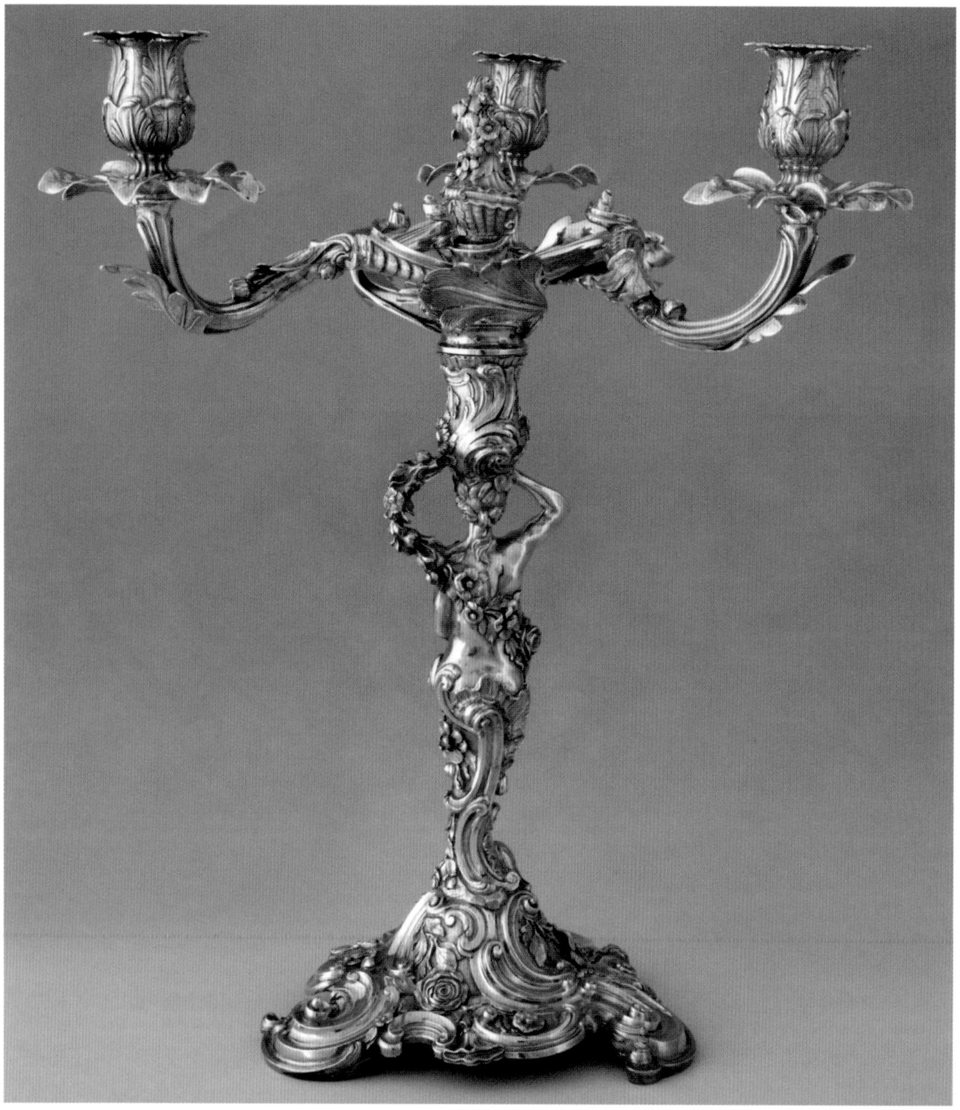

Reverse view of cat. 72 with three branches.

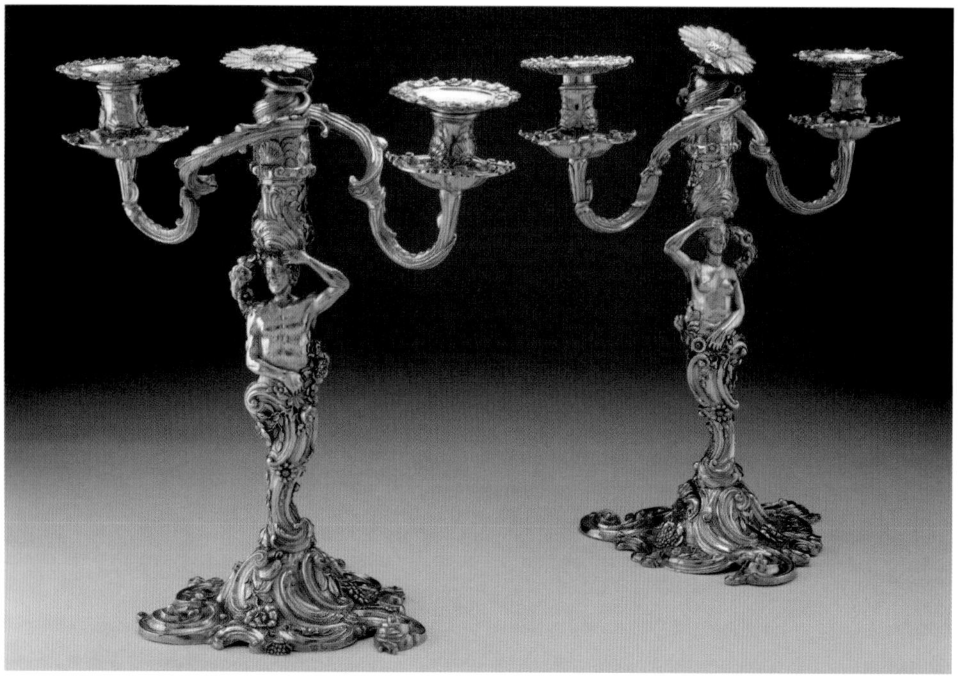

FIG. 100 / Male and female term candlesticks by Paul de Lamerie, London, 1748, with branches by Frederick Kandler, London, 1753. Silver: h. 30.6 cm (12 in); weight 1440 g (46 oz 6 dwt) and 1333 g (42 oz 17 dwt). Ashmolean Museum, Oxford.

The Ickworth set are extremely close in form to the female term of the de Lamerie/Kandler group though with subtle differences in the chased detail. The flower types are not in the same arrangement, the term's hair is more pronouncedly knotted at the back, there are marginal variations in the finishing of the scrolls and the base is slightly less flat to the ground. Most notably of all there is, in addition to the garland of flowers passing behind the term's back, a spray also extending over her chest, presumably for reasons of modesty. Nevertheless the overall conformation and scale[7] are close enough to be from the same moulds, or at least to have been created by someone who had an intimate knowledge of the earlier pieces.

Although all the Ickworth sticks bear the mark of Simon Le Sage, who presumably dealt with the bulk of the order rather than Kandler because of his position as Subordinate Goldsmith to the King, two (nos. 3 and 4) have also been punched by James Peltro and on others there is evidence of his mark being defaced or overstruck by Le Sage (nos. 2 and 8). Thus the sticks were almost certainly made by Peltro, or in his workshop, and supplied to Le Sage who was, fortunately, not wholly successful in his attempts to eliminate the evidence, the marks being extremely difficult to detect amongst the wildly contoured and roughly textured surfaces of the undersides. Could Peltro be the link, therefore, between the various groups of this model of candlestick produced during the 1750s? His mark is rarely found, perhaps because he was not a retailer and was exclusively supplying to others, but it does occur on the epergne and stand supplied to the future 1st Lord Scarsdale of Kedleston in 1755 by Thomas Harache (fig. 101).[8] This is a tour de force of chasing in high-rococo style, like the Ickworth sticks, and Peltro's strong connection with such high-quality workmanship is further shown by a set of four candlesticks of another rococo pattern, marked for 1753, which were sold at Bonham's, London, on 24 March 2005 (lot 69).[9]

There is no consistent form of branches associated with the various versions of these candlesticks but Lord Bristol's are undoubtedly the most magnificent, with their provision for up to four candles and their swirling, twisting form, embellished by leaves and with foliate sockets which complement but do not match those of the sticks. There is something in them of the intertwined branches of Thomas Germain's double satyr candelabra of 1732[10] and the Earl may have seen comparable examples in Turin given that Andrea Boucheron had trained with the Parisian master. Germain famously points to one of the candelabra in his portrait by Nicolas de Largillière (fig. 102) and when Boucheron came to be portrayed he had

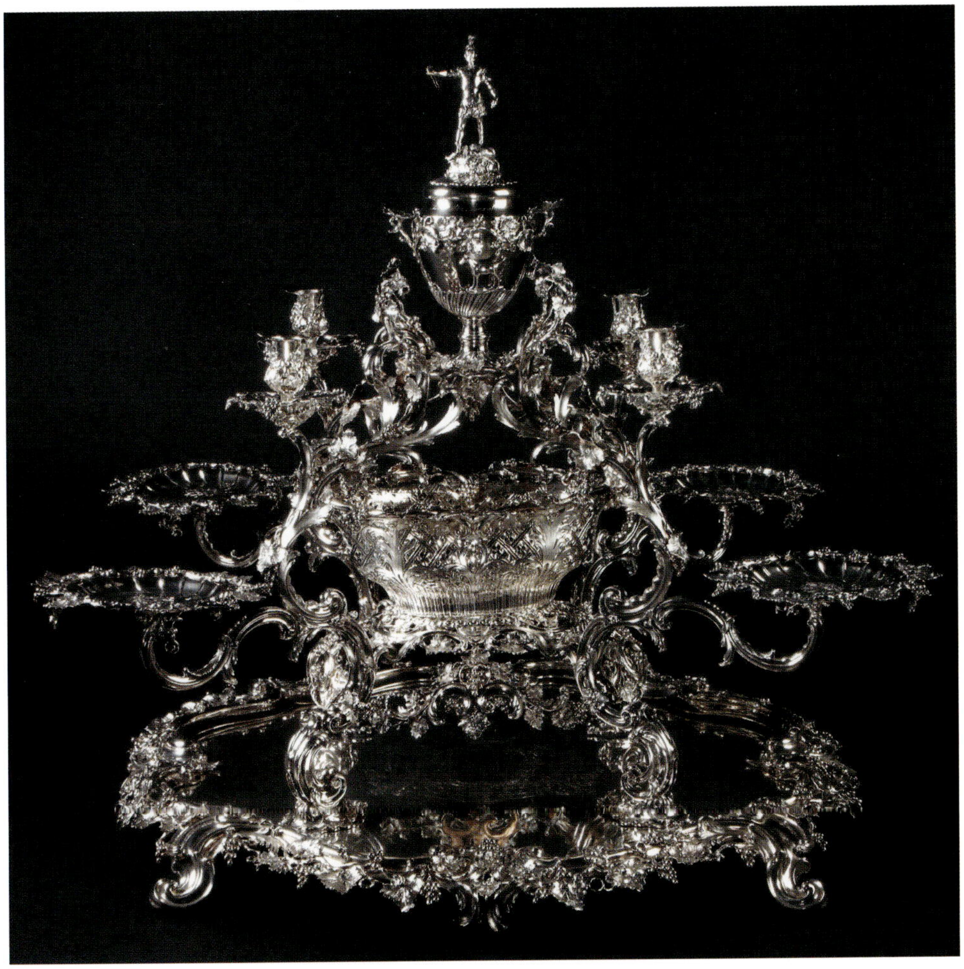

FIG. 101 / Epergne and stand by James Peltro, London, 1755. Silver: 70 x 66 x 55 cm (27½ x 26 x 21⅝ in). National Trust, Kedleston.

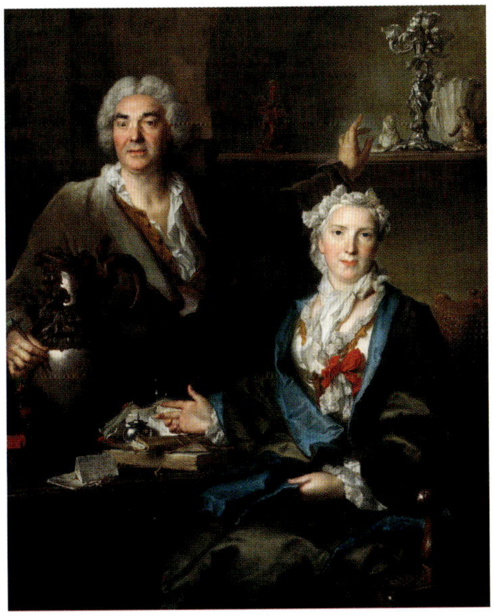

FIG. 102 / *Thomas Germain and his Wife* by Nicolas de Largilliere, 1736. Oil on canvas: 146 x 113 cm (57½ x 44½ in). Museu Calouste Gulbenkian, Lisbon.

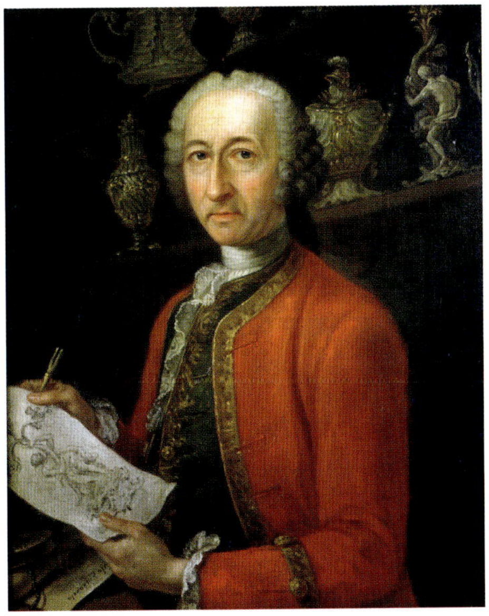

FIG. 103 / *Andrea Boucheron*, Italian, *c.*1750. Oil on canvas: 65 x 78 cm (25⅝ x 30¾ in). Palazzo Madama – Museo Civico d'Arte Antica, Turin.

himself depicted (fig. 103) holding a drawing of something very similar with the actual candelabrum in pride of place behind him. He could even have been involved with the design or manufacture of the satyr candelabra, having returned to Paris in 1728–9.[11]

The Ickworth candelabra are probably the earliest set of such a quality and quantity to survive intact, even down to all forty-eight of the nozzles. They can scarcely have been equalled at the time of their manufacture either, the Wickes ledgers only showing one larger set[12] in the mid-eighteenth century and very few others at all beyond the odd pair, such as those copying Germain's supplied to the future 1st Duke of Leinster in 1745.[13] Similarly, amongst allocations of perquisite plate from the Jewel Office the only grant coming close was that of twelve wrought candelabra received by Sir Charles Hanbury-Williams in 1756 as ambassador to Russia, but those had just two branches each.[14]

The Jewel Office allowed only 8s per ounce[15] for Lord Bristol's candelabra when in reality they are likely to have cost only slightly less than the Leinster pair which were charged at 16s 2d.[16] If taken at 15s 10d per ounce the cost would have amounted to the enormous sum of £1,435 of which the Earl would have had to pay about £710. His bank account (appendix 3) reveals only one payment to Le Sage, of £100 on 16 September 1758 via Lady Hervey, and that was a down payment insisted upon by the goldsmith,[17] probably largely allocated subsequently to a set of soup plates (cat. 78). Lord Bristol could have met the remainder by turning in further old plate but that must have been becoming thin on the ground and it is more likely that some of the items presented to the Jewel Office by Le Sage were not actually to be taken delivery of by the Earl. That could explain why the allocation included four dozen plates, which Lord Bristol could not possibly have wanted on top of the ten dozen he already had. There is no evidence of them ever having formed part of the Bristol silver and the same goes for the twelve each of oval and round dishes plus the eight salad dishes. All in all, the Jewel Office paid Le Sage £709 12s 11d for these items which is, very neatly, more or less what was required. Equally neat is the fact that they are the first four items for Lord Bristol listed in the delivery book.[18]

Though some of these candelabra have for many years now, and perhaps since the 1820s, bedecked the great dining room table at Ickworth for which they are perfectly scaled (fig. 104) they were not intended for such use. Dinner was still eaten in daylight hours and even at supper candelabra, especially Lord Bristol's with their profusion of branches, would not have mixed practicably with the

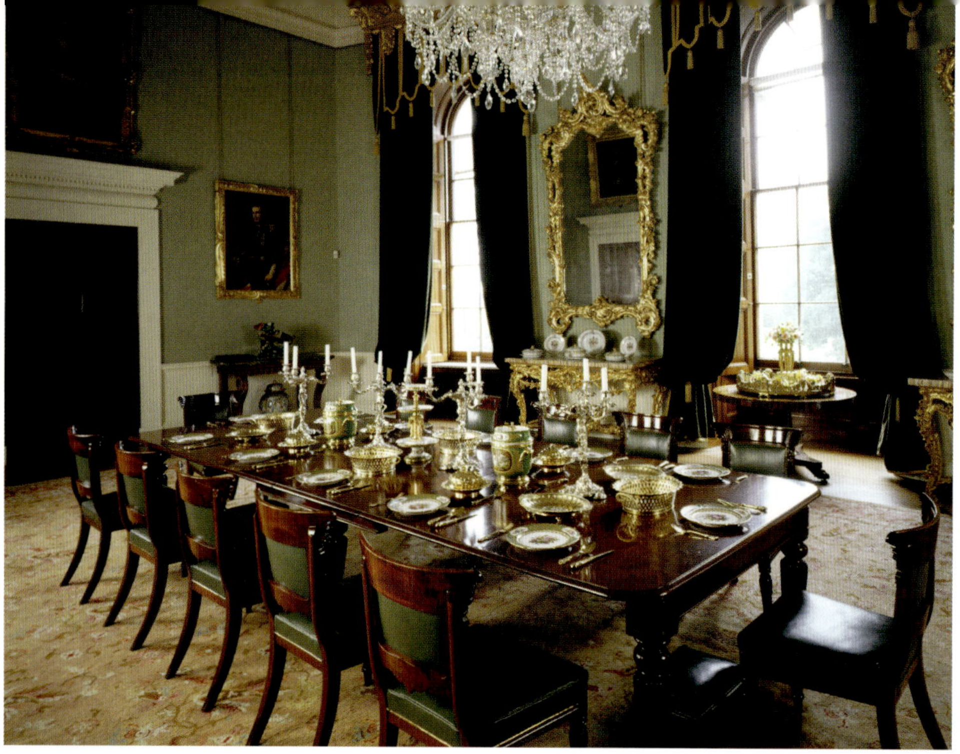

FIG. 104 / The dining room at Ickworth with some of the candelabra in place on the table.

need to change the dense array of dishes as the meal progressed. Michel-Barthélemy Ollivier's depiction of a supper given by the Prince de Conti at the Temple in 1766 (fig. 99) shows individual sticks in use, and Lord Bristol already had a substantial provision of those (cat. 62). Instead the candelabra would have been for a great entertaining room – a saloon or a gallery – where they would have been placed on torchères, side tables or brackets for use during evening entertainments. An excellent example is provided by Dunham Massey in Cheshire where in 1758 the Great Gallery had four three-branch silver candlesticks on gilt brackets, as well as fourteen silver sconces and a magnificent pair of six-branch chandeliers.[19] In total this allowed for thirty-eight candles in one room, which was prodigious enough, but Lord Bristol would have been able to muster an additional ten from the Le Sage/Peltro candelabra alone. This may seem wildly extravagant, but he was taking over the vast Monteleone Palace in Madrid from his predecessor, Sir Benjamin Keene, and having been sent plans he knew that the rooms were of gargantuan proportions (fig. 38). In addition, as Ambassador Extraordinary and Plenipotentiary it was expected of him to put on a show of magnificence and he was clearly very ready to do so.

A candlestick bearing only the maker's mark 'TH', possibly that of Thomas Holland, is identical in detail to the Ickworth sticks and was probably cast from a mould taken from one of them by Rundell, Bridge & Rundell in the early nineteenth century, whilst overhauling the Bristol plate.[20] Holland would be a good candidate as he was responsible for producing copies of a pair of Emick Romer candlesticks in 1809 for the future 1st Marquess (cat. 103).

1. One of the twelve finials was missing in 1956 when the collection was handed over to the National Trust and had been 'for some 20 years at least' before that, according to the butler. TNA, T 227/1245, ff. 192–3, report on an inventory check of the Ickworth contents by Douglas Davidson (NT), 5 April 1957.
2. Schroder 2009, cat. 185–6, pp. 476–485.
3. Most pertinent amongst examples from this period are those with female standing figures holding an arm up to support the sockets above their heads. See a pair marked for Augsburg, 1650, sold at Sotheby's, 11 February 1999, lot 46.
4. Culme 1999, cat. 2, pp. 36–41.
5. Schroder 2009, cat. 186, pp. 482–4; two pairs of male and female terms.
6. Museum of Fine Arts, Houston, nos. 2001.582–7 and 2001.620–1.
7. The Ashmolean group have a height range of 30.6 to 31.8 cm and the pair in the Virginia Museum of Fine Arts are 32.7 cm high. The Houston group are 32.1 cm high.
8. NT inventory no. 108946. See also Cornforth 1996, p. 129, fig. 4.
9. Also of 1753 and finely chased, though of a simpler rococo design, are two candlesticks by him which were with S.J. Phillips in December 2015, ref. 41604.
10. Detroit Institute of Arts, acc. no. 56.85.1.
11. Fina and Mana 2012, p. 223.
12. Wickes Ledgers, VAM 3 1747–50, f. 2, account of Mr. Chase: 'Nine pr [18] candlesticks & nozils & branches' weighing 1143 oz, 14 dwt. They must have been quite simple as only 3s per ounce was charged for fashion.
13. Wickes Ledgers, VAM 2 1740–8, f. 146, account of the Earl of Kildare. Another pair of the satyr form, by John Le Sage, 1744, were sold Christie's, 24 October 1990, lot 247.
14. Jewel Office Delivery Book 1732–93, f. 146.
15. Jewel Office Plate Book 1728–1767, f. 168.
16. Wickes Ledgers, VAM 2 1740–8, f. 146.
17. TNA, NA SP 94/252 Spain, supplementary 1755–60, letter from the Earl of Bristol to Joseph Richardson, 27 November 1758.
18. Jewel Office Delivery Book 1732–93, f. 165.
19. Lomax and Rothwell 2006, p. 19. Another example is provided by Temple Newsam where there were French plated candelabra for the eight giltwood torcheres of 1745–6 by James and Anne Pascall. Information from James Lomax.
20. Sold Sotheby's, 14 March 1996, lot 82. The mark is described as having a pellet between the letters so it may not be Holland's. The candlestick bears the arms of the 1st Duke of Buckingham and Chandos.

73. Eight dish covers

Silver / probably London / *c.*1758.

MARKS: None

SCRATCHWEIGHTS: Round 'N°-1 = 33=0'; 'N° 2 – 35=0'; 'N° 3 = 34=3'; 'N° 4 = 34=6'.

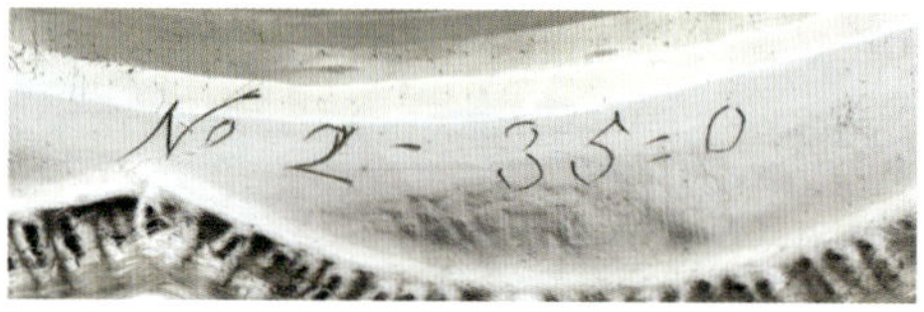

Octagonal 'N° 1 = 31=3'; 'N°-2 – 31=2'; 'N° = 3 32=5'; 'N°-4 – 32=0'.

MEASUREMENTS: Round h. 18.4 cm (7¼ in); diam 27 cm (10⅝ in). Octagonal h. 18.4 cm (7¼ in); w. and d. 25.4 cm (10 in).

INVENTORY: Round 852121.1.1–4. Octagonal 852115.1.1, 2.1, 3.1 and 4.1.

PROVENANCE: Jewel Office; allocated to the 2nd Earl of Bristol as Ambassador to Madrid 1758; discharged to Lord Bristol 9 April 1759 (see appendix 4); by descent to the 4th Marquess.

DESCRIPTION: The covers are raised and have stepped bases conforming to the dishes with which they are associated (cat. 36–7), four being octagonal and four being lobed and round. The bases terminate in a chased band of gadrooning and the covers rise as circular convex domes to another chased gadroon band, then rise again in reverse form to an applied flat top plate, the joint concealed by a cast and seamed moulding. The cast and chased tendril handles are capped by single flowers and held on by silver bolts and nuts.

HERALDRY: On the front of each cover are engraved the quartered arms of the Hanoverian monarchs (pre-1801) within the Garter and beneath an imperial crown flanked by the initials GR.

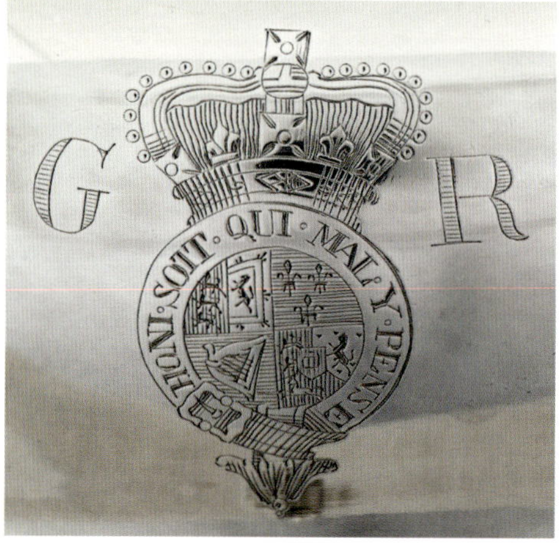

The Jewel Office allocation in 1758 (appendix 4) lists twenty dish covers as being delivered for Lord Bristol's use in 1758 and of these only the eight now at Ickworth survive. The absent twelve, which had gone by 1811 (appendix 5), are unlikely to have been part of the scheme to extract money for the excessive fashion cost of other items (see cat. 72) as they would have had to be specifically made for the dishes and to have matched the covers that do survive. Thus they could not easily have been taken from stock and then passed on to other clients once they had served their illicit purpose. They must therefore have been exchanged or lost at some point thereafter, or have been removed to Ireland by the Earl-Bishop and passed to the Bruce family. As they would have had to account for 935 ounces of silver they would have been for the larger sizes of dishes.

The covers would have been in place at the start of the meal and have been removed when the tureens were taken away to be replaced with the next set of principal dishes. In the painting of the coronation banquet of Joseph II as King of the Romans in Frankfurt in 1764 (fig. 30),[1] all the subsidiary tables are shown with their dishes still covered whereas at the high table the Imperial couple have commenced their meal and two attendants are removing the covers and passing them to footmen.

As dishes did not rest on the table in the same fashion for *service à la russe* the need for covers waned during the nineteenth century and many must have been turned in to be melted, making them rare today. They did still come into their own at breakfast, however, and one can be seen in use at Ickworth alongside dishes by Paul Storr in a photograph of *c.*1870 (fig. 48). Silver dish-covers were never commonplace in the aristocratic household anyway and many families had some or all of them in silvered brass or copper, or even as mere pewter. William Strode, for instance, acquired a 'Brass Dish Cover Silver'd' from Wickes and Netherton in 1753 for £2 including engraving (the same thing in silver, assuming a weight of 30 oz, would have cost at least £12) and the vastly wealthy Sir Jacob Downing, 4th Bt, when equipping himself with a dinner service in 1750, had seventeen pewter covers with his twenty silver dishes.[2] Lord Bristol may well have been thus equipped previously and have used the opportunity of the ambassadorial allocation to upgrade.

1. Studio of Martin II Mytens, Schloss Schönbrunn, Austria.
2. Wickes Ledgers, VAM 5 1750–4, f. 110 and VAM 3 1747–50, f. 57.

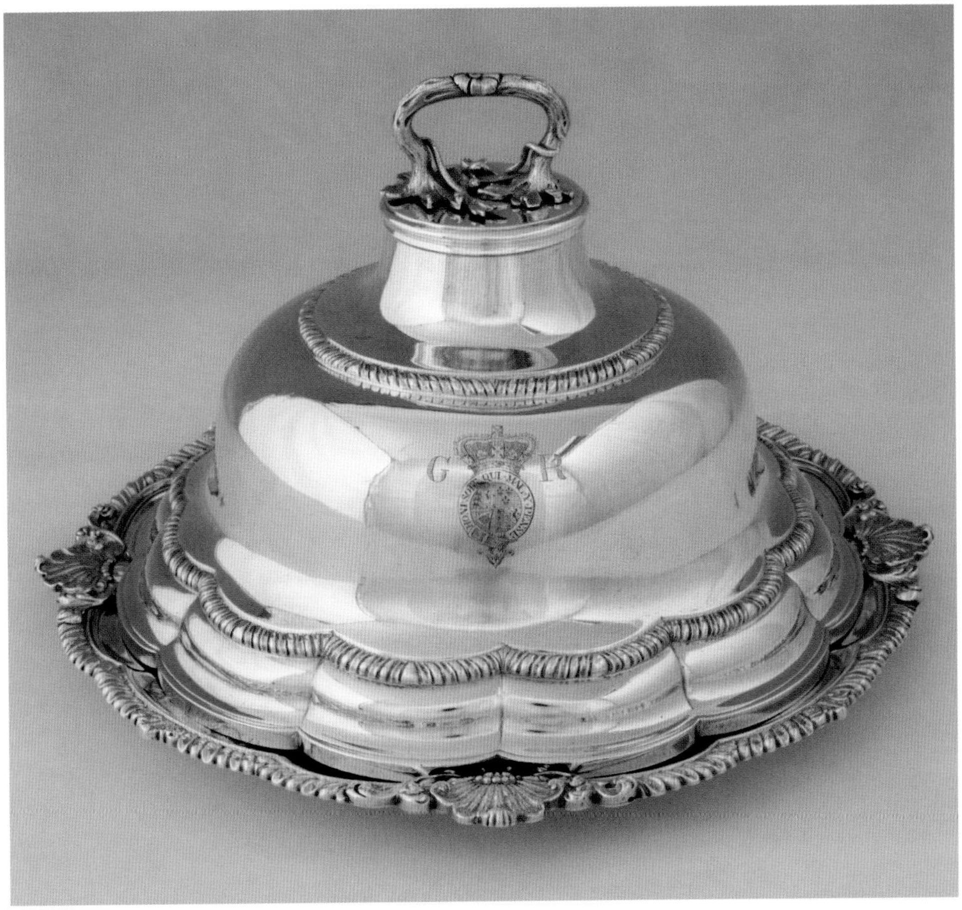

cat. 73 on cat. 36.

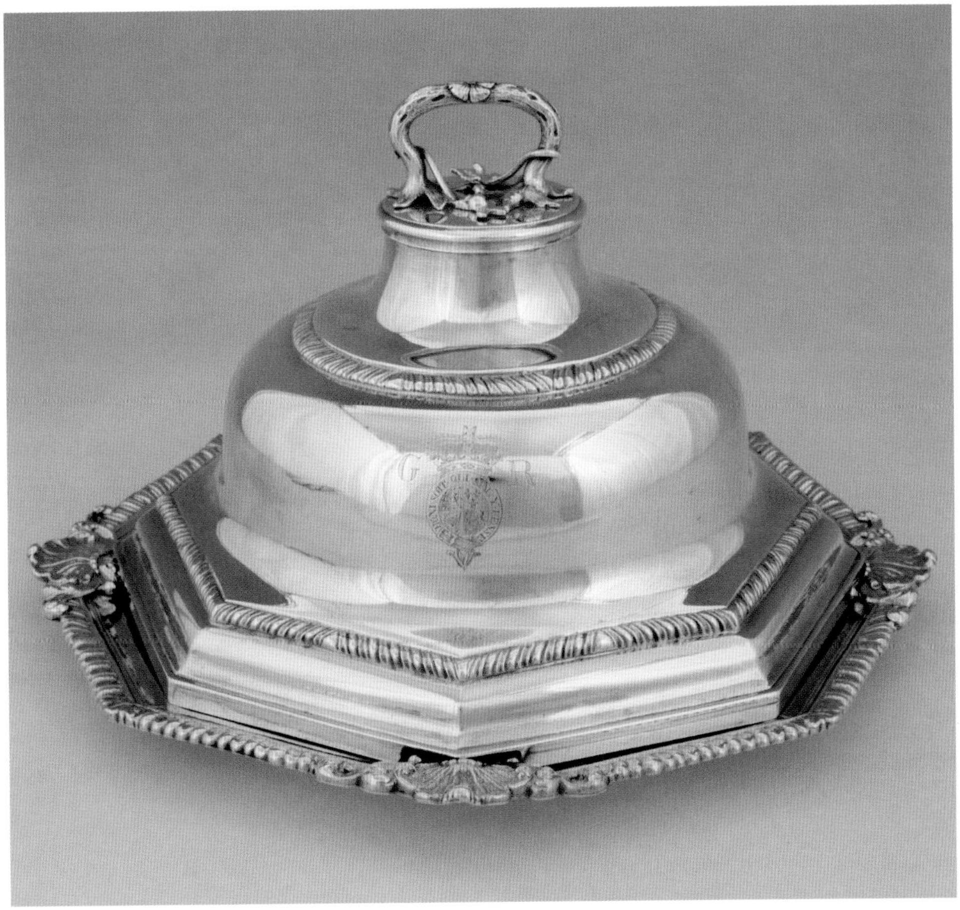

cat. 73 on cat. 37.

74. Dessert dish, subsequently alms dish

Sterling silver, gilded / **Frederick Kandler, London** / **1758/9**

MARKS: The dish is fully marked on the underside of the rim with date letter 'C', lion passant, leopard's head and maker's mark 'FK' in italics beneath a fleur-de-lis (Grimwade 1990, no. 692).

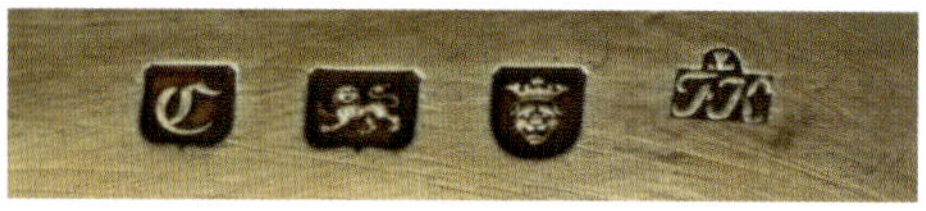

SCRATCHWEIGHT AND INSCRIPTION: 'N°2 [/] 32∧3' and 'Ickworth Church', both on the underside

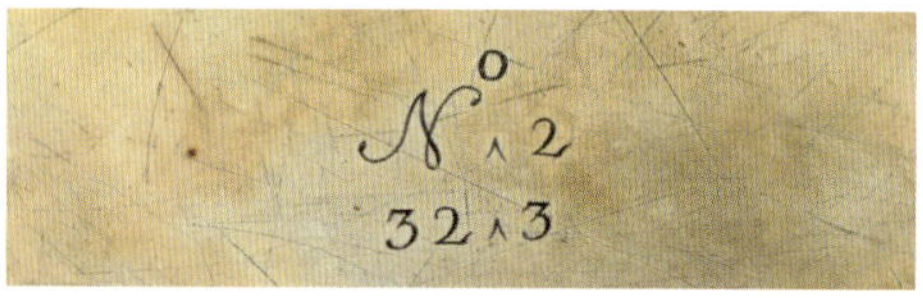

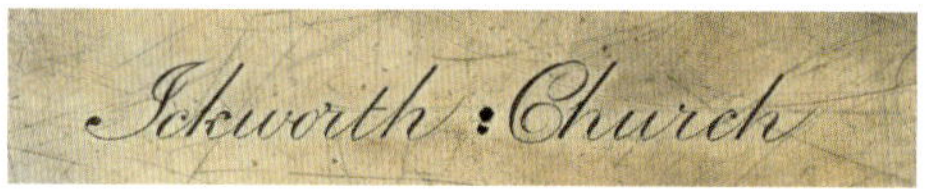

MEASUREMENTS: h. 2.5 cm (1 in); diam. 30.5 cm (12 in).

INVENTORY: 852905

PROVENANCE: Jewel Office; allocated to the 2nd Earl of Bristol as Ambassador to Madrid 1758; discharged to Lord Bristol 9 April 1759 (see appendix 4); by descent to the 3rd Earl; probably given by him *c.*1778 to the church of St Mary, Ickworth, as part of the Communion plate; transferred 1984 to St Leonard's, Horringer; on loan to the National Trust.

LITERATURE: Yates 2013, pp. 14–15, ill.

DESCRIPTION: The circular dish is raised and has a shallow well with ribbed sides and a broad rim to which is applied a moulded and gadrooned cast border.

HERALDRY: The rim of the dish was engraved in 1758 with the quartered arms of the Hanoverian monarchs (pre-1801) within the Garter and beneath an imperial crown. To this were added *c.*1778 the royal supporters and motto and an ermine mantling.

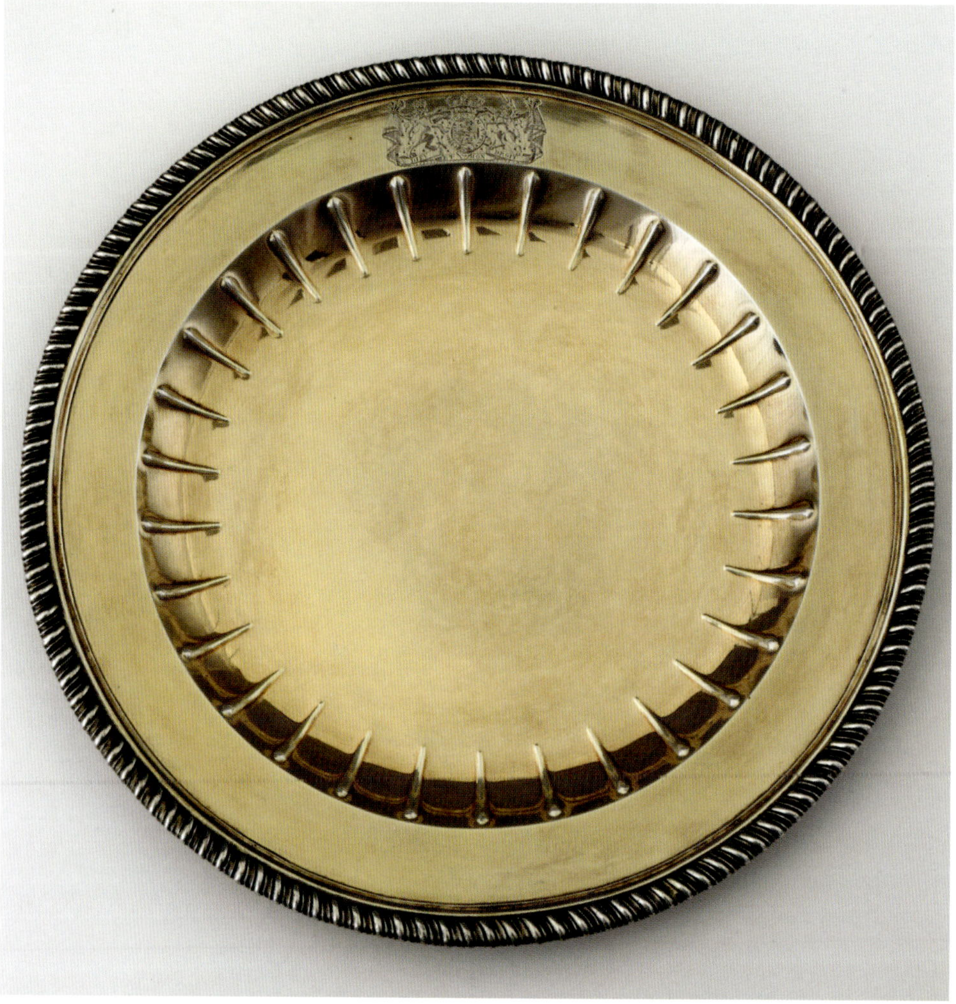

This is the only survivor of the twelve round, oval and octagonal silver-gilt dishes (four of each) which came from the Jewel Office in 1758. What happened to the others is not known but they are most likely to have been turned in for melting during the tenure of either the 3rd or 4th Earl of Bristol. The former is most likely as he probably gave this dish to Ickworth church following its restoration during his brief tenure of the estate.[1] The embellishment to the royal arms is by a different and far superior hand to that employed on the chalice (cat. 106) and paten (cat. 107) donated by the 5th Earl (future 1st Marquess) in 1810, suggesting that they were not all given at the same time. The gift of secular items for sacred use was common, particularly when they were no longer fashionable, and a pair of similar dishes, made in Newcastle in 1772, was given for use as alms dishes by the 7th Viscount Bulkeley to the churches of Llanfaes and Penmon on Anglesey in 1812.[2]

1. Yates 2013, p. 8.
2. Jones 1906, pp. xxxviii, 26 and 47.

75. Four covered sugar dishes and stands

Sterling silver, gilt / Frederick Kandler, London / 1758/9

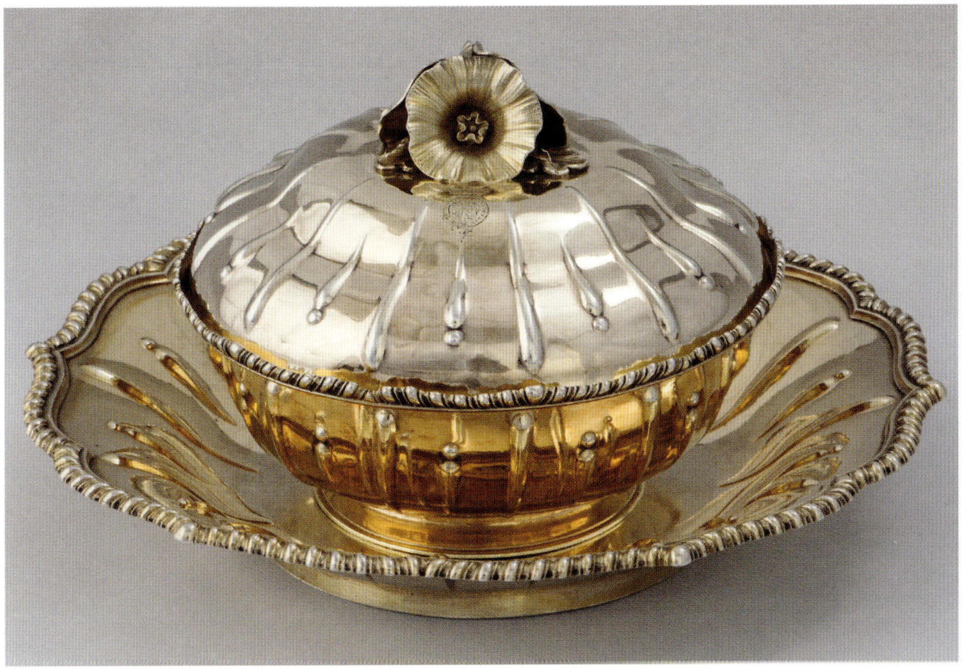

MARKS: Stands: Marked on their undersides. No. 1 has the date letter 'C' and part of another mark, illegible. No. 2 has date letter 'C', lion passant, leopard's head and maker's mark 'FK' in italics beneath a fleur-de-lis (Grimwade 1990, no. 692) for Frederick Kandler. No. 4 has the date letter 'C', lion passant and part of Kandler's mark. Dishes: All are fully marked on the underside of the rim with maker's mark (as above), lion passant, leopard's head and date letter 'C'. Covers: All are marked on their undersides with maker's mark (as above) and lion passant.

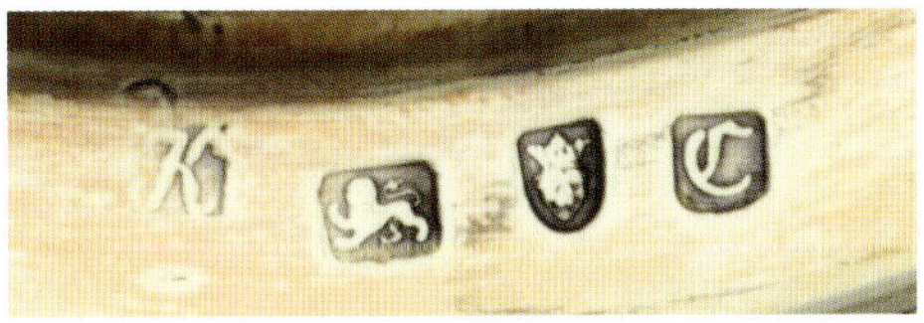

SCRATCHWEIGHTS: Stands 'Nº 1 [/] 18∧2'; 'Nº 2 [/] 17∧19'; 'Nº 3 [/] 18∧8'; 'Nº 4 [/] 18∧3'. Dishes (with covers) 'Nº 1 [/] 15∧4'; 'Nº 2 [/] 14 18'; 'Nº 3 [/] 14 [sic] 15∧2'; 'Nº 4 [/] 14 [sic] 14∧2'.

MEASUREMENTS: Stands h. 4.1 cm (1⅝ in); diam. 22.2 cm (8¾ in). Dishes h. (with covers) 10.8 cm (4¼ in); diam. 14.6 cm (5¾ in). Stand and dishes with covers h. (overall) 11.7 cm (4⅝ in).

INVENTORY: 852065.1.1–3, 2.1–3, 3.1–3 and 4.1–3.

PROVENANCE: Jewel Office; allocated to the 2nd Earl of Bristol as Ambassador to Madrid 1758; discharged to Lord Bristol 9 April 1759 (see appendix 4); by descent to the 4th Marquess.

LITERATURE: Penzer 1957a, I, p. 41, fig. VI and p. 43; Banister 1980, p. 794.

EXHIBITED: *Treasures from National Trust Houses*, Christie's, London, 1957–8, cat. 179 (one set); Society of the Four Arts, Palm Beach, Florida, 1959; *Ideal Home Exhibition*, London, 1960; *Silver from National Trust Houses*, Treasurer's House, York Festival, 1969 (two).

DESCRIPTION: The stands are raised in the form of deep, splayed bowls on seamed, plain foot rings. Their sides are chased with twelve ribs and twelve intermediary tear-drop ribs with additional single drops above. The shaped rims have applied gadroon and moulding borders which are cast. The dishes are circular and raised as steep-sided bowls with the same ribbing as the stands, a horizontal rim and applied, cast gadroon borders. The concave foot rings are raised and seamed. The ogee-domed covers are also raised and have ribbing to conform to the dishes and stands. Their handles are in the form of three convolvulus flowers with stalks and leaves beneath.

HERALDRY: The centre of each of the stands and the cover of each dish, adjoining the handle, is engraved with the quartered arms of the Hanoverian monarchs (pre-1801) within the Garter and beneath an imperial crown.

In the first half of the eighteenth century sugar was dispensed at meals from casters, such as the larger of those supplied with the Earl of Scarsdale's epergne in 1724 (cat. 11). This continued to be the standard practice in the 1750s and Lord Bristol's allocation of sugar dishes for use with dessert, rather than as part of the tea equipage, is one of the first recorded instances. It is likely that he was reacting to Continental custom and perhaps particularly that in Italy as the French were not such devotees of sugar as were the English and Italians.[1] A large number of *zuccheriere* of Turin manufacture survive from the period – probably more than any other category of plate – and many are ribbed or fluted and have floral finials for handles as do the covers of the Ickworth dishes.[2] It may be telling that although dishes for sugar did begin to appear more regularly in subsequent years in Britain, the next significant occurrence amongst ambassadorial plate was that of Sir James Gray, 2nd Bt, in 1767, and he had been stationed in Italy for much of the previous two decades.[3] Sir James, who was also destined for Spain, did not have stands, as did Lord Bristol, and nor did any of the other recipients of sugar dishes through the Jewel Office or from Wickes and Netherton or Parker and Wakelin. Many of the dishes were in fact in glass with silver mounts, as those supplied to the 4th Earl of Holderness in 1759 by Wickes and Netherton: '2 Cut Glass Bowls & Covers' at £2 16s, '2 silver mountings' weighing 12 oz, 18 dwt, at £6 14s and '2 Fine Sugar Spoons' at £5 1s 6d.[4] Thomas Robinson, 2nd Lord Grantham must have had an especially sweet tooth as he received eight silver gilt rims for basins on going to Spain as ambassador in 1771.[5]

1. Pinkard 2009, p. 149.
2. Fina and Mana 2012, pp. 177–203.
3. He received 'four Sucriers wth. Covers and Spoons' weighing 85 oz, 10 dwt, on being appointed ambassador to Spain. See Jewel Office Delivery Book 1732–93, f. 238.
4. Wickes Ledgers, VAM 6 1756–60, f. 201.
5. Jewel Office Delivery Book 1732–93, f. 264.

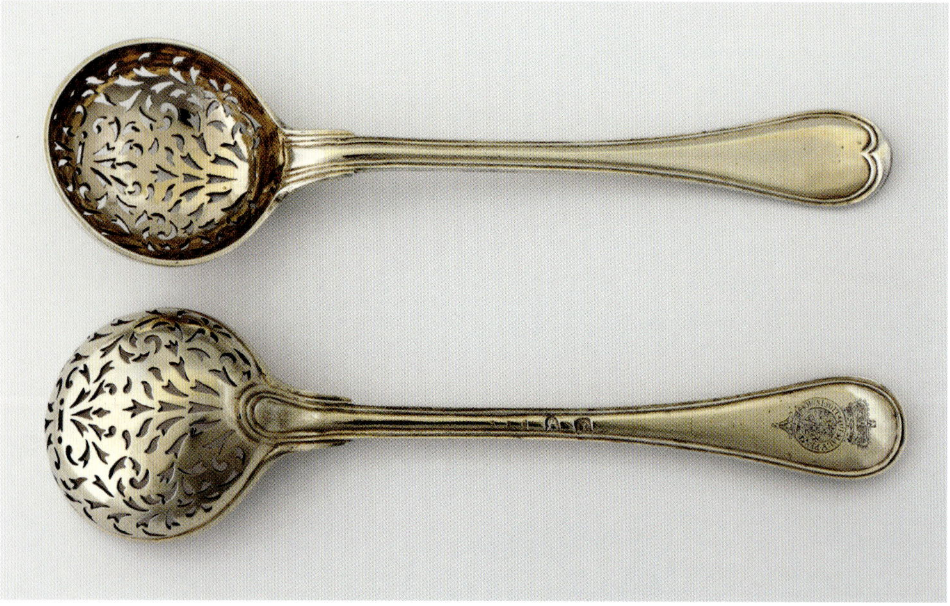

76. Four sugar ladles

Sterling silver, gilded / **London** / **1758/9**

MARKS: The ladles are marked on the rear of their stems. All are faint and on none is the maker's mark legible but three bear the date letter 'C' and the lion passant, and the leopard's head can be made out on all four.

SCRATCHWEIGHTS: None.
Actual weight (combined) 223 g (7 oz, 3 dwt).

MEASUREMENTS: l. 17.8 cm (7 in).

INVENTORY: 852196

PROVENANCE: Jewel Office; allocated to the 2nd Earl of Bristol as Ambassador to Madrid 1758; discharged to Lord Bristol 9 April 1759 (see appendix 4); by descent to the 4th Marquess.

LITERATURE: Penzer 1957a, I, p. 43.

EXHIBITION: Society of the Four Arts, Palm Beach, Florida, 1959 (two); *Ideal Home Exhibition*, London, 1960.

DESCRIPTION: The raised bowls are almost hemispherical and are pierced in a foliate and floral symmetrical pattern. The tapering handles with rounded terminals are forged and are of the double-reeded Hanoverian pattern with additional shouldering at the junction with the bowl.

HERALDRY: Each of the ladles is engraved on the reverse of the terminal with the quartered arms of the Hanoverian monarchs (pre-1801) within the Garter and beneath an imperial crown.

These ladles are much plainer than those Lord Bristol had already acquired in Turin, which makes their inclusion in his perquisite plate rather puzzling, unless he intended one or other of the sets to be used with porcelain sugar dishes (see cat. 59).

77. Eight dessert dishes

Sterling silver, gilded
Simon Le Sage, London / **1758/9**

MARKS: All the dishes are marked on their undersides with date letter 'C', lion passant, leopard's head and maker's mark 'S·L' in italics with a cup above and mullet below (Grimwade 1990, no. 2576).

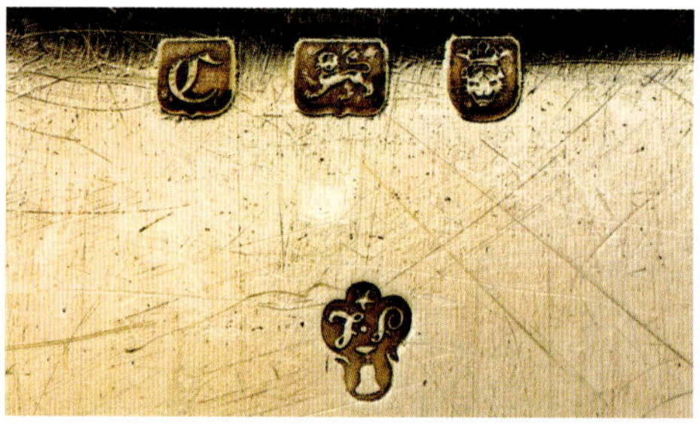

SCRATCHWEIGHTS: Pincushion dishes 'N^{o}.=1 [/] 21=5'; 'N^{o}.=2 [/] 23=8'; 'N°. 3 [/] 22=9'; 'N^{o}.=4 [/] 25=5. Round dishes 'N° 1 21=18' plus [old] faint '22 13' and '22'; 'N° 2 21=6' plus [old] faint 'oz 22=3'; 'N° 3 21=17' plus [old] faint '22'; 'N° 4 21=19' plus [old] faint '22"'.

MEASUREMENTS: Pincushion dishes h. 2.54 cm (1 in); w. 23.8 cm (9⅜ in); d. 21.3 cm (8⅜ in). Round dishes h. 3.5 cm (1⅜ in); diam. 23.5 cm (9 ¼ in).

INVENTORY: Pincushion 852067.1–4. Round 852101.1–4.

PROVENANCE: 2nd Earl of Bristol; by descent to the 4th Marquess.

EXHIBITED: *Treasures from National Trust Houses*, Christie's, London, 1957–8, cat. 176–7 (one of each).

LITERATURE: Penzer 1957a, I, pp. 42–3, figs. VII and VIII.

EXHIBITED: Society of the Four Arts, Palm Beach, Florida, 1959 (pincushion dishes); *Ideal Home Exhibition*, London, 1960 (one pincushion and two round dishes); *Silver from National Trust Houses*, Treasurer's House, York Festival, 1969 (two).

DESCRIPTION: The dishes are raised, four into an oblong form with concave sides and inverted corners and four into shaped circular, or cinquefoil form. They have cast moulded and gadrooned borders applied to the rims.

HERALDRY: The centre of each dish is engraved with the quartered arms of the Hanoverian monarchs (pre-1801) within the Garter and beneath an imperial crown flanked by the letters GR.

These dishes do not appear in the Jewel Office records and must represent some part of the machinations whereby Lord Bristol avoided having to pay the goldsmith for fashion charges beyond the official limits. Unlike the candelabra (cat. 72) and the soup plates (cat. 78) there is insufficient physical and archival evidence even to surmise about exactly what was entailed in this case.

Deep dishes of this form began to appear around 1750, almost certainly deriving from France (see cat. 48), and these are early examples.[1] Though they might have been used to serve nuts, fresh or candied fruit and other elements of the dessert[2] their deep sides made them particularly well suited to stewed or puréed fruit, prepared with sugar syrup. This is probably what led to the type becoming known as *compote* dishes, often anglicised to 'comport'. The earliest such reference in the Wickes and Parker and Wakelin ledgers is amongst purchases by the 4th Viscount Howe in October, 1766: '4 Hatt [triform] & 4 Pincushion Comport Dishes' weighing 162 oz and costing £62 2s. The 6th Earl of Coventry, in April 1770, acquired four each of pincushion and 'Round Gadroon' 'Compote Dishes', almost certainly of the same form as the Ickworth set and of a comparable weight at 193 oz in total.[3] Other shapes produced were ovals and triangles, and comport dishes were used for both dessert and, ungilded, for the earlier courses. By the end of the century the latter type were often being supplied with covers, as those by Paul Storr of 1795 at Mount Stewart in Northern Ireland.[4]

For additions to the set made by Frederick Kandler in 1769/70 see cat. 89.

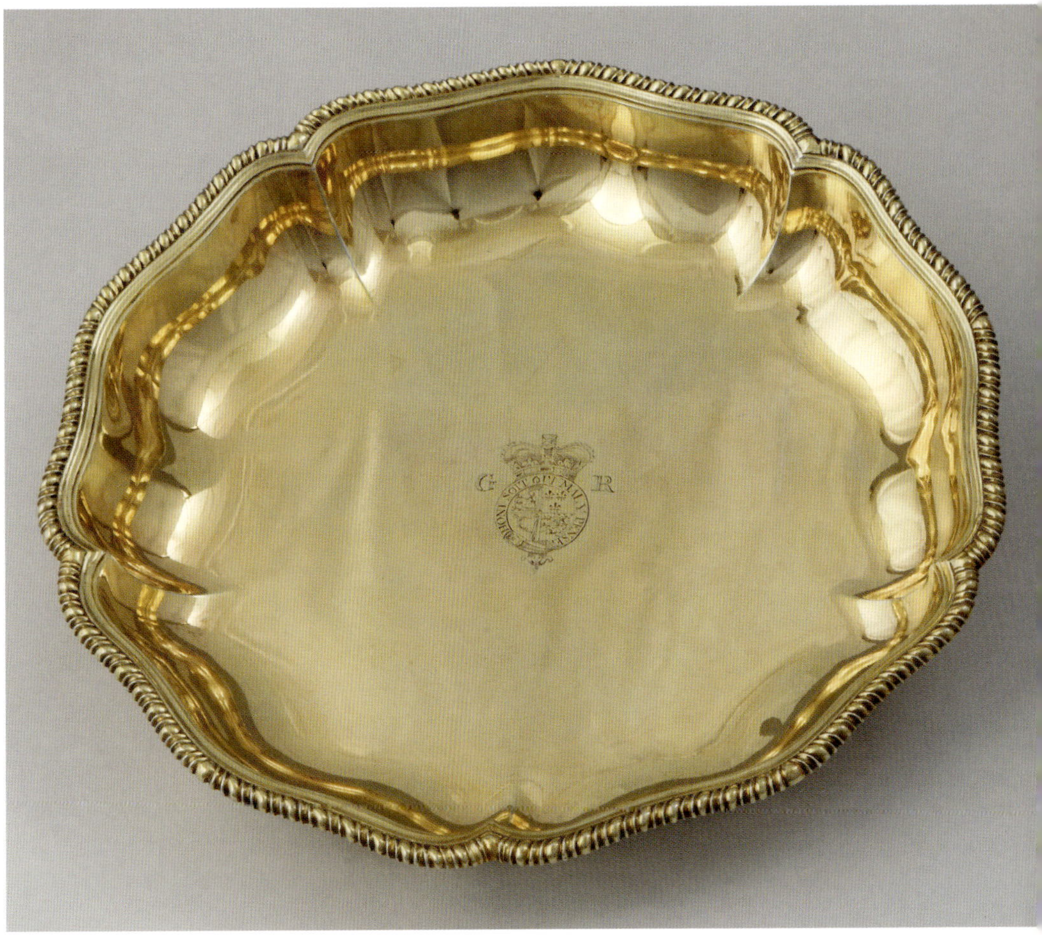

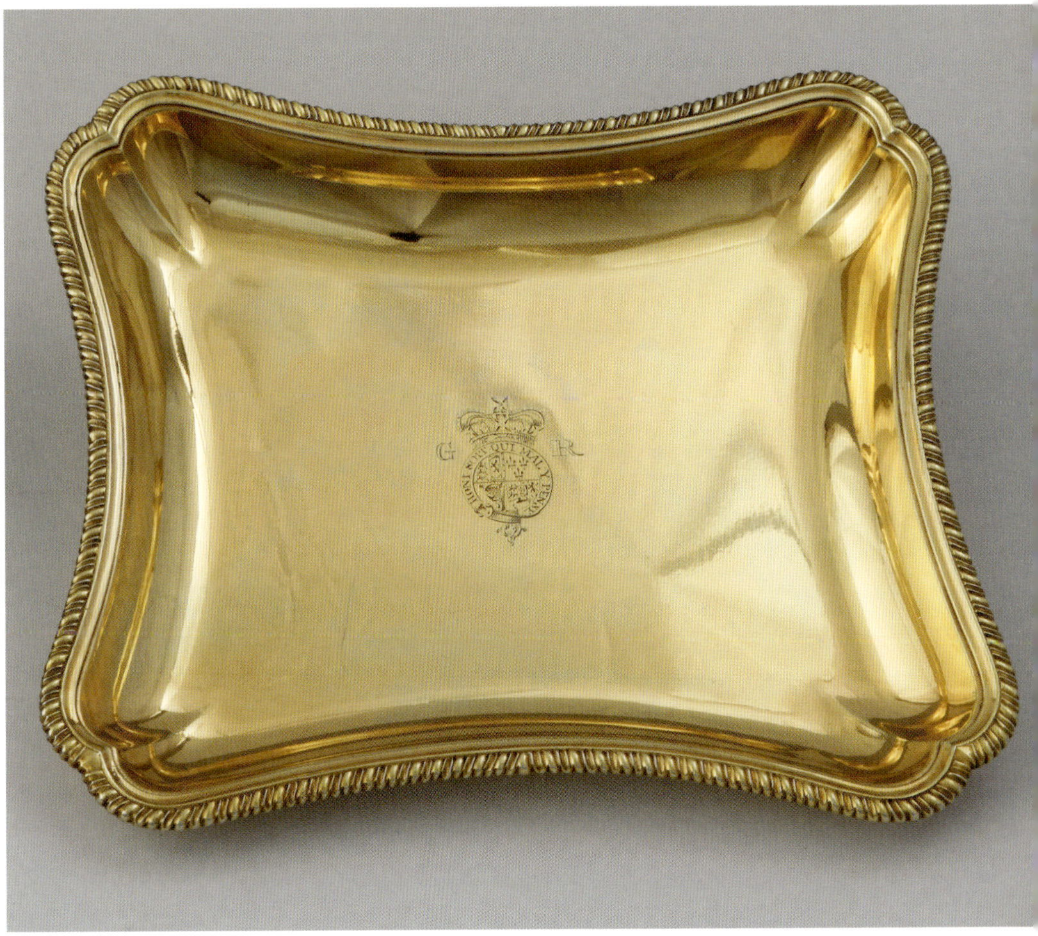

---

1. A pair of round dishes of this form by George Methuen, 1748, were sold by Sotheby's Zurich, 22 November 1978, lot 47.
2. See Paston-Williams 1993, pp. 260–1, for a discussion of dessert.
3. Parker and Wakelin Ledgers, VAM 7 1765–75, ff. 31 and 59.
4. Inventory no. 1656387.

78. **Twelve soup plates**

Sterling silver / **Simon Le Sage, London** / **1758/9**

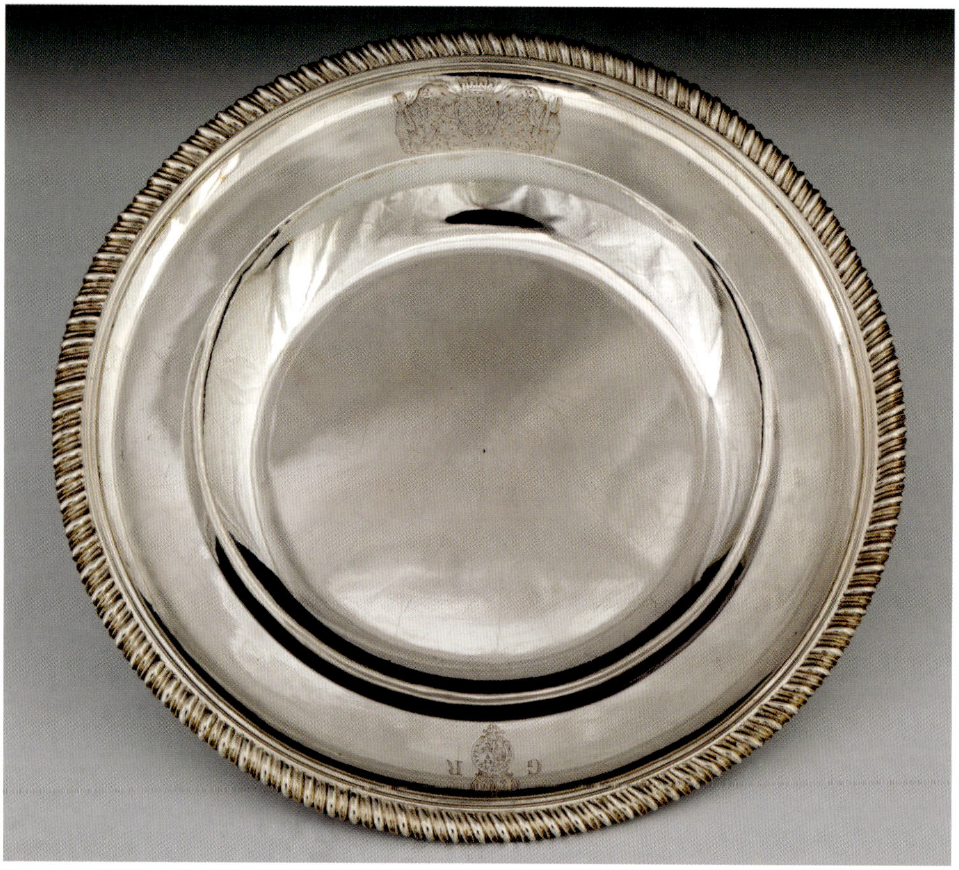

These are the only items amongst the 2nd Earl's plate that bear both the royal arms and his own, the latter almost certainly being executed in Spain by an engraver who was not used to English armorials as is particularly evident in the rendering of the coronets. The reason for the addition must be that these plates did not form part of the ambassadorial allocation and Lord Bristol wanted to make that very clear. They are not listed in the Jewel Office records and they were most probably purchased out of the £100 down payment that had been made in September 1758 to ensure that work started on the overall order (see cat. 72). They bear evidence of being formed out of other items, having old scratchweights and centring marks as well as distorted hallmarks. Le Sage may even have used some of the pieces presented to the Jewel Office to extract funding for the fashion of the candelabra, the old scratchweights tallying with the average weights of the dozen round dishes and the four dozen plates.[1] The simple form of these soup plates, not matching Lord Bristol's others, suggests that they were intended to form part of his everyday service of silver, rather than to be used on grand occasions.

1. These average weights are 39 oz, 18 dwt, and 17 oz, 17 dwt.

MARKS: Nos. 4, 6, 8, 10 and 12 have no hallmarks. The remainder are fully marked on their undersides with date letter 'C', lion passant, leopard's head and maker's mark 'S·L' in italics with a cup above and mullet below (Grimwade 1990, no. 2576).

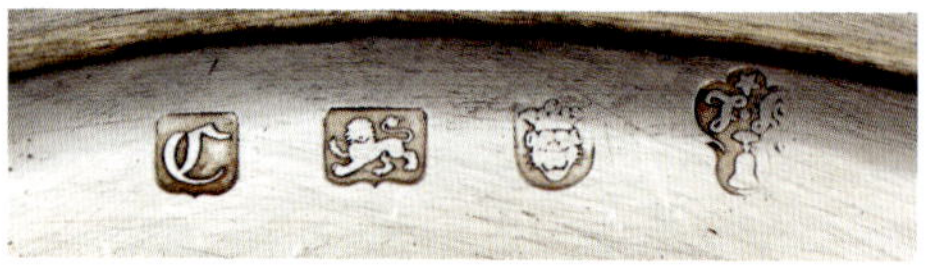

SCRATCHWEIGHTS: 'N° 1 [/] 19=0'; 'N° 5 2 [/] 18=19' plus old scratch 'N° 2 [/] [-] 5 –'; 'N° 3 [/] ~~18∧1~~ [/] 18=5 [faint] [/] 18=10 [actual scratchweight]'; 'N°. = 4 [/] 18=15'; 'N° 5 [/] 19=0'; 'N° 6 [/] 19=0'; 'N° 7 [/] ~~19∧8~~ [/] 19=6 [faint] [/] 18=15 [actual scratchweight]';

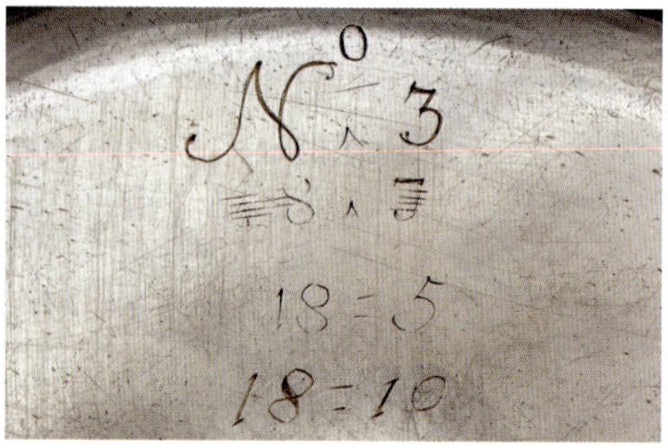

'N° 8 [/] 19=0'; 'N° 9 [/] 19∧18 [faint] [/] 18=16 [actual scratchweight]'; 'N° = 10 [/] 19=1'; 'N°. 11 [/] 19=3 plus [faint] 'N° 11 [/] ~~19∧11~~ [/] 19=13; 'N° 12 [/] 18=11' plus [faint] 'N° 3 [/] 39=10 [/] 38=16'.

MEASUREMENTS: h. 2.5 cm (1 in); diam. 24.8 cm (9⅞ in).

INVENTORY: 852125

PROVENANCE: 2nd Earl of Bristol; by descent to the 4th Marquess.

LITERATURE: Penzer 1957a, II, p. 137.

DESCRIPTION: The circular plates are raised with deep wells and broad rims to which have been applied moulded and gadrooned cast borders.

HERALDRY: Each plate is engraved on its rim with both the quartered arms of the Hanoverian monarchs (pre-1801) within the Garter and beneath an imperial crown flanked by the letters GR and, opposite, the quartered shield, supporters and motto of the 2nd Earl of Bristol in an ermine mantling and beneath an earl's coronet.

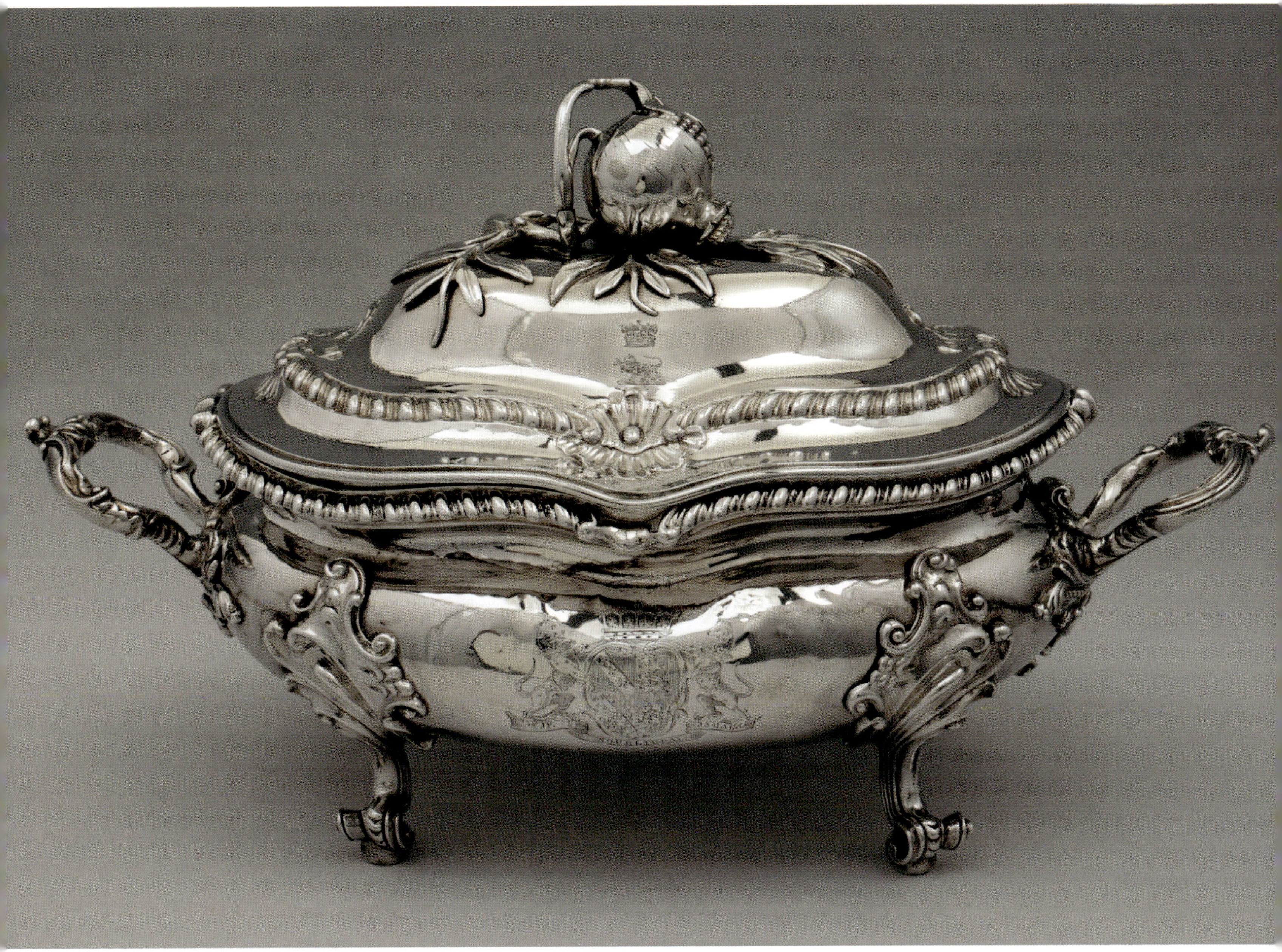

79. **Oval tureen**

Sterling silver / **William Cripps, London** / **1757/8**

MARKS: Fully marked on the underside of the tureen and on the bezel of the cover with the maker's mark 'WC' in a rectangular punch (Grimwade 1990, no. 3058), lion passant, leopard's head and date letter 'B'.

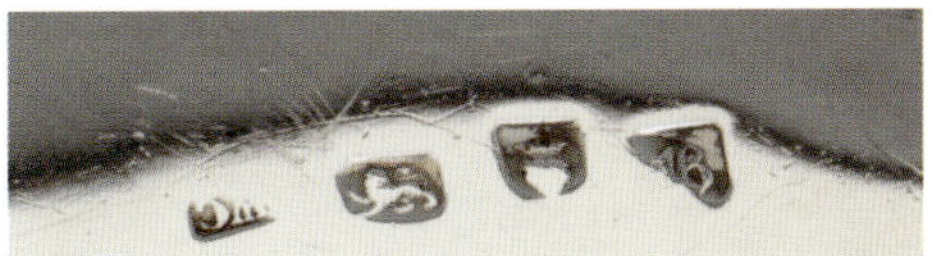

SCRATCHWEIGHT: '73 - 4'. This is over another which is only partially legible, '- =13'.

MEASUREMENTS: h. 21.3 cm (8⅜ in); w. 37.1 cm (14⅝ in); d. 18.4 cm 7¼ in).

INVENTORY: 852087

PROVENANCE: Probably 2nd Earl of Bristol; by descent to the 4th Marquess.

LITERATURE: Penzer 1957a, II, p. 137.

EXHIBITED: *Ideal Home Exhibition*, London, 1960; *British Week*, Milan and Frankfurt, 1965.

DESCRIPTION: The body of the tureen is raised and is of shaped oval *bombé* form with a cast gadroon-and-scroll border applied at the rim. It rests on four cast scroll-on-ball feet with scrolling cartouches extending onto the body of the tureen and there are two cast leaf-and-scroll handles. The domed cover is raised and conforms in shape to the base. It has a large wire applied at the rim, a seamed short bezel and an intermediary band of chased gadrooning with shells at the centre of all the sides. The handle is cast and is in the form of a pomegranate on a stalk with foliage asymmetrically arranged over the plain top of the dome.

HERALDRY: The tureen base is engraved on one side only with the quartered arms, supporters and motto of the 2nd Earl of Bristol. The cover has, also on one side, the Hervey crest beneath an earl's coronet.

This form of tureen derived from French designs of the 1730s and 1740s via Paul de Lamerie, George Wickes and other prominent London makers and was very popular in the 1750s and 1760s. Numerous examples survive by various makers including George Methuen, Frederick Kandler and Edward Wakelin.[1]

The coat of arms on the tureen could apply to the 2nd, 3rd or 4th Earls of Bristol but the rococo style of the engraving makes it most unlikely that it could post-date the 2nd Earl who must, therefore, have been the purchaser. As he already had at least six tureens, including the pair from the Jewel Office which do not survive, it might seem surprising that he felt the need to get another, and one that was definitely not up to sharing a table with the Kandler and Turin pairs (cat. 43 and 53). Traces of an erased crest issuing out of a ducal coronet[2] on both the body and the cover indicate a second-hand purchase, and the naïve character of the engraving[3] could not have come out of Kandler's workshop. It is therefore likely that the tureen was acquired provincially for use at Ickworth (the others being in London) and it probably came from the Bury St Edmunds retail silversmith, Peter Rogers. He had been regularly patronised by the 1st Earl (see cat. 15 and 16) and other members of the family were continuing to use him in the 1760s.[4] The purchase must have occurred after the 2nd Earl's return from Spain in 1762 and probably during his subsequent four years in the political wilderness when he spent long periods of time at Ickworth.[5]

1. See, for instance, the near identical pair marked by George Methuen, 1759, sold at Christie's, 3 July 1968, lot 86.
2. A 'ducal' coronet is purely heraldic and does not denote rank as does a 'duke's' coronet. Its form is, in fact, closer to that of a marquess. See Burke 1884, p. xxxiv, ill.
3. The arrangement is broadly copying that on Lord Bristol's plates and dishes, without the mantling, but is more crudely executed and the fourth quarter, for Felton, is heraldically incorrect, showing lions passant guardant when they should be just passant.
4. Payments to Peter Rogers from Lord Bristol's brother William in 1763 and his uncle Felton in 1761 appear in their bank accounts. Goslings Ledgers, 130/35, f. 144 and 130/31, f. 124.
5. If, however, the tureen was acquired by the future 3rd Earl and crudely engraved to match the rest of the silver after his succession, it could relate to the payment of £21 to the retail silversmith Thomas Harache on 19 June 1759. See Goslings ledgers, 130/29, f. 394.

80. Mirror plateau

Mirror glass and wooden base with sterling silver frame / London / 1766/7

MARKS: The frame is marked on one of the short sides with date letter 'L', lion passant, leopard's head and a maker's mark rendered indecipherable by wear.

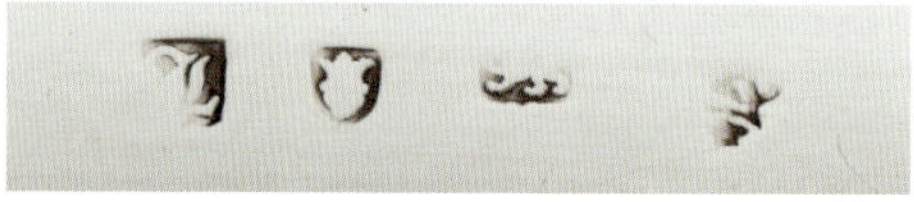

SCRATCHWEIGHT: '20=5'

MEASUREMENTS: h. 5.7 cm (2¼ in); w. 44.8 cm (17⅝ in); d. 40 cm (15¾ in).

INVENTORY: 852091

PROVENANCE: 2nd Earl of Bristol; by descent to the 4th Marquess.

LITERATURE: Penzer 1957a, II, p. 137.

DESCRIPTION: The frame, which rests on four cast reeded scroll feet, is rectangular with shaped, inverted corners. It is formed of seamed sheet silver and is secured to the wooden core by silver screws. The mirror plate is probably a replacement.

HERALDRY: On the front and back edges is engraved the royal crest of a lion passant guardant imperially crowned within the Garter and beneath an imperial crown.

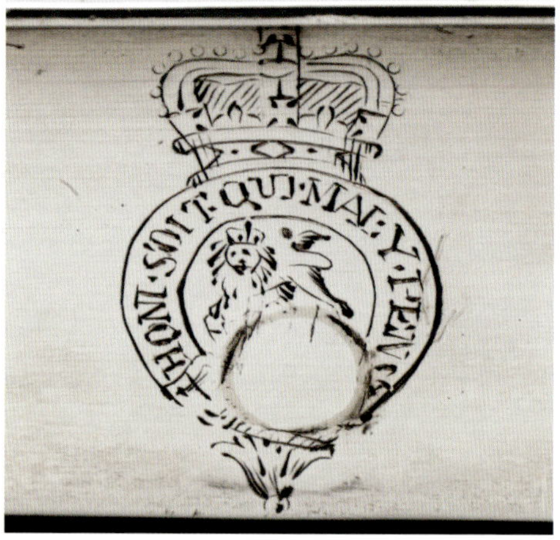

The acquisition of this mirror plateau or dessert frame (as it was called in 1811), which is possibly the earliest of English manufacture to have survived, was prompted by Lord Bristol's appointment as Lord Lieutenant of Ireland in 1766 and may in part be a reflection of his earlier sojourns in Turin and Madrid. Such plateaux were an important presence on Continental tables from at least the 1730s[1] whereas they do not appear to have taken hold in Britain until the middle of the century.[2] Other surviving London-made examples are few and far between and mostly from the Regency period and later.[3] The Earl would have seen magnificent Turinese plateaux with rich rococo frames whilst he was in Italy such as those of *c.*1755 now in the Chicago Art Institute and the Museo di Arti Decorative Accorsi-Ometto, Turin (fig. 105).[4] His is much plainer, in part because fashions had moved on but primarily because the plateau would have been placed at the centre of the elaborate table arrangements associated with mid-eighteenth-century dessert and did not in itself need to be decorative.

Although on a far grander scale than even Lord Bristol in semi-regal state as Lord Lieutenant would have aspired to, a sense of the fantastical creations of the period is given by the description of the dessert prepared for George III and

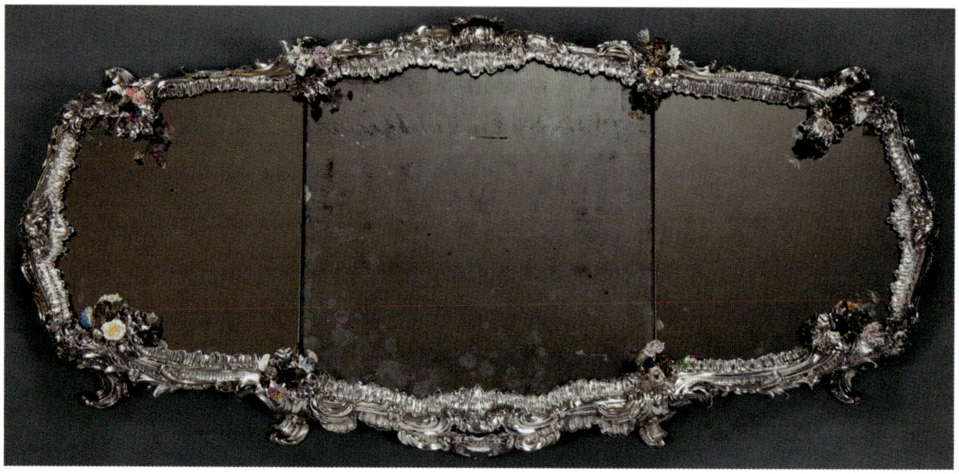

FIG. 105 / Mirror plateau, Turin, *c.*1755. Silver frame: 139 x 67 cm (54¾ x 26⅜ in). Museo di Arti Decorative Accorsi-Ometto, Turin.

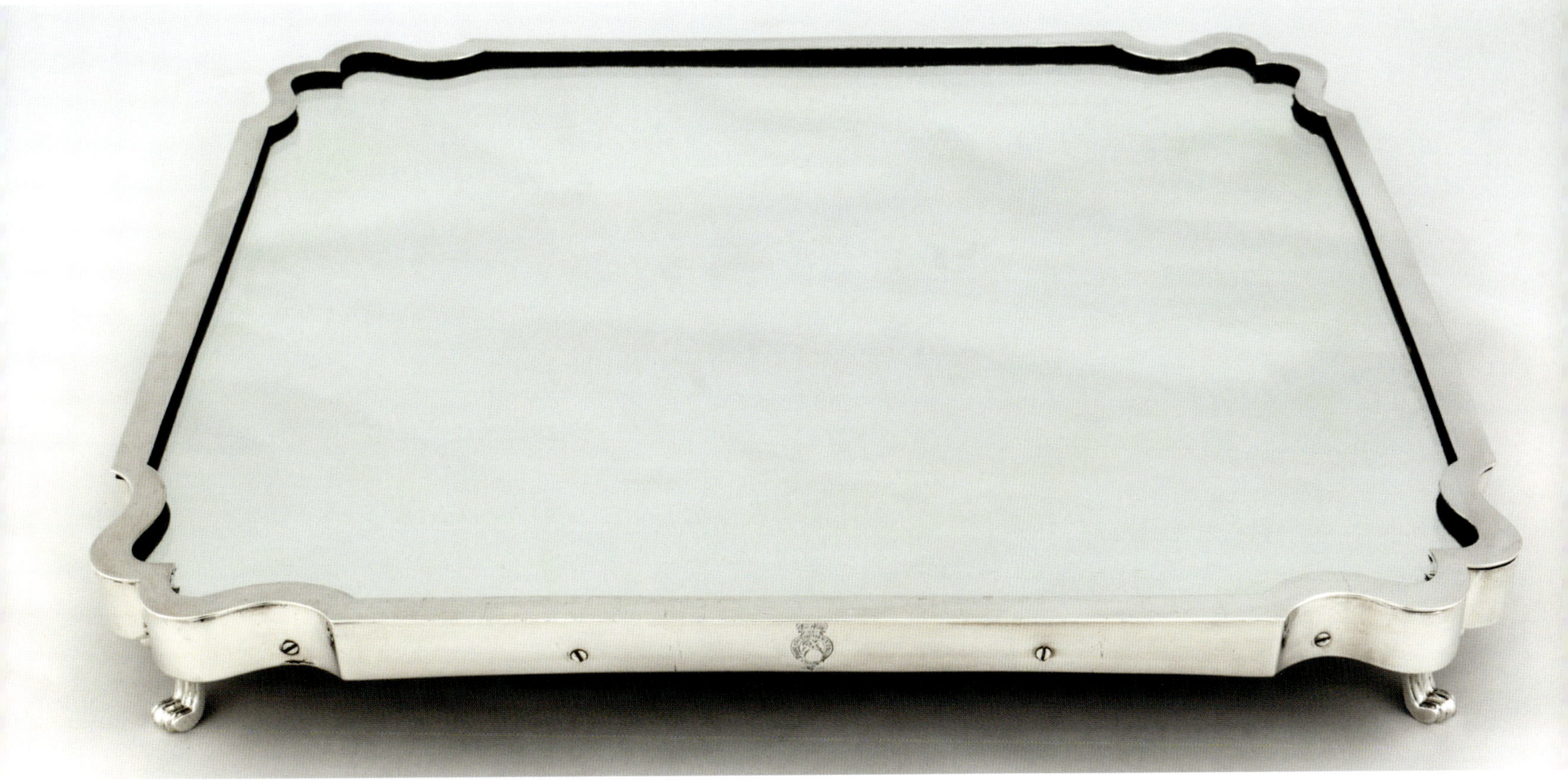

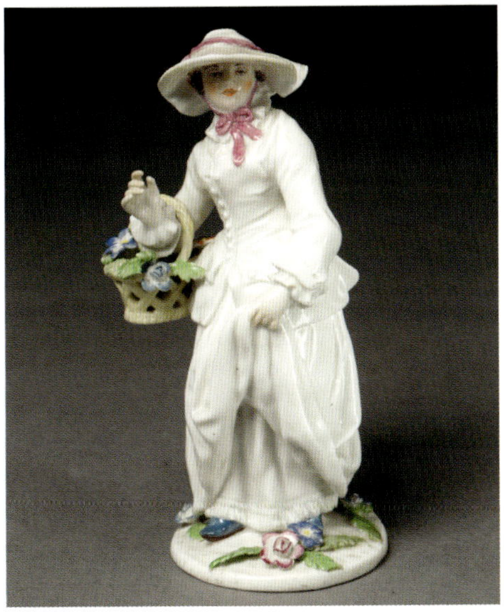

FIG. 106 / Figure of Spring from the *Rustic Seasons*, Chelsea porcelain, *c.*1755. Soft-paste porcelain, painted in enamel colours: h. 13.3 cm (5¼ in). Victoria and Albert Museum.

Queen Charlotte at the Guildhall in London in November 1761:

… the King's table was furnished with a desert of sweet-meats, which had a lively and grand appearance, representing in an expressive manner a large bay, in which the waves seemed to roll as if fanned by a gentle breeze. In the centre were seen Neptune and Amphitrite riding a car drawn by sea-horses, and surrounded by sea nymphs and myriads, with whales, dolphins, and other inhabitants of the watery element, who in a supportive manner seemed to play and throw up water, which to distant spectators appeared to flow as if from fountains. The bounds of the bay were composed of ornamented pastry, which served as a foundation on which the desert was placed. At proper distances laurels seemed to grow, extending their boughs over the centre, and bearing as fruit different sorts of sweet-meats, which formed in the whole a most pleasing prospect.[5]

Much use was made in such arrangements of porcelain figures and Lord Bristol had an impressive collection from the Bow and Chelsea manufactories to choose from including the Watermen series, the Rustic Seasons (fig. 106), Heathen Bustos, and male and female dancers. Some of these would undoubtedly have been displayed on the plateau and by 1768 Lord Bristol had added eighteen groups and individual figures in biscuit ware, subsequently described as 'White Seve [Sèvres] China Figures for Deserts'.[6] A set of Meissen wine-glass rinsers are the only survivors of the 2nd Earl's porcelain for the dessert table (fig. 107). By the mid-twentieth century the plateau had been put to rather more prosaic use, being found by Norman Penzer, the silver specialist who was writing up the collection for *Apollo* magazine, in use as a dressing-table mirror in one of the bedrooms.[7]

The presence on the plateau and on several other pieces of the same date (cat. 81–3) of the royal arms might suggest that Lord Bristol was receiving another tranche of perquisite plate from the Jewel Office on his appointment to Ireland but Lords Lieutenant were not, in fact, entitled to an allocation (see chapter 3 for a full discussion).

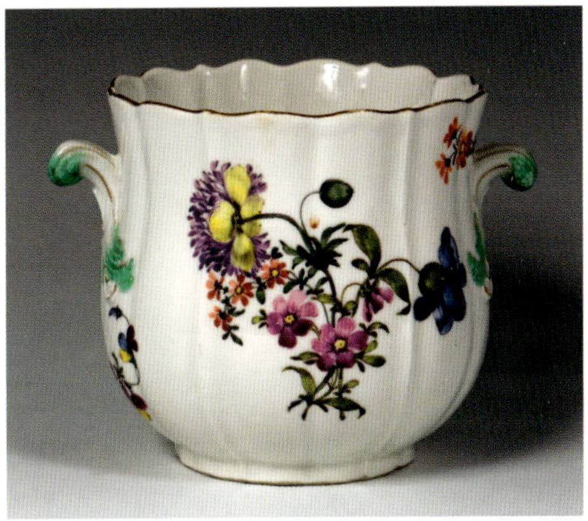

FIG. 107 / Wine glass rinser, Meissen, *c.*1750. Hard-paste porcelain: h. 12.5 cm (5 in). National Trust, Ickworth.

1. See, for instance, that of *c.*1730 from Augsburg previously in the Saxon royal collection sold at Christie's, 23 November 1973, lot 46.
2. They appear on table plans in the *circa* 1760 London publication *The modern method of regulating and forming a table explained and displayed*. Information from James Lomax.
3. One of 1821 by Paul Storr was sold by Christie's 26–7 November 2013, lot 474.
4. Both bear the assay mark of Bartolomeo Pagliani who was in post from 1753–75. See Fina and Mana 2012, pp. 53–7, figs. 19–20. Another, of *c.*1750 and possibly a royal commission, was sold Sotheby's Monte Carlo, 23–4 June 1976, lot 49.
5. *Public Ledger*, Monday 16 November 1761, issue 578.
6. Ferguson 2011, pp. 75–79.
7. Penzer 1957a, II, p. 137.

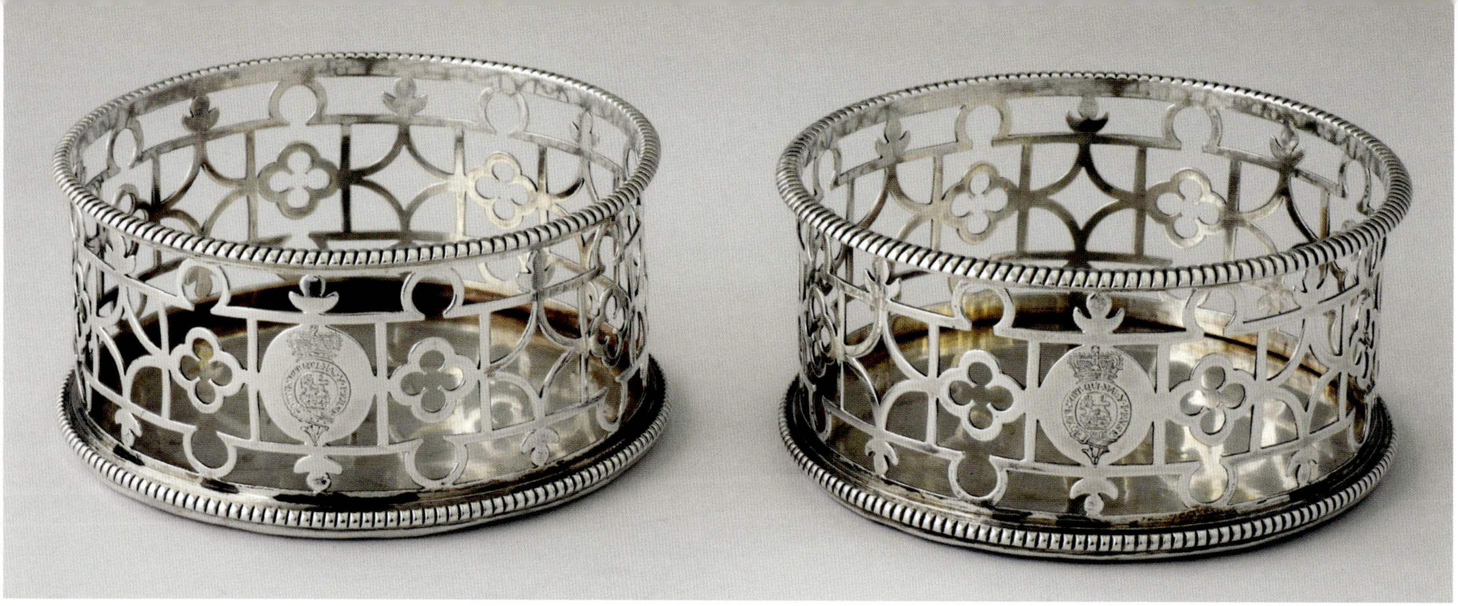

81. **Eight bottle stands**

Sterling silver / Elizabeth Aldridge(?), London / 1766/7 / mahogany bases

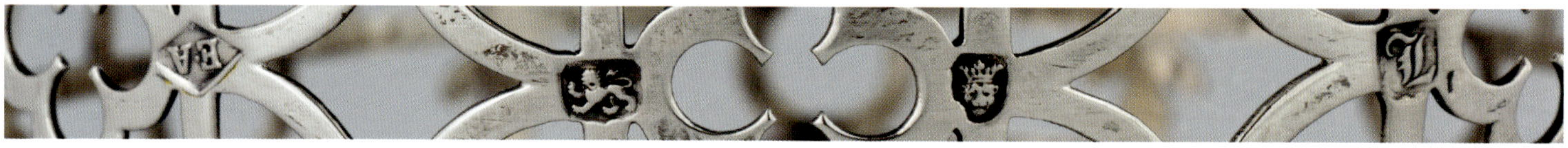

MARKS: The stands are marked on their sides, four with the lion passant, leopard's head, date letter 'L' and maker's mark 'E·A' in a lozenge-shaped punch probably for Elizabeth Aldridge (Grimwade 1990, no. 3530). The other four lack the maker's mark. The marks on all but one of the stands have been cut during piercing.

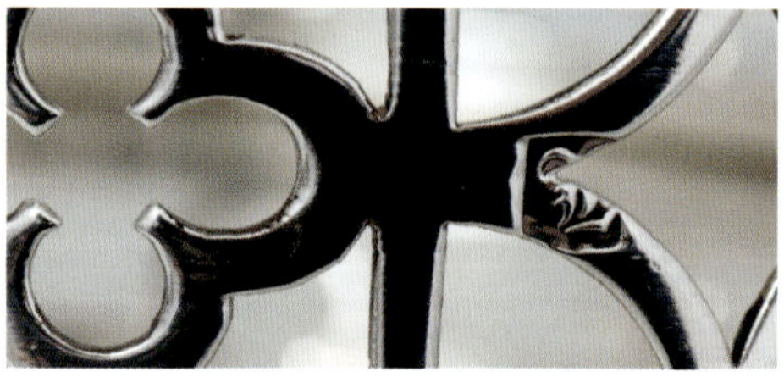

SCRATCHWEIGHTS: None. The 1811 plate list gives a combined weight of 46 oz, 16 dwt.

MEASUREMENTS: h. 5.7 cm (2¼ in); diam. 10.8 cm (4¼ in).

INVENTORY: 852058

PROVENANCE: 2nd Earl of Bristol; by descent to the 4th Marquess.

LITERATURE: Banister 1980, p. 794.

DESCRIPTION: The galleries of the stands are made from sheet silver seamed once and liberally hand-pierced with a central band of alternating rectangular and square panels containing respectively quatrefoils and indented lozenges. One of the square panels has a larger, plain disk for armorials. The central band is attached to the rim and foot, which have applied gadroon mouldings, via alternating open, broken circles and triform leaves. The bases of the stands are formed from flat sheet silver on top of polished mahogany discs.

HERALDRY: The gallery of each stand is engraved with the royal crest of a lion passant guardant imperially crowned within the Garter and beneath an imperial crown.

Bottle stands had been in existence since early in the eighteenth century though never, seemingly, in large numbers. The first reference to them in the Jewel Office records is in 1711–12 when they were the subject of a short-lived spate of enthusiasm. At that time they were known as 'fflaskes for botles' or 'frames for flasks' and within a fourteen-month period pairs were delivered to the 1st Earl Poulett as Lord Steward, Henry St John as Secretary of State, Henry Watkins as Secretary to the Utrecht embassy and Lord Lansdowne as Comptroller of the Household.[1] They would probably have been raised from a single sheet of silver with an applied, spreading foot like one of 1715 by Anthony Nelme,[2] which is perhaps the earliest survivor, and two others in the Ashmolean Museum, of 1723 by Augustine Courtauld and 1724 by Simon Pantin.[3] The bottles, or flasks, may well have been blown directly into the stands, as is suggested by the Courtauld example in which a later bottle survives, and as was certainly the practice with salts (see cat. 67).[4]

This early form of bottle stand probably persisted until about 1730, the final mention amongst perquisite plate being the two 'Flask Stands' weighing 39 oz, 15 dwt, delivered to Arthur Onslow as Speaker in March, 1727.[5] At around the same time the more flexible form with a pierced gallery, in which the bottle would sit loosely and did not have to be specially made, began to appear and a pair survives which sadly lacks hallmarks but has late *Régence* decoration and contemporary engraved arms.[6] The four 'saucers for Bottles' weighing 34 oz delivered to Charles Basset in 1736 by George Wickes[7] were perhaps of a flatter form but references to 'bottle stands' appear occasionally in the ledgers from 1741,[8] including the re-engraving of four belonging to the 6th Earl of Coventry in 1751.[9] There are few surviving examples, however, from before the mid-1760s, when it would appear that they became very much *de rigueur*. Having been entirely absent from the Jewel Office registers through the previous few decades a set of ten were allocated in 1763 to the 1st Earl (subsequently Marquess) of Hertford as ambassador to France, his successor, the Duke of Richmond, had eight in 1765 and Sir James Gray, 2nd Bt, took the same number to Spain in 1767.[10] Lord Bristol, who had always shown himself keen to be up with the latest fashions associated with the dining table, was thus in at the beginning.

The bottle stands would have been placed on the table at the moment in the meal described by the Swiss César de Saussure in 1727:

When everyone is done eating, the table is cleared, the cloth even being removed, and a bottle of wine with a glass for each guest is placed on the table. The King's health is first drunk, then that of the Prince of Wales, and finally that of all the Royal Family. After these toasts the women rise and leave the room, the men paying them no attention or asking them to stay; the men remain together for a longer or lesser time. This custom surprises foreigners, especially French-men, who are infinitely more polite with regard to women than are Englishmen; but it is the custom, and one must submit.[11]

The stands have wooden bottoms, originally covered with brown wool cloth (surviving on two) to ensure that they could slide on the table without catching or doing damage. By the 1770s the entire base was being made in turned mahogany as it was found that the flat silver plate could, if damp from the bottle or condensation, create a vacuum with the bottle and be lifted along with it, subsequently 'to fall with a clatter to the table'.[12]

The maker's mark on these bottle stands, 'E.A' in a lozenge, would have appeared in the lost register of 1758–73 and cannot be absolutely verified. Its similarity to that of Edward Aldridge and the fact that the Aldridges specialised in pierced wares of this fine quality make it highly likely, however, that it is that of Edward's widow, Elizabeth. Edward Aldridge and John Stamper's mark appears on a pair of pierced bottle stands of 1757 with similarly extensive piercing to the Ickworth set.[13] Hallmarking must have been carried out prior to piercing as some of the marks have been cut into or wholly lost (see image). This would have been done to avoid distortion to the delicate final structure and presumably the pattern must have been marked out to guide the placing of the punches.

1. Jewel Office Delivery Book 1698–1732, ff. 168, 170 and 173.
2. Brett 1986, p. 149, no. 558.
3. Schroder 2009, cat. 141–2, pp. 370–3.
4. Hennell 1986, p. 56, fig. 33.
5. Jewel Office Delivery Book 1698–1732, f. 300.
6. Christie's, 15 June 1983, lot 174.
7. Wickes Ledgers, VAM 1 1735–40, f. 74.
8. Unpublished analysis of object types in the first two Wickes ledgers by Elaine Barr, drawn to my attention by Philippa Glanville.
9. Wickes Ledgers, VAM 5 1750–4, f. 65.
10. Jewel Office Delivery Book 1732–93, ff. 207, 224 and 238. Sir John Cust, 3rd Bt also had a set of six as Speaker in 1769; ibid., f. 257.
11. Muyden 1902, pp. 222–3.
12. Hughes 1957, p. 128.
13. Christie's, 29 June 1977, lot 87. These stands also have a pierced base, a rare alternative way of avoiding suction to the bottle.

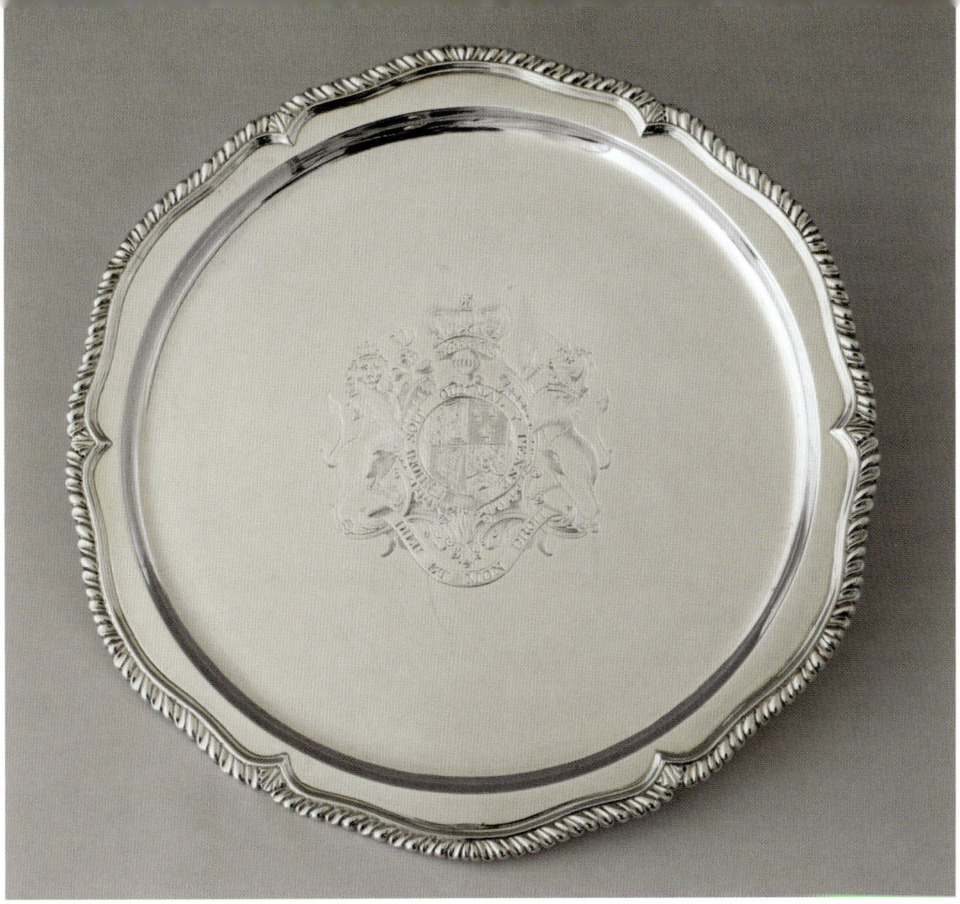

82. Four round waiters

Sterling silver / Frederick Kandler, London / 1766/7

MARKS: The waiters are fully marked on their undersides with date letter 'L', lion passant, leopard's head and maker's mark 'FK' in italics beneath a fleur-de-lis (Grimwade 1990, no. 692).

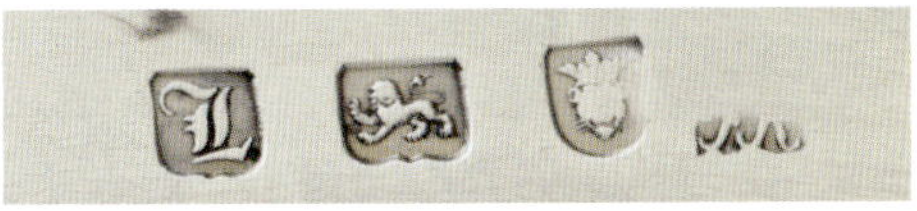

SCRATCHWEIGHTS: '41=7 [/] Nº 1'; '41=1 [/] Nº 2'; '41=16 [/] Nº 3'; '41=7 [/] Nº 4'.

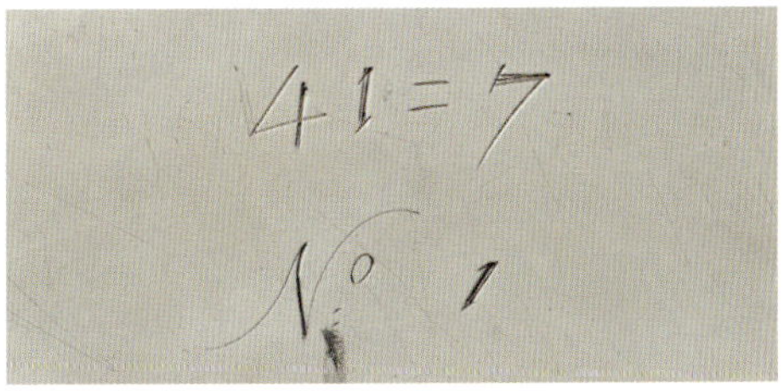

MEASUREMENTS: h. 3.8 cm (1½ in); diam. 34.6 cm (13⅝ in).

INVENTORY: 852120

PROVENANCE: 2nd Earl of Bristol; by descent to the 4th Marquess.

EXHIBITION: *British Week*, Milan and Frankfurt, 1965.

DESCRIPTION: The waiters, which have no feet, have shallow circular wells and narrow rims with shaped hexafoil moulded and gadrooned borders which are cast and applied.

HERALDRY: Each waiter is engraved at its centre with the quartered arms of the Hanoverian monarchs (pre-1801) within the Garter and flanked by the royal supporters, the motto below and a full-faced helmet and imperial crown above. The Garter is within a rococo cartouche and a rose and a thistle rise above each of the supporters.

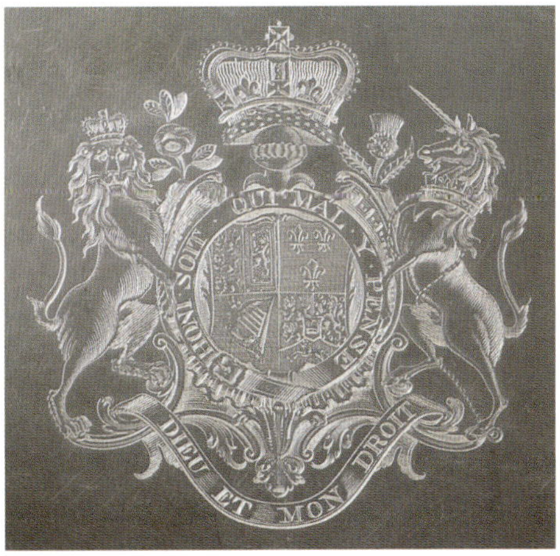

These pieces, like the plateau and bottle stands, were probably bought out of Lord Bristol's income as Lord Lieutenant of Ireland and hence they are engraved with the royal arms. The engraving is superbly executed and survives in excellent condition. The making of these pieces was also highly accomplished, since they do not have feet and thus have to be perfectly flat so as not to wobble on a table top. They are an unusual form and exactly how they were intended to be used is not clear. With such care lavished on their central engraving it seems unlikely that they would have been employed in the same fashion as the oval and other shallow dishes, all of which have the arms on their rims, and their lack of feet means that they would have been difficult to lift from the table during the meal. It is thus more likely that they were intended for waiting and could be placed on a side table with glasses on them, or they could even have been part of an intended buffet display which the Earl would have needed in his new, semi-regal state and does not appear to have owned previously. They are described as waiters in the 1811 plate list (appendix 5).

83. **Eleven table spoons**

Sterling silver / Thomas and William Chawner (?), London / 1766/7

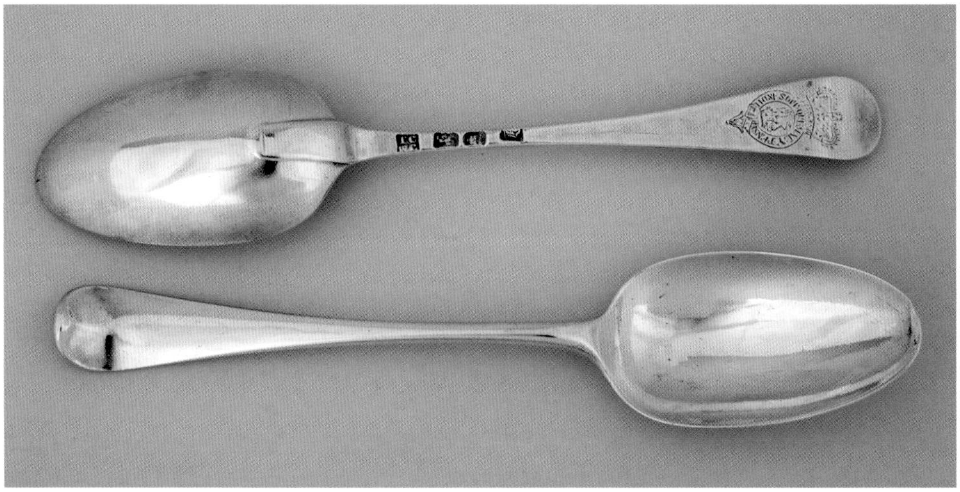

MARKS: Each fully marked on the reverse of the stem with date letter 'L', leopard's head, lion passant and makers' marks 'T·C' above 'W·C' (7 – Grimwade 1990, no. 3816) and 'TC' horizontally with 'WC' vertically as a cross (4 – Grimwade 1990, no. 3817).

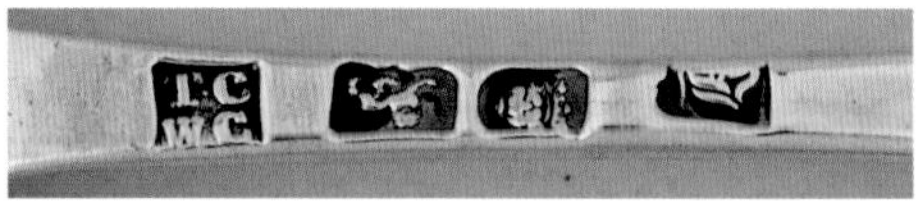

SCRATCHWEIGHTS: None.
Actual weight: (combined) 651 g (20 oz, 18 dwt).

MEASUREMENTS: l. 20.3 cm (8 in).

INVENTORY: 852099.19–29

PROVENANCE: 2nd Earl of Bristol; by descent to the 4th Marquess.

LITERATURE: Penzer 1957a, II, p. 136.

DESCRIPTION: The spoons are forged from single pieces of silver. They are of the Hanoverian pattern with raised egg-shaped bowls, plain, tapering stems and single drops at the junction with the bowl. The terminals are upturned on the bowl side with slight ribs.

HERALDRY: Each of the spoons is engraved on the reverse of the terminal with the royal crest of a lion passant guardant imperially crowned within the Garter and beneath an imperial crown.

These were made to match the existing spoons (cat. 26 and 69) and were either an augmentation or a replacement for losses that might have been endured in the rapid exit from Spain in 1762. The marks have been attributed to the Chawners by Arthur Grimwade and are very likely to be theirs but that cannot be proved for certain as the result of the loss of the register for 1758 to 1773.[1]

1. Grimwade 1990, pp. 4–5.

84. Two carving knives and two carving forks

Silver handles, steel blades and prongs / handles probably London / *c.*1766 / blades and prongs later

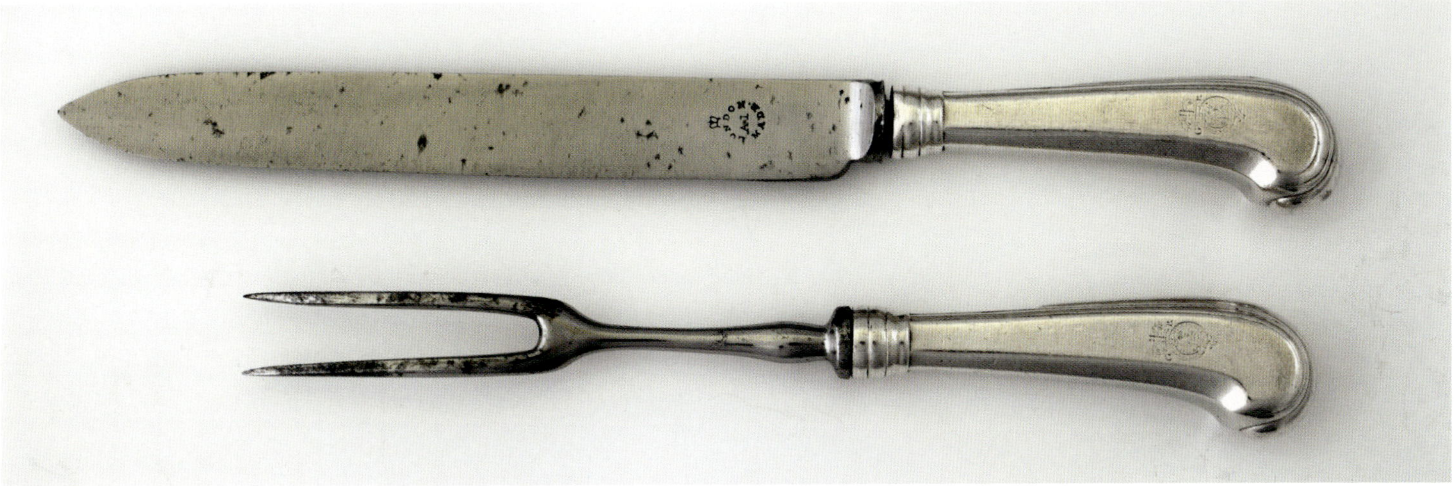

MARKS: No marks on the handles. The blades of the knives are stamped with a crown above 'LONDON MADE' in a circle around 'A1'.

SCRATCHWEIGHTS: None. A combined weight of 22 oz is given in the 1811 plate list.

MEASUREMENTS: l. of handles 11.4 cm (4½ in); l. of knives (overall): 29.8 cm (11¾ in); l. of forks (overall): 26.7 cm (10½ in).

INVENTORY: 852203.1–4

PROVENANCE: 2nd Earl of Bristol; by descent to the 4th Marquess.

DESCRIPTION: The cast, pistol-shaped handles are plain apart from round-moulded cappings. The steel forks have two prongs and the blades of the knives, also steel, are straight with pointed ends. They are probably early-twentieth-century replacements.

HERALDRY: Each handle is engraved on the left-hand side of the stem with the quartered arms of the Hanoverian monarchs (pre-1801) within the Garter and beneath an imperial crown flanked by the letters GR.

These were made to match the table service acquired as part of the ambassadorial allocation in 1758. That had not included carving knives and forks and those Lord Bristol already owned (cat. 42) were of a different pattern.

For a discussion of carving in the eighteenth century see cat. 42.

85. Two oval dessert dishes

Sterling silver, gilded / Frederick Kandler, London / 1766/7

MARKS: Both dishes are fully marked on their undersides with the date letter 'L', leopard's head, lion passant and maker's mark 'FK' in italics beneath a fleur-de-lis (Grimwade 1990, no. 692).

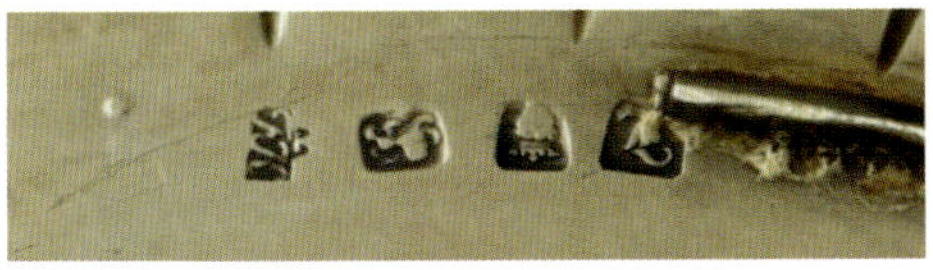

SCRATCHWEIGHTS: 'N^{o}.=3 [/] 32=10'; 'N^{o}.=4 [/] 32=9'.

MEASUREMENTS: h. 5.1 cm (2 in); w. 34 cm (13⅜ in); d. 29.8 cm (11¾ in).

INVENTORY: 852064.3–4

PROVENANCE: 2nd Earl of Bristol; by descent to the 4th Marquess.

LITERATURE: Penzer 1957a, I, pp. 41–2, fig. v; Banister 1980, p. 793.

DESCRIPTION: As cat. 13.

HERALDRY: The centre of each dish is engraved with the quartered shield, supporters and motto of the 2nd Earl of Bristol in an ermine mantling and beneath an earl's coronet.

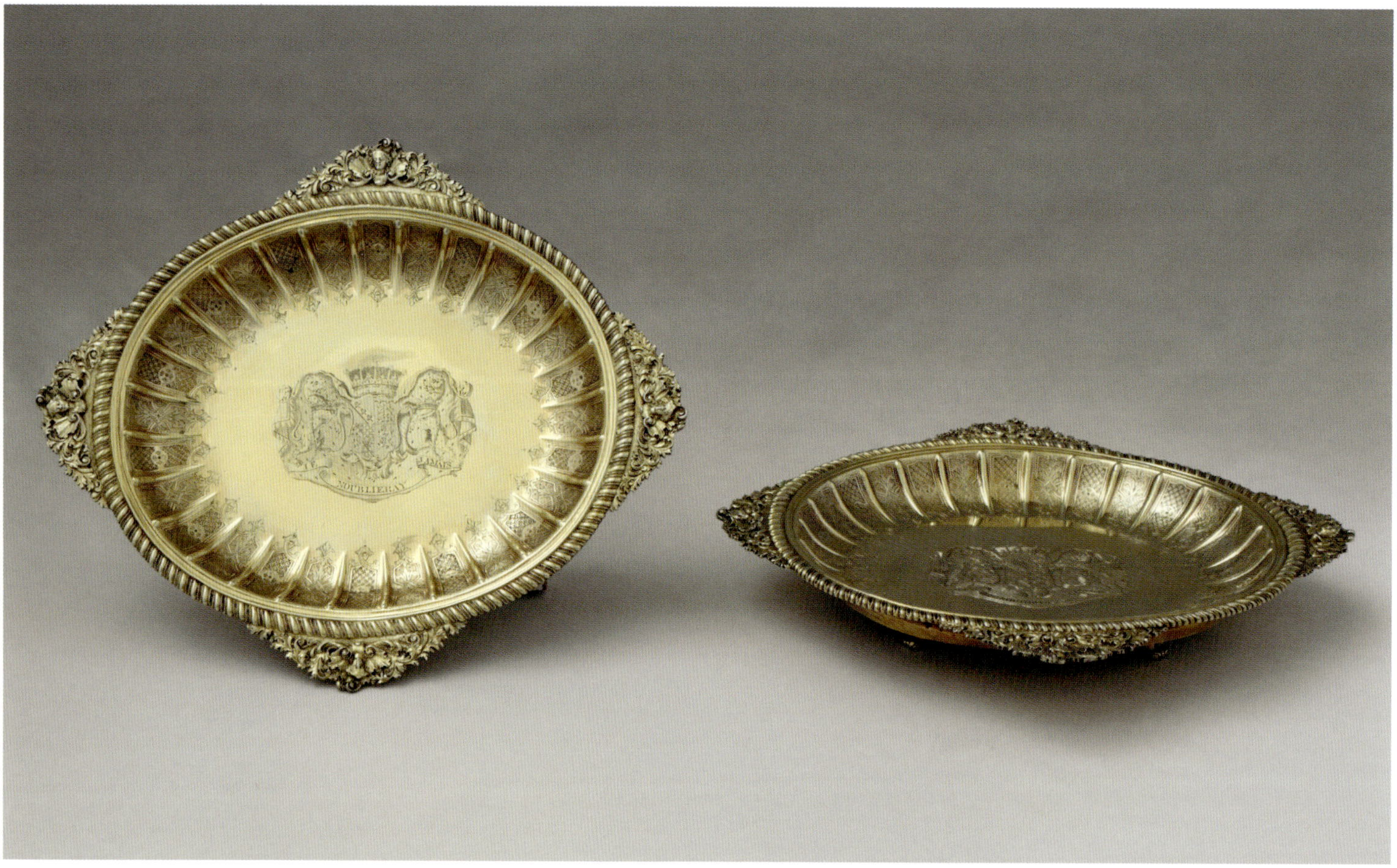

With the de Lamerie dish of 1724 (cat. 13) and that by Kandler of 1751 (cat. 28), this pair, which are near-exact copies, made up a set of four. It was probably at this point that all of them were gilded and turned over to use as part of Lord Bristol's now extensive dessert service. With dessert silver increasingly gilded, the number of dishes specifically allocated to the course increased. Thus in 1763 the Earl of Hertford received nine silver-gilt fruit dishes for his embassy to France, two years later his successor, the Duke of Richmond, had twelve and in 1783 the Duke of Manchester, on being dispatched to the same court, was allocated '20 Scollop'd Dest. [dessert] Dishes'.[1] Lord Bristol, from 1766, had twelve available and he was thus equipping himself for entertaining on an up-to-date ambassadorial scale whilst on the vice-regal throne. He was also assiduously keeping up with the rapidly changing dining fashions and he continued to do so, commissioning a further eight silver-gilt dishes in 1769–70 (cat. 89), bringing his total up to that subsequently to be received by the Duke of Manchester.

1. Jewel Office Delivery Book 1732–93, ff. 207, 238 and 317.

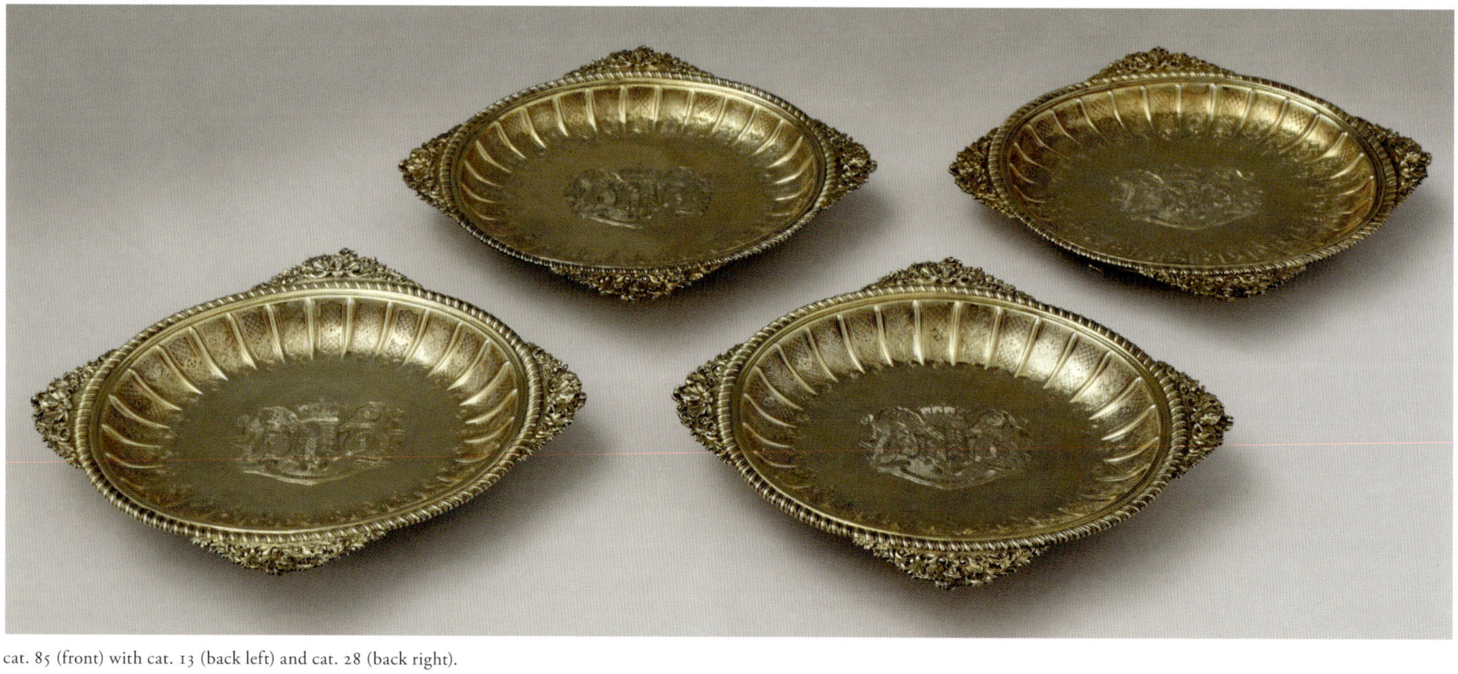

cat. 85 (front) with cat. 13 (back left) and cat. 28 (back right).

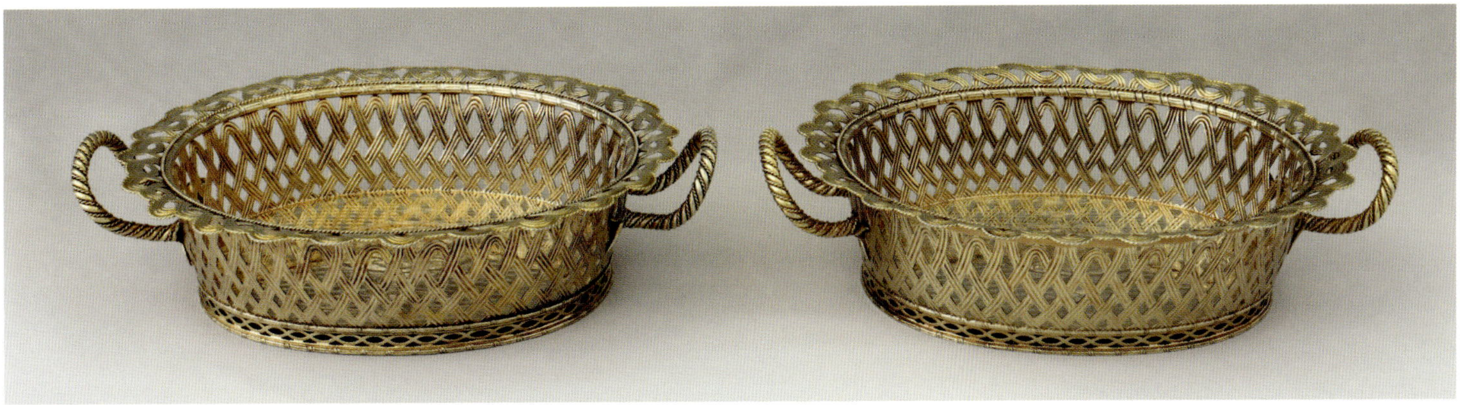

86. Two dessert baskets

Sterling silver, gilded / Frederick Kandler, London / 1768/9

MARKS: Each fully marked on the underside with date letter 'N', leopard's head, lion passant and maker's mark 'FK' in italics beneath a fleur-de-lis (Grimwade 1990, no. 692).

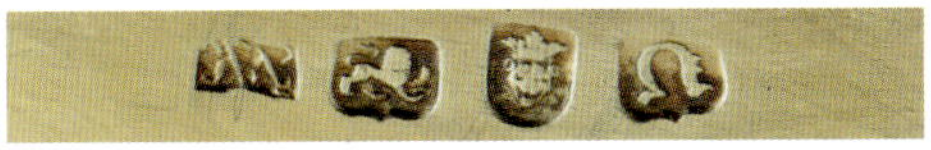

SCRATCHWEIGHTS: 'Nº 3 [/] 45=11'; 'Nº-4 [/] 45=14'.

MEASUREMENTS: h. 8.6 cm (3⅜ in); w. 30.8 cm (12⅛ in); d. 26.7 cm (10½ in).

INVENTORY: 852063.3–4

PROVENANCE: 2nd Earl of Bristol; by descent to the 4th Marquess.

LITERATURE: Penzer 1957a, I, p. 40, fig. III and p. 42; Banister 1980, p. 793.

EXHIBITED: *Ideal Home Exhibition*, London, 1960.

DESCRIPTION: As cat. 19.

HERALDRY: The centre of the floor of each basket is engraved with the quartered shield, supporters and motto of the 2nd Earl of Bristol in an ermine mantling and beneath an earl's coronet.

As he had done with the oval dishes (see cat. 85), Lord Bristol copied an existing pairing of de Lamerie (cat. 19) and Kandler (cat. 45) items to create his set of four silver-gilt dessert baskets. At the beginning of the eighteenth century the primary purpose of baskets was for fruit (see cat. 19), but from about 1720 that had changed and they are almost always thereafter referred to as for bread in inventories, the Jewel Office records and the Wickes ledgers. From the mid-1750s, however, baskets specifically for fruit re-emerged, though never in large numbers. The Countess of Pomfret received two from Wickes and Netherton in 1755 and the Countess of Mountrath one, gilded, in 1757.[1] Lord Bristol's provision was lavish and may have been occasioned by the introduction of the mirror plateau. With that in place in the centre of the table, it would not have been possible to accommodate the epergne, with its multiple baskets for fruit, and an alternative would thus have been needed.

1. Wickes ledgers, VAM 5 1750–4, f. 224 and VAM 6 1756–60, f. 115.

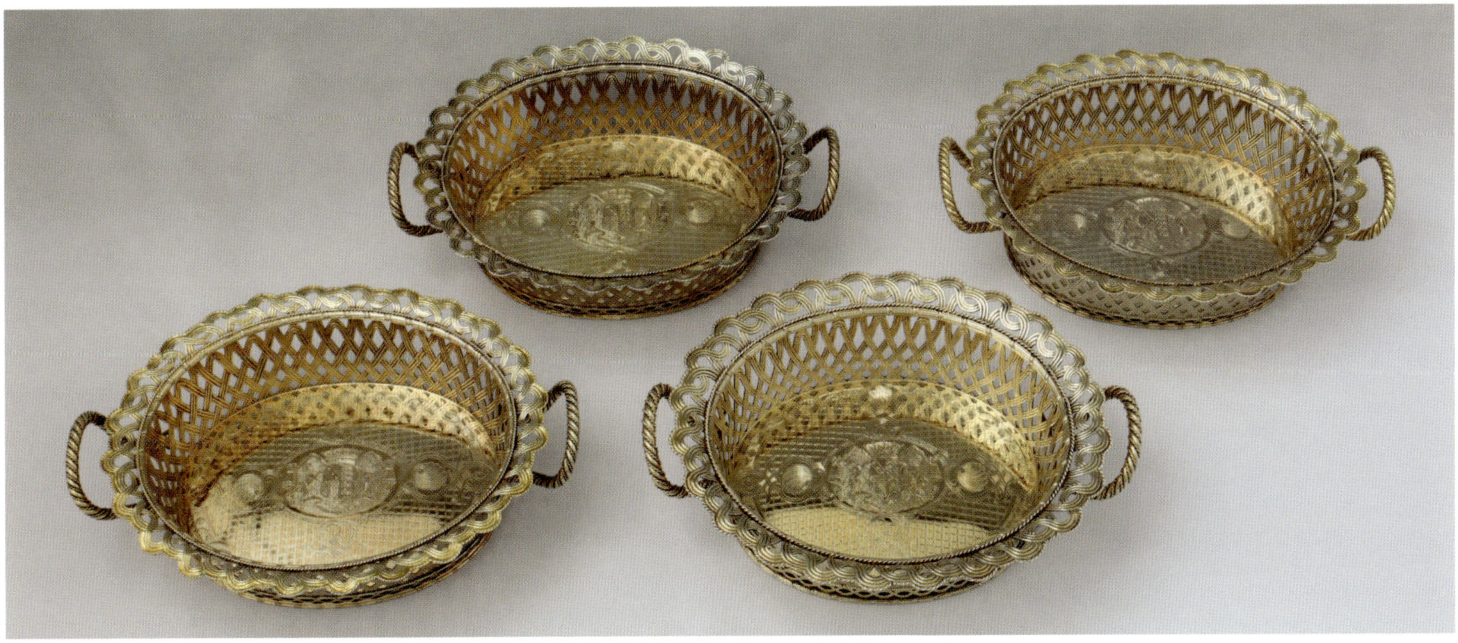

cat. 86 (front) with cat. 19 (back left) and cat. 45 (back right).

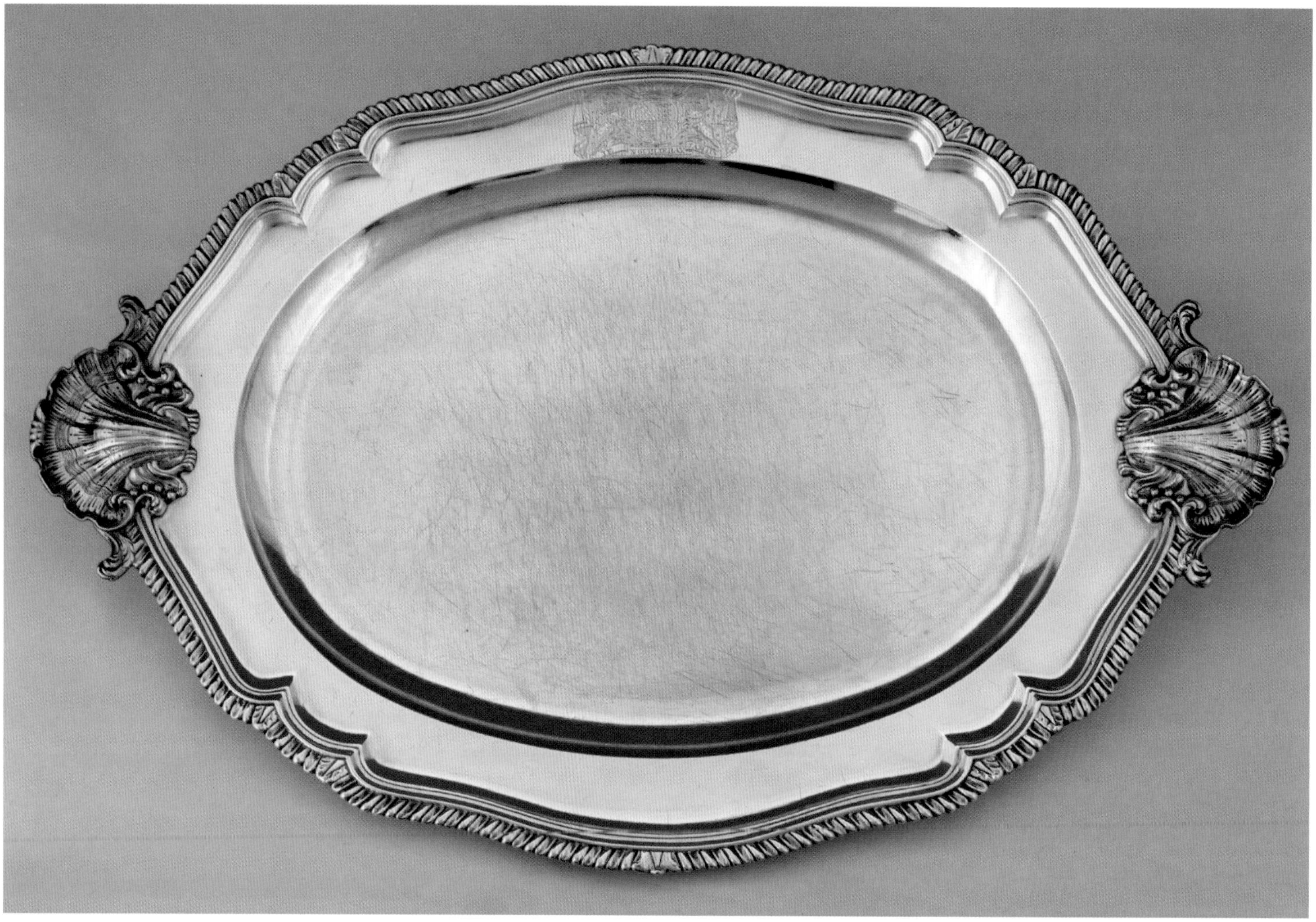

87. **Four large oval dishes**

Sterling silver / Frederick Kandler, London / 1768/9

MARKS: All are marked on the underside of the rim with date letter 'N', leopard's head, lion passant and maker's mark 'FK' in italics beneath a fleur-de-lis (Grimwade 1990, no. 692).

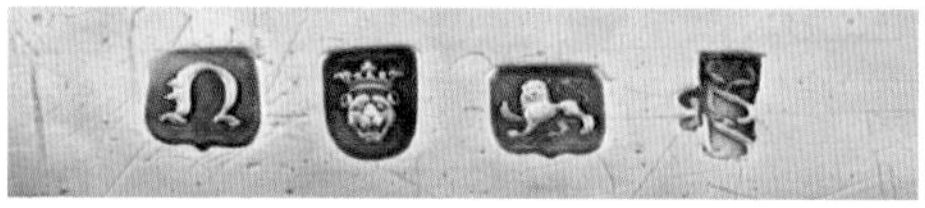

SCRATCHWEIGHTS: 'Nº =1 [/] 105=5'; 'Nº 2 [/] 104=17'; 'Nº 3 [/] 103=5'; 'Nº 4 [/] 100=18'.

MEASUREMENTS: h. 5.7 cm (2¼ in); w. 62.5 cm (24⅝ in); d. 42.9 cm (16⅞ in).

INVENTORY: 852095.3–6

PROVENANCE: 2nd Earl of Bristol; by descent to the 4th Marquess.

LITERATURE: Penzer 1957a, II, p. 137.

DESCRIPTION: The dishes are raised and have flat oval wells and broad rims with shaped borders applied with cast and chased gadrooning. Two large cast and chased shells are applied to each as handles.

HERALDRY: Each rim is engraved with the quartered shield, supporters and motto of the 2nd Earl of Bristol in an ermine mantling and beneath an earl's coronet.

These are the largest of Lord Bristol's dishes and they would have been used for the roasts which would have replaced soup during the first course of dinner, and also for the principal offerings of the second course. These at the 1st Viscount Jocelyn's dinner of 1 July 1747 were '6 Grous Poults Lard[ed] and Barded' at one end of the table and '4: feasant Poults: 2 Larded' at the other (fig. 96).[1]

Lord Bristol must have had a provision of large dishes prior to 1768, in addition to the two for which there were mazarines (cat. 33), and it would seem unlikely that they were lost in the evacuation from Madrid, as if so they would have been replaced earlier on. It could be that they were old anyway in 1751, adapted by the addition of shell handles, and that the heavy use in the subsequent two decades, plus long-distance transportation, led to the need to renew them. This is corroborated by the fact that the payment in Lord Bristol's bank account which must relate to these and to four dish covers (cat. 88), £85 6s to Frederick Kandler on 13 March 1770,[2] is only about a third of what would have been needed. The rest must have been made up with old plate.

1. Jocelyn Dinner Book, f. 216.
2. Goslings ledgers, 130/43, f. 95.

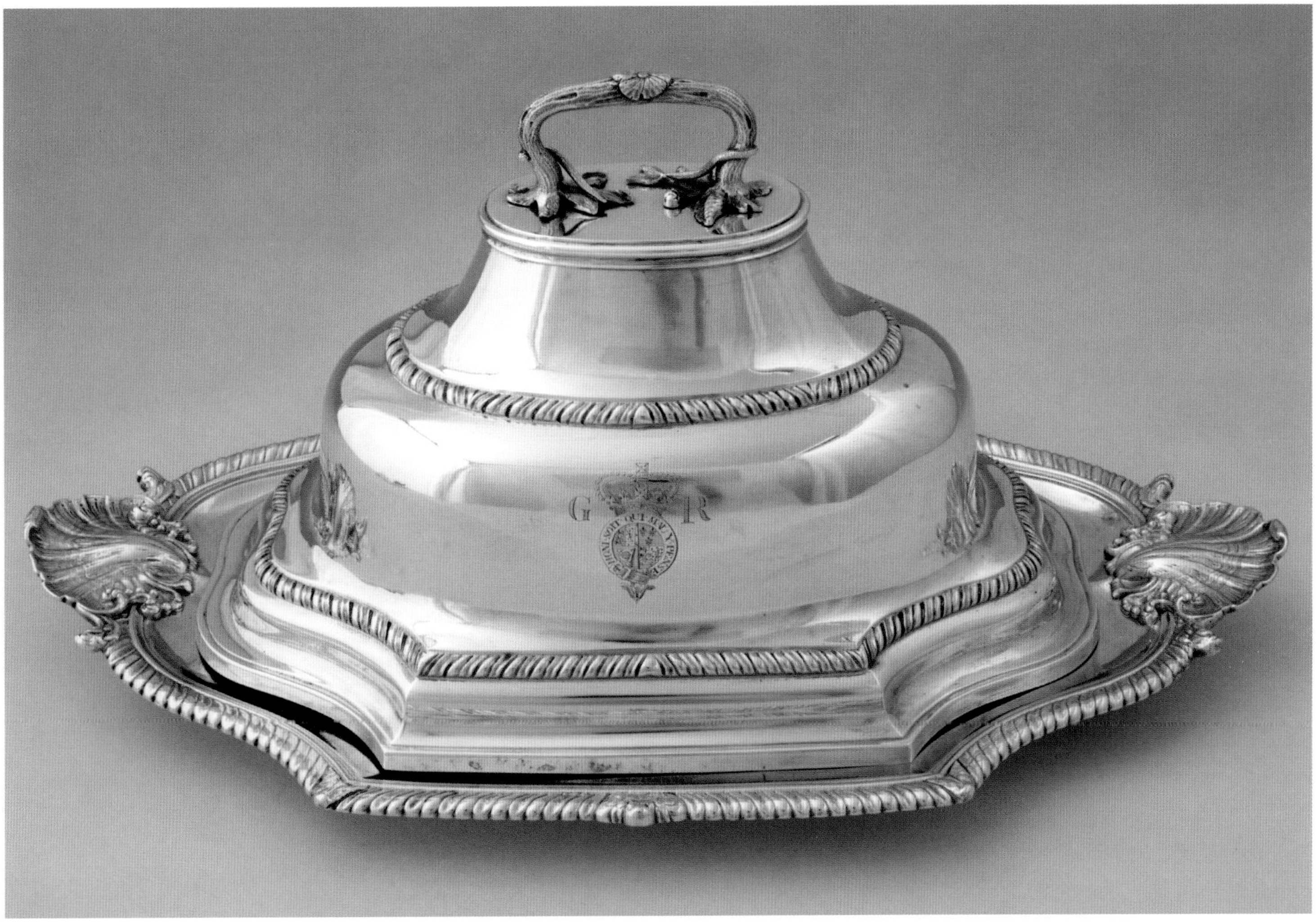

cat. 88 on cat. 38

88. **Four dish covers**

Sterling silver / Frederick Kandler, London / 1768/9

MARKS: All are marked on the external face of the rim of the covers with maker's mark 'FK' in italics beneath a fleur-de-lis (Grimwade 1990, no. 692), lion passant, leopard's head and date letter 'N'.

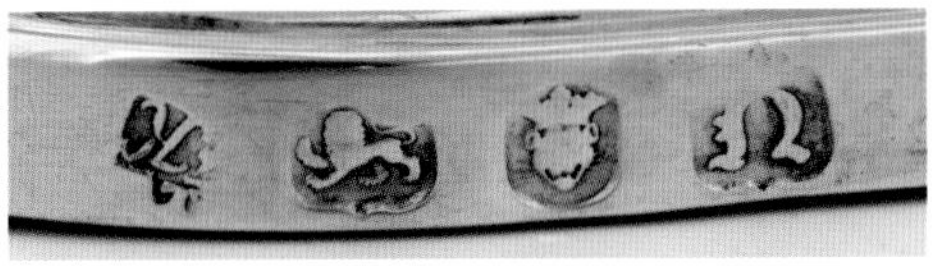

SCRATCHWEIGHTS: 'N° 1 = 33 6'; 'N° 2 = 32=12'; 'N° 3 = 33=5'; 'N°-4 - 33=7'

MEASUREMENTS: h. 4.4cm (1¾ in); w. 42.2 cm (16⅝ in); d. 25.4 cm (10 in).

INVENTORY: 852110.1.2, 2.2, 3.2 and 4.2.

PROVENANCE: 2nd Earl of Bristol; by descent to the 4th Marquess.

DESCRIPTION: The covers are raised and have stepped bases conforming to the lobed dishes with straight sides with which they are associated (cat. 38). The bases terminate in a chased band of gadrooning and the covers rise as oval convex domes to another chased gadroon band, then rise again in reverse form to an applied flat top plate, the joint concealed by a cast and seamed moulding. The cast and chased tendril handles are capped by single flowers and held on by silver bolts and nuts.

HERALDRY: The covers are engraved on one side only with the quartered arms of the Hanoverian monarchs (pre-1801) within the Garter and beneath an imperial crown flanked by the letters GR.

Given that only eight of the twenty covers supplied in 1758 survive, these four could be replacements for some of them, perhaps necessitated by damage or wear and tear. If that was the case it would explain the royal arms, but they could equally well have been engraved merely to match the existing covers.

89. Eight dessert dishes

Sterling silver, gilded / Frederick Kandler, London / 1769/70 (pincushion) and 1770/1 (round)

MARKS: All are marked on their undersides with maker's mark 'FK' in italics beneath a fleur-de-lis (Grimwade 1990, no. 692), lion passant, leopard's head and date letters 'O' (pincushion) and 'P' (round).

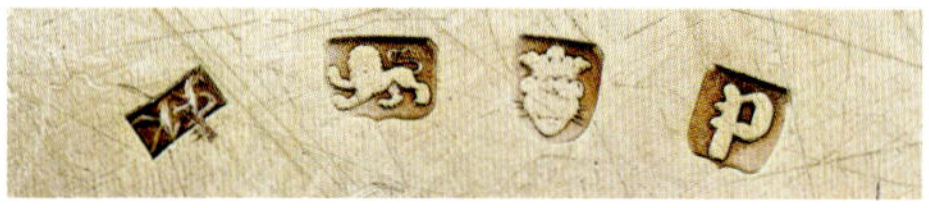

SCRATCHWEIGHTS: Pincushion dishes only 'N° 5 [/] 21=17'; 'N° 6 [/] 22=1'; 'N° 7 [/] 21=11'; 'N° 8 [/] 21=16'.
Actual weights: (round dishes) 599 g (19 oz, 5 dwt); 593 g (19 oz, 1 dwt); 596 g (19 oz, 3 dwt); 612 g (19 oz, 14 dwt).

MEASUREMENTS: Pincushion h. 2.5cm (1 in); w. 23.8 cm (9⅜ in); d. 21.3 cm (8⅜ in). Round h. 3.8 cm (1¼ in); diam. 23.5 cm (9¼ in).

INVENTORY: Pincushion 852067.5–8. Round 852101.5-8

PROVENANCE: 2nd Earl of Bristol; by descent to the 4th Marquess.

LITERATURE: Penzer 1957a, 1, p. 43.

DESCRIPTION: As cat. 77.

HERALDRY: The centre of each dish is engraved with the quartered arms of the Hanoverian monarchs (pre-1801) within the Garter and beneath an imperial crown flanked by the letters GR.

These match exactly the eight dishes made by Simon Le Sage in 1758 (cat. 77). As with the dish covers (cat. 88) they may have been exchanged for some of the ambassadorial plate, hence the royal arms. Certainly, the payment to Frederick Kandler which must relate to them, £29 3s on 30 March 1771, would not have been sufficient on its own.[1] They are likely to have cost at least 10s 6d per ounce, totalling £90 or so.[2]

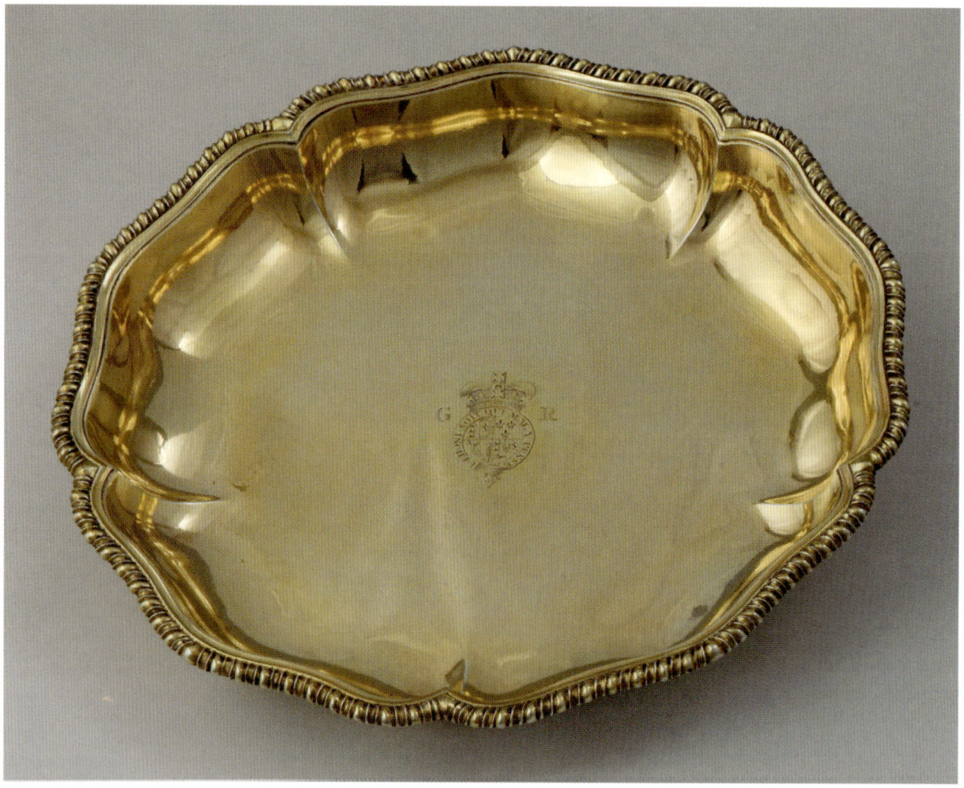

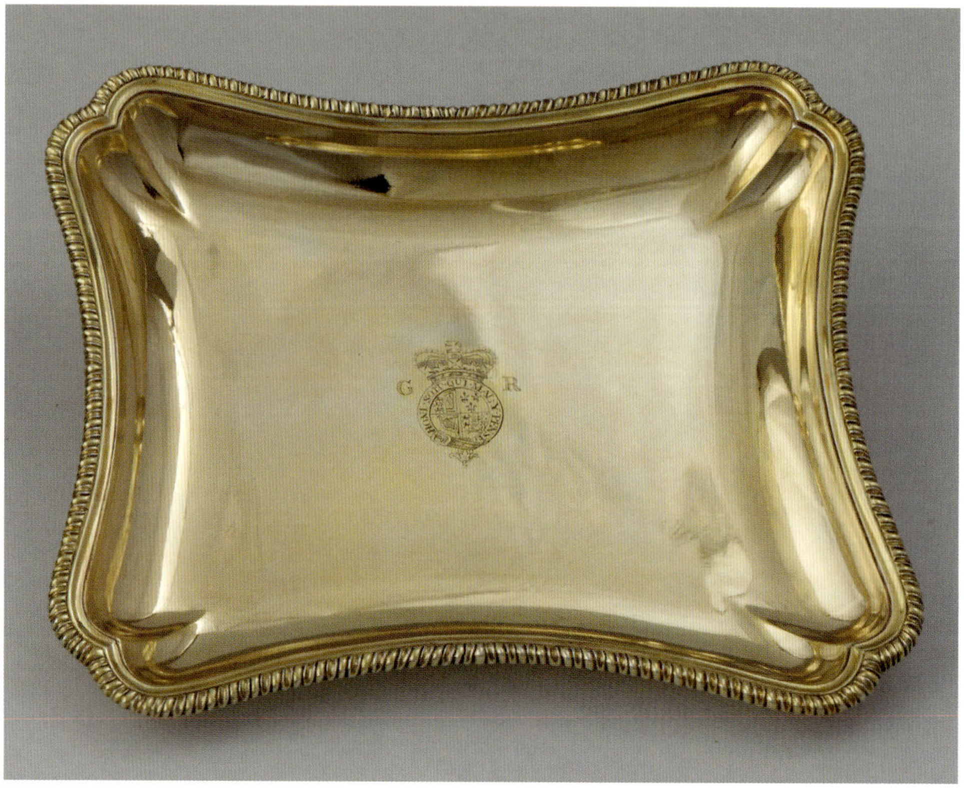

1. Goslings ledgers, 130/43, f. 97.
2. The Jewel Office paid 10 6d for Lord Bristol's silver-gilt in 1758. See Jewel Office Plate Book 1728–67, f. 166.

PART FOUR

SILVER OF FREDERICK HERVEY 4TH EARL OF BRISTOL (1730–1803)

90. **Six dessert knives**

Sterling silver hafts / London, 1790/1 / Twentieth-century steel blades

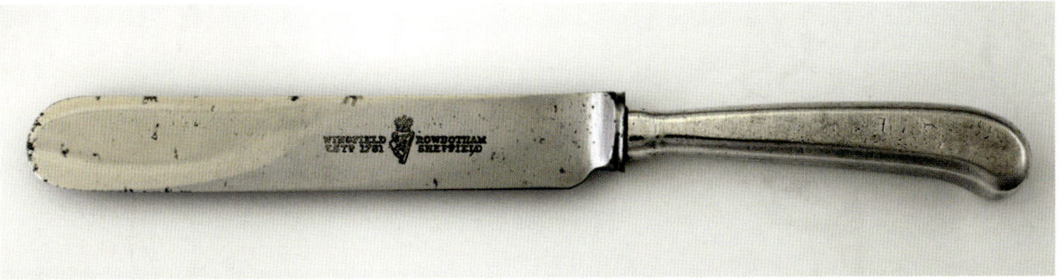

MARKS: Very worn but a full set is legible on one and comprises the lion passant, leopard's head, date letter 'p', monarch's head and maker's mark 'FH' in a heart-shaped punch (not identified). The blades are stamped with a harp flanked by 'Wingfield Rowbotham' and 'Estd – 1751 Sheffield'.

MEASUREMENTS: l. (of haft) 7.9 cm (3⅛ in).

INVENTORY: 852206

PROVENANCE: 4th Earl of Bristol; by descent to the 4th Marquess.

DESCRIPTION: Plain pistol-shaped hafts and later straight steel blades with rounded ends. They have been very well used and are in poor condition.

HERALDRY: Each haft is engraved on the left side with the Hervey crest beneath an earl's coronet. The engraving is very worn.

The pistol handles are very old-fashioned for 1790 and must have been specified by the 4th Earl, perhaps to match existing tableware commissioned in his youth. Twelve survive of which half passed to the National Trust in 1956.[1] The blades were made for far larger handles.

These are amongst the few items of silver commissioned by the 4th Earl of Bristol that passed to his son, the future 1st Marquess. As everything that could be left away from him was, passing with Downhill in Co. Londonderry to Sir Henry Bruce, 1st Bt, they must have been in England at the Earl's death in 1803 and treated as heirlooms.

1. Death duties list *c.*1951, p. 16.

91. Four chamber candlesticks

Sterling silver / John Scofield, London / 1791/2

MARKS: Fully marked on their undersides with the monarch's head, lion passant, leopard's head, date letter 'q' and maker's mark 'I·S' in a punch shaped as conjoined circles (Grimwade 1990, no. 1670). One lacks the maker's mark where repaired. Also marked on the nozzles (except on one which is a replacement) and on the extinguishers with the same marks except for the leopard's head.

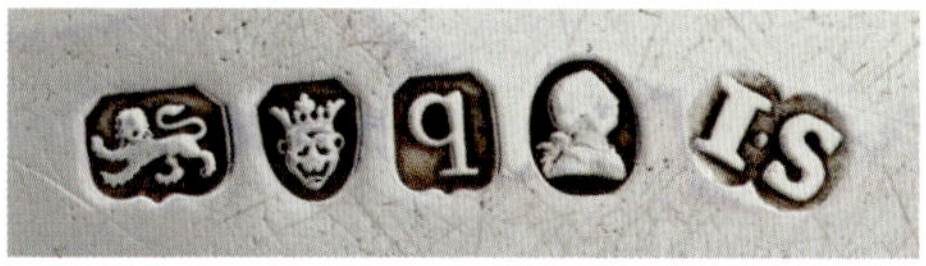

SCRATCHWEIGHTS: none.

Actual weights: 277g (8 oz, 18 dwt); 299g (9 oz, 12 dwt); 302g (9 oz, 14 dwt); 303g (9 oz, 15 dwt).

MEASUREMENTS: h. 8.9 cm (3½ in); diam. (of base) 14 cm (5½ in).

INVENTORY: 852189.7–10

PROVENANCE: Probably 4th Earl of Bristol; by descent to the 4th Marquess.

DESCRIPTION: The circular concave saucer bases are raised with applied cast borders of reeding, scroll handles and slightly domed centres. Concave profiled stems are formed of two cast sections between which is a slot for snuffers (missing) and support circular, vase-shaped sockets in which are seamed nozzles with concave drip pans. The sockets and drip pans have applied reeded borders as do the cone-shaped extinguishers topped by cast and applied vase-shaped finials. The extinguishers also have applied S-shaped scroll handles and L-shaped hooks by which they are secured into sockets attached to the thumb-pieces of the base handles. One of the nozzles is a replacement and has the reeded moulding applied beneath the rim.

HERALDRY: Each base, nozzle and extinguisher is engraved with the Hervey crest beneath an earl's coronet.

Chamber or hand candlesticks were intended for moving from room to room in the dark and seem to have been personal items in the first half of the eighteenth century, with which the owner would have travelled. Thus at Dunham Massey in 1750/54 there was only one 'Hand Candlestick' and that was part of the 2nd Earl of Warrington's own chamber plate. It does not survive, but his granddaughter's of 1754 by Magdalen Feline does and is inscribed underneath 'The Lady Mary Grey'.[1] By the late eighteenth century sets of chamber candlesticks began to be provided in wealthy households and the number available increased over time. These may well have been the first such set for the St James's Square house, in which Lord Bristol made occasional stays in 1791–2, between his protracted Continental wanderings.[2]

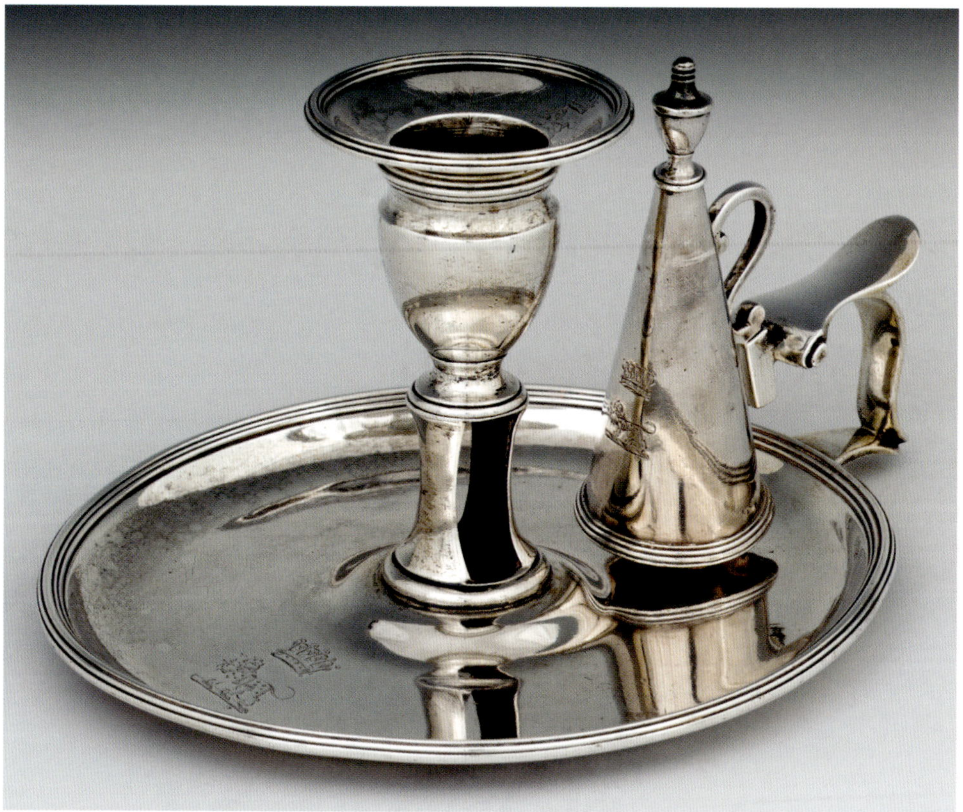

1. Lomax and Rothwell 2006, cat. 75, pp. 146–7.
2. Fothergill 1974, pp. 131–2, 147 and 149.

PART FIVE

SILVER OF JOHN AUGUSTUS, LORD HERVEY (1757–96)

92. Coffee pot

Sterling silver, gilded / Abraham Peterson and Peter Podio, London / 1788/9

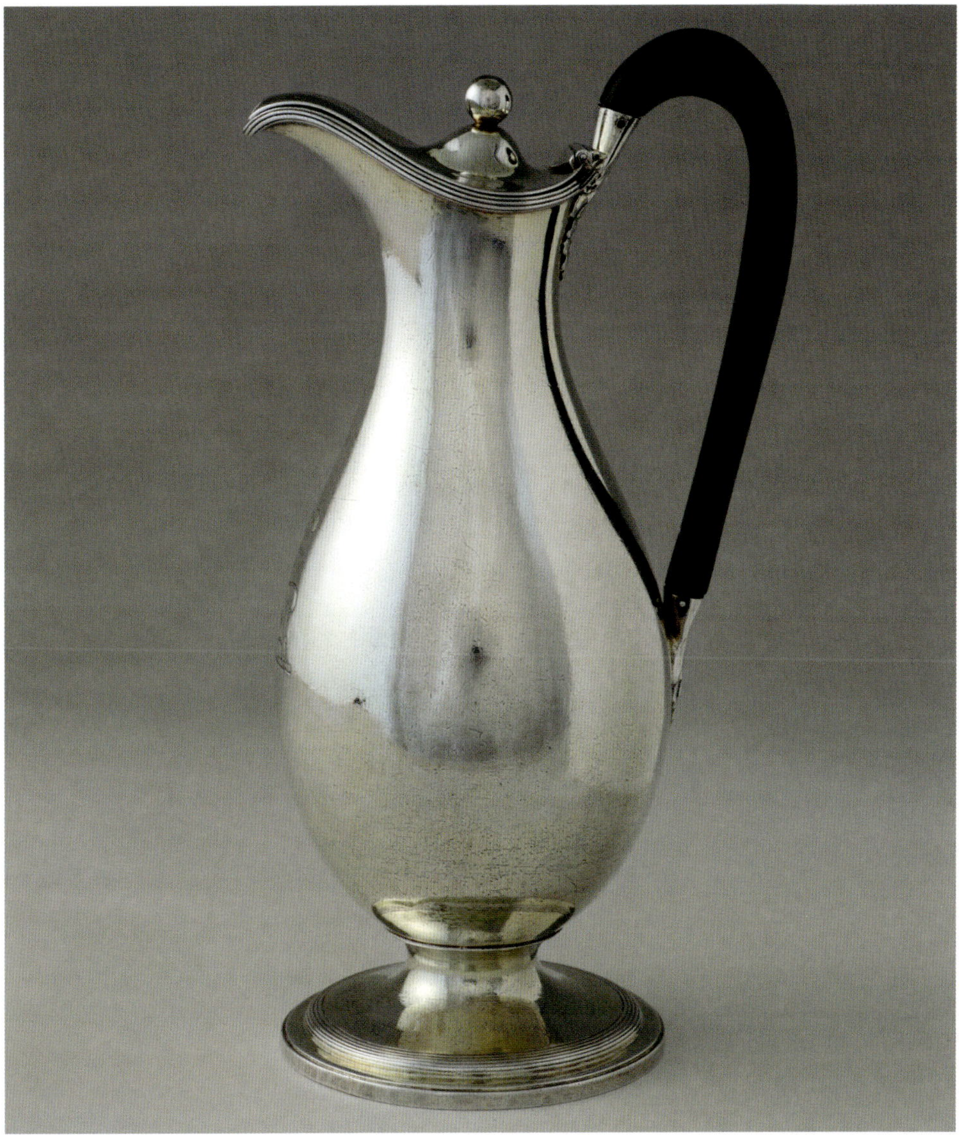

MARKS: Fully marked on the underside with maker's mark 'AP' over 'PP' in a square punch with cut corners (Grimwade 1990, no. 80), lion passant, leopard's head, date letter 'n' and monarch's head. The underside of the lid is marked with the same maker's mark and the lion passant.

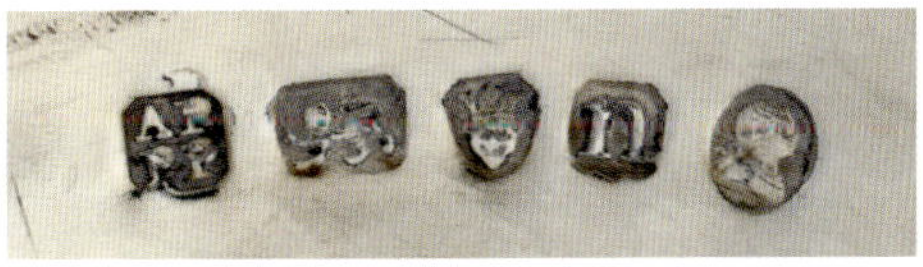

SCRATCHWEIGHT: None.
Actual weight: (incl. handle) 737 g (23 oz, 14 dwt).

MEASUREMENTS: h. 28.6 cm (11¼ in); w. (incl. handle) 14.6 cm (5¾ in); diam. 11.4 cm (4½ in).

INVENTORY: 852111

PROVENANCE: John Augustus, Lord Hervey; by descent to the 4th Marquess of Bristol.

LITERATURE: Penzer 1957a, II, p. 136.

DESCRIPTION: The pear shaped body is raised, splaying slightly at the top and being formed into a broad, beak-shaped pouring lip on one side. A cast reeded moulding is applied to the rim and the curved wooden handle is connected by two silver pinned sockets which terminate in cast acanthus leaves. The domed and curving lid is raised and has a cast ball finial and a five-part pin hinge connected to the rim. The circular, raised foot is stepped and has a cast reeded moulding. The gilding is badly worn and the exposed surface of the silver is pitted.

HERALDRY: The front of the pot is engraved with the Hervey crest beneath a baron's coronet for John Augustus, Lord Hervey (1757–96).

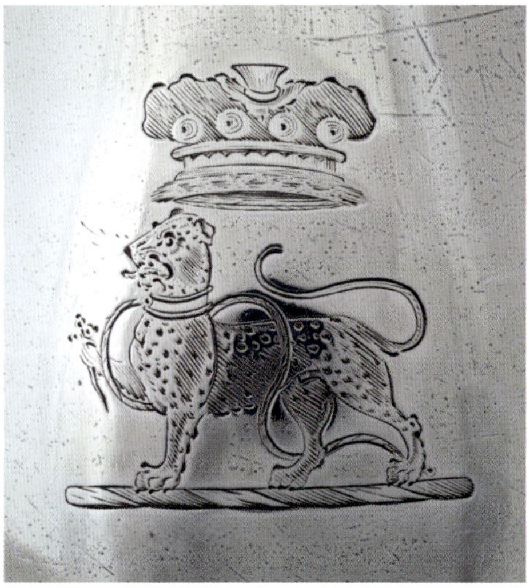

This handsome, neoclassical coffee pot must have been commissioned by Lord Hervey for use in Florence where he went as Envoy to the Grand Duchy of Tuscany in 1787. He stayed for seven years but his temper and indiscretions, including calling the Grand Duke a fool and his chief minister a knave, resulted in his recall in 1793. His brother, the future 1st Marquess, was given special permission by William Pitt the Younger to deliver the news to the temperamental Lord Hervey personally so as to soften the blow, and he may have arranged for the silver, including this coffee pot, to be returned to England.[1]

The pot can be seen in use in the *c.*1870 photograph of the family at breakfast in the library at Ickworth (fig. 48).

1. Fothergill 1974, pp. 155–7.

93. Dessert service

Sterling silver, gilded / George Smith III and William Fearn, London / 1788/9

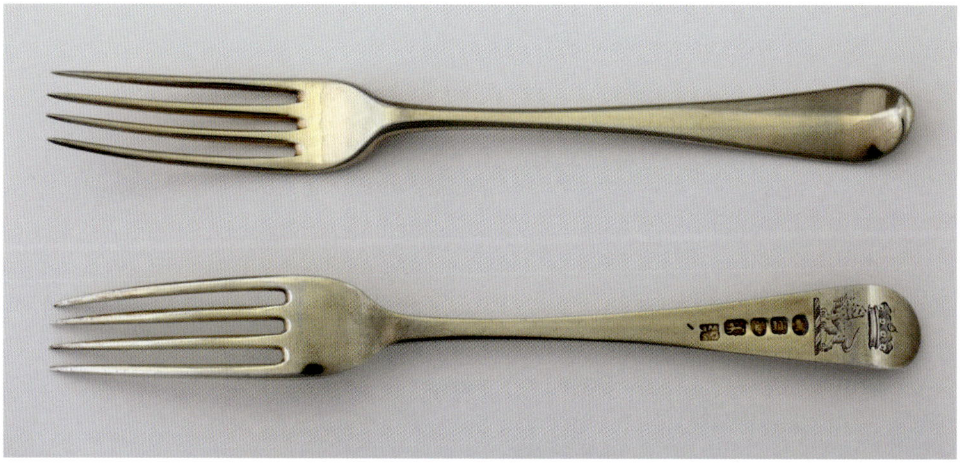

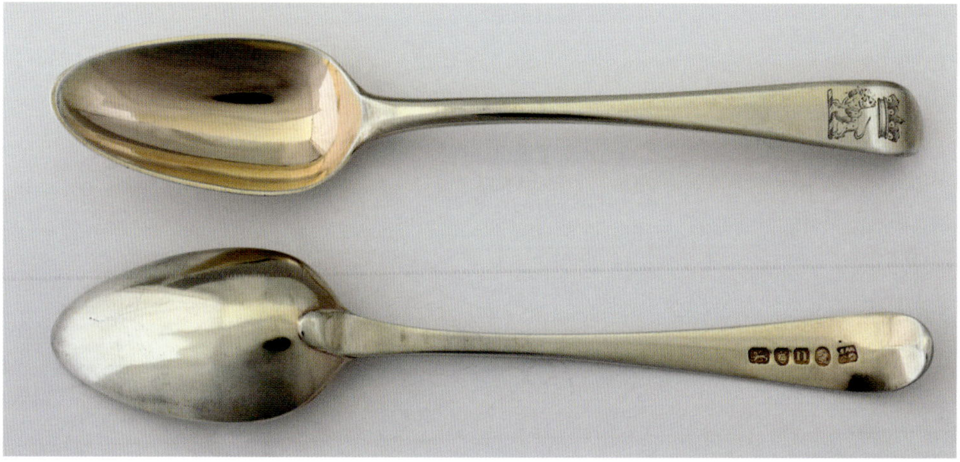

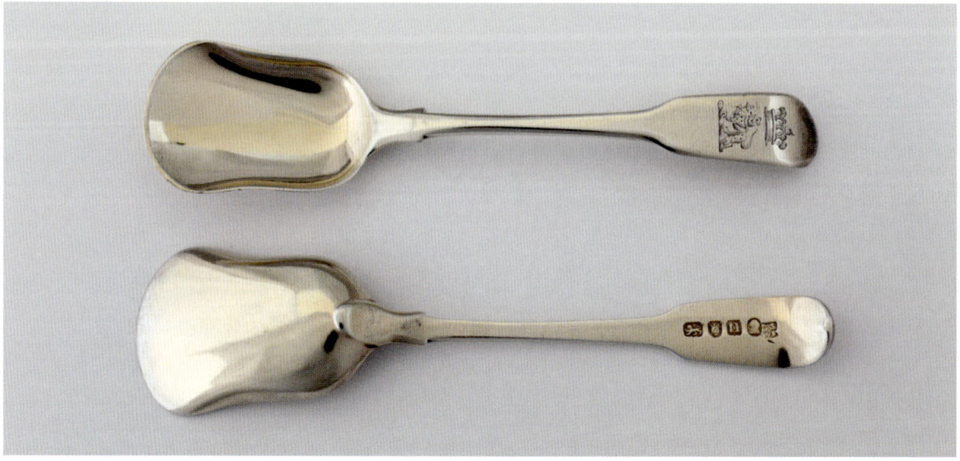

MARKS: Each piece is fully marked on the reverse of the handle at the terminal end with lion passant, leopard's head, date letter 'n', monarch's head and maker's mark 'GS' over 'WF' in a square punch (Grimwade 1990, no. 910).

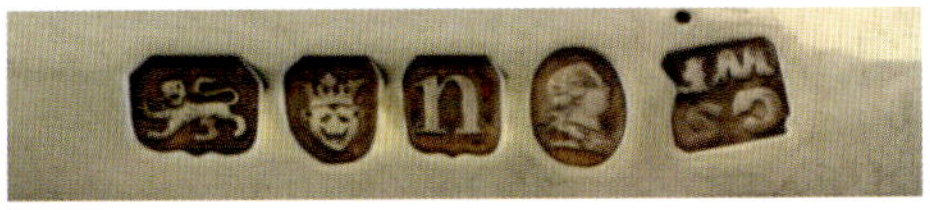

SCRATCHWEIGHTS: None. This is combined with the 1803 service (cat. 100) in the 1811 plate list so it is not possible to extrapolate a weight from that document.

MEASUREMENTS: (l.) forks 17.8 cm (7 in); spoons 17.8 cm (7 in); ice spades 14.3 cm (5⅝ in).

INVENTORY: 852198.7–12 (forks), 852198.1–6 (spoons) and 852201 (ice spades).

PROVENANCE: John Augustus, Lord Hervey; by descent to the 4th Marquess of Bristol.

LITERATURE: Penzer 1957a, I, p. 43.

DESCRIPTION: The service consists of six each of silver-gilt dessert forks and spoons of plain Old English pattern and six ice spades of fiddle pattern.

HERALDRY: The front of the terminals of the spoons and the reverse of the forks are engraved with the Hervey crest beneath a baron's coronet for John Augustus, Lord Hervey.

In 1811 these formed part of a mixed service of four dozen spoons and forks and thirty ice spoons or spades. Most were probably of this date and pattern plus some of fiddle thread which were added with the knives in 1803 (see cat. 100). This would have allowed for up to forty-eight guests at dinner or, perhaps more likely for such a large number, at a ball supper or other evening entertainment. The spades were for eating ice creams and sorbets which had become increasingly popular during the course of the eighteenth century. They seem to have been made from around 1780 and these are some of the earliest surviving examples. None are recorded in the Jewel Office records before 1784 when the 3rd Duke of Dorset as ambassador to France received two dozen 'Ice Ladles'. Thereafter they were a staple part of diplomatic allocations and later the same year the term 'ice spades' was used for the first time for the set of sixteen taken to The Hague by the brilliant diplomatist, Sir James Harris (later 1st Earl of Malmesbury).[1]

Since the 2nd Earl of Bristol had acquired his dessert flatware in 1758 it had become fashionable to lay spoons with the bowl upwards and those of this service are consequently engraved on the front of the terminal. Forks, however, continued to be laid with the tines facing down so the location of their engraving, on the reverse of the terminal, did not change. This meant that for a while both pieces of flatware were arranged in the position in which they were to be used, but by the mid-nineteenth century forks too were reversed, probably in order to prevent damage to the linen and the polished surface of the table as the tines were made, and kept, much sharper than is the custom today.

Lord Hervey acquired a matching table service at the same time, but that and the rest of the dessert service were retained by the family in 1956.[2]

1. Jewel Office Delivery Book 1732–93, ff. 320–1.
2. Probate valuation 1952, p. 28. At that time there were 17 spoons and 11 forks in the table service. Much of the remainder of the dessert service was sold Sotheby's Suffolk, 11–12 June 1996, East Wing Ickworth, lot 324.

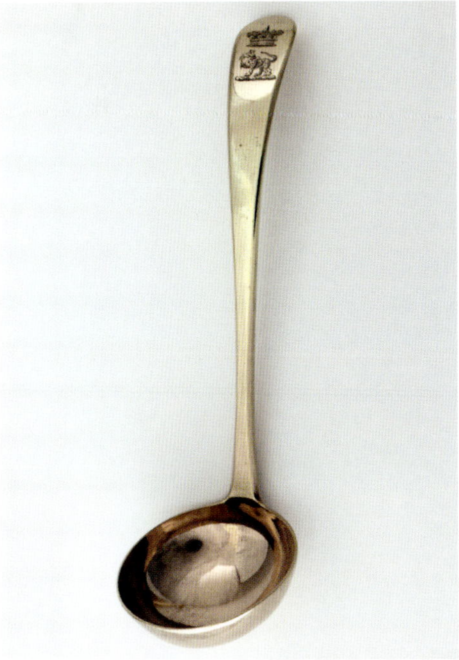

94. Cream ladle

Sterling silver, gilded / Wildman Smith, London / 1788/9

MARKS: Marked on the reverse of the stem with date letter 'n', monarch's head and maker's mark 'W·S' in an oval (Grimwade 1990, no. 3316).

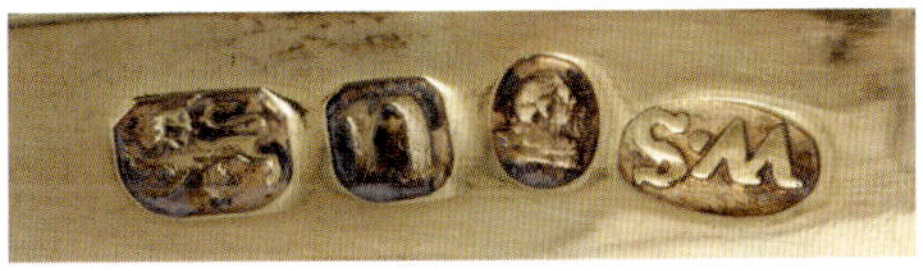

SCRATCHWEIGHT: None.
Actual weight: 18 g (0 oz, 12 dwt).

MEASUREMENTS: l. 12.7 cm (2.54 in).

INVENTORY: 852200

PROVENANCE: John Augustus, Lord Hervey; by descent to the 4th Marquess of Bristol.

LITERATURE: Penzer 1957a, I, p. 43.

DESCRIPTION: A near hemispherical raised bowl is from the same rod of silver that was forged into the plain, Old English pattern handle.

HERALDRY: The front of the handle terminal is engraved with the Hervey crest beneath a baron's coronet for John Augustus, Lord Hervey.

This ladle, with two others listed in 1811, formed part of Lord Hervey's dessert service.

PART SIX

SILVER OF FREDERICK WILLIAM HERVEY, 5TH EARL AND 1ST MARQUESS OF BRISTOL (1769–1859)

95. **Two chamber candlesticks**

Sterling silver / John Edwards III, London / 1795/6 and 1798/9

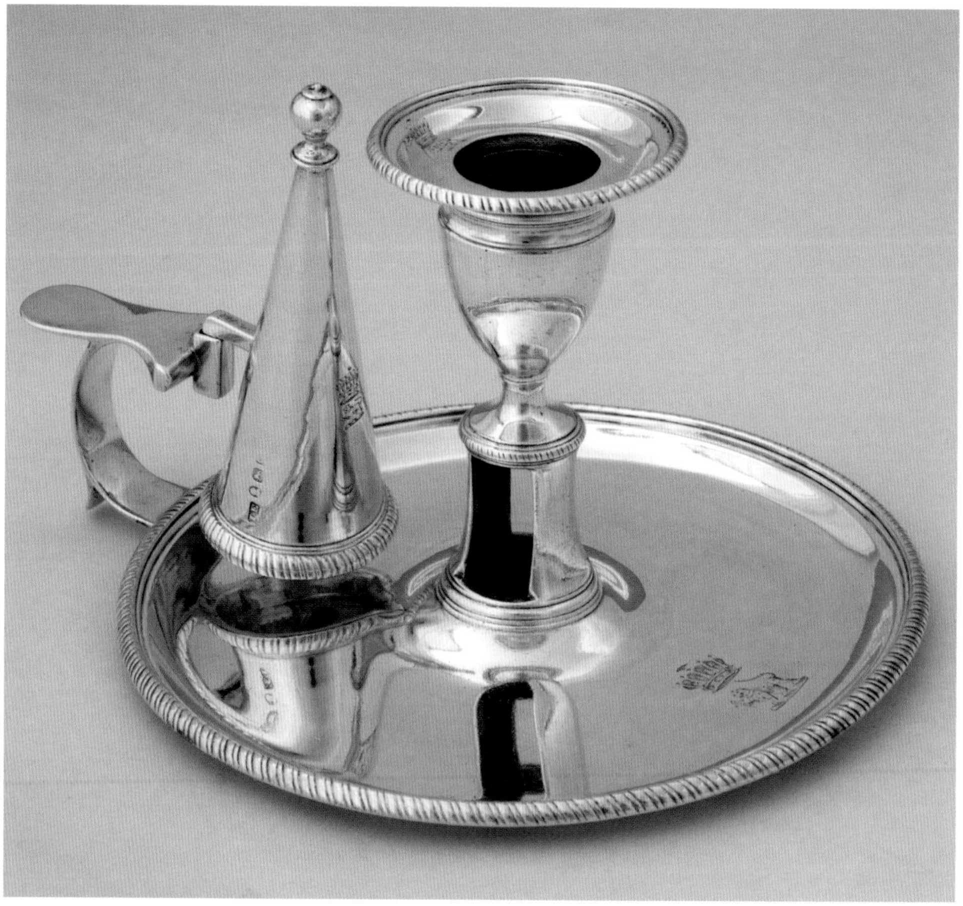

MARKS: Both are fully marked on the underside of the saucer with maker's mark 'I·E' in a rectangular punch with cut corners (Grimwade 1990, no. 1273), lion passant, leopard's head, date letters 'u' and 'C' and monarch's head. The extinguishers and nozzles all have the same marks excepting the leopard's head. The socket rims, nozzle sleeves and extinguish-ers have either one or two notches to indicate the correct groupings.

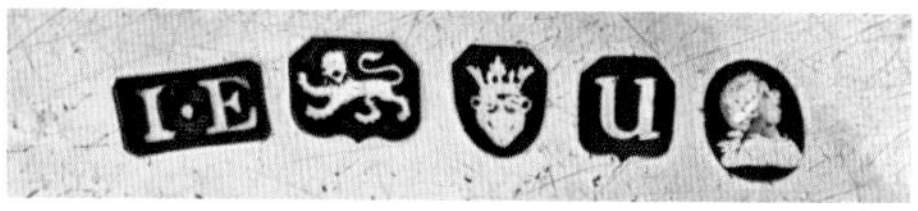

SCRATCHWEIGHTS: None.
Actual weights: 343 g (11 oz, 1 dwt); 349 g (11 oz, 4 dwt).

MEASUREMENTS: h. 9.5 cm (3¾ in); w. (with handle) 15.9 cm (6¼ in); diam. (of saucer) 14 cm (5½ in).

INVENTORY: 852189.1–2

PROVENANCE: 1st Marquess of Bristol; by descent to the 4th Marquess.

DESCRIPTION: The circular concave saucer bases are raised with applied cast gadroon borders, scroll handles and slightly domed centres. The concave profiled stems are formed of two cast sections between which is a slot for snuffers (missing) and support cast circular, vase-shaped sockets with chased gadrooning to their feet. The seamed nozzles have concave drip pans with applied cast gadroon borders. The cone-shaped extinguishers with cast ball finials and gadrooned rims also have applied L-shaped hooks by which they are secured into sockets attached to the thumb-pieces of the base handles.

HERALDRY: Each saucer, nozzle and extinguisher is engraved with the Hervey crest beneath an earl's coronet.

These were probably bought from stock by the 5th Earl shortly after inheriting in 1803, either to augment the set of four acquired by his father in 1791 (cat. 91) for St James's Square or for use at Ickworth. Apart from their gadrooned borders they are of the same form. An additional eight chamber sticks were acquired in 1811 (cat. 110).

96. Inkstand

Sterling silver / John Emes, London / 1798/9

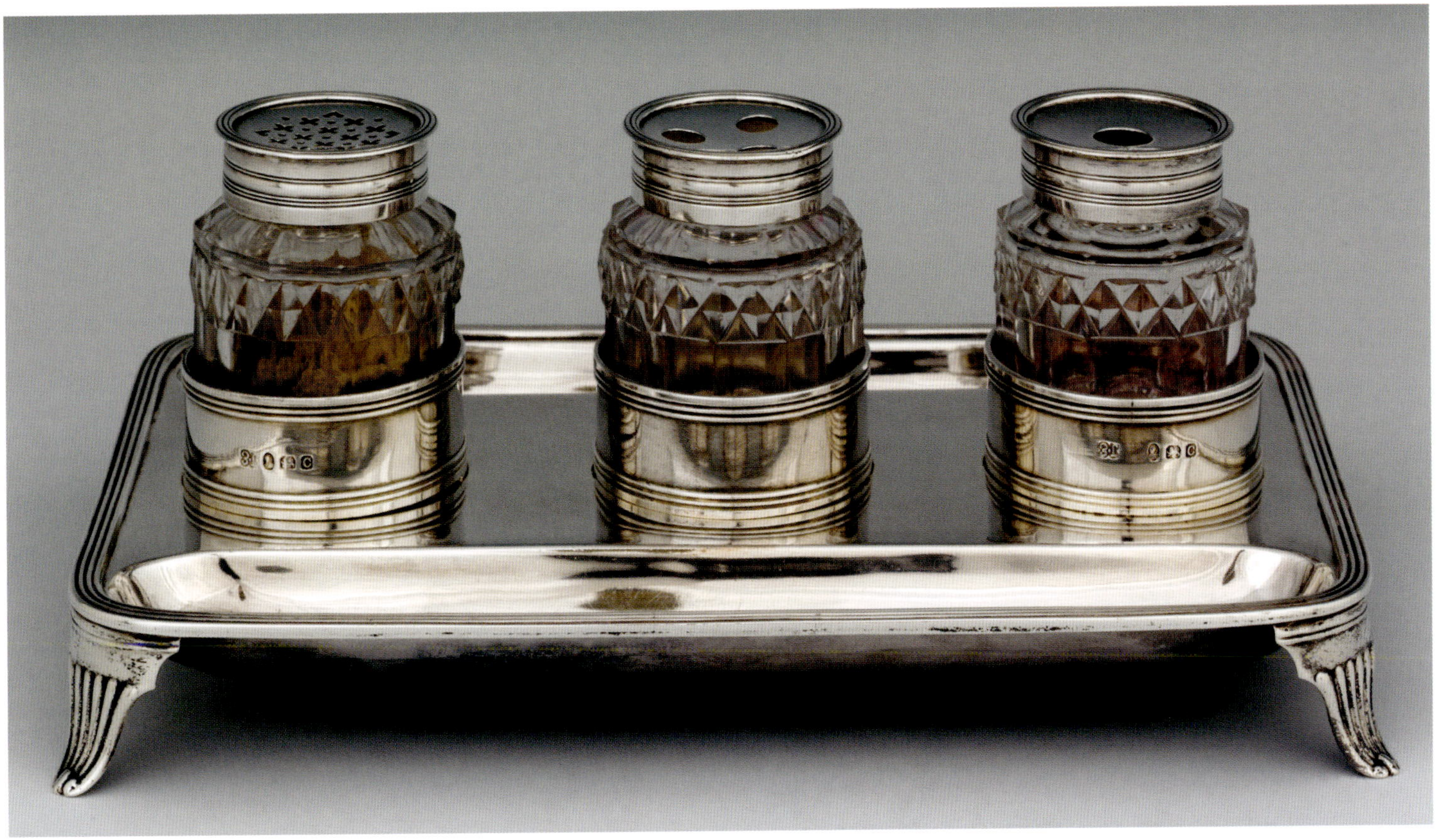

MARKS: Fully marked on the underside with maker's mark on base 'J·E' in a shaped punch (Grimwade 1990, no. 1807), lion passant, leopard's head, date letter 'C' and monarch's head. The holders for the three bottles are marked on their sides with the maker's mark, date letter 'C' and the lion passant and the bottle tops have the same plus the monarch's head.

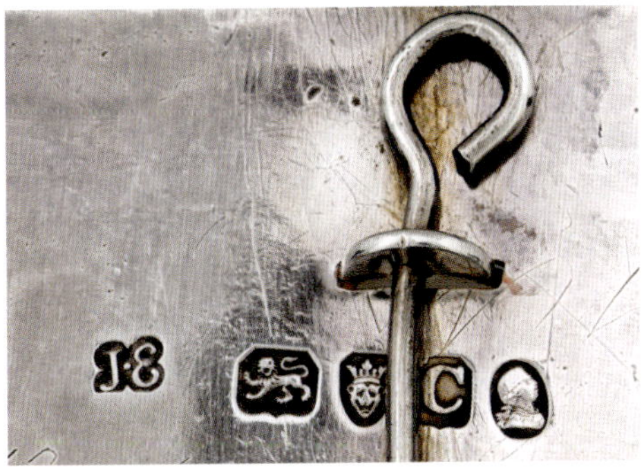

SCRATCHWEIGHT: '13"19'

MEASUREMENTS: h. 7.9 cm (3⅛ in); w. 21 cm (8¼ in); d. 14.6 cm (5¾ in).

INVENTORY: 852188

PROVENANCE: Elizabeth Albana Upton, Lady Hervey (subsequently Countess and Marchioness of Bristol) (1775–1844); by descent to the 4th Marquess.

LITERATURE: Penzer 1957, II, p. 136.

DESCRIPTION: The inkstand is formed of a plain rectangular tray with rounded corners which is raised and has two inverted pen trays. It rests on four cast reeded and scroll feet and has three bottle holders made of seamed sheet with applied reeded mouldings top and bottom. The three cut-glass bottles (for pounce, ink and shot for quill cleaning)[1] have seamed silver mounts over which the tops push on. They are also seamed and have applied reeded mouldings and dished tops, pierced in a diaper pattern on that for the pounce pot and with one and three circular holes for the other two. The bottle holders are secured in place by staples which penetrate to the underside and have two long pins passing through them. Being Lady Bristol's personal property the inkstand is not listed in either the 1811 or 1826 plate lists.

HERALDRY: Engraved in one of the pen trays is the monogram EAH beneath a baron's coronet for Elizabeth Albana, Lady Hervey, subsequently Countess and Marchioness of Bristol.

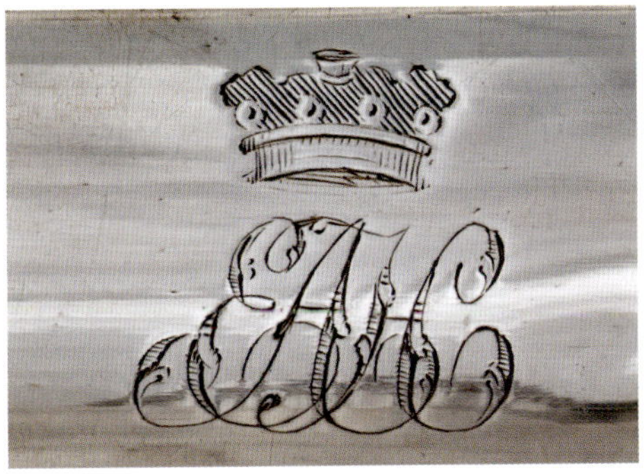

Seventeen ninety-eight was the year of Elizabeth Upton's marriage to the future 1st Marquess and this inkstand could have been a wedding present, perhaps even from her husband.

1. Hughes 1957, p. 150.

97. Tea pot

Sterling silver / **Henry Nutting, London** / **1801/2**

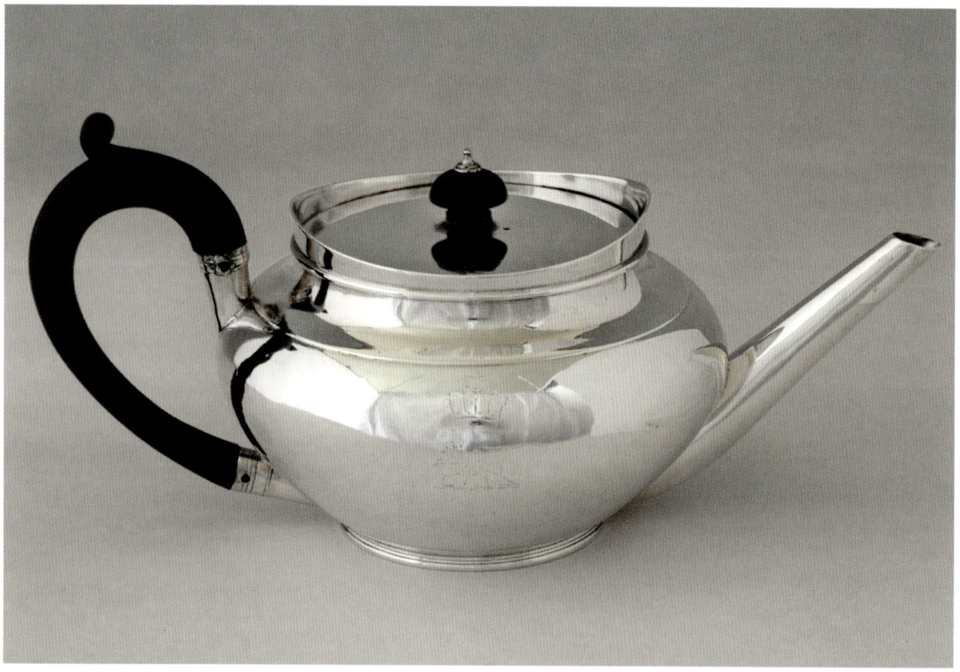

MARKS: Fully marked on the underside with maker's mark 'HN' in a rectangular punch (Grimwade 1990, no. 1036), date letter 'F', lion passant, monarch's head, leopard's head. The bezel of the lid is marked with the lion passant only.

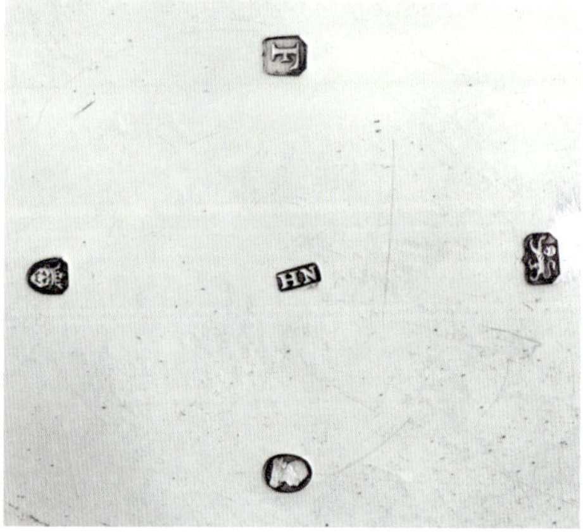

SCRATCHWEIGHT: None.
Actual weight: 598 g (19 oz, 5 dwt).

MEASUREMENTS: h. 13.3 cm (5¼ in); w. 27.9 cm (11 in); diam. (of base) 8.6 cm (3⅜ in).

INVENTORY: 852106

PROVENANCE: 5th Earl (subsequently 1st Marquess) of Bristol; by descent to the 4th Marquess.

DESCRIPTION: The compressed spherical body is raised in two pieces, the concave curved neck-piece being separate and applied and having a waved profile at the rim. Inside and outside the neck are applied wire mouldings, the inner one supporting the raised, slightly domed lid which has an applied, seamed bezel, a turned ebony knop with cast silver finial and a drilled steam hole. The carved ebony loop handle with scrolled thumb-piece is pinned to two seamed tubes of silver with chased lines that are soldered to the body. The straight, tapering spout is seamed and applied. The body is pierced behind the spout to act as a strainer.

HERALDRY: The side of the pot (with spout to the right) and the lid are engraved with the Hervey crest beneath an earl's coronet.

The 5th Earl probably acquired this tea pot from stock shortly after his inheritance. He could have exchanged an old tea pot or there may not previously have been tea pots in silver (see cat. 20). The form is a development of the bullet shape of the early eighteenth century and though larger, it is not as substantial as was becoming general in the nineteenth century.

98. Four casserole dishes and covers

Sterling silver / William Pitts(?), London / 1801/2 / Silver-plated liners/moulds

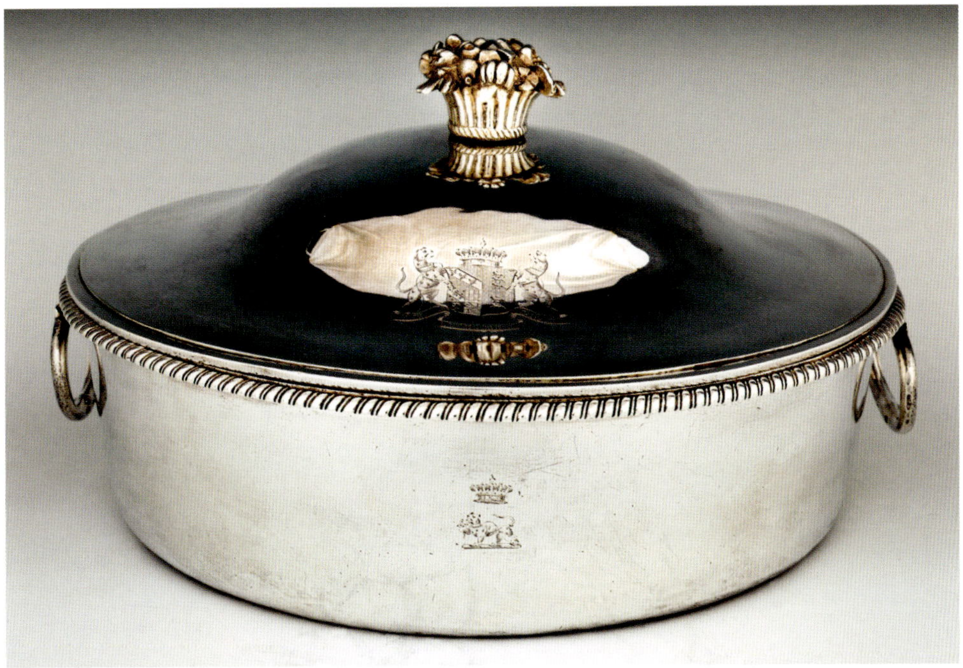

MARKS: Each is fully marked on its underside with maker's mark 'W·P' in an oval punch, lion passant, leopard's head, monarch's head and date letter 'F'. The mark given by Arthur Grimwade (1990, no. 3263) does not have a pellet but one is present in Pitts' shared mark with Joseph Preedy (no. 3272). There are no marks on the plated liners/moulds.

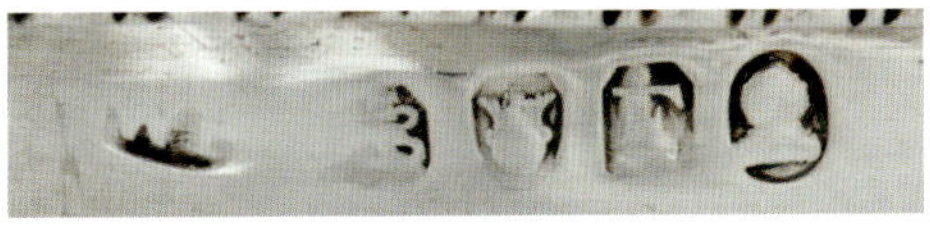

SCRATCHWEIGHTS: None.
Actual weights: (excluding liners) 1214 g (39 oz, 1 dwt); 1224 g (39 oz, 7 dwt); 1245 g (40 oz); 1263 g (40 oz, 12 dwt).

MEASUREMENTS: h. 12.4 cm (4⅞ in); diam. 22.5 cm (8⅞ in).

INVENTORY: 852187

PROVENANCE: Probably the 5th Earl (subsequently 1st Marquess) of Bristol; by descent to the 4th Marquess.

LITERATURE: Penzer 1957a, II, p. 137.

DESCRIPTION: The flat-bottomed circular dishes are raised and each has two oval reeded drop handles and a cast gadroon border applied at the rim. The covers are raised in the form of flat ogee domes and have handles in the form of a fruit basket bolted through at the apex. The plain, plated liners conform to the dish. Each of the dishes and covers is engraved, on the rims and the bezels, with numbers from 1 to 4 to identify the correct pairings.

HERALDRY: Each dish is engraved on its side with the Hervey crest beneath an earl's coronet and the covers have the quartered shield, supporters and motto as borne by the 2nd, 3rd and 4th Earls of Bristol beneath an earl's coronet.

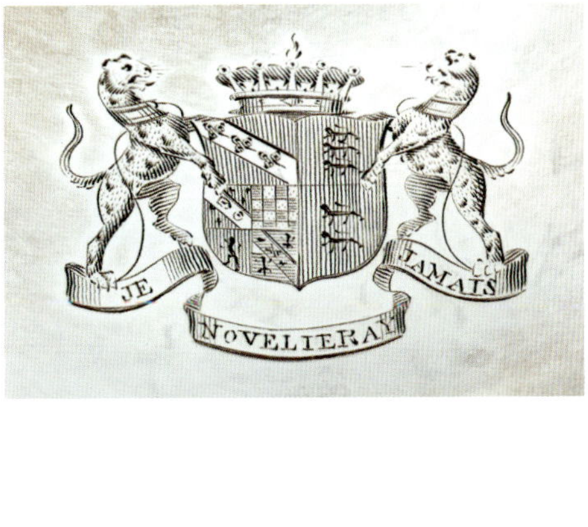

The quarterings on these dishes are the same as those borne by the 4th Earl and his elder brothers, yet he was not in England again after 1792 and it seems hardly likely that he would have commissioned silver at a distance in his last years of ever more purposeless wandering. It is more probable that they were acquired from stock by his son shortly after inheriting and were engraved before he had settled on his own favoured quarterings.

The dishes are recorded as casseroles in the 1811 plate list (appendix 5) and the word then had a very different culinary meaning to what is understood of it now. A casserole in the early nineteenth century was a rice dish moulded to the shape of the container and combined with various fillings,[1] such as the 'Casserole au Ris, with Giblets' which was regularly prepared for the Marquess of Buckingham's table by his cook, John Simpson:

Boil a quarter of a pound of Carolina rice in broth, until it becomes stiff; then line a mould (according to the shape of the dish the casserole is wanted for); butter the mould ... do the rice well over with egg and smooth it with the back of a spoon; put in the oven to set the egg; when the egg is set put in the giblets; (they should be stewed until very tender;) take all the bones from the wings, cut the gizards in slices, put a little coulis to them, and put them in the mould; cover it with paste [pastry]; put it in the oven for an hour, turn it out a few minutes before it is wanted ...[2]

The liners are too large to fit correctly and it is possible that they are, in fact, moulds intended for setting the casserole before placing it in the dish.

Specific dishes for casseroles had first appeared in England around 1770 and perhaps the earliest reference in the Parker and Wakelin ledgers is the '4 Casteroles [sic] & Covers' weighing 152 oz, 14 dwt, which were delivered to the 1st Earl Harcourt in March, 1769.[3] The combined weight of the Ickworth set is not dissimilar at around 160 oz.

1. Larousse 1990, p. 231.
2. Simpson 1806, pp. 100–1.
3. Parker and Wakelin Ledgers, VAM 7 1765–75, f. 119.

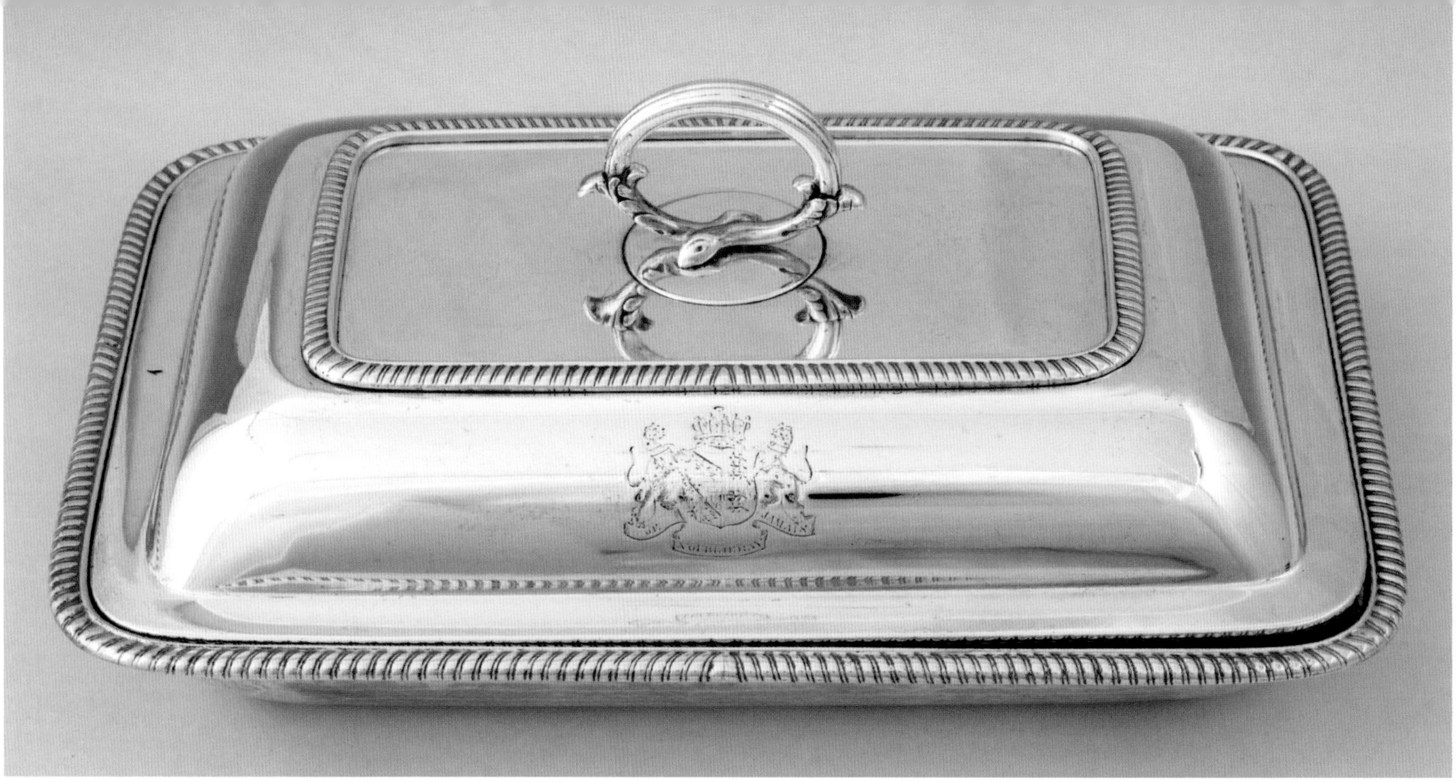

99. **Two oblong covered dishes**

Sterling silver / Richard Cooke, London / 1802/3

MARKS: The dishes and covers are all fully marked on their left-hand sides with maker's mark 'R·C' in a shaped punch (Grimwade 1990, no. 2289), lion passant, leopard's head, date letter 'G' and monarch's head. Each of the dishes and covers is engraved, on the rims, with numbers 1 or 2 to identify the correct pairings.

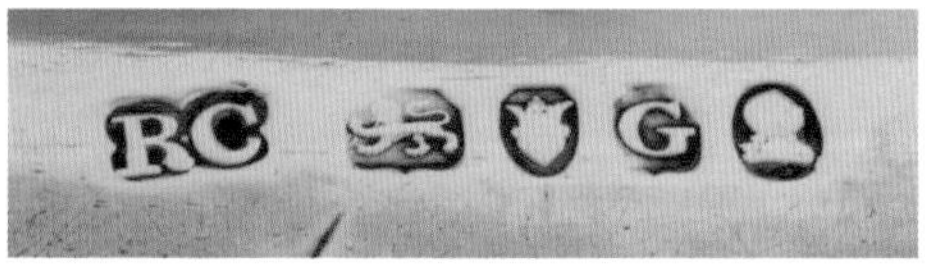

SCRATCHWEIGHTS: None.
Actual weights: 1835 g (59 oz); 1882 g (60 oz, 10 dwt).

MEASUREMENTS: h. 11.4 cm (4½ in); w. 29.2 cm (11½ in); d. 21 cm (8¼ in).

INVENTORY: 852190

PROVENANCE: Probably the 5th Earl (subsequently 1st Marquess) of Bristol; by descent to the 4th Marquess.

LITERATURE: Penzer 1957a, II, p. 137.

DESCRIPTION: The oblong dishes with rounded corners are raised and have narrow horizontal rims with applied borders of cast gadrooning. The covers are domed in the same manner that the base is dished, with an applied border of gadrooning on the inside of the rim and a further band of cast gadrooning on the exterior at the edge of the flat of the dome. The foliate and reeded ring handles are applied to flat circular plates and are detachable by turning.

HERALDRY: The fronts of the covers are engraved with the quartered shield, supporters and motto as borne by the 2nd, 3rd and 4th Earls of Bristol beneath an earl's coronet. Both the dish and the inside of the cover are engraved on their rear edges with the Hervey crest beneath an earl's coronet.

Like the casserole dishes (cat. 98) and in spite of their arms these dishes were most probably commissioned by the 5th Earl. They are described in 1811 as double dishes and each one can either be used with its cover on or, by the removal of the handle, as two separate receptacles. That is why the crest is engraved on the back edge of each. Their form is an updated version of the pincushion dishes of the mid-eighteenth century (see cat. 48 and 77).

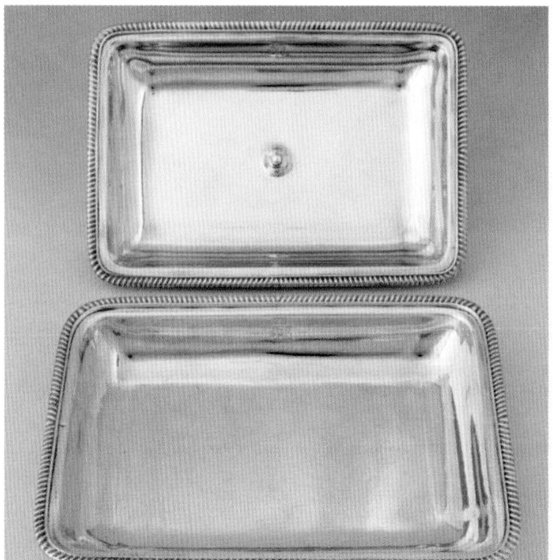

100. **Dessert service of knives, forks and spoons**

Sterling silver, gilded

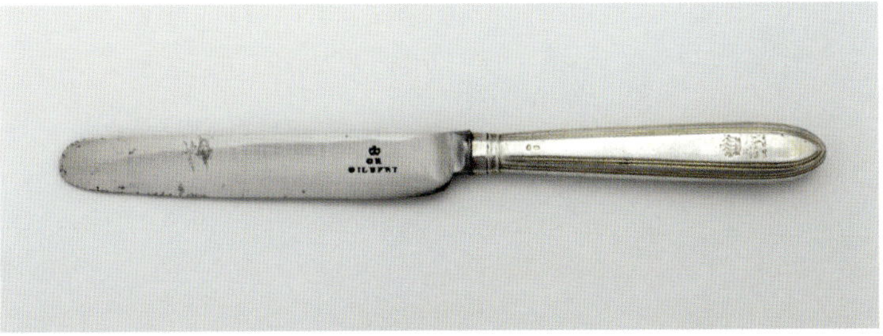

A. **Dessert knives with steel blades (x 12)**
William Abdy II (?), London / 1803/4

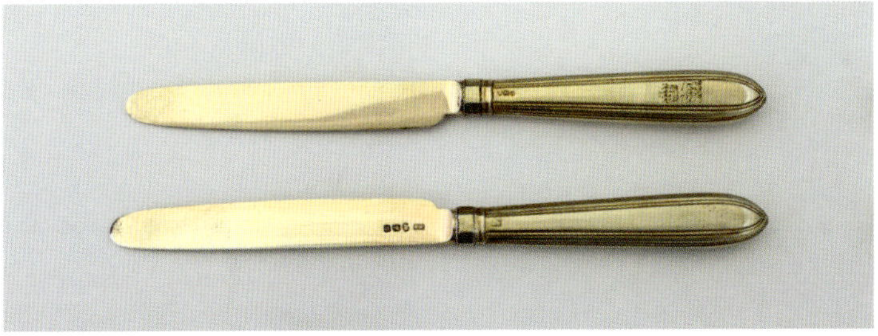

B. **Dessert knives with silver-gilt blades (x 12)**
Moses Brent, London / 1803/4

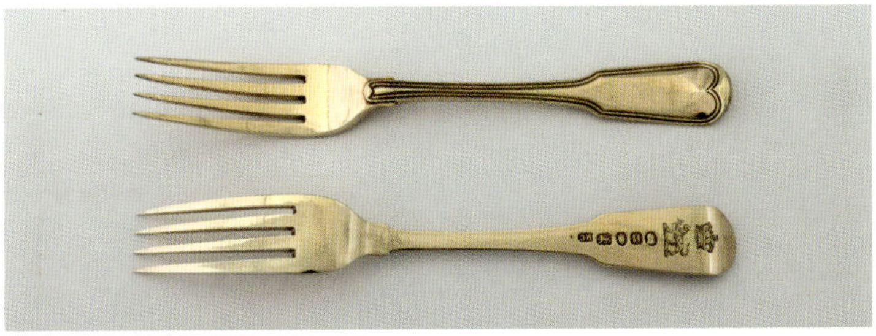

C. **Dessert forks (x 6) / Richard Crossley / 1803/4**

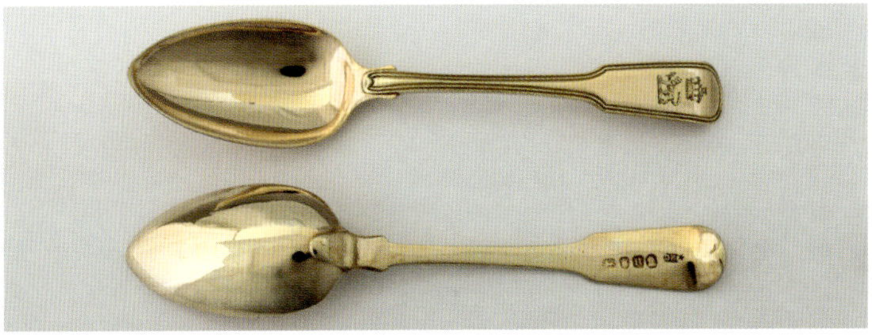

D. **Dessert spoons (x 6) / Richard Crossley / 1803/4**

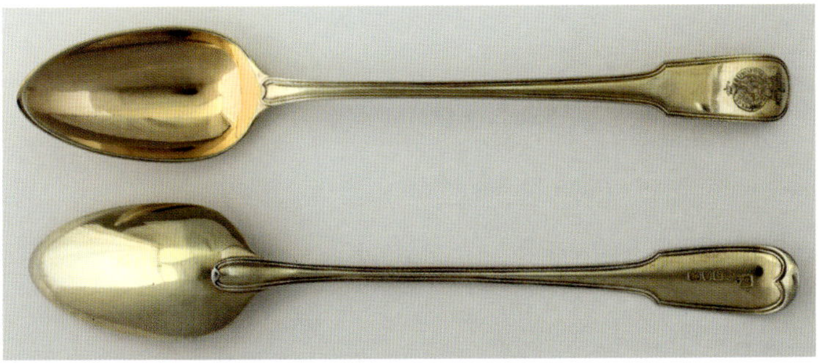

E. **Gravy spoons (x 6) / George Smith III & William Fearn / 1794/5 and William Eley I & William Fearn / 1803/4**

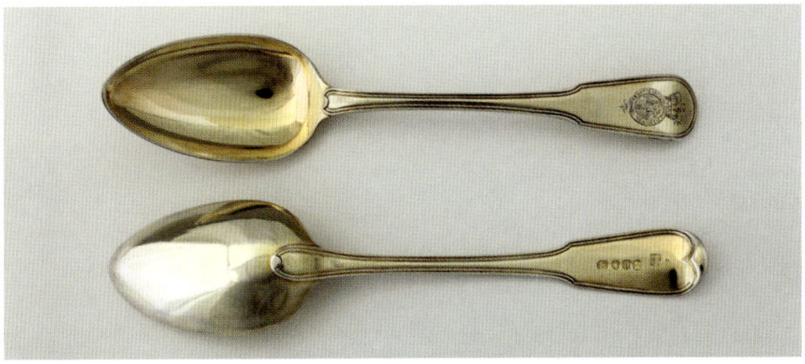

F. **Table spoons (x 6) / William Eley I & William Fearn / 1803/4**

MARKS AND MEASUREMENTS:

A. Dessert knives with steel blades. All have the monarch's head and lion passant on the left side of the handle and four also have the date letter 'H'. On the reverse side, worn off on many, is the maker's mark 'WA' in a rectangular punch (probably Grimwade 1990, no. 3004 though that has a pellet between so perhaps he was using his father's mark, no. 3003). The steel blades are stamped with an imperial crown above 'GR [/] GILBERT'. l. (of handle) 10.2 cm (4 in); l. (overall) 24.8 cm (9¾ in).

B. Dessert knives with silver blades. All marked on the left side of the handle with the monarch's head, lion passant and date letter 'H' and on the back with the maker's mark 'M·B' in a rectangular punch (Grimwade 1990, no. 2000).

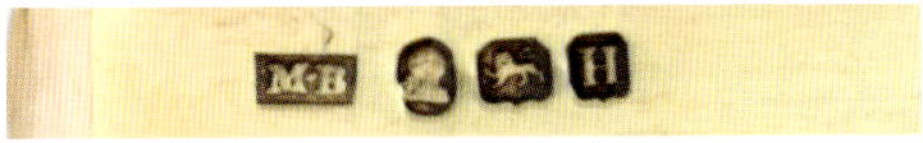

The reverse side of each blade has the same marks. l. (of handle) 10.2 cm (4 in); l. (overall) 21.6 cm (8½ in).

C. and D. Dessert forks and spoons. All fully marked on the reverse of the handle with maker's mark 'RC' in a rectangular punch (Grimwade 1990, no. 2288), lion passant, leopard's head, date letter 'H' and monarch's head. l. (of forks) 16.2 cm (6⅜ in); l. (of spoons) 17.8 cm (7 in).

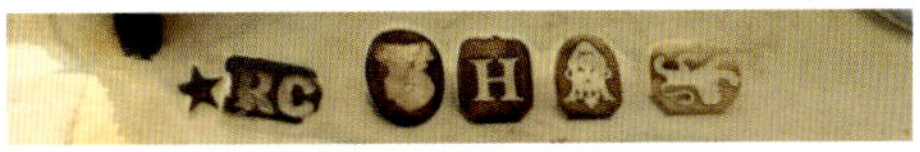

E. Gravy spoons: All fully marked on the reverse of the handle with lion passant, leopard's head, monarch's head and maker's marks 'GS' over 'WF' in a square punch (Grimwade 1990, no. 910) and 'WE' over 'WF' in a square punch (Grimwade 1990, no. 3112), four with the date letter 't' and two with 'H'. l. 27.3 cm (10¾ in).

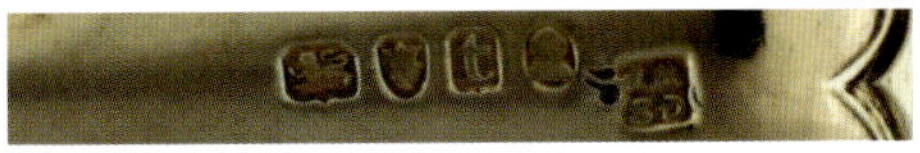

F. Table spoons: All fully marked on the reverse of the handle with lion passant, leopard's head, date letter 'H', monarch's head and maker's mark 'WE' over 'WF' (as above). l. 21.6 cm (8½ in).

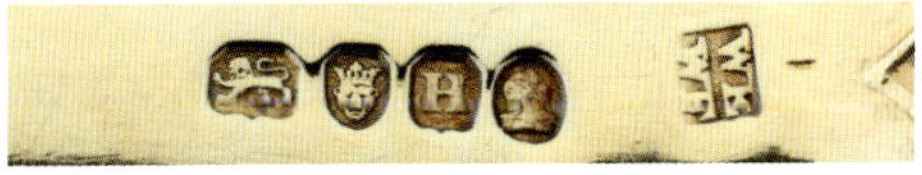

SCRATCHWEIGHTS: None. The combined weights for the gravy spoons and table spoons given in the 1811 plate list (appendix 5) are 23 oz, 2 dwt, and 15 oz, 14 dwt. Four dozen of each of the silver bladed knives, the steel bladed knives, the forks and the spoons were, respectively, 74 oz, 16 dwt; 24 oz, 18 dwt; 68 oz, 1 dwt; and 58 oz, 18 dwt.

INVENTORY: A. 852193; B. 852202; C. 852199.7–12; D. 852199.1–6; E. 852195.1–6; F. 852195.7–12

PROVENANCE: 5th Earl (subsequently 1st Marquess) of Bristol; by descent to the 4th Marquess.

LITERATURE: Penzer 1957a, I, p. 43.

DESCRIPTION: The dessert spoons and the forks are of the fiddle thread pattern,[1] the forks with four tines. The serving and table spoons are French-style fiddle thread.[2] The knife handles, which are reeded, have pointed ends and stems tapering towards the blade with octagonal ferrules. Both the silver and contemporary steel blades are slightly tapering with rounded ends.

HERALDRY: All the knives (A and B) are engraved at the top of the left hand side of the handle with the Hervey crest beneath an earl's coronet. The dessert spoons (C) are engraved on the front of the terminals and the forks (D) on the underside of the terminals with the Hervey crest beneath a baron's coronet. The serving and table spoons (E and F) are engraved on the front of the terminals with the quartered arms of George III (as borne 1801–16) within the Garter and beneath an imperial crown.

This dessert service, which augmented that of John Augustus, Lord Hervey (cat. 93), would have been supplied by the 1st Marquess's favoured goldsmiths, Rundell, Bridge & Rundell. It demonstrates how a visually coherent whole could be made up of components by a number of different makers, in this case five. The complete service numbered nine dozen dessert knives (five dozen with steel blades, the rest silver-gilt), four dozen each of dessert spoons and forks, thirty ice spoons, six serving spoons and six table spoons (see appendix 5). The typical size of a grand dessert service in the mid-eighteenth century had been three dozen knives, spoons and forks and very often, as with the 2nd Earl's (cat. 71), they were not gilded. By 1800, however, the taste for gilding had burgeoned, partly egged on by the Prince of Wales and his set, and there had also been a substantial increase in the scale of entertaining and the quantity of household plate held by Britain's aristocracy. Lord Bristol was to go on to acquire a complete additional service of the same size in 1823 (cat. 114), plus a third in ungilt silver extending to 18 each of knives, forks and spoons (cat. 113). This may have been with the intention of fully equipping himself in London, at Ickworth and at his house in Brighton. If so this more old-fashioned service would have been likely to be the one allocated to Ickworth, the most up-to-date style being needed in London, whereas Brighton was a retreat where gilding and huge quantities were not required.

The service must have been in the process of manufacture at the death of the 4th Earl of Bristol in Italy on 8 July 1803. Thus the dessert forks and spoons are engraved with a baron's coronet and the new Earl must have taken the pragmatic decision not to have them re-engraved. The knives were presumably yet to be engraved, however, and they all have an earl's coronet. The royal arms on the serving and table spoons do not denote another tranche of perquisite plate, the future 1st Marquess never having held a position that would have entitled him to that. It is probable, therefore, that he had exchanged a few pieces of the 2nd Earl's ambassadorial plate and was acknowledging that in the armorials of the new pieces. He did the same on a larger scale with the additional table and dessert services acquired in the 1820s (cat. 120 and 119 respectively), though in those cases he was probably recognising ambassadorial pieces lost or alienated during the tenures of the 3rd and 4th Earls.

1. Pickford 1983, pp. 114–5, fig. 153.
2. Ibid., pp. 114–5, fig. 155.

101. **Two sugar ladles**

Silver-gilt / probably Rundell, Bridge & Rundell, London / *c.*1803

MARKS: There are vestiges of marks, all indecipherable, on the backs of the stems but these are probably from the mould taken of the 1758 ladles of which these are copies.

SCRATCHWEIGHTS: None. The 1811 plate list (appendix 5) gives a combined weight of 3 oz, 8 dwt.

MEASUREMENTS: l. 16.5 cm (6½ in).

INVENTORY: 852197

PROVENANCE: Probably the 5th Earl (subsequently 1st Marquess) of Bristol; by descent to the 4th Marquess.

DESCRIPTION: The ladles are cast and have almost hemispherical bowls pierced in a foliate and floral symmetrical pattern. The tapering handles with rounded terminals are of the double-reeded Hanoverian pattern with additional shouldering at the junction with the bowl.

HERALDRY: None.

These are copies of the set provided to the 2nd Earl as part of his ambassadorial silver in 1758 (cat. 76). They were presumably acquired as part of the 5th Earl's expansion of his table services on inheriting in 1803. The gilding is probably a reapplication from the early 20th century.

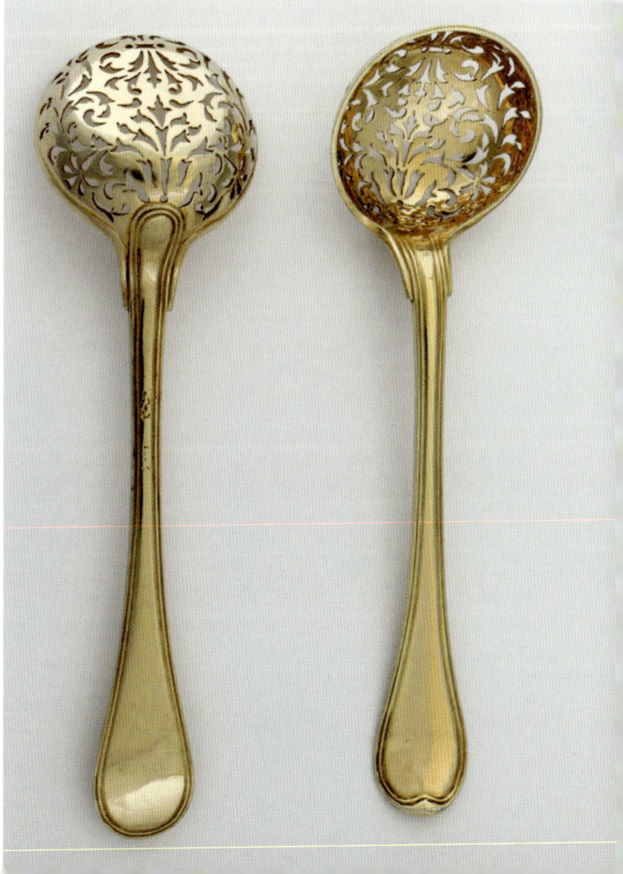

102. **Six table knives**

Sterling silver hafts / Moses Brent, London / 1803/4 / Stainless steel blades, *c.*1920

MARKS: The knife hafts are all marked on their right-hand sides with the monarch's head, lion passant and date letter 'H'. Two are also marked (very worn) on their left-hand sides with the maker's mark 'M.B' in a rectangular punch (Grimwade 1990, no. 2000). The stainless steel blades, which are replacements of *c.*1920, are stamped with an imperial crown above concentric circles, the outer inscribed 'BUTLER SHEFFIELD. ENGLAND', the inner 'REGD.', and beneath '"NON-STAIN"'.

SCRATCHWEIGHTS: None. The weight given in 1811 (appendix 5) for nine dozen was 135 oz, which gives an average of 1¼ oz per haft.

MEASUREMENTS: l. (of handle) 12.7 cm (5 in). l. (overall) 29.5 cm (11⅝ in).

INVENTORY: 852207

PROVENANCE: 5th Earl (subsequently 1st Marquess) of Bristol; by descent to the 4th Marquess.

DESCRIPTION: The silver handles are of the hour-glass pattern[1] with ball-on-stem finials and the stainless steel blades are slightly tapering with rounded ends.

HERALDRY: The left hand side of each haft is engraved near the terminal with the Hervey crest beneath an earl's coronet.

These knives, the pattern of which had been developed in eighteenth century France,[2] are the only representatives surviving at Ickworth of an enormous table service commissioned by the future 1st Marquess on his succession in 1803 (see appendix 5). There were 108 knives and forks, sixty spoons, twelve gravy or serving spoons and six pairs of carving knives and forks. Some were sold by the executors of the 7th Marquess in 1999.[3] It is probable that the knives were erroneously thought in the 1950s to be associated with the 1820s service of which all components except knives are represented at Ickworth (see cat. 120).

As he had done for dessert (cat. 93, 100, 114 and 119), the Marquess eventually equipped himself with table services for all his principal houses (see also cat. 69 and 120), this one probably being used in St James's Square up to the delivery of a new service in 1823 when it is likely to have been allocated, as second best, to Ickworth.

Moses Brent was a specialist maker of silver knife hafts and blades and met almost all of Rundell, Bridge & Rundell's commissions in the late eighteenth and early nineteenth centuries.[4]

1. Pickford 1983, pp. 120–1, figs. 163–5.
2. Ibid., p. 120.
3. Sotheby's Summers Place, 14–16 September 1999, lot 1174.
4. Grimwade 1990, pp. 447–8.

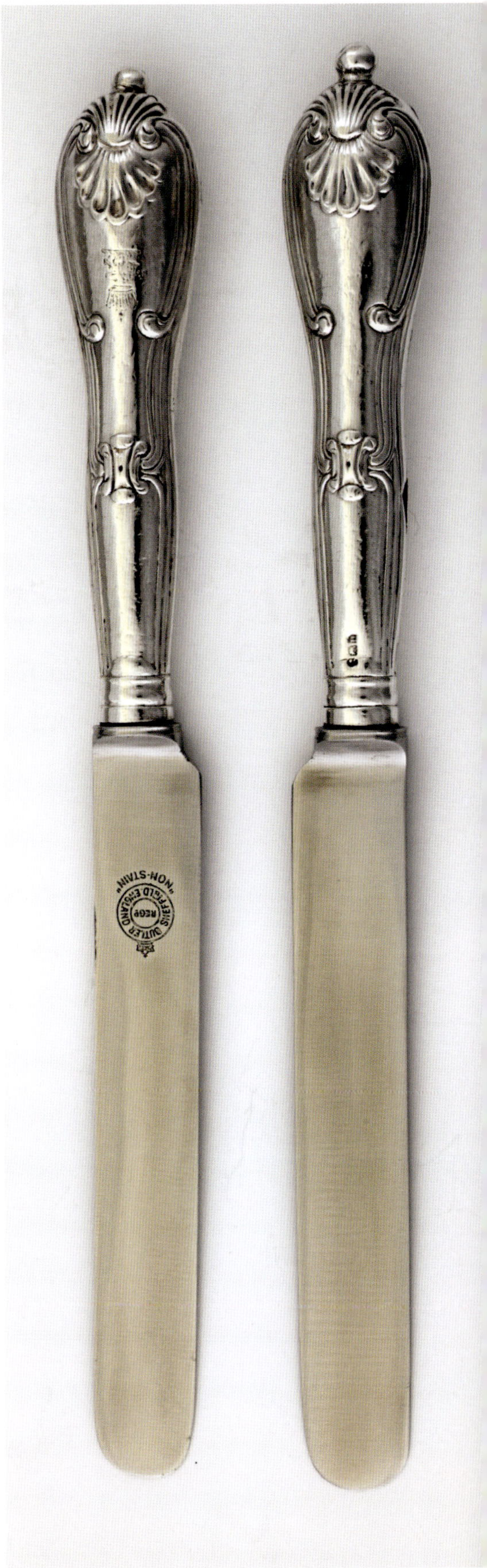

103. **Six candlesticks**

Sterling silver / **Emick Romer, London (x 2)** / **1763/4**
Sterling silver / **Thomas Holland II (x 4)** / **1809/10**

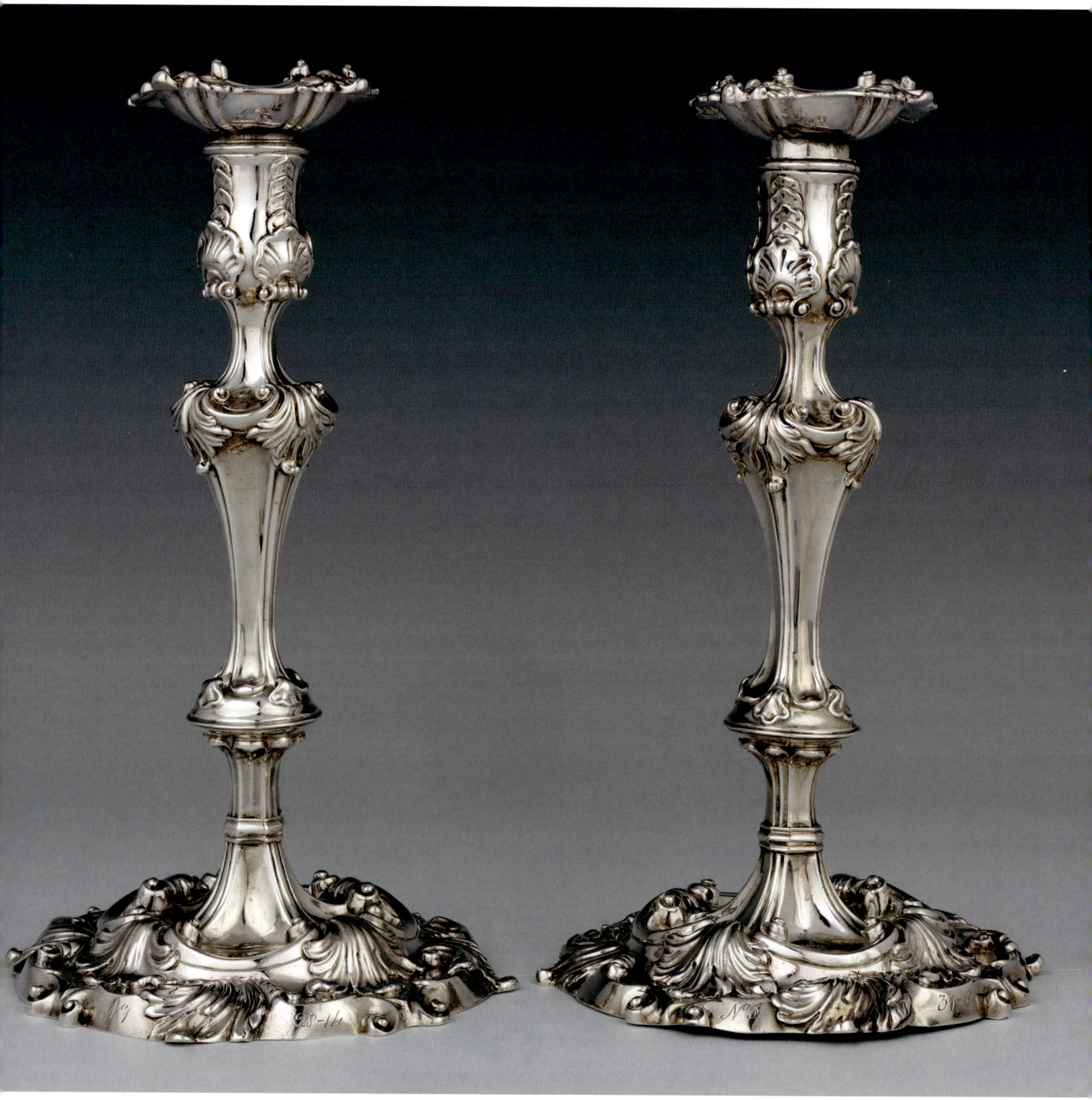

Romer left, Holland right

MARKS: Candlesticks 1 and 4 are fully marked on their undersides with date letter 'h', leopard's head, maker's mark 'ER' in a shaped punch (Grimwade 1990, no. 638) and lion passant. They also have the lion passant on their sockets. Nos. 2, 3, 5 and 6 are fully marked on the outside of the foot rim with the lion passant, leopard's head, date letter 'O', monarch's head and maker's mark 'TH' in a rectangular punch (Grimwade 1990, no. 2789). Five of the nozzles are marked on their sleeves with the monarch's head, lion passant, date letter 'O' and the 'TH' maker's mark (as above). The sixth (No. 1) has a sterling lion and the remnants of a maker's mark ending in 'C'.

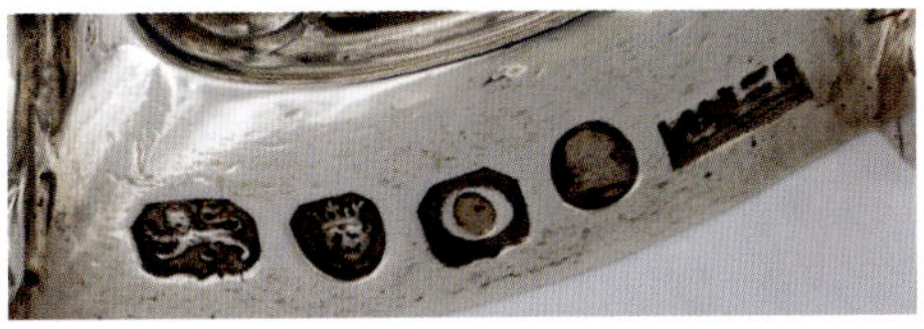

SCRATCHWEIGHTS AND INSCRIPTIONS: On the outside of the foot rim: 'No 1 28-14'; 'No 2 31 "'; 'No 3 31 18'; 'No 4 29-3' plus 'oz 58' [this is the old, combined scratchweight for the two 1763 sticks]; 'No 5 31-6'; 'No 6 31-6'. The nozzles are marked from 1-6 to identify the correct pairings with the sticks.

MEASUREMENTS: (without nozzles) Nos. 1 and 4 (Romer): h. 25.4 cm (10 in); diam. (of base) 15.2 cm (6 in). Nos. 2, 3, 5 and 6 (Holland): h. 24.1 cm (9½ in); diam. 15.1 cm (6 in).

INVENTORY: 852093

PROVENANCE: 5th Earl (subsequently 1st Marquess) of Bristol; by descent to the 4th Marquess.

LITERATURE: Penzer 1957a, II, p. 133 (erroneously all given to Romer); Banister 1980, p. 794.

EXHIBITED: *Ideal Home Exhibition*, London, 1960; *British Week*, Milan and Frankfurt, 1965.

DESCRIPTION: The candlesticks are cast and chased and have shaped circular feet with shell, leaf and scroll decoration rising at the centre as stiff leaves bound in an octagon by a moulded ring. Above is a compressed spherical knop from which the stem rises as shaped, octagonally arranged leaves to a shoulder with alternate shells and scrolls, further scrolls extending upwards to the sockets which are embellished with shells and overlapping leaves. The nozzles have seamed sleeves applied to cast scrollwork drip-pans.

HERALDRY: The feet and drip pans are all engraved with the Hervey crest beneath an earl's coronet.

The two Romer sticks are typical of the best of cast and chased examples from the 1750s and 1760s. They are firmly rococo in style and their sinuous, irregular decoration twists and froths and has something of the auricular in it too. The design derives from the shouldered candlesticks of the 1740s and was in production in this exact form from at least 1751, when a set of four plus another pair by Alexander Johnston were marked.[1] They measure the same as the Ickworth pair, have matching drip pans and are likely to be from the same moulds, still being used twelve years later.

To create his mould for the 1809 copies Thomas Holland took a cast of one of the Romer pair, as is evident from the shadow of the old hallmarks visible on their undersides and from their fractionally smaller scale. The pattern proved as popular in the Regency as it had been in the mid-eighteenth century and by 1813 it had been taken up by Sheffield makers, being found on a set of sticks by Kirby, Waterhouse & Co of that year and on another by John Watson of 1818–20.[2]

Although it is possible that the 2nd Earl of Bristol owned the Romer pair, the fact that the engraved crests and coronets are consistent on all six suggests the contrary, as does the lack of any relevant payments in his bank account. The engraving is of a very poor quality and not up to that executed for the 2nd Earl in Kandler's workshop.

1. Set of four sold Sotheby's, 19 June 1986, lot 60, the pair sold Sotheby's, 22 June 1967, lot 95.
2. The 1813 set were sold at Christie's 13 May 1992, lot 195, those by John Watson also Christie's, 23 July 1980, lot 118.

104. **Pair of tea urns**

Sterling silver / **Paul Storr, London** / **1809/10**

MARKS: The underside of the bases are fully marked with maker's mark 'P.S' in a shaped punch (Grimwade 1990, no. 2235), lion passant, leopard's head, date letter 'O' and monarch's head. The bezels of the covers have the same maker's mark, lion passant and date letter 'O'. The extending tubes beneath the finial have the lion passant and same maker's mark (small version) only. The charcoal chambers within the urns have the same maker's mark, lion passant and king's head on their rims and the bezels to the lids have the lion passant, date letter 'O' and same maker's mark (small version).

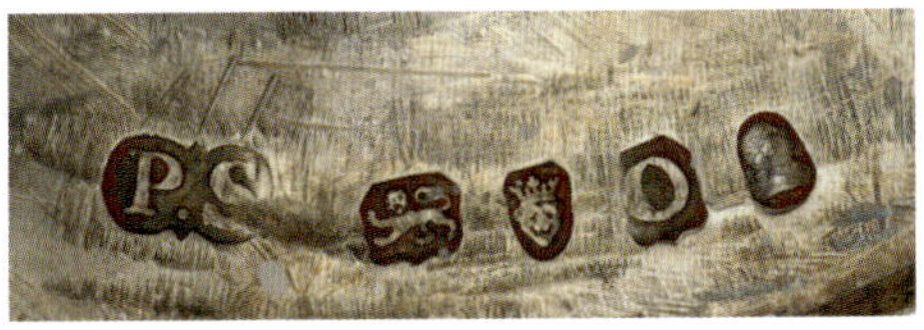

SCRATCHWEIGHTS AND INSCRIPTIONS: 'Nº 1. 191, 10,'; 'Nº 2, 197"'. The bezels of the covers and the charcoal inserts are marked either '1' or '2' to identify the correct groupings of component parts.

MEASUREMENTS: h. 36.5 cm (14⅜ in); w. (incl. handles) 38.1 cm (15 in); d. (incl. spout) 40.6 cm (16 in); diam. (of body) 29.8 cm (11¾ in); w. (of square base) 15.2 cm (6 in).

INVENTORY: 852129

PROVENANCE: 5th Earl (subsequently 1st Marquess) of Bristol; by descent to the 4th Marquess.

LITERATURE: Penzer 1957a, II, p. 136.

DESCRIPTION: On each urn four cast leaf-capped lion's paw feet flanked by scrolls and anthemions support a plain square base constructed of seamed sheet silver. Above this is a raised, domed foot with a prominent chased band of gadrooning applied to a raised hemispherical bowl forming the body of the urn with an applied and seamed moulded wire and two applied cast reed-and-tie handles emanating from pairs of cast lion masks. A seamed tube projects horizontally from the body to a cast and chased rectangular spigot, the sides decorated with flower heads on matted grounds, a cast swan's head projecting forwards as the spout and an ivory anthemion

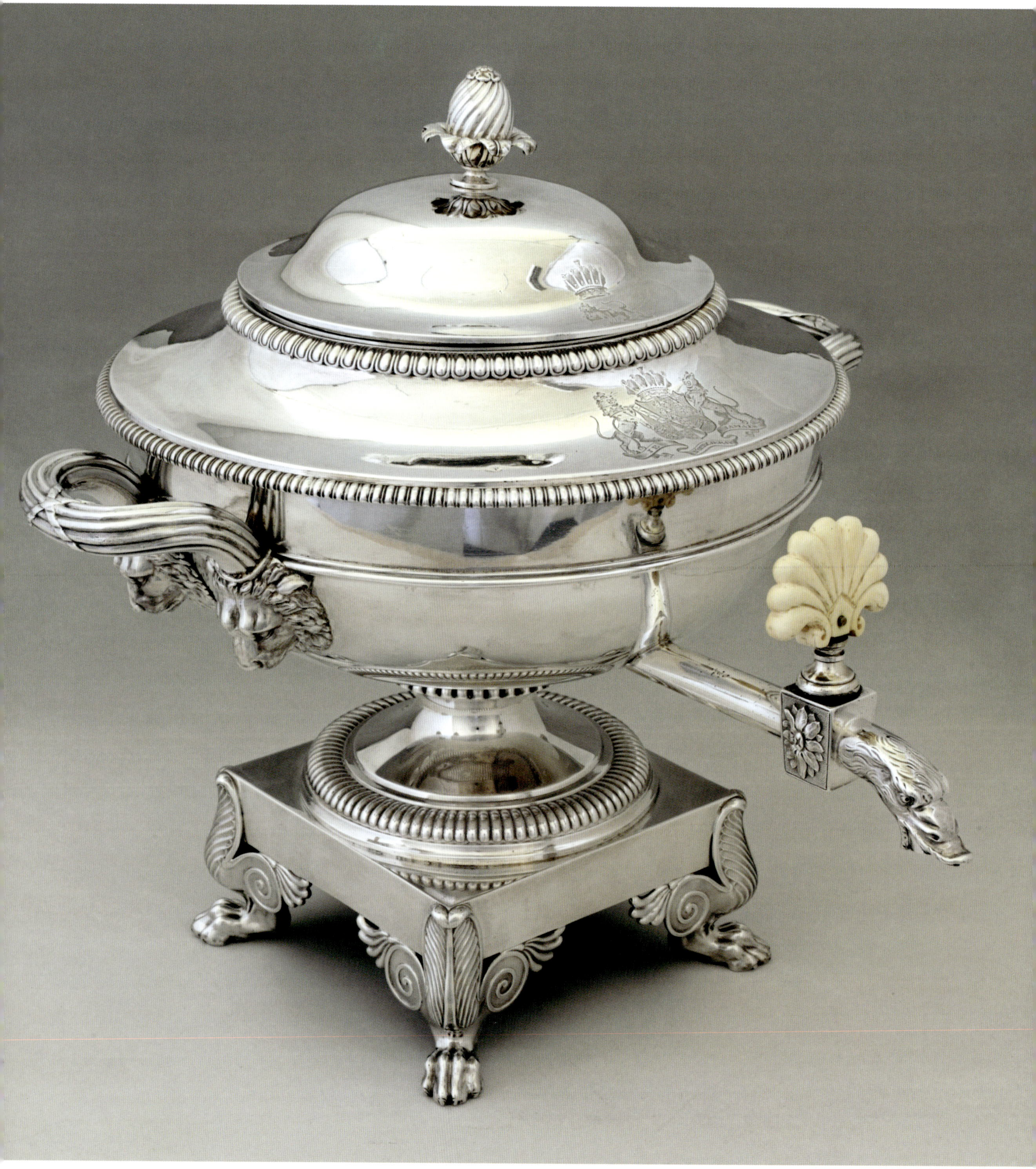

on a circular silver foot forming the tap handle. The bowl of the urn is closed in by a wide, concave rim which is raised and has a cast gadroon moulding applied at its base and a cast egg-and-cable moulding at the lip. The shallow ogee-domed cover is raised, has a seamed bezel and is plain apart from the cast flower-bud-and-calyx finial which is attached to a retractable seamed tube punched with multiple holes to allow the release of steam. Within the urn is a second cover with a broad, flat rim pierced with stylised flowers and a central circular hole beneath which is applied a vertical circular, seamed sleeve (intended to hold a heated iron bar), its simple lid formed of sheet with a seamed applied bezel and a ring-pull handle. Both urns are in excellent condition.

HERALDRY: The front of each urn, above the tap, is engraved with the quartered shield, supporters and motto of the 5th Earl of Bristol beneath an earl's coronet and the covers have the Hervey crest beneath an earl's coronet.

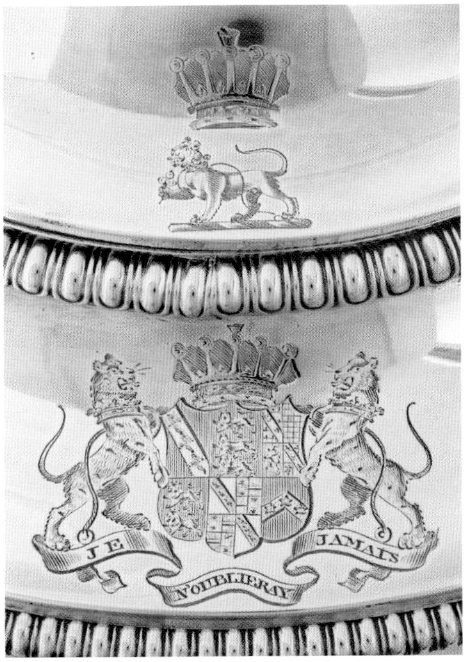

The popularity of tea had continued to burgeon throughout the eighteenth century, helped by a significant reduction in price, and in the Regency period it would still be offered to those visiting at different times of the day as had previously been the case. Its principal, formal appearances, however, were at breakfast (fig. 48), which in the early nineteenth century commenced at around ten o'clock and consisted only of tea and toast, perhaps with the occasional boiled egg, and after dinner.[1] House parties were generally larger and more frequent, requiring greater quantities of tea to be dispensed, and there was also an increased sensitivity to the presence of servants. Both were factors in the early-nineteenth-century spike in enthusiasm for tea urns for dispensing hot water, which had greater capacity than kettles and could be operated by the lady of the house or whichever member of the company was presiding.

Silver tea urns had first appeared in significant numbers in the 1760s and they were then generally ovoid in shape.[2] They became more attenuated as the Neoclassical took hold in the 1770s, having an appearance and proportions close to that of the large racing trophies of the period.[3] The 'Tea Vase' received from the Jewel Office by the 4th Viscount Galway on being appointed Comptroller of the Household in 1784[4] was probably of this form which continued to be made into the nineteenth century. By far the most popular shape by 1810, however, was the hemispherical-bodied urn, as already widely adopted for soup tureens and as chosen for the Ickworth pair. Paul Storr made many such urns during the first twenty years of the century but a commission for two matching must have been rare, and their survival today in the house for which they were acquired is possibly unique.

Urns were either designed to have a spirit lamp beneath, in the same fashion as eighteenth-century kettles and plate frames, or like this pair they were provided with an internal cavity into which a heated iron rod could be placed to keep the water warm. This method, which avoided the complications of a lamp failing to operate successfully, being knocked or even setting light to the linen, had been patented in 1774 by John Wadham.[5]

1. Pettigrew 2001, p. 98.
2. See for instance that of 1766 by Louisa Courtauld in the Metropolitan Museum of Art, New York, accession no. 66.192.1.
3. For example that of 1780 by Richard Carter at Wallington, Northumberland; NT inventory no. 584866.
4. Jewel Office Delivery Book 1732–93, f. 321
5. Schroder 1988b, p. 337.

105.
Four first-course dishes

Sterling silver / Paul Storr, London / 1809/10

MARKS: All the stands are fully marked on one of their sides and all the dishes on their undersides with maker's mark 'P.S' in a shaped punch (Grimwade 1990, no. 2235), lion passant, leopard's head, date letter 'O' and monarch's head. The covers are marked on their bezels with the same maker's mark, lion passant and date letter 'O'.

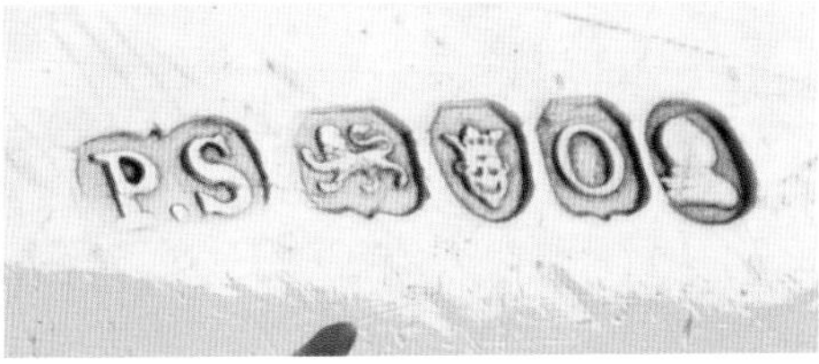

SCRATCHWEIGHTS AND INSCRIPTIONS: On the undersides of the stands: 'Nº 1 [/] oz dwt [/] 123„5„'; 'Nº 2 [/] oz [/] 123„–„'; 'Nº 3 [/] oz [/] 122„–„'; 'Nº 4 [/] oz [/] 124„–„'. Each stand, dish and cover is numbered from 1 to 4 to identify the correct groupings of component parts.

MEASUREMENTS: h. 20 cm (7⅞ in); w. 31.4 cm (12⅜ in); d. 22.9 cm (9 in).

INVENTORY: 852103

PROVENANCE: 5th Earl (subsequently 1st Marquess) of Bristol; by descent to the 4th Marquess.

LITERATURE: Penzer 1957a, II, p. 136; Hartop 2015, p. 76, fig. 77.

DESCRIPTION: The square stands with indented corners are raised, each having four bun feet on circular pads, a plain rectangular moulding on the underside and an applied moulding at the lip plus cast and chased scallop shells on the sides, their tops angled horizontally to accommodate the handles of the dishes. The dishes conform to the shape of the stands and are raised with indented corners, plain seamed bezels and narrow horizontal rims with applied cast gadrooning enriched by shell decoration at the corners and by central leaves front and back. Applied to the centres of the sides are prominent cast scallop shell handles. The covers are raised as square domes and have bases with indented corners to fit the dishes. The flat circular tops are applied, surrounded by a band of cast gadrooning and have leaf, reed and tie handles springing from leopard masks and feet. The handles are bolted through to the underside and each is secured by two silver nuts.

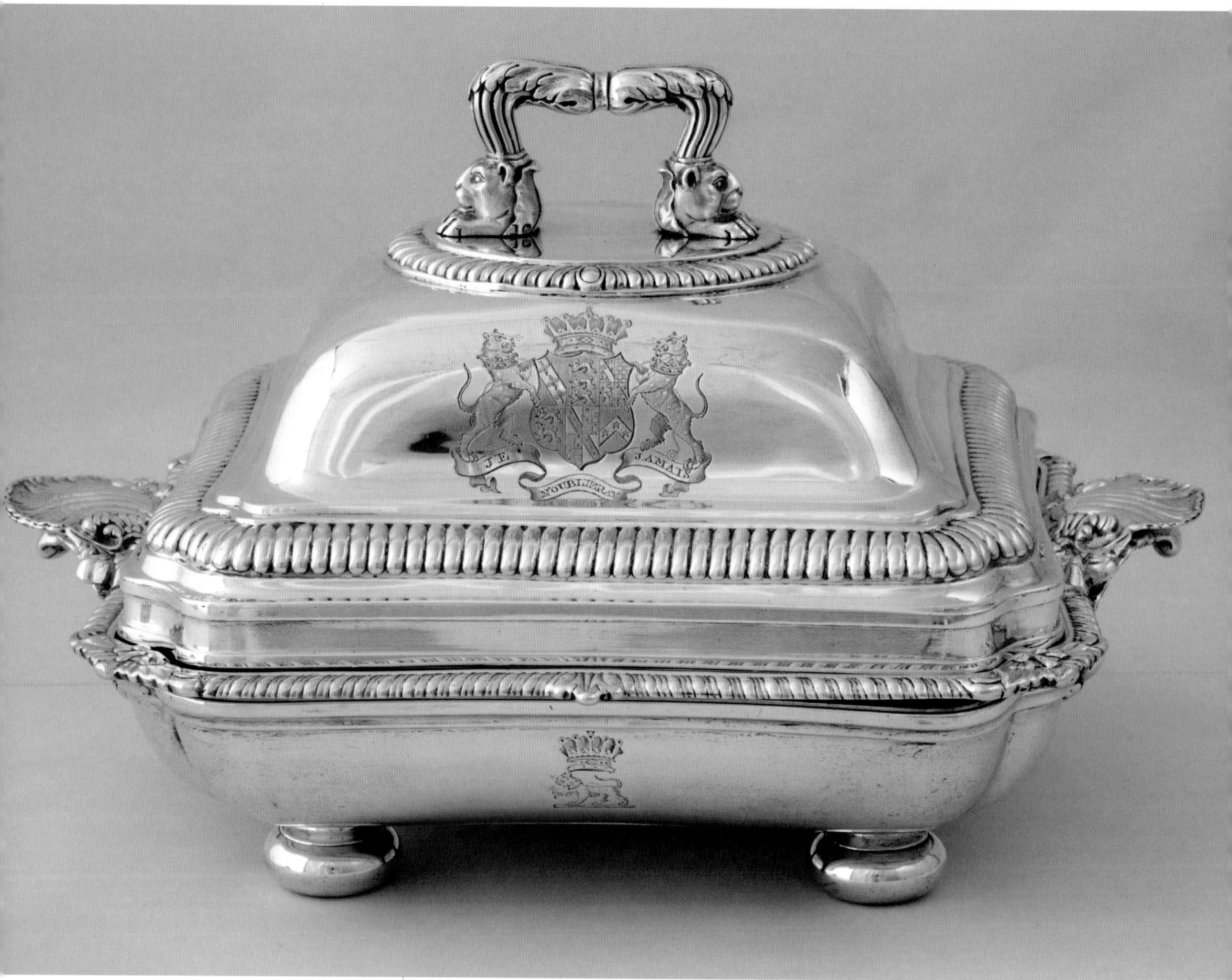

HERALDRY: Each cover is engraved on the front and back with the quartered shield, supporters and motto of the 5th Earl of Bristol beneath an earl's coronet. The stands are engraved front and back with the Hervey crest beneath an earl's coronet. Each dish has the crest and coronet in the centre.

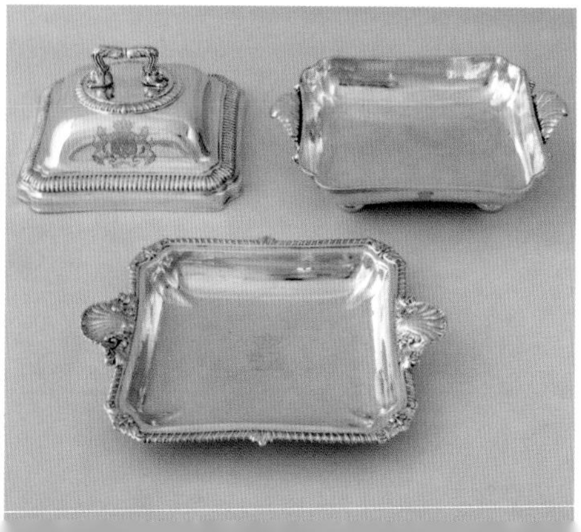

These dishes, supplied with stands which would be filled with hot water to help keep the food warm, are in a conventional pattern for the period particularly associated with Paul Storr.[1] In order to blend them with Lord Bristol's inherited dinner service, however, the cast shell handles which so prominently mark it out have been copied and applied to the sides of the dishes and stands. Furthermore, in place of the usual lion masks on the cover handles there are leopards, presumably intended to represent the Hervey crest and thus to make a nod to the Kandler tureens and their Turin counterparts (cat. 43 and 53). The variant cover handles do not seem to have been used again, clients presumably preferring the more showy lions, but the shells appeared at least once more, on a pair of dishes of 1819.[2]

As with their eighteenth-century antecedents these dishes were provided in pairs or sets of four so that they could be arranged symmetrically on the table. They would have been in place at the commencement of dinner, to be uncovered and the contents partaken of once the tureens had been removed. With the development of a more substantial breakfast menu with hot dishes later in the nineteenth century they were put to good use for that meal too and one can be seen on the sideboard in the photograph of the family at breakfast, *c.* 1870 (fig. 48). As a consequence they have been well used and have considerable wear though the very heavy gauge of silver has saved them from any serious denting.

1. Hartop 2015, p. 76.
2. Christie's New York, 17 May 2011, lot 153.

106. **Chalice**

Sterling silver, gilded / **John Cramer, London** / **1810/11**

MARKS AND INSCRIPTION: fully marked on the outside of the foot rim with maker's mark 'I·C' in a rectangular punch (Grimwade 1990, no. 1217), lion passant, leopard's head, date letter 'P', monarch's head. On the underside of the chalice is engraved 'Ickworth Church'.

SCRATCHWEIGHT: None.
Actual weight: 279 g (8 oz, 19 dwt).

MEASUREMENTS: h. 15.6 cm (6⅛ in); diam. (at rim) 8.3 cm (3¼ in).

INVENTORY: 852904

PROVENANCE: 5th Earl (subsequently 1st Marquess) of Bristol; given by him to the church of St Mary, Ickworth, as part of the Communion plate; transferred 1984 to St Leonard's, Horringer; on loan to the National Trust.

LITERATURE: Yates 2013, p. 14, ill.

DESCRIPTION: The domed foot is raised and has an applied stiff-leaf band. It terminates in a moulded band and a short ring stem. The straight sided circular cup with a slightly flared rim is raised, has an incised line at the rim and a broad matted band.

HERALDRY: The foot is engraved with the quartered arms of the Hanoverian monarchs (pre-1801) within the Garter plus the royal supporters and motto, all against an ermine mantling and beneath an imperial crown.

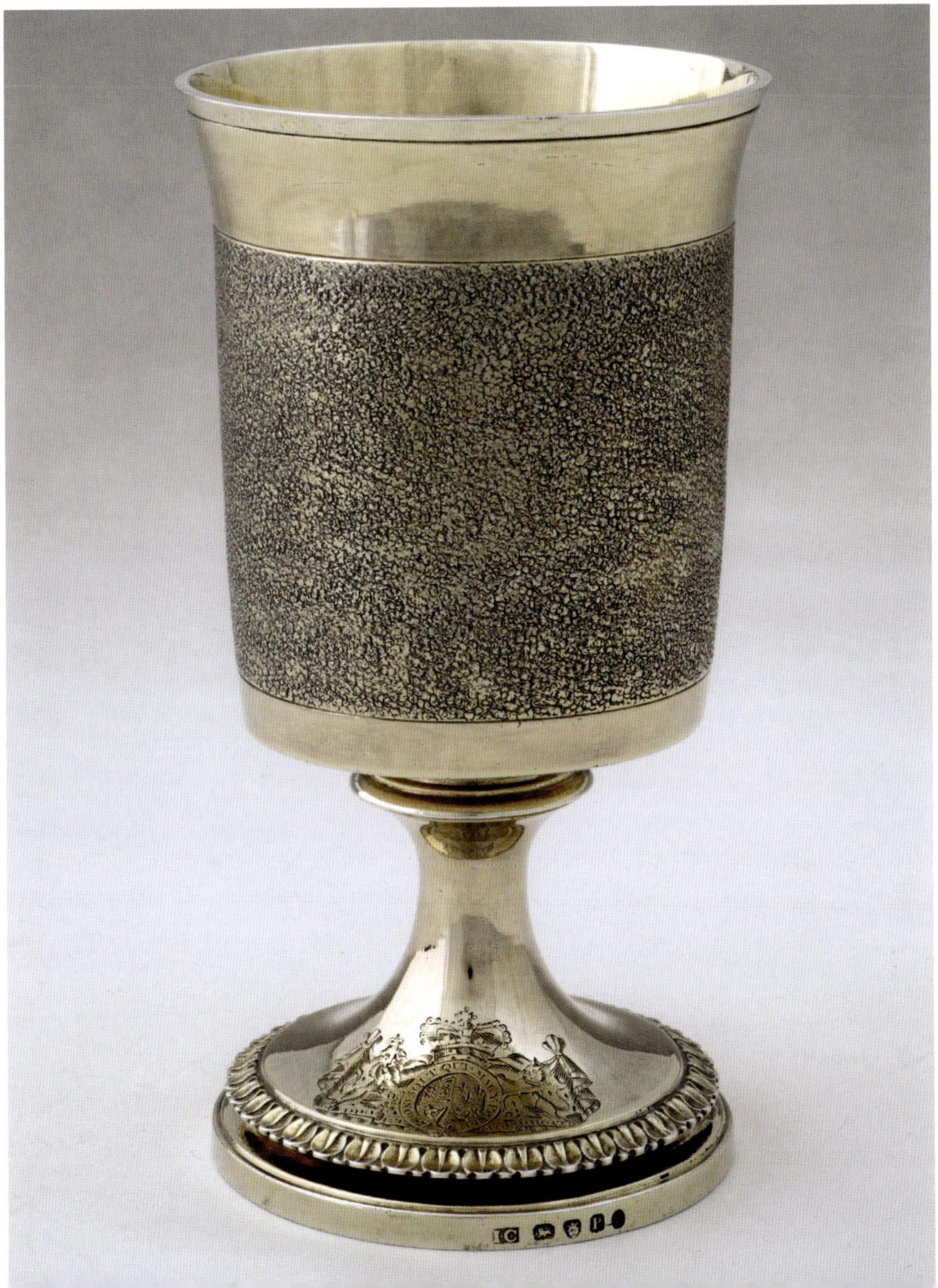

The broad matted band is typical of the treatment of beakers of the late seventeenth century from Germany and Switzerland, presumably to assist with grip as well as for decorative effect.[1] There are contemporary English examples too, such as a London-made tumbler cup of 1689,[2] and though the treatment continued to be applied occasionally thereafter[3] it was in the early nineteenth century that the most noticeable revival occurred, probably prompted by antiquarianism. It is possible that the cup of this chalice is a reused beaker, but if any hallmarks exist on it they are hidden by the foot.

The pre-1801 royal arms have been engraved on the piece in order to match with the alms dish probably given by the 3rd Earl of Bristol *c.*1778 (cat. 74). The other pieces of Ickworth church plate on loan from Horringer church are the flagon of 1705 by John Jackson I (cat. 6) and the French paten (cat. 107).

1. See for instance three Augsburg-made beakers of *c.*1680 and 1700 sold at Sotheby's, 26 February 1976, lots 77–9.
2. Sotheby's, 1 February 1968, lot 98.
3. A set of four beakers of 1714 has the same treatment, sold Sotheby's, 24 October 1968, lot 112.

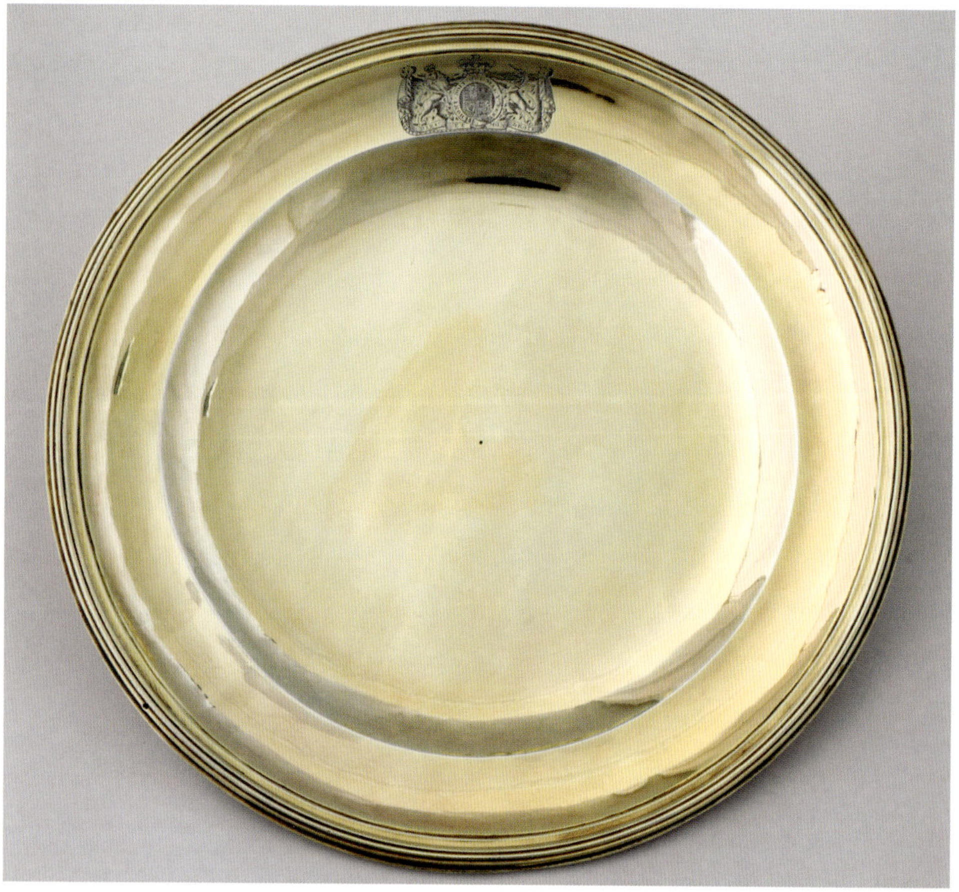

107. Paten

Silver-gilt / Jean François Nicolas Carron, Paris / 1787/8

MARKS AND INSCRIPTION: The underside of the rim is stamped with the maker's mark of a pistol above 'C' flanked by 'I' and 'F' and below a crowned fleur-de-lis between two pellets (Nocq 1926–31, vol. 1, p. 223), the Paris charge mark of a crowned 'A' for 1783–9 and the warden's mark of a crowned 'P' with 87 for 1787–8. The fourth mark, a covered cup under a fleur-de-lis, appears to be an Orléans countermark.[1] Engraved on the underside 'Ickworth Church'.

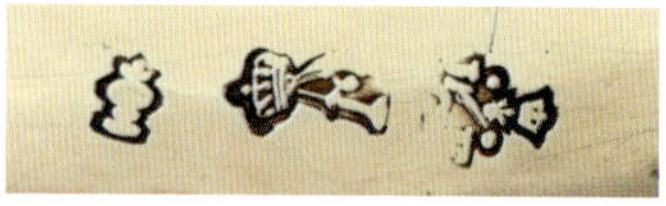

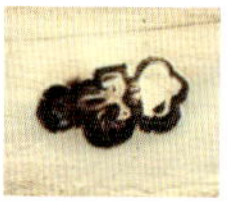

SCRATCHWEIGHT: None.
Actual weight: 294g (9 oz, 9 dwt).

MEASUREMENTS: diam. 23 cm (9 in).

INVENTORY: 852906

PROVENANCE: Probably 5th Earl (later 1st Marquess) of Bristol; given by him to the church of St Mary, Ickworth, as part of the Communion plate; transferred 1984 to St Leonard's, Horringer; on loan to the National Trust.

DESCRIPTION: The circular paten is raised and has a shallow well with a broad rim and an applied moulded border.

HERALDRY: The rim is engraved with the quartered arms of the Hanoverian monarchs (pre-1801) within the Garter plus the royal supporters and motto, all against an ermine mantling and beneath an imperial crown.

This piece, which must have been made as a small plate for domestic use, could have been acquired by the 4th Earl of Bristol or by John Augustus, Lord Hervey when passing through France in the 1780s or 1790s, but it could equally well have entered the stock of Rundell, Bridge & Rundell via a French émigré.

The paten forms part of the Ickworth church plate and was probably given in 1810–11 by the future 1st Marquess along with the chalice (cat. 106). The style of the engraving matches. For the other associated pieces see cat. 6 and 74.

1. Information from Christopher Hartop.

108. Pair of ice pail liners

Sterling silver
William Fountain, London / 1810/11

MARKS: Both of the liners are marked on their outer sides with maker's mark 'WF' italics in a rectangular punch (Grimwade 1990, no. 3127), lion passant, date letter 'P' and monarch's head. The rims are marked on the rear of the bezels with the lion passant, date letter 'P' and the same maker's mark.

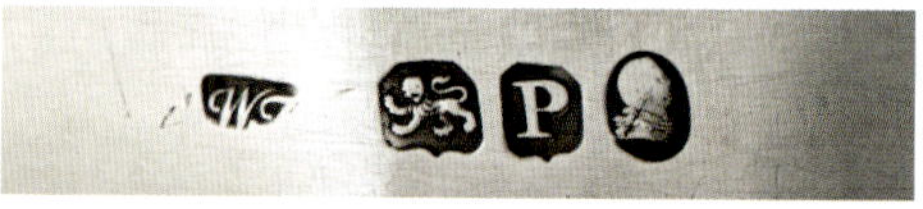

SCRATCHWEIGHTS: None.
Actual weights: 1. 1036 g (33 oz, 6 dwt); 2. 988 g (31 oz, 15 dwt).

MEASUREMENTS: h. 15.6 cm (6⅛ in); diam. (of liner sleeve) 13.3 cm (5¼ in); diam (of rim) 21.3 cm (8⅜ in).

INVENTORY: 852069.3–6

PROVENANCE: 5th Earl (later 1st Marquess) of Bristol; by descent to the 4th Marquess.

DESCRIPTION: Each circular sleeve is seamed with plain square wires top and bottom and is soldered to a flat base plate which has a larger diameter in order to rest against the sides of the pail. The plain rims are raised and have dished profiles, narrow flat outer edges and wide central openings conforming with applied seamed bezels. A rectangular seamed wire is applied under the outer edge of each rim to give strength and to secure it in position in the pail. The liners and one of the rims have punch marks (one and two) as do the pails, to identify the correct compositions.

HERALDRY: None.

These pieces were made for the pair of ice pails of *c.*1730 by Philip Rollos II (cat. 18). Sleeve liners do not seem to have been provided in the early eighteenth century, there being no mention of them in the Jewel Office records, whereas liners for tureens are recorded if supplied. There are, however, removable pierced plates, or drainers, surviving in pails of 1718 and *c.*1720 by David Willaume and in Paul Crespin's 1728/9 pair.[1]

Ice would have been packed in the base of the pails, and on top of the drainers if they were provided, with the bottles placed above, their broad bottoms ensuring sufficient contact to chill the wine. The width of the bottles of the period and the excellent conductivity of silver would also have ensured a sufficiently cool atmosphere in the upper section of the pail. By the turn of the eighteenth century, however, the increasingly slender form of wine bottles would have made cooling in this fashion less effective and many old pails were provided with sleeve liners, such as these, to narrow the aperture and to provide a void for ice.

1. See Hartop 1996, cat. 60, pp. 263–7, Sotheby's New York, 22 April 1998, lot 325 and Christie's, 3 July 1996, lot 100.

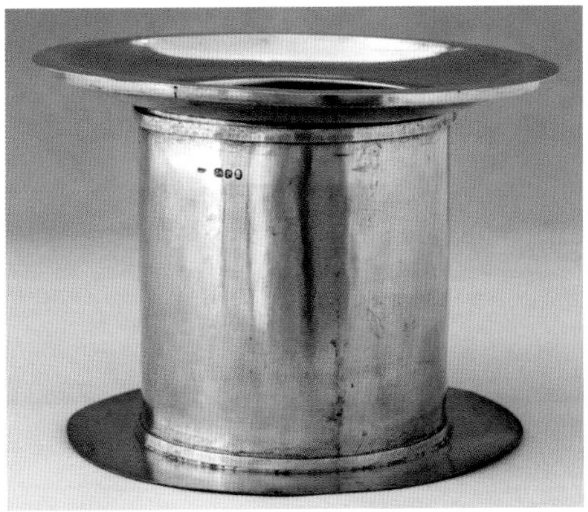

109. **Two inkstands**

Sterling silver / John Cramer, London / 1810/11 and 1811/12

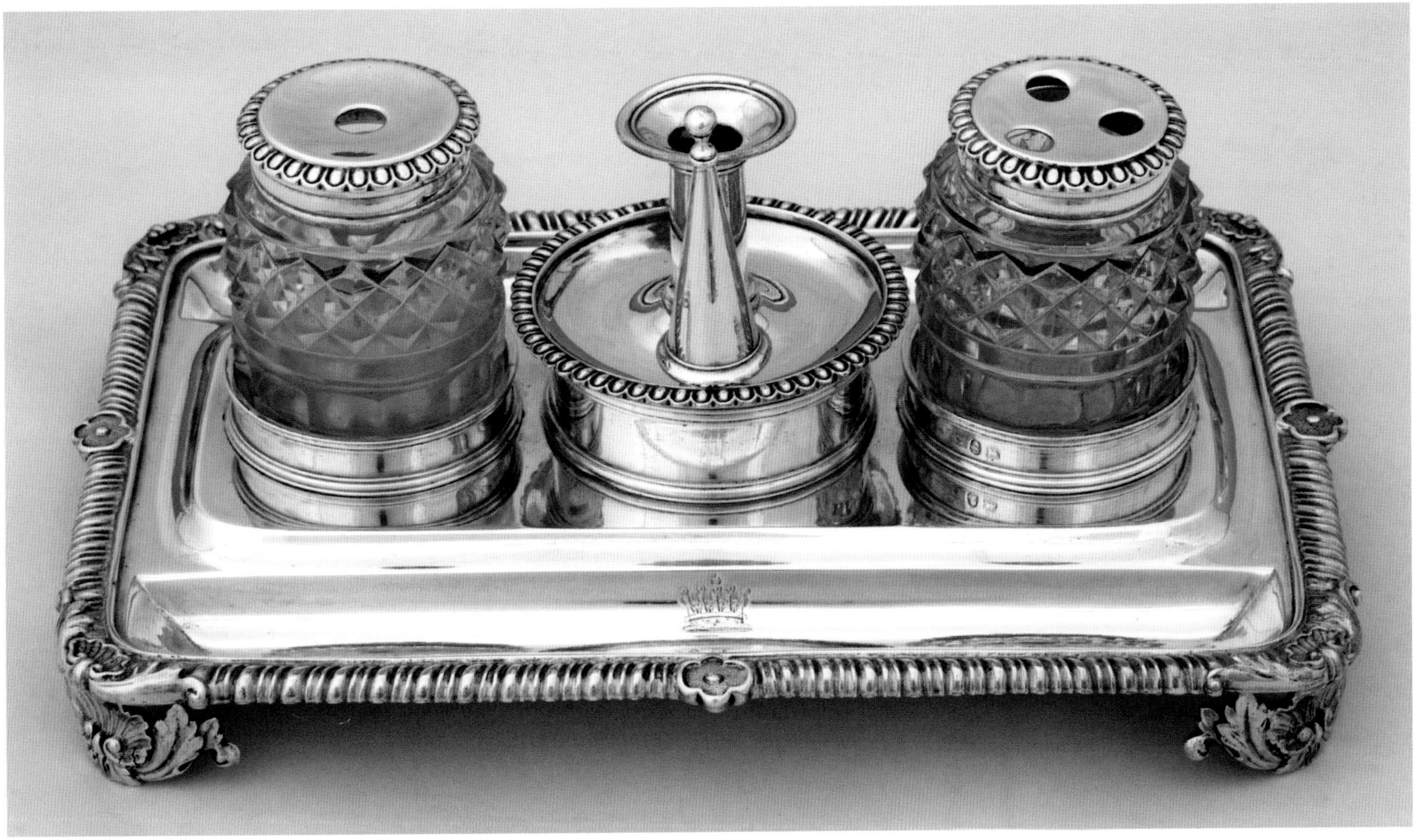

MARKS: The undersides of the stands are fully marked with the monarch's head, lion passant, leopard's head, maker's mark 'I·C' in a rectangular punch (Grimwade 1990, no. 1217) and the date letters 'P' and 'Q'. Partial sets of conforming marks are found on the tapersticks, extinguishers, bottle holders and bottle tops.

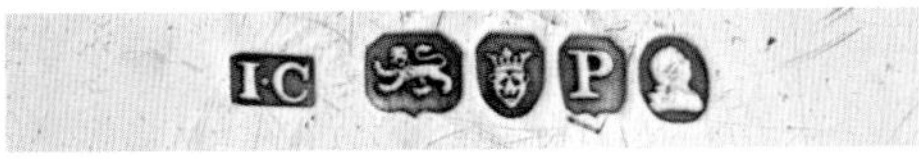

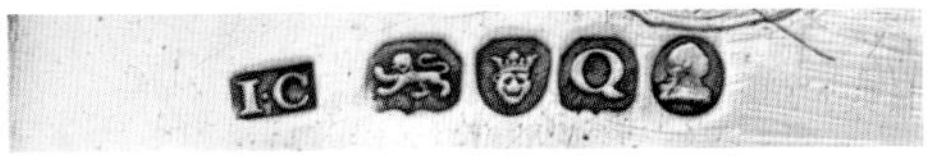

SCRATCHWEIGHTS: Very faint – 'Oz [/] 21„9' (1810) and 'Oz – 22„0' (1811)

MEASUREMENTS: 1810 inkstand h. 9.5 cm (3¾ in); w. 21.5 cm (8½ in); d. 15.6 cm (6⅛ in). 1811 inkstand h. 9.5 cm (3¾ in); w. 22.2 cm (8¾ in); d. 15.2 cm (6 in).

INVENTORY: 852117 and 852118

PROVENANCE: 5th Earl (subsequently 1st Marquess) of Bristol; by descent to the 4th Marquess.

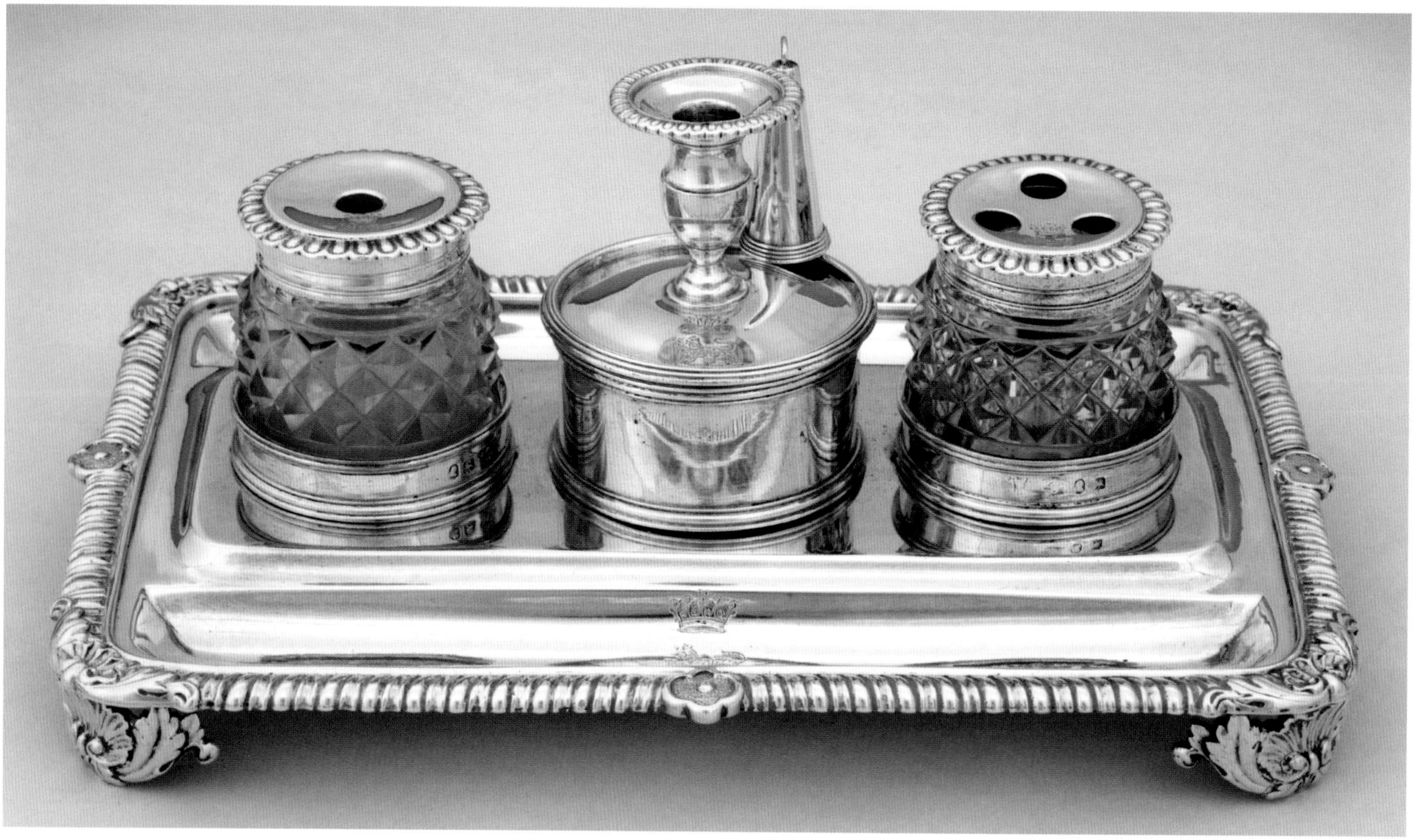

DESCRIPTION: The rectangular stands with curved corners are raised and each has two full length concave-profiled pen wells and cast gadroon borders with central quatrefoils, the corners decorated with shells and scrolling leaves. The four cast feet are also formed of shells and scrolling leaves. On top of each stand are three seamed circles of silver with reeded mouldings top and bottom and flat base plates, bolted through to the underside of the stand. Two contain cut glass bottles, for ink and quill-cleaning shot, which have silver covers formed of seamed sheet applied to dished tops pierced with one and three holes and with cast tongue-and-cable mouldings. The central, larger containers, for sealing wax and wafers, have as their lids the raised dishes of tapersticks, that of 1810 with a cast tongue-and-cable moulding to the rim and the other with reeding. Both tapersticks have vase-shaped sockets but their cast drip pans differ. That of 1810 is fixed with a simple moulded rim whilst that of 1811 is detachable and has a tongue-and-cable rim The tapering extinguishers vary slightly too, one (1810) having a ball finial and a moulded rim and the other a ring finial for an attaching chain (missing) and a reeded rim.

HERALDRY: Both of the inkstands are engraved with the Hervey crest beneath an earl's coronet in one of the pen wells and on the taperstick saucer. The 1811 stand has the same engraving also on the two bottle tops.

These inkstands are quite typical for the period. They were acquired shortly after the listing of Lord Bristol's plate in May, 1811 (see appendix 5), being included amongst 'plate added' on the same document. The fact that they do not exactly match would not have mattered as one was intended for St James's Square and the other for Ickworth, as recorded in both the 1811 and 1826 plate lists.[1]

1. Bristol plate list 1826–7. They are recorded as 'Ickworth Ink Stand' and 'London Ink Stand'.

110. **Four chamber candlesticks**

Sterling silver / John Mewburn, London / 1811/12

MARKS: The base of each saucer is fully marked with maker's mark 'IM' in a rectangular punch (Grimwade 1990, no. 1528), lion passant, leopard's head, date letter 'Q' and monarch's head.

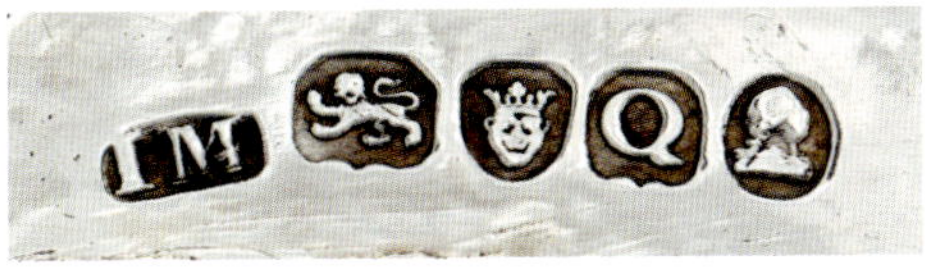

SCRATCHWEIGHTS: 'N 3 13"15'; 'N 5 13"6'; 'N 6 13"6'; 'N 7 13"1'

MEASUREMENTS: h. 9.5 cm (3¾ in); w. (incl. handle) 17.8 cm (7 in); diam. (of base) 14.6 cm (5¾ in).

INVENTORY: 852189.3–6

PROVENANCE: 5th Earl (subsequently 1st Marquess) of Bristol; by descent to the 4th Marquess.

DESCRIPTION: The circular concave saucer bases are raised with applied cast gadroon borders, scroll handles and slightly domed centres. The concave profiled stems are formed of two cast sections between which is a slot for snuffers (missing) and support cast circular, vase-shaped sockets with chased gadrooning to their feet. The seamed nozzles have concave drip pans with applied cast gadroon borders. The cone-shaped extinguishers with cast vase finials and gadrooned rims also have applied L-shaped hooks by which they are secured into sockets attached to the thumb-pieces of the base handles.

HERALDRY: The saucers, drip pans and extinguishers are all engraved with the Hervey crest beneath an earl's coronet.

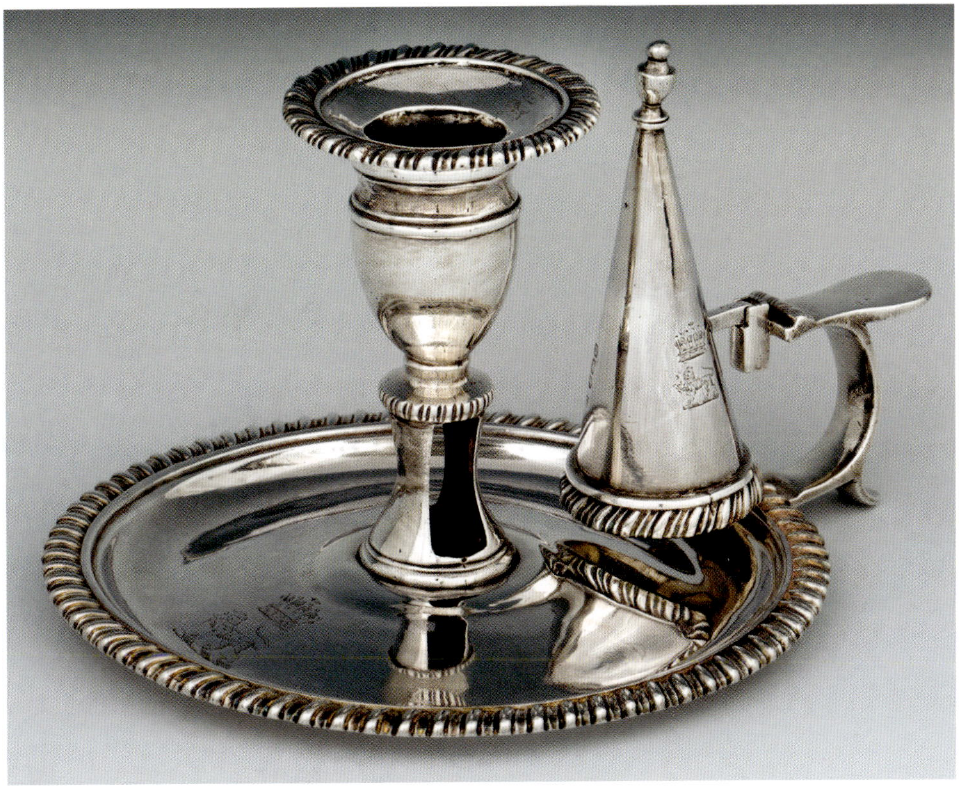

This set originally extended to eight and was probably intended for St James's Square, the previous mismatched sets (cat. 91 and 95) being combined at Ickworth. The acquisition was made in November 1811, according to a note in the copy plate book of that year.[1] Of the four retained by the family in 1956 two were sold from the East Wing in 1996. They bore the same hallmarks, were numbered 1 and 2 and had scratchweights of 13-1 and 13-3.[2]

1. SRO, 941/75/1, Copy Plate Book 1811.
2. Sotheby's Suffolk, 11–12 June 1996, East Wing Ickworth, lot 341. Hammer price £2,400.

111. **Tea pot**

Sterling silver
John Mewburn, London / 1813/14

MARKS: Fully marked on the underside with maker's mark 'IM' in a rectangular punch (Grimwade 1990, no. 1528), lion passant, date letter 'S', monarch's head and leopard's head. Also marked on the bezel of the lid with the same maker's mark (mis-struck), lion passant and date letter 'S'.

SCRATCHWEIGHT: None.

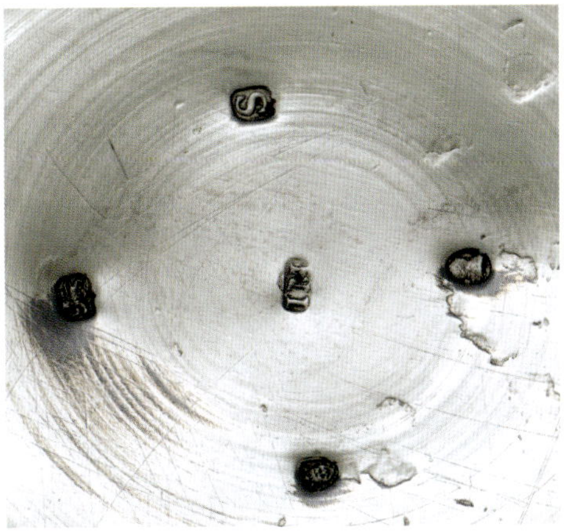

Actual weight: 734 g (23 oz, 12 dwt).

MEASUREMENTS: h. 12.7 cm (5 in); w. 28.9 cm (11⅜ in); d. 16.5 cm (6½ in).

INVENTORY: 852107

PROVENANCE: 5th Earl (subsequently 1st Marquess) of Bristol; by descent to the 4th Marquess.

DESCRIPTION: The compressed spherical body is raised in two pieces, the concave curved neck-piece being separate and applied as is the seamed, wave-profiled rim.

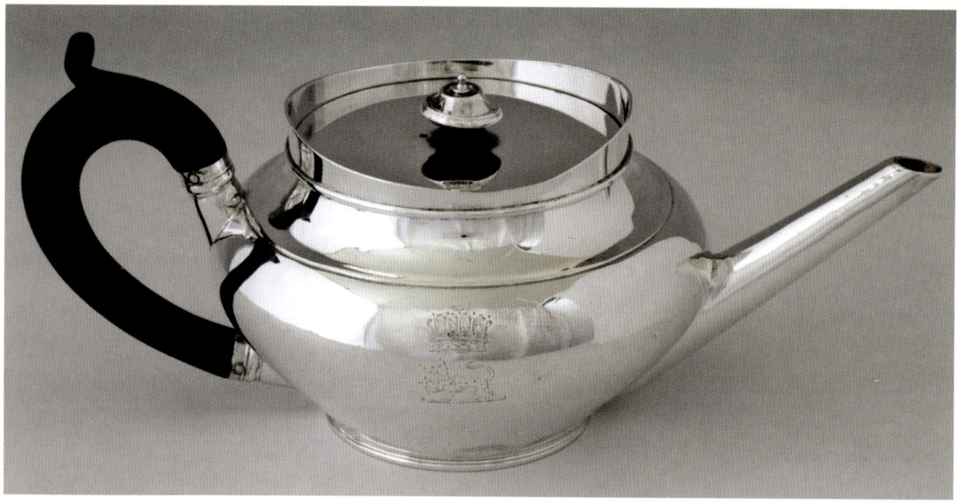

Inside and outside the neck are applied wire mouldings, the inner one supporting the raised, slightly domed lid which has an applied, seamed bezel, drilled steam hole and turned wooden knop with raised silver cap and cast urn finial to silver bolt. The carved ebony loop handle with scrolled thumb-piece is pinned to two seamed tubes of silver with chased mouldings that are soldered to the body. The straight, tapering spout is seamed and applied. The body is pierced behind the spout to act as a strainer.

HERALDRY: The side of the pot (with spout to the right) and the lid are engraved with the Hervey crest beneath an earl's coronet.

This is almost identical to the 1801 teapot by Henry Nutting (cat. 97) and was probably acquired to be used alongside it.

112. **Pair of grape scissors**

Sterling silver / William Eley I, William Fearn and William Chawner II, London / 1813/14

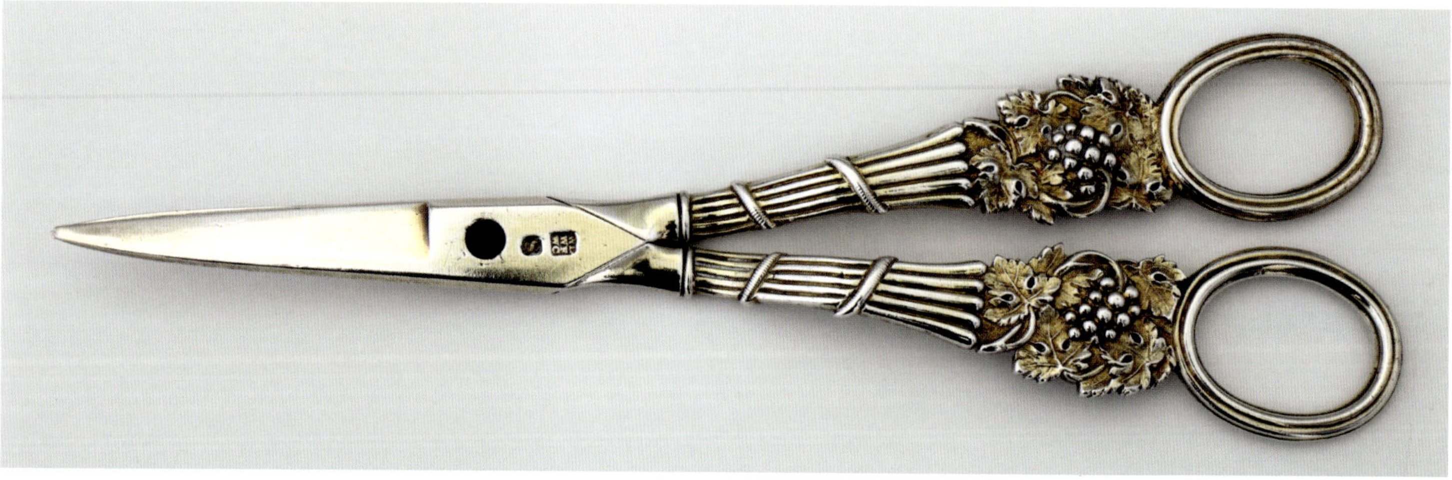

MARKS: Marked at the top of the blades, on the front with the date letter 'S' and maker's mark 'WE' over 'WF' over 'WC' (Grimwade 1990, no. 3114) and on the back with the monarch's head and lion passant.

SCRATCHWEIGHT: None. The 1811 plate list (appendix 5) gives a combined weight of 7 oz for this and the 1820 pair (cat. 116).

MEASUREMENTS: l. 18.8 cm (7⅜ in).

INVENTORY: 852102.210

PROVENANCE: 5th Earl (subsequently 1st Marquess) of Bristol; by descent to the 4th Marquess.

LITERATURE: Penzer 1957a, I, p. 43.

DESCRIPTION: The sharply pointed scissor blades have cast and chased reed-and-tie lower stems above which are grapes and vine leaves against matted grounds with applied oval reeded handles.

HERALDRY: None

These were supplied in 1815 (see appendix 5) and must therefore have been from stock. They are more elaborate than many of the period and they are particularly finely cast and chased. Grape scissors were amongst the plethora of new articles in silver produced in the decades around 1800. None appear in the Jewel Office Delivery Book finishing in 1793 and it is probable that they began to be made in the first decade of the nineteenth century, quickly becoming very popular and an essential accoutrement for a fashionable household. There are few examples surviving of such an early date as these, two others of 1809 and 1812 in the Ashmolean Museum showing the progressive elaboration of treatment of the stems of the handles.[1] They, like the Ickworth pair, have straightforward scissor blades whereas within a few years there had been a development which allowed the cut stalk to be held once severed (see cat. 116).

1. Schroder 2009, cat. 403–4, pp. 931–2.

113. Dessert service

Sterling silver knifes (x 6) with silver blades / Moses Brent, London / 1815/16 (x 1) / and Robert Peppin, London / 1818/19 (x 5)
Sterling silver forks (x 6) and spoons (x 6) / Robert Peppin, London / 1821/2, 1822/3 and 1823/4

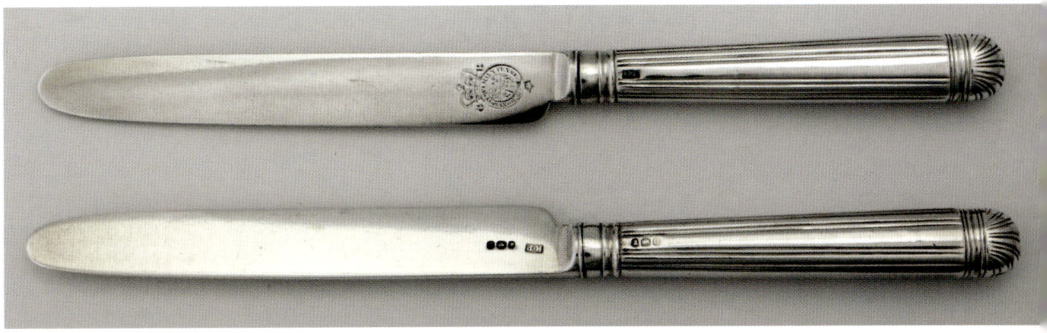

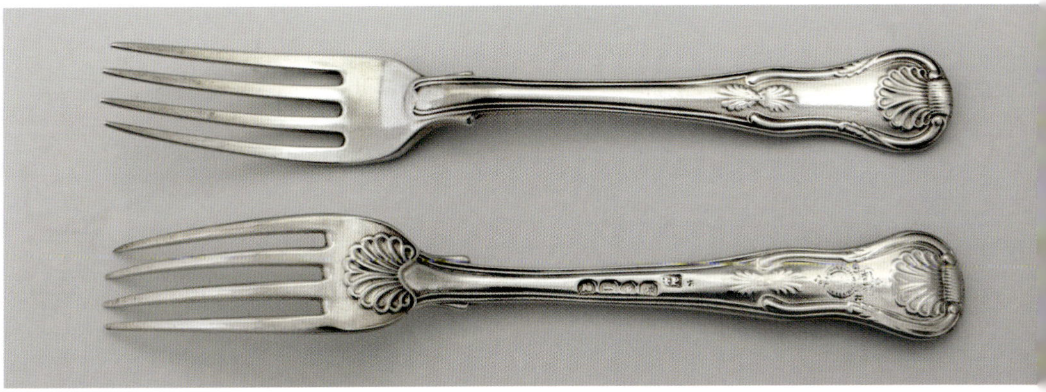

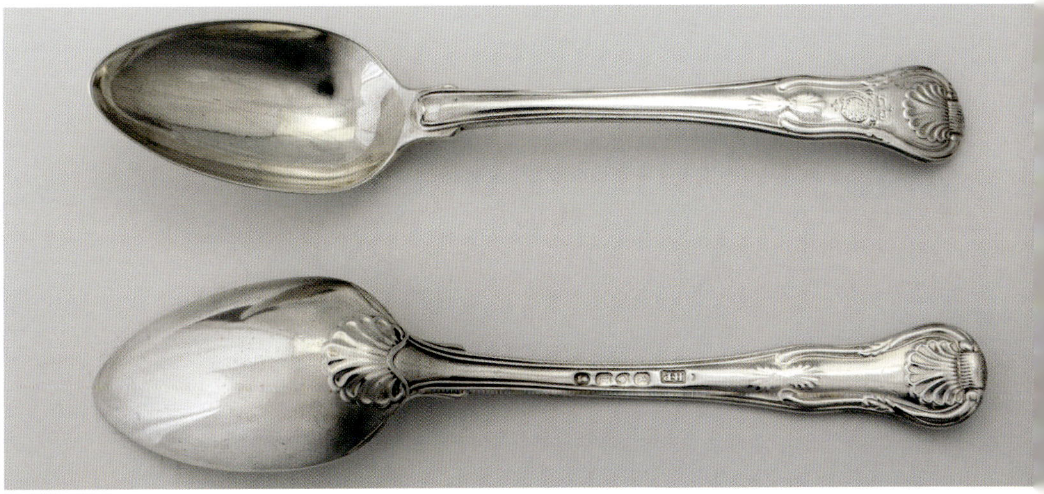

MARKS: One of the knives has on its blade the maker's mark 'M·B' in a rectangular punch (Grimwade 1990, no. 2000), monarch's head, lion passant and date letter 'U' and on the haft the lion passant only. The other five are marked on both their hafts and blades with maker's mark 'R·P' in a rectangular punch (Grimwade 1990, no. 2413),[1] monarch's head, lion passant and date letter 'c'. The spoons and forks are all fully marked on the reverse of the stem with monarch's head, date letters 'f' (three forks), 'g' (all the spoons and two forks) and 'h' (one fork), leopard's head, lion passant and maker's mark 'R·P' in a rectangular punch (Grimwade 1990, no. 2413).

SCRATCHWEIGHTS: None. The 1811 plate list (appendix 5) gives overall weights for 18 spoons and forks of 38 oz, 6 dwt, and 37 oz, 9 dwt, respectively.

MEASUREMENTS: (l.) knives 20.3 cm (8 in); forks 17.4 cm (6⅞ in); spoons 18.4 cm (7¼ in).

INVENTORY: Knives 852194.
Forks 852184.7–12. Spoons 852184.1–6

PROVENANCE: 5th Earl (subsequently 1st Marquess) of Bristol; by descent to the 4th Marquess.

DESCRIPTION: The knife hafts are of the double thread and shell pattern[2] with slightly tapering blades. The forks, which have four tines, and the spoons are of the King's pattern with union shell heel.[3]

HERALDRY: Each knife blade is engraved on its left side, each fork on the reverse of its terminal and each spoon on the front of its terminal with the quartered shield of the Hanoverian monarchs (pre-1801) within the Garter and beneath an imperial crown flanked by the initials GR.

These pieces were acquired in 1823 according to a note of additions on the 1811 plate list (appendix 5) and were originally part of a table and dessert service which had eighteen each of dessert knives with steel blades, dessert knives with silver blades and dessert forks and spoons. Nothing of the table service, which was more extensive, survives at Ickworth having been retained by the family in 1956.

Substantial quantities of such popular patterns of flatware and cutlery as these must have been kept in stock by Rundell, Bridge & Rundell, and hence the varying dates and makers of this service. The preponderance of pieces by Robert Peppin suggests that he may well have taken over from his near-neighbour in Hatton Garden, Moses Brent, as the principal supplier of knives to Rundell, Bridge & Rundell. Although a date of death has not yet been ascertained for Brent there do not appear to be any pieces bearing his mark of later than 1818.

The Earl would have had to request specifically the engraving of the pre-1801 royal arms and in doing so he was almost certainly putting right the loss of over 1,000 ounces of heirloom plate during the tenures of his uncle and father, the 3rd and 4th Earls. He was not, however, going to the extent of replacing exactly what had gone, as in 1823 all of the 2nd Earl's dessert service of 1758 survived. The intention may well have been to augment that service, albeit in a different pattern.

1. This is without a pellet but Grimwade notes that he also had marks incorporating one.
2. Pickford 1983, pp. 50–1, fig. 43e.
3. Ibid., p. 122, fig. 166.

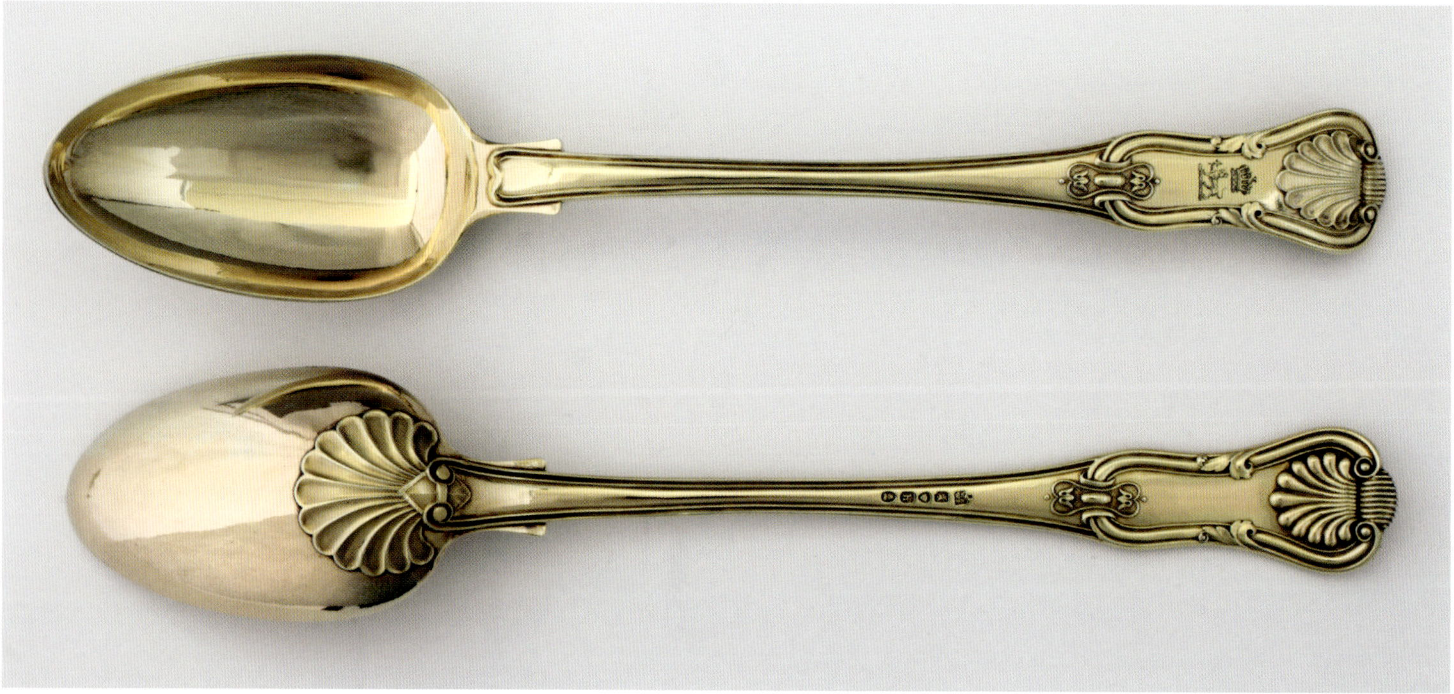

114. **Dessert service**

Sterling silver, gilded / William Eley I and William Fearn, London / 1823/4

MARKS: The silver-bladed knives are fully marked on their blades with the maker's mark 'WE' over 'WF' in a square punch (Grimwade 1990, no. 3112), monarch's head, lion passant, date letter 'h' and leopard's head. Their hafts and those of the steel-bladed knives have the same except for the monarch's head. The steel blades are stamped with an imperial crown flanked by 'GR' over 'GILBERT'. All the spoons and the forks are marked on the underside of their stems with same marks as found on the blades of the silver-bladed knives.

SCRATCHWEIGHTS: None. The weight given for the service in the 1811 plate list (appendix 5) is 384 oz, 19 dwt.

MEASUREMENTS: (l.) knives 21.5 cm (8½ in); ice spoons 30.8 cm (12⅛ in); table spoons 22.3 cm (8¾ in); dessert forks 17.2 cm (6¾ in); dessert spoons: 17.3 cm (6¾ in).

INVENTORY: 852102.1-208

PROVENANCE: 5th Earl (subsequently 1st Marquess) of Bristol; by descent to the 4th Marquess.

LITERATURE: Penzer 1957a, I, p. 43.

DESCRIPTION: The service consists of four serving or ice spoons, twelve table spoons and forty-eight each of silver-gilt bladed knives, steel-bladed knives, forks and spoons. It is of the hour-glass pattern, the silver-gilt knife blades being cast and chased with husks issuing from tentacles and scrolling around flower-heads. All the blades, which are contemporary, are slightly tapering with pointed ends.

HERALDRY: The left-hand side of the fork hafts, the front of the spoons and the rear of the forks are all engraved on their terminal with the Hervey crest beneath an earl's coronet.

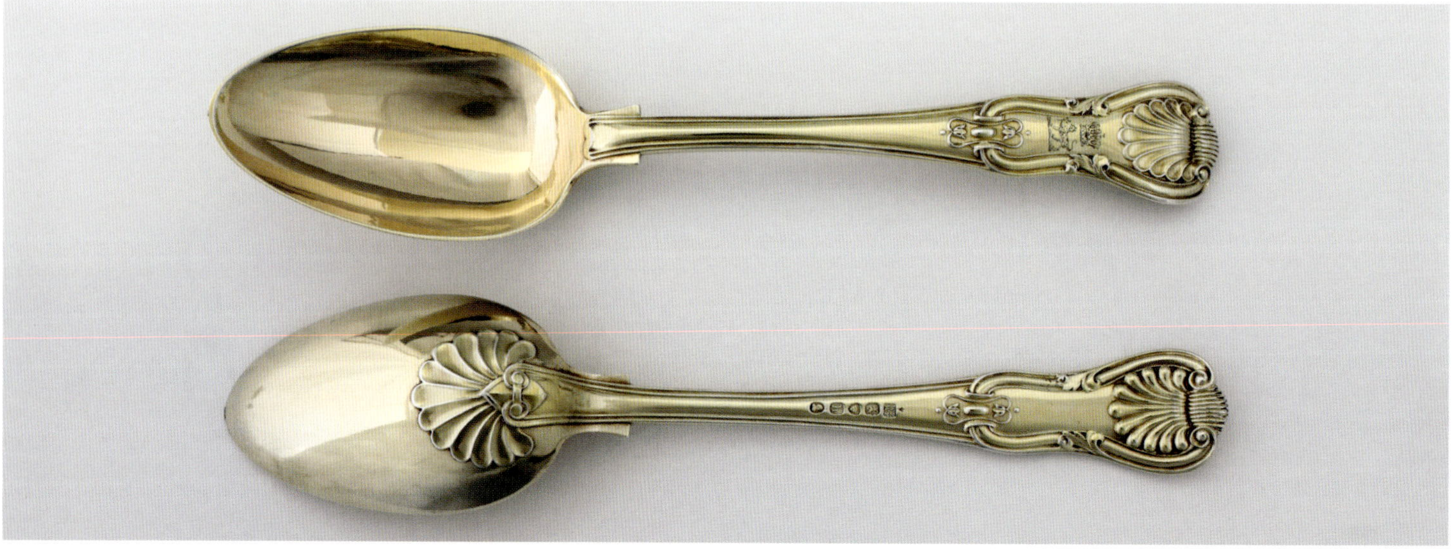

Although almost all the table and dessert services listed in the 1811 and 1826 plate lists are still represented at Ickworth this is the only one that is complete. A note in the 1811 list confirms that it was delivered in 1823, the year it was marked, and unlike the ungilt dessert service which came at the same time (cat. 113) it is of a consistent date and by a single maker. It may well have been ordered specifically from Eley and Fearn by Rundell, Bridge & Rundell to fulfil Lord Bristol's commission. As the finest of the dessert services available it would almost certainly have been intended for the London house and it is listed there in 1874.[1] It is in near-perfect condition.

1. Bristol Plate Lists 1874.

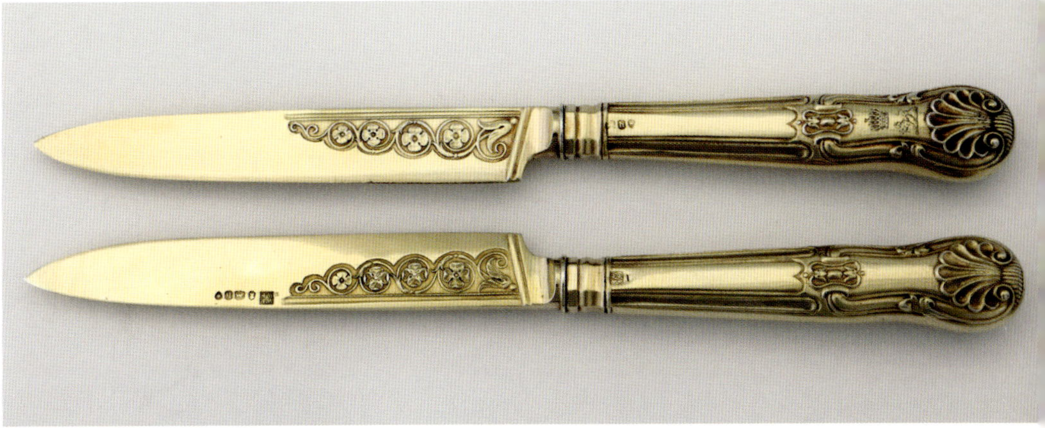

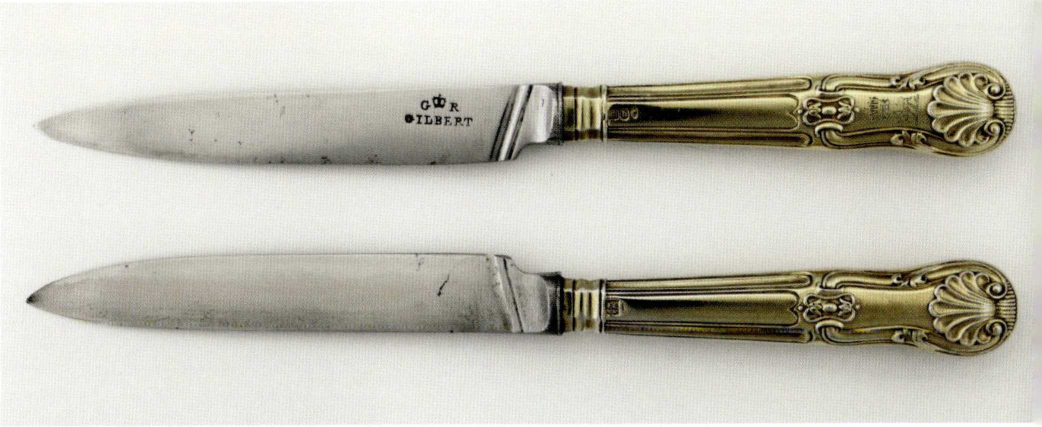

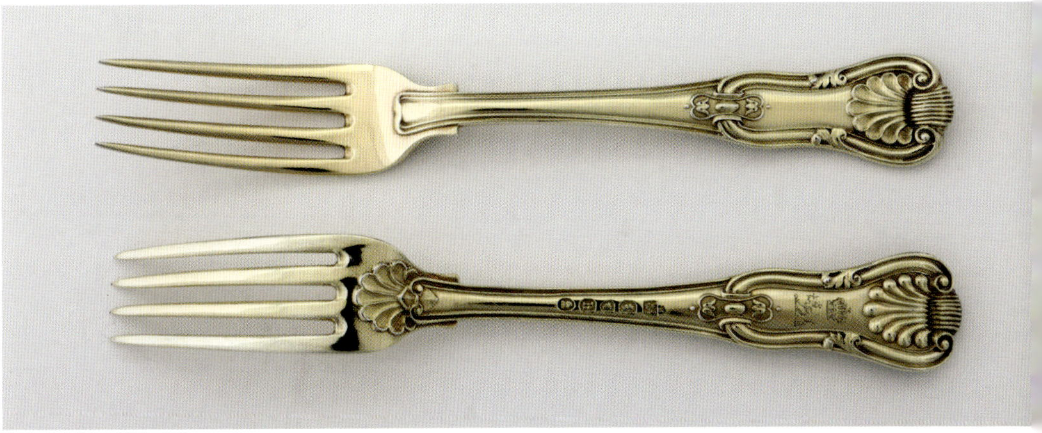

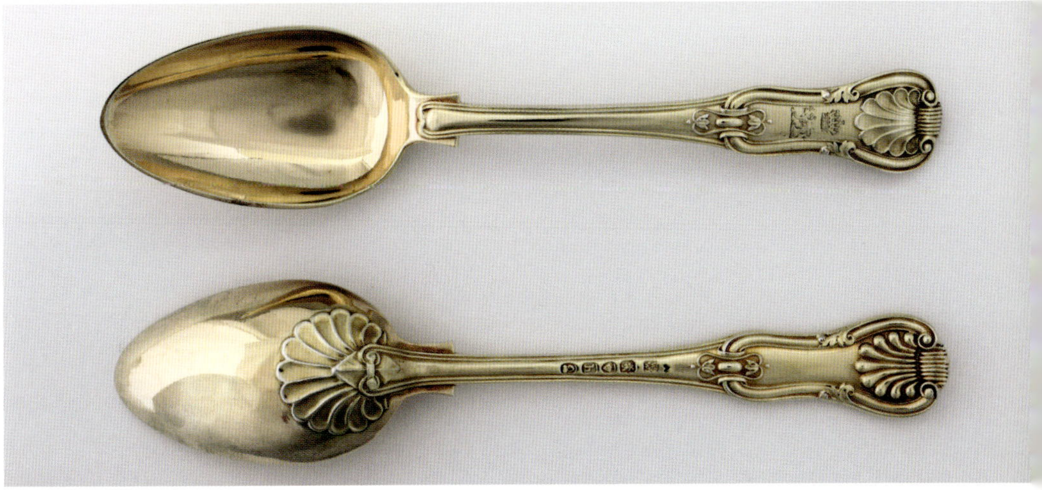

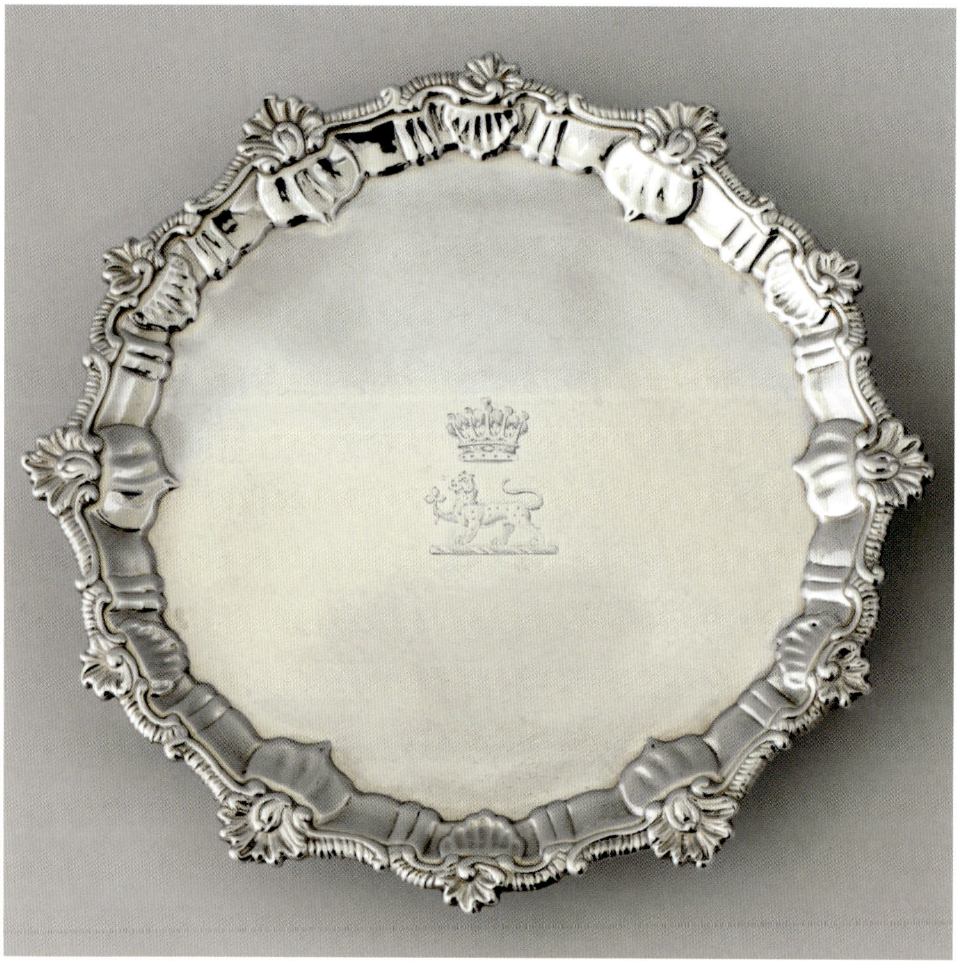

115. Two waiters

Sterling silver / Ebenezer Coker, London / 1755/6

MARKS: Each is fully marked on its underside with maker's mark 'E·C' italics in a shaped punch (Grimwade 1990, no. 556),[1] lion passant, leopard's head and date letter 'U'.

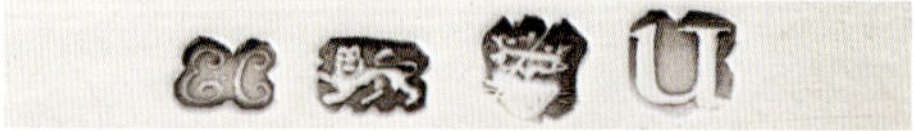

SCRATCHWEIGHTS: None.
Actual weight: 272 g (8 oz, 15 dwt); 285 g (9 oz, 3 dwt)

MEASUREMENTS: h. 2.5 cm (1 in); diam. 18.7 cm (7⅜ in).

INVENTORY: 852123

PROVENANCE: 5th Earl (subsequently 1st Marquess) of Bristol; by descent to the 4th Marquess.

DESCRIPTION: Each of the circular waiters is on three cast claw-and-ball feet and is raised with a chased shaped border and an applied cast gadroon, scroll and shell border.

HERALDRY: The centre of each salver has been re-engraved *c.*1823 with the Hervey crest beneath an earl's coronet.

These waiters must be the pair recorded in the 1811 plate list as having been added in 1823, their weight roughly tallying and the engraving appearing to be early nineteenth century (see appendix 5). In 1874 the same pair, then in the St James's Square house, are described as 'Shell' waiters. The revived interest in mid-eighteenth-century styles would have made them quite acceptable seventy years after their manufacture and they would not have been seen as outmoded.

Whether Lord Bristol was merely charged for the metal, and not fashion, as would have been the case with second-hand plate in the eighteenth century, is unknown.

1. Grimwade shows the mark without a pellet but Pickford 1989, p. 200 shows it as here. This is probably an unregistered version of his standard mark.

116. Pair of grape scissors

Sterling silver, gilded
William Eley I and William Fearn / 1820/1

MARKS: On the inside faces of the blades are punched the monarch's head, lion passant, date letter 'e' and maker's mark 'WE' over 'WF' in a square punch (Grimwade 1990, no. 3112).

SCRATCHWEIGHTS: None. The 1811 plate list (appendix 5) gives a combined weight of 7 oz for this pair and that of 1813.

MEASUREMENTS: l. 16.6 cm (6½ in).

INVENTORY: 852102.209

PROVENANCE: 5th Earl (subsequently 1st Marquess) of Bristol; by descent to the 4th Marquess.

DESCRIPTION: The handles are the same as those on the 1813 pair (cat. 112) but the pivot is circular, with a cast knurled surround to the tightening screw, and the blades are slightly curved, together giving the appearance of a bird's head. The blades are thick and one has an applied, right-angled cutting edge.

HERALDRY: None.

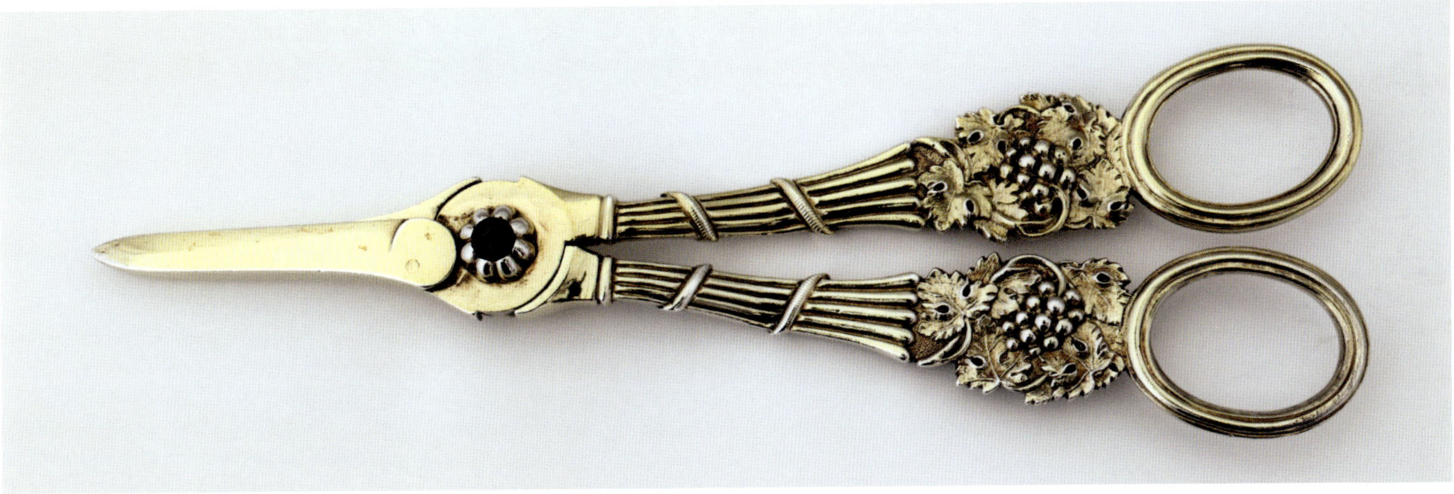

According to notes in the 1811 plate list (appendix 5) relating to subsequent additions to the collection these were acquired in July 1824 so, as with the earlier pair, they must have come from stock. Since 1813 (the date of the earlier pair – see cat. 112) the scissor form had developed and the addition of a right-angled cutting edge to one of the blades allowed the severed stalk to be clamped between the blades and the grapes brought to the diner's plate without falling onto the table, provided of course that they were used the right way round.

117. **Pair of grape scissors**

Gilded silver-plate / ***c.*1825**

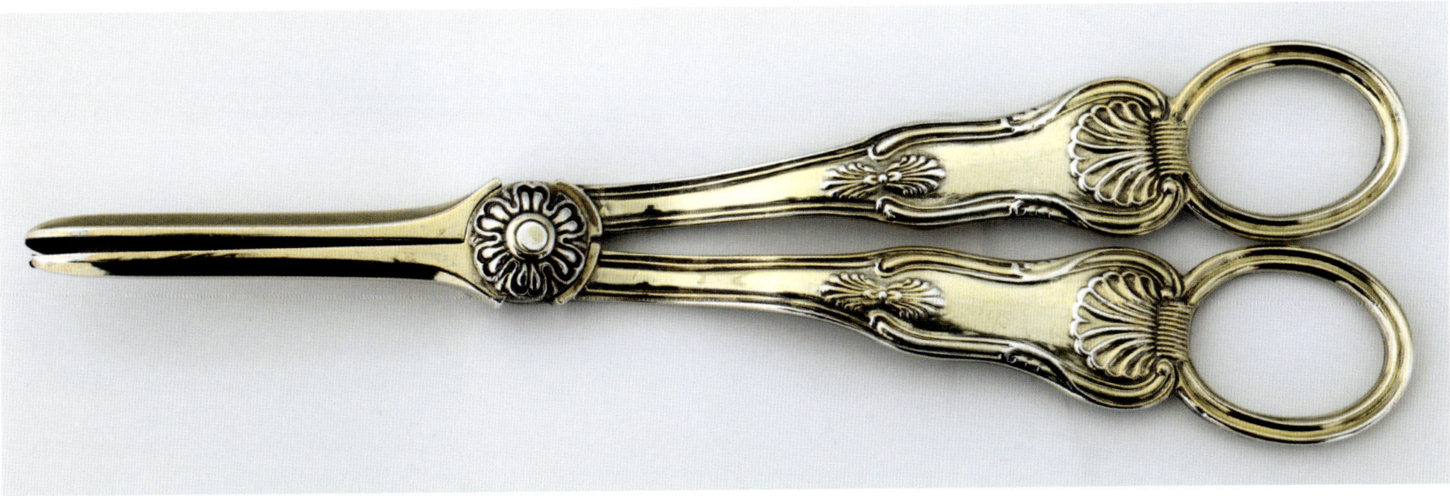

MARKS: The inside edges of the blades are stamped with 'Z' aping a date letter, two other indistinguishable punches, 'B', another indistinguishable mark and '22' in conjoining circles.

SCRATCHWEIGHTS: None

MEASUREMENTS: l. 18.3 cm (7¼ in).

INVENTORY: 852102.211

PROVENANCE: Probably 5th Earl (later 1st Marquess) of Bristol; by descent to the 4th Marquess.

DESCRIPTION: The scissors have beak-shaped blades with a right-angled steel cutting edge, circular pivot with knurled tightening nut, King's Pattern stems and oval, fluted handles.

HERALDRY: None.

Grape scissors were often supplied in gilded silver-plate and numerous examples survive in National Trust collections. These ones may have been acquired to accompany the King's Pattern dessert service of the early 1820s (cat. 113). As they were not solid silver they were not included in either of the 1st Marquess's plate lists.

118. **Lincolnshire Tenants Candelabrum**

Sterling silver / John Bridge, London / 1826/7

MARKS: Fully marked on the underside with the maker's mark 'I·B' under an imperial crown (Grimwade 1990, no. 1172), lion passant, leopard's head, date letter 'l' and monarch's head. There are further, conforming marks on other components of the piece.

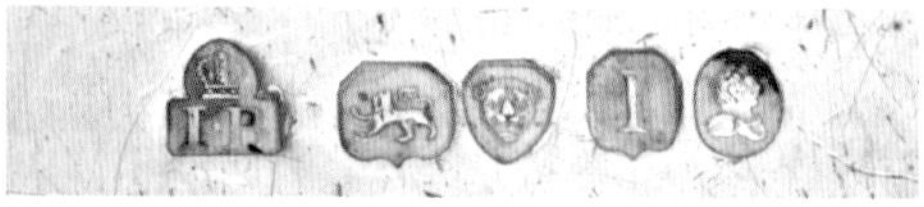

SCRATCHWEIGHT: '298 oz..s 8 dwt..s'.

MEASUREMENTS: h. 70 cm (27½ in); w. 43 cm (17 in); diam. (of base) 25 cm (10 in).

INVENTORY: 852057

PROVENANCE: Given to the 5th Earl (subsequently 1st Marquess) of Bristol 1827 by his Lincolnshire tenants; by descent to the 4th Marquess.

DESCRIPTION: Three cast and chased lion's paw and acanthus foliage feet interconnected by scrollwork and palmettes support a circular waved and ribbed platform with an inner acanthus leaf band. Above is a circular drum on which is engraved on one side a lengthy inscription and on the other a coat of arms (see below). The base of the drum has a cast band of stylised, fluted leaves and there is a pulvinated guilloche frieze. From a plain, flat circular plate on top of the drum rises a cast and chased column with profuse acanthus foliage interwoven with grape-bearing vines and populated by perching and feeding birds. Around the base of the column are three dancing *ballerini* in neoclassical dress and hand in hand (see image overleaf). From the plain capital of the column emanate a calyx of chased drooping acanthus leaves and six reeded, scrolling branches with applied acanthus leaves and flowers which terminate in cast and chased lotus flower sockets. A seventh, conforming socket is on a flaring stiff-leaf stem rising from the centre of the capital. The drip pans are formed as waterleaf coronas.

HERALDRY: On one side of the drum is engraved a rococo shield showing the arms of Hervey impaling Upton (sable, a cross moline or)[1] with the Hervey supporters and motto beneath an earl's coronet for the 5th Earl of Bristol. Each of the drip pans is engraved with the Hervey crest and an earl's coronet.

INSCRIPTION: On the opposite side of the drum to the arms of the 5th Earl of Bristol in various scripts and in upper and lower case:

This piece of Plate was Presented in the Year 1826 [/] to the Right Honble Frederick William Earl of Bristol, by the Tenants on his Lordship's Lincolnshire Estates, as a testimony of the very high sense they have of his virtues [/] and as a standing memorial of their attachment and gratitude for his noble act of generosity [/] in a reduction of 20 pr. Cent on their respective Rents [/] (to those under Lease as well as others) [/] during many years of extreme and unprecedented agricultural distress [/] and continuing that relief one Year after those difficulties had ceased.

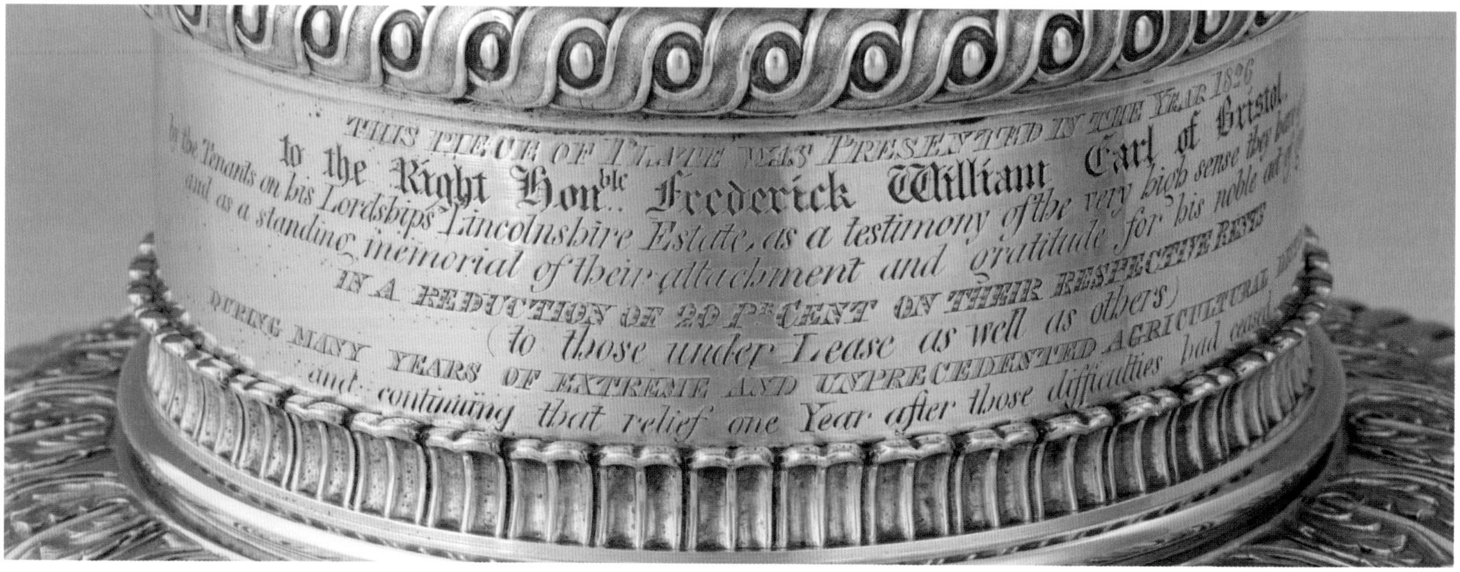

For two decades following the Napoleonic wars there were successive periods of agricultural depression and the worst of these was in the years 1820–4 when not only was the wheat price substantially reduced by good harvests and consequent massive overproduction but a general deflation also affected stock and dairy farmers.[2] Large landowners often reduced rents in such circumstances but Lord Bristol's response on his 14,000 acre Lincolnshire estate[3] seems to have been particularly generous. His reduction of 20 per cent compares favourably, for instance, with the Duke of Bedford's 17 on his Thorney estate on the Lincolnshire–Cambridgeshire border[4] and Lord Bristol also went further than many landowners in both applying the reductions to all his tenants, irrespective of the terms under which they held their land, and extending the reduction for a year beyond the end of the crisis in 1824. The tenants, to show their gratitude and no doubt also to encourage similar action in any future depressions, commissioned the candelabrum through the Earl's goldsmiths, Rundell, Bridge & Rundell. Details of the mechanics of this commission, which was presumably effected through the Earl's steward and with his own knowledge and influence on design, have yet to come to light. Testimonials had become enormously popular during the later, triumphant years of the Napoleonic wars and they continued so in peacetime, their subjects being great landowners, intellectuals, artists and industrialists in place of admirals and generals.

The candelabrum bears the mark of one of the principals of Rundell, Bridge & Rundell, John Bridge (1755–1834), and its sophisticated design and superb modelling and chasing are testament to the highly skilled artists and craftsmen assembled by the firm. The celebrated sculptor John Flaxman (1755–1826) had been supplying designs since 1805 and his former pupil, Edward Hodges Baily (1788–1867),

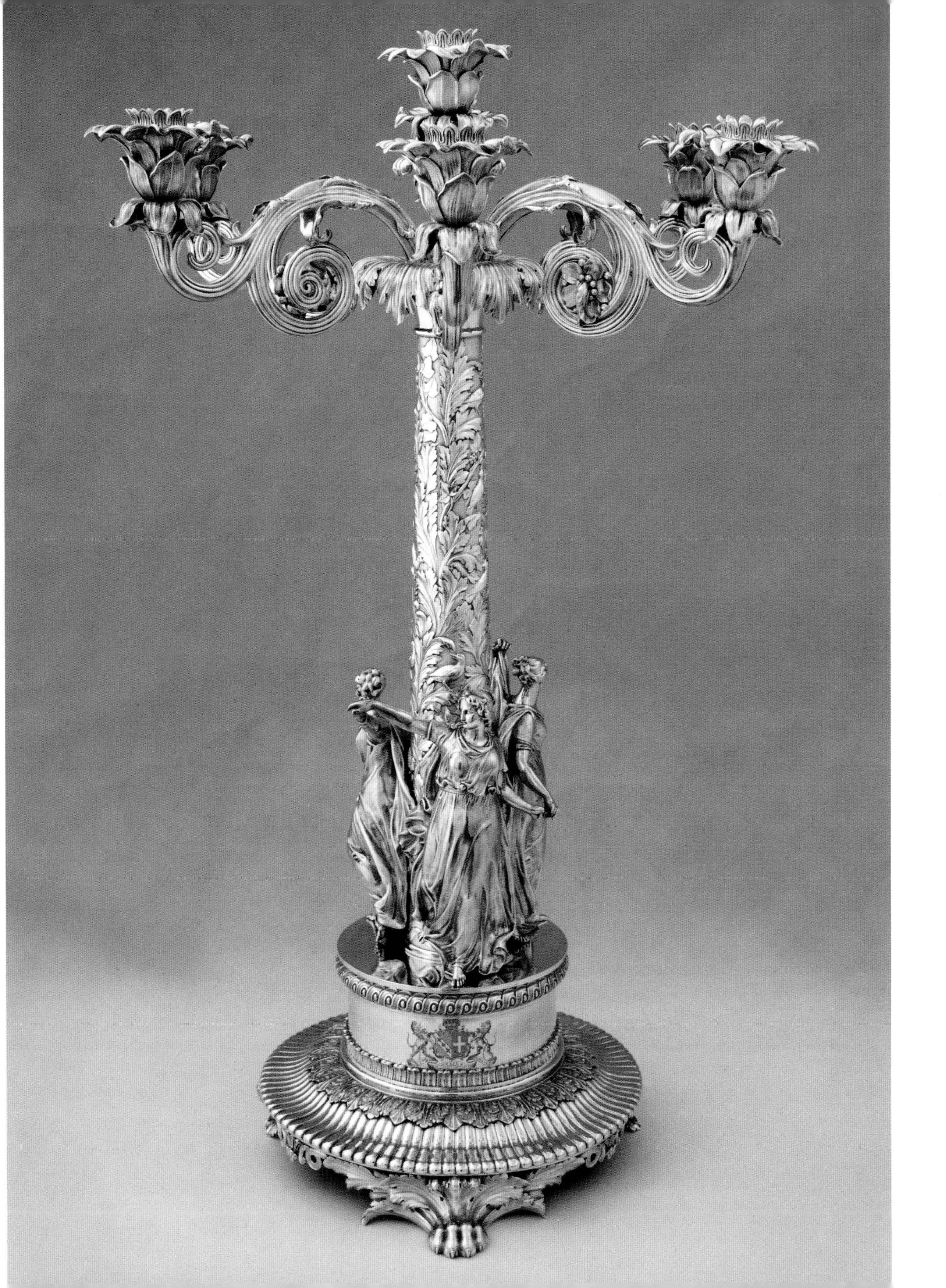

presided over modelling from 1815 until 1833.[5] The Ickworth candelabrum is probably Baily's work, drawing on Flaxman and others plus the plethora of published material that Rundell, Bridge & Rundell had at their disposal through the collection of John Gawler Bridge (1787–1849), the elder John's nephew and the partner in charge of the firm's artistic output from 1817.[6]

The *ballerini* in classical costume dancing hand-in-hand around the column of the Ickworth candelabrum are one of the truest interpretations in silver of the figures in the celebrated 2nd–3rd century AD Roman marble relief now in the Louvre and known as *Les Danseuses Borghèse* (the Borghese dancers) (fig. 108).[7] Their costume and posture is more convincingly antique than that of Benjamin Smith's decidedly Regency versions, as seen on a centrepiece of 1822,[8] or those designed for Barnard and Sons by Richard Freebairn and present on centrepieces of theirs from at least 1832.[9] Flaxman is very likely to have provided Rundell, Bridge & Rundell with the design for the trio on the Ickworth candelabrum, having produced the 'Dancing Hours' version of the relief for use on Josiah Wedgwood's ceramics as early as the 1770s.[10] The column itself is also of antique inspiration, probably deriving from the foliate friezes and columns shown in Piranesi's 1778 *Vasi candelabri cippi sarcofagi*. An album from the Rundell, Bridge & Rundell workshop in the Victoria and Albert Museum includes a drawing (no. 48) of birds and foliage which may well be related, and the columns of candelabra of 1815 and 1819 bearing Paul Storr's and Philip Rundell's marks respectively have similar, but not identical treatment.[11]

The Lincolnshire Tenants Candelabrum must have been engraved just before the marquessate was conferred on 30 June 1826 as the inscription refers to the 'Earl of Bristol' and an earl's coronet is shown on the coat of arms. It was presumably not fully completed until the following year, a note in the 1811 plate list (see appendix 5) recording that it was 'Sent home by Rundel & Bridge July 1827', 'home' probably meaning Ickworth. By 1874, however, it had returned to London, being in the St James's Square house.[12]

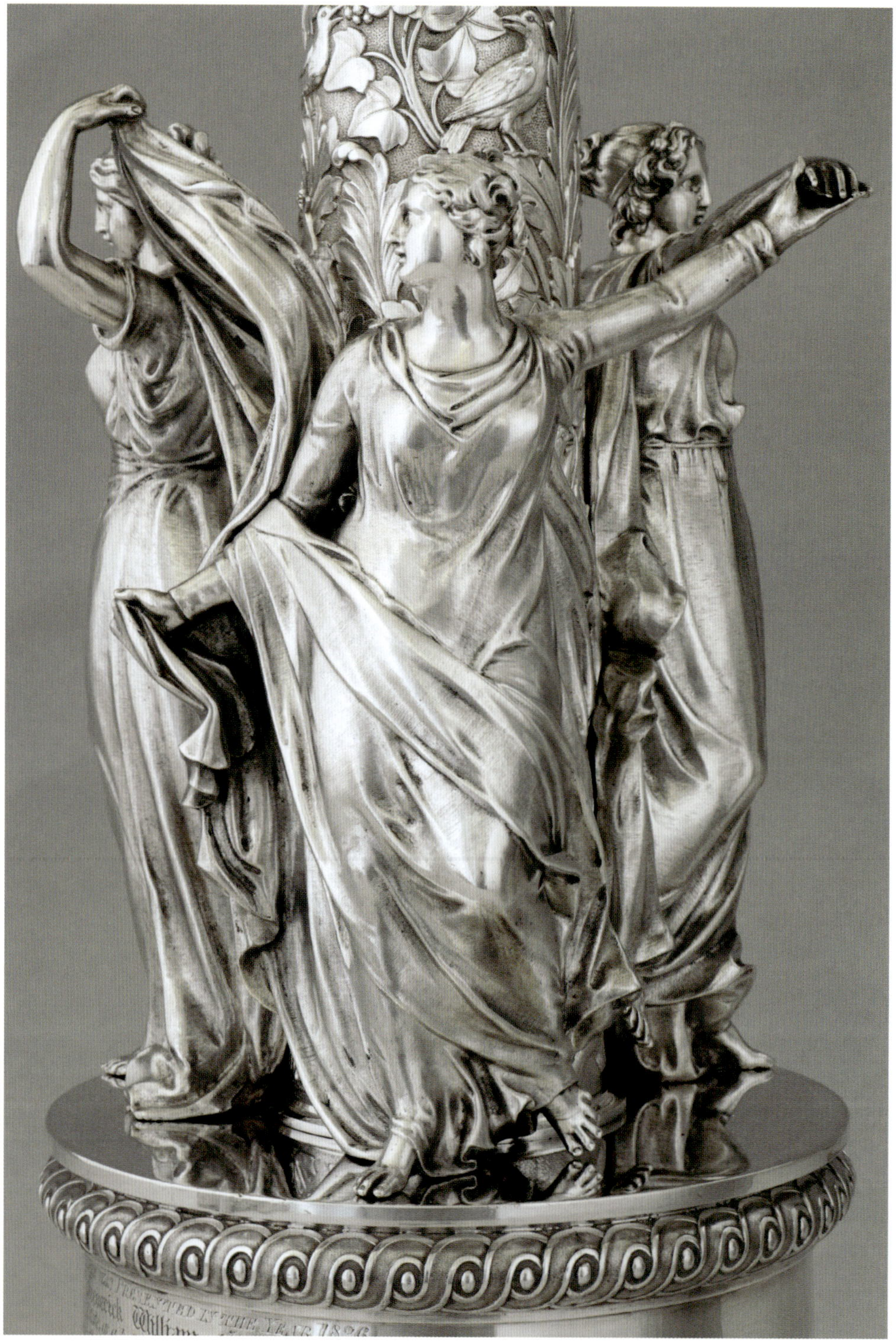

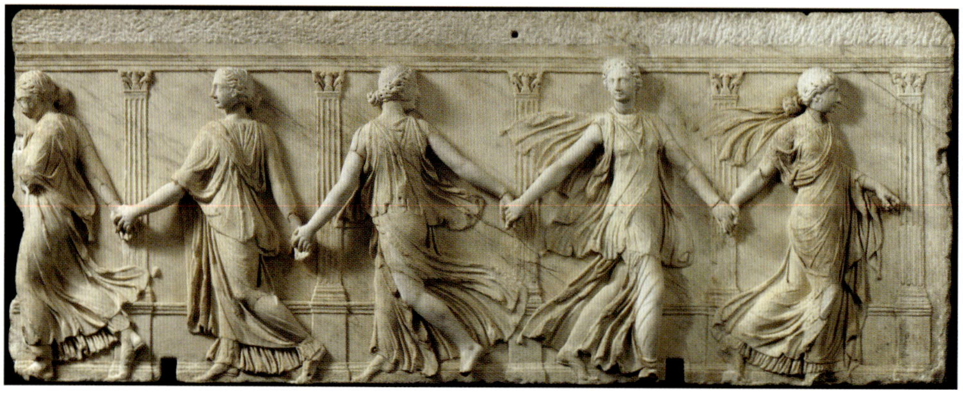

FIG. 108 / *Les Danseuses Borghèse*, Roman, 2nd century A.D. Marble relief: 73 x 185 cm (28¾ x 72⅞ in). Musée du Louvre, Paris.

1. Burke 1884, p. 1045.
2. Thompson 1963, p. 231.
3. Bateman 1883, p. 57.
4. Thompson 1963, p. 235.
5. Hartop 2005, pp. 103–5.
6. Ibid., pp. 13 and 102.
7. Louvre, Paris, inventory no. MR 747.
8. Sotheby's, 23 April 1970, lot 88.
9. Sotheby's New York, 23 October 2014, lot 449.
10. I am indebted to Ann Eatwell for sharing with me her research on sculptural models for a forthcoming publication on Barnard and Sons.
11. Christie's 12 April 1967, lot 64 and 8 July 1992, lot 133.
12. Bristol plate lists 1874, List of plate at 6, St James's Square, May 1874.

119. Dessert forks and spoons

Sterling silver (x 3 forks) / William Chawner II, London / 1826/7
Sterling silver (x 3 forks and x 6 spoons) / Charles Eley, London / 1826/7

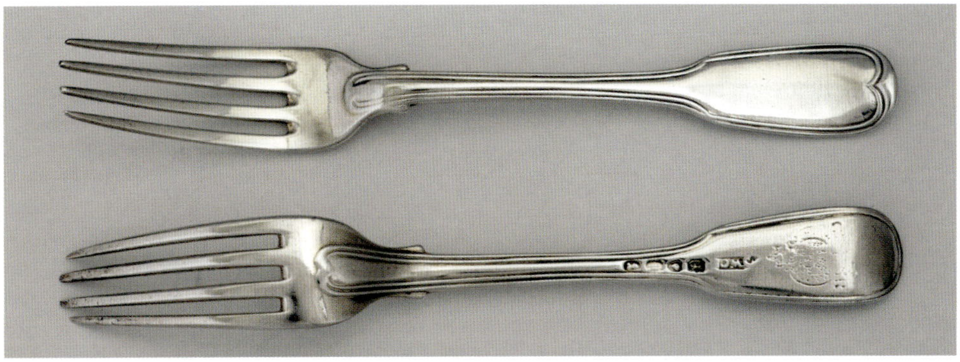

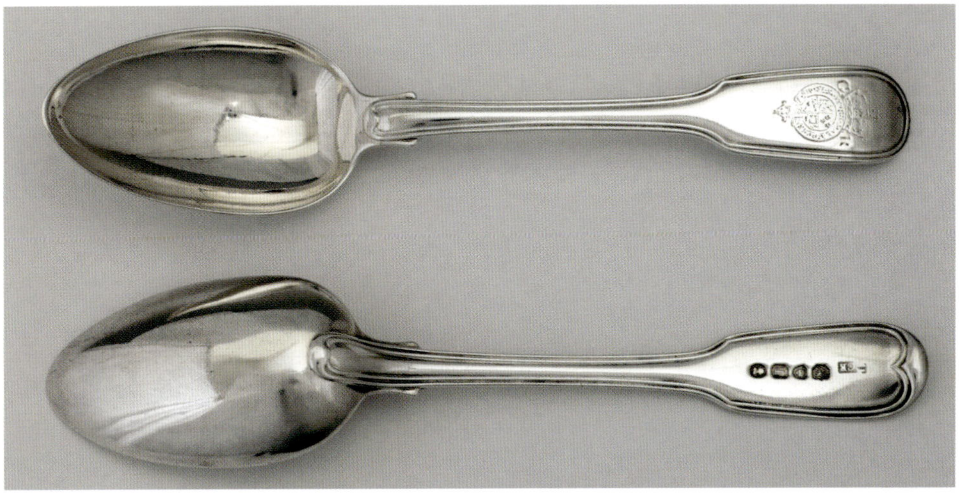

MARKS: All the forks and spoons are marked on the reverse of their handles with the monarch's head, date letter 'l', leopard's head, lion passant and makers' marks 'WC' in a rectangular punch (Grimwade 1990, no. 3069) and 'CE' in a rectangular punch (Grimwade 1990, no. 298).

SCRATCHWEIGHTS: None.
Actual weights: Forks 294 g (9 oz, 9 dwt). Spoons 298 g (9 oz, 12 dwt).

MEASUREMENTS: (l.) forks 16.8 cm (6⅝ in); spoons 17.5 cm (6⅞ in).

INVENTORY: 852185.13–24

PROVENANCE: 1st Marquess of Bristol; by descent to the 4th Marquess.

DESCRIPTION: Six each of forks and spoons of the French-style fiddle thread pattern.[1]

HERALDRY: The backs of the fork terminals and fronts of the spoon terminals are engraved with the quartered shield of the Hanoverian monarchs (pre-1801) within the Garter and beneath an imperial crown flanked by the initials GR.

These represent an augmentation of the 1758 ambassadorial dessert service, hence the pre-1801 royal armorials. In the 1811 plate list, against the addition of twelve each of these spoons and forks, it is noted that they are 'to match the old ones with the Kings arms'. They must have been chosen as the closest form amongst contemporary patterns to the reeded Hanoverian of the 1758 forks and spoons (cat. 71).

1. Pickford 1983, pp. 114–5, fig. 155.

120. **Table forks and spoons**

Sterling silver / John, Henry and Charles Lias, London / 1829/30

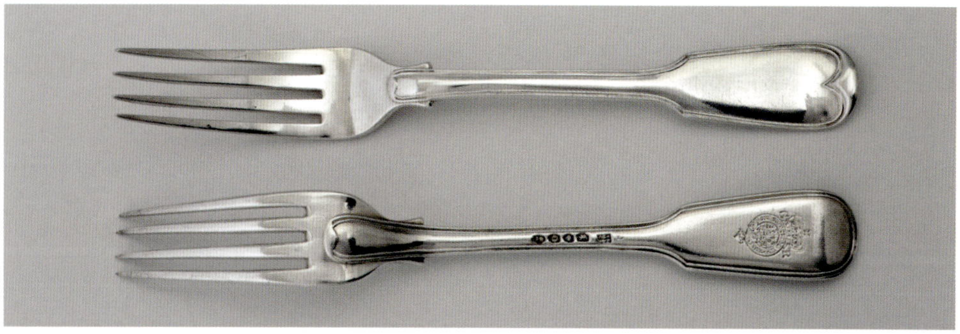

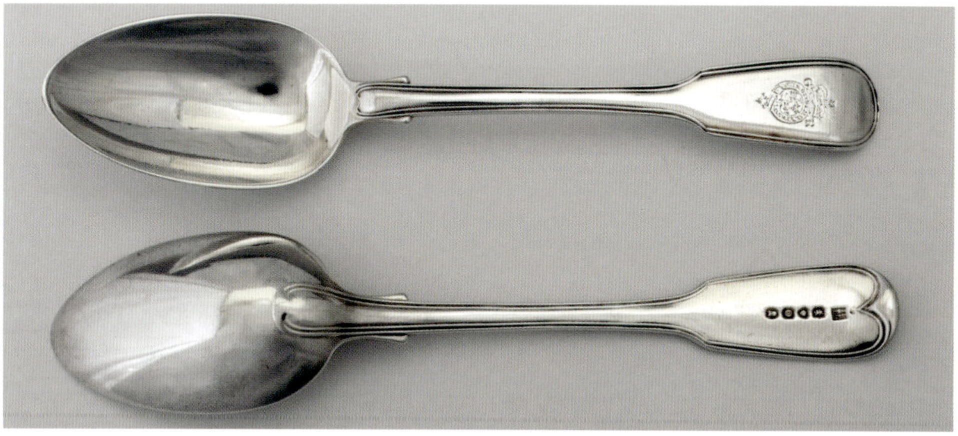

MARKS: The backs of the stems of the forks and of the terminals of the spoons are punched with the monarch's head, date letter 'o', leopard's head, lion passant and maker's mark 'IL' over 'HL' over 'CL' (Grimwade 1990, no. 1495).

SCRATCHWEIGHTS: None.
Actual weights: Forks 629 g (20 oz, 5 dwt). Spoons 581 g (18 oz, 14 dwt).

MEASUREMENTS: (l.) forks: 21.3 cm (8⅜ in); spoons 22.4 cm (8⅞ in).

INVENTORY: 852185.1–12

PROVENANCE: 1st Marquess of Bristol; by descent to the 4th Marquess.

DESCRIPTION: Six each of table forks and table spoons of the French-style fiddle thread pattern.[1]

HERALDRY: The backs of the fork terminals and fronts of the spoon terminals are engraved with the quartered shield of the Hanoverian monarchs (pre-1801) within the Garter and beneath an imperial crown flanked by the initials GR.

These are not recorded in either of the 1st Marquess's plate lists but must, like the matching dessert flatware (cat. 119), have been acquired as an augmentation of the table service that formed part of the 2nd Earl of Bristol's ambassadorial allocation in 1758 (cat. 69). They are thus engraved with the pre-1801 royal arms. There are likely to have been a dozen of each originally, plus knives. They could have been given to Earl Jermyn on his marriage in 1830 by his father, the 1st Marquess of Bristol, which would explain their absence from the otherwise meticulously kept records of his plate.

1. Pickford 1983, pp. 114–5, fig. 155.

121. **Suffolk and Essex Tenantry Candelabrum**

Sterling silver
Benjamin Smith III, London / 1840/1

MARKS: The base is fully marked behind one of the groups of animals with maker's mark 'BS' in a quatrefoil stamp (Grimwade 1990, no. 231), lion passant, leopard's head, date letter 'E' and monarch's head. Each of the nozzles is marked on its neck with the lion passant, leopard's head and the same maker's mark. The basket is marked on its underside with the maker's mark, monarch's head, lion passant and date letter 'E'. Beneath the oak leaf frieze of the base is stamped 'B SMITH DUKE S^{T} LIN^{N} INN FIELDS'.

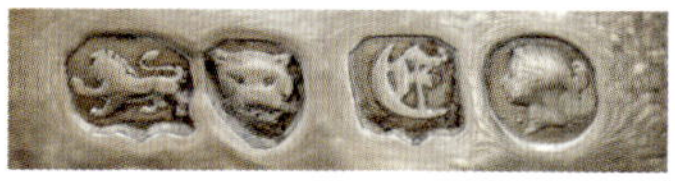

SCRATCHWEIGHT: None. The weight is given in additions to the 1811 plate list (appendix 5) as being 482 oz, 15 dwt.

MEASUREMENTS: h. 82 cm (32¼ in); w. 50 cm (19⅝ in).

INVENTORY: 852056

PROVENANCE: Given to the 1st Marquess of Bristol 1840 by his Suffolk and Essex tenantry; by descent to the 4th Marquess.

DESCRIPTION: Three cast and chased shell, scroll and acanthus leaf feet support an indented triangular base with cut corners in the form of a pulvinating band of cast and chased oak leaves, acanthus leaves at the corners. On the ledge above the feet rest cast and chased cattle, sheep, horses and pigs. The irregular hexagonal plinth with concave sides has three short plain panels behind the farm animals and three slightly recessed long panels, one with a lengthy inscription (see below) and the other two with chased views of Ickworth House and church. Above is a stepped cornice on top of which are cast and chased figures of a shepherd holding a crook and carrying a lamb, his dog and a beehive at his feet, and a preacher between a kneeling farm labourer holding a sickle and a sheaf of wheat and his wife with two small children, further wheat being amongst them. The figures surround a reeded and fluted stem with an acanthus leaf capital from which emanate six S-scroll reeded branches terminating in campana vase sockets with removable gadrooned nozzles. A central, vertical stem rises above the sockets and supports a circular basket with a fluted base and flaring wirework sides terminating in a cast and chased foliate rim.

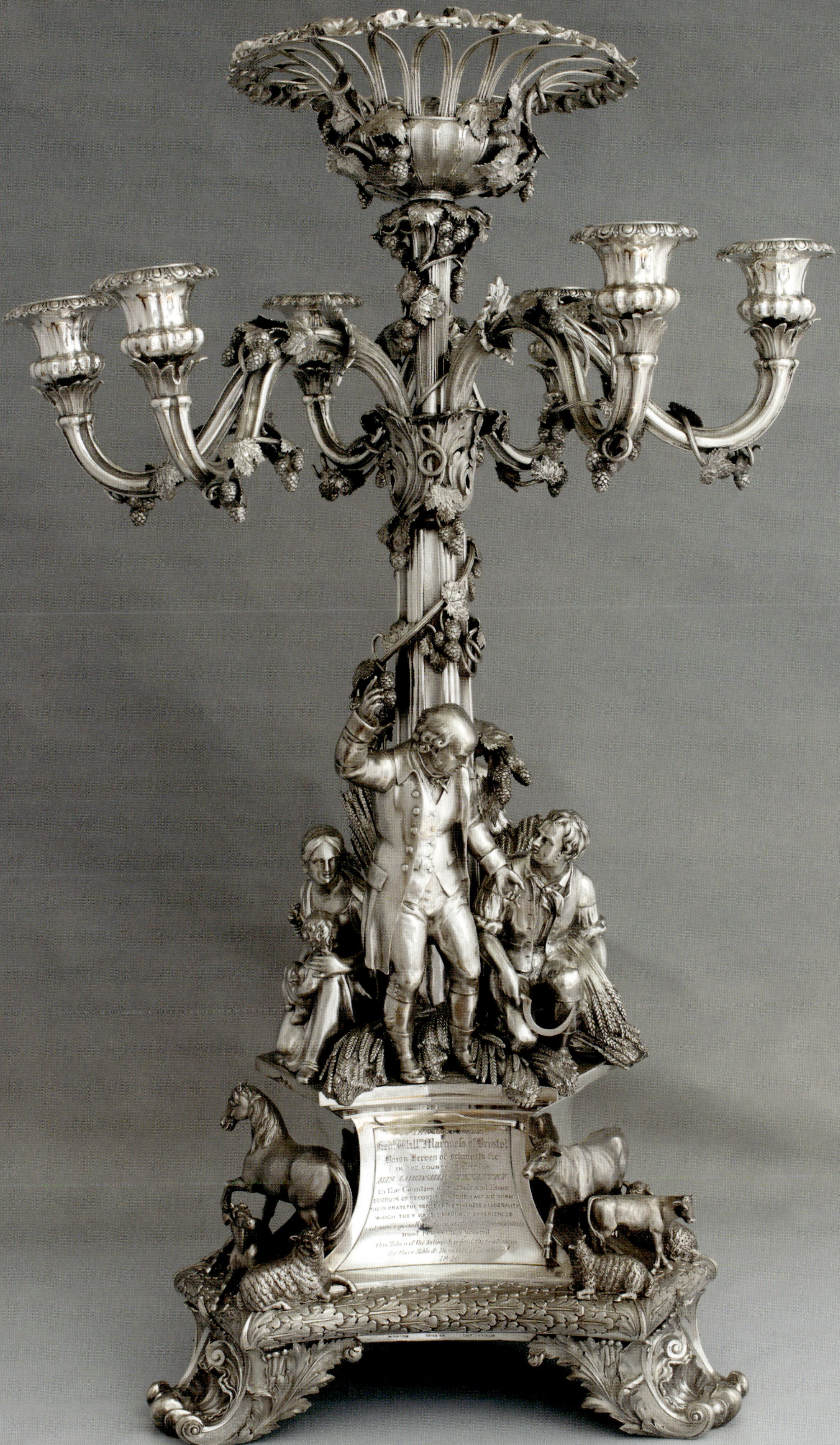
Marquess of Bristol
in the Counties of
WHICH THEY HAVE UNIFORMLY EXPERIENCED

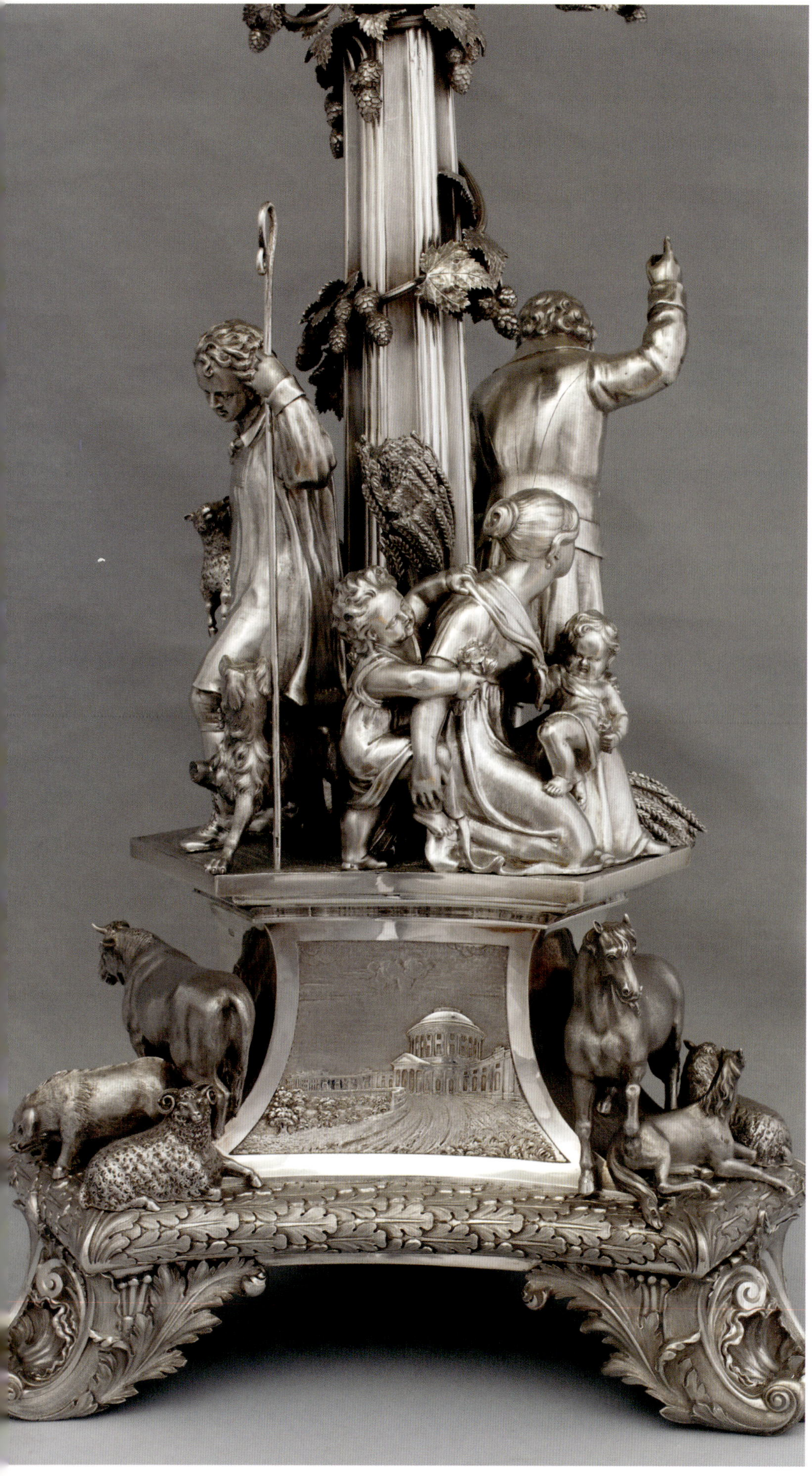

Twining round the upper and lower stems, the branches and the basket is a hop bine in flower.

HERALDRY: None.

INSCRIPTION: On one panel (see above):

To the Most Noble [/] Fredk. Willm. Marquess of Bristol [/] Baron Hervey of Ickworth &c [/] in the county of Suffolk [/] His Lordships Tenantry [/] in the Counties of Suffolk and Essex [/] desirous of recording in some lasting form [/] their grateful sense of the kindness & liberality [/] which they have uniformly experienced [/] and more especially in Seasons of difficulty and distress [/] most respectfully present [/] this Token of the feelings & regard they entertain [/] for their Noble & Benevolent Landlord [/] 1840

A run of bad harvests in the last years of the 1830s finally brought increases in grain prices after fifteen years of instability and there was, for a time at least, a return to agricultural prosperity.[1] Evidently Lord Bristol had been helping the beleaguered tenants on his 18,000 acres in Suffolk and Essex,[2] and they, as their Lincolnshire counterparts had done previously (see cat. 118), acknowledged their landlord's actions through a testimonial candelabrum. By 1840 Rundell, Bridge & Co. was on its last legs and the commission was given instead to the younger Benjamin Smith who had the services of the accomplished designer and modeller, Charles Grant. Grant was also responsible for the testimonial of 1841 to the acclaimed actor, William Macready, which was shown at the Great Exhibition of 1851, and he went on to work for Barnard and Sons and Elkingtons.[3]

For the tripod at the centre of the Suffolk and Essex Tenantry Candelabrum Grant drew on the antique sources that had become popular in the years around 1800 but he did not combine that with classical figures as might a designer of twenty years earlier (see cat. 118). He was described in census returns as a 'designer modeller of the human figure' and he put his exceptional skills in that sphere to good effect on the naturalistic and contemporary figural groupings around the base of the candelabrum. Within a few years the rococo would supplant the antique for the core of such centrepieces, as on the candelabra presented to Wilbraham Egerton of Tatton in 1848 and the 8th Marquess of Tweeddale in 1849, both marked by John S. Hunt and designed by Alfred Brown.[4] Though the Ickworth candelabrum is a weighty and massive piece of silver at nearly 500 ounces and two and a half feet tall, it is dwarfed by the 1,355 ounces and four feet of the Tweeddale Testimonial.

As well as no doubt being touched by this mark of appreciation from his tenants, Lord Bristol was also able at long last to put a line, quite literally, under his efforts to return the family plate to the weight left by the 2nd Earl of Bristol in 1775: 16,700 oz, 11 dwt. Lord Bristol had noted this in 1811 (see appendix 5) against the total then of 15,201 oz, 1 dwt: 'Deficient – oz: 1, 398=10'. By 1829 he was within one hundred ounces of achieving his goal but it was the Suffolk and Essex candelabrum that finally achieved that and the Marquess was able to record the weight of the family plate as being 17,130 oz, 19 dwt. It is typical of his quietly determined character that he had persevered over all those years and that, slowly and surely, he had set things right for his heirs.

1. Thompson 1963, pp. 238–9.
2. Bateman 1883, p. 57.
3. I am indebted to Ann Eatwell for sharing her researches on Charles Grant and for drawing my attention to the Macready Testimonial.
4. Sotheby's 25 February 1971, lot 145 and Christie's, 22 May 1991, lot 6.

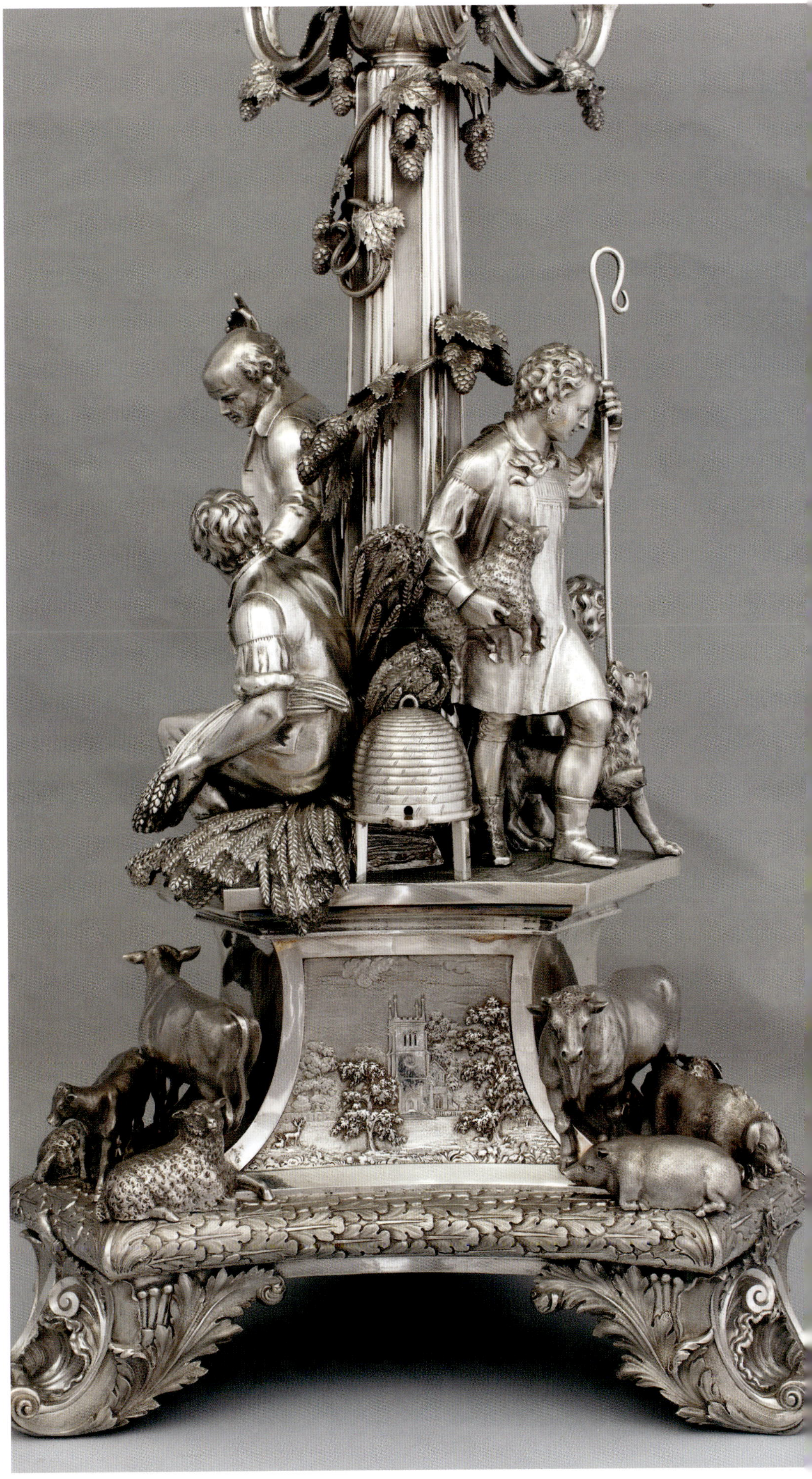

122. **Pocket inkwell**

Sterling silver / John Reily, London / 1815/16

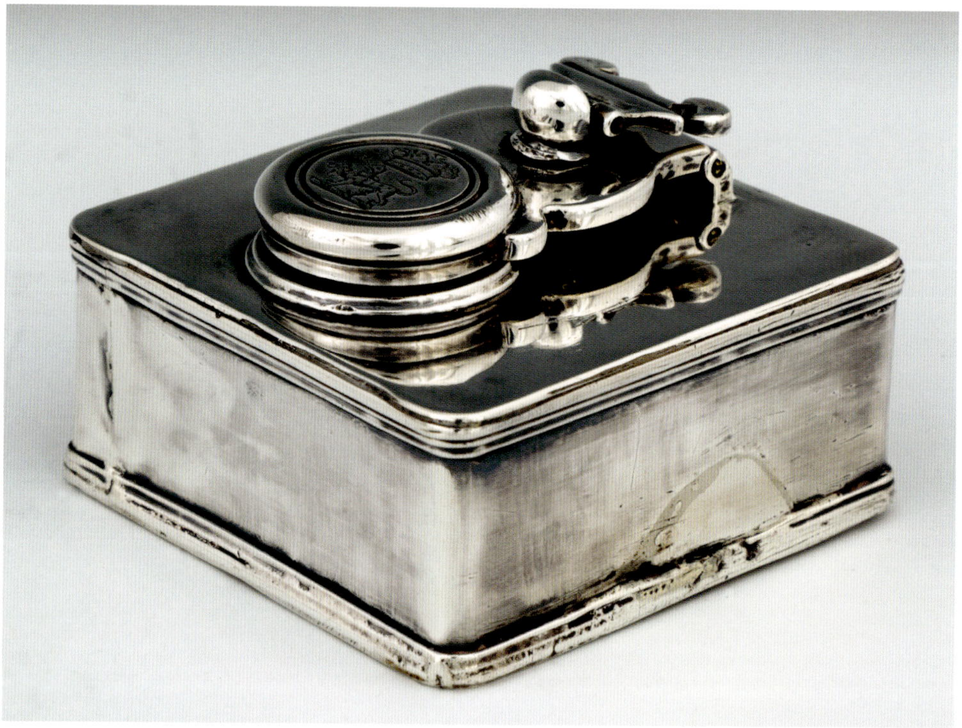

MARKS: Fully marked on the side of the inkwell with maker's mark 'IR' in a rectangular punch (Grimwade 1990, no. 1627), lion passant, leopard's head, date letter 'U' and monarch's head. Also marked on the underside of the cap flange with the same maker's mark, lion passant and date letter 'U'.

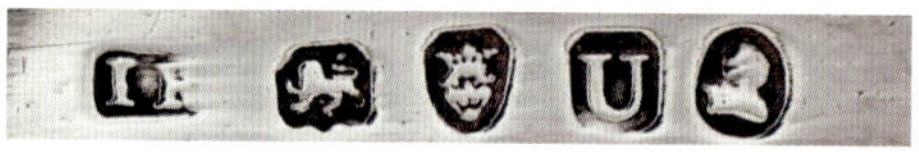

SCRATCHWEIGHT: None.
Actual weight: 100 g (3 oz, 4 dwt).

MEASUREMENTS: h. 3.2 cm (1¼ in); w. and d. 5.1 cm (2 in).

INVENTORY: 852798

PROVENANCE: Frederick, Lord Hervey (subsequently Earl Jermyn and 2nd Marquess of Bristol); by descent to the 4th Marquess.

DESCRIPTION: The inkwell is square, the sides formed of seamed sheet with applied mouldings at the junctions with the top and bottom which are of plain sheet. A circular hole in the top has an applied cast rim and a seamed tube bezel over which the cast round cap fits. The cap is applied to a shaped flange which has a three-part pin hinge operating from the top of the inkwell. It is secured in the closed position by a screw mechanism attached to the flange and with a hinged drop handle of shaped form.

HERALDRY: Engraved on the cap is the Hervey crest beneath a baron's coronet for Frederick, Lord Hervey (subsequently Earl Jermyn and 2nd Marquess of Bristol).

Judging by the number of items surviving with his mark John Reily seems to have been a prolific producer of small and intricate wares including boxes of various kinds, grape scissors, bottle labels, spirit flasks and pocket or travelling inkwells such as this one.[1] He presumably supplied Rundell, Bridge & Rundell, from whom Lord Bristol is likely to have acquired the piece for his eldest son. The inkwell, which has been well used, probably accompanied Lord Hervey on the family's protracted tour of Europe from July 1817 to May 1821.[2]

1. Two other pocket inkwells by Reily, of 1819 and 1824, were recently with Steppes Hill Farm Antiques (www.steppeshillfarmantiques.com/silver-and-porcelain/d/george-iii-silver-travelling-inkwell-with-wafer-seal-compartment/98920, last accessed 18 March 2016) and Henry Willis Antique Silver (http://www.henrywillis.co.uk/antique-english-silver-dealer/2011/george-iv-travelling-inkwell-42, accessed same date).
2. Strachey 1998, p. 46.

123. **Coffee pot**

Sterling silver / **John Parker I and Edward Wakelin** / **1772/3**

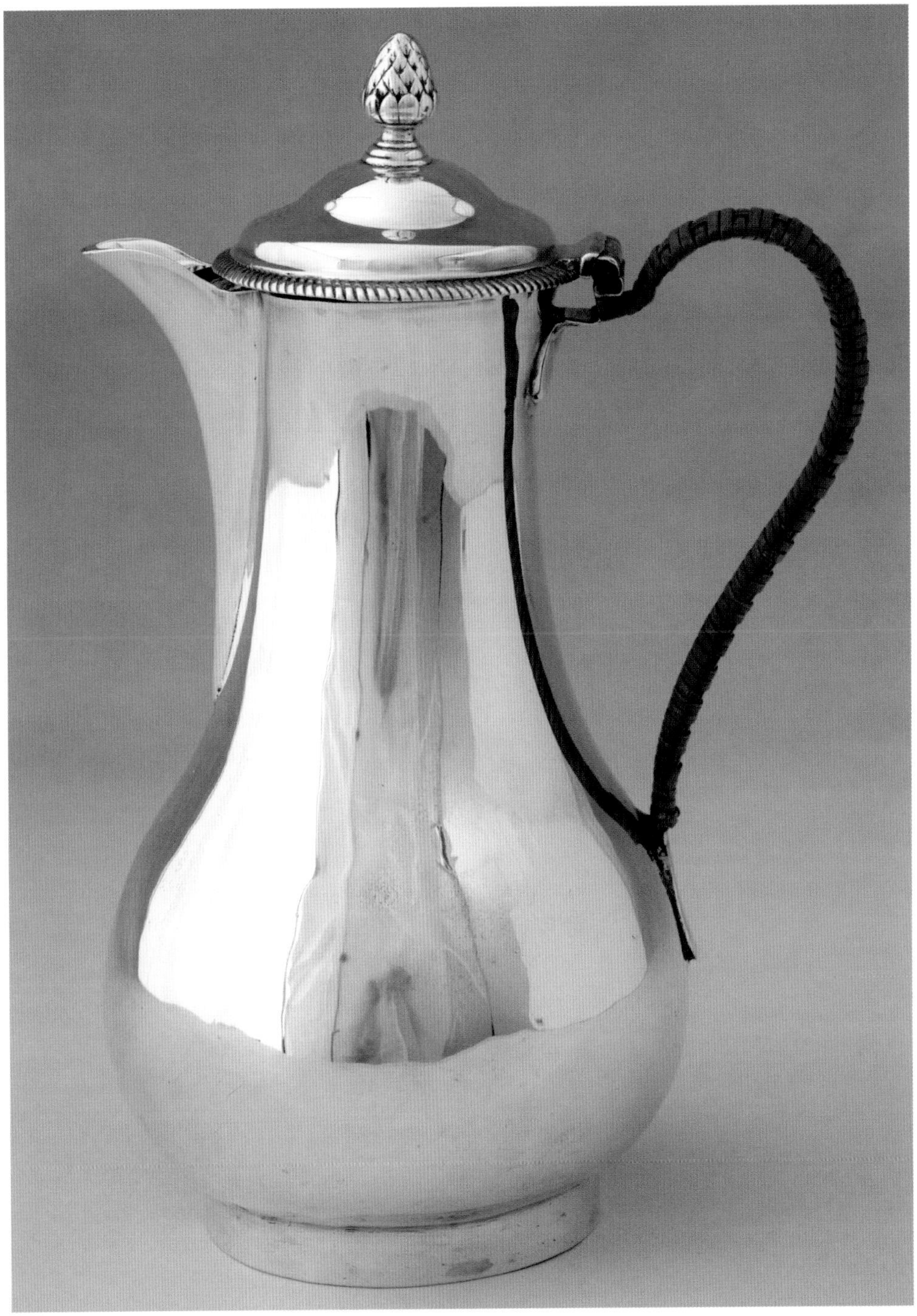

MARKS: Marked on the underside with maker's mark 'I·P' over 'E·W' surmounted by a fleur-de-lis issuing out of an open crown, lion passant, leopard's head and date letter R.

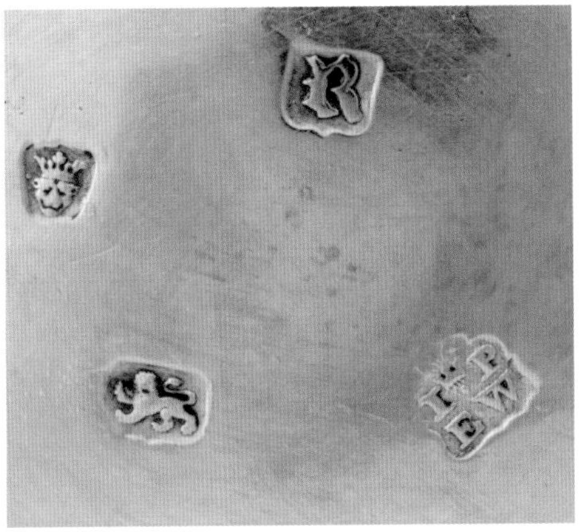

SCRATCHWEIGHT: '11=15'

MEASUREMENTS: h. 20.3 cm (8 in); w. (incl. handle and spout) 13 cm (5⅛ in).

INVENTORY: 852060

PROVENANCE: Probably acquired second-hand by Earl Jermyn (subsequently 2nd Marquess of Bristol); by descent to the 4th Marquess.

DESCRIPTION: The elongated pear-shaped body, which is raised, splays towards the rim and has an applied, beak-shaped spout, also raised. The flattened base has an applied and seamed foot ring and the handle is formed of a curved strip of sheet silver, wickered. A five-part pin hinge is fixed to the handle. The domed cover is raised and has a cast and chased gadroon rim, a seamed bezel and a cast pineapple finial.

HERALDRY: The front of the cover has been re-engraved *c.*1830 with the Hervey crest beneath an earl's coronet.

As this coffee pot does not appear in the plate lists of the 1st Marquess of Bristol and the engraving looks to be early nineteenth century, it is likely that it was acquired second-hand by Earl Jermyn, perhaps on his marriage in 1830. Parker and Wakelin, one of the principal retailing goldsmiths of the late eighteenth century, were never patronised by the Herveys and this is the only piece representing the prolific partnership at Ickworth. It is of almost identical form to Lady Hervey's coffee pot of 1762 by Frederick Kandler (cat. 22).

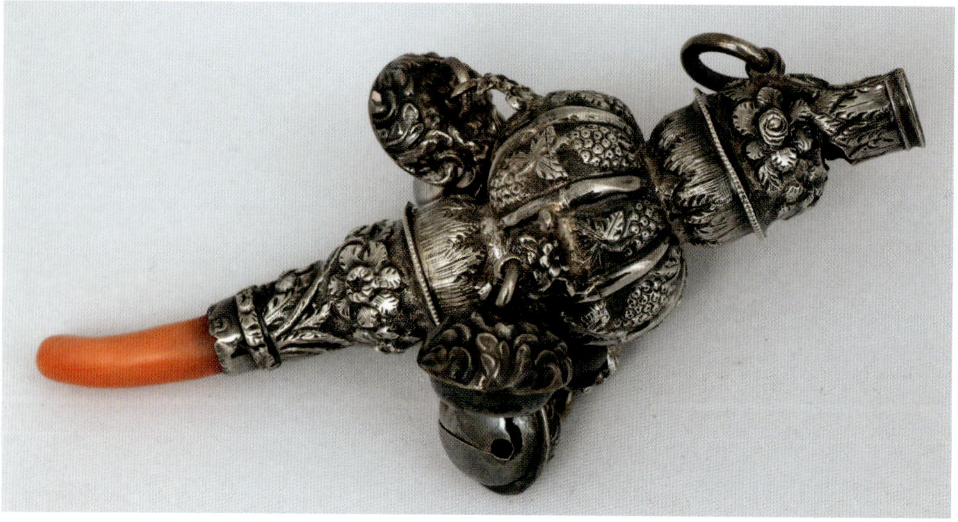

124. **Teething coral**

Silver / **George Knight, London** / ***c*.1825**

MARKS: The body of the rattle at the junction with the coral has part of the maker's mark 'GK' in a rectangular punch (Grimwade 1990, no. 840)

SCRATCHWEIGHT: None.
Actual weight: 31 g (1 oz).

MEASUREMENTS: l. 9.4 cm (3¾ in); w. 5 cm (2 in).

INVENTORY: 852799

PROVENANCE: Probably Frederick Hervey, Earl Jermyn (subsequently 2nd Marquess of Bristol); by descent to the 4th Marquess.

DESCRIPTION: The bulbous body is raised in two parts and seamed and is chased in segments with the leaves and fruit of strawberries. At one end is a lambrequin collar and a hemispherical cap with foliate chasing above which is a circular whistle and at the other end is a tapering, seamed stem chased with strawberry flowers and holding a piece of coral. Attached to the sides of the body by chain links are four hemispherical, chased bells. A ring for a lace is attached to the underside of the whistle.

HERALDRY: None.

This coral, or baby teether and rattle, is of the typical form for the eighteenth and early nineteenth centuries and was made by one of the principal producers of such pieces in the latter period, George Knight. It was probably acquired for the children of Frederick Hervey, Earl Jermyn (subsequently 2nd Marquess), the first of whom, Lady Elizabeth Hervey, was born in 1832.

PART EIGHT

SILVER OF FREDERICK WILLIAM JOHN HERVEY, 3RD MARQUESS OF BRISTOL (1834–1907)

125. **Waiter**

Sterling silver / **John Tuite, London** / **1738**

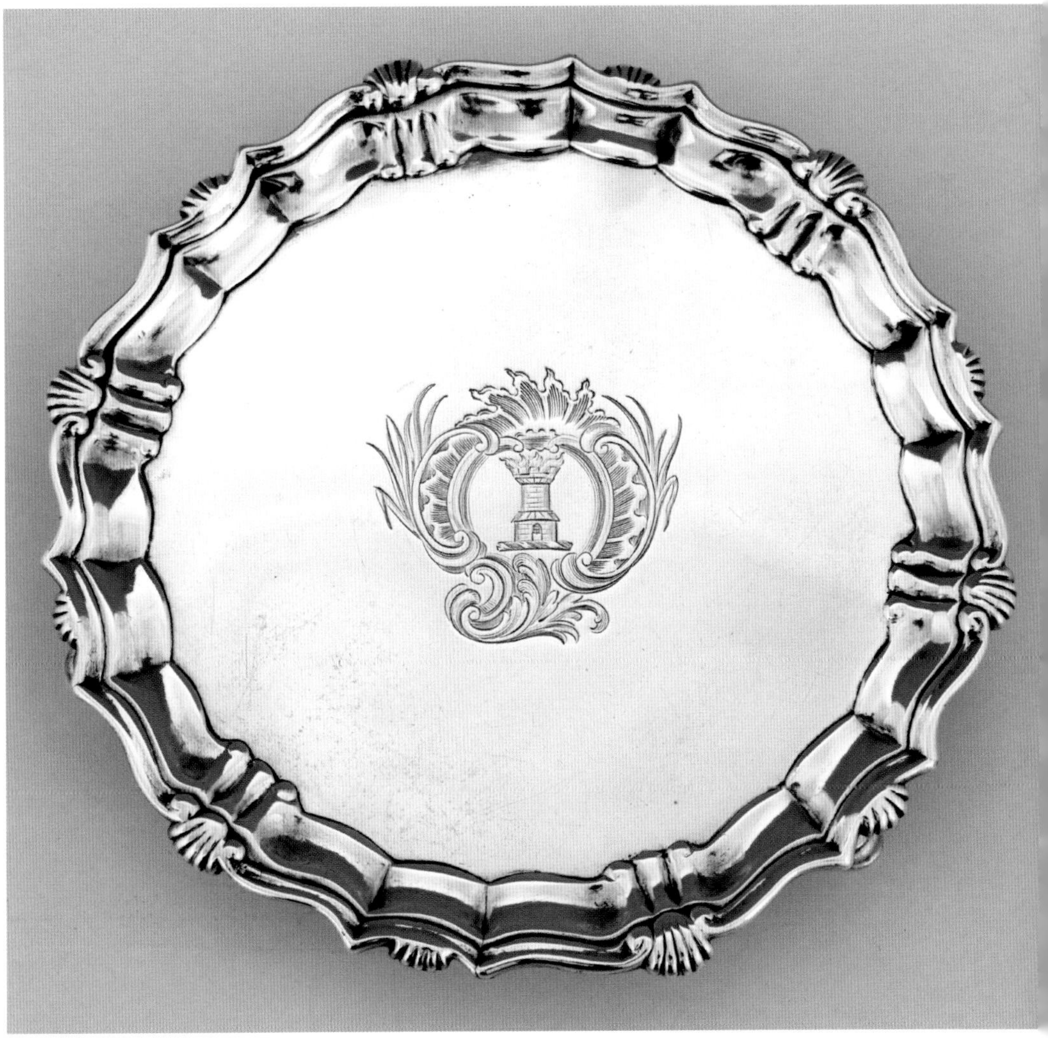

MARKS: Fully marked on the underside with maker's mark 'IT' italic either side of a ewer (Pickford 1989, p. 182, Tuite's Dublin registered mark), lion passant, date letter 'C' and leopard's head.

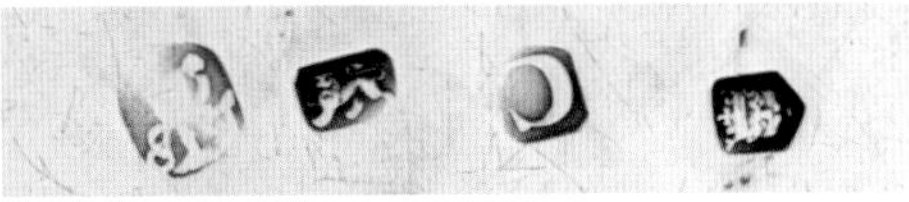

SCRATCHWEIGHT: None.
Actual weight: 249 g (8 oz).

MEASUREMENTS: h. 2.5 cm (1 in); diam. 16.2 cm (16⅜ in).

INVENTORY: 852088

PROVENANCE: Possibly acquired second-hand by General Lord Henry Percy (1817–77) and bequeathed by him to the 3rd Marquess of Bristol; by descent to the 4th Marquess.

DESCRIPTION: The waiter is raised and has a shaped circular rim with multiple creases and an applied cast border with scrolled mouldings and shells. There are three hoof feet.

HERALDRY: The centre of the waiter is engraved with the crest of a flaming crenellated tower within a rococo cartouche. This could relate to a number of families including Castell, Crosse of Somerset and Paddon of Norfolk (none with obvious connections to the Herveys).[1]

What connection this waiter has with the Herveys and how it came into their possession is uncertain, but it does not appear in the plate lists of the 1st Marquess of Bristol so its introduction is likely to post-date him. It could be one of the two waiters that are recorded in the 1874 copy plate list as being added in 1878 and coming from Lord Henry Percy.[2] The youngest son of the 5th Duke of Northumberland, he was a distinguished soldier who was awarded the Victoria Cross in 1857 for outstanding bravery at the Battle of Inkerman and rose to the rank of general.[3] As he died in 1877, the year before the waiters plus a coffee pot, a 'round tray' and an inkstand came to Lord Bristol, it is likely that they were a bequest. The engraved crest, however, remains a conundrum, as it does not appear to relate to the Percys any more than it does to the Herveys.

1. Fairbairn 1905, plate 118, no. 15. Note that only the crests of some of the families listed against this plate had fire emanating just from the top of the tower.
2. Bristol plate list 1874b.
3. G.C. Boase, 'Percy, Lord Henry Hugh Manvers (1817–1877)', Rev. Roger T. Stearn, *Oxford Dictionary of National Biography*, Oxford University Press, 2004 (http://www.oxforddnb.com/view/article/21942, accessed 21 Dec 2015).

126. **Inkstand**

Sterling silver, gilded / Edward and John Barnard, London / 1857/8

MARKS: Fully marked on the underside of the stand and on the caps and rims of the bottles with lion passant, leopard's head, date letter 'b', monarch's head and maker's mark 'EB' over '&' over 'JB' in a quatrefoil (Culme 1987, nos. 2904–6). The sockets for the bottles are marked with the same maker's mark, the monarch's head and the lion passant. The underside of the stand is also stamped 'B' and '993'.

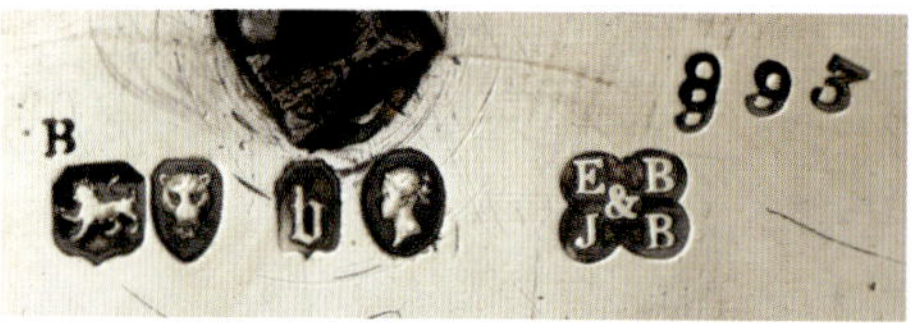

SCRATCHWEIGHT: None.
Actual weight: (excluding glass bottles but including bottle caps) 1474 g (47 oz, 8 dwt).

MEASUREMENTS: h. 12.7 cm (5 in); w. 37.1 cm (14⅝ in); d. 25.4 cm (10 in).

INVENTORY: 852191

PROVENANCE: Charles Manners, 6th Duke of Rutland (1815–88); probably given by him to his nephew, the 3rd Marquess of Bristol; by descent to the 4th Marquess.

DESCRIPTION: The rectangular stand with rounded corners and elevated central platform is raised and rests on four foliate scroll and floral cast and chased feet which merge with the conforming cast and chased border. The platform is fitted with two circular raised and chased scrollwork sockets which are bolted through to the underside and which hold two hexagonal bellied and faceted cut-glass bottles for ink and pen cleaning with seamed and raised rims. The covers to the bottles have seamed necks with engraved reeding, cast foliate rims and raised tops which are dished and ribbed as hexafoils and have one and three circular holes.

HERALDRY: The centre of the stand is engraved with the shield (or, two bars azure a chief quarterly of the last and gules, in the 1st and 4th two fleurs-de-lis, and in the 2nd and 3rd, a lion passant guardant, all or),[1] supporters, motto, duke's coronet and crest of Manners, Duke of Rutland, for Charles Cecil John, 6th Duke (succeeded January, 1857, died 1888).

This inkstand must have been commissioned by, or for, the 6th Duke of Rutland shortly after his inheritance in 1857 and was presumably given by him to his nephew, the 3rd Marquess of Bristol (son of the 2nd Marquess by his wife, Lady Katherine Manners), prior to 1874 when it is recorded at Ickworth.[2] The piece was acquired in the first place through R&S Garrard, the Crown Jewellers, and appears in the Edward Barnard and Sons order book for January 1858 as follows:

R & S Garrard, Harrison. A 14 In[ch] rich chased Louis XIV Inkstand (foliage scroll & mounted flower), scroll flower edge ink boxes & mounts pd SColes cut glass Inks, no wafer box or centre ornam[ent]ing. Sent to them for gild[in]g.
993 [£]47 4[s] 12[d]

A taper stick was provided to match at a cost of £9 18s 3d which, though it is probably that listed in 1874, did not pass to the National Trust in 1956.[3] Engraving, as well as gilding, must have been carried out by Garrards.

The numbers stamped on plate produced by Barnards have been suggested to relate to customers[4] but that cannot be the case here as the inkstand bears the number '993' and the taper stick is recorded as '167'. Whether or not, instead, they are to do with patterns remains to be proved, but the only surviving pattern books, both of 1808, do contain a rococo centrepiece numbered '953'. Although described as 'Louis XIV' by Barnards the style of the inkstand is obviously derived from mid-eighteenth-century rococo designs which had been part of the repertoire of the firm since the early nineteenth century, and there is a related design in the pattern books, sadly not numbered (fig. 109).[5]

1. Burke 1884, p. 656.
2. Bristol plate lists 1874, 'List of Plate at Ickworth', June, 1874. This must be the larger of two gilt inkstands, the smaller being noted in the copy plate list of the same year as being Lady Bristol's. Bristol plate list 1874b.
3. I am indebted to Ann Eatwell for finding the Edward Barnard and Sons order book entry and for her comments on the inkstand.
4. Culme 1977, p. 53.
5. V&A, Barnard pattern book, f. 69.

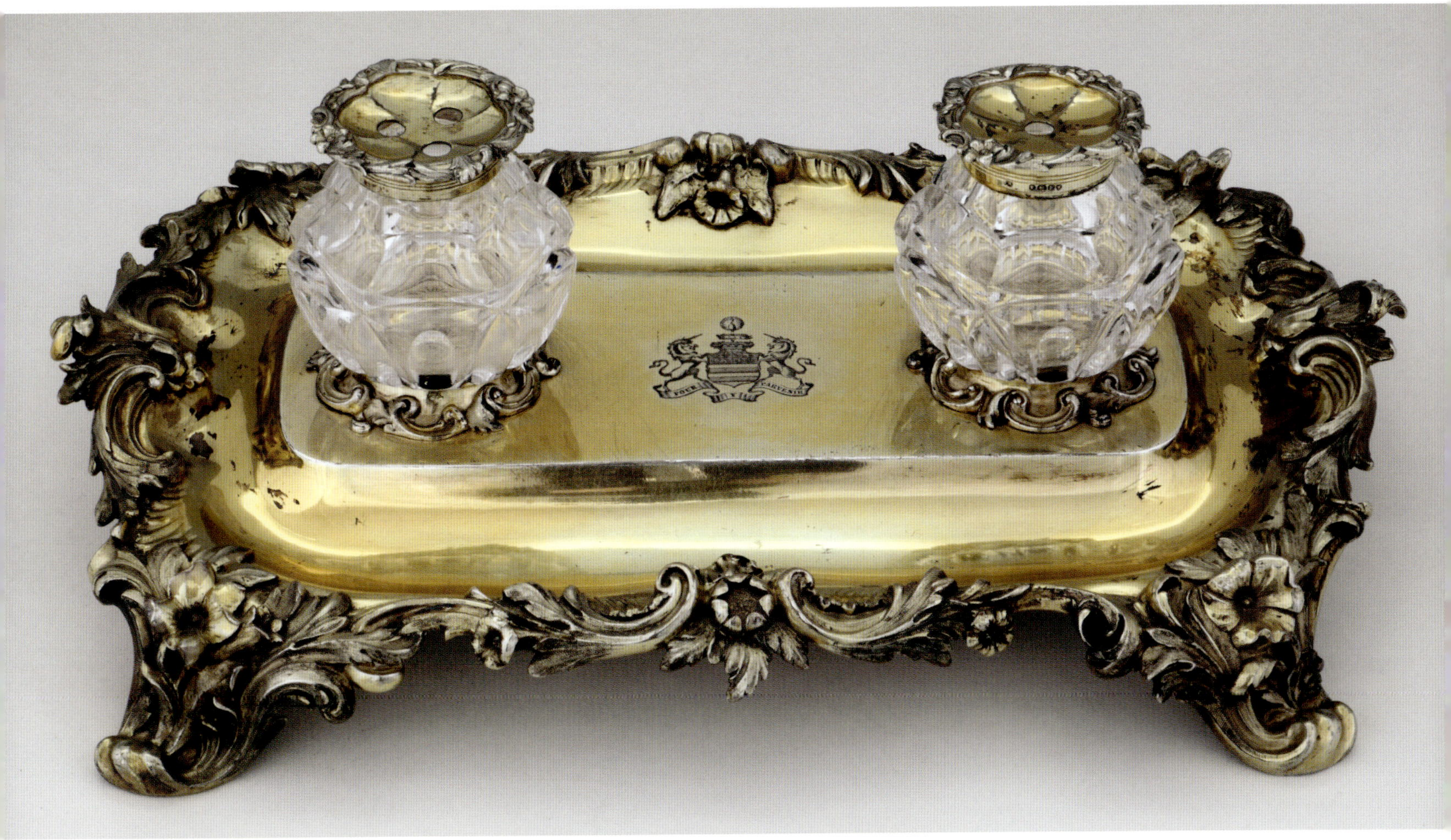

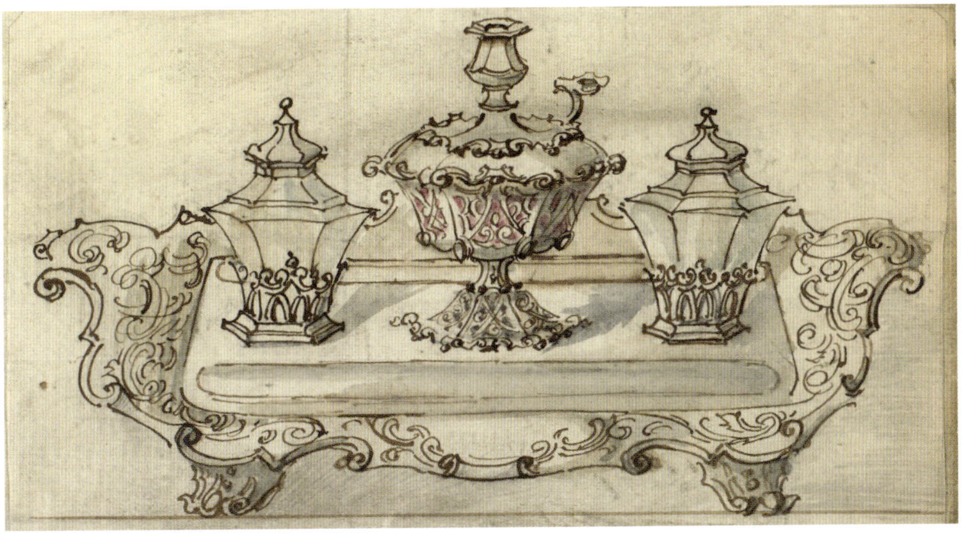

FIG. 109 / Rococo inkstand design from the Barnards pattern books, early 19th century. Victoria and Albert Museum.

PART NINE

SILVER OF FREDERICK WILLIAM FANE HERVEY, 4TH MARQUESS OF BRISTOL (1863–1951)

127. **Salver**

Sterling silver / **William Brown, London** / **1837/8**

MARKS: Fully marked on the underside with lion passant, leopard's head, date letter 'B', monarch's head and maker's mark 'W·B' in a punch of interlocking circles (Grimwade 1990, no. 3039).

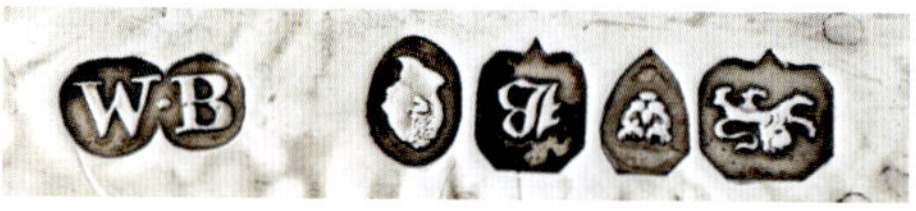

SCRATCHWEIGHT: None.
Actual weight: 3047 g (97 oz, 19 dwt).

MEASUREMENTS: h. 5.1 cm (2 in); diam. 51.3 cm (20¼ in).

INVENTORY: 852100

PROVENANCE: James Hodnett; Colonel William Hodnett; his daughter, Lady Augustus Hervey; her son, the 4th Marquess.

EXHIBITED: *Ideal Home Exhibition*, London, 1960.

DESCRIPTION: The salver has four cast scroll and leaf feet and is raised with a shaped, chased border and an applied cast shell, scroll and leaf border. Around the edge of the field is a broad, flat-chased band of C-scrolls, scrolling foliage, flowers, trelliswork and fish scales on a matted ground.

HERALDRY AND INSCRIPTION: The centre of the salver is engraved with a rococo shield bearing quarterly per fesse indented argent and gules a label of five points azure, the ancient arms of the Hoddenet family,[1] beneath a lion rampant crest and within a circular inscription: 'Presented to James Hodnett Esqre. as a mark of esteem, by the Gentlemen of the Island of St Vincent. 1836.'

This salver is likely to have been inherited by the 4th Marquess from his mother, Lady Augustus Hervey (Mariana), who was the daughter of Colonel William Hodnett. He in turn was presumably the son of James Hodnett to whom the salver is inscribed. It is unlikely that this family was entitled to bear the ancient arms of the Hoddenets, as engraved on the salver, nor the lion rampant crest which was borne by many families but none named Hodnett.[2] The form of the salver is typical of the mid-nineteenth-century revival of interest in the rococo, and the broad, flat-chased border was clearly inspired by the decoration of tea tables of the 1740s, such as those surviving at Dunham Massey in Cheshire.[3]

1. Burke 1884, p. 495.
2. Fairbairn 1905, plate 67, no. 5.
3. Lomax and Rothwell, cat. 37–8, pp. 88–93, coffee table by James Shruder, 1741 and tea table by David Willaume II, 1741.

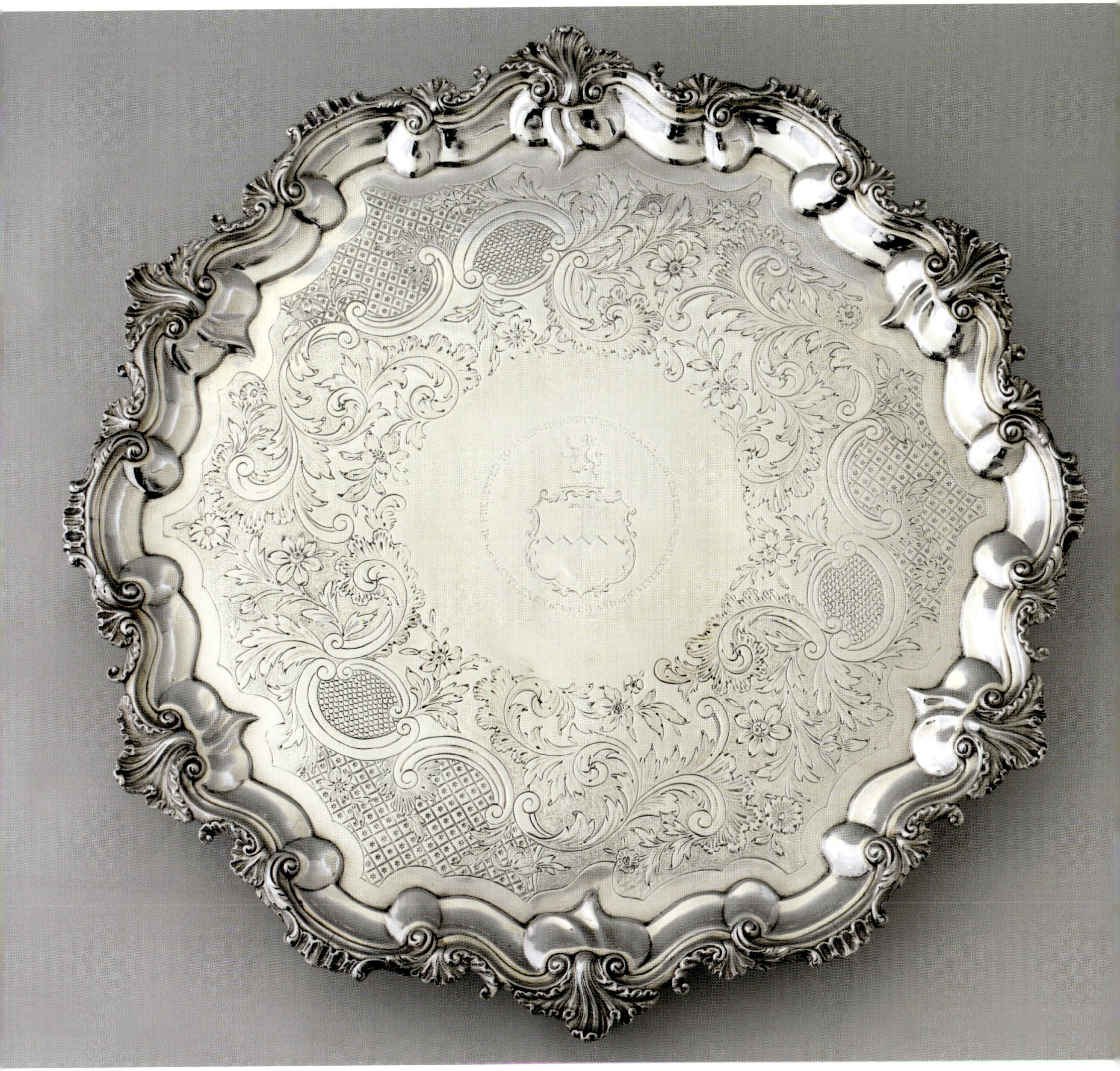

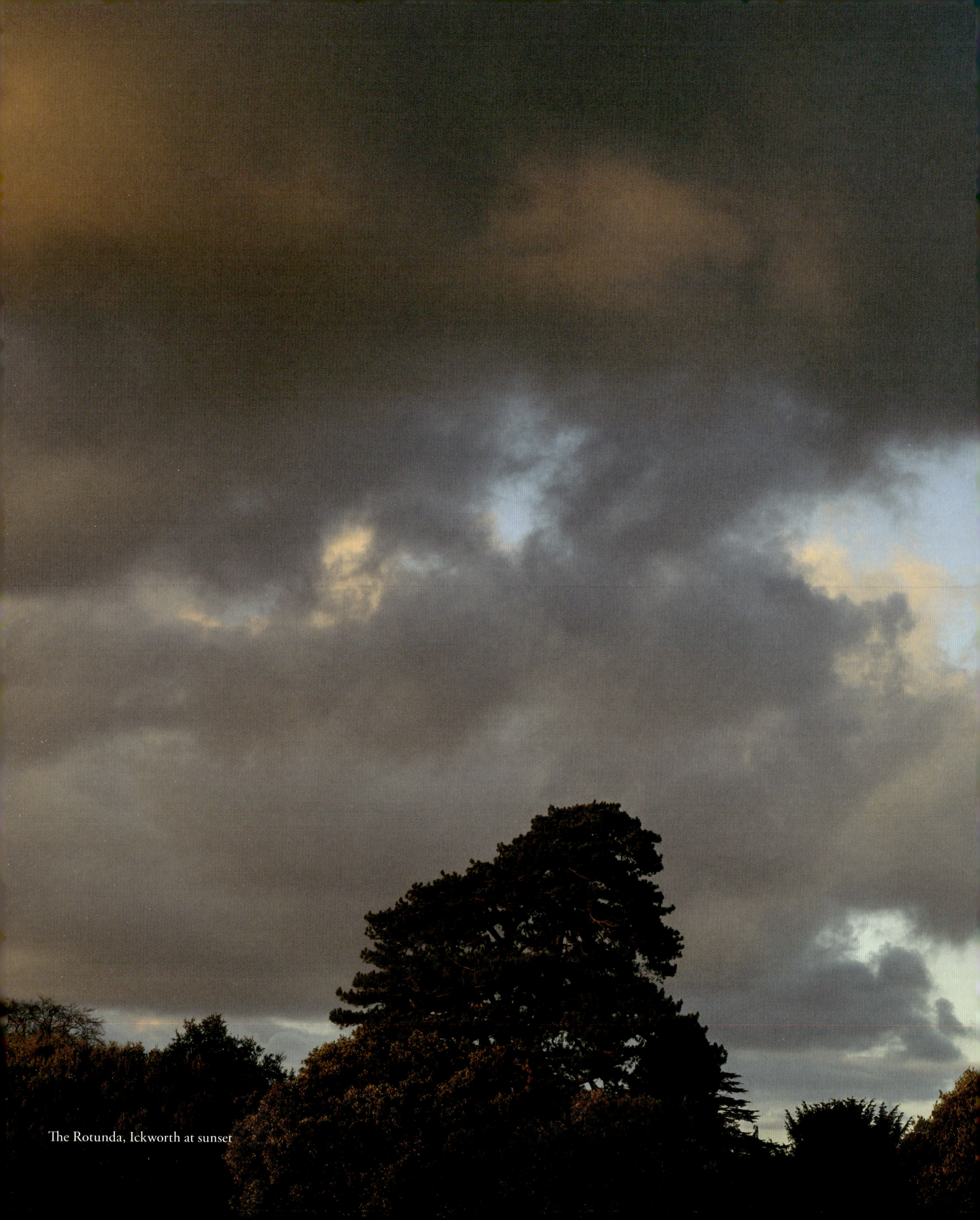

The Rotunda, Ickworth at sunset

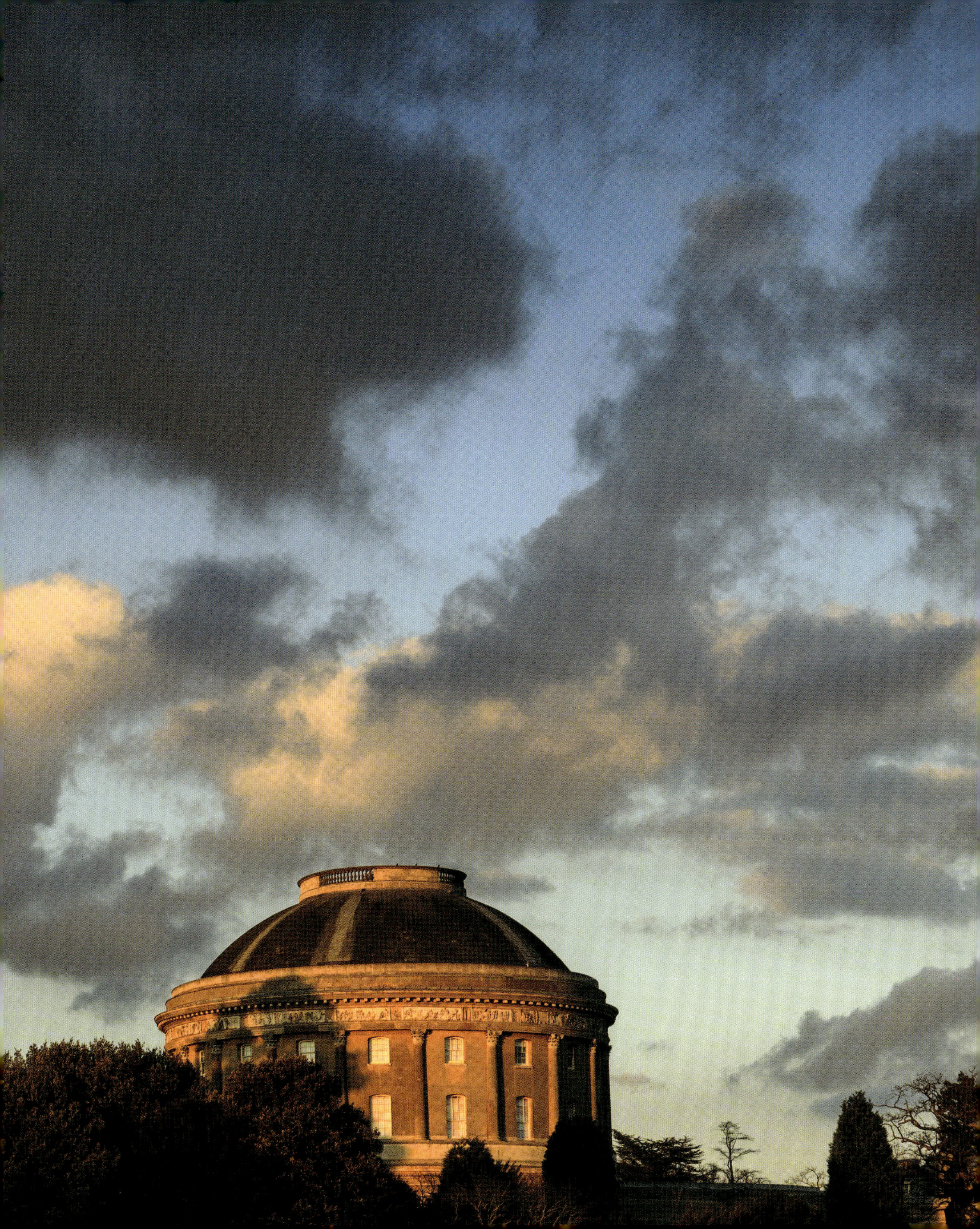

APPENDICES

APPENDIX ONE

REFERENCES TO SILVER AND GOLD IN THE 1ST EARL OF BRISTOL'S ACCOUNTS

The 1st Earl's accounts are contained in two volumes, covering 1688–1742 and 1742–51, plus a third, sub-book, for 1742–4. They are held in the Suffolk Record Office at Bury St Edmunds (ref. 941/46/13–14). In addition to entries relating to plate, references to jewellery and precious metal in the form of fringes and other embellishments to upholstery, costume and saddlery or harness have also been included. Most of the silver references from the first volume were included in the Rev. Sydenham Hervey's 1894 publication, *The Diary of John Hervey, first Earl of Bristol. With Extracts from his Book of Expenses, 1688 to 1742* (Hervey 1894a), under 'Miscellaneous'. A selection up to 1727 were also reproduced in the appendix to *John Hayward's 1959 Huguenot Silver in England 1688–1727* (Hayward 1959), pp. 81–4.

Biographical references for the goldsmiths and toymen mentioned below are given in appendix two.

VOLUME 1, 1688–1742 [SRO, 941/46/13]

My Book of Expences and Disbursements begining the 1st. Novbr. 1688 and ending at Lady Day 1742.

1688		
	My whole Expenses beginning from 1 November, 1688; on wch day, & in wch year I married my dearest wife Mrs Isabella Carr.	
1688/9		
February 19	For ye Change of my Gold watch –	005=10=00
1689		
May 25	Paid Hutchinson ye sadler at Charing Cross for a Crimson silver & gold Hoose, & Holster Capps }	010=00=00
October 1	Paid Frenoye [Paul du Fresnoy, see chapter 1] ye fringe maker in part of his Bill of 216 l, wch he has agreed to take 205 l for	050=00=00
October 4	Paid for a silver hanging candlestick for the nursery, weighing 17 ounces 10 penny weight	005=11=00
October 12	Paid Frederick Sadier a Goldsmith for boyling my wifes Plate, Plate, & in full of all other accts –	001=01=06
October 13	Paid Mr Abrey for varnishing my wifes plate	000=15=00
October 16	Paid then to Mr Paul Clowdsley in full for 15 yds & ½ of orange & Silver stuff, a scarlet lining, & three yds of scarlett Satin, & all other Accounts – 044=01=06	044=01=06
October 31	Remain yet Due to Frenoye [Paul du Fresnoy, as above], ye silk man, for ye Fringe of ye Bed, Edging for the window Curtains, & c	155=00=00
	made even all Accts with [Abraham] Chambers the 6th Novbr 89 Due to Chambers for ye Change of my shaving Pott, for a new shaving Bason & Pott –	013=00=00
November 6	Paid Abr. Chambers for a silver Candlestick & then made even all the Accounts between us –	003=12=00
December 24	Paid to Ben: Ray[e][1] mercer at ye Black Lion in Pater Noster Row for a Brown & Silver westcoat, & a Lining for it, & a Coat }	007=15=00
December 24	Paid for Six dozen of Princes metal[2] Buttons	001=10=00
1689/90		
January 13	Due to Mr Morton for gold and Crimson fringe for ye India Bed Quilt }	017=00=00
January 24	Paid for a pair of Silver Andirons for my dear wife her Closett Chimney	013=05=00
January 24	Paid then for a Gold Snuff box, which be it here remembered, ye Goldsmith Mr Howerd of whom I bought it, is obliged whenever I return it, to allow me for it again six pounds, & a Crown	006=10=00
January 30	Paid then to a french man for a Silver Snuff Box [see cat. 2]	001=10=00
February 3	daer cosen donn [John Hervey] gave me a sillver ege thing worth tenn ginnes [hand of Isabella Hervey]	010=15=00
March 14	paid then to Abr: Chambers for a Corrail Sett in Gold & then I made even all other Accts with him	0001=10=00
1690		
May 6	Paid then to Mr Frampton for 3 years Contribution mony to Newmarkett Plate ended this last Aprill at five guineys a year	0012=18=00
December 19	Paid Mrs Harache for a Silver Standish	0015=10=00
1690/1		
January 17	Paid Mr Hornbault for Setting dear wives Ear-rings	0000=15=00
1691		
April 17	Paid for my black sadle with silver Galloone & ye furniture	0001:07:00
April 25	Paid for ye Leaden Sadle I rode for ye Plate with …	0000:11:06
May 1	Paid John van Colina [Collema] for Gilding, and mending dear wives standish And at ye same time I paid him for a ffan I gave my sister Elwes …	0001:01:06
June 17	Paid Ric: Wheigham a sadler for a plate furniture, and a sadle, Hoose, Capps, and baggs, with Silver galloone & fringes	0040:00:00
1692		
May 4	To ye ffringe-maker for Silk-Lace & c for ye great Coach	0002:03:05
May 31	Gave Welch Tom[3] for a Little Diamond Ring	0000:08:00
December 10	Paid John Deards (by Ditto [Thomas Walsh, John Hervey's valet de chambre[4]]) for a silver headed Cane	0001:15:–
December 16	Paid Mr Robert ffowle in full for a pair of large Andirons, and a silver pair of scales	0088:5:6
December 17	Paid Mr Morton for ye change of my silver fringd Gloves	0002:0:–
1692/3		
February 9	Paid Mr Robert ffowle in full of his Bill for several pieces of Plate & all other demands whatsoever –	0420:–:–
1693		
April 27	Paid Mr Hornbault ye Jeweller for Rings, Locketts & c	0020:–:–
April 29	Paid ffr: Kercher [Frances Kershaw[5]] for hair Rings [for mourning, mourning, following the death of Isabella Hervey], & c. ten pounds	0010:–:–

[There is then a gap in the accounts, following the death of his first wife. They begin again in June 1695.]

1695		
June	Paid Charles Mather (ye Cane-man in ffleet Street) for a silver snuff box, a Table-Book, a Pockett Case & a silver wove-Hatband, by Bill on Chambers	015:–:–
December 7	Paid Mr ffrancis Ferris, (for ye use of his master, Mr Thomas Tompion,[6] ye sume of sixty pounds in full for a gold repeating watch for my dear wife	060:–:–
1696		
April 22	Paid Mr Tompion for ye gold Chain of my dear wifes repeating watch	007:15:00

May 6	Paid Mr [James] Chambers & Partnr[7] in full of their Bill for Plate exchanged & made for me to this Day [see cat. 3] – £115 ~~in gold~~ – [note in left margin] Plate Paid this 115 in gold out of my pockett so never ought to Acct by exch	0115:–:–
May 18	Paid Mr James Seamer ye Goldsmith for 2 Table Stands	0015:–:–
May 18	Allow'd Mr James Chambers & partner upon Accompt this Day stated, for an other Dozen of silver Plates	0062:02:6
May 23	Paid Mr James Seamer ye Goldsmith for eight diamond Buckles, which I gave my dear wife (for Bodies [bodice?] – 51£	0051:–:–
June 12	Paid Mr Edward Waldegrave ye Goldsmith for a Bason & Ewer weighing 244 ounces & a half, at 5 shills 2 pence pr ounce	0063:03:02
June 23	Paid Mr Chambers & Partnr in full of their Bill for ye silver stand, & salvers &c thirty pounds –	0030:05:–
October 7	Paid Mr James Seamers (ye Goldsmith's) man Tho. Outlaw, for ye great silver chasd Baskett, weighing 128ou:04dwt, at 5s:5d pr ounce	0034:10:–
October 17	Paid Mr James Seamer for a monteth weight 75 ou, at 5s:4d pr ou & a Chafindish wtt 24ou 15dwt at 6s:6d pr ou together 28:05:00 – [His first son by his second wife was christened on the 25th having been born on the 15th]	0028:05:–
November 5	Paid Mr Rich Hoar ye Goldsmith for a pair of branch Candlesticks weighing 78 ounces 2 dwt, & for a pair of Gilt Sconces weighing 46 ounces 14 dwtt, both at 7s:6d per ounce	0046:15:06
November 7	Paid Mr Edw: Waldegrave, a Goldsmith in Russel Street, for Eleven Dishes, 1 dozen of Plates, a Coffee Pott & a porridg Ladle weighing 802 ounces, at 5s:3d¼ pr ounce & for ye Graving [note in margin] £7 3s in mony, ye rest in old plate of my dear Fathers	0211:07:–
November 19	For 2 Dishes made by Mr Chambers weighing 154ou:½ at 4d pr ounce fashion, & 10s for graveing them, & ye Plate at 05s:02d pr ounce [note in left margin] gave him ye wt in old Plate,	0042:19:09

1697

May 7	Paid Mr Duncombe & Mr Pigeon (as Execs: of Mr Bapt May) for a large silver Cystern, 2 Dozen of nurld plates, 1 large Cup & Cover, 1 Bason, 1 Chamber pott, 1 Ladle & 1 Skimer, all weighing – 1128 ounces 15 peny weight which at 5s:4d p ounce came to 301 £	0301:–:–
June 4	Paid Charles Mather (as by a bill of Particulars)	0009:16:–
July 1	Paid Mr Jam: Chambers in full of his bill for Plate & c –	0096:–:–

1698

June 23	Paid Mr Chambers in full of his Bill for Buckles & c. –	0004:07:–
July 15	Paid Charles Mather in full of his Bill	0006:15:–
December 7	Paid Mr Chambers his Bill in full for a Tea-Kettle & Lampe wt. 90 ou, 11 dwtt at 6s. 2d. & for a Chafin Dish with a Candle-Heater, wtt. 51 ou. 18 dwtt at 5s. 6d p ou in all –	0042:19:10
December 31	Paid Watt Compton Goldsmith in Lincoln's Inn ffields for 2 pair of Andirons & 2 little Knobbs for Tongs & Shovel weighing 307ou:14dwtt at 5s4d p ounce	00082:01:–

1698/9

January 17	Paid David Williams [Willaume I] for ye silver Borders for 8 Glass Sconces for ye drawing Room weighing 231 ou 13 dwtt	00075:15:–
January 20	Paid Ditto for a pair of ye same Borders for ye Chimney Sconces all of silver weighing 53oz.:13dwtt: at 6s:6d, & for a Pair of Chimney Sconces all of silver weighing 90 oz. 03 dwtt at 7s p ounce; in all –}	00047:6:–
February 21	Paid David Williams [Willaume I] for ye 8 great Silver Sconces weighing 491 ounces at 7s p ounce 171:17 & for graving & c, in all 175£ in full of all Demands - - -	00175:-:-

1699

May 8	Paid Pet[er] du Fresnoye ye fringemaker in full	00160:–:–

1699/1700

January 27	Paid Geo: Lewis, Silversmith, for 2 pair of Plate Andirons, being French Plate at 5s.5d p ounce intrinsick valu, & 1d fashion, in all 5s 6d p ounce, ye large pair weighd 135ou:2dwtt:, ye Doggs 28ou:09dwt cost	00045:–:–

1700

July 6	Paid Williams [David Willaume I] ye french silversmith for 2 pottage & 4 ragow spoons	015:15:–
October 26	Paid [Samuel] Lanseter for 2 silver Jarrs & c. delivered Bury ffair 99	003:09:–

1702

April 29	Paid Mr [Henry] Tatlocke ye Lace man for silver ffringe for my padd saddle & in full of all other Demands	0020:–:–
December 11	Paid Mr Chambers for ye Present of Plate I gave Mr Vanbrook [John Vanbrugh]	0065:00:–

1703

June 23	Paid Mr Chambers & Comp in full of their Bill for new Plate (beside 1236 ounces they had of me in old Plate), 209:16:00 ye 22 new Dishes & 3 Doz: of Plates weighed in all 1668ou:05dwtt at 10d ffashion	0209:16:–
December 21	Paid Coll Parsons for an antique Seale a Head of Socrates	00005:–:–

1703/4

January 24	Paid Dan Dargent for dear wifes Jewels, Loopes & Buttons	00125:10:00

1704

June 22	Paid Bouquet for ye Egg-marine stone for my seale …	00007:–:–

1704/5

	[bound in at this page is a receipt] For the Right Honourable my Lord Hervey [then added in Lord Hervey's hand] for the Plate he gave to be runn for at Bury, wch he won, & gave to the corporation there 1 Monteth weight 134oz:13d at 6s:9d ye oz – 45:9:0 [,] & A Tankard of 22oz:14d at 6s:3d ye oz – 07:2:0 [Then reverting to merchant's hand] April 25 1705 [,] Received then of the Right Honourable John Lord Hervey the sum of fifty two pounds & Eleven Shillings in full of this Bill by me John Chamberlain. [On the reverse, in Lord Hervey's hand] Mr Chamberlains Bill & Receipt for Bury plates 23 Apr: 1705	52:11:0
February 21	Paid Mr Chambers for 12 Spoons, 12 fforkes & 12 Knives & c	29:13:–

1705

July 9	Paid Charles Mather in full for my Seale, Chessboard &c	20:0:0
September 22	Paid Morgan Herbert[8] for ye Gold Watch I gave Aunt Poley[9]	22:10:–

1706

July 5	Paid Chambers in full of his Bill for Ick: Church fflagon [see cat. 6] &c	19:–:–

1707

December 17	Paid Mr Chambers for ye two new Pair of Candlesticks [see cat. 4], & for a dressing weight for dear wife &c	20:10:–

1707/8

March 9	Paid Mr Tho: Brydon for a pair of Candlesticks, Snuffers & Stand which I made a present of to Monsieur Masson	16:13:6

1708

April 5	Paid Anthony Harrison[10] for my silver watch	11:16:6
December 2	Paid Mr Chambers for a great silver nurld Dish & c in full	18:15:7
December 2	Paid Charles Mather in full for my Pocket Case of Knife Cizers & c	3:4:6

1708/9

January 1	Paid Pierre Platel ye french silver-smith, more than ye office allowd for Nanns silver frame & ye 5 covers to it [christening gift]	63:10:–

1709

April 12	Paid Mr Alderman Chamberlain for thirty eight mourning Rings which I gave to the Corporation of Bury, their Recorder & Town-Clerk, upon ye Death of their Burgess Sr Thomas Felton [4th Bt, John Hervey's father-in-law]	37:10:–

June 16	Paid Mr Chambers for ye 3 gold medalls of ye Princess Sophia, ye Elector of Hannover her son, & ye Prince Electoral his son [a note has been inserted after the 'Elector of Hannover her son'] wch I exchanged for a larger of him & paid 12£:14s more for it, so they cost in all 62£:14s	50:15:–
October 6	allowd Sr Compton ffelton upon Accompt, as Executor to Sr Tho: ffelton, for a parcel of old Plate at 5s.1d p ounce 29:08:07½ [115 oz 15 dwt] allowd Ditto for Household Goods apprizd at Whitehal …	125:08:6
	allowd Ditto for Household Goods yt were in ye Lodgings at Windsor	21: 01:6

1710

June 27	Paid Mr Chambers in Exchange for ye Elector of Hannover's gold meddal.	12:14:–
August 10	Allow'd Mr Chambers upon Accot. for ye Candlesticks & Snuffers Carr [Hervey] gave to Clare Hall in Cambridg, when he came away	17:14:–

1711

July 26	Paid Mr Chambers for mending ye Silver Toaster	1:02

1712

April 25	Gave ye Poor at Newmarket, when my Horse call'd Ickworth wonn ye Queens Plate of 100 Guineys value there	00005:–:–

1713

May 27	Paid Charles Mather, in full for dear wife's Snuff-Box [gold, as recorded in published version, is not specified in original] & all Demands	20:–:–

1713/14

March 2	Paid Charles Mather for my new Gold Snuff Box	22:06:–

1714

October 19	Paid Charles Mather for a gold Snuff-Box for my Son Carr	19:14:6
October 19	Paid Ditto for a pair of gold-Buckles for my self	6:01:10
October 19	Paid Louis Cuny for my Earls Coronet fourteen pounds	14:–:–
October 27	Paid Lord Wharton & Mr Childers my two Subscriptions to Quainton & Newmarket great stake-Plates wch. they won	43:–:–
December 24	Paid Mr [John] Hasell[11] ye silk-man for ye triming of my travelling Coat and ye additional gold to my Parliament-Robes	10:15:–

1716

August 29	Paid Mr Chambers for a silver stew-pan weighing 67 ozs. 14 dwt., for a Silver Chamber Pott weighing 30 OZs. bothe at 6s:6d p ounce, & for graveing them & c in all 32:07s:03d	32:7:3

1717

May 24	Paid F: Harris, servant to Tho: Alexander for the Silver Trimming I gave my Daughter Betty	15:–:–

1718

November 29	Paid Danl Delander[12] in full for my gold Chain & sniffles [?]	5:–:–

1718/19

January 1	Paid Angel Burket for a new silver-sword for Will . .	3:10:–

1720

October 14	Gave my Son Mr John Hervey, to buy him silver Plates & Dishes when he went to Housekeeping, 300 Guineas	315:–:–

1721

May 27	Paid Ant: Nelme, & Co. in full for mending & boyling plate, & altering ye Coronets of my Plates & Dishes.	5:05:–
September 23	Subscription to ye Plate [at Bath] [on separate sheet with expenses of Bath trip]	01:01:–
September 25	Paid for an Etuy for a Fairing at Bath for Mrs. Bradshaw	2:02
September 27	Paid for ye Ring I gave Lady Lucy for a Fairing	1:11:6
October 17	Paid [Thomas] Alexander ye Lace-Man for Wills [William Hervey, Lord Bristol's son] Silver Galloon	5:15:6

1723

June 16	Paid my Son Henry wch. he laid out … 3£ 11s more for a Fuzee, & Silver shoulder Knott for his red-regimental Cloaths	
July 7	Paid Benjamin Brooke ye Gun-Smith in full for a Pair of Pistols made up with Silver Knobbs & c 10 Gin.	10:10:–
July 12	Paid Walter Turner for my son Henrys Silver Lace for his Regimentall Hatt & Cloaths, & for a Scarlet Sash &c	6:05:–
August 30	Paid Nicholas Olivier ye Taylor, in full for my son Wills Brown cloath suite Trim'd with gold orris, & all other Demands	10:06:6
December 13	Paid Eus: Treganey ye Sadler in full for my son Harrys Crimson velvet Hoose & Pistol-baggs, embroiderd wth. gold & gold Fringe six pounds twelve shillgs. six pence	6:12:06

1724

May 20	Paid Ben: Godfrey,[13] for ye use of his master John Craig in full for ye silver Tea-Pott I gave Mrs Sellars of Sleaford.	4:10:–

1724/5

February 24	Paid John Vickers for 18 yards of Pink-colour & silver stuff, which I gave dear Nann [Lady Ann Hervey, daughter of the 1st Earl] for her Birth-day Cloaths to Dance at Court in ye 10 March next	27:–:–
March 19	Paid Temple ye Bury-Taylor in full of his Bill for my son Henrys Brwon suite trimmed with silver & all Demands	17:–:–

1725

June 17	Paid Val[entine] Grimstead for Play-things for ye Children	1:01:–
July 8	Paid Mr Thomas Hinchliffe ye mercer in full for my Daughter Bettys gold & silver manteau & Pettycoat & all other Demands to this day fivety six pounds 10 shills.	56:10:–

1725/6

February 26	Paid Mr David Willaume ye silver-smith in full for ye dozen of silver plates I gave my son Lord Hervey	78:–:–

1726

March 26	Paid Richard Hill, servant to Walter Turner Lace-man in full for 17 yards of Gold Galloon for Will's new suite.	4:–:–
April 6	Paid David Willaume ye silver-smith in full: his Bill for a new Tea-kettle & Lamp [see cat. 14], a Cruet & Frame, a Case for a Dozen Spoons, Knives & Forks for my son Will, boyling & mending & c in all	67:–:–
April 9	Paid John Sibthorp in full for a Copy of Rubens's Bacchanal 5£, 10 black leather Chairs at 12£:03s: a sett of Knives & Forkes at 18s; a Case of 12 Agatt handled Knives, 12 Forkes Ditto, & 12 silver spoons at 10£:10s in all 28£ 11s bought at Brigadier Mundens Auction of Goods	28:11:–
October 14	Paid Dardes [John Deards, toyman] for a gilt Etuy for Mrs Williams 2 Guineas ½	2:11:06
October 21	Paid for a Snuff-Box I gave Mrs Saint Hayes	1:10:–
December 7	Gave John Frost ye Lady Howard of Effingham her servant when he brought me ye gold Cupp, as a Present from Her which she desir'd I would accept to remember her by silver plates I gave my son Lord Hervey	1:01:–

1726/7

January 21	Paid for ye silver Cistern I gave my Son, & Daughter Hervey weighing 317 ounces at 5s. 02½d pr ounce . . [second-hand from Lady Howard of Effingham's estate, see below 23 April 1727]	82:11:–

1727

April 13	Paid Andrew Regnier[14] ye Taylor, in full of his Bill for my own, and my son Wills doubled-breasted Cloaths wch. were Trim'd with Gold, my camlett surtout &c to this day	17:10:–
April 17	Paid David Willaum ye silversmith for ye ye [sic] Case of 12 gilt Knives, 12 Spoons & 12 Forks, weighing 131 ounces at 5s.8½d bought at ye Ds. of Shrewsburys sale at 36:17:06 & for boyling & mending old Plate in all	37:10:–
April 23	Paid & allow'd for ye several Pieces of Plate I bought which were Lady Effinghams (besides ye Cistern of 82£:11s I gave my son Ld Hervey & chargd before) in all 58£:04s, which made ye whole I was chargeable for 140£:15s;	58:04:–

	Paid & allow'd for other Goods, as Linnen, Beds & Bedding, an Iron Hearth, Sconces & c in all amounting to 37£	37:–:–
May 13	Paid Robert Leigh ye Cabinet-maker in full for putting in new Glasses to ye silver sconces, & Indiacutt jappan Frame, & for a dumb-waiter, & all other Demands	10:10:–
1728		
June 20	Paid David Willaume ye silver-smith in full of his two Bills, one for new snuffers & pan, ye other for mending worke	6:13:9
1728/9		
January 23	Paid Paul Girard ye Toy-man in full for Rings & c for Harry [son of the 1st Earl]	30:–:–
February 14	Paid Chas: Alingham[15] his Bill for spoons & c [William] Mathews[16] had of him	:12:4
1729		
April 21	Paid Edwd. Hooke for 2 Bitts, silver Bosses & Headstack [?] in all	3:–:–
1731		
November 6	Paid Mrs Margaret Marsh in full of her Bill, & what she laid out for my Daughter Louisa her white & gold Lustring at 23s/p for ye wedding her Silver Handkerchief, shoemakers Bill, Fann &c, in all 34:09:00	34:09:–
1731/2		
March 3	Paid Samuel Trenoweth in full of my Daughter Louisa her Silver wedding Triming &c and all Demands	34:–:–
1732		
April 3	Paid David Willaume silver-smith in full of his Bill & all Demands	7:–:–
October 16	Paid my wife by a Bill she drew on my Banker Fowler 23 August 1732 payable to Guillaume [David Willaume II] ye silver-smith for 75£, in full of her quarterly Allowance due & ending at Midsummer last 1732	75:–:–
1733		
April 6	Paid George Wickes & Mr [John] Craig for a Silver Coffee-Pott at 5s. 9d & all Demands [41 oz, 8 dwt]	11:18:–
April 25	Paid E[dward]. Scarlet[t] for ye Perspective Glass & Handle of my Cane trimm'd wth. Gold	3:13:–
1734		
March 5	Repaid Lord Hervey what he laid out for ye Gold Lace of my Cloaths	6:18:–
1735		
April 27	Paid Mr Peter Rogers of Bury for a silver Coffee-Pott [cat. 15] & is in full of all Demands	6:18:–
October 17	Paid Peter Rogers for a silver mugg I gave [Mrs Mary] Williams[17] for a Bury-Fairing	3:10:–
1736		
November 10	Paid Mr Peter Rogers of Bury for Williams her Silver Coffee Pott & other things	7:05:–
1737		
April 1	Paid Christopher Cock ye Auctioneer in full for a silver Epargne weight 497 ounces, 12d weight at 6s.08½d pr ounce, bought at Ld Scarsdales sale [see cat. 11–13]	166:17:–
April 18	Paid my wife for the Silver standish I gave to Lord Hervey	34:14:10
1737/8		
February 5	Repaid Lady Hervey wch. she paid for Georges shoe & Knee Buckles	4:–:–
1738		
November 22	Paid Mr Rogers of Bury for a Pair of Silver Candlesticks I gave Lady Anne [Hervey, 1st Earl's daughter]	13:04:06
1739		
December 24	Paid John Hopkins for a silver sugar canister I gave Williams for a Fairing	5:13:6
1740/1		
January 30	Paid Matt Cutler for a gold Hankerchief I gave to Lady Hervey 5 Pounds	5:–:–
February 21	Paid Richard Gurney & Comp for four Gaudroned silver Dishes weighing 155 ounces 7 d weight at 7s.6d pr oz, ingraving at 5s. each	59:05:3
1741		
January 25	Paid Lady Hervey for the two pots-pourris [silver?] which I gave her	28:18:6

VOLUME 1A, 1742–4 [SRO, 941/46/13A]

The By-Book of Disbursements at Ickworth for Oats, Coals, Day-Labourer's Wages, Bury Trades-mens Bills & c Enter'd in gross Sumes from Time to Time in my Great Book of General Disbursements Beginning from the 6th of Janry. 1741/2.

1742		
October 27	Paid Mr Rogers in full of his Bill to this day	1 4 11
1744		
October 22	Paid Mr. Peter Rogers silver smith in full –	15[s] 01[d]

VOLUME 2, 1742–51 [SRO, 941/46/14]

My Book of Expences & Disbursements beginning at Lady Day 1742

1742		
May 6	Repaid her [Lady Hervey] also for the Desert Frames & Glasses	4 18 6
1743		
July 14	Paid Nicholas Spramont [Sprimont] for two Pair of Silver Candlesticks [see cat. 62] in full of all Demands 25£.04s.04d	25 04 04
September 9	Paid Mr Peter Rogers in full of his Bill for the new Silver Sauce Boats, Salt Shovels & all Demands	11. 05. 06
1744/5		
January 21	Paid Mr E. Jordens Silversmith for a Sett of Casters, I made a Present of to Mrs Williams upon her Accepting, at my request, the Office of a Housekeeper, it being much beneath Her Birth or other Excellent Qualitys	15 16 08
1745		
April 13	Paid Mr Peter Rogers, Silversmith, one pound thirteen shillings & two pence, in full of his Bill	01 13 02
April 18	Paid Mr Plampin of Fornham two Guineas, which I subscribed to the Gentlemans Plate, which is to be Run'd for on Bury new Cours on Wednesday next	02 02 00
November 27	Paid Mr Richard Rayment[18] ten pounds twelve Shillings & one penny in full of his Bill for a New Silver Watch Braziers work & all other Demands to ye 4th of October last inclus	10 12 01
November 27	Paid Mr Peter Rogers two pounds one Shilling & sevenpence in full of his Bill for Silver-Smith Glasses & all other demands to ye 7th Octr: last	02 01 07
1745/6		
January 3	Paid Mr Peter Rogers of Bury for Six Silver Spoons given to Mrs Mary Williams for a Bury Fairing four pounds seventeen Shillings & sixpence	04 17 06
March 15	Paid Mr Peter Rogers of Bury five pounds eight Shillings and four pence in full of his Bill for exchanging a Silver Sauspan [see cat. 16] & c – – and all demands to this Day	05 08 04
1746		
May 22	Paid Mr Peter Rogers of Bury four Pounds, four Shillings and eight pence in full of his Bill for six three-pronged Silver Forks Mrs Mary Williams Bought of him ye 9th Instant by my Order	04 04 08
May 24	Paid Philip Hinterflood two Guineas, which was my Contribution to Gentlemens-Plate at Bury which was Run'd on Wednesday ye 21st Instant	02 02 00
September 24	Paid Mr Peter Rogers of Bury four Pounds & one Shilling in full of his Bill for six Silverhafted Knives I gave Mrs Williams for a Bury Fairing	04 01 00

October 29	Paid Mr Peter Rogers of Bury two Pounds Fourteen Shillings & Elevenpence in full of his Bill for Silversmiths Goods & all other demands	2 14 11
1747		
April 25	Paid Mr Peter Rogers of Bury a Bill in full of all Demands six Pounds & nine shillings	6 9 –
October 24	Paid Mr Peter Rogers of Bury Twelve Shillings & six pence in full of his Bill for Glasses & all other Demds	– 12 6
October 31	Repaid my Grandson the Lord Hervey Fourteen Shillings which he paid for Cleaning & Repairing my Gold repeating Watch	– 14 –
November 12	Paid Mr Peter Rogers of Bury Twenty Five Pounds Sixteen Shillings in of his Bill for a New Silver Nurl'd Slalver [sic], weight 66oz=&1Pwt. at 7s/8d P ounce, which I Presented Mrs Mary Williams with for the Unparallell'd Service She hath render'd me in Twenty four years Servitude & my late Wife	25 16 –
1747/8		
January 31	I put Twenty Guineas into Mrs M: M: Herveys [Mary Hervey, his granddaughter?] Hands to Buy a piece of Plate for me to make a Present to Mrs Masculine [Maskelyne]	21 – –
1748		
April 9	Paid Mr Peter Rogers of Bury one Pound, one Shilling & one Penny halfpenny in full of his Bill for Glasses & c & all other Demands	1 1 1½
October 26	Paid Peter Rogers of Bury six shillings & nine pence in full of his Bill for Glass & c and all other Demands	– 6 9
1748/9		
January 11	Repaid my Son Felton (by an order on my Banker) seven Pounds, Seventeen Shillings & sixpence which he paid for a Hair-Ring	7 17 6
1749		
May 6	Paid Joshua Cobham of Bury five Shillings in full for a Plate Basket & all other Demands	– 5 –
July 17	Paid Mr Benjamin Gray[19] Eighteen Shillings in full of his Bill for Mending, Cleaning & Puting a new Spring to my Gold Repeating Watch & all other Demands	– 18 –
August 28	Repaid my Footman Will Fenton two Pounds & one Shilling, being what he had laid out with Mr Rogers for three Silver Spoons which he gave his Aunt Plumb	2 1 –
October 27	Paid Mr Peter Rogers, of Bury, four Pounds, Eighteen Shillings & sixpence in full of his Bill for a KnifeCase, Glasses & all other Demands	4 18 6
December 15	Paid Mr Dickenson of Bury one Pound & Seven Shillings in full for an Etuey for my Grand-Daughter Smyth	1 7 –
1749/50		
February 17	Paid Philip Winterflood, of Bury, three Guineas for my Subscription to the Hunters Plate which is to be Run'd for on Bury Raceground on the 14th June next	3 3 –
1750		
April 18	Paid Mr Peter Rogers Silversmith of Bury one Pound, two Shillings & fourpence halfpenny in full of his Bill & all Demands	1 2 4½
October 17	Paid Mr Peter Rogers of Bury, one Pound, Nineteen Shillings & threepence halfpenny in full of his Bill for Silver Ware, Glasses & all other Demands	1 19 3½

[The 1st Earl of Bristol died on 20 January 1751]

1. He was also patronised by the 6th Earl of Dorset. See Beard 1997, p. 93.
2. This is a type of brass, the yellow colour of which imitated gold. It was named after Prince Rupert of the Rhine. See Wikipedia article on 'Brass', accessed 3 February 2016.
3. John Hervey's servant. See Hervey 1894a, p. 185. 'Welch Tom' may have been Thomas Aubrey who served the family for fifty years and is buried in Ickworth churchyard.
4. Hervey 1894a, p. 184.
5. She was the wife of Edmund Kershaw, chaser. See TNA C 11/467/6 Kershaw v Wilson. I am grateful to Vanessa Brett for this information.
6. 'The father of English clock making'. See Britten 1904, pp. 269–82.
7. I have not been able to identify the name of James Chambers' partner at this date. There is no reference to him in Matthews and Tuke 1926.
8. See Britten 1904, p. 627.
9. Dorothy Felton (d.1713), aunt of John Hervey's second wife Elizabeth Felton. She was married to Sir John Poley (d.1705) of Boxted Hall, Suffolk.
10. See Britten 1904, p. 623.
11. He provided the fringe for the furniture used at the coronation of George II. See Beard 1997, p. 146.
12. Clock and watch maker in London. See Britten 1904, p. 593.
13. This is presumably the goldsmith Benjamin Godfrey, for whom Arthur Grimwade found no record of apprenticeship or freedom. See Grimwade 1990, p. 524.
14. He was tailor to the 1st and 2nd Earls of Bristol and there are regular payments to him in the bank accounts of both.
15. Not identified.
16. Lord Bristol's valet de chambre. See Hervey 1894a, p. 184.
17. She entered Lady Bristol's service, presumably as a lady's maid, in 1723, and was appointed housekeeper in January 1745. See Hervey 1894a, p. 185. Lord Bristol's subsequent purchases of silver for her, commissioning of a portrait and purchasing and furnishing of a house in Bury St Edmunds, may suggest that there was a more intimate connection between the two.
18. A well-known Bury St Edmunds clockmaker who specialised in lantern clocks. See Britten 1904, p. 680.
19. Of Pall Mall, the father-in-law of Justin Vulliamy. See Britten 1904, pp. 347–8.

APPENDIX TWO

SUPPLIERS OR REPAIRERS OF SILVER AND GOLD IN THE 1ST EARL OF BRISTOL'S ACCOUNTS

Only those who dealt with plate, or were toymen, are included in this list. They are placed in the order in which they first appear in the accounts. References to 'Heal' and 'Grimwade' are to Heal 1935 and Grimwade 1990 (see Bibliography).

FREDERICK SADIER 'a goldsmith' – 7/10/1689. Not in Heal or Grimwade.

MR ABREY – 13/10/1689. Not in Heal or Grimwade. Varnishing plate.

ABRAHAM CHAMBERS – 6/11/1689, 14/3/1689/90. Heal, p. 122, 'goldsmith; Three Squirrels, over against St Dunstan's Church, Fleet street. 1683–93, killed by highwaymen', and Matthews and Tuke 1926, p. 82. Will proved 22/5/1693, TNA, PROB 11/414/387.

MR HOWERD – 24/1/1689/90. Not in Heal or Grimwade, unless he is the John Howard, pawnbroker, King's Arms, Hatton wall, near Hatton Garden, recorded as giving up trade in 1707 by Heal, p. 178. A William Howard, Goldsmith, was recorded in Gutter Lane in 1721, Heal, p. 178.

MRS HARACHE – 19/12/1690. Heal, p. 169, 'silversmith, corner of Great Suffolk Street. 1699'. Grimwade, p. 533, sub Peter Harache I. Julian Cousins (*Silver Studies*, vol. 19, 2005, p. 74) suggests she may be Ann Harache, wife of Peter I and acting on his behalf.

JOHN VAN COLINA [COLLEMA] – 1/5/1691. Repairing and gilding. China and Indiaware merchant. See Ferguson 2016, p. 116. Will proved 19/9/1737, PROB 11/685/124, in which he describes himself as dealing in 'Chinaware and Lacquerware'.

JOHN DEARDS [or DEARD] – 10/12/1692 (silver headed cane), 14/10/1726 (gilt etui). Heal, p.138, 'toyman & goldsmith (?), Fleet Street, (died) 1731' and Grimwade, p. 487 under William Deard/s, his son, also goldsmith and toyman, opposite St Dunstan's Church, Fleet Street. See also Brett 2004 and 2014, p. 37.

ROBERT FOWLE [or FOWLES] – 9/2/1692/3. Heal, p. 154, 'goldsmith & jeweller; Queen's Head, Fleet Street. 1675. Black Lion, Fleet Street. 1693–1705'. See also Mitchell 1994. Will proved 14/9/1705, PROB 11/484/175.

ffr: KERCHER [? FRANCES KERSHAW] – 29/4/1693, for hair rings. She was the wife of Edmund Kershaw, chaser. See TNA, C 11/467/6 Kershaw v Wilson, 1720. I am grateful to Vanessa Brett for this information.

CHARLES MATHER – June, 1695 ('ye Cane-man in ffleet Street', silver snuff box), 2/12/1708 (pocket scissors), 27/5/1713 (snuff box), 2/3/1713/14 (gold snuff box), 19/10/1714 (gold snuff box and gold buckles). He is described as 'an eminent toyman in Fleet-street', near the Temple, in Chalmers 1822, p. 243, note y. Mather retired to Teddington and called himself a gentleman in his Will which was proved 26/7/1738 (PROB 11/690/440) and included a bequest for the founding of a parish library at his place of birth, Preston Gubbals in Shropshire.

JAMES CHAMBERS [brother of Abraham] – 6/5/96. 18/5/1696, 23/6/1696, 19/11/1696, 1/7/1697, 23/6/1698, 7/12/1698, 11/12/1702, 23/6/1703, 21/2/1704/5, 5/7/1706, 17/12/1707, 16/6/1709, 27/6/1710, 10/8/1710, 26/7/1711, 29/6/1716. Heal, p. 122, 'goldsmith; Three Squirrels, over against St Dunstan's Church, Fleet street. c.1680–1714'. See also Matthews and Tuke, p. 82. Will proved 27/9/1733, PROB 11/661/197.

JAMES SEAMER [or SEYMOUR] 'ye Goldsmith' – 18/5/1696, 23/5/1696, 7/10/1696, 17/10/1696. Heal, pp. 239–40, 'goldsmith; Flower-de-Luce, near Serjeant's Inn, Fleet street. 1695–1709. Three Flowers-de-Luces, Fleet street. 1701–(deceased) 1739'. As James Seymour, 'goldsmith; Flower-de-Luce, corner of Mitre court, Fleet street. 1693–1734'.

EDWARD WALDEGRAVE 'a Goldsmith in Russel Street' – 12/6/1696, 7/11/1696. Heal, p. 262, 'goldsmith; anchor & Crown, Russell street, Covent Garden. 1690–1721.

[SIR] RICHARD HOARE 'ye Goldsmith' – 5/11/1696. Heal, p. 175, 'goldsmith & banker; ... Golden Bottle, Fleet Street. *c.*1690–(died) 1719'. See also Hutchings 2005, pp. 8–31.

MR [SIR CHARLES?] DUNCOMBE and MR [CHARLES?] PIGEON – 7/5/1697, as executors of Baptist May, selling plate to John Hervey. Heal, p. 145, for Sir Charles Duncombe; 'goldsmith and banker, Grasshopper, Lombard Street. 1672–(retired) 1695. (died) 1711'. The Will of Charles Pigeon of Gray's Inn was proved 27/3/1701, PROB 11/459/403.

WALTER COMPTON 'Goldsmith in Lincoln's Inn ffields' – 31/12/1698. Heal, p. 129, 'goldsmith; Duke [Sardinia] street, over against the lower end of Great Wild Street. 1695–1712. Strand. (Insolvent) 1719.

DAVID WILLIAMS/WILLAUME [I] 'ye french silversmith' – 17/1/1698/9, 20/1/1698/9, 21/2/1698/9, 6/7/1700, 26/2/1725/6, 6/4/1726, 17/4/1727, 20/6/1728. Heal, p. 269, 'goldsmith & banker; ... Golden Ball, Pall Mall. 1697–1712'. Grimwade, pp. 703–4.

GEORGE LEWIS 'Silversmith' – 27/1/1699/1700. Heal, p. 195, 'plate-worker; Angel (or Angel & Crown or Golden Angel & Crown), over against New Exchange, Strand. 1697–1714'. Grimwade, p. 581.

SAMUEL LANSETER 'of Bury' – 26/10/1700. He was the son of John Lanseter, mercer, of Bury St Edmunds, and appears to have carried on his father's business. He was a churchwarden of St James's Church, Bury and died on 11 September 1731, aged 88. See Morton 1958, pp. 49 and 53.

JOHN CHAMBERLAIN – 23/4/1705 (Bury stakes plate), 12/4/1709 (as 'Mr Alderman Chamberlain' for mourning rings. Heal, p. 122, 'goldsmith; St Edmondsbury. 1704–12' and, as John Chamberlen, 'plate-worker; Maiden Lane. 1704'. Grimwade, p. 461, 'mark entered as largeworker, 2 March, 1704'.

THOMAS BRYDON – 9/3/1707. Heal, p. 116, 'plate-worker; St Martin's-le-Grand. 1697–1702'. Grimwade, p. 453, large-worker, from Bury St Edmunds.

PIERRE PLATEL 'ye french silver-smith' – 1/1/1708/9. Heal, p. 224, 'plate-worker; over against the Duke of Schomberg's, in Pall Mall. 1699–1707.' Grimwade, p. 627.

LOUIS CUNY [or CUGNY] – 19/10/1714 (earl's coronet). Heal, p. 135, 'plate-worker; Three Crowns, corner of Panton street and Hedge lane, near Leicester fields. 1703–27.' Grimwade, p. 482.

ANGEL BURKET – 1/1/1718/19 ('silver-sword'). Possibly the Burkitt 'silversmith' recorded by Heal, p. 117, at 'Two White Friars, Fleet Street 1716'.

ANTHONY NELME – 27/5/1721. Heal, 'goldsmith; Golden Bottle, Amen corner, Ave Mary lane, 1685–(died) 1722.' Grimwade, pp. 605–6.

JOHN CRAIG – 20/5/1724. Heal, 'goldsmith; corner of Norris street, Haymarket. 1714–1735. Grimwade, p. 477 sub Ann Craig.

VALENTINE GRIMSTEAD – 17/6/1725, children's playthings. Not in Heal but recorded elsewhere as a toyman of St Paul's Churchyard – information from Vanessa Brett. Will proved 5/4/1750, in which he is described as a fletcher, TNA, PROB 11/778/111.

JOHN SIBTHORP – 9/4/1726. Brigadier Munden's auction. Presumably the auctioneer.

PAUL GIRARD 'ye Toy-man' – 23/1/1728/9 'for Rings'. His Will, 'Translated out of French', was proved 11 March 1745. He was of the parish of Saint Anne, Soho. PROB 11/738/285. Paul Crespin's father, Daniel, was Girard's nephew. Perhaps related to Noah Girard, recorded by Heal, p. 160, as a jeweller in Lothbury court, Throgmorton street in 1706 and in French court, Broad street in 1708.

DAVID WILLAUME [II] – 3/4/1732, 16/10/1732. Heal, p. 269, Grimwade, p. 704. No distinction is made in the accounts between David Willaume senior and junior but Grimwade suggest that David senior retired in about 1728 so these two later purchases have been given to his son. The commission to Edward Jordens (q.v.) in 1737 suggests Lord Bristol continued to patronise the Willaume business.

GEORGE WICKES & MR [JOHN] CRAIG – 6/4/1733. Heal, p. 133, 'goldsmiths & jewellers; corner of Norris Street [Haymarket]. c.1730–(Partnership dissolved) 1735'. See also Barr 1980, pp. 22–6.

E[DWARD] SCARLET[T] – 25/4/1733, gold cane handle. He was an eminent optician. Several examples of his trade card survive. See http://www.antiquespectacles.com/trade_cards/scarlett/scarlett.htm (last accessed 18 March 2016).

PETER ROGERS 'of Bury' – 27/4/1735, 17/10.1735, 9/9/1743, 22/10/1744, 13/4/1745, 27/10/1745, 3/1/1745/6, 15/3/1745/6, 22/8/1746, 24/8/1746, 29/9/1746, 29/10/1746, 25/4/1747, 24/10/1747, 12/11/1747, 26/10/1748, 9/11/1748, 27/101749, 18/4/1750, 17/10/1750. Rogers was a retail silversmith in Bury St Edmunds in the mid-eighteenth century. By the time of his death he must have been retired and was describing himself as a gentleman. Will proved 9/4/1791, TNA, PROB 11/1204/46.

CHRISTOPHER COCK 'ye Auctioneer' – 1/4/1737, Scarsdale epergne. He was a famous and prolific auctioneer in the early eighteenth century.

JOHN HOPKINS – 24/12/1739. Heal, p. 177, 'goldsmith; Golden Cup and Cover, near Fleet bridge in Fleet street. 1736–1763'. Grimwade, p. 551; he specialised in second hand plate.

RICHARD GURNEY & Company – 21/2/1741/2. Heal, p. 165, 'plate-workers; Foster Lane. 1734–1750.' Grimwade, p. 530.

NICHOLAS SPRAMONT [SPRIMONT] – 14/7/1743. Heal, p. 247, 'plate-worker; Compton Street, Soho. 1742–(died) 1770'. Grimwade, p. 668.

E[DWARD] JORDENS 'Silversmith' – 21/1/1744/5. Will proved 6/2/1766, PROB 11/916/73. Jordens was closely connected to Ann Tanqueray and David Willaume II and supplied much silver to the widow of the 4th Duke of Beaufort and her son the 5th Duke from the 1740s to the 1760s. See Goodway 2004 and Sale 1995. Jordens entered Willaume's third mark at Goldsmiths' Hall in 1739 (Grimwade, p. 704) 'by Verteu of a Letter of Eturney' and he probably ran the retail business thereafter though without ever entering his own mark.

APPENDIX THREE

REFERENCES RELATING TO THE ICKWORTH SILVER IN GOSLINGS AND HOARE'S BANK LEDGERS UP TO 1775

The Goslings ledgers are preserved in the Barclays Group Archives, Dallimore Road, Wythenshawe, Manchester M23 9JA. Hoare's Bank archives are at C. Hoare & Co., 37 Fleet Street, London EC4P 4DQ. Almost every member of the Hervey family had an account with Goslings and their predecessors in the eighteenth century. John, Lord Hervey and his eldest son also had accounts at Hoare's. The few references to silver in the accounts of the 3rd and 4th Earls of Bristol are referred to where relevant in the main text. The early-nineteenth-century ledgers, relating to the tenure of the 1st Marquess of Bristol, have not been examined in the preparation of this work as the 1811–40 plate list (appendix 5) records most of his purchases.

NICHOLAS LEKE, 4TH EARL OF SCARSDALE

(d.1736) (Goslings ledgers)

Lord Scarsdale commissioned the epergne from Paul de Lamerie which was purchased at auction in 1737 following his death by the 1st Earl of Bristol. The casters, cruet frames and central dish survive at Ickworth (cat. 11–13).

LEDGER 130/8 / f. 276 / 1725

August 26	To Paul Delamerie	150 –

LEDGER 130/8 / f. 338 / 1725/6

March 4	To Mr. Lemerie	100 –
March 18	To Mr. Lemerie	50 –

JOHN HERVEY, 1ST EARL OF BRISTOL

(1665–1751) (Goslings ledgers)

The ledgers commence in 1718 but the first entries for Lord Bristol are dated 1719, the account having been carried forward from a previous, lost volume. The account was held up to his death.

LEDGER 130/7 / f. 441 / 1725/6

March 4	To David Willaume	16 – –[1]
March 26	To Engraving a Large Spoon wth Crest [possibly cat. 41]	– 1 –

LEDGER 130/7 / f. 442 / 1726

April 19	To David Willaume	145 – –[2]
April 27	To a Scollop Plate new Sterlg. wtt. 21 oz 19 @ 6/2 p oz Silver & duty & 1/6 p oz fashion 8.8.4[.] Engraving 5[s]	8 13 4
Contra credit April 27	By 14 oz. 12 Old Silver @ 5/9 p oz	3 17 10

LEDGER 130/9 / f. 135 / 1726/7

March 4	To Mr. Panton [Simon Pantin?]	105 – –[3]

LEDGER 130/12 / f. 367 / 1730

July 31	To Davd. Willaum[e] ordr. my Lady	125 – –[4]

LEDGER 130/12 / f. 368 / 1730

November 21	To Mr. Williams [David Willaume] ordr. my Lady	30 – –

LEDGER 130/14 / f. 21 / 1731

October 25	To David Williams [Willaume] ordr. of my Lady	10 10 –
November 4	To Davd. Willaum[e] ordr. of my Lady	75 – –

LEDGER 130/14 / f. 23 / 1732

September 1	To Davd. Wiiliams [Willaume] ordr. of my Lady	75 – –
September 19	Do. ordr. of Do.	15 – –

LEDGER 130/19 / f. 10 / 1743

July 16	To Nichs. Spramont [see cat. 62]	25 4 4[5]

JOHN, LORD HERVEY

(1696–1743) (Hoare's Bank ledgers)

Account opened July, 1728 and held up to his death. Lord Hervey also held an account with Goslings but it was scarcely used and there are no payments to goldsmiths.

LEDGER 38 / f. 218 / 1740

October 1	To Jno. Curghey[6] as over rec'd of him ye 19th Sepr. for a Cupp	– 7 –
Credit September 19	By a Gold Cupp sold for (to Jno. Curghey)	69 17 6

LEDGER 42 / f. 239 / 1741

Credit December 18	By Jno. Kerly [Curghey?] junr. (p hand) of Jno. Marsh in full for prize mony due to Jno. Hervey Esqr.	971 12 –[7]

MARY LEPEL, LADY HERVEY

(1706–68) (Goslings ledgers)

Account opened January, 1745 and held up to her death.

LEDGER 130/23 / f. 244 / 1752

July 31	To Fredk. Kandler	219 4 –
November 29	To Mr Kandler	32 – –

LEDGER 130/23 / f. 244 / 1753

May 17	To Fredk. Kandler	40 – –

LEDGER 130/25 / f. 218 / 1754

April 8	To Fredk. Kandler	22 13 –

LEDGER 130/25 / f. 218 / 1756

February 17	To Fredk. Kandler	105 – –
July 6	To Fredk. Kandler	38 5 –

LEDGER 130/27 / f. 185 / 1757

March 26	To Frederick Kandler	23 2 –
July 13	To Fredk. Kandler	78 12 –

LEDGER 130/27 / f. 185 / 1758

April 14	To Fredk. Kandler	72 6 –

LEDGER 130/41 / f. 404 / 1768

July 9	To Fredk. Kandler	34 – –

GEORGE WILLIAM HERVEY, 2ND EARL OF BRISTOL

(1721–75) (Goslings ledgers)

As the Hon. George Hervey and from 1743 as Lord Hervey, the Earl had an account with Hoare's Bank from August 1738 to June 1748. This is primarily concerned with his travels abroad from 1738–41 and there are no payments to goldsmiths. His bank account with Goslings was opened in July 1744 and held until his death.

LEDGER 130/21 / f. 192 / 1749/50

March 12	To Elizh Chenevix[8]	14 12 6

LEDGER 130/23 / f. 74 / 1752

July 29	To Fredk. Kandler	263 13 5
November 13	To Fredk. Kandler	171 8 6

LEDGER 130/23 / f. 75 / 1752

December 12	To Fredk. Kandler	11 11 –

LEDGER 130/25 / f. 77 / 1755

March 22	To Fredk. Kandler	100 – –
April 26	To Fredk. Kandler	51 – –
April 29	To Insurance on Plate &c to Genoa	76 4 6

LEDGER 130/25 / f. 80 / 1757

February 9	To Edwd. Scarlett[9] ord Lady Hervey	12 12 –

LEDGER 130/27 / f. 65 / 1758

September 16	To Mr. [Simon] Le Sage [see chapter 3] order Lady Hervey	100 – –

LEDGER 130/39 / f. 84 / 1767

March 7	To Fredk. Kandler	81 7 –

LEDGER 130/41 / f. 90 / 1769

July 17	To Duty on Plate	10 – –[10]

LEDGER 130/43 / f. 95 / 1770

March 13	To Fredk. Kandler	85 6 –

LEDGER 130/43 / f. 96 / 1770

July 21	To Duty on Plate	10 – –

LEDGER 130/43 / f. 97 / 1770

March 18	To John Deards [junior][11]	17 – –
March 30	To Fredk. Kandler	29 3 –

LEDGER 130/46 / f. 106 / 1771

July 17	To Duty on Plate	10 – –

LEDGER 130/46 / f. 107 / 1772		
July 17	To Duty on Plate	10 – –

LEDGER 130/49 / f. 120 / 1773		
July 19	To Duty on Plate	10 – –

LEDGER 130/49 / f. 121 / 1774		
July 18	To Plate Duty	10 – –

1. This does not appear to relate to any of the payments recorded in the 1st Earl's account. It may perhaps have been a cash withdrawal from Willaume, who also acted as a banker.
2. This is the combined total of the payments to Willaume recorded in the accounts for 26 February 1725/6 and 6 April 1726. Willaume presumably presented the two cheques simultaneously.
3. This may relate to the acquisitions from the estate of Lady Howard of Effingham, see accounts (appendix 1) 21 January 1726/7 and 23 April 1727. The overall cost of those transactions, however, was £177 15s.
4. This and the following entries relate to Lady Bristol with-drawing her allowance and other cash sums from David Willaume as a banker, his premises in St James's Street being convenient for the Herveys in St James's Square.
5. This is for the candlesticks entered in the accounts (appendix 1) two days earlier.
6. John Curghey was a toyman based in Fleet Street, right next to Hoare's Bank. Information from Pamela Hunter. Heal 1935 records him as 'goldsmith; Ship, corner of Crane court, near Fetter lane, Fleet street. 1734–49' and 'Opposite St Dunstan's Church, Fleet street. 1752'.
7. Given the reference to John Hervey Esq., this must relate to an old debt, incurred before 1723 when he became Lord Hervey. Perhaps plate or other valuables had been turned in to Curghey, the toyman, by the debtor.
8. Toyshop owner in Suffolk Street, London. See Brett 2014, p. 16 and Heal 1935, p. 124, note 1. She leased Strawberry Hill at Twickenham before Horace Walpole.
9. Spectacle maker (see appendix 2). These were presumably for Lord Bristol, ordered on his behalf by his mother. London-made spectacles were evidently considered superior to what could be obtained in Turin as the Earl of Rochford, Lord Bristol's predecessor, had also requested two pairs to be sent by a Mr Watkins whilst there. One was to be 'mounted in silver in the neatest manner possible. They are for a Lady between Thirty and Forty, and are not to magnify and help the Sight, but meerly to preserve it.' The other was 'a Pair of the neatest Spectacles from the same hand, but not mounted in Silver. They are for the Nose of a Lady that has smelt Sixty Winters and more, and who has no other defect in her Eyes than what is owing to the Wear & Tear of Time. Mr. Watkins knows what will suit her age. And put them up in the same form as the former pair in a plain neat Shagreen Case.' State Papers Turin, SP 92/90, ff. 64 and 87, George Charles to Mr Payzant at Whitehall, 17 November 1751 and 26 January 1752, Turin.
10. This is the duty on plate charged to owners between 1756 and 1777. £10 was the maximum rate, for 4,000 ounces and upwards. See Sale 2008, p. 114. No payments are recorded prior to 1769 but neither does Lord Bristol appear in the register of defaulters 1757–68.
11. Toyman in London, see Brett 2015, p. 93.

APPENDIX FOUR

DOCUMENTS RELATING TO THE 2ND EARL OF BRISTOL'S DIPLOMATIC PLATE

Set out below are all the entries relating to the plate allocated to the Earl of Bristol on going to Madrid in 1758 as Ambassador Extraordinary and Plenipotentiary. As such he was entitled to 5,893 ounces of white plate and 1,066 ounces gilt. In theory this was a loan but by the early eighteenth century it had become accepted practice for it to be discharged absolutely to the recipient (see chapter 3 for a full discussion). The relevant documents are all in the National Archives at Kew.

1. WARRANT FOR ISSUE OF PLATE, 22 JUNE 1758

LC 5/110, Jewel Office Warrant Book 1732–1762, f. 302.

These are to Signify His Majestys pleasure that You provide and deliver to the Earl of Bristol His Majestys Ambassador Extraordinary and Plenipotentiary to the Catholick King [the King of Spain] the Quantity of Five Thousand Eight Hundred and Ninety three Ounces of White Plate and One Thousand Sixty six Ounces of Gilt Plate, being the Usual Allowance on Such like Occasions And for so doing this shall be your Warrant Given this 22d day of June 1758. in the Thirty Second Year of His Majestys Reign.

Devonshire [Lord Chamberlain]

To the Hon.[ble] S.[r] Richard Lyttleton K.[t] of the Bath Master of His Majesty's Jewel Office

This Warrant will amount unto Two Thousand Nine Hundred and fifty Pounds or thereabouts [.] £2950

E Yardley

Let this Warrant be executed Whitehall Treasury Chambers 6th. July 1758.

Holles Newcastle [First Lord of the Treasury]
Duncannon [Lord Commissioner of the Treasury]
J[ames] Grenville [Lord Commissioner of the Treasury]

2. PAYMENTS TO GOLDSMITH, PROBABLY DECEMBER 1758

LC 9/48, Jewel Office Accounts and Receipts Book 1728–1767, ff. 166–8

1758 Earl of Bristol

Itm Reced two dozen of gilt Plates knurl'd wt 434 oz at 10s & 6 p oz	227·17·6
Itm Reced twelve gilt Dishes knurl'd wt 481 oz. 5 at 10s & 6 p oz [cat. 74 (one)]	252·13·1
Itm Reced four gilt Sugar Dishes wth. Covers wt 59 oz. 11 at 10s & 6d p oz [cat. 75]	31·5·3
Itm Reced four gilt Stands for them knurl'd wt. 72oz. 13 at 10s & 6d p oz [cat. 75]	38·2·9
Itm Reced four gilt Sugar Strainers wt. 7 oz. 3 at 10s. & 6d p oz [cat. 76]	3·15·0
Itm Reced one small gilt Waiter wt. 12 oz at 10s & 6d p oz	6·6·0
Itm Reced four dozen of Plates. wt. 857 oz 15 at 7s & 3d p oz	310·18·8
Itm Reced twelve round Dishes wt 478 oz. wt 478 oz. 15 at 7s p oz	167·11·3
Itm Reced twelve oval Dishes wt. 444oz.2dwt at 7s p oz	155·8·8
Itm Reced eight sallet Dishes rib'd wt. 186oz.16dwt at 8s p oz	74·14·4
Itm Reced two Tureens and Covers wt. 203oz.5dwt at 8s. p oz	81·6·0
Itm Reced two Tureen Ladles wt. 15oz.15dwt at 8s p oz [cat. 63]	6·6·0
Itm Reced six ragou Spoons wt. 22oz.13dwt at 7s p oz [cat. 64]	7·18·6
Itm Reced one Epargne wt. 157oz.10dwt at 8s p oz	63·0·0
Itm Reced four Sauce-boats and Spoons wt 77oz.17dwt at 8s p oz [cat. 65–6]	31·2·9
Item Reced six Salts and Spoons wt. 26oz at 8s p oz [cat. 67–8 (six salts and four spoons)]	10·8·0
Item Reced three dozen of Knife hafts wt. 90oz.10dwt at 5s & 9d p oz & 3s & 8d Each Fashion [cat. 69 (six)]	32·12·4
Itm Reced three dozen of Forks and three dozen of Spoons [.] wt 179oz at 5s & 9d p oz & 3s & 8d Each Fashion [cat. 69 (nine forks and seventeen spoons)]	64·13·3
Itm Reced three marrow Scoops wt. 4oz.18dwt at 8s p oz [cat. 70 (two)]	1·19·2
Itm Reced two dozen of desert Knife hafts with silver blades [.] wt. 59oz.12 at 5s & 9d p oz & 5s Each Fash: [cat. 71 (six)]	23·2·8
Itm Reced two dozen of desert Forks and two dozen of desert Spoons [.] wt. 78oz. 1 at 5s & 9d p oz & 3s Each Fash: [cat. 71 (twenty three of each)]	29·12·9
Itm Reced six pair of wrought Candlesticks wt 725oz.2 at 8s. p oz [cat. 72]	290·0·9
Itm Reced six pair of Branches wth. four Nozels each wt. 1087oz.7 at 8s. p oz [cat. 72]	434·18·9
Itm Reced twenty covers for Dishes wt. 1198oz.10dwt at 8s p oz [cat. 73 (eight)]	479·8·0
	[Total 2,825·1·5]

3. JEWEL OFFICE ACCOUNT SUMMARY FOR THE HALF YEAR TO CHRISTMAS, 1758

LC 5/110, Jewel Office Warrant Book 1732–1762, f. 307.

Midsummer 1758 to Christmas following. Febry 1 1759 allowed this Account Richard Lyttleton [Master of the Jewel Office] £3555.4.7

The Particulars of the within mentioned Account are as follows

Gold works

[none]

Gilt plate

To the Right Hon.ble Earl Gower } Christening Plate } 130[oz] · 0[dwt]	68·5·0

To the Right Hon.ble the Earl of Bristol } in full of his Warrant for Gilt Plate } w.t 1066[oz] · 12 [dwt]	599·19·1

White plate

To the Said Earl of Bristol in full of } his Warrant for White Plate } w.t 5893[oz] · 8 [dwt]	2265·1·10[1]
To the Governor of the Bahamas } Islands Chapel Plate } w.t 179[oz] · 5 [dwt]	71·14·10

4. NOTICE OF DELIVERY OF THE PLATE, 9 JANUARY 1759

LC 9/45, Jewel Office Delivery Book 1732–93, f. 165.

1759 January 9

Delivered to the R.t Hon.ble the Earl of Bristol His Majesties Ambassador Extraordinary and Plenipotentiary to the Catholick King, the following Particulars of Plate for the use of his Table to be returned on demand to wit

White plate

Impris four dozen of Plates	w.t 857[oz] . 15-[cwt]
Itm twelve round Dishes	w.t 478[oz] . 15[cwt]
Itm twelve oval Dishes	w.t 444[oz] . 2[cwt]
Itm eight sallet Dishes rib'd	w.t 186[oz] . 16[cwt]
Itm two Tureens and Covers	w.t 203[oz] . 5[cwt]
Itm two Tureen Ladles [cat. 63]	wt 15[oz] . 15[cwt]
Itm six ragou Spoons [cat. 64]	wt 22[oz] . 13[cwt]
Itm one Epargne	wt 157[oz] . 10[cwt]
Itm four Sauce-boats and Spoons [cat. 65–6]	wt 77[oz] . 17 [cwt]
Itm six Salts and Spoons [cat. 67–8]	wt 26[oz] . –
Itm three dozen of Knives, Forks and Spoons [cat. 69 (part)]	wt 269[oz] . 10 [cwt]
Itm three marrow Scoops [cat. 70 (two)]	wt 4[oz] . 18[cwt]
Itm two dozen of desert Knive hafts wth. silver blades [cat. 71 (six)]	wt 59[oz] . 12[cwt]
Itm two dozen of desert Forks and Spoons [cat. 71 (twenty-three of each)]	_ 78[oz] . 1[cwt]
Itm six pair of wrought Candlesticks [cat. 72]	wt 725[oz] . 2[cwt]
Itm six pair of Branches with 4 Nozels Each [cat. 72]	wt 1087[oz] . 7[cwt]
Itm twenty Covers for Dishes [cat. 73 (eight)]	wt 1198[oz] . 10[cwt]
Total white plate	oz 5893 . 8[cwt]

Gilt plate

Impris two dozen of Plates	wt 434[oz] . _
Itm four round Dishes [cat. 74 (one)]	wt 128 oz . 10[cwt]
Itm four oval Dishes	wt 187[oz] . 15[cwt]
Itm four Dishes, Octagons	wt 165[oz] : –
Itm four Sugar Dishes w.th Covers and knurl'd Stands [cat. 75]	[wt] 132[oz] . 4[cwt]
Itm four Sugar Strainers [cat. 76]	wt 7[oz] . 3[cwt]
Itm one small Waiter	wt 12 oz
Total gilt plate	oz 1066 . 12[cwt]

[In a different hand] John Turner for the Earl of Bristol

12.th Apr. 1759. Discharged by Privy Seal dated 9 Apr. 1759 and Enter.d in the Warrant Book fol 311.

[The whole entry is crossed through to indicate that the plate has subsequently been discharged: see below]

5. NOTICE OF ABSENCE OF PLATE FROM THE JEWEL OFFICE, 25 FEBRUARY 1759

LC 5/110, Jewel Office Warrant Book 1732–1762, f. 310

These are to certify that there hath been delivered out of His Majestys Jewel Office for the Rt Hon.ble the Earl of Bristol His Majestys Ambassador Extraordinary and Plenipotentiary to the Catholick King by an Indenture bearing date the 9.th day of January last past Signed by Joseph Richardson Esq.r [sic. Actually John Turner] Agent to the Said Earl the quantity of 5893 ounces and Eight peny weights of White Plate and 1066 ounces and 12 penyweights of Gilt Plate which being Valued the White Plate at Six Shillings and Eight pence by the ounce and the Gilt plate at 10 Shillings by the ounce do amount unto the Sum of 2497£.15s.4d[2] No part of which Said Plate hath been returned into the Said Office dated the 27.th day of February 1759

Robt Mathew Clerk

6. DISCHARGE OF PLATE, 9 APRIL 1759

LC 5/110, Jewel Office Warrant Book 1732–1762, f. 311.

The Earl of Bristols Discharge of Plate

George the Second by the Grace of God of Great Britain France and Ireland King Defender of the Faith & So Forth. To the Commissioners of our Treasury Chancellor and Under Treasurer, Barons Chamberlains and all other Officers and Ministers of Our Exchequer now being, And to Our High Treasurer Commissioners of our Treasury Chancellor and Under Treasurer Chamberlains Barons and all other Officers and Ministers of Our Exchequer that hereafter shall be and to the Master and Treasurer of Our Jewels and Plate now and for the time being and to all others whom this may Concern Greeting Whereas there hath been delivered out of our Jewel Office by an Indenture or Receipt bearing date the Ninth day of January last. unto our Right Trusty and Right Wellbeloved Cousin George William Earl of Bristol Our Ambassador Extraordinary and Plenipotentiary to the Chatholick [sic] King the Quantites [sic] of Five Thousand Eight Hundred Ninety three Ounces and Eight penyweights of White Plate and One Thousand Sixty six Ounces and twelve penyweights of Gilt Plate which being valued the White Plate at Six Shillings and Eight pence by the Ounce and the Gilt Plate at Ten Shillings by the Ounce doth amount unto the Sum of Two Thousand four Hundred Ninety Seven pounds fifteen Shillings and four pence No part of which Said Plate hath been returned into Our Said Jewel Office And Whereas We are graciously pleased in Consideration of the many good and acceptable Services performed unto Us by the said George William Earl of Bristol to grant unto him the aforesaid plate and to discharge him from the same Know ye therefore that We of Our especial Grace certain knowledge and meer motion have given and granted and do by these Presents for Us Our Heirs Executors and Administrators give and Grant unto the Said George William Earl of Bristol the Said Several Quantities of White and Gilt Plate amounting to Six Thousand Nine Hundred and Sixty Ounces and Valued at Two Thousand four Hundred Ninety Seven pounds fifteen Shillings and four pence and every part and parcel thereof to his own use without any account or other matter or thing to be rendred [sic] to Us Our Heirs and Successors for or in respect of the same or any part thereof Our Will and Pleasure therefore is and we do hereby direct Authorize and Command Such of You to whom it appertains to cause the said George William Earl of Bristol his Heirs Executors and Administrators to be forthwith acquitted exonerated and discharged of and from the Said Several Quantities of White and Gilt Plate and every part and parcel thereof and of and from all Suits Prosecutions Troubles and Demands whatsoever for touching and concerning the same or any part thereof And that you the Master and Treasurer of Our Jewels and Plate do forthwith upon Sight hereof do forthwith deliver or cause to be delivered up the said Indenture or Receipt whereby the said George William Earl of Bristol his Heirs Executors and Administrators and his or their Lands Goods and Chattels are or might be charged or chargeable with the Same or any part thereof if these presents had not been made And these Our Letters of Privy Seal being first entred [sic] in the Office of Our Remembrancer in the Court of Our Exchequer shall be to You and every of You a Sufficient Warrant and Discharge And these Our Letters Shall be Your Sufficient Warrant and Discharge in this behalf Given under our Privy Seal at our Palace at Westminster the Ninth day of April in the Thirty Second Year [1759] of Our Reign.

Examined
Sam Wilson Dep.y
Enrolled among the Records of His Majestys

Court of Exchequer at Westminster to wit among Records of Easter Term in the Thirty Second Year of the Reign of His Majesty King George the Second kept and Registered in the Custody of His Said Majesty's Remembrancer there Roll

[J] Price one of the Sworn Clerks

1. These figures are marginally more than in the Accounts and Receipts book, perhaps allowing for knife blades, cases and such like.
2. The rates and total used in the notice of absence and the discharge are different from those in the actual payments (Accounts and Receipts book) and in the accounts. For certain official documents it would appear that the lower rates and limit had to be stated but it was to the higher limits, as in the initial warrant and the delivery notice, that the allocation was made.

APPENDIX FIVE

LIST OF PLATE BELONGING TO THE 5TH EARL AND 1ST MARQUESS OF BRISTOL, 1811–40

Suffolk Record Office, ref. 941/75/1, list of plate in 1811 with additions up to 1840, plus copy plate book of the same dates. Catalogue numbers adjacent to the entry (eg. cat. 77) denote that the pieces survive at Ickworth. References to catalogue numbers in italics (eg. *see cat. 32*) indicate that the pieces are not at Ickworth but are referred to in the relevant catalogue entry.

[1] GILT PLATE	oz.	dwt	no.	
A Gadroon'd Pincushion Dish	21	5	1	[cat. 77]
A do do do	23	8	2	[cat. 77]
A do do do	22	9	3	[cat. 77]
A do do do	25	5	4	[cat. 77]
A do do do	21	17	5	[cat. 89]
A do do do	22	1	6	[cat. 89]
A do do do	21	11	7	[cat. 89]
A do do do	21	16	8	[cat. 89]
4 do Round Shap'd do	77	2	4	[cat. 89]
A Gad^{d} Sallad Dish	21	18	1	[cat. 77]
A do do	21	6	2	[cat. 77]
A do do	21	17	3	[cat. 77]
A do do	21	19	4	[cat. 77]
Fruit basket	43	13	1	[cat. 19]
do do	43	17	2	[cat. 45]
Carried forw^{d} oz	431	4		

[2] BROUGHT FORW^{D}	oz.	dwt	no.	
Fruit Basket	43	11	3	[cat. 86]
do do	45	14	4	[cat. 86]
Oval Chased Bason	31	7	1	[cat. 13]
do do	32	3	2	[cat. 28]
do do	32	10	3	[cat. 85]
do do	32	9	4	[cat. 85]
Sugar Dish & Cove	15	4	1	[cat. 75]
do do	14	18	2	[cat. 75]
do do	14	15	3	[cat. 75]
do do	14	14	4	[cat. 75]
Stand to do	18	2	1	[cat. 75]
do do	17	19	2	[cat. 75]
do do	18	8	3	[cat. 75]
do do	18	3	4	[cat. 75]
4 Sugar Ladles	7	15	4	[cat. 76]
4 do do	8	10	4	[cat. 59]
Carried forw^{d} oz	797	6		

[3] BROUGHT FORW^{D}	oz.	dwt	no.	
2 Sugar Ladles	3	8	2	[cat. 101]
Coffee Pot / Suppose/	12			[cat. 22]
do do	22	12		[cat. 92]
6 Gravy Spoons	23	2	6	[cat. 100]
6 Table do	15	14	6	[cat. 100]
4 Doz^{n} Dessert Knives (all Silver)	74	16	48	[cat. 100 (12)]
4 Doz^{n} do do (Steel Blades)	24	18	48	[cat. 100 (12)]
1 do do do (Suppose)	18	16	12	
4 Doz^{n} do Forks	68	1	48	[cat. 93 (6) and 100 (6)]
4 do do Spoons	58	18	48	[cat. 93 (6) and 100 (6)]
30 ~~Tea~~ Ice do	29	15		[cat. 93 (6)]
12 Tea do	6	12		
1 Sugar Tongs	1	3		
6 Bottle Labels	2	15		
6 do Stoppers	2	2		

[crossed through in Copy Plate Book, 1811.
2 pair of Grape Scissors added in, see below,
plus 'Oct: 1840} one pair of Grape Scissors added}']

Examined May 3^{d} 1811	1161	18
B. [ristol]		

[4–6] BLANK

[7] DINNER SERVICE	oz.	dwt	no.	
1 Gadroond Table Plate	17	6	1	[cat. 35]
" do do	17	5	2	[cat. 35]
" do do	17	18	3	[cat. 35]
" do do	16	5	4	[cat. 35]
" do do	18		5	[cat. 35]
" do do	16	17	6	[cat. 35]
" do do	18	4	7	[cat. 35]
" do do	17	14	8	[cat. 35]
" do do	18	2	9	[cat. 35]
" do do	18	8	10	[cat. 35]
" do do	18	15	11	[cat. 35]
" do do	17	19	12	[cat. 35]
" do do	18	13	13	[cat. 35]
" do do	17		14	[cat. 35]
" do do	16	18	15	[cat. 35]
" do do	16	11	16	[cat. 35]
Carried forw^{d} oz	281	15		

[8] BROUGHT FORW^{D}	oz.	dwt	no.	
Gadroon'd Table Plate	18	7	17	[cat. 35]
do do	17		18	[cat. 35]
do do	17	14	19	[cat. 35]
do do	18	9	20	[cat. 35]
do do	18	9	21	[cat. 35]
do do	17	17	22	[cat. 35]
do do	17	12	23	[cat. 35]
do do	18	6	24	[cat. 35]
do do	17	11	25	[cat. 35]
do do	18	16	26	[cat. 35]
do do	19		27	[cat. 35]
do do	19	9	28	[cat. 35]
do do	18	12	29	[cat. 35]
do do	18	3	30	[cat. 35]
do do	18	1	31	[cat. 35]
do do	18	1	32	[cat. 35]
Carried forw^{d} oz	573	2		

[9] BROUGHT FORW^{D}	oz.	dwt	no.	
Gadroond Table Plate	17	16	33	[cat. 35]
do do	17	9	34	[cat. 35]
do do	17	16	35	[cat. 35]
do do	17	8	36	[cat. 35]
do do	16	3	37	[cat. 35]
do do	18	13	38	[cat. 35]
do do	17	12	39	[cat. 35]
do do	18	18	40	[cat. 35]
do do	16	19	41	[cat. 35]
do do	19	6	42	[cat. 35]
do do	18	2	43	[cat. 35]
do do	18	14	44	[cat. 35]
do do	18	6	45	[cat. 35]
do do	17	17	46	[cat. 35]
do do	17	1	47	[cat. 35]
do do	16	13	48	[cat. 35]
Carried forw^{d} oz	857	15		

[10] BROUGHT FORW^{D}	oz.	dwt	no.	
Gadroond Table Plate	18	6	49	[cat. 35]
do do	16	7	50	[cat. 35]
do do	17	17	51	[cat. 35]
do do	19	3	52	[cat. 35]
do do	19	4	53	[cat. 35]
do do	18		54	[cat. 35]
do do	17	10	55	[cat. 35]
do do	17	13	56	[cat. 35]
do do	18	4	57	[cat. 35]
do do	18	4	58	[cat. 35]
do do	17	16	59	[cat. 35]
do do	18	10	60	[cat. 35]
do do	17	19	61	[cat. 35]
do do	17	3	62	[cat. 35]
do do	17	15	63	[cat. 35]
do do	17	7	64	[cat. 35]
Carried forw^{d} oz	1144	13		

[11] BROUGHT FORW^{D}	oz.	dwt	no.	
Gadroond Table Plate	18	4	65	[cat. 35]
do do	17	6	66	[cat. 35]
do do	18	8	67	[cat. 35]
do do	18	5	68	[cat. 35]
do do	19	4	69	[cat. 35]
do do	18	11	70	[cat. 35]
do do	18	3	71	[cat. 35]
do do	17	13	72	[cat. 35]
do do	16	4	73	[cat. 56]
do do	16	1	74	[cat. 56]
do do	16	15	75	[cat. 56]
do do	16	7	76	[cat. 56]
do do	16	1	77	[cat. 56]
do do	16	14	78	[cat. 56]
do do	16	1	79	[cat. 56]
do do	16		80	[cat. 56]
Carried forw^{d} oz	1420	10		

[12] BROUGHT FORW^{D}	oz.	dwt	no.	
Gadroond Table Plate	15	18	81	[cat. 56]
do do	16	7	82	[cat. 56]
do do	15	15	83	[cat. 56]
do do	15	15	84	[cat. 56]
do do	17	2	85	[cat. 56]
do do	17	4	86	[cat. 56]
do do	16	18	87	[cat. 56]
do do	16	16	88	[cat. 56]
do do	17	10	89	[cat. 56]
do do	16	19	90	[cat. 56]
do do	17	5	91	[cat. 56]
do do	17	10	92	[cat. 56]
do do	17	9	93	[cat. 56]
do do	17	7	94	[cat. 56]
do do	16	16	95	[cat. 56]
do do	17	6	96	[cat. 56]
Carried forw^{d} oz	1690	7		

[13] BROUGHT FORW^{D}	oz.	dwt	no.	
Gadroon'd Table Plate	16	16	97	[cat. 56]
do do	16	4	98	[cat. 56]
do do	17	5	99	[cat. 56]
do do	17	10	100	[cat. 56]
do do	15	16	101	[cat. 56]
do do	15	13	102	[cat. 56]
do do	18	7	103	[cat. 56]
do do	18	12	104	[cat. 56]
do do	17	17	105	[cat. 56]
do do	17	6	106	[cat. 56]
do do	17	19	107	[cat. 56]
do do	18	4	108	[cat. 56]
do do	17	11	109	[cat. 56]
do do	16	10	110	[cat. 56]
do do	17	18	111	[cat. 56]
do do	17	11	112	[cat. 56]
Carried forw^{d} oz	1967	6		

[14] BROUGHT FORWᴰ	oz.	dwt	no.	
Gadroond Table Plate	18	9	113	[cat. 56]
do do	17	15	114	[cat. 56]
do do	17	9	115	[cat. 56]
do do	17	14	116	[cat. 56]
do do	17	13	117	[cat. 56]
do do	19		118	[cat. 56]
do do	17	15	119	[cat. 56]
do do	17	17	120	[cat. 56]
Gadroon'd Soup do	19	17	121	[cat. 57]
do do	19	12	122	[cat. 57]
do do	21	1	123	[cat. 57]
do do	19	1	124	[cat. 57]
do do	21	5	125	[cat. 57]
do do	21	7	126	[cat. 57]
do do	20	4	127	[cat. 34]
do do	20	18	128	[cat. 34]
Carried forwᵈ oz	2274	3		

[15] BROUGHT FORWᴰ	oz.	dwt	no.	
Gadroon'd Soup Plate	20	12	129	[cat. 34]
do do	20	4	130	[cat. 34]
do do	20	14	131	[cat. 34]
do do	20	2	132	[cat. 34]
do do	20	12	133	[cat. 34]
do do	20	14	134	[cat. 34]
do do	20	19	135	[cat. 34]
do do	20	15	136	[cat. 34]
do do	20	19	137	[cat. 34]
do do	20	5	138	[cat. 34]
do do	20	19	139	[cat. 34]
do do	20	6	140	[cat. 34]
do do	21	5	141	[cat. 34]
do do	20	11	142	[cat. 34]
do do	20	3	143	[cat. 34]
do do	20	10	144	[cat. 34]
Carried forwᵈ oz	2603	13		

[16] BROUGHT FORWᴰ	oz.	dwt	no.	
Gadroon d Soup Plate	19		145	[cat. 78]
do do	18	19	146	[cat. 78]
do do	18	10	147	[cat. 78]
do do	18	15	148	[cat. 78]
do do	19		149	[cat. 78]
do do	19		150	[cat. 78]
do do	18	15	151	[cat. 78]
do do	19		152	[cat. 78]
do do	18	16	153	[cat. 78]
do do	19	1	154	[cat. 78]
do do	19	3	155	[cat. 78]
do do	18	7	156	[cat. 78]
Oval Table Dish 25 by 17	105	5	1	[cat. 87]
do do "	104	17	2	[cat. 87]
do do "	103	5	3	[cat. 87]
do do "	100	18	4	[cat. 87]
Carried forwᵈ oz	3244	4		

[17] BROUGHT FORWᴰ	oz.	dwt	no.	
Gadroon'd Table Dish 23½ by 14½	92	15	1	[cat. 32]
do do	93	10	2	[cat. 32]
do do 22½ by 14½	73	11	3	[cat. 55]
do do	73	15	4	[cat. 55]
do do 18 by 12	43	9	1	[cat. 40]
do do "	46	[?]	2	[cat. 40]
do do "	49	12	3	[cat. 40]
do do "	50	2	4	[cat. 40]
do do 16½ by 10	38	14	1	[cat. 38]
do do "	39	9	2	[cat. 38]
do do "	40	7	3	[cat. 38]
do do "	41	3	4	[cat. 38]
do do "	34	6	1	[cat. 39]
do do "	34	7	2	[cat. 39]
do do "	34	13	3	[cat. 39]
do do "	34	19	4	[cat. 39]
Carried forwᵈ oz	4064	16		

[18] BROUGHT FORWᴰ	oz.	dwt	no.	
Irregular Shape Dish	67	7	1	[cat. 55]
do do	68	7	2	[cat. 55]
Pincushion Dish	28		1	[cat. 48]
do do 10 by 8¾	28	6	2	[cat. 48]
do do	29	6	3	[cat. 48]
do do	29	18	4	[cat. 48]
Octagon Dish	33	10	1	[cat. 37]
do do	34	16	2	[cat. 37]
do do	34	14	3	[cat. 37]
do do	35	9	4	[cat. 37]
Round Shaped Dish	32	19	1	[cat. 36]
do do	34	2	2	[cat. 36]
do do	34	14	3	[cat. 36]
do do	34	15	4	[cat. 36]
do do	23	13	1	[cat. 49]
do do	24	3	2	[cat. 49]
Carried forwᵈ oz	4638	15		

[19] BROUGHT FORWᴰ	oz.	dwt	no.	
Round Shaped Dish	24	5	3	[cat. 49]
do do	24	5	4	[cat. 49]
2 Oblong Double Dishes	127	18		[cat. 99]
4 Cassaroles & Covers	166	10		[cat. 98]
1 Rich 1st Course Cassarole ['made to keep warm with hot water', Copy Plate Book 1811]	123	5	1	[cat. 105]
" do do	123	-	2	[cat. 105]
" do do	122	-	3	[cat. 105]
" do do	124	-	4	[cat. 105]
Sallad Dish	25	11	1	[cat. 31]
do do	26	11	2	[cat. 31]
do do	26	17	3	[cat. 31]
do do	26	18	4	[cat. 31]
Oval Mazareene, 17 by 11	28	11	1	[cat. 33]
do do "	30	18	2	[cat. 33]
Oval Dish Cover	33	6	1	[cat. 88]
do do	32	12	2	[cat. 88]
Carried forwᵈ oz	5705	2		

[20] BROUGHT FORWᴰ	oz.	dwt	no.	
Oval Dish Cover	33	5	3	[cat. 88]
do do	33	7	4	[cat. 88]
Round Dish Cover	33		1	[cat. 73]
do do	35	-	2	[cat. 73]
do do	34	3	3	[cat. 73]
do do	34	6	4	[cat. 73]
Octagon Dish Cover	31	3	1	[cat. 73]
do do	31	2	2	[cat. 73]
do do	31	5	3	[cat. 73]
do do	32		4	[cat. 73]
Oval Tureen wᵗʰ Cover	231	15	1	[cat. 43]
do do	236	5	2	[cat. 43]
Round do	194	2	1	[cat. 53]
do do	199	7	2	[cat. 53]
Small do	73	4		[cat. 79]
Sauce Boat	18	6	1	[cat. 65]
Carried forwᵈ oz	6986	12		

[21] BROUGHT FORWᴰ	oz.	dwt	no.	
Sauce Boat	18	3	2	[cat. 65]
do do	18	4	3	[cat. 65]
do do	18	10	4	[cat. 65]
Sauce Boat	23	2	1	[cat. 30]
do do	23	3	2	[cat. 30]
do do	24	2	3	[*see cat. 30*]
do do	24	16	4	[*see cat. 30*]
Sauce Boat	17	2	1	[cat. 29]
do do	17	13	2	[*see cat. 29*]
do do	19	14	3	[*see cat. 29*]
do do	19	15	4	[*see cat. 29*]
Gadroon'd Salt	4	14	1	[cat. 67]
do do	4	~~14~~17	2	[cat. 67]
do do	4	14	3	[cat. 67]
do do	4	17	4	[cat. 67]
do do	4	16	5	[cat. 67]
Carried forwᵈ oz	7234	~~6~~14		

[22] BROUGHT FORWᴰ	oz.	dwt	no.	
Gadroon'd Salt	4	12	6	[cat. 67]
do do	9	5	1	[cat. 46]
do do	9	16	2	[cat. 46]
do do	10	3	3	[cat. 46]
do do	10	5	4	[cat. 46]
do do	10	5	5	[cat. 46]
do do	9	18	6	[cat. 46]
do do	10	1	7	[cat. 46]
do do	10	2	8	[cat. 46]
do do	8	16	9	[*see cat. 46*]
do do	9	6	10	[*see cat. 46*]
do do	9	6	11	[*see cat. 46*]
do do	9	12	12	[*see cat. 46*]
4 Salts[1]	22	15		
Cruet Frame	20	11		[cat. 12]
do do	20	13		[cat. 12]
Carried forwᵈ oz	7420	~~2~~0		

[23] BROUGHT FORWᴰ	oz.	dwt	no.	
Soy Frame[2]	11	10		
Castor	14	8	1	[cat. 11]
do	12	15	2	[cat. 11]
do	24	16	3	[cat. 11]
do	12	6	4	[cat. 11]
do	12	12	5	[cat. 11]
do	23	-	6	[cat. 11]
4 Cruet Mounts wᵗʰ Handles	12			[cat. 12]
Ice Pail	168	-	-	[cat. 18]
do do	168	18		[cat. 18]
New Linings & Tops to do.	65	-		[cat. 108]
Bread Basket	42	16		[cat. 50]
do do	42	-	-	[cat. 50]
Round Waiter 13½ Inchs [sic]	41	7	1	[cat. 82]
do do "	41	1	2	[cat. 82]
do do "	41	16	3	[cat. 82]
Carried forwᵈ oz	8154	~~7~~5		

[24] BROUGHT FORWᴰ	oz.	dwt	no.	
Round Waiter 13½ Inch	41	7	4	[cat. 82]
do do 7 Inch	9	7	1	[cat. 51]
do do "	9	12	2	[cat. 51]
do do "	8	19	3	[cat. 51]
do do "	9	5	4	[cat. 51]
do do "	9	2	5	[cat. 51]
do do "	9	7	6	[cat. 51]
8 Pierced Bottle Stands	46	16		[cat. 81]
4 Plain do do[3]	13	17		
6 Escallop Shells	25	10		[cat. 61]

	oz.	dwt	no.	
Cistern	314	15		[cat. 1]
108 King's Pattern Table Knives	135	-		[cat. 102 (6)]
6 do do Carving Knives	8	6		[*see cat. 102*]
6 do do Forks	29	-		[*see cat. 102*]
108 do do Table Forks	322	5		[*see cat. 102*]
60 do do do Spoons	170	2		[*see cat. 102*]
Carried forw^d oz	9316	~~17~~15		

[25] BROUGHT FORW^D	oz.	dwt	no.	
[all subsequent dwt totals altered by 2]				
12 King's Pattern Gravy Sp^ns	64	10		[*see cat. 102*]
60 threaded Table Knives	60	19		
60 Plain do Forks (Suppose)[4]	145	-		
48 do do Spoons do	105	-		
12 do Gravy do	46	-		
48 Pistol Handle Table Knives (suppose)	73			[cat. 69 (6)]
48 Table Forksdo	120	-		[cat. 69 (9)]
['Plain', Copy Plate Book] do	120	-		[cat. 69 (9)]
36 do Spoons do	88	-		[cat. 26 (1), 69 (17) and 83 (11)]
12 Gravy do do	41	-		[cat. 52 (4) and 64 (6)]
2 Carving Knife & Fork Hafts	22			[cat. 84]
2 Carving Knife Hafts	3	14		[? cat. 42]
2 do Forks	9	3		
2 do Knife Hafts	4	4		
2 do Forks	7	8		
2 Travelling Knives	3	2		
2 do Forks	4	6		
Carried forw^d oz	10114	1		

[26] BROUGHT FORW^D	oz.	dwt	no.	
Travelling Spoons	4	5		
2 Spoons for Confectioner	5	-		
2 Soup Ladles	28	14		[cat. 54]
2 do do	23	11		[cat. 44]
2 do do	16	16		[cat. 63]
4 Sauce do	10	11		[cat. 66]
8 do do	21	1		
6 Salt do	1	8		[cat. 68 (4)]
12 do do	3	19		[cat. 47 (4)]
2 Sugar do	8	17		
12 Wine Labels	7	2		
6 do do	2	5		
6 Corks	2	6		
4 do	1	10		
10 Skewers	4	13		
9 do	7	9		
Carried forw^d oz	10263	8		

[27] BROUGHT FORW^D	oz.	dwt	no.	
2 Mustard Ladles	-	18		
3 Marrow Spoons	3	8		[cat. 70 (2)]
['2' in Copy Plate Book but same weight given]				
24 all Silver Desert Knives	59	12		[cat. 71 (6)]
24 Desert Forks	39	8		[cat. 71 (23)]
24 do Spoons	38	13		[cat. 71 (23)]
Candlestick wth Branch	147		1	[cat. 72]
do do	145		2	[cat. 72]
do do	147		3	[cat. 72]
do do	146		4	[cat. 72]
do do	149	5	5	[cat. 72]
do do	148		6	[cat. 72]
do do	153	10	7	[cat. 72]
do do	151	15	8	[cat. 72]
do do	154		9	[cat. 72]
do do	156	10	10	[cat. 72]
do do	159	10	11	[cat. 72]
Carried forw^d oz	12062	17		

[28] BROUGHT FORW^D	oz.	dwt	no.	
Cand^k wth Branch	153		12	[cat. 72]
Table Candlestick	17	3	1	[*see cat. 3*]
do do	17	3	2	[*see cat. 3*]
do do	16	17	3	[*see cat. 3*]
do do	15	13	4	[*see cat. 3*]
do do	16	7	5	[*see cat. 3*]
do do	17	6	6	[*see cat. 3*]
do do	16	9	7	[*see cat. 3*]
do do	17	15	8	[*see cat. 3*]
do do	16	16	9	[cat. 4]
do do	17	10	10	[cat. 4]
do do	17	6	11	[cat. 4]
do do	17	13	12	[cat. 4]
do do	14	8	1	[cat. 7]
do do	15		2	[cat. 7]
do do	14	9	3	[cat. 3]
Carried forw^d oz	12463	12		

[29] BROUGHT FORW^D	oz.	dwt	no.	
Table Cand^k	14	6	4	[cat. 3]
do do	14	10	5	[cat. 3]
do do	14	17	6	[cat. 3]
do do	15	15	7	[cat. 9]
do do	16	2	8	[cat. 9]
do do	16	1	9	[*see cat. 3*]
do do	16	3	10	[*see cat. 3*]
do do	16	6	11	[*see cat. 3*]
do do	16	10	12	[*see cat. 3*]
do do	14	14	13	[cat. 8]
do do	15	17	14	[cat. 8]
Table Candlestick ['Rich Table Candlesticks' in CopyPlate Book]	28	14	1	[cat. 103]
do do	31		2	[cat. 103]
do do	31	18	3	[cat. 103]
do do	29	3	4	[cat. 103]
Carried forw^d oz	12755	8		

[30] BROUGHT FORW^D	oz.	dwt	no.	
Table Cand^k	31	6	5	[cat. 103]
do do	31	6	6	[cat. 103]
6 Hand Cand^ks ['suppose'	-	-		[cat. 91
(weight) in Copy Plate Book]	66	-	-	and 95]
Preserving Pan	57	18		[cat. 10]
Saucepan	36	-	1	[cat. 16]
do	15	5	2	
Orange Strainer ['orange' erased in Copy Plate Book]	2	10		
Inkstand & 3 Boxes	65	4		[cat. 27]
2 Nutmegraters	6	-		[cat. 2 and 17]
Desert Frame	20	5	-	[cat. 80]
Large Tea Tray	235		1	[cat. 58]
do do	235	6	2	[cat. 58]
Tea Urn	191	10	1	[cat. 104]
do do	197		2	[cat. 104]
Carr^d forw^d oz	13945	18		

[31] BROUGHT FORW^D	oz.	dwt	no.	
Tea Kettle & Lamp	52	6		[cat. 14]
Triangular Stand to do	13	18		[cat. 25]
Coffee Pot	17	10		[cat. 15]
Chocolate Pot	28			[cat. 5]
Tea Pot	19	-	-	[cat. 97]
89 Tea Spoons & 2 Tea Tongs (suppose)	43			
24 threaded fid Tea Spoons ['Fiddleheaded threaded' according to Copy Plate Book]	16	3		
3 do do Sugar Tongs (suppose)	4	8		
	13945	18		
[in Lord Bristol's hand]				
Examined May 18th 1811 Bristol				
Gilt Plate [in Lord Bristol's hand]	1161	18		
Total oz	15302	1		

[Copy Plate Book: 'Carefully Examined & compared with the original May 18th, 1811 Bristol'] The total quantity of Plate left by George Earl of Bristol was – oz 16700=11

Quantity as per Book – oz 15,302=1
Deficient – oz 1, 398=10

Memorandum as to the state of the family Plate }
May 1811 Bristol

[32] BROUGHT FORW^D	oz.	dwt	no.	
[From this point forward all in Lord Bristol's hand]				
8 Hand Candlesticks with Gadroon Edge				
No. 1 – 13:1:0	106	10	12	[cat. 110 (4)]
No. 2 – 13:13:0				
No. 3 – 13:15:0				
No. 4 – 12:14:0				
No. 5 – 13:6:12				
No. 6 – 13:16:0				
No. 7 – 13:1:0				
No. 8 – 13:4:0				
['Added Nov^t 1811' according to Copy Plate Book]				
Coffee Pot	24	8		
/Ickworth/ Ink Stand	25	8		[cat. 109]
/London/ Ink Stand	22	0		[cat. 109]
Tea=Pot	22	15		[cat. 111]
One Tea Pot made at Lyons[5] about	20	0		
oz	15,519	2	12	

[33] ADDED IN 1823	oz.	dwt	no.	
Kings Pattern:				
3 Dozen Table Forks _	129	0		[*see cat. 113*]
2 Dozen Table Spoons _	83	16		[*see cat. 113*]
Not weighed 2 Dozen ½ Table Knives (about)	40	0		[*see cat. 113*]
oz	15,771	18	12	
" 1 Dozen ½ Desert Knives Steel blades				[*see cat. 113*]
" 1 Dozen ½ Do silver blades				[cat. 113 (6)]
1 Dozen ½ Do Spoons _	38	6		[cat. 113 (6)]
1 Dozen ½ D~~o~~ Forks _	37	9		[cat. 113 (6)]
2 small Waiters	18	13		[? cat. 115]
3 Pair Sugar Tongs	5	0		
~~2 Pair of Grape Scissors added~~ one ~~July 1815~~ [,] ~~one July 1824~~ ~~weight about seven ounces~~	~~7~~	~~0~~		
[Crossing through endorsed 'B.']				
oz	15,871	6	12	
Kings Pattern Gilt Desert Set:				
4 Dozen Desert Spoons	89	19		[cat. 114]
4 Dozen Desert Forks	99	18		[cat. 114]
4 Dozen Do Knives silver blades	90	16		[cat. 114]
4 Dozen Do Knives steel blades	36	4		[cat. 114]
1 Dozen large Spoons	42	17		[cat. 114]
4 Ice Do	25	5		[cat. 114]
oz	16,256	5	12	

[33] ADDED JUNE 1824	oz.	dwt	no.
1 Dozen Tea Spoons	9	5	
2 Carving Knives & forks steel Prongs	5	13	
2 Carving Spoons	13	15	
1 Dozen Kings Pattern Knives	11	19	
1 Dozen Kings Pattern Forks	39	19	

[33] MAY 1826	oz.	dwt	no.
1 Pair of Asparagus Tongs	6	0	
oz	16,342	16	12

[34]	oz.	dwt	no.
Total Quantity of Plate left by George Earl of Bristol (see four pages back)	16,700	11	

[35] BROUGHT OVER	oz.	dwt	no.	
oz	16,342	16	12	
2 Pair Grape Scissors omitted one July 1815, one July 1824	7	0	0	[cat. 112 and 116]
TOTAL OZ	16,349	16	12	

27 May 1826,
Bristol

January 1827

One dozen Tea Spoons}	9	19	
One Large Branch Candlestick given by the Lincolnshire Tenants. Sent home by Rundel & Bridge July 1827	298	8	[cat. 118]
oz	~~16,448~~	~~4~~	~~12~~
oz	16,658	=3	=12

['16,648 4 12' in the Copy Plate Book]

Bristol July 25th 1827

[35] ADDED 4 APRIL 1827

['August 4 1827', Copy Plate Book]

One dozen desert Spoons [cat. 119]

One dozen desert Forks (6 of each)]
['to match the old ones with the Kings arms', Copy Plate Book]

one Sugar Tongs [no weight given]
B[ristol], 20 July 1829

ADDITIONAL PAGE IN COPY PLATE BOOK

oz [all in Lord Bristol's hand]	16,648	=4	=12	
Suffolk & Essex Tenantry, gave me 1841 one large Candlestick with figures & ornaments	482	15	0	[cat. 121]
oz	17,130	19	12	

The dozen desert forks & spoons mention'd at the Bottom of the last Page, which were added August 1827 [cat. 119 (6 of each)]

1. Four oval salts 'Continental, late 18th century' are listed in the Probate valuation 1952, p. 25.
2. Probably that of 1802 listed in the Probate valuation 1952, p. 27.
3. Retained by the family in 1956. By John Emes, 1799, engraved with Hervey crest and baron's coronet. Probate valuation 1952, p. 25.
4. This is probably the Old English pattern service recorded in the Probate valuation 1952, p. 28. There were then only 11 forks (1786 and 1790), 17 spoons (1788) 7 gravy spoons (six of 1803, one of 1790) and no knives.
5. Probate valuation 1952, p. 24, 'A French compressed spherical teapot with corded rib around body, early 19th century'.

HERVEY OF ICKWORTH
Selective family tree

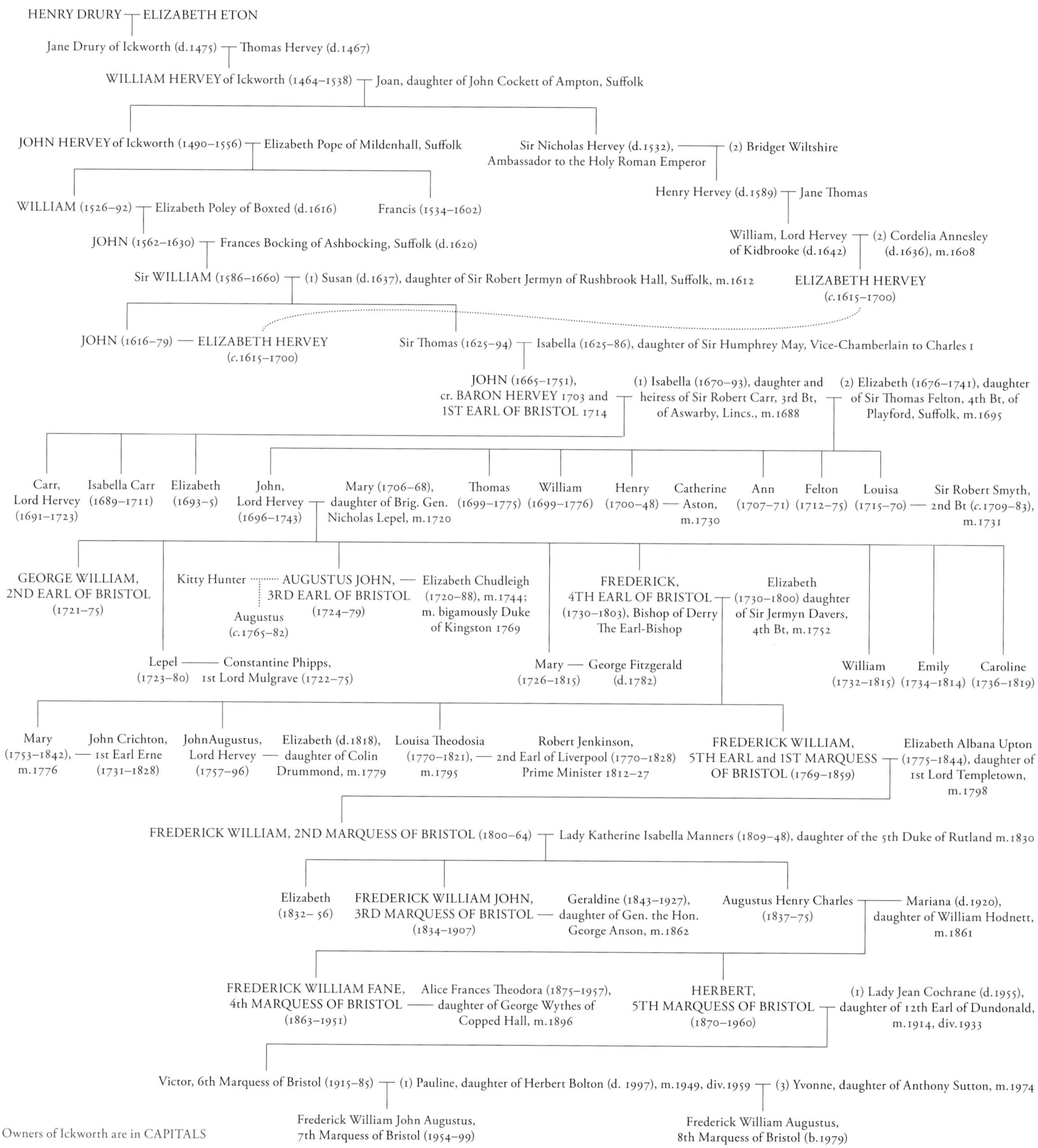

Owners of Ickworth are in CAPITALS

BIBLIOGRAPHY

ABBREVIATIONS

AST: Archivio di Stato di Torino, Sezione Corte, Archivi Juvarriani, Piazza Castello, 209, Torino, Italy.
BGA: Barclays Group Archives, Dallimore Road, Wythenshawe, Manchester M23 9JA.
BL: British Library, 96 Euston Rd, London NW1 2DB.
DRO: Derbyshire Record Office, New Street, Matlock, Derbyshire DE4 3FG.
HBA: Hoare's Bank Archives, C. Hoare & Co., 37 Fleet Street, London EC4P 4DQ.
HRO: Hampshire Record Office, Sussex St, Winchester, Hampshire SO23 8TH.
NAL: National Art Library, Victoria & Albert Museum, Cromwell Road, London SW7 2RL.
NRO: Northamptonshire Record Office, Wootton Hall Park, Northampton NN4 8BQ.
ODNP: *Oxford Dictionary of National Biography*, Oxford, 2004.
SRO: Suffolk Record Office, 77 Raingate Street, Bury St Edmunds, Suffolk, IP33 2AR.
TNA: The National Archives, Kew, Richmond, Surrey TW9 4DU.

ARCHIVES

Lady Mary Booth 1730 | National Trust, Dunham Massey, Cheshire, ref. CL.L.7.8, Lady Mary Booth (subsequently Countess of Stamford), 'Receits Transcribed from a Book of the Right Honourable Earl of Warrington's To which is added Tables of From 4 to 33 Dishes 1730'.
Bristol accounts 1688–1742 | SRO, 941/46/13, 1st Earl of Bristol's diary and disbursements 1688–1742.
Bristol accounts 1742–51 | SRO, 941/46/14, 1st Earl of Bristol's diary & disbursements 1742–51.
Bristol plate list 1811 | SRO, 941/75/1, 'List of Plate May 4th 1811', belonging to the 5th Earl (later 1st Marquess) of Bristol, with amendments dated 1823 to 1829.
Bristol plate list 1826–7 | SRO, 941/75/2, List of plate dated 15 April 1826 with additions of 25 May 1826, 25 July 1827 and August 1827.
Bristol plate lists 1874 | SRO, 941/75/3, 'List of plate [at St James's Square] May, 1874', 'June 1874 List of Plate at Ickworth' and 'Putney Plate', undated.
Bristol plate list 1874b | SRO, 941/75/4, 'Ickworth & 6 St Jamess Square Copy of Inventory of Plate May 1874'.
Chatham papers | TNA, PRO 30/8, Papers of William Pitt, 1st Earl of Chatham.
Death duties list *c.*1951 | SRO, HA 507/9/21, List of silver etc offered in lieu of death duties following the death of the 4th Marquess of Bristol, typescript, n.d.
Goslings ledgers | BGA, 130/1–151, customer ledgers of Gosling and Sharpe's Bank and its predecessors 1718–1809.
Great Wardrobe Bills 1757–8 | TNA, LC 9/303, Great Wardrobe Bills, October 1757 to October 1758.
Hoare's Bank accounts | HBA, customer ledgers 2–13 for Nicholas Lepel, 30–44 for John, Lord Hervey and 39–48 for George, Lord Hervey (later 2nd Earl of Bristol).
Holderness correspondence | BL, Egerton MS 3464. Correspondence of the Earl of Holderness with English diplomatic representatives.
Jewel Office Delivery Book 1698–1732 | TNA, LC 9/44, Jewel Office Delivery Book, September 1698 to February 1731/2.
Jewel Office Delivery Book 1732–93 | TNA, LC 9/45, Jewel Office Delivery Book, March, 1732 to 1793.
Jewel Office Plate Book 1728–1767 | TNA, LC 9/48, '1728 to 1767 Plate Book or Goldsmiths Book'.
Jewel Office Warrant Book 1732–62 | TNA, LC 5/110, Jewel Office Warrant Book, 1732 to 1762.
Jocelyn Dinner Book | The Winterthur Library, Folio 219, Dinner Book of Robert, 1st Viscount Jocelyn, October 1740 to November 1751.
Letters to admirals, consuls etc 1759–61 | SRO, HA 507/7/2, George William, 2nd Earl of Bristol, correspondence, Madrid, letters to Admirals, Consuls etc (copies), 1759–1761.
Letters from admirals, consuls etc 1755–9 | SRO, HA 507/7/3, George William, 2nd Earl of Bristol, correspondence, Turin and Madrid, letters from Admirals, consuls etc., 1755–59.
Letters from admirals, consuls etc 1760–1 | SRO, HA 507/7/4, George William, 2nd Earl of Bristol, correspondence, Madrid, letters from Admirals, consuls etc (1760–1).
Letters from Secretaries of State 1755–9 | SRO, HA 507/7/5, George William, 2nd Earl of Bristol, correspondence, Turin and Madrid, letters from Secretaries of State, 1755–9.
Letters from Secretaries of State 1759–61 | SRO, HA 507/7/6, George William, 2nd Earl of Bristol, correspondence, Madrid, letters from Secretaries of State, 1759–61.
Newcastle papers | BL, Add MS 32686-32992, official correspondence of Thomas Pelham-Holles, Duke of Newcastle, 1697–1768.
Parker and Wakelin Ledgers | NAL, Garrard Ledgers, VAM 7, 8 and 10, John Parker and Edward Wakelin 1765–76, gentlemen's ledgers.
Plate tax list 1757–62 | TNA, T 47/5, Yearly lists of persons paying plate duties 1756–62.
Plate tax defaulters 1757–68 | TNA, T 47/6, Plate Duty – Actual and suspected defaulters 1757–68.
Probate valuation 1952 | National Trust office, Westley Bottom, Suffolk, photocopy of probate valuation of the Ickworth silver carried out by Christie, Manson & Woods Ltd, April, 1952.
State Papers Spain | TNA, SP 94, State Papers for Spain.
State Papers Turin | TNA, SP 63, State Papers for Turin.
State Papers Venice | TNA, SP 99, State Papers for Venice.
Wickes Ledgers | NAL, Garrard Ledgers, VAM 1–3, George Wickes 1735–1750 and VAM 4–6, George Wickes and Samuel Netherton 1747–1760, gentlemen's and stock ledgers.
Wilmot Papers | DRO, D 3155, correspondence of Sir Robert Wilmot, 1st Bt, as English Secretary to the Lords Lieutenant of Ireland 1740–72.

PUBLICATIONS

Abel 1960 | Abel, Deryck, *The House of Sage 1860–1960*, company centenary pamphlet (1960).
Alcorn 2000 | Alcorn, Ellenor M., English Silver in the Museum of Fine Arts, Boston, Volume II: Silver from 1697 (Boston, 2000).
——2006 | Alcorn, Ellenor M., *Beyond the Maker's Mark Paul de Lamerie Silver in the Cahn Collection* (Cambridge 2006).

Banister 1980 | Banister, Judith, 'Rococo silver in a neo-classical setting: the Bristol family silver at Ickworth', *Country Life*, vol. 168 (4 September 1980), pp. 792–4.
Bargoni 1963 | Bargoni, Augusto, 'Argenti' in volume 3 of Vittorio Viale (ed.), *Mostra del Barocco Piemontese*, 3 vols (Turin, 1963).
Barr 1980 | Barr, Elaine, *George Wickes: Royal Goldsmith 1698–1761* (London, 1980).
Bateman 1883 | Bateman, John, *The Great Landowners of Great Britain and Ireland* (London, 1883).
Beard 1997 | Beard, Geoffrey, *Upholsterers and Interior Furnishing in England 1530–1840* (London, 1997).
Beard and Gilbert 1986 | Beard, Geoffrey and Christopher Gilbert, *Dictionary of English Furniture Makers 1660–1840* (Leeds, 1986).
Belvoir Castle *c.*1990 | *Belvoir Castle Leicestershire* [guide book], n.d. (*c.*1990).
Billings, E.R., *Tobacco: Its History, Varieties, Culture, Manufacture and Commerce, with an account of its various modes of use, from its first discovery until now* (Hartford, Connecticut, 1875).
Bimbenet-Privat & Mitchell 2003 | Bimbenet-Privat, Michèle and David Mitchell, 'Words or Images: descriptions of plate in England and France 1660–1700', *The Silver Society Journal*, no. 15 (2003), pp. 47–62.
Black 1999 | Black, Jeremy, *The British Abroad: The Grand Tour in the Eighteenth Century* (London, 1999)
Brett 1986 | Brett, Vanessa, *The Sotheby's Directory of Silver 1600–1940* (London, 1986).
——2004 | Brett, Vanessa, 'The great (and lesser) toyshops', *Silver Studies*, no. 16 (2004), pp. 117–123.
——2014 | Brett, Vanessa, *Bertrand's Toyshop in Bath: Luxury Retailing 1685–1765* (Wetherby, 2014).
Britten 1904 | Britten, F.J., *Old Clocks and Watches and Their Makers* (London, 1904).
Brown 1978 | Brown, Peter Douglas, *William Pitt, Earl of Chatham: The Great Commoner* (London, 1978)
Burke 1884 | Burke, Sir Bernard, *The General Armory of England, Scotland, Ireland and Wales* (London, 1884).
Butler 2009 | Butler, Margaret R., '"Olivero's" painting of Turin's Teatro Regio: toward a reevaluation of an operatic emblem', *Music in Art*, vol. 34 no. 1–2 (2009), pp. 137–51.

Cameron 1996 | Cameron, Peter, 'Henry Jernagan, the Kandlers and the client who changed his mind', *Silver Society Journal*, no. 8 (1996), pp. 487–99.
Chalmers 1822 | Chalmers, Alexander (ed.), *The Tatler*, 4 vols (London, 1822).
Clarke 1763 | Clarke, Rev. Edward, *Letters concerning the Spanish nation written at Madrid in the years 1760 and 1761* (London, 1763).
Clayton 1971 | Clayton, Michael, *The Collector's Dictionary of the Silver and Gold of Great Britain and North America* (London, 1971)
Coke 1889–96 | *Lady Mary Coke, Letters and Journals 1756–74*, 4 vols (London, 1889–96).
Copinger 1911 | Copinger, W.A., *The Manors of Suffolk*, volume 7 (Manchester, 1911).
Copper pamphlet 1755 | Anonymous, *Serious reflections on the manifold dangers attending the use of copper vessels, and other utensils of copper and brass, in the preparations of all such solids as are designed for food to human bodies: in a letter to a friend* (London, 1755).
Cornforth 1996 | Cornforth, John, 'A splendid unity of arts [the silver at Kedleston Hall, Derbyshire]', *Country Life*, vol. 190, (13 June, 1996), pp. 128–31.
——1999 | Cornforth, John, 'Ickworth, Suffolk – I', *Country Life*, 19 August, 1999, pp. 40–5.
Cousins 2005 | Cousins, Julian, 'Pierre Harache I and II: a challenge to current attributions', *Silver Studies*, no. 19 (2005), pp. 71–7.
Craven and Stanley 2004 | Craven, Maxwell and Michael Stanley, *The Derbyshire Country House* (Ashbourne, 2004)
Croker 1821 | Croker, J.W. (ed.), *Letters of Mary Lepel, Lady Hervey* (London, 1821).
Culme 1977 | Culme, John, *Nineteenth Century Silver* (London, 1977).
——1987 | Culme, John, *The Directory of Gold and Silversmiths, Jewellers and Allied Traders, 1838–1914* (London, 1987).
——1999 | Culme, John, *English Silver: The Jerome and Rita Gans Collection, Addendum I* (Richmond, Virginia, 1999).
——2015 | Culme, John, *British Silver Boxes 1640–1840: The Lion Collection* (Woodbridge, 2015).

Davis 1976 | Davis, John D., *English Silver at Williamsburg* (Williamsburg, Virginia, 1976).
Dennis 1960 | Dennis, Faith, *Three Centuries of French Domestic Silver: Its Makers and its Marks* (New York, 1960).
Dobson 1896 | Dobson, Austin, *Eighteenth Century Vignettes*, Third Series (London, 1896).
Dove 2007 | Dove, Anthony, 'Plate duty. Its origins, marks

and variations', *Silver Studies*, no. 22 (2007), pp. 105–16.
Dutens 1806 | Dutens, Louis, *Memoirs of a Traveller now in Retirement*, 5 vols (London, 1806).

Earwaker 1884 | Earwaker, J.P. (ed.), *Lancashire and Cheshire Wills and Inventories at Chester* (Manchester, 1884).
Emmerson 1992 | Emmerson, Robin, *British Tea Pots and Tea Drinking* (London, 1992).
Erskine 1953 | Erskine, David (ed.), *Augustus Hervey's Journal* (London, 1953).

Fairbairn 1905 | Fairbairn, James, *Fairbairn's Crests of the Leading Families in Great Britain and Ireland* (London, 1905).
Fennimore and Halfpenny 2000 | Fennimore, Donald L. and Patricia A. Halfpenny, *Campbell Collection of Soup Tureens at Winterthur* (Winterthur, 2000).
Ferguson 2011 | Ferguson, Patricia, 'Digby, Tollemache and Hervey: three aristocrats and their ceramics', *English Ceramic Circle Transactions*, vol. 22 (2011), pp. 49–87.
—2016 | Ferguson, Patricia, '"Japan China" taste and elite ceramic consumption in 18th-century England: revising the narrative' in Jon Stobart and Andrew Hann (eds), *The Country House: Material Culture and Consumption* (Swindon, 2016), pp. 113–122.
Fina 2002 | Fina, Gianfranco, *L'argenteria Torinese del Settecento* (Turin, 2002).
Fina and Mana 2012 | Fina, Gianfranco and Luca Mana, *Argenti Sabaudi del XVIII Secolo* (Milan, 2012).
Fortescue 1927 | Fortescue, Hon. Sir John, *The Correspondence of King George the Third from 1760 to December 1783*, 6 vols (London, 1927).
Fothergill 1974 | Fothergill, Brian, *The Mitred Earl: An Eighteenth-Century Eccentric* (London, 1974).
Frégnac 1965 | Frégnac, Claude (ed.), *Les grands orfèvres de Louis XIII à Charles X* (Paris, 1965)

Gage 1822 | Gage, John, *The History and Antiquities of Hengrave in Suffolk* (London, 1822).
—1838 | Gage, John, *The History and Antiquities of Suffolk. Thingoe Hundred* (London, 1838).
Germain 1748 | Germain, Pierre, *Éléments d'orfèvrerie* (Paris, 1748).
Glanville 1990 | Glanville, Philippa, *Silver in Tudor and Early Stuart England* (London, 1990).
—1992 | Glanville, Philippa, 'Boughton silver' in Tessa Murdoch (ed.), *Boughton House: The English Versailles* (London, 1992), pp. 152–7.
—1996 | Glanville, Philippa (ed.), *Silver* (London, 1996).
Glasse 1747 | Glasse, Hannah, *The art of cookery made plain and easy* (London, 1747).
Goodway 2004 | Goodway, Eileen, 'Ongoing research', *Silver Studies*, no. 16 (2004), p. 124.
Grimwade 1974 | Grimwade, Arthur, *Rococo Silver 1727–1765* (London, 1974).
—1990 | Grimwade, Arthur, *London Goldsmiths 1697–1837: Their Marks and Lives* (3rd edn, London, 1990).
Gordon 1830 | Gordon, Pryse Lockhart, *Personal Memoirs*, 2 vols. (London, 1830).

Hackenbroch 1963 | Hackenbroch, Yvonne, *English and other Silver in the Irwin Untermeyer Collection* (London, 1963).
Halsband 1973 | Halsband, Robert, *Lord Hervey: Eighteenth-Century Courtier* (Oxford, 1973).
Hare 1990 | Hare, Susan (ed.), *Paul de Lamerie, At the Sign of the Golden Ball: An Exhibition of the Work of England's Master Silversmith (1688–1751)* (London, 1990).
Hartop 1996 | Hartop, Christopher, *The Huguenot Legacy: English Silver 1680–1760* (London, 1996).
—2005 | Hartop, Christopher, *Royal Goldsmiths: The Art of Rundell & Bridge 1797–1843* (Cambridge, 2005).
—2010 | Hartop, Christopher, *The Classical Ideal: English Silver, 1760–1840* (Cambridge, 2010).
—2013 | Hartop, Christopher, 'Sir Robert Walpole's silver', *Silver Studies*, no. 29 (2013), pp. 24–83.
—2015 | Hartop, Christopher, *Art and Industry: The Silver of Paul Storr* (Cambridge, 2015).
Hayward 1959 | Hayward, J.F., *Huguenot Silver in England 1688–1727* (London, 1959).
Heal 1935 | Heal, Ambrose, *The London Goldsmiths* (Cambridge, 1935).
Hennell 1986 | Hennell, Percy, *The Hennell Salt Cellars 1736 to 1876*
Hernmarck 1977 | Hernmarck, Carl, *The Art of the European Silversmith*, 2 vols (London, 1977).
Hervey 1857 | Hervey, Rev. Lord Arthur, 'Ickworth and the family of Hervey', *Proceedings of the Suffolk Institute of Archaeology and Natural History*, vol. 2, part 6 (1857), pp. 291–429.
Hervey 1894a | Hervey, Rev. S.A.H., *The Diary of John Hervey, First Earl of Bristol. With Extracts from his Book of Expenses, 1688 to 1742* (Wells, 1894).
—1894b | Hervey, Rev. S.A.H., *Letter-Books of John Hervey, First Earl of Bristol*, 3 vols (Wells, 1894).
—1906 | Hervey, Rev. S.A.H., *Journals of the Hon. William Hervey, 1755–1814* (Bury St Edmunds, 1906).
Holmes 1996 | Holmes, Michael, *Augustus Hervey: A Naval Casanova* (Bishop Auckland, 1996).
Hughes 1957 | Hughes, G. Bernard, *Small Antique Silverware* (New York, 1957).
Hughes 2000 | Hughes, Graham, *Treasures at Salters' Hall* (Alfriston, 2000).
Huguenot Society 1891–3 | *Proceedings of the Huguenot Society of London*, vol. IV. 1891–1893 (Lymington, 1894).
Hutchings 2005 | Hutchings, Victoria, *Messrs Hoare Bankers: A History of the Hoare Banking Dynasty* (London, 2005).

Jackson 1911 | Jackson, Sir Charles James, *Illustrated History of English Plate Ecclesiastical and Secular*, 2 vols. (London, 1911).
—1921 | Jackson, Sir Charles James, *English Goldsmiths and their Marks* (London, 1921).
Jacobsen 2012 | Jacobsen, Helen, *Luxury and Power: The Material World of the Stuart Diplomat, 1660–1714* (Oxford, 2012).
Jenkins 2005 | Jenkins, Susan, '"An Inventory of His Grace the Duke of Chandos's Seat at Cannons taken June the 19th 1725" by John Gilbert', *The Walpole Society*, vol. 67 (2005), pp. 93-192.
Jones 1906 | Jones, E. Alfred, *The Church Plate of the Diocese of Bangor* (London, 1906).
—1935 | Jones, E. Alfred, *Catalogue of Plate Belonging to the Duke of Portland KG GCVO at Welbeck Abbey* (London, 1935).
—1938 | Jones, E. Alfred, *The Plate of Eton College* (London, 1938).
—1939 | Jones, E. Alfred, *Catalogue of the Plate of Clare College, Cambridge* (Cambridge, 1939).
Jones and Garibaldi 2006 | Jones, Katherine and Christopher Garibaldi, 'Crespin or Sprimont? A question revisited', *Silver Studies*, no. 21 (2006), pp. 24–32.
Jourdain 1926 | Jourdain, Margaret, 'Cisterns, wine coolers and cellarets', *Country Life*, (12 June 1926), pp. 853–854.

Kersey 1708 | Kersey, John, *Dictionarium Anglo-Britannicum: or, a general English dictionary* (London, 1708)

La Chapelle 1733 | La Chapelle, Vincent, *The modern cook* (London, 1733)
—1736 | La Chapelle, Vincent, *The modern cook*, 2nd edition (London, 1736).
Larousse 1990 | *Larousse Gastonomique* (London, 1990).
Leadam 1909 | Leadam, I.S., *The History of England from the Accession of Anne to the Death of George II* (London, 1909).
Lee and Ryrie 2008 | Lee, Sophie and Alec Ryrie, 'The Tudor Reformations' in Timothy Schroder (ed.), *Treasures of the English Church: A Thousand Years of Sacred Gold & Silver* (London, 2008), pp. 28–39.
Lewis 1937–83 | Lewis, W.S. (ed.), *The Yale Edition of Horace Walpole's Correspondence*, 48 vols (New Haven, 1937–1983).
Lodge 1933 | Lodge, Sir Richard (ed.), *The Private Correspondence of Sir Benjamin Keene* (Cambridge, 1933).
Lomax 1992 | Lomax, James, *British Silver at Temple Newsam and Lotherton Hall* (Leeds, 1992).
—1999 | Lomax, James, 'Royalty and silver: the role of the Jewel House in the eighteenth century', *The Silver Society Journal*, no. 11 (1999), pp. 133–9.
—2014 | Lomax, James, 'The Ambassador's plate revisited' in Patrick Eyres and James Lomax (eds), *Diplomats, Goldsmiths and Baroque Court Culture: Lord Raby in Berlin, The Hague and Wentworth Castle* (Barnsley, 2014), pp. 64–91.
Lomax and Rothwell 2006 | Lomax, James and James Rothwell, *Country House Silver from Dunham Massey* (National Trust Books, 2006).
London, Seaford House 1929 | *Queen Charlotte's Loan Exhibition of Old Silver*, Seaford House, London. exh. cat. (London, 1929).
Lopato 2015 | Lopato, Marina, *State Hermitage Museum Catalogue, British Silver* (New Haven and London, 2015).

Mason 1787 | Mason, Charlotte, *The Lady's Assistant for regulating and supplying the table*, 6th edition (London, 1787).
Massialot 1702 | Massialot, François, *The court and country cook* (London, 1702).
Mazza and Piccoli 2011 | Mazza, Emilio and Edoardo Piccoli, '"Disguised in scarlet". Hume and Turin in 1748', *I Castelli di Yale*, no. 11 (2011), pp. 71–108.
Matthews and Tuke 1926 | Matthews, P.W. and Anthony Tuke, *History of Barclays Bank Limited* (London, 1926).
Mitchell 1994 | Mitchell, David, '"Mr. Fowle Pray Pay the Washwoman": the trade of a London goldsmith-banker, 1660–1692', *Business and Economic History*, vol. 23, no. 1 (Fall 1994), pp. 27–38.
Mortlock 1997 | Mortlock, D.P., 'Thomas Coke and the family silver', *Silver Society Journal*, no. 9 (1997), pp. 552-8.
—2007 | Mortlock, D.P., *Aristocratic Splendour: Money and the World of Thomas Coke, Earl of Leicester* (Stroud, 2007).
Morton 1958 | Morton, A.L., 'John Lanseter of Bury', *Proceedings of the Suffolk Institute of Archæology*, vol. 28, part 1 (1958), pp. 29–53
Moxon 1753 | Moxon, Elizabeth, *English Housewifry. Exemplified in above four hundred and fifty Receipts, giving directions in most parts of cookery*, 4th edition (Leeds, 1753).
Murdoch 2006 | Murdoch, Tessa (ed.), *Noble Households: Eighteenth Century Inventories of Great English Houses* (Cambridge, 2006).
—2010 | Murdoch, Tessa, 'The great silver wine cistern of Thomas Wentworth', Expert Adviser's Statement, Export Reviewing Committee, Case 11 2010–11, unpublished report downloaded from http://www.artscouncil.org.uk/media/uploads/pdf/case_11_expert_statement.pdf.
Muyden 1902 | Muyden, Madame van (ed.), *A Foreign View of England in the Reigns of George I & George II: The Letters of Monsieur César de Saussure to his Family* (London, 1902)

Nichols 1822 | Nichols, John, *Illustrations of the Literary History of the Eighteenth Century*, vol. 4 (London, 1822).
Nocq 1926–31 | Nocq, Henry, *Le poinçon de Paris*, 5 volumes (Paris, 1926–31).
Noël-Waldteuffel 1993 | Noël-Waldteuffel, Marie-France, 'Manger à la cour: alimentation et gastronomie aux XVIIe et XVIIIe siècles', in *Versailles et les tables royales en Europe XVIIème–XIXème siècles* (Paris, 1993), pp. 69–84.
Norton 1980 | Norton, Lucy (ed.), *Saint-Simon at Versailles* (London, 1980).

Oman 1957 | Oman, Charles, *English Church Plate 597–1830* (London, 1957).
—1966 | Oman, Charles, 'The plate of the chapel of the Sardinian embassy', *The Burlington Magazine*, vol. 108 (1966), pp. 500–503.

Paston-Williams 1993 | Paston-Williams, Sara, *The Art of Dining, A History of Cooking and Eating* (London, 1993).
Penzer 1957a | Penzer, N.M., 'The Hervey silver at Ickworth', *Apollo*, vol. 65 (February and April 1957), pp. 39–43 and pp. 133–137.
—1957b | Penzer, N.M., 'The Great Wine Coolers', Parts I & II, *Apollo*, vol. 66 (August and September 1957) pp. 3–7 and 39–46.
Pettigrew 2001 | Pettigrew, Jane, *A Social History of Tea* (London, 2001).
Phillips 1935 | Phillips, P.A.S., *Paul de Lamerie, Citizen and Goldsmith of London: A Study of His Life and Work A.D. 1688–1751* (London, 1935).
Piccoli 2016 | Piccoli, Edoardo, 'A "little known" country and its capital: British residents and travellers in Turin and Piedmont, 1747–48', in *Turin and the British in the Age of the Grand Tour* (Cambridge, 2016).
Pickford 1983 | Pickford, Ian, *Silver Flatware: English Irish and Scottish 1660–1980* (Woodbridge, 1983).
—1989 | Pickford, Ian (ed.), *Jackson's Silver and Gold Marks of England, Scotland and Ireland* (Woodbridge, 1989).
—1998 | Pickford, Ian, *Antique Silver* (Woodbridge, 1998).
Pijzel-Dommisse 2014 | Pijzel-Dommisse, Jet, 'Ambassadorial plate, embassies and the Dutch Republic' in Patrick Eyres and James Lomax (ed.), *Diplomats, Goldsmiths and Baroque Court Culture: Lord Raby in Berlin, The Hague and Wentworth Castle* (Stainborough, 2014), pp. 93–110.
Pinkard 2009 | Pinkard, Susan, *A Revolution in Taste: The Rise of French Cuisine 1650–1800* (New York, 2009).
Pollak 1991 | Pollak, Martha D., *Turin 1564–1680* (Chicago and London, 1991).
Proceedings in Parliament 1743–74 | *The history, debates, and proceedings of both Houses of Parliament of Great Britain from the year 1743 to the year 1774*, 7 vols (London, 1792).

Raffald 1769 | Raffald, Elizabeth, *The experienced English house-keeper, for the use and ease of ladies, house-keepers, cooks, &c.* (Manchester, 1769).

Robinson 2012 | Robinson, John Martin, *James Wyatt: Architect to George III* (London, 2012).

Rothwell 2012 | Rothwell, James, 'The Trail of Gold', *Apollo*, vol. 175, no. 599 (June, 2012), pp. 62–9.

Rowell 2009 | Rowell, Christopher (ed.), '2008–2009 Acquisitions', *The National Trust Historic Houses and Collections Annual 2009*, pp. 30–7.

Rutherford 2015 | Rutherford, Sarah, 'Where is Capability Brown at Ickworth?', unpublished report for the National Trust (2015).

Sadie 1990 | Sadie, Julie Anne (ed.), *Companion to Baroque Music* (Berkeley and Los Angeles, 1990).

Sale 1995 | Sale, Anthony, 'Records of plate of the Beaufort family in the Badminton House archives and elsewhere', *Silver Studies*, no. 7 (1995), pp. 381-91.

——2008 | Sale, Anthony, 'Plate tax', *Silver Studies*, no. 23 (2008), pp. 114–5.

Schroder 1988a | Schroder, Timothy, *The National Trust Book of English Domestic Silver 1500–1900* (Middlesex, 1988).

——1988b | Schroder, Timothy, *The Gilbert Collection of Gold and Silver* (Los Angeles, 1988).

——2009 | Schroder, Timothy, *British and Continental Gold and Silver in the Ashmolean Museum*, 3 vols (Oxford, 2009).

Simón 2012 | Simón, Victoria Chisbert, 'Del Palacio de Monteleón a la Plaza del Dos de Mayo Arco de Monteleón y Escultura de Daioz y Velarde', unpublished thesis, Universitat de València (2012).

Simpson 1806 | Simpson, John, *The complete system of cookery … being one year's work at the Marquis of Buckingham's from the 1st January, to the 31st December, 1805* (London, 1806).

Sinsteden 2008 | Sinsteden, Thomas, 'Household plate of the dukes of Ormonde', *Silver Studies*, no. 23 (2008), pp. 123–34.

Sitwell 1960 | Sitwell, Major-General H.D.W., 'The Jewel House and the Royal Goldsmiths', *Archaeological Journal*, 117 (1960), pp.131–55,

Smith 1907 | Smith, Guy Oswald, 'Silver nutmeg graters or spice boxes', *The Connoisseur*, vol. XIX (September–December 1907), pp. 169–173.

Storrs 2000 | Storrs, Christopher, 'Savoyard diplomacy in the eighteenth century (1684–1798)', in Daniel Frigo (ed.), *Politics and Diplomacy in Early Modern Italy* (Cambridge, 2000), pp. 210–53.

Strachey 1998 | Strachey, Hon. Nino, *Ickworth* (London, 1998).

Stuart 1936 | Stuart, Dorothy Margaret, *Molly Lepell, Lady Hervey* (London 1936).

Swift 1745 | Swift, Jonathan, *Directions to servants* (London, 1745).

Temple Newsam 1992 | *Country House Lighting 1660–1890* (Leeds, 1992).

Thompson 2011 | Thompson, Andrew C., *George II* (New Haven and London, 2011).

Thompson 1963 | Thompson, F.M.L., *English Landed Society in the Nineteenth Century* (London, 1963).

Trusler 1775 | Trusler, Rev. John (ed.), *Principles of politeness and of knowing the world; by the late Lord Chesterfield … with additions by the Reverend Dr. John Trusler* (London, 1775)

——1788 | Trusler, Rev. John , *The honours of the table, or, rules for behaviour during meals with the whole art of carving illustrated by a variety of cuts* (London, 1788).

Verral 1759 | Verral, William, *A complete system of cookery. In which is set forth, a variety of genuine receipts, collected from several years experience under the celebrated Mr. de St. Clouet, sometime since cook to his Grace the Duke of Newcastle* (London, 1759).

Versailles 1993 | *Versailles et les tables royale en Europe XVIIème–XIXème siècles* (Paris, 1993).

Visser 1991 | Visser, Margaret, *The Rituals of Dinner* (New York, 1991).

Waterson 1994 | Waterson, Merlin, *The National Trust: The First Hundred Years* (London, 1994).

Watts and Shirley 1929 | Watts, W.W. and Andrew Shirley (eds.), *Queen Charlotte's Loan Exhibition of Old Silver*, catalogue of the exhibition at Seaford House, 1st May to 8th June (London, 1929).

Wees 1997 | Wees, Beth Carver, *English, Irish & Scottish Silver at the Sterling and Francine Clark Art Institute* (New York 1997).

Westman 2013 | Westman, Annabel, 'New Light on the Textiles at Ham House' in Christopher Rowell (ed.), *Ham House: 400 Years of Collecting and Patronage* (London, 2013), pp. 248–61.

Wheaton 1983 | Wheaton, Barbara Ketcham, *Savoring the Past* (New York, 1983).

Woolf 1961 | Woolf, S. J., 'English public opinion and the Duchy of Savoy' in *English Miscellany: A Symposium of History, Literature and the Arts*, vol. 12 (1961), pp. 211–58.

Yates 2013 | Yates, Kate, *Ickworth Church: A History* (Ickworth, 2013)

PHOTOGRAPHIC CREDITS AND COPYRIGHT

Unless otherwise indicated all photographs are
National Trust Images/Robert Thrift

pp. ii, 60–1: National Trust Images/David Kirkham
Fig. 1: National Trust Images/Angelo Hornak
Figs 2, 4, 6, 7, 15, 16, 23, 26, 34, 35, 36, 41, 43, 44, 49, 52, 53, 58, 69, 72: National Trust Images
Figs 3, 18, 24, 57: National Trust Images/Sue James
Fig. 5: © The Rosalinde and Arthur Gilbert Collection on loan to the Victoria and Albert Museum, London
p. iv, figs 8, 73: National Trust Images/Andrew Butler
Fig. 9: Barclay's Group Archives
Figs 10, 38, 45: Suffolk Record Office, Bury St Edmunds
Figs 12, 13: Clare College, Cambridge
Figs 14, 51, 65, 86a: Sotheby's London
Fig. 17: © Historic England
Figs 19, 20, 74, 80, 83, 86, 89, 90, 92: © Christie's London Images Ltd
Fig. 21: National Portrait Gallery, London
Fig. 25, 93: The Trustees of the British Museum
Figs 27, 56, 104: National Trust Images/Andreas von Einsiedel
Fig 28, 98: The Provost, Fellows and Scholars of The Queen's College, Oxford
Fig. 29: Scala, Florence/Museo Civico d'Arte Antica, Turin
Fig. 30: © Bundesmobilienverwaltung, Hofmobiliendepot, Möbel Museum Wien, Photographer: Edgar Knaack
Fig. 31: © The Metropolitan Museum of Art/ Art Resource/Scala, Florence
Figs 32, 105: Private Collection/Fondazione Accorsi-Ometto, Museo di Arti Decorative
Figs 33, 106, 109: Victoria and Albert Museum
Figs 37, 48, 88, 107, cat. 2, 4 (detail), 12 (main), 17, 35 (details), 39 (detail), 49, 51 (reverse), 52, 53 (hallmark), 54 (hallmark), 55 (hallmark), 56 (hallmarks), 65, 72 (hallmark), 77 (detail), 78, 88 (detail), 89 (detail), 91, 96, 98, 103, 110, 122: National Trust Images/Robert Morris
Fig. 39: Fundación Lázaro Galdiano
Figs 40, 78, 94, 97: © British Library Board
Fig. 46: National Trust Images/Ray Dale
Fig. 50: National Trust Images/John Hammond
Fig. 54: National Trust Images/Rupert Truman
Fig. 55: National Trust Images/Christopher Hurst
Fig. 60: © Country Life Picture Library
Fig. 61: National Trust Images/Phil Mynott
Fig. 67: Groeningemuseum, Bruges
Fig. 68: © The Governor and Company of the Bank of England
Figs 70, 100: Ashmolean Museum/University of Oxford
Fig 71: Courtesy of Lowell Lisbon Ltd
Fig. 76: National Museums & Galleries of Wales
Figs 77, 81, 82: Leeds Museums and Galleries (Temple Newsam)
Fig. 79: The State Hermitage Museum, Russia
Fig. 84: Norfolk Museums Service (Norwich Castle Museum & Art Gallery)
Fig. 85: National Gallery of Ireland
Fig. 87: Reproduced by kind permission of the Society of Dilettanti, London © Photographic Survey, The Courtauld Institute of Art, London
Fig. 91: National Trust Images/Brenda Norrish
Fig. 95: Museum of Fine Arts, Boston
Fig. 96: Courtesy, The Winterthur Library: Joseph Downs Collection of Manuscripts and Printed Ephemera
Fig. 99: Musée national des châteaux de Versailles et de Trianon/Bridgeman Images
Fig. 101: Andrew Patterson
Fig. 102: Museu Calouste Gulbenkian, Lisbon/ Fundacao Caloutse Gulbenkian
Fig. 103: © Fondazione Torino Musei
Fig. 108: RMN-Grand Palais (musée du Louvre)/ Hervé Lewandowski
pp. 224–5: National Trust Images/Justin Minns

Shell handle of round tureen dish (Turin, *c.*1756, see cat. 55) from the silver of George William Hervey, 2nd Earl of Bristol

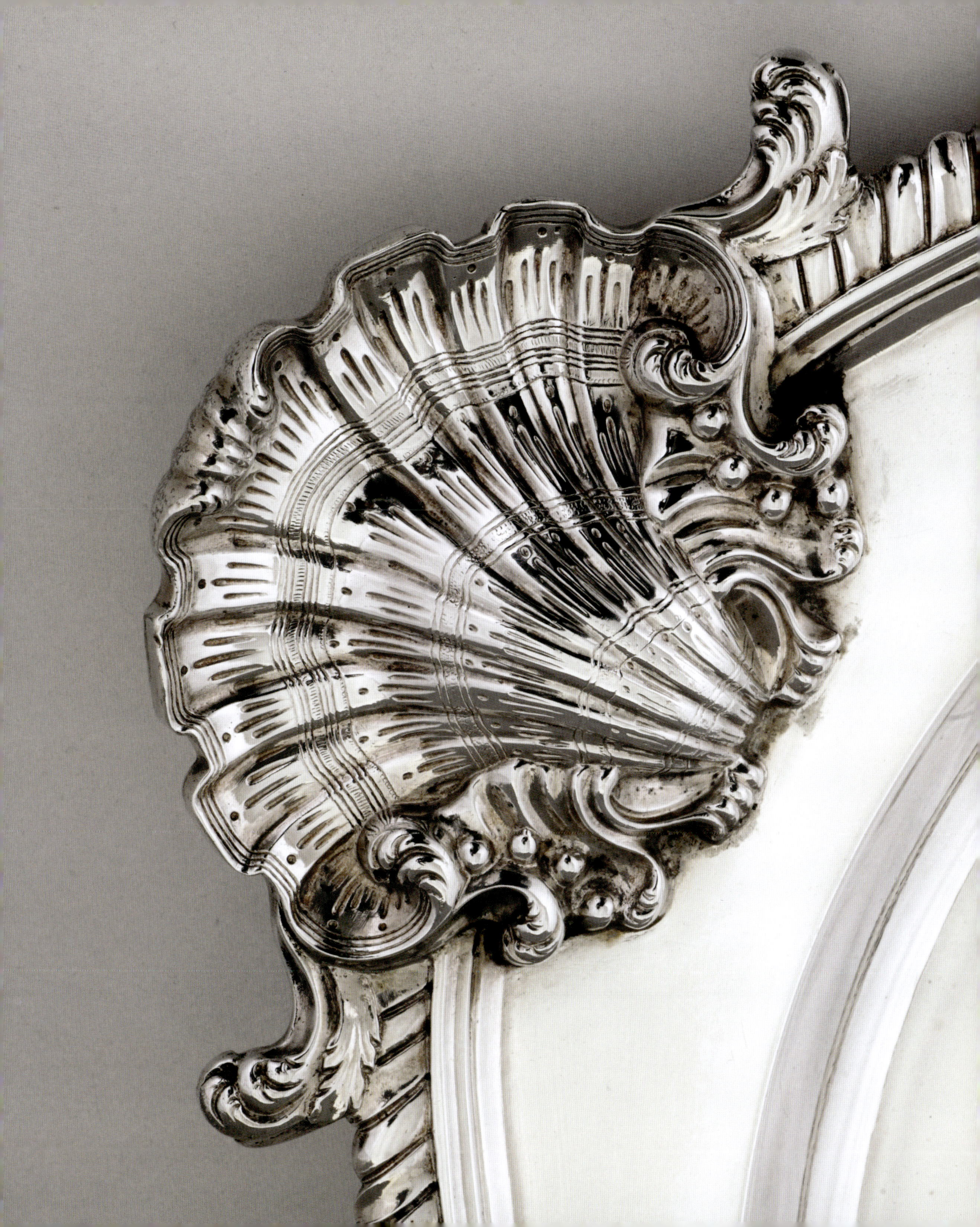

INDEX

Page numbers in *italics* are figures; with 'n' are notes.

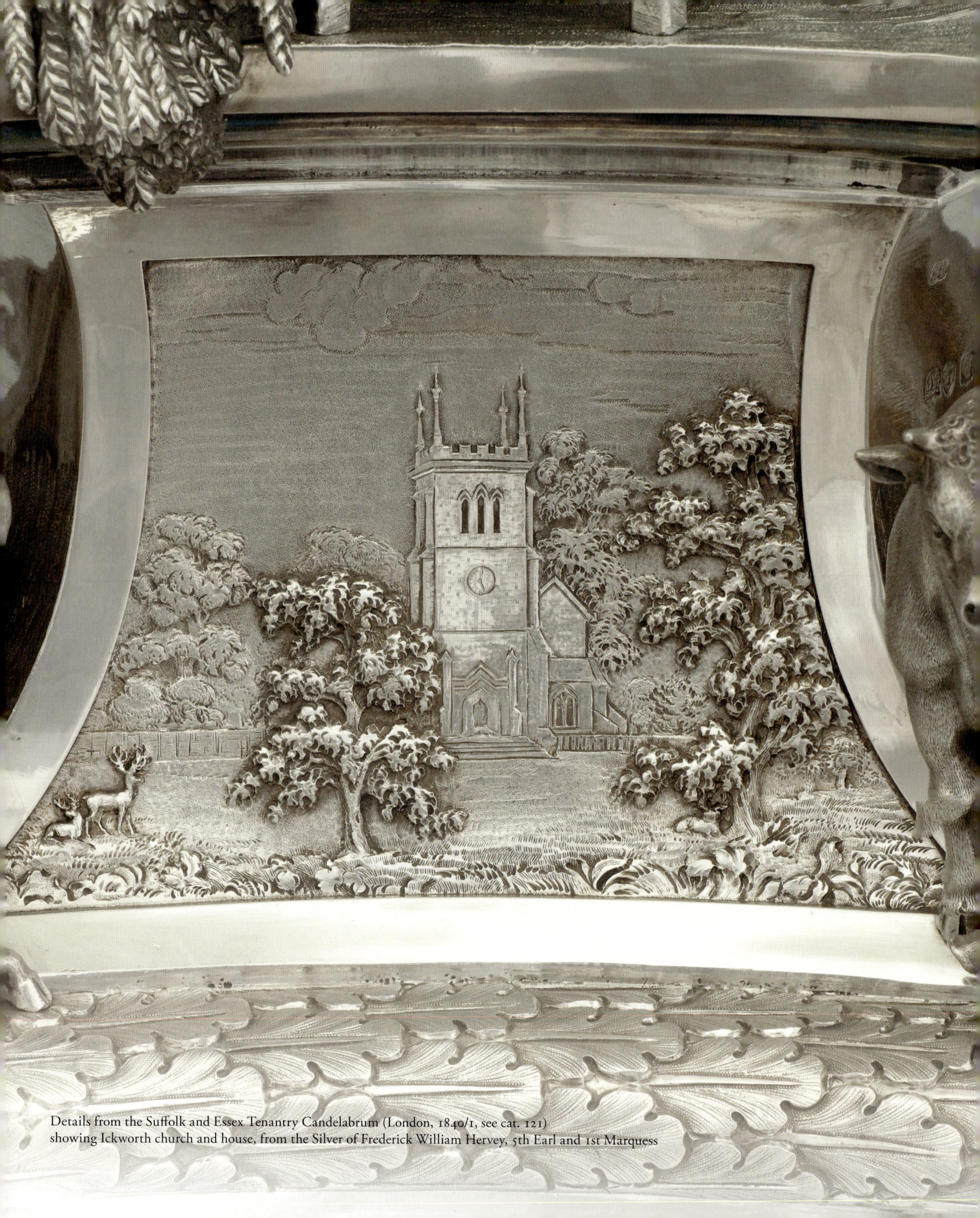

Details from the Suffolk and Essex Tenantry Candelabrum (London, 1840/1, see cat. 121) showing Ickworth church and house, from the Silver of Frederick William Hervey, 5th Earl and 1st Marquess

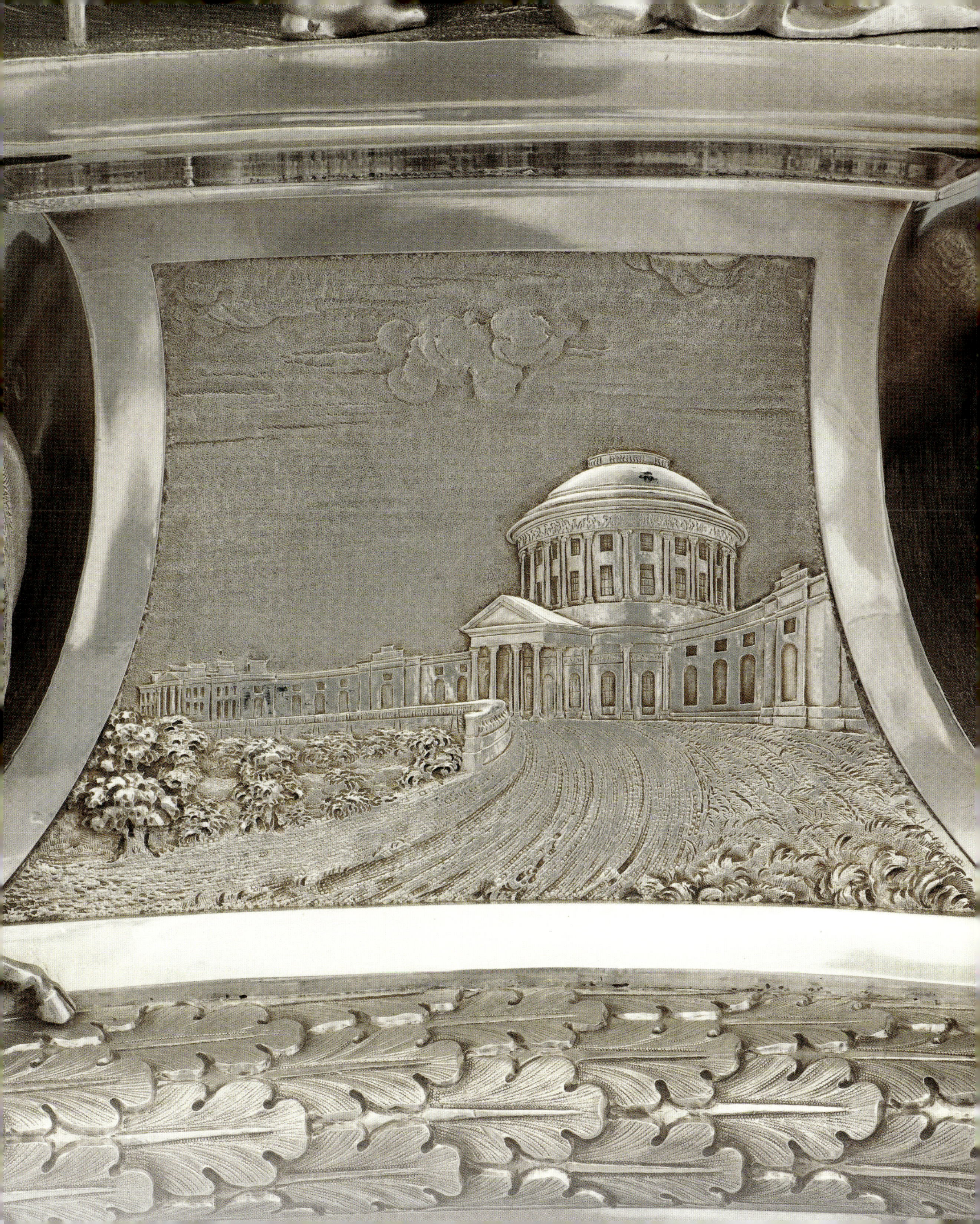

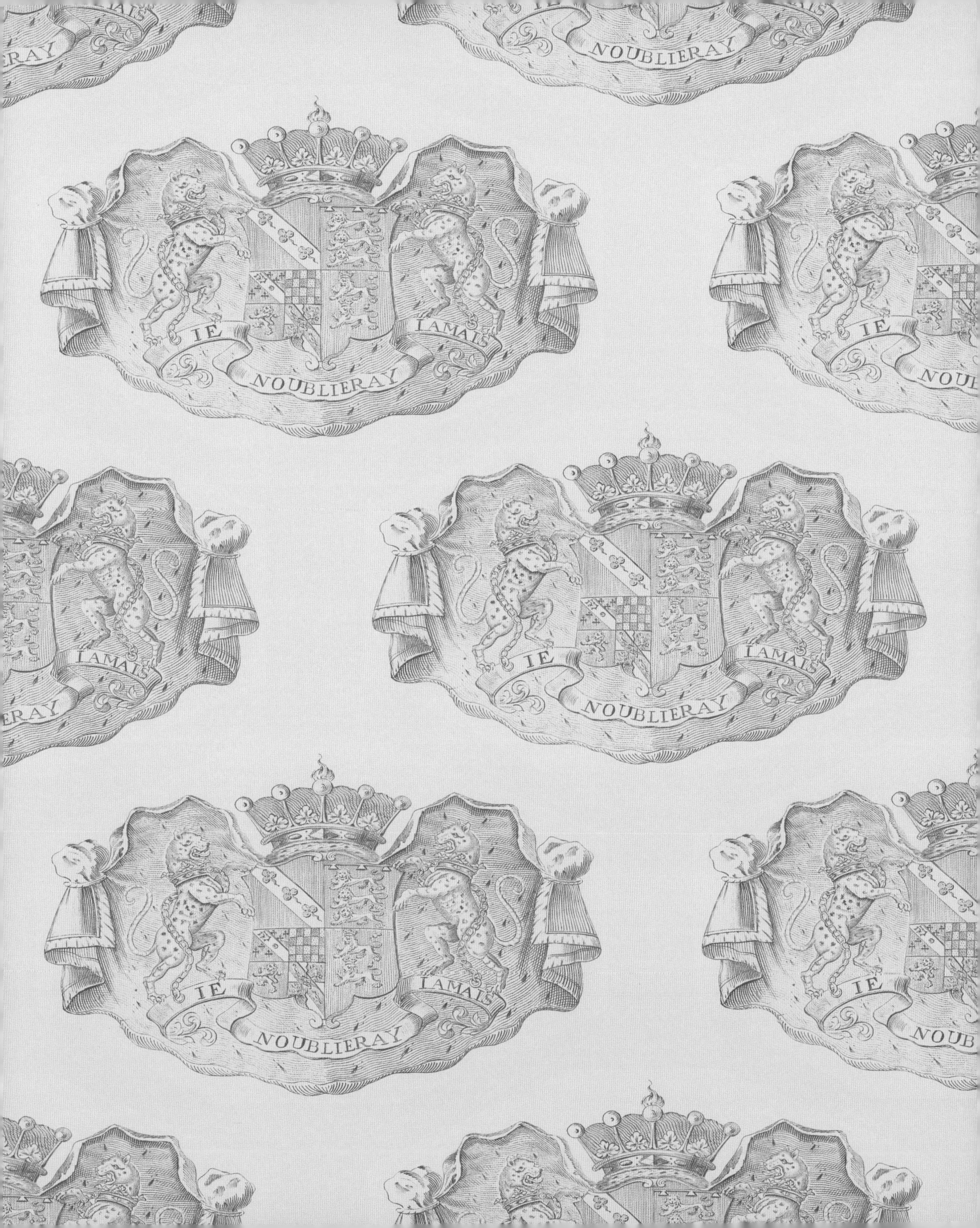
NOUBLIERAY
IE
IAMAIS
NOUBLIERAY
IE
IAMAIS
IE
IAMAIS
NOUBLIERAY
IE
IAMAIS
NOUBLIERAY
IE

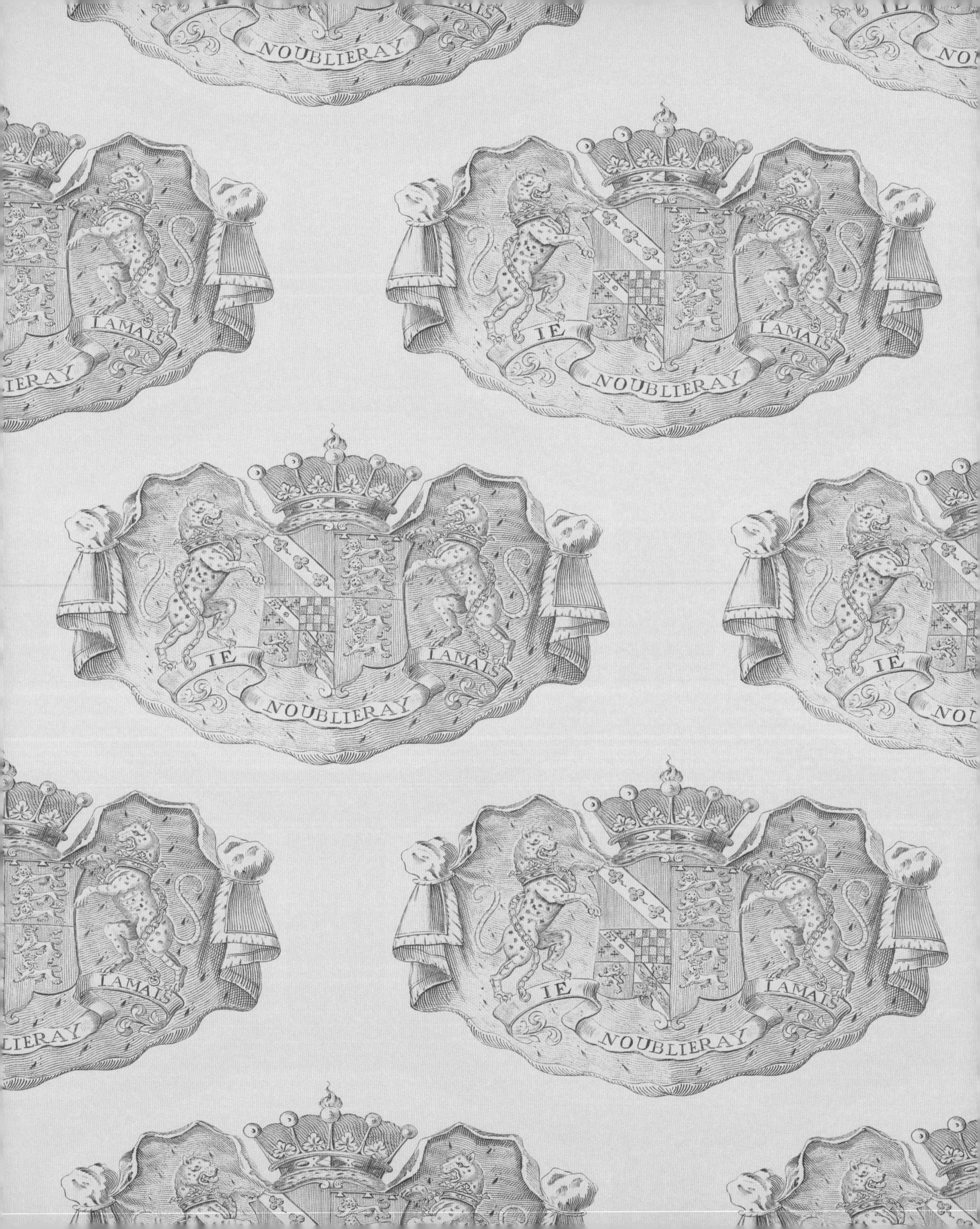
IE
IAMAIS
NOUBLIERAY

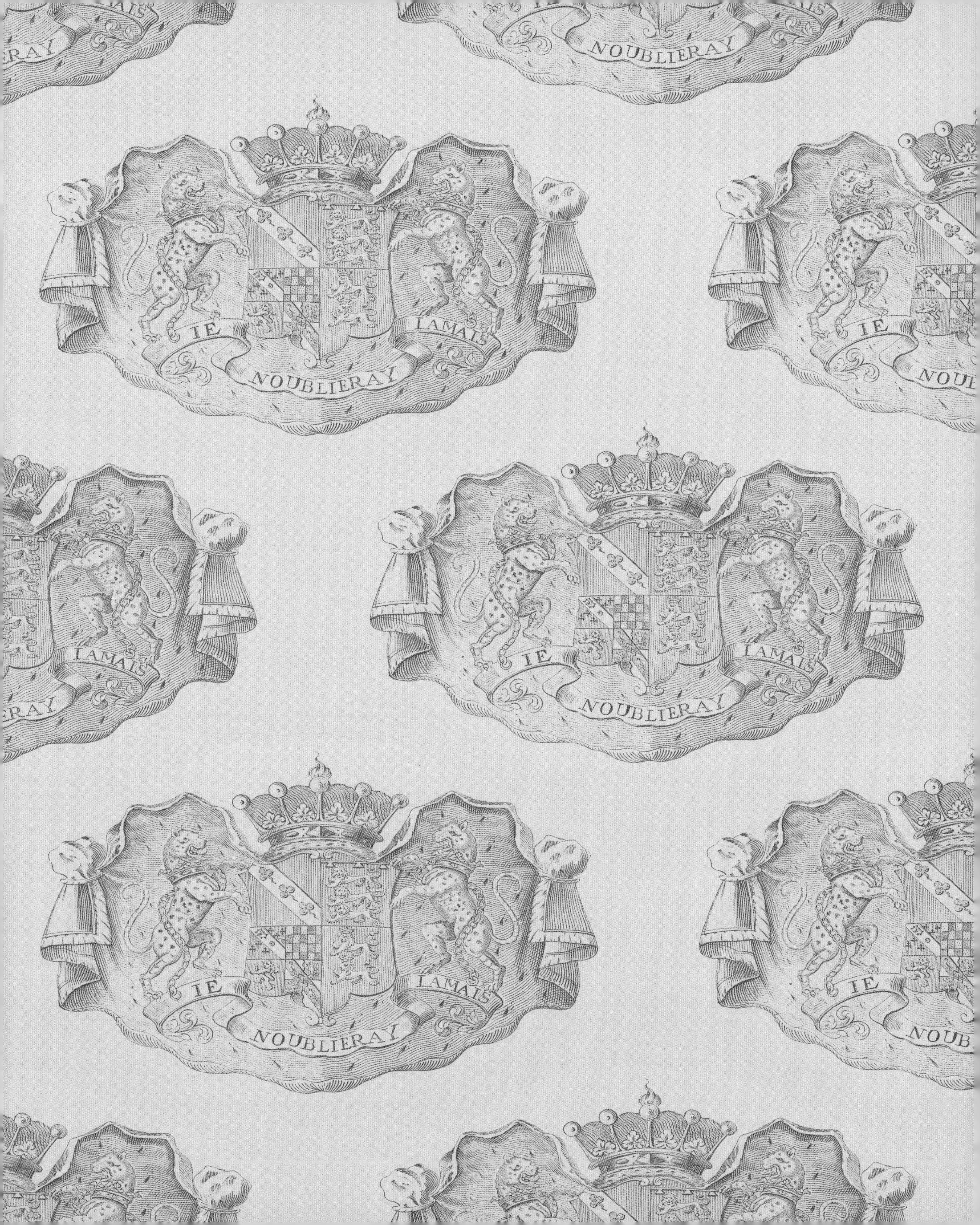
IE
IAMAIS
NOUBLIERAY

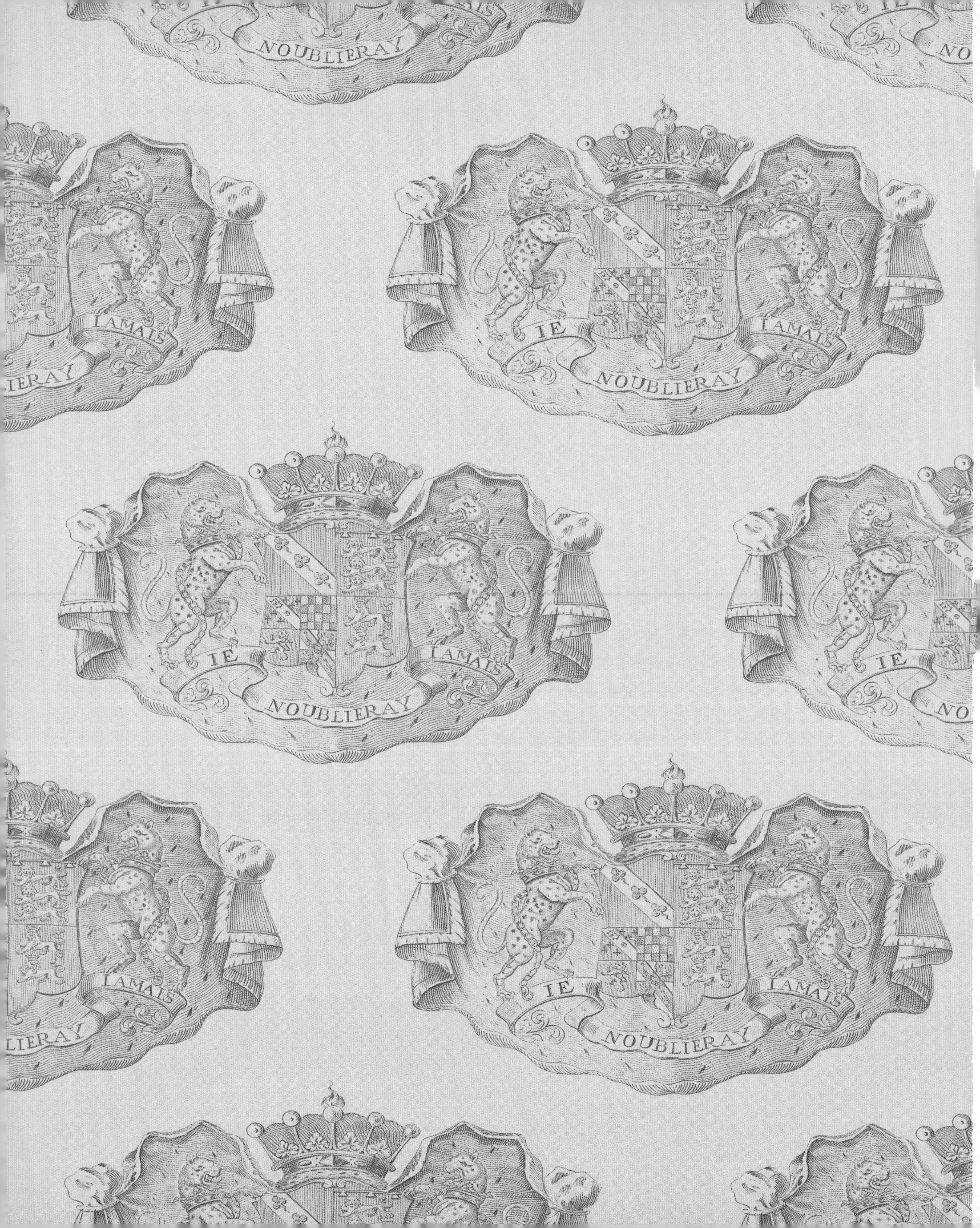
IE
IAMAIS
NOUBLIERAY